Robert Hahn

Conduct and Constraints

Testing the Limits of the Harm Principle

Tenth Edition

Pearson Learning Solutions, 501 Boylston Street, Suite 900, Boston, MA 02116
A Pearson Education Company
www.pearsoned.com

Printed in the United States of America

35 2023

000200010271892990

EEB/KE

ISBN 10: 1-269-89261-4
ISBN 13: 978-1-269-89261-2

COPYRIGHT
ACKNOWLEDGMENTS

FOR ZOË AND CHAVA

I hope someday you will read this book
and find something useful in it.

CONTENTS

ACKNOWLEDGMENTS

Thanks are gratefully offered to all those friends, students, and colleagues who discussed with me the contents of this book and who read parts of the manuscript at various stages over the years. These kind persons provided me with criticisms, corrections, and in the process saved me from some embarrassing mistakes. The significant improvements in the new sixth edition are due to the editorial expertise of Ms. Margot Schlipp, a former student and now a professor of English. Special thanks are due to Shane Stroup, one of our excellent graduate students, who has helped me make significant revisions for the seventh edition. I would like to thank Eric Thomas Weber for excellent suggestions and proposed revisions that have been incorporated into this new eighth edition. And I would like to add special thanks to Mike Jostedt, Jr. for his revisions to the ninth edition. In preparation of extensive revisions for this new 10th edition, I would like to acknowledge the valuable assistance I received from my graduate assistants Joseph Smith and Shannon Griffen, and most especially, from Jared Kemling.

SECTION I

Self-Identity, Self-Interest, and Strategies for Conduct

Chapter 1

Conduct and Constraints: Introduction

A. AN OVERVIEW OF SECTIONS I, II, AND III

This study entitled *Conduct and Constraints* is intended to challenge readers to discover a moral meaning of their self-identity and to unfold their own strategies for moral decision-making. In order to introduce the readers to this range of ethical thinking, we divide our study into three parts:

Section I: Self-Identity, Self-Interest, and Strategies for Conduct
Section II: The Morality of Killing
Section III: Sexual Morality

In each section of the course we will raise the question "Who am I?" and in each section we will propose, broadly, a different answer. In Section I our answer will be that "I am a rationally self-interested creature who is trying to overcome alienation." In Section II our answer will be that "I am the creature with a serious right-to-life." And in Section III our answer will be "I am a consenter."

Section I aims to challenge the readers to raise questions about their sense of who they are, and urges them to seek a meaning in the context of their conduct. We begin by advancing a thesis that all of our actions are motivated by self-interest. Indeed, not just any kind of self-interest but what we shall call *rational* self-interest. We pursue the argument that the overall goal of all of our actions is happiness, and we consider what that might mean. We argue that whenever we have the choice, we always choose to engage in that action whereby we seek to maximize our own best interests. In order to decide which course of action offers the likelihood of a better result, we perform a kind of calculation, weighing

3

the anticipated benefits and deficiencies against each other. The alternative that we choose is a particular expression of our self-interest calculated rationally. Certainly, at times, we make mistakes, we choose courses of action that do not bring us the happiness that we desire and that motivates our action, but the important point is that our choice reflects our best assessment of what we *believe* to be in our own best self-interest.

Even if the reader accepts this descriptive analysis of *how* we tend to behave, it still remains for us to explain *why* we behave that way. The thesis that we offer is a theory about alienation. Human beings, ontologically speaking, are deficient or imperfect creatures. One way to understand all of our actions is to see each one as a constructive response to the consciousness that something is lacking or missing in our lives, that each of our actions seeks to overcome life's obstacles and challenges in order to become more whole or complete. In a word, the human condition is *alienated,* and all of our actions may be interpreted purposefully as the attempt to overcome that alienation. Pursuing our self-interests is a way of expressing our human purpose to overcome alienation.

The reader is reminded that there are many ways to organize our experiences and that theories about rational self-interest and alienation are only two ways among many. This accords well with another thesis that operates throughout, namely, that human beings are *meaning-makers*. We need to discover meaning for our lives to be worthwhile, and there are many ways to chisel out a sense of meaningfulness in our lives. The readers are invited to challenge our approach and to discover a more useful or more adequate framework in which to grasp their own meaning.

Having set out the theses of rational self-interest and alienation, we turn to examine that broad domain in which individuals experience interference with their self-interests. Since we advance the argument that the pursuit of self-interest seeks happiness as its goal, and that happiness is identified with unalienated experience, we turn to focus on conditions that interfere with the realization of our self-interests because they pose threats to the happiness that we granted everyone desires. The theses of rational self-interest and alienation lead us to see human life in the context of flourishing. For our lives to flourish, to reach the happiness that we have hypothesized everyone is seeking, we must be prepared to promote maximum freedom, maximum liberty, so that each person can achieve the specific requirements for his/her own happiness. To promote flourishing we must be prepared to promote freedom—in this sense, our theory is a very "liberal" one in the sense that it is committed to the promotion of "liberties."

Everyone wants to be happy, but in a world of so many people there is invariably a conflict among (self) interests. To help everyone achieve happiness we must promote freedom, but what shall we do when one person's happiness interferes with the happiness of another? This should be our starting point. Are there any exercises of freedom that we should oppose? What if someone needs more money to be happy and decides to rob a bank? What if someone is opposed to his/her government and decides to blow up a building to achieve happiness? What if a person is unhappy with their boss and believes he/she will be happy if only they would come to work one day and shoot the boss! In all these cases, and in the countless other examples that they suggest, it should become clear that not every exercise of freedom and liberty should be permissible even though we acknowledge that everyone is always trying to pursue and maximize their own happiness.

To take on this difficult challenge, we advance the ideal of a *harm principle*. The ideal of a harm principle is part of a proscriptive, not prescriptive, strategy for assessing moral conduct. The prescriptive strategy quite literally "prescribes" or recommends conduct—you ought to do so and so. On the contrary, our proscriptive strategy only "proscribes" or recommends against conduct—you ought not to do so and so. When should conduct be proscribed? Conduct should be proscribed or recommended against whenever it violates the harm principle.

We begin, then, by defining the *harm principle* as "harmful wrongdoing" and reflect upon it first as formulated as a principle of law. Accordingly, we distinguish *Harm-to-Others, Harm-to-Self,* and *Impersonal Harms.* We insist that *harm to others,* that we define as a *wrongful setback to the interests of others,* is impermissible conduct and deserves constraint. This will be our paradigm principle of immoral conduct. However, we challenge the readers to determine what kinds of constraints, if any, are required in cases of *harm to self,* where no other person's interests are wrongfully set back, and *impersonal harms,* where no one is harmed directly, neither others nor the actors themselves, but the community comes to regard the conduct as harming its standards of acceptable conduct. We separate the unmistakably impermissible conduct of harms to others from the questionably impermissible harms to self and impersonal harms by appealing to what we shall call the *Volenti* maxim: Where there is consent, there is no wrongdoing. We shall certainly accept that where actions are performed with the consent of the parties that participate in them, there *may* be harmful results, but the maxim invites us to consider that where there are consensual (adult) acts, there can be no wrongdoing. The principle that is in our central focus—the *harm principle*—is interpreted to mean *harmful wrongdoing.* Our debate over the impermissibility of harms to self and impersonal harms will turn on the question of whether or not they properly constitute *wrongdoing* even *if* they cause harm. And if they are judged to still be wrong, we must explore others senses in which consensual adult actions might nevertheless be wrong. What good reasons could be proposed to explain and clarify such a view?

The more liberal positions tend to insist that while harms to others merit liberty-limiting principles, in those cases where the actors harm only themselves or no one is directly harmed, liberty-limiting constraints are unacceptable. The more conservative positions tend to agree that harm to others is always impermissible but advise, in varying degrees, additional constraints in the cases of harms to self and impersonal harms. The conservative positions tend to endorse what we may call the *enforcement of morality*, that not all conduct that is consensual is still morally permissible; the liberal positions recommend that people be left alone to live their own lives when there is no harm to others. The readers are challenged to discover how liberal or conservative their own views may be, and upon further reflections whether they are sustainable.

The investigation of the harm principle follows directly from the thesis that individuals seek to maximize their own self-interests. The clear line of demarcation is the *wrongful* setback of another's interests, for such conduct deserves constraint: *harm to others*. We began by offering a descriptive theory about human nature that committed us to a vision of human *flourishing*. Humans seek to grow and develop, attempt to overcome alienation, and however possible, promote liberties to achieve these aims. Thus, in general, our thesis commits us to promote liberties and therefore regards the restriction of liberties as evil. But, it is also clear that certain behavior is regarded as harmful and therefore must itself constitute an evil. Our problem will be to determine when the evil of actions is so great as to outweigh the evil of limiting liberties. And this is no easy task.

The orientation of our thesis presents us with a formidable shortcoming. The harm principle offers guidance, at best, only when certain conduct deserves constraint. When conduct can be judged to constitute harmful wrongdoing, it deserves liberty-limiting principles. But this approach is incapable of instructing us about *what* conduct is wise and desirable. It offers us no insight into what conduct to recommend. It offers no guidance for prescribing conduct. Indeed, the shortcoming of the harm principle is that while it offers some clarity about what not to do, it does so at the price of being unable to tell us what to do.

To partially remedy this deficiency, we turn next to explore three strategies for action that have traditionally offered guidance in *prescribing* or *recommending* conduct as both wise and desirable: deontological, utilitarian, and command theories. What does it mean to say that some conduct is *right*? Each of these strategies recommends a way to distinguish right from wrong conduct. The deontologist insists that an action is right if it is in accord with an appeal to a principle that will withstand the test of universalizeability; if some action is the kind that everyone, in the same general situation, agrees ought to be done then it is judged to be right action. The deontologist never considers the consequences of an action as the moral ground for his/her decision of its morality; the right thing should be done without regard to assessed consequences. In this sense, the deontologist argues that the rightness of conduct is in accord with duty, or obligation. Our sense of obligation arises when we come to be aware that something or other should be done. We create a maxim or rule for action, and if that maxim proves to be capable of being universalized, that everyone in the same general situation ought to do that thing, then it is the right thing to do, a moral law. The utilitarian objects to the simple appeal to a universalizeable principle, insisting instead that only by appeal to anticipated consequences can right from wrong be distinguished. The utilitarian objects that the well-intentioned action, appealing to lofty principles, is not right if the suffering that it produces outweighs the happiness that would have likely been produced by another course of action. An action is right, according to the utilitarian, if it produces the greater good for the greater number of people. Thus, the utilitarian endorses means-ends reasoning; the utilitarian is a consequentialist and calculates the right course of action by appeal to reckoning the likelihood that better consequences will result for more people. Thirdly, the command theorist disputes both the deontologist and utilitarian. The command theorist, usually the orthodox religious person, insists that right and wrong can only be distinguished by appeal to the commandments of our creator who has made morality by willing it to be so. Any other effort to identify right and wrong proves, ultimately, to be merely arbitrary and capricious. The right thing to do, says the command theorist, is whatever God commands, either in scripture or through some other kind of divine revelation. By examining these three strategies, our sense of the complexities that challenge our interpretation of the harm principle is enhanced. For it is the harm principle that proves to be the liberty-limiting principle that guides our recommendation of constraints, and hence the interference for individuals to achieve the happiness that we granted each person self-interestedly pursues.

Finally, in Section I, we make concrete the ideal of constraints by focusing on the question: What is the appropriate social response to those who violate the harm principle? The familiar response seems to be: *punish* those who harm others. Our moral problem is to see if we can find a fitting answer to the question: "Do two wrongs make a right?" Here's the problem. If we agree that harming others is, ordinarily, a bad thing since harming others makes them worse off than they were before, and we agree that, all things being equal, it is not a good idea to make others worse off than they were before because such actions clearly set back one's self-interest, then we will need a moral defense of the institution of punishment. This is because punishment requires the infliction of harm, and harm makes others worse off than they were before. Thus, we need a persuasive argument that shows why we should permit the state to engage in the very same (harmful) conduct that we declared impermissible in the first place. To justify the institutionalization of punishment we must show that the familiar arguments against harming others can be overridden. We consider two arguments, each of which displays a different strategy to override the usual prohibition of the harm principle, a deontological and utilitarian defense. And in this way, the readers have a chance to discover under what conditions liberty-limiting constraints may be defended against those impulses to perform certain kinds of conduct, and further, precisely what kinds of argument and strategies are adequate for such a defense. By reflecting on these issues, it is anticipated that the readers will discover more deeply both their own positions and the reasons that compel them to defend their views.

Section II is aimed to *test* the methodologies and theses introduced in the first section. We examine the *Morality of Killing* and investigate both non-human animal killing and human killing in the cases of abortion, infanticide, euthanasia, suicide, and capital punishment. In each case, we test the harm principle and its limits. We challenge both the liberal and conservative interpretations of the harm principle by contrasting the objections against harming others with comparable claims about harming one's self. In this way, the readers have the chance to reflect upon and review earlier positions on the harm principle and the appropriateness of liberty-limiting constraints on conduct.

The analysis proceeds from the point of view that a "person" is a *domain* expressed in/by rights. The deprivation of a right is the deprivation of one's rightful domain; the deprivation of one's rightful domain is the deprivation of one's essential nature, and it is in this sense—the *wrongful* deprivation of one's essential nature—that we discover the central meaning of *immoral* conduct. Immoral conduct is an expression of gross disrespect. The *Volenti* maxim is central to each issue debated although it is not always clear who has the right of consent in conflicting cases. In each case, we are to inquire whether or not there is a violation of the harm principle and test the principle that where there is consent there is no wrongdoing, and hence no impermissible conduct. And if we still regard that something wrong has been committed or attempted, and yet consent is present, we must now wonder if there is some other compelling principle that is at play—that I discuss as "free-floating evils"—or rather that our moral sentiment is instead unfounded.

Our problem is deepened by forcing us to decide whether moral rights, that affirm our essential nature, are alienable or inalienable. That is, we are forced to decide whether or not one may forfeit a right and under what conditions. This is particularly difficult with regard to problems about the morality of killing. In order to make clear the range of conundrums, we look at abortion, infanticide, euthanasia, capital punishment, and suicide. We try to determine under what conditions the killing of human animals is not impermissible. This requires that we determine the conditions under which killing can or cannot be justified. The reader must determine whether or not there is a single strategy that can be applied to these diverse cases of killing or whether each of them is to be resolved by appeal to a distinct principle. By setting these dilemmas together the reader can determine if and how they are connected.

The reader is first challenged to reflect upon right-to-life issues by formulating policies concerning *rights* as they apply to non-human animals. It is interesting and significant to note that, for most of us, the time we have devoted to reflect on the permissibility of killing non-human animals is negligible in comparison to the time that we have agonized over and debated the problems of human killing. We must reflect upon why this so and be prepared to defend our views. This proves to be no easy task.

While many persons are horrified by cruelty to animals, many of those same persons assent to animal "testing" (torture?) for human medical purposes, and cheerfully eat meals consisting of animals. In both cases, we become accomplices to such killing, certainly, when we eat animal products, but also when we purchase products made from animals, and products whose safety is tested by means of experiments involving non-human animals, the further results of which are the harming and subsequent destruction of those animals. We all may have strong emotional feelings about animals, but our challenge is to develop a rational discourse in which persuasive arguments are advanced to defend our feelings and practices. To those who object that non-human animals do not and *should not* have rights since they cannot make a claim, demand those rights, or file a petition in a court to uphold them, we are at once reminded that the same can be said of the fetus, the infant, the comatose, and severely impaired human animals. Most people would not for a moment believe that they were not *entitled* to rights even if they were unable to make a claim, demand a right, or file a petition. The purpose of this discussion is not only to raise questions about how we behave and why but also to press ourselves to discover if we have thought through deeply interconnected issues concerning the permissibility of killing in cases about which many of us have powerful and emotionally charged feelings, such as abortion.

Our discussion and debate continues by turning to the domain of human killing. First of all, we examine the controversial matter of abortion. Here the reader must decide what conditions, if any, ought to stand in order to deny a woman's request to abort. The question for female readers is not "What would you elect to do or not do?" While I very much hope that female readers will wonder about just these things, our focus will be on a slightly different question: Are there good grounds to stand in the way of some woman who requests an abortion, and if so, what are they? In this sense, everyone is welcome to hold whatever moral positions seem right for them, and to them. No reasons are required, in my estimation, to justify your positions *for you.* But moral feeling is inadequate to stand in someone else's way and to recommend liberty-limiting principles to stop them from pursuing their selected course of action. And so, if your religious beliefs, your horoscope, your absolute acceptance of the prophecy of the Magic 8 Ball, sways you, you are welcome to hold whatever view on whatever grounds. But these grounds are insufficient, unsupportable, and uncompelling to stand in the way of someone else and instruct them about the right thing to do.

Some cases are initially more troubling than others, but we will look at many kinds of cases in order to see what principle of conduct seems applicable, and whether or not that conduct requires constraint. We begin with a hypothetical case concerning the right-to-life that seeks to helps us distinguish between biological and moral aspects of the issue. We consider the case of deciding which inhabitants on a distant planet have the right-to-life and on what grounds: Welcome to the Planet Zeldar. If none of the creatures on this planet in any way resembles any creature on Earth, by appeal to what condition(s) shall we determine which creatures, if any, have a serious right-to-life? What counts as a *moral* reason to decide the issue, one way or another?

With this broad framing of the moral issue introduced, we turn to the Supreme Court case, *Roe v. Wade,* to understand the current state of the legal debate. Then, we consider a range of hypothetical cases in order to test and deepen our understanding of the complexity of the issue: the case of the woman who becomes pregnant as a result of being raped, the expectant mother whose physical frailties place her life in danger if she attempts to carry the fetus to term, the woman who finds herself pregnant after carefully using birth control, and the woman who finds herself pregnant without having used birth control. Is abortion permissible in any or all of these cases and why? The question is not whether you support or endorse abortion; the question is whether you have any good and compelling reasons to proscribe that conduct for the woman who requests it.

No matter how liberal persons may be on the issue of abortion, very, very few seem to find permissible the termination or killing of a newborn, that is, the termination of the fetus after having been born: infanticide. What shall we do, then, in the case of severely defective newborns? Babies born without brains? Terminally ill newborns? How does the argument for or against active euthanasia work in these cases?

The issue of dealing with terminally ill newborns runs up against the general, and related issue, of euthanasia or "mercy-killing." Under what conditions shall we condone the practice of active as opposed to passive euthanasia. Passive euthanasia ordinarily involves the refrain from us or subsequent removal of life-support devices from the terminally ill. The permissibility of the practice is usually defended by an appeal to mercy. After a certain and irretrievable state of bodily decay or mental deterioration, some argue that there is no acceptable standard of life worth preserving. But, if mercy motivates the policy, can it not be argued that in some cases of terminal illness, active euthanasia indeed seems more merciful? A lethal injection administered at the request of a terminally ill 90-year-old grandmother, in excruciating pain, surely seems more merciful than insisting that her suffering be needlessly prolonged. If under such circumstances, should she request a lethal injection to end her hopeless suffering, what good reasons do we have to interfere, to stand in her way, and to insist that she may not proceed—or have another intercede on her behalf—in fulfilling her wish? If and when must her request be proscribed? According to current practice, sanctioned by the American Medical Association and most states' laws, active euthanasia is forbidden, while passive euthanasia is permissible. Is the policy consistent? Is it justifiable? How does the *Volenti* maxim affect this policy? How should it?

In summary, Section II again raises questions about our nature and identity, about our conduct and the appropriateness of constraints. In terms of the morality of killing, the moral meaning of being a person is further explored. Persons are those creatures with rights; perhaps the most fundamental right is the right-to-life. Which animals, or which living creatures in general, are entitled to be classified as *persons* and thus be entitled to the right-to-life? Under what conditions must we recognize the right-to-life? Under what conditions may that right be forfeited? Is the right-to-life, and hence the meaning of being a person, restricted to "humans"? What good reasons do we have to justify these positions?

Section III is aimed, again, to test afresh the methodologies and theses introduced in the first section. We examine *Sexual Morality* and investigate the cases of rape, marriage and monogamy, adultery, pornography, sodomy, and sexism and racism. In each case we try to test the harm principle and its application to determine which conduct deserves to be proscribed. We challenge both the liberal and conservative interpretations of the harm principle by contrasting our objections against harm to others with arguments supporting the imposition of liberty-limiting constraints in the cases of impersonal harm and harm to self.

We begin Section III by pursuing our discussions of conduct and constraint in terms of the domain of persons. We continue to accept the argument framework that persons are defined as domains expressed in/by rights. To deprive another person of a right is to deprive another person of his/her rightful domain. To deprive another person of his/her rightful domain is to deprive another person of their very nature. To deprive another person of his/her very nature *unjustly* is immoral. Thus, our point of departure offers a clarification on what counts as moral conduct through our understanding of immoral conduct. This perspective will prove useful throughout the remainder of the course; it is particularly instrumental in helping us distinguish right from wrong with respect to specific conduct—not just right and wrong for each of us, but moreover what is right and wrong when other's choose to engage in different choices quite their own. Central to every debate will be the *Volenti* maxim, both in regard to harms to self and to issues concerning constraint of impersonal harms. Is conduct that harms no one directly deserving of liberty-limiting constraints? You and I might choose not to engage in certain activities but are our reasons compelling to constrain others?

The specific conduct we examine is diverse. We begin by asking what is wrong with rape. I think that no one has trouble anymore understanding that there is something seriously wrong with rape. But not everyone agrees as to what is specifically wrong with it. We will try to work out conflicting views and their consequences. We then turn to examine marriage and monogamy. Marriage is the only contractual relation, in the English language at least, that cannot be abrogated by the parties who make it. Why does permission to dissolve the marriage contract rest with the State? Why is the State interested? If one takes the point of view that marriage is legalized intercourse tacitly interwoven into a social fabric whose strands include parenting and children, what good reasons are there for the institution? Because marriage, in the United States at least, is by definition, monogamous, we shall wonder about that necessary restriction. And we shall wonder what consequences might follow if the centrality of the nuclear family is not taken as an axiom for social systems.

In order to think this through further, we turn to investigate what is wrong with adultery. Since extramarital sexual conduct is so widespread in our social organization, it behooves us to consider the good reasons that may be proposed for legislating conduct that makes so many citizens violators of the marriage vows and law. We shall see how our answers to these moral dilemmas accord with the positions developed in the first section of the course.

The next topics of specific conduct we address are pornography and, utilizing recent Supreme Court decisions, sodomy. In both cases, we are not interested in debating whether such conduct is either wise or desirable. The discussion focuses exclusively upon the question of whether or not we ought to constrain such practices, whether in ourselves or others. We will follow the general strategy here, as elsewhere, of formulating a "harm" principle. Where a violation of that principle can be shown—which is another way of stating that *someone* has been *unjustly* deprived of his/her rightful domain, and thus the conduct is immoral—restraint or interference with the conduct of others may be permissible and even desirable. Our problem is to determine where, when, how, and to whom, the harm has been perpetrated. Based on fact finding, remedial procedures can be outlined.

If pornography entails written, visual, or audible depictions of sexual conduct whose overwhelming purpose is to excite sexual impulses, and if the Supreme Court's decisions on sodomy concern the permissibility of private consensual sexual conduct between adults, our task is not to determine whether we should recommend against—proscribe—such practices. Our concern is merely to determine if, when, and by virtue of what good reasons, we ought to stand in the way of others and object to and prosecute them for making decisions about the most intimate kinds of personal conduct. Clearly, an attempt to constrain the consensual behavior of others on the grounds that such behavior seems disgusting and repulsive is surely, by itself, an unacceptable reason. It's a good enough reason for each of us who feels that way not to do it, but is that revulsion adequate to proscribe the conduct of others? Let's see if we can make this point more clearly.

Let's say I despise eating snails. I find the eating of them to be loathsome. That is surely a good enough reason for me to refrain from eating them. But before I stand in your way and tell you not to eat them, I must have a better reason than that I am disgusted by them. If certain kinds of sexual conduct are found by you to be revolting, then by all means refrain from those practices. But before standing in someone's way and constraining them from those private, consensual adult activities, a better reason than personal offense must be given. Of course, if it can be shown that other kinds of harm are engendered, then serious objections might well be raised. But, note, this is a different kind of argument and, again, allows us to test the *Volenti* maxim and the formulation of free-floating evils.

We then turn to issues concerning racism and sexism. We investigate what is wrong with such practices, making every effort to compare and contrast the social activities associated with them.

B. NAVIGATING A MORAL PATH BETWEEN TWO UNACCEPTABLE EXTREMES

The orientation of this investigation into moral reasoning is not prescriptive. It is not our objective to recommend certain conduct as wise or desirable. The reader will not be advised of the "right" thing to do. There are two important reasons for this. First of all, we operate under the presumption that there are no simple, absolute answers to moral dilemmas. There are no simple "do's" and "don'ts." Moral decisions are always made with regard to the specific details of a circumstance in question, and since the details invariably differ from circumstance to circumstance, no absolute answers can be soundly arrived at in advance. Secondly, we offer no particular prescriptions for specific conduct; we are concerned not with recommending certain practices but rather raising the question, "Under what conditions ought we to constrain conduct, whether our own or that of others?" This proscriptive strategy calls for further comment.

Having supposed that there are no absolute answers to moral dilemmas, by which I mean that specific solutions to moral issues cannot be made in advance, as if in a vacuum, but always with regard to the specific details of circumstances, then how can we think about moral decisions at all? We undertake the task of navigating a course midway between two unacceptable extremes. On the one hand, absolute moral answers are rejected; on the other, we must avoid the consequence of being left with the position that "anything goes."

Absolute Answers vs. "Anything Goes" Relativism

Many persons have held the view that if there are not absolute answers, there can be no answers at all. If there are no moral "absolutes," then every decision is merely an individual's opinion, and since it is generally supposed that one person's opinion is not inherently superior to any other's, then there can be no meaningful constraints on conduct. The moral absolutist wants to argue for everything or nothing, and we reject that position as a starting premise. However, it is clear that we do not succumb to a doctrine of "moral relativism" that undermines the meaningfulness of moral restraint. Thus, one way of describing the difficulty here is to take on the task of navigating a course between these two extremes. Rejecting moral absolutes, we at once reject the "anything goes" of an extreme moral relativism. Our problem is to determine how meaningful standards are possible in a world so conceived.

C. THE IDEA OF RATIONAL DISCOURSE AND THE PRIVILEGE OF DOUBT

In order to proceed with this general task, we shall adopt a strategy for approaching moral issues. We will call this strategy *rational discourse* or *rational argumentation* and its distinguishing feature is its form. We shall distinguish:

(i) a position or thesis for which we intend to argue: WHAT

(ii) the reason(s) for holding that position: WHY

This strategy is indispensable to coherent and productive discussion. To hold a position or opinion without being able to produce the reason(s) for subscribing to that position is unacceptable for our purposes. Equally unacceptable is to hold an opinion for reasons irrelevant to the position in question. We seek to promote rational discourse. That means that whenever a position is advanced, it will be necessary to defend or justify that position with reasons. To insist upon an opinion without reasons brings a meaningful and rational discourse to an abrupt halt. We will then be left with something of a garden-party conversation where everyone presents thoughts and feelings, and no constructive and thoughtful disagreement can proceed. The central question "Who am I?" is fundamental to answering moral dilemmas; and the strategy of steering a course, in answering these moral challenges, between absolute standards and no standards at all will be achieved through the technique of rational discourse that requires that we distinguish between opinions/positions, on the one hand, and reasons for holding those opinions, on the other.

Rational discourse involves the thoughtful strategy of learning how to justify your moral positions with adequate reasons, engaging in a debate with others, and yourself, as to precisely what reasons are sufficient to defend your opinions.

This book offers an opportunity to have the *privilege of doubt* as serious questions are raised about self-identity and conduct. Each reader brings with him/her a host of opinions, many of which have not been submitted to careful scrutiny. Each of us carries "received" opinions from parents, teachers, clergy, friends, television, internet, social media and so on. Each reader is invited to submit that wide assortment of views to the most careful re-examination. It is not necessary to abandon any of these views, but it will be salutary to critically examine them before returning them to the intellectual repository in which they reside. It is advisable to replace opinions that cannot be defended with more adequate positions that are better able to be defended. And it should be kept in mind that all of these views, new or old, are always capable of being tested by new challenges, and new experiences, which call into question the adequacy of our moral stances.

D. SOME REFLECTIONS ON REFLECTING ON SELF-IDENTITY

"Who am I?" There are many ways to answer this question. A response would largely depend upon the context in which a person were asked. If one is being interviewed as a prospective candidate for an advanced degree at a university, one's response would be one thing. If one were an applicant for some job or other, the answer would no doubt differ. If a policeman investigating a crime asks a person who they are, again, the response would bear little resemblance to the one proposed to a

15

prospective employer. And if a date asks the same question, the answer would be very different indeed. In all of these cases, a person's response to the general question "Who am I?" would be more or less distinct. What does this suggest about our nature?

We begin with the supposition that human identity is multifold and multifaceted. A person is a complex set of characteristics, activities, dispositions, and so on. Our identity is different in different contexts. In each context the story we tell about who we are is different, and that is not, ordinarily, because we are confused about our own personal identity. Identity is a relation and thus we have as many different identities as we have relations. Invariably, however, there is a web of connections that holds together these divergent stories, a web which connects these multifarious strands. Let's investigate this claim more closely.

We are commonly asked, and in many different ways, to account for ourselves. At a social event, someone may start up a conversation in which you are asked, however vaguely, to identify yourself. You might say "I am from Kalamazoo, Michigan, and my dad does this, and my mother does that, and I have so many brothers and sisters, and I went to a certain high school." You might respond differently. You might say "My name is such and such, and I am a sophomore, and I major in English." Or, again, you might say "I'm a person who likes to play tennis, and go to the theater, and I like to eat spicy food," and other such things. In each case, you identify yourself by a description; you are a set of stories. You repeat these stories, and often, to each and every person who in their different ways asks you to account for yourself.

Granting the variety of kinds of stories we tell in the process of identifying ourselves, readers shall seek to perfect a certain kind of storytelling. The story is very specific, inasmuch as it applies to each person, and yet very general, inasmuch as it also applies to everyone. Just what sort of story is it? The answer to the question "Who am I?" which we shall pursue is first proposed as "I am a human being." I am a *homo sapiens*. I am a certain kind of animal, distinguishable from other kinds of animals. And despite the fact that each of us has a different personal history, it may be truly said that we are all human beings. The first section of the book tries to show that this framing of our task is anything but vacuous, that although the initial answer to our question of self-identity sounds very general, it proves to be significant, informative and, curiously enough, intimately personal.

Some views are going to be put forth as convincingly as possible. But, the reader must be on guard at all times, critically scrutinizing the views expounded with no less care than the introspection of your own. The reader need not accept the points of view advanced here; the reader who deeply understands will be capable of formulating rational arguments. The reader is then invited to criticize those views.

Let the reader also be warned that many find this kind of thinking particularly strange at the outset. An investigation of the question "Who am I?" immediately reveals the peculiarity of the enterprise. This is a feature of all self-investigation or introspection. The object of our inquiry is the human mind, and yet the tool we are employing for this investigation is at once the object into which we are inquiring. The mind we are investigating is at once the instrument doing the investigation. And we must be cognizant that the process of uncovering human identity, the manner of investigation, will be decisive in determining the identity of the object we pursue.

Let the thesis be stated right from this very first chapter that human beings are the creatures who are self-investigating. Humans, by their very nature, want to know, and find happiness or satisfaction in both the pursuit and acquisition of this sort of knowing. And if that thesis is sound, then by engaging in such inquiries and discussions, we fulfill our very nature, by—as curiously as it sounds—coming to be what we are. If human beings are fundamentally intellectual and moral creatures—thinking creatures—then by engaging in such thinking activities we affirm our very nature. We come to realize ourselves. And if self-realization, or affirming one's own essential nature, is fulfilling or satisfying, then despite the difficulties, the activity will prove to be deeply rewarding; it ought to make us happy. The reader may thus anticipate this investigation to be a great deal of fun.

Section I: Week 1: Introduction

Name_____ TA _____

Section #_____

1) In your opinion, what is involved in the study of Philosophy?

2) In your opinion, what is involved in the study of Ethics?

3) Do you already have an ethical system? If so, what is that system, and how did you come to believe in it?

Chapter 2

Self-Identity and Rational Self-Interest

A. THE IDEA OF RATIONAL SELF-INTEREST

Any attempt to formulate a moral theory concerning conduct requires, first of all, a conception of a self, an adequate answer to the question: Who am I? We must determine, first of all, who we are, the kind of creatures that we are, in order to adequately begin to assess what kinds of conduct are unacceptable, and why.

Unfortunately, this is not an easy task. This question cannot be adequately answered in one chapter, or perhaps even a dozen. Nevertheless, we can begin on that road to self-discovery and continue our reflection throughout, keeping in mind the challenge that any penetrating understanding about conduct, and any adequate moral theory, requires first of all a deep understanding of human nature.

Let us begin with the hypothesis that we are fundamentally self-interested creatures, and that one profitable approach to an analysis of human behavior can begin with the supposition of *Rational Self-Interest*: we are motivated to act in such a way that we seek to maximize our own (self) interests. The "rational" ingredient finds expression in the following sense: when given a choice between, let's say, two courses of action, 'A' and 'B', all things being equal, we, the agents or actors, are naturally inclined to choose the one alternative that we believe will best promote our interests. It is, of course, true that we may choose 'A' and then find ourselves disappointed afterwards. There is nothing to guarantee that our choice will, in fact, maximize our own interests. What the theory claims is only that we believe 'A' to offer us the better chance for the fulfillment of our interests when we choose it.

To illustrate this point, let's say that we have a choice for employment, or a choice for a date, or any other choice of action for that matter: 'A' or 'B'. Each of us, then, reflects on each opportunity. We perform a kind of calculation in assessing each—sometimes called the "hedonic calculus"—adding up the advantages and disadvantages of each choice, so far as we are able. At the end of the calculation, we make a decision, let's say choosing 'A' over 'B'. In that case, we have decided that job 'A' or date 'A' offers us the likelihood of a better experience (admitting, of course, that each of us may define "better" differently). We then accept the job or go out on the date. Afterwards, we may judge that the job or date was not the "better" experience that we hoped it would be. We might have misassessed details about the job, its requirements, its benefits, and so on, or even how important some factors were in our choice (for instance, how far the office was from our home in rush-hour traffic, or the personality of our supervisors, etc.), or even misevaluated our own interests, perhaps discovering that certain kinds of work were really not as fulfilling as we supposed. So also for the date. We may have discovered that we misappraised the person we felt attracted to, or our own needs and desires. In all cases, the theory in no way guarantees the satisfaction of our interests; it only declares that our choices, all things being equal, reflect our best guess about what we believe to advance our self-interests.

Even if we hold that human activities, like those of other animals, are broadly motivated by self-interest, there are several variations in which this theory may be expressed. Let us consider a few:

Hedonistic Theory (or Psychological Egoism): The best course of action is the one that leads to the agent's greatest happiness.

Desire-Fulfillment Theory: The best course of action is the one that leads to the fulfillment of the agent's desires throughout the whole life.

Objective List Theory: The best course of action is the one that leads to the realization of as many good things as possible and the suffering of as few bad things as possible (as if we could clearly distinguish between experiences so as to be sure what things were good and what things were bad).

These few examples in no way pretend to exhaust the range of possible theories that more particularly express our self-interested behavior. The examples are intended to make the point that when we reflect on our naturally self-interested inclinations to action, there are many subtle (and not so subtle) variations that come into play when we try to express more precisely the patterns exhibited by our behavior. Of the three variations given above, happiness and pleasure would seem to constitute a central part of our self-interest, and this is because happiness and pleasure, as opposed to misery and pain, seem to be central to our experience when life goes as well as possible for us. And it is the aim of our self-interested behavior for life to go as well as possible for us.

But to claim that it is in all of our interests that "life goes as well as possible" in no way stipulates the particular ingredients that constitute such an experience. For surely, there may be as many conceptions of happiness and pleasure as there are readers of this book. So, how is it possible to discuss, in general, human nature and conduct given the facts of each person's differences?

What kind of a discourse makes it possible to speak of everyone's behavior in *general* while granting everyone's choices to be different *in specifics*? We shall try to achieve this general analysis by advancing our theory of self-interest in terms of a general theory of happiness. Let us formulate an argument. Each person, of course, will test whether the analysis illuminates a central aspect of his/her experience. And in this, the confirmation or refutation of the theory consists.

The Happiness Argument

Everyone desires to be happy. Purposeful actions result from desires and those desires express a wish, the fulfillment of which is intended to produce happiness. Now, it so happens that every desire, when it is fulfilled, does not produce the desired or intended happiness. So let us distinguish between two kinds of desire:

(i) mere *wants*, the fulfillment of which does not produce the intended happiness, and

(ii) genuine *needs*, which, because these desires are directed toward something substantial in me, do produce the intended happiness when they are fulfilled.

If everyone desires to be happy and acts in order to produce this happiness, then everyone desires that not all of his/her desires will be satisfied. If some desires, when fulfilled, produce the intended happiness while others do not, then evidently what we really desire is to have all of our needs (= genuine desires) satisfied, but not all of our wants (= mere desires). What we really desire is what we really need and not what we merely want. And this is another way of affirming that what we genuinely desire is happiness.

Difficulties arise when we try to distinguish between these two kinds of desire: (i) mere wants, and (ii) genuine needs. Question: What do I really desire? Answer: I really desire *what I really need*. We must now turn to consider what constitutes real needs thereby securing a strategy for action in order to achieve the *happiness* that we agreed everyone desires.

23

Let's try this reasoning again. We began by supposing that human beings desire to be happy. We engage in actions when we become conscious that there is something we desire. The actions are intended to fulfill that desire and by fulfilling that desire we expect to become happy, or at least happier than we were before we engaged in the action. Thus, why do we act? Because there is something that we desire; we are conscious that something is missing or lacking and we believe that by attaining that end we will achieve happiness. The problem arises here when it becomes clear that although the general intention of all our actions is to secure satisfaction or happiness, not every desire, when fulfilled, produces satisfaction or happiness. In these cases, we often feel regret. We believed that acting in a certain way would produce satisfaction but in the case of mere wants, we find ourselves unhappy—or at least not fully happy—with the result of our successful action. That is, we find ourselves dissatisfied. But because we agreed that everyone really desires to be happy and that fulfilling all desires does not produce the intended happiness, then we must admit that what we really desire is *not* to have *all* of our desires fulfilled but only those which will produce the intended satisfaction. The desires which will produce happiness we call needs, as opposed to those desires which don't produce happiness which we call wants. Our new strategy is to act, whenever possible, only on those desires which are genuine needs. The difficulty is to determine within the structure of desire how to distinguish genuine needs from mere wants. This is a formidable task. Indeed, it is a task that properly requires guidance from a psychologist and sociologist and is beyond the scope of this book. However, the converse task is within our grasp. Whereas the specific things we truly need are difficult to delineate, we can instead try to consider the general range of things that we do NOT need. Each and every action that produces a result that we do NOT need is an action that fails to contribute to our interest or that defeats our interests. In future reflection, we can pass over all of those actions that fail to contribute to our "real" interests; what will concern us primarily is the range of actions that positively defeat our interests. We will try to identify one and all such actions in terms of the *Harm Principle* and we will discuss that shortly.

For the time being, we should note that our approach to action is end-oriented. This is another way of introducing a consequential theory of human conduct. All human actions are assessed in terms of the ends or consequences that they intend to produce and, specifically in terms of maximizing the happiness of the agent or actor. We begin this way because it seems *prima facie* obvious and acceptable, but later we shall challenge this strategy. The approach we begin with is generally known as *utilitarian* and later it will be challenged by objections from an approach called *deontological*. The deontological strategy begins with the supposition that human conduct ought not be assessed, first and foremost, in terms of "ends," but rather from "duty"; that is, human beings affirm their moral agency by pursuing acts because they *ought* to be done irrespective of consequences. The utilitarian insists that all actions can be meaningfully assessed only and ultimately with regard to the happiness they can be expected to produce. Usually, however, the utilitarian insists that happiness is not measured individually, but rather in terms of the greatest good for the greatest number of persons. We shall pursue these conflicting strategies later. For the time being, it is more useful to this introductory stage to follow through on a consequentialist strategy.

Connected with this issue is the difficulty of stating clearly what "happiness" or "satisfaction" is. Is happiness a feeling that results from achieving a certain end or is it more properly identified with a quality of activity? For example, sometimes people are happiest in goal-directed actions but when they achieve the desired goal, they cease to be happy. In dating relations, many people report that the pursuit or chase is fun, exciting or, in a word, a happy experience, but the happiness seems to dissipate when the desired person is "caught." In such cases, happiness seems to be identified more closely with a quality of experience in activity as opposed to the achievement of some goal through the action.

At this stage of the discussion, we grant that there are as many different definitions of happiness as there are readers of this book. What is relevant to this argument is that however each person defines happiness, it is the obscure object of desire that motivates each person's actions. One person may desire a high paying job, another desires ice cream and cake, still another desires a wonderful lover and so on. But in each and every case, the general object of our desire is happiness. How can we account for this commonly pursued strategy?

In the next chapter, a theory will be put forth that attempts to account for our strategies. For now, we will raise objections to this analysis: What reasonable objections should be raised to the thesis of rational self-interest?

B. OBJECTIONS TO THE THEORY OF RATIONAL SELF-INTEREST: ALTRUISM

Objections can be raised against the thesis of rational self-interest. Central among those objections might be some version of the doctrine of *altruism*. The thesis of rational self-interest maintains that everyone always acts, when given the choice, according to their own assessment of what is in their best interest. Some contend that all *self-interested* action must also be *selfish,* and since some acts seem to be genuinely unselfish, then the general theory of self-interest must be wrong.

Altruism is the principle or practice of selfless concern for the welfare of others, a disinterested and selfless concern for the well-being of others. It offers a vision that we can be motivated to act for purely selfless reasons, to extend care to others without any personal rewards for doing so. To act with the prospect of any personal reward or benefit undermines the claim that we have acted altruistically.

Altruism is not simply a way to describe human motivations when we act but is part of a totalizing, moral world view. Altruism is sometimes identified with acts of kindness, good will, and respect for others—and so they may be. But more precisely, the altruist holds that only acts done for the exclusive sake of others' benefit are good; any actions done for one's own sake are not. Thus, one way to see the theoretical foundation of altruism is to consider that we have no right to exist for our own sake but only to be of service to others. Seen in this light, self-sacrifice is our highest virtue for it is our duty, the very meaning of our being. By acting altruistically, we affirm our human nature, our meaning for being.

The altruist wants to maintain not only that there are genuinely selfless acts broadly motivated by unselfish motives but moreover that moral life truly begins only with such unselfish acts. Thus, challenged by altruistic objections, the proponents of rational self-interest must address two main points: (i) Are all actions that are motivated by self-interest necessarily selfish? and (ii) If moral life requires unselfish acts and all human acts are motivated by self-interest, is "morality" even possible?

One reply by proponents of rational self-interest is to introduce an important distinction between two kinds of self-interest: (a) *Un*enlightened, and (b) Enlightened.

First of all, it certainly seems true that most of our daily decisions are both self-interested and selfish. For most of us, our choices of orange juice over grapefruit juice, the white shirt over the blue shirt, to mow the lawn today over mowing tomorrow, are both self-interested and selfish. These choices are expressions of our own preferences and do not, by themselves, suggest objectionable behavior to the altruist. Nor does the theory of rational self-interest fail to realize that some persons extend their self-interested choices narrowly into other domains justifiably identifying themselves as selfish persons. Such persons would exhibit behavior that might be called self-interested but *Unenlightened*.

Secondly, the version of this theory that will provisionally embrace is one that shares a similar proclivity with the altruist's, namely, in understanding the importance of care or concern for *The Other* (i.e. for the time being, I mean "others" in general; next chapter I shall develop this concept). Unlike the central tenet of altruism, the theory of rational self-interest maintains that all human actions are fundamentally rooted in self-interest. We can outgrow mere selfishness when we recognize that

The Other is genuinely a part of our deepest interest because we share a world together. Nevertheless, our motivations are always rooted in self-interested calculations. However, as a person grows and matures, a person discovers that it is genuinely in his/her interest to care for The Other, to include concern for others as fundamental to his/her own calculation of self-interest. This is the ideal of *Enlightened Self-Interest*. Let's consider an example in order to make the point clearer.

Take the case of someone like Mother Teresa, the well-known Nobel Prize winner for Peace, who devoted her whole life to the difficult and largely thankless task of helping the world's neediest and most destitute persons. Mother Teresa's behavior would seem to be not only emblematic of the ideal of selflessness but also a counter-example to the thesis of rational self-interest. After all, how can one account for loving care extended to colonies of lepers, the diseased and despairing, on the supposition that individuals are motivated to secure their own self-interests?

Proponents of rational self-interest reject the altruist's description of genuinely and exclusively selfless action, while nevertheless applauding Mother Teresa for extraordinary and unselfish conduct. The thesis of self-interest insists that everyone is always motivated to act by self-interest, hence Mother Teresa's actions were also expressions of her self-interestedness. But how shall we understand this? Mother Teresa found tremendous self-satisfaction in the actions that she pursued and found worthy; had she not, she never would have pursued these actions. On this account, Mother Teresa's general strategy was identical with that of everyone else. BUT, the significant difference in her distinguished and laudable behavior was the degree to which her conduct was "Other" oriented. She, like everyone else, gained satisfaction pursuing those things most important to her but she recognized that The Other was a fundamental ingredient in her own assessment of self-interest. Her strategy commands our greatest admiration and respect. She discovered the meaning of *Enlightened Self-Interest;* she learned to find her deepest satisfaction in the satisfaction of Others. When a person discovers happiness by helping others, life offers endless opportunities for happiness. But, from the perspective of the theory of rational self-interest, her behavior was no less self-interested for it.

Thus, this reply by proponents of rational self-interest to the proponents of altruism, really seeks to challenge the very possibility of truly altruistic acts. The objection is that an altruistic act requires no personal reward extrinsic or intrinsic. Thus, no acts of sacrifice or sharing can count as genuinely altruistic so long as the actor gains an extrinsic reward such as some benefit as the motivating ground for the act, or any intrinsic reward, including the personal gratification for behaving selflessly. The proponents of rational self-interest claim that in cases such as Mother Teresa, the actor receives

27

deep gratification for selfless acts, and consequently, the actor "benefits" personally from such acts, and thus vitiates the claim that the acts are truly altruistic. To decide this important matter, we must decide whether such intrinsic rewards qualify as "benefits," hence personal gain, and hence the fulfillment of the kind of self-interest that undermines the claims of altruism. The proponents of rational self-interest claim it does.

When one gains deep satisfaction from The Other's satisfaction, the world bursts forth as a field that offers the prospect for unlimited happiness—because everyone delights in the realization that the actions of others are compatibly motivated to bring to fruition their own self-interests as well.

Another way to think about this idea is to see Enlightened self-interest as a cooperative strategy. In the next chapter, we will explore friendship and love as two strategies to promote rational self-interest. There, genuine friendship and love are cooperative activities that allow an individual to promote his/her self-interest in the mutual process of promoting the interests of the Other simultaneously. So, let it be emphasized that enlightened self-interest expresses cooperative actions that while fostering conditions for one's own happiness fosters also the interests of the Other at the same time.

The altruist wants to insist that other-oriented behavior is requisite for moral life—actions that show a selfless care for the welfare of others. The thesis of rational self-interest, introduced here, shares a similar disposition. Other-oriented actions that display a recognition and respect for Others and express care and concern for them are essential to an understanding of moral life. The self-interested thesis presumes that all actions are motivated by self-interest whether the self-conception is enlightened or *un*enlightened. *The crucial point to focus on is not self-interest but rather the kind of self in which we are interested.* As we grow, we discover ever more clearly that we live in a shared world and that our own experience and happiness is complexly interwoven with the lives of Others. We care for Others as an enlightened expression of our mature self-interest—because our own happiness depends upon it—but we do not cease to be self-interested on that account.

Chapter 3

Self-Identity and Alienation

A. SELF-INTEREST AND THE OTHER: THE OTHER HOLDS THE KEY TO WHO I AM

So far, the argument has proposed the claim that all of our actions are motivated by our assessment of self-interest. If we believe that one course of action will more likely produce a greater satisfaction of our interests, all things being equal, then we naturally choose that course of action. Why is this so? The answer we have so far proposed is that such a course of action is deemed more likely to produce happiness and everyone desires to be happy.

If we compare and contrast experiences of happiness can we find a common ingredient in them? Do all of our "happy" experiences share some factor that allow us to describe our state of feeling as "happy" despite the differences in circumstances? Let me ask the same question in slightly different ways: What does it *feel* like when you have successfully completed a big project, such as graduating from high school? What does it *feel* like when you have had an exceptionally delicious meal? What does it *feel* like when you have seen the best movie ever? The best vacation ever with your best friends? When you just had the best date ever? Do all these *feelings* of happiness have something in common? Do they share the same structure of feeling? In this chapter we shall consider and explore the hypothesis that they do. All of our feelings of happiness share the same common structure: *the overcoming of alienation.* In the course of this chapter we shall connect the experience of happiness, as the goal of all our actions, with the overcoming of alienation.

What we now propose to offer is an account of human nature knowing full well that this is only one way of describing our experience. We do not pretend that this way of illuminating our behavior is exclusive;

surely, there are other ways to account for our dispositions, but I offer it as one way of helping to make sense of our self-interested motivations, to help make clearer what sort of human nature might be presupposed by it.

Our thesis begins with the claim that *The Other holds the key to who I am*. What we are trying to show is that one way we identify ourselves is in terms of descriptive stories—narrative stories—that we tell about ourselves. An important constraint on that kind of storytelling is our understanding, from past experiences, of the reaction of others when we tell them our stories. In ways both gross and subtle, each one of us detects a reaction from others about the way we try to describe ourselves, portrait ourselves, and the degree to which they accept or reject our self-descriptions. In this important sense, who I am is conveyed in a descriptive story, and that story has been regulated by my own assessment of who The Other will allow me to be. It is in this respect that "The Other holds the key to who I am."

As a reader, then, what would it be like to describe *yourself* now. You might begin by saying things like: My name is so-and-so, I live in such and such a town, my major field of study is this, or the kind of work I do is that, and so on. And this sort of description is perfectly appropriate on many occasions. But what this sort of descriptive story amounts to is a narrative of the specific features that *distinguish you from everyone else*. For our purposes, however, I would like to help us start a narrative story that *identifies us all together*, rather than separates us, a story that could be told truly of each and every one of us, a story that we share in common.

I now ask you to adopt a different stance, both unusual and more general than the familiar one to which you have grown accustomed. The next time somebody asks you "Who are you?" (in whatever specific manner the question is actually phrased), you might reply "I am a not-This." What will be the result? The reaction might be anything from a strange look to utter dismay. But one way that we can all describe our experience is to say that we are "not-This" and we are "not-That." Let us develop this idea.

If we were standing outside, we could say that we are not-That building, we are not-That tree, not-That cloud, and so on. It would not take us long to realize that there are an infinite number of things which we are not. This is not the only way to describe ourselves, of course, but we *could* describe ourselves in this way. Unlike the familiar narrative story that . . . I come from this town and I study that subject and I like these foods and have those hobbies . . . all of which set me off and apart from everyone else, this narrative story can be told by everyone and provides a way of seeing our identities as sharing something in common. Fundamentally, one and all of us are a not-This. But what does it mean to be a not-This?

In all of these ways, anything and everything that reminds us of what we are not—not-This, not-That—I shall call *The Other*. Who is The Other? The Other is anything and everything that can say "no" to me, anything and everything that—for me—is a not-This, and that reminds me that I am limited and restricted.

Each of us can envision the world in terms of a series of obstacles. These challenges remind us that we are limited or restricted. Fundamentally, we understand ourselves negatively. By "negatively" I mean that we can understand ourselves as limited, imperfect creatures who overcome these 'nots' as we grow. Thus, on this account, we come to grasp our self-identity as descriptions, narrative stories, that convey a certain range of experience the limits of which are those points where the world says "no" or we believe the world will say "no."

In many ways, when we encounter The Other as the world of many tasks and obstacles, we often expect it to say "yes," and often it does. But, often enough, we encounter our world and it says "no." The car won't start; The Other has just said "no." It's raining on the day we've planned a picnic; The Other said "no." Your boss denies you a raise that you asked for; The Other just said "no." You've just been turned down for a date, you just missed the plane, the concert tickets ran out before you reached the box office; in all these ways you have encountered The Other, and The Other has said "no." Your desire has been thwarted. Each of us has an idea about how far we can engage The Other before we expect to hear "no." We have an idea of our range of personal ability, an idea of the limits of power we have as persons. This is another way of speaking of a person's sense of *self-confidence*. This self-confidence might be called one's *power-range*: how far one can interact with The Other before one thinks that The Other will say "no." How do we come to formulate that power-range?

A *person* arrives at a conception of his/her self-confidence by a complex operation of experience and reflection. We try out for the tennis team at school. If we make the team, our self-confidence is enhanced since The Other has said "yes." Next, we might enter a tournament to test our skills. At each stage of success, our self-confidence grows as we overcome the obstacles and challenges set by The Other(s). If there is a job we would like, we can apply for that job. If we are hired, our power-range—our sense of our own capability—is augmented. If we are promoted and advanced in responsibilities and benefits, our sense of self is commensurably increased. If the employer says "no" to our application, we might be more reluctant to apply the next time. If we lose early in the tennis tournament, we might be reluctant to enter another. If several potential dates turn us down, we might feel more insecure, less self-confident, and thereby more uneasy to ask out the next person whom we find interesting and attractive. The important and central point here is that *The Other holds the key to who I am*, for it is

31

The Other's "yes" or "no" to which we react that constitutes the fundamental ingredient for developing our narrative story, our description of ourselves.

B. SELF-INTEREST AND THE PROJECT OF OVERCOMING THE OTHERNESS OF THE OTHER

Now let us reintroduce self-interest into this discussion. If we have the opportunity to pursue a course of action that we believe offers a better prospect rather than a course of action we believe offers a worse prospect, would we choose, all things being equal, the better or the worse? We all naturally prefer the opportunity that we suppose offers something better. If we suppose that one employer offers a better job than another, or we suppose one entree at a restaurant offers a better taste treat than another, or one vacation package offers a better holiday experience than another, then surely we would be inclined to choose the "better" job, entree, holiday, whatever. The point is that whenever we have the prospect for something better, the prospect for something more fulfilling to our interests, we naturally prefer better over worse, more over less. But let us also be clear that we might choose one job opportunity over another and feel dissatisfied, we might choose one entrée over another (tasting the other entrée from our friend's plate) and conclude we chose the wrong alternative, but none of these familiar experiences challenge our statement of strategy. We are motivated to select whatever we judge to offer "better" over "worse" though we may mis-assess the alternatives, indeed, we may judge poorly. Nevertheless, our strategy is in no way compromised by what turns out to be faulty evaluation.

Now, if this is so we may ask how we might best account for it. Granting that we prefer opportunities for what we believe to be to our advantage, why do we prefer better over worse, more over less? Our theory offers the following sort of reply: We naturally prefer that which is in our own interests; we want to be happy and find happiness in the satisfaction of the self-interests that motivated our choice of action in the first place. Thus, whenever we have the opportunity to act in such a way that we believe it is in my/our own best interest, we are naturally inclined to pursue that course of action.

The thesis we are arguing is that the meaning of "better" is defined expressly in terms of maximizing what is my own appraisal of self-interest: if an experience is supposed to more significantly further my self-interest, then that experience is judged to be "better." Stated differently, the "better" experience is the one that enhances my self-interest, and the meaning of "self-interest" fundamentally reduces to happiness. This happiness is pleasurable but it is not simply pleasure. This happiness is a consequence of the experience of growth; it is the feeling we have when we grow. Growth, then, produces the feeling of satisfaction or happiness.

By "satisfaction," however, I do not mean merely a completed state. Rather, I mean an activity or quality of an activity. The purpose of every action, on this theory, is the realization of a desire; each desire is an expression of self-interest. When we have a desire what has happened is that we have become aware that something is lacking or missing in our lives; the desire is the mental activity that precedes our action to overcome that lack and find satisfaction. The desire may be for a meaningful job, or improved health, or simply something everyday such as something to eat for dinner this evening. Happiness is a realization of any desire, it is the realization of our self-interest but it is not merely a reflection of a specific accomplishment. *Happiness is an activity* or a quality of our experience that pervades the activity.

On this hypothesis, by contrast, unhappiness is suffering. It is the consciousness of the *Otherness* of The Other. Let us explore this idea. Unhappiness is dissatisfaction. When we desire something and are thereby conscious that something is lacking, we act in order to overcome that lacking; if The Other says "no," we fail to overcome that lacking, fail to satisfy what our self-interest directs us to accomplish and thus are painfully aware of our own limitations and inadequacies. We are, in failure, painfully aware of the otherness of The Other. We are, in failure, aware of that aspect of The Other that challenges us and can destroy us, psychologically, emotionally, and even physically. Our motivation is to *grow,* to overcome the *Otherness* of The Other, to gain satisfaction. Our success in overcoming the otherness of the other may be the successful action of a tennis player in winning a tournament, but it is *not* just adversarial. *Our happiness may result in the overcoming of otherness through cooperative and harmonious interaction with the Other.* And we shall explore these strategies further.

C. ALIENATION AND THE GROWTH-TO-HAPPINESS: THE *ONTOLOGICAL* THEORY

Another way to describe all our experiences is *to say* that each of us is a kind of expanding and growing energy. Having discovered that we are incomplete, un-whole, and unfulfilled, all human actions can be interpreted as attempts to overcome that incompleteness; all of our actions can be viewed as attempts to overcome obstacles and challenges. In a phrase, all human activity can be viewed as having as its purpose: overcoming of alienation through *growth*. Growth means the overcoming of these challenges, increasing our power-range, overcoming The Other. Indeed, it would be better and more precise to restate this last claim. Growth and happiness are not consequences of the overcoming of The Other as such but rather the overcoming of the *Otherness* of The Other, that is, the aspect of The Other that confronts us and reminds us that we are vulnerable, that we are a not-This, and hence becoming increasingly happy, whole, fulfilled. As we become more successful in our strategies for growth we naturally enjoy an invigorated self-confidence, more success in meeting one challenge after another.

The more we grow, the more we experience openness. We feel ourselves to be less insecure because our growth has rendered us less vulnerable. Whenever an experience makes us feel more confident, we experience ourselves as an expanding energy. It is this feeling of expansion that is characteristic of the experience of overcoming the *alien* nature of The Other, that aspect of The Other that causes us to feel insecure, vulnerable, threatened: The Other's *Otherness*.

Thus, according to this theory, the desire for happiness proves to be a desire for wholeness, completeness. In short, this means that human experience is constituted by the consciousness of being incomplete, cut off from that wholeness. And everything that we do, each and every action, according to this theory, attempts to make us whole. *The fundamental human condition is alienation. The human project is to grow, to overcome that alienated condition.*

The thesis just advanced is an *ontological* theory. The term "ontological" refers to an exploration of and an account of the *being* of things, the reality of things. Broadly speaking, ontology investigates terms such as being, existence, becoming, and reality, and various classifications of things that can be said to exist. Now some things are thought to be eternal things, and within this classification we can identify mathematical objects such as "triangles" and even abstract ideas such as "justice." We can classify non-eternal things such as plants and animals—things that come-and-go, live and die, things that perish. We can refer to the idea of a being we call "God," a being who exists eternally, never-changing, a being neither created nor capable of being destroyed. For our concerns, our ontological account is of the status of human *being*. The ontological part of our theory offers to show us our essential nature, the kind of being that we are. We are deficient, imperfect, mortal beings—beings who live only a short amount of time when viewed in the context of a universe billions of years old. Human lives can be viewed as activities that are motivated with the purpose of making ourselves complete, whole, and perfected. Stated differently, we are *alienated* creatures and each of our self-interested actions is calculated, consciously and unconsciously, to overcome our alienated condition.

D. FRIENDSHIP AND LOVE AS STRATEGIES TO OVERCOME ALIENATION: THE *INTEREST* IN SELF-INTEREST

Regardless of the activity undertaken, it seems largely uncontested that persons prefer to avoid *boredom*. No one likes to be bored. What shall we make of this obvious claim? We might gain better insight into boredom if, instead, we consider the state of experience opposite of boredom, the state that everyone seeks to embrace rather than avoid. What shall we call it, boredom's opposite? We might call it *interest*.

The experience of interest is one in which our attention is fully absorbed in an activity. When we are bored, our attention drifts; we become aware of other things around us, chores and appointments, irritations and distractions, momentary delights and amusements. But, when we are fully interested in the activity we are undertaking, we are remarkably unaware of countless distractions. The experience of interest is opposed to boredom and characterizes our *unalienated* experience. When we are interested we feel less alienated, less distanced from our world; we feel happier.

When are we interested? What ingredient characterizes all those experiences in which our interest is intense as opposed to scattered, and fragmented? Or, asked differently, what do interesting experiences have in common? One way to describe that common ingredient is to call it *growth*. Whenever we believe that we are gaining from an experience, whenever we believe that we are benefiting by paying attention, there we shall find an experience deserving to be called "growth."

Each activity that produces happiness reduces alienation, is an occasion for growth, and will maximize self-interest. In order to illustrate this ideal, let us turn to consider *friendship*, one powerful life-strategy to overcome alienation. But as we do, please note that overcoming alienation is not simply competition—one side winning only when the other side loses such as in an athletic contest, a football game, an Olympic race, the running of a marathon. Reflecting on friendship and love as ways we become whole and complete, shows that human interactions often enough produce deep happiness, shows that cooperation and congeniality may lead to harmonious accord. These blossoming friendships, and the many ways that love enters our lives, help us emphasize that overcoming alienation does not simply require that one wins while the other loses as we grow to completeness and the happiness of wholeness. Cooperation and harmonious interaction are powerful strategies to overcoming the *otherness* of The Other.

There are many different kinds of friendship. The relation we share with our parents may properly be characterized as friendship (or maybe not in some cases). With our acquaintances at the university or at work, we experience varying degrees of friendship. Certainly, we experience different levels of friendship. In each and every case, we might organize the degree of friendship in terms of the degree of *interest*, the degree to which the relation helps us overcome Otherness, overcome alienation; in each case, we can ask which relations help us to feel more whole and complete. We can ask which relations produce in us the experience of greater *growth*? Which produce greater *interest*? Thus, friendship can be seen as one of life's activities that serves the purpose of overcoming alienation, and thereby promoting our happiness.

Some of our friendships deepen and become more special than others. In some of these cases, friendship turns into love. For the moment, the reader is invited to reflect on "love" as the deepest degree of friendship, the deepest degree of interest. Let us, for the moment, consider the initial stages of being in love as *undivided interest*. As such, the experience offers the most complete, if only temporary, prospect for overcoming alienation. But let us examine the experience in greater detail.

We sometimes describe the experience as "falling in love." When we say that we have fallen in love, we often describe the experience in terms of the uniqueness of the individual for whom we care. Let's say 'A' loves 'B'.

According to our analysis of the theory of rational self-interest, what implications are there for our understanding of this friendship that has deepened into love?

As the friendship develops, we are accustomed to say that it may blossom into an experience of love. But whenever discussion turns to love, a topic so many consider central to any deep understanding of the nature of human experience, most feel rather at a loss to clearly articulate what it is they mean when they refer to it. We now turn to examine the nature of love, as another step in which friendship blossoms in our project of overcoming the otherness of The Other, of overcoming alienation, and hence promoting our own happiness.

First of all, if human activity is motivated principally by one's assessment of what is in one's own self-interest, falling in love, like any other activity, must be self-interested. We have to ask, then, if this means that all love is fundamentally selfish, and thus we return to the question of whether all self-interested acts reduce to selfishness. There is what we may call a romantic vision that love is not selfish. Love, like all other activities—on the theory of rational self-interest—is fundamentally self-interested. But it still remains for us to determine whether "self-interest" is extensionally identical with "selfish" in this case. For it might be that falling in love is always an expression of *un*enlightened self-interest. I have no doubt that the experience of falling in love for many people is by and large an experience of *selfish*-interest, but from this it does not follow that *all* (or most) experiences of love are selfish. But it may be the case and so this is for us to consider.

For the purposes of our discussion, let us consider the first powerful moments of falling in love, the hours, days, weeks, and perhaps months, when people express the feelings that they have. And let us discuss this by defining the experience of falling in love as a powerful and *undivided interest*. Whenever we believe something to offer the prospect for growth, we are interested. The more substantial the prospect for growth, the more undivided is our attention to that which offers the prospect. A friend may hold our interest. We grow in his or her company. And if that growth attains a quality in which our attention becomes undivided because we become so deeply convinced that The Other offers us the prospect for tremendous growth, we find ourselves in love. Since our theory affirms that we are alienated creatures who seek a wholeness available only by overcoming all the things which can annihilate us by their "no's," whosoever can capture our undivided interest has provided a means, even more powerful than friendship, for realizing the desired completeness. In this experience, then, consists the special value of love.

The initial experience of falling in love is undivided interest. In the development of friendship, the interest has to be held but it does not have to be entirely undivided. In the ideal case of love that we are now considering, our attention or interest must find such satisfaction in the presence of The Other that we do not experience ourselves in an alienated world. The Other helps us forget about our alienation. The more deeply The Other helps us to forget about everything and anything that reminds us of what we are not, to that degree we are in love, and that means—in our theory—to that degree we have overcome our alienated state. In this important sense, friendship and love can be seen as life strategies whose purpose, like every other action, is designed to overcome alienation. Here is an illustration.

> Suppose you go to the movie theater and watch a film. Let's say that you get so tuned in to the movie that you forget you are there. It should strike you on a moment's reflection that your experience of time has become disoriented. And not only is the experience of the passage of time disoriented, but it is specifically disoriented by the astonishing rate at which time has evidently passed. As the credits come up at the end of the movie in which you were totally absorbed, you might glance at your watch and be rather amazed at how quickly the time seems to have passed—"time flies when you are having fun." When we feel bored, on the other hand, time drags by at an excruciatingly slow rate.

The experience of time, in terms of boredom, is a reflection of how disengaged we are from The Other. The more aware we are of The Other, the slower the time passes. It is the disengagement, or disconnectedness, which makes us feel bored and therefore painfully aware that time slowly trudges on. But as soon as we feel connected, as soon as our interest is held, time slips right by. This accords well with our theory of interest.

Our interest is held when we think we are getting something, when we think we are benefiting by paying attention. The more our attention is held comfortably, the more we feel growth; and conversely, the more we feel growth, the more comfortable it is for us to continue to hold our attention. The experience of falling in love arises, then, when non-alienating friendship becomes the condition for undivided interest.

I have suggested that falling in love might be characterized by the experience of undivided interest. Does that mean you could be in love with your job, your car, your pet, your religion, even an idea? Sure you could. When our attention is undividedly interested, we feel open. When we feel like we are growing, we feel more whole or complete. That is what we desire because that is what we really need. We need the experiences that lead us to an unfoldment, but we do not want to feel too vulnerable. It is not the experience itself which is positive or negative, it is the context in which that experience transpires. It has to do with the value of the experiencer, *per se*. It is not a matter of the content of that experience itself.

Every time we grow we move from where we are to where we are not. Thus growth always involves some ingredient of risk and vulnerability. The delight we take in growth is a reflection of our venturing out into a new domain, a place where we were not before. If we are in a program of studies leading to medicine, we may well have to pass through the challenging course of Organic Chemistry. The course is very difficult, and often serves as a gate-keeper to allow the most serious and competent students to pass while channeling the less talented away from this path. Naturally, the student feels much pressure, much vulnerability, when the course begins. But as the student masters the difficult materials and grows in and through such mastery, the successful achievements visits happiness upon the student.

Now, if what we have been saying makes some sense, we seem to have a problem. Let us go through the argument again. All activity is motivated by our assessment of what we think is in our self-interest. We act by virtue of what we think is going to provide growth, to give us something we regard as benefit. So the activity of love, like any other activity, is motivated by self-interest. Is that the case? Does that mean that all love is fundamentally selfish? Ordinarily, the meaning of love connotes a kind of a sharing. But as soon as we think that the person we love does not have anything to offer us anymore—so the theory seems to go—we say that we are no longer in love. Let us become clearer about this analysis. To achieve this end, I now turn to analyze, on our theory, the simple expression "A loves B."

When we say "A loves B" what do we mean? When we say that we love someone, in the initial stages at least, that person is the occasion for our growth. The presence of that person makes us feel expanded and undivided in our interest. As long as that experience is there—the undivided interest that characterizes the experience of the overcoming of our alienated state along with the positive realization of wholeness—we claim to be in love. But—and this is the crucial turn—as soon as we feel that condition is no longer fulfilled, we claim that we no longer are "in love." The idea of being in love with someone does not seem to be the right analysis. It almost seems that we are in love *with love,* that is, the experience of growth, unfolding, opening up, *undivided interest,* overcoming alienation.

We do not want to be loved just for our money, or just for our body. Somehow, even if we do not know exactly what we mean, we want to be loved for who/what we truly are. But, if "A loves B" means that 'B' is the occasion for 'A's' own significant growth—and that is why 'B' holds 'A's' undivided attention—then at whatever point 'B' no longer provides the occasion for 'A's' growth, 'A' would correctly declare that 'A' no longer loves 'B.' At this stage, the analysis reveals that 'B' seems incidental or accidental to 'A's' growth, and when 'B' no longer provides the occasion for that growth, 'A' might claim that 'A' outgrew 'B.'

This analysis is troubling, precisely because it suggests that love is not only self-interested—like all other actions—but is also selfish (a position to which our theory of rational self-interest does *not* subscribe). This question of whether love, although self-interested, is necessarily selfish, deserves thoughtful consideration from the reader. The task is to determine if something is wrong with the argument, and if so, precisely what. Or, perhaps a different kind of analysis is required to clarify our position.

Our analysis of love has been couched in the broader context of the human condition. Like every other activity, it represents a strategy to overcome alienation. Each person, of course, will be the best judge of the adequacy of this account, by attempting to apply it to his/her own experiences and see if it illuminates the details of interaction.

The "friend" is distinguished from the vast array of alien Others. In the presence of what is alien, we exercise caution because this Other is unknown and therefore unpredictable. The Other who becomes our friend, who becomes non-alien, reassures our comfort, permits us to put down our defenses, to open up and expand. The friend ushers us into an area of substantial growth by creating a new horizon, a new and expanded context in which we come to identify ourselves by enlightening our self-interest.

Earlier, we distinguished between "unenlightened self-interest" (which we equated with selfishness) and "enlightened self-interest." Enlightened self-interest we identified in terms of how one pursues goals holding The Other to be a fundamental part of one's own care and concern, and thus of one's own happiness. An important problem is to determine if, while remaining a self-interested action, the loving experience can prove to be an illustration of "enlightened" self-interest.

E. IS OUR EXPERIENCE FUNDAMENTALLY UNHAPPY? SELF-IDENTITY: PROBLEMS

We have now considered, in cursory fashion, a general theory concerning self-identity. We briefly attempted to answer the question "Who am I?" We arrived at the ontological position that human *being* is itself deficient, incomplete, *alienated*. The thesis invited us to see all of our actions as motivated by our own assessment of self-interest, the ultimate aim of which is to become whole, complete, unalienated. Growth and happiness characterize unalienated or perfected experience while unhappiness and dissatisfaction characterize the alienated condition in which we tend to find ourselves.

First, we can reject this ontological account of human being—the alienation theory. Second, we can reject the theory of conduct—rational self-interest. Third, we can accept these descriptions of how we are and how we tend to behave and still insist that we can overcome these natural dispositions and inclinations; we can become genuinely altruistic. These are some of the ways that the positions introduced can, and should, be challenged. Indeed, there are many different kinds of objections that can and must be raised by the reader before coming to a conclusion about our very nature and the kinds of motivations that find expression in our actions.

If, however, the reader will, for the moment, entertain the theories of alienation and rational-self-interest, we find ourselves with a difficult problem that requires an answer. The position we have advanced identifies human being with a kind of unhappy consciousness. Our alienated condition is fundamentally an expression of our natural, inherent self-dissatisfaction. By acting successfully, we overcome that alienation more and more and hence achieve happiness more and more. But, since we continue to act throughout our lives, it might be that human existence is fundamentally unhappy since our continual consciousness consists in the formal awareness that something is lacking, missing, or defective and which, in turn, motivates desires and actions. Does this mean that happiness is unattainable, or at best temporary? Does this mean that falling in love, like all other actions, is not merely self-interested but also selfish? The reader must think deeply about these concerns.

Chapter 4

The Harm Principle: Part I
The Idea of Harming[1]

PRELIMINARY REMARKS ABOUT THE "HARM PRINCIPLE"

Chapters 2 and 3 provided a vision of human behavior. In Chapter 2, we considered a descriptive theory of human conduct starting with the presumption that the goal of all action is happiness. We considered *rational self-interest* as a description of one way in which all human actions can be organized. The doctrine of rational self-interest avers that whenever we have a choice among competing alternatives, we always select that alternative that we believe will best maximize our self-interest, and thus promote the happiness that we have assumed everyone is pursuing. Of course, we might come to regret our selection, as a result of being unhappy after securing our course of action. In this case, we might conclude, in retrospect, that the choice of action did not accrue the benefits that motivated our hopeful selection. But in any case, the selection itself was motivated by our best guess of how to maximize our self-interests. Whenever we can choose to act, our choice reflects our exercise of rational self-interest, and that amounts to the promotion of our happiness.

In Chapter 3 we introduced the idea of *alienation*. The idea of alienation, in this discussion, is that the central, shared feature of all human choices is that "self-interest" amounts to "overcoming alienation." When we overcome alienation, we experience happiness. The feeling of being alienated, by contrast, is the feeling that we are lacking, separated from our goals, disconnected from our world. In its extreme, we feel depressed, powerless, and hopeless; in its lesser manifestations,

41

alienation is experienced as failure, the inability to achieve our goals. When, however, we maximize self-interest, we experience growth, expansion, wholeness, the overcoming of vulnerability and limitations; we feel joyous. When we overcome alienation, we feel happy.

One way to explore further this idea of happiness as the overcoming of alienation is to ask all the readers to imagine how they "feel" when they are happy. When you have accomplished a great task, had a delicious meal, watched a superb film or listened to a favorite song, do the experiences of happiness share a common feature? The theory of our last chapter offers the claim that they do; each happy experience offers a degree of overcoming alienation. The happier the experience, the more we overcome alienation, the more whole or complete we feel.

Thus Chapters 2 and 3 set the stage for our ethical dilemma. We granted that everyone is pursuing their own happiness and for each of us that means different particular things. One person wants to become a physician, another an athlete, and another proficient in business. One person is happier when enjoying a meal at a Chinese restaurant, while another prefers Italian or French cuisine. One person is happier with their bedroom walls painted yellow, while another prefers white, and another green. One person enjoys a vacation by the beach while another prefers skiing on a mountain. And so the material conditions for each of our happiness differs. Now, since we began with the presumption that each person is trying to maximize their own self-interest, and thus maximize their happiness (and each person experiences happiness as the "overcoming of alienation" regardless of the particular choices), our analysis forces us to conclude that central to human strategies for happiness is the promotion of freedom or liberty. We are compelled to advocate an extremely liberal theory. But note, the term "liberal" is not being used to juxtapose "democrats" with "republicans" but rather to take quite literally the importance of "maximizing freedom," that is, liberty. And it seems to me that democrats and republicans all extol the virtues of freedom and liberty.

Each of us needs the freedom, the liberties, to make those choices that we believe will make us happy. It is here that our ethical problem has its root, for we will see that many times our choices to secure our own happiness come into conflict with the pursuit of happiness by others, and when this happens we must determine under what conditions we must restrict or constrain individual freedom. But since our happiness requires the freedom to pursue those particular choices, it would seem that the diminishment of freedoms must be an evil.

Chapters 2 and 3 combine to advocate a theory of *human flourishing*. Humans are pursuing happiness, and since the happiness for each of us has very different material particulars, we find ourselves advocating the freedom or liberty to make choices and so secure the happiness that we already assumed each person was seeking. But let us consider an extreme choice to make our point as clearly as possible. Let's say one person's happiness is to make a colorful garden of flowers in their front yard, while another person's happiness is to conduct a drive-by shooting at someone at that house! It must be immediately clear to (almost) everyone that while the making of a garden poses no real or substantial dangers to others, the drive-by shooting most certainly does. But when we recommend that the gardener should have the freedom to make the garden but the drive-by shooter should be stopped, we are confronted by the general question: under what circumstances should we recommend the limiting of liberties?

Let's press such an example further to make sure we are all clear about what is at stake. When some fellows were distressed by certain actions taken by our federal government, in response and retaliation, they blew up the Federal Building in Oklahoma City killing 168 people and injuring more than 600 others. Their happiness consisted in blowing up a building, and anyone who was nearby, too bad for them. This exercise of freedom is as outrageous as it is impermissible, but how shall we make clear why this exercise of liberty is impermissible while others are permissible? When a middle schooler is distressed by his classmates, and in order to become happy he elects to exercise his freedom by shooting them with a rifle during recess, or when two high school students were distressed by the bullying they felt from their school chums, and replied by entering school and killing thirteen students before killing themselves as they exercised their freedom to find a happiness that they believed meant something important to them, such conduct is impermissible. But, again, how shall we distinguish between the exercise of liberty that is permissible from the exercise that is not? When should the exercise of freedom be constrained even though it is designed to promote the happiness that we agreed everyone is seeking? While we must seek to open freedoms to others so that people will flourish in their pursuit of happiness, the drive-by, the blowing up of buildings, the attacks in school are clearly unacceptable exercises of freedom. But what is the best way to frame an account for a position that seems *prima facie* to make so much sense? How do we draw a line, as it were, to distinguish which exercises of freedom are permissible and which are not?

The theory of human flourishing is a theory about promoting liberties to achieve happiness. And so, from this theoretical perspective, the limiting of freedoms must count as an evil, because to limit freedoms means to interfere with the pursuit of happiness. But we can also see by these hyperbolic examples, that there are clear cases when the limiting of liberties, by contrast to the consequences of not doing so, is a good. Thus, while the promotion of liberties is usually a good, there are cases when such liberties unconstrained are more evil than good. In such cases, then, we must be prepared to show that while the limiting of liberties is usually an evil, there are cases when the limiting of liberties is a good and so overrides an injunction that, stated simply, is not to promote evils. So, while liberty-limiting restrictions may be an evil, pro forma, such limitations override the prohibitions against them, as the case of the drive-by shooter and others considered, make abundantly clear.

How should we determine, then, if and when liberty limitations are to be recommended? How shall we decide when the unrestrained promotions of freedom constitute an evil? We shall formulate a principle that we shall call the *harm principle*. We shall be cautious about how we formulate it, and we shall be mindful about those difficulties when we test it. But our project will be to formulate a principle that offers ethical guidance about when the exercise of freedom, crucial to the realization of our happiness, deserves to be constrained. And then we shall test a range of conduct to see if it does or does not violate the harm principle. Conduct that violates the harm principle will be deemed "immoral" and that means it is conduct that deserves to be constrained.

A. INTRODUCTION: THE "HARM PRINCIPLE" AND THE PROSCRIPTIVE APPROACH

Moral decision-making is a complex operation precisely because there can be no general rules that adequately cover the extraordinarily diverse and specific choices of action that confront each of us. Although general rules can be offered to help us gain clarity in our moral deliberations, the particular situations in which we find ourselves commonly contain contingencies that escape the organization established by such general rules.

In the history of philosophical writing on ethics, on the contrary, the familiar model was one in which general rules were declared, and then individual acts of conduct were assessed in terms of whether or not some particular action properly fell under the jurisdiction of that rule. This strategy is part of what we shall call a "juridical or judicial approach." For example, the general rule: *Thou shalt not kill* might be put forth. Then, some persons might wonder whether or not the killing of some person or other was permissible. And then the result of the deliberation might be announced.

Moral Principle: Thou shalt not kill.

Particular Action: Should I kill 'X'?

Moral Decision: I should NOT kill 'X'.

In this model, it is supposed that we can formulate general rules, and those rules can indeed illuminate the sound choices for our moral reasoning. Unfortunately, many cases of moral reasoning cannot be reasonably accommodated within this model. For example, we may accept the general rule *Thou shalt not kill* but find ourselves confronted by the complication that one is presently being attacked by a knife-wielding assailant. Or, one might be in a situation in which one were a member of the armed forces caught in a military conflict with the exchange of unfriendly fire. In short, one might accept the general rule while rejecting the application of that principle in particular situations. We might all agree that *Thou shalt not lie* is a good, useful, and helpful moral prescription. But, if we are sitting at home with our family and someone bursts through the door brandishing a firearm, points it menacingly at us and demands "Where's your mama?" the reply that—granting we think it's a good idea to be a truth-teller—she's in the room down the hall on the left, seems perfectly ludicrous. Now, if I may be sarcastic I might interject here that such a reply would only come from someone who is presently having some very serious difficulties with their mother! Surely our sense of things is not to tell the truth about where our mother is, despite our reasonable demeanor to regard truth-telling in general as a good thing to practice. To reject the general rule in particular situations is, in some important sense, to reject not only the rule but also the model itself, the very idea that there can be general rules at all. Recent writings by philosophers have taken these numerous exceptions to be fatal blows to the traditional model and have been proposing alternative approaches.

The effort to assist individuals in developing skills for deciding moral issues is honorable but admits many difficulties. Rather than advise or recommend a specific course of conduct—which would be a "prescriptive approach"—the disposition adopted here is to avoid a kind of prescriptive ethics. A prescriptive ethics would be one in which recommendations were advanced to undertake certain actions. The difficulties are exceedingly great to see how to advise individuals with specific recommendations to act since the particular circumstances invariably need to be considered to see what principles might apply. The complexities of particular situations pose such great challenges to the very idea of general rules or principles.

Rather than recommend the performance of certain conduct, we instead adopt a "Proscriptive approach" and ask: *Is there any good reason why certain conduct ought NOT be performed or permitted?* That is, should we constrain the impulse within ourselves to perform some action, and should we recommend that others who are inclined to perform such actions be constrained? We shall not focus on the question of whether or not some course of conduct is either wise or desirable but rather only whether or not the conduct is *impermissible*. Conduct that can be judged to be impermissible we shall judge to be immoral, and immoral conduct deserves to be constrained. Such conduct deserves to be *proscribed*.

What conduct is "impermissible" or "immoral"? We shall identify immoral conduct with behavior that can be judged to be wrong, we shall regard wrong behavior as impermissible, and we shall identify impermissible behavior with conduct that causes or seeks to cause *harm wrongfully: The Harm Principle.* Thus, let us define the 'Harm Principle' as 'harmful wrongdoing.'

This idea should seem sufficiently straightforward. Conduct that causes harm, or is intended to cause harm, is conduct that deserves to be constrained. And thus the burden of our inquiries shall be to determine what, if any, harm has been done or was intended. But it immediately becomes obvious that we can be harmed in many ways: we can be harmed by an assault, we can be harmed in an automobile accident in a parking lot, we can be harmed by being fired from a job. Since the fender-bender in the parking lot is likely an unintentional accident, we need to distinguish the harm that results without the intention to set-back interests from the harm that is expressly intended to set-back our interests. The intentional harm is more than a case of harming, it is a case of wronging. In our judicial system, unintentional harms are remanded to the Civil Courts while intentional harms are remanded to the Criminal Courts. To violate the harm principle, to behave "immorally" one must both harm and wrong.

A person who assaults another, not in self-defense, is a person who has harmed another. The person who has committed rape has certainly harmed another. Such actions are wrong and deserve to be constrained; they constitute clear Harm to Others. Why is such harmful conduct *wrong*? Because the harming has resulted from acts for which there was no consent from the other, interests have been set-back without the victim's consent.

But there are many other cases where individuals are accused of "harming" and these cases are of a different sort and require a different analysis. In the case of [self-] euthanasia or suicide, an individual is being harmed but the person who causes the harm is identical with the one who suffers it. This is also true of the one who abuses alcohol or other chemical substances. In these cases we confront a different issue of harm: *Harm to Self.* And we must be prepared to state in what senses the harm(s) consists, and what, if anything, deserves to be done in response to it. Is such conduct harmful? We must ask afresh whether the harmful conduct also counts as wrongful. Let's consider it this way: Suppose we agree that it is. Is this conduct, too, impermissible, because it is wrong, and wrong because it is harmful, and because harmful therefore immoral? In what senses do harms-to-self count as wrong? This debate is often argued legally under the rubric "Legal Paternalism," namely, that it is necessary to prohibit certain conduct in order to prevent harm—physical, psychological, economic—to persons who commit such actions to themselves. Are we morally (as opposed to legally) obliged to constrain individuals from doing harm to themselves? Why? In what cases, if any, is the conduct not impermissible?

We may also distinguish another range of behaviors believed by some to be wrong without causing harm to anyone directly: *Impersonal Harm*. In this class of actions should be included questions dealing with the permissibility of pornography and questions concerning whether or not certain sexual practices engaged in private by consenting adults are impermissible. These practices, as diverse as masturbation and sodomy, prostitution and gambling, are supposed to cause harm but in many cases not to anyone in particular. Such matters are often debated under the legal classification of "Legal Moralism." Legal Moralism is a position that argues that it is legitimate to prohibit conduct on the grounds that it is inherently immoral even though it causes neither harm nor offense to the actor or to others. It is sometimes argued that such conduct causes a kind of abstract harm to the community. While not directly harming a specific person, nor the actor, it is nevertheless maintained that certain conduct is inherently degrading and debasing and thereby harms the community in some indirect, abstruse, but real fashion.

The organization of kinds of potentially objectionable conduct in terms of: (i) Harm to Others, (ii) Harm to Self, and (iii) Impersonal Harm, makes no claim to offer an exhaustive analysis of kinds of behavior. Rather, these distinctions are introduced with the hope that they will lend clarity to our reflections upon our own behavior, that of others, and the views expressed in our culture, explicitly and implicitly, by individuals and (through) institutions.

Thus, rather than debate general rules for conduct, whether they be the Ten Commandments or some other list of do's and don'ts, our approach will be to inquire whether certain conduct is wrong and is thus impermissible, and therefore deserving of constraint. At no point will our strategy recommend certain actions as wise or desirable; we will focus, instead, on the question of whether or not the conduct is impermissible. In order to accomplish this end, we will examine a range of actions to determine if they commit harm, and if so, what sort of harm. And we will also have to examine a range of actions that some suppose to be wrong even where no direct harm can be shown, as it can certainly be exhibited in the clearest cases of *harm to others*.

B. ORGANIZING HARMS

When an important thinker like Joel Feinberg discusses the *harm principle*, he does so in order to understand, recommend, and defend legal practices. For him this amounts to a debate over when, if ever, encroachments on our liberty can be justified. In his efforts to understand legal statutes, he examines the conditions under which liberty-limiting principles or laws may be imposed. Our debate is moral, not legal, and yet since the law constantly reflects, echoes, and amplifies moral sentiments, such an analysis proves useful for and illuminating to our purposes. We must keep in mind, however, that the law is fundamentally part of an institution that offers to reach compromises among conflicting claims; stated differently, in the United States, the law is not a moral institution, though is affected by moral sentiments. We do not suppose moral issues, ordinarily, to be resolved by compromise. And we must keep this important distinction in mind, as we proceed. Feinberg lists a range of possible justifications for liberty-limiting principles:

(1) [a] the private harm principle: prevent harm to others

   [b] the public harm principle: prevent harm to essential institutions

(2) the offense principle: prevent offense to others

(3) legal paternalism: prevent harm to self

(4) legal moralism: prevent sin or enforce morality

(5) extreme paternalism: benefit self

(6) the welfare principle: benefit others.

In this interesting list, the reader can begin to discover how liberal or conservative are his/her proclivities. The most liberal positions resist liberty-limiting encroachments; personal liberty is of primary importance. The most liberal positions, those recommending minimalist constraints only, draw the line above (1), by liberals like J.S. Mill, who argued that harm to others is the only ground for legislation, include only (1) [a] and [b]. Thus, those who oppose enacting laws to limit liberty tend to find behavior that harms others to be unacceptable, but allow an individual to lead his or her own life, risking self-harm. When harm to another or oneself cannot be shown, as in the cases of impersonal harm (= legal moralism), the more liberal sentiments oppose restrictions while the more conservative endorse liberty-limiting restrictions.

C. THE IDEAS OF *PERSONS* AND *RIGHTS*

In order to think through the idea of the *harm principle,* to determine when conduct is wrong and precisely why, two important ideas or concepts must be considered: *persons* and *rights.* It has been a familiar doctrine in political and legal philosophy to suppose that "persons" and "rights" are terms that can be properly applied only to human beings. These terms are employed to suggest the domain of duties and obligations; in general, one harms another when one violates another's rights.

First of all, who or what is a "person?" The term, and even the concept of, "person" is ambiguous. It is used in a variety of ways in common language and even in philosophical discourse. A person can be contrasted with a (mere) thing, a usage developed especially by the eighteenth century philosopher, Immanuel Kant. Kant insisted that human beings are persons, not things. Things have an instrumental use and can be used as means to an end; their worth is commensurate with their utility. Persons, on the other hand, have an unconditional worth, and are ends-in-themselves, not merely means to other ends. Thus, while persons have value in their own right, things acquire a value in terms of their usefulness alone.

A person, in our discussions, is intended to convey the idea of a moral agent. The term "human being," in contrast, is at root a biological term, derived from identifying the genus, and more particularly, the species from which we have descended. Identifying human genetic materials, an analysis of DNA, cannot provide a moral argument for identifying our moral status, though this is sometimes embraced or attempted, explicitly or implicitly. When we attempt to identify "person" with "human DNA" we have evaded the moral question of what it is that makes "human DNA" worthy of respect and protection and instead only identify the creatures for which the protection and respect is extended. Instead, what we need to answer is this: what is it about any creature that shows it deserves protection and respect, and then connect the argument to show why/that creatures with human DNA deserve such protections and respect. To help achieve this clarity, we shall employ the term "person"—not "human"—whenever we ask about the moral status of a creature or entity.

The idea of personhood is also enmeshed in discussions about self-consciousness. Some have argued, like Kant, that persons are creatures who are conscious of their identity through time. Indeed, the philosopher Leibniz made the point that this inward consciousness of ourselves is the basis of the justification for reward and punishment. Thus, "person" characterizes a creature with a kind of self-consciousness that makes it possible to ascribe praise or blameworthiness for actions and responsibility for conduct. It is the peculiar kind of self-consciousness that persons have that accounts for their moral standing, not their DNA nor a biological argument.

The term "person" is often used to identify those creatures deserving of rights. And since personhood and rights are deeply intertwined, we turn now to consider the idea of rights in order to more deeply grasp the domain of persons.

The idea of rights has been a focus for legal and political philosophy since the seventeenth century. At that time, one central concern was the debate over *natural rights*. Were there certain aspects of human life that demanded respect and protection? Were these aspects that demanded respect and protection acquired at birth, and henceforth became somehow inalienable and sanctified so as to transcend the authority of written laws?

Discussions of rights are familiar from legal disputes and it is not, therefore, surprising that the idea of rights is embedded in such discourse. When a person claims to have been harmed, or offended, that person claims to be deprived of that to which he/she had a right. To acknowledge a right was to acknowledge a power a person could exercise over another, or a power of acting to realize something that the community believed to be a good.

Subsequently, some have held that a right is a claim upheld by a court. This has led to the objection that persons may have rights to which they never make claim, and produces the difficulty of deciding whether infants, for example, have rights since they are incapable of making claims. Some have responded by insisting that to have a right is not a matter of *making* a claim so much as it is a matter of *having* a claim whether one makes it or not. In such a case, an individual could be said to have a right to something when such a claim could be defended whether or not one actually demands the right.

There are those, such as Jeremy Bentham, who tried to define *rights* in terms of *duties*. One has a legal duty to do something only where the law authorizes a punishment for *not* doing it. In this context, one has a right to something only where one is obliged to act in a certain way. This view has been criticized by those who point out that while one's duty is what one is required to do, a right implies only what persons may do if they choose to do so. Thus, rights are distinguished from duties though may be interconnected with them.

To offer a view of rights requires that we make a distinction between legal and moral rights. We might say, as does H.L.A. Hart, that to ascribe a legal right to a person is to reach a conclusion of law. But a moral right cannot be justified in this fashion. When we shall debate whether there is a moral right to abort or not abort a fetus, or a moral right of the fetus to not be aborted; we are not asking what ought to be done but only what is the relevant *claim* to be made. We will be asking whose interests are at stake and how mediation should proceed among the persons who claim a conflict of interests.

We shall not pursue the idea of rights in terms of claims made or demanded, exercised or asserted, waived or surrendered. To say that a creature has a *right* to something will mean to say that a creature has an interest in that thing, that a creature desires that thing, and that it would be wrong for others to deny the creature that thing in which an interest or desire is expressed or implied. In the legal context, that interest would, or should, be protected by law. But, in a moral context, that interest amounts to what the creature desires or what would be its advantage to have.

D. PROBLEMS

In Chapters 2 and 3, an ideal of a "person" was advanced, central to which was the notion of *flourishing*. Persons are creative creatures with wide avenues for possible growth and unforeseeable horizons for happiness. In order to promote human flourishing, we seek to promote liberties. For in a world where all things were equal, a condition where liberties were promoted would be a better one than that in which liberties were restricted. By promoting liberties, we are directly committed to promoting human happiness, a condition that can be realized through human flourishing.

The argument that we must keep in mind is that if the promotion of liberties is a good thing, then the constraint of behavior, in the form of liberty-limiting principles, must be, all things being equal, an evil thing. In order to favor liberty-limiting principles, we must be able to show that the evil inherent in restricting liberties can be outweighed by the harm caused by the actor(s). It is not enough to show that the acts of others are harmful, it must further be shown that the harmfulness is so great as to override the ordinary prohibitions against restricting liberties. Thus, to take extreme examples such as those who engage in drive-by shootings, blow up buildings, or shoot their classmates during recess at school, while they are exercising their liberties, the harm caused by their acts overrides any claim that such persons make for the freedom to behave in such a fashion. These objections to the enactment of freedoms are clearest in cases of *harm* to *others*. But can this kind of case be made in the multifarious incidents of *harm* to *self* and *impersonal harms*?

We must also be prepared to meet a host of difficulties that surround the ideas of *persons, rights,* and *harm*:

1. Even if we grant that self-conscious human beings are members of the class of persons, and thereby capable of blame and praiseworthiness, we can wonder whether or not any other animals are entitled to be included within this class, whether any other animals fulfill the conditions of being *persons*. And we must be prepared to answer why or why not.

2. We must reach a conclusion as to whether or not a creature can have rights without also having the right-to-life. For those who reach the conclusion that other animals are not entitled to the right-to-life, it remains for us to determine whether they have any claim to any rights, and we must be prepared to offer good reasons for our position.

3. We must be able to answer the question of whether or not the fetus is a *person* (and not just a human being, not being mislead merely by biological arguments that point to human DNA).

4. We must decide what happens to the status of *persons* who become comatose? Can they lose or forfeit those domains to which they previously had rights? So also for the case of capital punishment; can one forfeit the right-to-life? Are rights alienable?

5. What kinds of harm result in the violation of rights? Without debating what kinds of harm are unwise or undesirable, can we state clearly the harm that is *impermissible*? What reasons can we offer?

NOTE

[1] This chapter draws on Joel Feinberg's *Social Philosophy*, Englewood Cliffs, New Jersey: Prentice Hall, 1973, Ch. 2.

Name_____ TA _____

Section #_____

1) What is the goal of a rationally self-interested creature?

2) Is it beneficial to have *all* of your desires fulfilled? How can we tell if a desire is a "need" or merely a "want"?

Name_____ TA _____

Section #_____

3) Does the "altruist" *agree* or *disagree* with the theory of rational self-interest? Why?

4) What is the difference between "Unenlightened" and "Enlightened" self-interest?

Name_____ TA _____

Section #_____

5) Describe "alienation" and give an example of how it might occur.

Name_____ TA _____

Section #_____

6) Define the word "harm" in the context of "the Harm Principle." Can you have a harm "above the line"?

7) What is a "right? What kind of being can be said to have "rights"?

Chapter 5

The Harm Principle: Part II
Harm to Others and
Harm to Self[1]

A. HARM TO OTHERS

The idea that harming others is both inappropriate and unacceptable has few detractors. It is generally agreed that persons are entitled to basic protections from harm, that each of us has a *right* not to be harmed, and that others who harm us or intend to harm us should be constrained. Therefore, actions that intend to harm others may broadly be declared to be wrong. In the domain of legal discourse, no one doubts that murder, assault, and theft are kinds of conduct that result in one person's harm of another unjustly. But, more precisely, in what sense(s) are they wrong? Or, asked differently, what does it mean to "harm wrongfully"?

When we discuss the idea of harm, we mean two things: (i) setback to interests, and (ii) wrongdoing. Let us consider these two senses of harm:

(i) *Harm as a Setback to (Self) Interests:* We have already considered the idea of self-interest. Each individual, we argued, tends to choose that course of action that is believed to offer the opportunity for better consequences, the prospects for something more, or stated simply, more happiness. Given the choice of pursuing action 'A' or action 'B', all things being equal, the agent chooses the one that is believed to provide the greatest happiness. If you have the opportunity for employment 'A' or 'B', or the chance to spend an evening with date 'A' or 'B', the theory of rational self-interest maintains that you will choose the one that you believe will maximize your own interests—maximize your happiness. Of course, each person may have different interests and would not choose the same job or friend. And, naturally, each person makes choices by appealing to different criteria. The theory only advises that that choice, all things being equal, is motivated by the assessment of which job or person, for instance, is believed more likely to promote self-interests. In this central sense, we argued, human conduct is fundamentally rationally self-interested.

But, we also noted that to claim individuals are self-interested in no way settles the question about the "self" in which they are interested. As we grow and develop, our self-conception changes and so does our assessment about what is and what is not in our own interest. Thus, claiming that we are basically self-interested does not, in itself, decide the issue of who we are, nor does it decide the question of whether we are selfish or not. Self-interest does not stand in opposition to selfishness, and yet in each case we must determine their interrelation. We distinguished between two kinds of self-interested conduct: (i) enlightened self-interest and (ii) unenlightened self-interest, and only the latter did we identify with selfishness.

Within this frame of reference, we can say that a person has been harmed when that person's interests have been set back, or has been challenged by actions that intended to set-back interests. By "set back" we mean to thwart, defeat, diminish, undermine, damage, one's goals and aspirations. When a person has an interest in something, let's call it 'X', we mean that such a person has a stake in 'X'. When a person has a stake in something, he/she is at risk, whether it be in terms of energy or money, to gain or lose depending upon the nature or condition of 'X'.

> Let's say I have an interest in my classic car (= 'X'). I have a stake in maintaining its excellent working order and its appearance. I have risked energy and money in caring for, repairing, and preserving this classic automobile. I stand to gain or lose when I choose to sell the car or enter it into a competition, depending upon the car's condition. If someone damages my car, then I have been harmed since what I have an interest in now is diminished in value. In this real sense, I have had a set-back of my interests, and hence have been harmed.

Note that we sometimes speak as if one can harm a car, that the paint could be harmed by salts in the road (leftover from safety procedures enacted during winter snowstorms), or that the windshield could be harmed by a prankster roving through the neighborhood with a pellet gun. This sense of 'harm' is not what is meant here. The windshield may be broken and the paint damaged, but inanimate objects cannot be "harmed."

(ii) *Harm as Wrongdoing:* When 'A harms B' we tend to mean not only that A sets-back B's interests or acts in such a way to intend to set-back B's interests, and thus that 'A wrongs B', and this means that A has treated B unjustly. To be treated wrongly, hence unjustly, A's action must set-back B's interests. But setting back interest alone does not adequately explain the wrong that has been caused. Thus, 'A harms B' may mean that 'A's actions have unjustifiably and inexcusably violated 'B's *rights*.

When we say that a person has a right to something, we mean that the person has an interest in that thing and it would be wrong for others to deny the person that thing. In this sense, and as a legal matter, to have a right is to *have a claim* either for specific assistance (repayment of a debt, compensation for losses, and so on), or for noninterference in one's private affairs. And such a claim may be directed against a particular individual or against an institution, including the state. In the domain of *legal* rights, the person who has a right may also have a claim to the legal enforcement of a valid claim against an individual or institution. Does this legal view extend to moral debates, and if so, how?

It may be argued that harming is wrong because it *injures*, but this identification is too narrow for moral debates. Injury is most often identified with the infliction of damage to one's health or body. But in cases such as theft, we may say that a person has been harmed without claiming that a person has been injured; for while we are accustomed to saying that theft harms a person's economic interests, we would not usually say that a person is injured by a monetary loss. When a professor fails to have a manuscript accepted for publication, the professor has clearly been harmed but not injured; so also for the political candidate who loses the election, the loss is harmful without being an injury. Thus, although injury is a kind of harm it is not coextensive with it.

Harm to others may involve injury or it may not. The *wrongness* of the harm, however, requires that it involves moral indefensibility. That is, conduct that harms another can be said to be wrong only when the wrongdoing was unexcused and unjustified. And so we focus again upon the intentions of the actors; and in just this way, harm in the public sphere is remanded to the criminal or civil court. When one has a minor traffic accident in the parking lot of a shopping mall, certainly one person may be found negligent or inattentive and hence the cause of the damage. That person appears, when challenged, in the civil court and if found guilty pays the cost of repairing the other's car. In such a case, the damage has been accidental; neither party intended to hit the other's car—it was an accident. But, had the circumstances been different, had one person been accused of intentionally trying to hit the other's car, then the matter should be referred to the criminal court because there was "criminal intent"—the intention was to cause harm. Thus, if the harm results without some person(s) being at fault then

we shall say only that someone has been harmed but not wronged—
it was an accident. In such a case we will grant that some person has
suffered a setback to their interests. But to claim further that he/she
has been wronged, we must be prepared to show that the harm was
*the result of a voluntary act that cannot be justified, that caused the
harm or intended to cause harm.*

It is clear that a person may be harmed by others, even when he or
she voluntarily consents to actions by others. One may consent to bungee
jump off a bridge and be permanently maimed or die. One may consent
to a boxing match and become severely impaired. One might consent
to drive in an auto race and be gravely injured, consent to a whipping
by a prostitute and suffer humiliations and physical trauma, consent
to smoke cigarettes and risk lung cancer, consent to gamble and lose
all one's money. In all these cases it is clear that a person, with full
consent, may be harmed by others. The interesting question for us is
whether or not they can also be *wronged* in the process.

There is a well-known negative principle of law and morality,
expressed in an ancient maxim of Roman law: *Volenti non fit injuria*
("To one who has consented no wrong is done.") Earlier, Aristotle, in
Book 5 of the *Nicomachean Ethics,* held the theory that one person
wrongs another only when that person inflicts harm upon him voluntarily. A harmful act is voluntary whenever it is not the result of compulsion. Thus, no injustice is committed, no wrong is enacted—though
of course one may be harmed—as a result of a voluntary or consensual act.

In legal discussions, the debaters want to get clear on the nature of
harm and the extent of wrongdoing so that they will better understand
how to authorize coercion or liberty-limiting laws. For the time being,
we are trying to understand when harmful acts are wrong because we
want to determine whether conduct is impermissible. When one has
been deprived of that to which one has a right *without consent* then one
has been not just harmed but wronged. To be wronged and hence
harmed is impermissible. We need not labor over the issues of showing
how murder, assault, and theft are harmful and wrong and thus impermissible because in all these cases the set-back to interests is *without*
consent. But we must be prepared to reasonably defend and criticize a
wide selection of actions.

In our reflections on the problems entailed in harm to others, we
must also consider the range of conduct often called *offenses to others.* For it is clear that not everything that we dislike and wish to avoid
is harmful to us. Receiving a rude comment on the highway in the stress
of a traffic jam or enduring a monumentally boring lecture, we find ourselves distressed, offended, or irritated without having our interests
harmed. In much the same way, eating a poorly prepared meal will be
unpleasant without being harmful so long as the food is not spoiled.

In a myriad of ways, we are challenged by experiences that hurt and offend our feelings, that produce unpleasant mental states such as nausea in the confrontation with revolting smells or grating noises, mild disappointments, wounds to our pride, guilt and shame, boredom, disgust, frustration, anger, and so on. In all these cases, our main concern is simply to avoid these distressing experiences; they do not themselves cause harm but only momentary displeasure.

However, were we forced to endure these discomforts for a prolonged amount of time, we might then argue that these *offenses* interfered with our interests. Thus, the grating noise that we dislike takes on a different character when it persists throughout the night and interferes with our sleep. We might argue that the disruption of our sleep caused our health or our ability to function at work to be impaired. And if the offense continues long enough unchecked the mental suffering may become incapacitating or debilitating and therefore *harmful*. When we consider the idea of moral wrongdoing, we must keep in mind that offensive behavior can cause harm and therefore may be subject to critical assessment as a harm to others.

Let me emphasize again one more important distinction in the criminal law, and consider its implications for moral deliberations. When one has been harmed by an intentional act—rape, murder, assault, theft—this is customarily handled as a criminal offense. But when one has been harmed unintentionally—by an accident—this is customarily handled as a civil matter. Thus, a person who in anger intentionally drives his/her car at someone and hits them, the matter is referred to the criminal court. When someone accidentally has a fender-bender in the parking lot at a mall, disputes are handled by civil courts. The crucial element in distinguishing criminal from civil is "intention" or volition. And thus we emphasize that both the causing of harm unjustly, and the intention to cause harm unjustly, are both emblematic of violations of the harm principle.

B. HARM TO SELF

While few fail to recognize that harm to others is wrong because it deprives others of that to which they have a right unjustly and in the process sets back their interests, the issue of deciding whether self-harm is wrong is much more contentious. *Paternalism* wishes to address this issue and maintains two things: (i) that if we can agree that certain kinds of conduct *to others* is harmful then that same conduct administered *to oneself* must also be harmful in the same fashion; and (ii) a person needs to be protected from his/her own self-administered, harmful behavior. Legal paternalism is the doctrine that maintains the support of legal prohibitions when those restrictions are deemed necessary to prevent harm (physical, psychological, or economic) to the actor him/herself.

61

Liberal positions tend to reject paternalistic interference, insisting that where there is no harm to others, a person should be able to live his/her own life, and make his/her own choices even if it results in their own suffering and self-harm. More conservative positions insist that society has a duty to protect persons even from themselves, from their own folly. Our problem is to determine when, if ever, others have a right to interfere with our conduct, that, although leaving us (the agent or actor) at risk, poses no danger or harm to anyone else. And we must be prepared to offer good and cogent reasons in defense of our position.

The term "paternalism" may itself be infelicitous but it invites us to consider the nature of the relation that is invoked when we consider interfering in the process of an actor's conduct toward him/herself. In such cases, the outside individuals, or the state, stand to the actor as parents stand to children (i.e. dependent minors). The child is supposed to be insufficiently competent to make decisions about how to behave, and the parents step forward, being the responsible parties, to constrain the conduct of the child. Thus, to accept the permissibility of paternalism, we must be prepared to argue that others, or the state, may have the right to treat normal adults as if they were children, a view that many find to be unacceptable. Nevertheless, a central tenet of paternalism is that others have a right, a duty, to protect persons from their own folly. And a substantial underlying issue to be resolved is how to make sense of the claim that others know better what is or is not in our own interest.

We should be very clear that there are countless matters in which no one would reasonably disagree that others do indeed know better than each of us what specifically is or is not in our own interests. The certified mechanic knows better how to fix the brakes on our car, the surgeon knows better how to take out our appendix, the cosmetologist knows better how to cut our hair, and so on. But the far-reaching question is whether it makes any sense to assert that anyone else really knows what is or is not in my own best interest for securing happiness. Legal paternalism asserts that the state does know better than each of us, should we seek to pursue certain activities. Does it make moral sense, and if so, how?

There are cases regarded by many as justifiable interference, especially those that involve attempts at suicide. But we must also consider cases of self-euthanasia, in the face of terminal diseases, and the permissibility of suicide under a variety of circumstances that include great duress. Our strategy is not to advise that a course of action is either wise or desirable but only whether or not it is impermissible. We may not choose to encourage self-euthanasia and suicide but we might conclude that it is not impermissible if another steps forward and expresses the intention to do so. What good reasons do we have to tell others that they must not do so? We will identify an act as impermissible if it denies a person a right *unjustly*, and where there is consent it is difficult to show in so many cases of harms to self that the denial is unjust.

The harm to others principle commits us to the position that when a person wrongs another, that is, deprives a person a right unjustly, then the behavior is unacceptable and deserves to be restricted. But, a motivating factor in advocating this position was the recognition that, in harming another, the person harmed has *not consented* to the harm, the harm has not arisen through voluntary action of the person harmed and in that condition consists the wrongfulness of the action. When the issue of consent is removed, the *Volenti* condition would seem to become operative and consequently the self-imposed action is fully voluntary, then to what good reasons can we reasonably appeal to justify interference in a person's private choices for action?

> What is at stake in the debate over the moral issues surrounding harm to self is really flushed out in the question "Whose life is it, anyway?" By appeal to what reasons are others entitled to instruct us what to do with our own life? On what grounds can someone deny us our own *autonomy*, our right to live our own life, make our own choices, and suffer the consequences of our own actions?

Some cases look like the principle of harm to self is operating alone but prove to be indirect cases of harm to others. For example, the seatbelt laws and the requirements to wear motorcycle helmets both seem initially to be simply paternalistic. The argument is sometimes offered that the state is interested in protecting the lives and well-being of its citizens and the implementation and enforcement of these laws, laws that are clearly liberty-limiting principles, are designed to further that objective. But the argument is also made that persons who fail to wear seatbelts or fail to wear protective headgear on motorcycles are much more likely to risk serious injury, injuries that will require emergency treatment (treatment that cannot be denied and the cost of which is exorbitant)—that affects the insurance rates that everyone pays. Although these laws, then, seem merely paternalistic, they might prove to be defensible instead on the principle of harm to others. Failure to comply with these laws results in the set-back to (economic) interests of other people and thus causes harm wrongfully. What we shall try to get clear on is whether any cases can be isolated to self-harm, and then ask what good reasons can be offered for their prohibition.

Later, we will examine in detail cases involving self-euthanasia and suicide. For now, two other illustrative cases as divergent as drug use and masturbation will be considered briefly. The case of drug use is complex. First, we certainly need to distinguish among drugs in order to produce thoughtful policies about what conduct is harmful, why and how. We need to ask how our positions are complicated when we consider the nexus of harms to others that has emerged as a direct consequence of the drug trade, and to ask which issues of drug use for oneself can be separated from questions regarding the drug trade. For instance, in discussions of harm, we may want to distinguish soft drugs like marijuana from hard drugs like heroin. We may want to distinguish homegrown marijuana that is not necessarily dependent upon the drug trade from heroin and methamphetamine that require sophisticated and dangerous chemical preparations. Or, we may decide under some other line of reasoning that all drugs should be grouped together, either by advocating their permissibility or impermissibility, one and all. Regardless of which strategy we take on the question of whether persons are entitled to live their own lives, and hence entitled to use substances that are presently controlled, we will also have to get clear about less controlled substances such as alcohol and cigarettes. Let us make no mistake about it, alcohol and nicotine are drugs, and addictive drugs at that. As we reflect on the limits of permissible conduct, we may want to distinguish between the current legal debate and the question of moral acceptability. The discussions may converge, but they also may prove to be quite different. With the new changes in laws concerning legalizing marijuana for recreational use, like alcohol, we observe changing opinions about prohibited and controlled substances in our society. I urge the readers to enter the debate more broadly, to ask whether or not an individual is morally entitled to intoxication? Is it permissible to become intoxicated—if so, why so, if not, why not—and then, we should explore what limits if any should be placed on the kinds of intoxication that should or should not be morally permissible.

The case of masturbation is still invoked by some as a moral rather than a private issue. Sometimes the case of masturbation is treated simply as an inherently immoral act rather than a harm to self but still considered as a case of harm to self. What good reasons, if any, can be offered for interference? For many people, practices engaged in private and alone cannot count as a wrong, though this line of thought can be called upon to argue for the permissibility of drug use as well. If we regard drug use for oneself to be wrong—and not simply unwise and/or undesirable—we must be prepared to offer reasons in the case of masturbation as well. There was a well-publicized case of an actor Pee-Wee Herman involved a case of masturbation at an adults-only entertainment center, but his conduct violated statutes for conduct in a public place. It is hard to argue, however, that his conduct was anything but a victimless offense; indeed, what do patrons expect to find at the kind of adults-only entertainment center that he attended? Was his behavior deemed to be offensive or harmful to patrons there, other than vice squad police who waited undercover as part of a sting operation? In another strange legal case, (May 1994), James Van Arx, age 41, who had been on probation for child molestation in Wausau, Wisconsin, was jailed after he refused court-ordered sex therapy designed to induce interest in adult erotic images.

He argued that such therapy was unconstitutional because it required him to masturbate, which is against his religion. In such a case, ironically, moral and legal questions are juxtaposed.

Under what conditions, if any, ought we to constrain or authorize the constraint of conduct when we judge that conduct to be harmful to the person against himself/herself?

NOTE

[1] This chapter draws heavily on two works by Joel Feinberg; *Harm to Others,* Oxford University Press, 1984, and *Harm to Self,* Oxford University Press, 1986.

Chapter 6

The Harm Principle: Part III Impersonal Harming[1]

A. HARM TO OTHERS, SELF, AND IMPERSONAL HARMING

One way of interpreting the principle of rational self-interest—that each of us naturally tends to act in such a way as to maximize our own interests—is to see it as a principle of maximizing liberties. In order to maximize our interests, we should be cautious about the imposition of restraints upon each other. In order to justify liberty-limiting principles, we must be prepared to offer good and weighty reasons whereby the right to pursue our self-interests may be overridden. In the last chapter, we advanced the claim that harm to others, the wrongful set-back of the other's interests, is sufficient to justify liberty-limiting principles. Such conduct we judged to be impermissible, and thereby deserves to be constrained. But the case of harm to self could not be answered so easily or unambiguously. Let us recall why.

When an agent or actor places him/herself at risk voluntarily, that agent has not been wronged when that agent suffers from the choice of action. The agents, indeed, may have their interests set back—may be harmed—without having any rights violated, and with no rights violated are not entitled to claim that he/she has been wronged. Still, some may argue that society has a vested interest in the well-being of its citizens and must restrict liberties and constrain actions that might place the agent at risk from serious harm, and that this interest outweighs a self-interested demand for maximizing liberties. The principles at stake seem to be two-fold: (i) while consent is necessary to justify the exercise of adult liberties, is it also sufficient? (ii) if consent is present, and hence the charge for "wrongfulness" is discharged provisionally, if the conduct still *seems* wrong (suicide?), is there some other principle that, replacing or joining "consent," is also a factor in determining whether conduct is "wrongful"?

These problems require further elucidation. To claim that consent is "necessary" is to insist that it must be present for harmful conduct to escape the charge of wrongfulness; when harm results even though the actions are consentful—bungee jumping off a bridge—the harm that might result was not intentional and the jumper knew the potential risks and "signed off" acknowledging them, and so the possibility of wrongful harm is, prima facie, dismissed. If we claim that consent is necessary and sufficient to escape the charge of immoral conduct when harm results, then "consent" must be present *and is also enough* (= sufficient) to escape that charge. But, a persistent matter that has yet to be resolved emerges if we still come away with a feeling, a sense, that some conduct still seems wrong even though the individual who has been harmed consented. And we will encounter the same problem with a range of *Impersonal Harms* including gambling, prostitution, consensual fighting-in-the-cage, and many other cases. If consent is present and yet the conduct still seems wrong, perhaps, there is yet another factor or factors that need to be considered, along with consent, to clarify when harmful conduct is also wrongful.

The reader will determine how liberal or conservative a position to adopt. The decision concerning paternalism rests prominently on the interpretation of the *Volenti* maxim, specifically how far to extend its reach. The liberal insists that where there is consent, there can be no wrongdoing (although there can be harm in the sense of set-back to interests), and where there is no wrongdoing, liberty-limiting principles cannot be justified. Stated differently, the most liberal views commit each person to the position that no one is better situated to make judgments about the meaning of the good life than the person whose life it is; and thus no one else is better situated to tell anyone how to live his/her own life. Of course, anyone can select to take the advice of others but this is still to affirm that each person is best suited to determine what is and is not in their own best interests, and responsible for the choices made and their outcomes, good or bad. The conservative argues, to the contrary, that where an action is deemed unacceptable by the harm it may likely cause, then any agent deserves to be restrained whether or not the agent or actor is simultaneously the victim. Thus the conservative argues that people need to be protected from their own folly. The liberal emphasizes the question of *consent* in interpreting wrongdoing; the conservative focuses upon harm irrespective of consent and in some strong sense does not accept extending indefinitely the *Volenti* maxim but rather equates harm with wrongdoing directly. Thus, the more conservative a stance we are inclined to adopt, the more we will argue that while consent is necessary to make permissible choices of conduct, it is not sufficient—it is not enough. The issue that each of you must resolve, in the question of harms to self, is the matter of *personal sovereignty*: To what extent is one's own life a matter of one's own sacred domain beyond the reach of others' intervention?

B. IMPERSONAL HARMING: HARMING TRADITIONAL VALUES AND ENFORCING MORALITY

Now we turn to a broad range of issues under the rubric of *moralism* that offer to supply just those factors that might, in addition to consent, clarify why it is that some cases of harming are still wrong even though the conduct is carried out consentfully. With regard to the law, these questions are referred to as issues of "legal moralism." The legal debate is intended to defend laws that "enforce morality" or, broadly, prohibit actions that ostensibly cause neither harm nor offense to anyone but constitute or cause evils of other kinds. Our debate is focused more on the idea of determining whether or not conduct is impermissible, and deserves to be constrained, irrespective of the particular legal statutes that are in existence. In our study later, we shall examine issues of pornography and censorship and the permissibility of consensual adult sexual practices engaged in private. These issues are framed in such a way in order to ask if liberty-limiting principles are appropriate in cases of consensual adult conduct, undertaken in private and not in public, and which harm or offend neither the actor nor anyone else *directly* but are judged to somehow harm *indirectly* and consequently are evils or wrongs. Sometimes these actions are referred to as *free-floating evils*, that is, conduct deemed to be immoral while directly harming no one. Often the complaint is that such conduct, while not harming any person directly, nevertheless harms the community or offends the community's standards. The conduct is judged by some to be immoral and wrong, depraved and degrading, regardless of the fact that it constitutes neither harm to others nor oneself, but rather provides a kind of *impersonal harm*.

The support for moralism, according to Joel Feinberg in *Harmless Wrongdoing*, comes from one of several arguments and includes: (1) the need to preserve a traditional life-style, (2) the need to enforce morality, (3) the need to prevent wrongful gain, and (4) the need to elevate or perfect the human character. The supporter of legal moralism finds such reasons adequate to recommend liberty-limiting laws on these grounds that there are certain acts that are inherently immoral and deserve to be prohibited even if such conduct is enacted in private and harms no party directly. These would all be among several factors that claim to show why consent, though necessary, is not sufficient to justify the permissibility of certain kinds of harmful conduct. There are times and circumstances in which conduct is regarded as immoral although the consent of the adult parties participating in it are present, and yet there is declaration from some quarters of our population that the conduct is nevertheless immoral. Are these cases violations of the harm principle? Let us become clearer about these arguments.

The argument that certain conduct undermines traditional life-styles reminds us of the offense principle. Some may regard unmarried persons living together under the same roof as evil, undermining and insulting to the institution of marriage that has been central to the life-style within our culture. But unlike other offenses that we considered with regard to our discussion of harm to others, this situation is not like the grating noise from the musicians next door who practice throughout the dead of night and prohibit a good night's sleep. In that case, one is confronted directly with offensive conduct which unchecked might very well become debilitating. In the case of the cohabitation of unmarried persons, the disturbed party is troubled only by the very idea of conduct which is largely unobserved except perhaps for the coming-and-going of the couple as they leave for work in the morning and return in the evening. When we identify these cases of impersonal harm we must clearly distinguish them from cases in which there is direct harm or offense to others.

The argument that communities need to preserve morality might be analogous to the need to preserve minimum civil codes for the appearance of houses in a municipality and the inspection of a home prior to sale. The principles that regulate housing codes are, in part, motivated to bolster the value of the homes and secure the desirability of the properties *in the entire neighborhood*, everyone benefitting from or being diminished by the collective care and appearance. In just this way, a community has an interest in enforcing certain standards of conduct to ensure the quality of life for its citizens. Thus, if a community deems that specific conduct falls beneath the threshold of acceptability— failure to mow the lawn in the summer, to paint a house falling into unseemly disrepair, storing dilapidated old cars in the front yard of the property, and so on—that community may, through legislation, enact statutes to safeguard a certain kind of life in that community. The argument for preserving a traditional life-style and the need to enforce morality are supposed to be morally coextensive. For morality turns out to be expressed in terms of the traditional life-style defined by a minimum threshold of rules and practices. What is central, however, to this second argument is the commitment to prohibit practices on the grounds that certain behavior is evil even if undertaken in private and harming no one directly. And in this important sense, the argument for enforcing morality directly challenges the *Volenti* maxim. Consent may be necessary to justify a practice but it is not sufficient, and these other factors help us to understand other grounds for recommending the diminishment of liberties. Let us consider the following examples.

Some have argued that the sport of boxing is inherently immoral. The object of the "sport" is to "knock out" one's adversary, to render one's opponent unconscious. Since the sport is marked by ingredients of brutality, some oppose the conduct outright. Advocates of boxing, however, are quick to counter these charges. One interesting line of rebuttal is that the prize fighters freely consent to enter the ring and engage in the fight and are compensated according to a prior mutual agreement. Fans pay considerable costs to view the contest and presumably receive their money's worth since patrons continue to attend. Also, no one is forced to watch. Hence, the rebuttal can be made that there is nothing immoral at stake since no rights are transgressed and all parties participating in the sporting event are consenting adults. Consent, according to the rebuttal, is both necessary and sufficient to justify the practice.

But how does the argument go from here? Suppose adults choose to pay for some other spectacle such as a live sex show—perhaps for a sadomasochistic display. We might now ask does a person have the right to submit to sadomasochistic treatment? Does the issue of compensation or public viewing affect the issue? Our question is whether anyone has the right to interfere with how consenting adults take their pleasure? Against the liberal reply that opposes interference on the grounds of the *Volenti* maxim, the conservative objector may insist that a community has the right to define and then suppress obscenity, deeming a range of conduct unacceptable. Doesn't a community have the right to establish minimum standards of decency whether those standards be in the form of repressing sadomasochistic sex shows, gladiatorial contests, or restricting "thong" bathing suits from the public swimming pools in some municipalities? Ordinances that regulate bathing attire are usually not framed in terms of averting depravity but in terms of an offense principle such as those that prohibit persons from parking damaged and rusting automobiles in their front yards, or penalize homeowners for failing to mow their lawn. Residents may complain that certain sights are "eyesores," offensive displays within their neighborhoods.

Perhaps we must take our hypothetical examples even further as a way of testing the *Volenti* maxim. One philosopher has invited us to consider the possibility of turning a major baseball park into a spectacle of gladiatorial splendor. What if entrance tickets were sold exclusively to consenting adults to watch a competition in which every contest resulted in someone's death. And let's say that each contestant gave full and free consent. With cable TV rights, prizes of two million dollars would go to the winners while prizes of one million dollars would go to the estates of the losers. Everyone has consented to watch or participate. Is anything wrong? Most of us, I believe, would be initially horrified to contemplate such a spectacle. But if one believes that consent is always necessary and sufficient to justify adult practices—the *Volenti* maxim—then it is not immediately clear how we will show—on what grounds—that such conduct is wrong and impermissible.

And there are many, many more such cases. Quite a few years ago, there were rumors that the Italian movie director Federico Fellini paid someone $10,000 in the movie *Satyricon* to have his hand cut off in a crucial scene. The rumor had it that the man desperately needed the money and in the 1960s, $10,000 represented a considerable sum for a voluntary act. The rumors proved false, yet the question of the permissibility remains. We may be horrified by many individual choices of action without articulating the reason that certain conduct is wrong. And we can imagine, the way daytime TV is going, that we might yet see someone agree to commit suicide on live broadcast for a price. Many persons find such behavior reprehensible because it seems utterly indecent. But our problem is to meet the challenge of the *Volenti* maxim, or find some other factor that clearly shows why some harmful conduct is nevertheless wrong. On what grounds does anyone acquire the moral authority to tell someone else how to live his/her own life, even if it is filled with potentially risky, self-harmful behavior?

Another area concerning enforced morality that is sure to loom large in the upcoming decades is the issue of whether or not persons may consent to sell body parts. Evidently, we find it acceptable for someone to work at minimum wage on tasks that seem inhuman, degrading, and dangerous. Why should we find it depraved if such a person agrees to sell a kidney to a wealthy patron for $100,000? If we suppose that the donor and the recipient freely agree to the transaction, where is the harm, and in what sense is it wrongful? How shall we specify the "wrong"? A very similar case might be constructed on behalf of prostitution. Why should we not allow adults to consentfully provide sexual services to adult patrons who solicit them? The prostitute might argue that despite the risks to health and person, $100 for half an hour or an hour's work might be preferable to an eight-hour day at minimum wage. It might not be acceptable to you or I but what good reasons do we have to stand in the way of these adults to make their consentful decisions? Perhaps these are cases of free-floating evils but we must be prepared to show which consenting adult transactions are impermissible and *why*. If we can specify "why" clearly enough, we will have shown the reasons to urge liberty-limiting principles because the conduct has then been shown to be wrong, and hence a violation of the harm principle.

Later in our discussions, we will focus on legal cases that reached the highest court in our land. When the United States Supreme Court decided *Bowers v. State of Georgia (Hardwick)* in 1986, the so-called "Sodomy Case," it supported the State of Georgia's legal interference with sexual practices of two consenting adult males in the privacy of their own home. The Court's reasons were: (a) the need to preserve a traditional way of life, (b) the need to respect long traditions of law and morality that opposed such practices, (c) the need to insist that not all conduct engaged in private is immune from prosecution, and (d) the need to emphasize that the general sentiment of the people of Georgia, as expressed through their legislature, was a sufficient condition to permit the enforcement of this conception of morality. In 2003 in the case of *Lawrence and Garner v. the State of Texas,* the Supreme Court reversed its decision in *Bowers v Hardwick.* What shall we conclude about private consensual adult sexual practices? How does this conclusion affect our position on the questions of consenting gladiatorial contests or the consensual selling of body parts? Asked differently, how shall we go about defining the meaning of obscenity or depravity? To what extent is "consent" necessary *and sufficient* to guide moral decision-making? These specific questions we shall explore further later on.

For now, let's contrast this situation with one other recent legal matter in order to reflect on the problem of allowing communities to define the meaning of immoral conduct, and to appeal to traditional values as sufficient to justify a law. When a state legislature passes a law and that law is determined to be unconstitutional at the level of the lower courts, the state is obliged to appeal the judicial decision as an act of defending the state's wisdom and pride in governing the lives of its citizens. The case of *Bowers v. Hardwick* was just such a case. When the Federal Appeals court declared the Georgia law unconstitutional, Attorney General Bowers, as a matter of course, appealed to the Supreme Court which agreed to hear the case. In Mississippi, an unusual departure from the common procedure resulted when the Federal Appeals court ruled the Mississippi law on miscegenation (marriage, cohabitation, or interbreeding between people of different races) to be unconstitutional. That law maintained that it was illegal and impermissible for persons of different races to marry. Several interracial marriages had been performed in Mississippi and one of those couples challenged the constitutionality of the law on the grounds that they had a legal standing and were in danger of arrest since they had violated the law. The state government in Mississippi was placed in an awkward position. If state government acted as was customary, they would be required to appeal the ruling of the Federal Appeals Court and thus would be required to petition the Supreme Court. But embarrassed at the prospect of perpetuating further the ideal of Mississippi as a racist state whose attitudes and laws were at variance with federal law, the state government chose instead to place the matter before the electorate in a plebiscite. If more than fifty-percent of the Mississippi state residents voted to declare the law null and void, an appeal to the Supreme Court could be avoided, along with the anticipated embarrassment. As it turned out, the vote in the late 1980s supported the measure but by a mere fifty-one-percent, having exacerbated the antagonism of both whites and blacks in the state. The point is, however, that if an appeal to traditional values is alone sufficient to justify a practice, then we must be prepared to resurrect the institutions of racist culture, and perhaps also slavery, since those institutions, too, can boast a long and traditional heritage. I am hoping that readers see the folly of such arguments.

C. IMPERSONAL HARMING: WRONGFUL GAIN AND PERFECTING CHARACTER

The case against free-floating evils is sometimes argued as a case against *wrongful gain*. In a wide range of cases, some have objected to kinds of conduct that, while not directly harming anyone, nevertheless allow one or more parties to gain from actions of dubious moral worth. When one or more persons benefit from such conduct, some conclude that these persons have gained wrongfully. Most often the objections to these kinds of behavior are couched in deploratory terms accusing persons of harmful *exploitation*.

The term "exploitation" has at least two main senses, one positive and laudatory, the other pejorative and deploratory. For example, we may encourage someone to exploit their talents or resources, that is, make the most of a situation, positively. No one is commonly troubled when urged to exploit a natural ability to sing, or an aptitude for mathematical skills, or athletic prowess. In these cases, we encourage someone to put to good use or advantage an ability or disposition rather than waste it or let it remain undeveloped.

It is the negative sense of "exploit" that concerns us here. In the pejorative and deploratory sense, "exploitation" refers to a relation between two or more persons or parties, in which someone is used for another's ends in a manner which is wrong or blameworthy, whether it wrongs that person or not. The issue of exploitation in the negative sense is extremely complex and we shall consider only the main point here. Let us illustrate this main point.

Prostitution is a familiar example some point to in the attempt to discredit as wrongful gain. Some have judged prostitution to be inherently immoral; the liberal objectors might challenge this view by pointing out that the parties to the action are consenting adults (N.B. I am not interested here in debating problems that arise when the parties include minors; the situation with minors must be addressed differently because we do not regard minors to be competent to give consent. In this case, with minors, the *Volenti* maxim is not operative). Certain persons desire sexual conjugation and find suitable partners who agree to provide the desired services for an agreed-upon price. Such an arrangement is identical in form to other widely accepted business practices. So, where's the harm? (For the time being, I pass over the many forms

74

in which prostitution may involve coerced behavior; but, then, where there is coercion, there is harm to another and hence the issue is decided to be a wrong deserving of constraint.) The massage parlor which offers illicit and illegal sexual services is another comparable institution that may claim to be harming no one directly but still receives the charge that the conduct perpetuated is immoral.

The conservative arguments might insist that although no one is harmed directly, persons are being exploited unfairly and wrongful gain is the consequence. These arguments might emphasize that the prostitutes are being exploited by their "pimps" who secure their services by a kind of coercive threat to limb and liberty. Or the argument might be against the prostitutes for economically benefiting from sexual conjugation outside the institution of marriage. Each time the reader debates an issue, however, the reader must be clear about where exploitation occurs and to whom. And should exploitation count as harm—how and why?

Another group of persons so maligned are magazine models, women and men who pose in ways expressly designed to sexually stimulate the viewers, and those women and men who perform in erotic videos. Sometimes the objections are given that these actors and models are being exploited. This argument is challenged by those who contend that the models and actors are not being exploited since they have chosen freely to participate, that they are compensated (sometimes) with substantial amounts of money, and that long lines of understudies are eagerly waiting to replace them. And it cannot be the publishers or producers who are exploiting them since they have freely offered employment and agreed to pay, often, thousands of dollars for a day's work. The readers/viewers cannot be said to be exploited since they have freely consented to purchase the magazine or purchase/rent the video. To the counterobjection that the models and actors are being exploited because they are being degraded and humiliated by their work, the rebuttal might well be that many jobs are degrading and humiliating and an enormous compensation overrides the set-back caused by degradation and humiliation. Finally, those who object to pornography on moral grounds (i.e. that in itself it is sinful or otherwise wrong) might argue instead that the persons who are exploited are not the models and actors who appear in these media but rather all women or all men (though usually the objection is framed with specific regard to women), who, even while not seen in magazine photos or in videotaped scenarios, nevertheless come to be viewed as sexual playthings and thus are subject to harms, indirectly. This objection suggests that pornography fosters an atmosphere that denigrates women and men and creates a social climate that tolerates harmful and deplorable acts toward women and men. The objection argues that making such conduct permissible fosters a dangerous social climate, and that that is intolerable.

Another argument for moralism, that is, for declaring impermissible free-floating evils (conduct that harms no one directly but still is somehow immoral) is the debate over blackmail. Blackmail may be regarded as another case of wrongful gain. Some cases concerning blackmail are easy to dismiss from this classification. For instance, the case of a person who tries to extract payment or goods from another on the promise not to assault him is clearly a case of criminal coercion and hence a (threatened) harm to another. In this case, a person demands payment for not doing what he has no legal right to do, that is, he threatens to do something that is illegal. A person who blackmails on the threat of future damage is involved in extortion and is threatening or harming others. Again, this is a case of someone demanding payment for not doing what he has no legal right to do in the first place, that is, he, too, threatens to do something illegal. So much for the obvious cases that deserve to be classified under harms to others and thus prohibited.

We can also imagine that person 'S' knows that a person 'G' has committed a crime and threatens to disclose this fact unless he receives a payment. This is a case of misprision; someone threatens not to do what he has a legal duty to do. Thus, the person who commits misprision offers to not honor his legal duty for a price. What shall we say about the harm here? Ought anyone really be required, on threat of punishment, to report another's alleged wrongdoing? If so, on what grounds? In the infamous case of Kitty Genovese, a case that we shall discuss later in regard to the abortion question, dozens of people in Queens, New York witnessed her murder; she was stabbed repeatedly on a city street in broad daylight and not one person called the police to report an emergency. Not a single one of them was ever brought up on charges of failing to honor their civic duty by failing to report a crime (in progress!).

Finally, let us consider what might be the most interesting case: Paradoxical Blackmail. Person 'S' threatens to reveal a damaging truth about person 'G' to the public unless 'G' pays a fee to 'S' or 'S' offers *not* to reveal to the public a damaging truth about 'G' if 'G' pays a fee. In this case, 'S' demands payment for not doing what he has a legal right to do, that is, 'S' may disclose or not disclose as he sees fit, legally speaking. From a legal standpoint, both 'S's threat and offer are to do something legally permitted. Nevertheless, the conduct is constrained by law. Should we judge it to be impermissible on moral grounds? And if so, why? Some have suggested that the case of paradoxical blackmail is a case of a free-floating evil, a case of wrongful gain.

Or the case of paradoxical blackmail may involve 'S's threat to disclose or offer *not* to disclose a damaging truth about 'G' and in return will accept employment in the form of a desirable job appointment. In this case, again, 'S' has a right to disclose or not to disclose as he sees fit. And 'S' has a right to seek employment. Each of these conditions is permissible within the law, but together are unlawful and perhaps immoral. What good grounds can we offer to defend such a practice?

Finally, some have argued against the permissibility of what we have called free-floating evils, or *impersonal harms,* on the grounds that the failure to develop an elevated character is itself the commission of an evil. From this perspective, the prevention of an evil is a powerful ground from which to defend the constraint of action. But, does it carry great enough weight to override the self-interested principle of promoting liberties? At what point is the limitation of liberty more odious than the evil the restriction seeks to prevent in the first place? The difficult truth is that we do not live in a black or white world. Invariably we must decide between infelicities, choosing the lesser evil. The prevention of an evil through the imposition of liberty-limiting laws or injunctions may be worse than the specific evil deed itself.

Some conservative proponents, in recognizing the fact that we are social beings, wish to see society as obliged to promote excellence of character. The liberal proponent, generally, agrees that excellence of character is a good thing for a society to cultivate. The problem is to determine how such a desirable result may be effected. The liberal tends to oppose interference from others. For how can a person be coerced to be fair, honest, trustworthy, dutiful, caring, loving, warm-hearted, generous, courageous, loyal, and so on? The conservative tends to counter this objection by insisting that, for the good of the whole society, others (perhaps the government and hence the law) are obliged to protect the populace and define public virtue. Quality of life depends upon a social environment that enriches individual life, and—in the name of enhancing the greatest good for the greatest number of people—this society must sanction institutions and coercive actions as a means of making people good. The liberal finds such techniques inappropriate for achieving excellence in character because manipulative techniques treat persons as means-to-an-end rather than as ends-in-themselves. To treat a person as a means, regardless of how worthy the end, is to reduce a person to a mere utility, a thing to be used like any other thing. The liberal accuses the conservative of a moral contradiction to which no one is entitled: one cannot coerce a person to be good. The conservative charges the liberal with risking the safety and well-being of the community by allowing each person to simply "do his/her own thing," and this diminishes the quality of life for each person and the community as a whole.

Thus, we are left with a series of challenges in assessing morally impermissible behavior. Even if we grant that harmful conduct deserves to be constrained, we have discovered that identifying and articulating harms is no simple matter. Harms to others are clearly unacceptable when persons' interests are set-back wrongfully. But what about harms that agents or actors cause to themselves? And what about the free-floating evils, or impersonal harms, which harm neither someone in particular nor the agent, but which still may be argued to be immoral? Are these harms also wrongful? What policy shall we recommend?

NOTE

[1] This chapter draws heavily on Joel Feinberg's *Harmless Wrongdoing*, Oxford University Press, 1988.

Section I: Week 3: Ch 5–6

Name_____ TA _____

Section #_____

1) Can an inanimate object be "harmed"? Why or why not?

Name_____ TA _____

Section #_____

2) Give an example of a "wrongful" harm. Give an example of a harm which *is not* "wrongful."

3) Describe the ancient Roman law known as the "Volenti Maxim."

Name_____ TA _____

Section #_____

4) What is the goal of "Legal Paternalism"? Which of the
   3 types of harms is it concerned with?

5) What is the goal of "Legal Moralism"? Which of the
   3 types of harms is it concerned with?

Name_____ TA _____

Section #_____

6) What is the definition of "exploitation" (in the negative sense)? Give an example of a situation which might be exploitative.

Chapter 7

Deontological Strategies[1]

A. PROSCRIPTIVE VS. PRESCRIPTIVE STRATEGIES FOR ETHICAL DECISION-MAKING

In the last three chapters we explored the idea of the 'harm principle' as a way to distinguish right from wrong conduct. Conduct that violates the harm principle—cases of harmful wrong-doing—were judged to be immoral. Such conduct was identified as being "wrong." We have appealed to the law—criminal vs civil—as a way to think again about what we regard as wrongful conduct and why. When we 'harm' others—set-back interests—we are liable to pay restitution and compensation for the harm we have caused; in such cases we have imagined "accidental harm" such as the unintentional fender-bender in parking lots. When the harm is caused intentionally, such acts are referred to criminal courts where the penalties are more grave. We have been exploring, by reflecting on this model, that "immoral conduct" is a term that applies to actions that set-back interests *wrongfully,* whereas accidental harms are not moral wrongs. Moral wrong-doing requires "immoral intention" in much the same sense that criminal wrong-doing requires criminal intent.

Some philosophers regard the business of ethics to concern recommending or "prescribing" conduct—you should do 'X' or 'Y' or even avoid doing 'X' or 'Y'. The approach we have adopted, by contrast, while it invites each person to wonder what he/she would/should do, raises a different question, namely, if John or Mary chooses to do some action 'V', are there any good reasons to stand in their way, oppose their selection of such acts, and advocate liberty-limiting principles if they do not? The proscriptive approach we are exploring allows each person to embrace their own choices of conduct without being compelled to justify them; you may follow the advice of your horoscope, Tarot Cards, the wisdom of the 8-Ball, your religion, or even the Sam-the-dog next door. In all the cases I am referring to, I mean that you are entitled to embrace whatever sources compel you to accept their wisdom without having to defend your views. But, these sources are insufficient as grounds to stand in the way of others and prohibit or constrain their choices. To stand in their way, to recommend liberty-limiting principles, we must be prepared to offer reasons. Our ethical explorations have invited us to consider what could count as good reasons.

Let me try to make this point clearer still. Suppose you are a vegetarian who opposes both the killing of non-human animals and their consumption, and you are horrified by the slaughter of animals. When John or Mary seek to find a hamburger, while your vegetarianism is a good enough reason for <u>you</u> not to eat one, or even patronize dining establishments that serve them, this, by itself, is not a sufficient reason to stand in the way of others and seek to constrain their pursuit of hamburgers. Of course you would be welcome to voice your opinion if asked, and perhaps also if not, but your revulsion at some action or other is not by itself sufficient grounds to merit liberty-limiting principles on the conduct of others. In terms of our discussion of the harm principle, your argument must establish, or try to establish, that animal killing and consumption are cases of harmful wrongdoing. Now perhaps you will argue that raising animals for food, besides being viscerally troubling is a poor way to manage our limited natural resources with a growing population, and we can better feed the bursting population with vegetable proteins and nutriments? Here we have the start of an "argument" and not merely assertion. Or you might want to argue that animals have, or should have right, as we take them for ourselves, and those include the right-to-life. Again, here is a position that must be argued for. If someone's religious beliefs commit them to the view that cows are reincarnated human souls, and thus by eating beef burgers one is not merely complicit in a murder but also a cannibal, such a view is sufficient to regulate the conduct of the person who holds such faithful beliefs. But, by itself, it is insufficient as grounds to regulate the beliefs of others who do not hold the same eschatological views. How precisely will we show that humans have a soul, that it continues after the death of the body, and that cows have the same souls? Until and unless we can convincingly demonstrate such claims, these sorts of claims must be regarded as testimonies of faith; testimonies of faith are good and compelling reasons for the faithful to abide, but not everyone shares the same faithful views.

Now we shall turn to explore three different "prescriptive" strategies that offer to instruct us of the "right thing to do." In these sections, you will be urged to distinguish "right" from "wrong" as prescriptions for action. As we continue through Part II and III, we will adopt a proscriptive approach but will make use of, and adapt, the strategies here for those proscriptive purposes.

B. THE IDEA OF A STRATEGY FOR ACTIONS

Having considered the defining mark of impermissible conduct—the *harm principle*—and a range of difficulties entailed in identifying what kinds of behavior deserve to be constrained, we now focus on this issue from a different perspective. In the preceding chapters, we focused on the defining mark of what we could regard as objectionable. Now, we will reflect upon a range of *strategies* or methods that might impel our actions to a salutary result. Whereas before we offered no recommendations about how to promote wise or desirable conduct, we will now consider some traditional formulas for promoting such conduct. In Chapters 7, 8, and 9, we will examine three strategies that claim to test the mark of wise and desirable conduct. In advancing this discussion, difficulties naturally arise when we try to test individual actions by appeal to these strategies. For once we agree on the general rule of the deontological, utilitarian, or command theory strategies, we are still faced by the arduous task of determining whether a specific action is in conformity with or in violation of those rules.

Our debate will be focused upon the question of whether conduct falls beneath the threshold of the *harm principle*. If it does, we can regard that conduct as immoral and impermissible, and thereby deserving of constraint. In these next three chapters, we will consider some efforts to identify rules for positively recommending conduct. The approach we offer has its shortcomings, most notably that we must tolerate a wide range of behavior that has nothing to recommend it. We must accept the proliferation of conduct neither wise nor desirable because, however unsuitable it may be, it does not violate the harm principle and thus does not fall below the threshold of impermissible conduct.

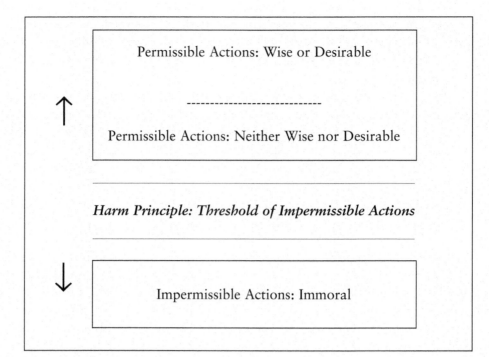

In this chapter I shall set out a deontological strategy for action, and distinguish it, provisionally, from a utilitarian strategy. I shall follow the line of thinking presented by Kant in the essay entitled the "Categorical Imperative," in order to articulate the deontological argument.

The overriding concern is to determine, from a strategic standpoint, how we shall best distinguish between what we commonly call right and wrong, or in our discussion, permissible from impermissible behavior. The deontologist and the utilitarian both provide us with criteria to distinguish between the two since both elaborate conditions for determining the rightness of an action. When these criteria are clear, we will then be in a position to review our provisional conclusions concerning the wrongness of conduct and hence a deeper meaning of the harm principle.

C. DEONTOLOGICAL MOTIVATIONS: NON-CONSEQUENTIAL

Let us distinguish, provisionally, between two strategies for action by responding to the question: Is the rightness of an action determined either by appeal to a principle independent of consequences, or by appeal to a principle that governs consequences? Let us more clearly distinguish the strategies as follows.

Deontological Strategy: The rightness of an action is determined by the fact that it ought to have been done, independently of any consideration of consequences.

Utilitarian Strategy: The rightness of an action is determined by the fact that the anticipated consequences are more likely to produce the greatest good for the greatest number.

The deontologist advises that the rightness of an action is never estimated by any appeal to consequences. The determining ground for conduct is an appeal to duty, whether or not the action in principle ought to be done. The deontologist views each action as an end-in-itself rather than as a means to some other end or consequence. If an action is determined to be obligatory, then the action ought to be done, even if unsuitable consequences are likely to arise from that conduct.

The utilitarian advises that the rightness of an action is always estimated by an appeal to consequences. An action which seems desirable in principle, but whose consequences are likely to produce tremendous unhappiness for a great number of persons, is deemed by this strategy to be inadvisable. Thus, the utilitarian regards all actions as means to ends. Where it can be demonstrated that the likelihood of a certain conduct will lead to the greater good for the greater number of people, that is the right thing to do.

Let us consider the following situation. I will propose two different dispositions toward action. In the case selected, I propose two scenarios which involve two agents, one a deontologist and the other a utilitarian. Both perform the same action, but, strategically speaking, from two different perspectives.

An elderly person appears stranded next to a car with an obvious flat tire.

Person A (Deontologist) stops and helps because this person believes that one ought to help others when they are in need. This person might receive a reward, or might not, but the concern for possible consequences does not enter into this person's moral deliberation about whether to stop and help. Person A changes the tire.

Person B (Utilitarian) stops and helps because this person hopes to gain some reward. This person presumes that the elderly person is unable to repair the tire, is stranded, helpless, and vulnerable, and will be most grateful for the assistance. The utilitarian might inquire first about a reward, or might simply hope that a reward will be forthcoming, but, in any case, it is the prospect for a reward that motivates this person's moral decision to stop and help. Person B changes the tire.

In both cases, persons A and B perform the same action of changing the tire. But, in both cases, the motivation for the conduct, and the criteria which enter into the moral deliberation, are quite distinct. In this scenario, the utilitarian seems to appear crude in comparison with the deontologist. This is a result of trying to make the point as favorably as possible to the deontological strategist whose defense we are focusing upon in this chapter. But, the utilitarian might have stopped to help in the name of promoting an example of kindness which, in the long run, might indeed be calculated to produce a greater good for a greater number of people. It would be misleading to suggest that utilitarians are greedy persons. This need not be the case, though it indeed might be so. The important point to emphasize is that the moral deliberation of the utilitarian consists in an appeal to consequences, however these consequences are conceived. The deontologist, on the other hand, never appeals to consequences, real or imagined, in order to determine the rightness of conduct.

Both the deontologist and the utilitarian regard human beings to be fundamentally moral. This means that both agree that human meaning is expressed in the exercise of reason over human action. And both regard the exercise of reason over action to be the central and fundamental characteristic that distinguishes us from every other creature. Thus, moral action affirms our ultimate human identity. Engaging in moral conduct is the resolution to our question: Who am I?

D. DEONTOLOGY'S CATEGORICAL IMPERATIVE

Let us examine the deontological strategy in greater detail. In order to do this, we will follow the position outlined by Kant in his discussion of the Categorical Imperative.

For the deontologist, the rightness of action is expressed by any conduct that affirms our moral nature. That moral nature consists in our acting for the sake of duty alone. The word "deontology," from the Greek *deontos,* means "ought." Moral action is an expression of what we ought to do, that is, our duty.

However, to be moral, one must not just act in accordance with duty. One must act for duty's sake alone. Thus, to do the "right" thing out of selfish motives would not be to act for the sake of duty. To act for the sake of duty is an exercise of reason. That is, it involves rational thinking. If an agent is to act rationally, the agent must act in accordance with a rule. If an action conforms to a moral rule, a rule which offers instruction on moral conduct, then that action is right. According to Kant, the general rule that distinguishes between right and wrong is called the categorical imperative. This means that there is an unconditional or exceptionless (categorical rule) imperative to which an agent appeals, and follows, if that agent is to act rationally.

According to Kant the general statement of the rule is as follows:

I must never perform an act unless I can consistently will that the maxim of my act become a universal law.

By "maxim" Kant means any rule for action. If the rule in question is suitable in a particular circumstance, but not in general, then the conduct cannot be recommended unconditionally. But if the maxim for action is of such a sort that anyone in that general predicament ought to follow that rule for conduct, then that maxim or rule has bestowed upon it the certification of a universal law.

This means that every time a person feels the obligation that something ought to be done, that person formulates a maxim or rule for action. If that rule can be universalized, then that maxim is declared to be unconditional. It is thus considered a categorical imperative. By willing in accord with the categorical imperative, a person affirms his/her nature as a moral agent. A moral agent engages in rational thinking and, following the dictates of rational thinking, conforms his/her conduct to a rule, and thus engages in right action. In this process, according to Kant, persons affirm their humanity by engaging in rational conduct and thereby distinguishing themselves from all the other creatures on the Earth.

As we began the text, we insisted that the goal of every action is happiness. This view required that we envisage all human conduct as goal-directed and invited us to consider what strategies would most effectively realize the happiness that we granted everyone desired. This was a suitable way to begin for two reasons. First, the strategy to act in the name of happiness has a common-sense appeal and certainly permits plausible confirmation by reflecting upon a wide assortment of our actions. Secondly, proposing something other than happiness as the goal of human action would be more difficult to take seriously at the outset. Now, however, we must consider the deontological critique of our very point of departure. The deontological position does not in itself undermine the claim that human motivations are fundamentally self-interested. In fact, Kant's brand of deontology also accepts this claim. But Kant's system is committed to the view that all other animals are also self-interested and that human beings can rise above self-interested animality by willing in accordance with the moral law. Kant's deontology offers one important challenge to the doctrine of self-interest. For, according to Kant, genuinely self-affirming behavior consists in obeying a law that persons impose upon themselves only because that kind of willing affirms an essential human nature.

We might offer the following counter-objection to Kant's position. This objection allows us to utilize Kant's strategy while retaining our claim that all human conduct is always motivated by self-interest, sometimes enlightened, sometimes unenlightened. Rather than view moral willing as a repudiation of self-interest, we might see it as the highest expression of self-interest, that is, of self-affirmation. By obeying a universal law that we have imposed upon ourselves, we will have realized our moral nature—and this is in our deepest self-interest to do.

The utilitarian views happiness as the goal of action. The deontologist, however, objects to that strategy for it fails to distinguish us from the rest of the brute animals who pursue the very same strategy, even if it is merely by instinct. The goal of action for the deontologist is moral. That is, all action provides the opportunity to rise above the other creatures through the exercise of reason in action. That exercise consists in reasoning for the sake of duty alone. The rational thinking that affirms our identity as moral agents is the moral purpose of action and it is the indispensable condition for being worthy of happiness. Thus, the deontologist does not pursue *eudaimonia* or happiness as the goal of action but rather pursues morality, and hence the worthiness to be happy.

This strategy follows from the presumption that "good" is ultimately defined in terms of the exercise of reason in accord with the categorical imperative or moral law. Kant's opening sentence in a work entitled the *Foundations of the Metaphysics of Morals* makes the point:

> *Nothing can possibly be conceived in the world, or even out of it, which can be called good without qualification except a Good Will.*

Thus, the meaning of "good" is identified with the rational exercise of the will in human conduct. An action is right when it follows from this moral disposition of the will. The will is moral when it is in conformity with the "moral law." Let us become clearer about this.

Kant distinguishes between two kinds of maxims, or rules, for action. The first kind may be called a "mere maxim" and is in no way morally binding. The second kind of maxim is a rule which is capable of being universalized. Maxims which are capable of universalization are called moral laws.

Maxims are either hypothetical or categorical.

(a) Merely subjective: "I ought to drink Pepsi." Everyone will grant that people have different tastes and thus there can be no way to suppose that everyone ought to agree with this rule of conduct.

(b) Objective—Moral Laws: "I ought to keep my promise." The maxim can be universalized. Failure to do so is self-stultifying (or self-contradictory).

Every rule for action, that is, every maxim, is either merely subjective or objective. The test is whether or not the maxim permits of universalization, if any agent in that general circumstance ought to will in accordance with the prescribed maxim. If the maxim is universalizable, then that maxim has been demonstrated to be a moral law. It is this exercise of rational thinking which is the mark of moral agency and is fundamental to human identity.

Kant distinguishes the subjective maxim from the moral law in terms of a technical distinction in the kind of willing in which the agent engages. The agent who wills the subjective maxim engages in goal-oriented behavior: this willing Kant calls *heteronomy*. The agent who pursues the objective maxim wills in accordance with the moral law: this willing Kant calls *autonomy*.

In the case of heteronomy, the law or rule for conduct comes from outside the self. In the case of autonomy, the law or rule for conduct comes from within myself. *Autonomy* literally means a law given to oneself. Our moral disposition conforms to principles which we impose upon ourselves for no other reason than that acting in accordance with the moral law affirms our fundamental nature.

In a series of three propositions, Kant makes clearer our moral nature:

> First Proposition: To have moral worth an action must be done from duty.

> Second Proposition: That an action done from duty derives its moral worth, not from the purpose which is to be attained by it, but from the maxim by which it is determined, and therefore does not depend on the realization of the object of action.

> Third Proposition: Duty is the necessity of acting from respect for the law.

In each of these propositions, moral conduct affirms our moral nature, and our moral nature appears in a disposition of our moral deliberations. In no way does that deliberation rest on anticipated consequences. Even the attainment of the object of action plays no moral role in assessing the worthiness of conduct. Thus, Kant can argue that the deontological test for rightness in action consists exclusively in an appeal for universalizability of the maxim, or autonomy. He insists that:

> *Act only on that maxim whereby one can at the same time will that it should become a universal law.*

And in order to make his case as clear as possible, he turns to examine four circumstances in order to test this thesis. The four test cases Kant calls upon are:

  (i) suicide

 (ii) lying to borrow money

(iii) developing natural talents

(iv) caring for others

In each case Kant will ask about the status of a maxim that calls upon us to engage in certain kinds of conduct. If the maxim appears to be of limited application or have self-stultifying (that is, self-contradictory) consequences, then the test will have shown that these particular maxims can, at best, have the status of being merely subjective. In all four cases, Kant believes that the status of the moral law becomes clearer.

In the case of suicide we are confronted by a person who wonders whether he can will to end his life when it suits himself to do so. Perhaps the individual has endured great suffering or perhaps the individual simply does not care to prolong a life which he/she finds meaningless. The specific circumstances Kant finds irrelevant to the issue. The problem is whether one may do with oneself as one pleases. Kant finds this unacceptable. This is because Kant holds that persons are subjects and agents. They are neither things nor properties. And unlike things and properties with which one may do as one pleases, persons must be treated with respect. Persons may never be treated as means to an end; they must always be treated as ends-in-themselves. For example, Kant regards slavery to be absolutely impermissible because persons cannot be the property of anyone else. But, by the same reasoning, persons cannot be their own property either. In the case of suicide, the individual comes to regard himself as his own property and thus can do with himself as he wills. But, in order to will this maxim consistently, one would have to concede that persons could be property which is inadmissible. Thus, suicide is impermissible. The maxim that a person may do with himself as he wills is rejected on the grounds that to accept the maxim, persons would at once have to be declared property, which is ruled out of hand.

In his *Lectures on Ethics,* Kant discusses many topics including a range of sexual activities classified under the Latin expression *crimina carnis contra naturam.* His view which offers a very conservative perspective that we shall examine when we discuss the institution of marriage, holds that sexual conduct outside of the marriage contract is an evil; it represents an indulgence and misuse of sexuality. Kant identifies a range of sexual practices to be a crime against nature including masturbation, homosexuality, and bestiality. He proclaims masturbation to be a greater evil than suicide because it places us below the nature of brute animals. Since Kant maintains that persons are not properties and, therefore, cannot do with themselves as they please, he judges many kinds of conduct to be degrading and debasing and hence impermissible on these grounds.

Lying in order to borrow money presents a similar circumstance similar in kind. When one is in need, it may become necessary to gain assistance from others. Invariably, persons are willing to be of assistance when they receive assurances that the remedies proposed will cause only temporary inconvenience. Many people are willing to help others in time of need but only on the promise that their loan will be repaid. Let us consider the status of a promise which is an intentional lie as a maxim for action.

A person claims to be in terrible financial trouble and can extricate himself from this dilemma if only you will lend him $500. For many this is a substantial and difficult request. But let us say that you wish to help this person, and you have the means, but just barely. The person says that he/she will pay you back—perhaps even with interest—in two weeks time if only you will loan them the much-needed money. If the $500 represents a considerable sum, and you wish to help, you will do so, but only on the grounds that you accept the promise. The promise is not a vague intention to repay at some indefinite time in the future. The promise is an absolutely binding agreement to repay at a definite and clearly agreed upon day. And it is essential to understand that you would never lend so great a sum, even to a friend in need, without the unambiguous assurance that you would be repaid as agreed.

The maxim for action in this case runs something like: "One ought not to keep one's promise—that is, one ought to lie—whenever one feels like it." It should be immediately clear that such a maxim could never attain the status of a universal law of nature. The maxim is self-stultifying or self-defeating. Why? At some point in time all of us are in need of assistance, sometimes financially. The only grounds on which a bank or an individual will ordinarily agree to help rests upon our promise to repay a loan. If the "promise" were assumed to be non-binding, no one would ever lend money needed in the first place. But sometimes financial assistance is desperately needed. Unless the promise to repay is regarded as absolutely binding, no one would ever be willing to provide the desperately needed help. Thus, lying to borrow money is self-defeating. Such a maxim for action could never be justified. This conceptual test, Kant believes, shows that such a principle is self-defeating and is thereby unsuitable to serve as a moral maxim.

Kant points out that there are contradictions inherent in the very conceptions of suicide and lying to borrow money. These two examples also make clear that he regards harm to others as impermissible and under certain conditions, harm to self impermissible as well. In the last two tests, he tries to show that there are contradictions, not in the conceptions, but in the willing itself.

In the third test Kant considers the maxim that we are under obligation to develop our natural talents. To develop our natural talents in order to realize our ends, certain talents are required and further, we are bid by the moral law to realize these ends. However, if we fail to universalize that maxim we shall find ourselves caught in a bind. On the one hand, we will be compelled by our moral nature to realize certain ends, but by laziness we would have failed to develop the natural talents indispensable to realize those ends. Thus, Kant can conclude that failure to universalize the maxim to realize our natural talents will place us in the contradictory position of willing the ends we must, while at the same time being unable to fulfill those demands for lack of talent. If one wills the ends one must also will the means.

In the fourth test, Kant examines the maxim of willing to care for others. He wonders about the consequences which would follow if we fail to universalize that maxim. He understands the consequences to be self-contradictory. Why? He grants that everyone at some time in his/her life will need assistance from others. Our lives may rely at some point on others' care. But, if we fail to universalize the maxim that we ought to care for others, we will find ourselves at some time both needing that care and unable to count on the care that we must have for our survival. This Kant understands to be self-contradictory, namely, to fail to will that a certain conduct, indispensable for our own survival, should become a universal law of nature.

E. SUMMARY OF THE DEONTOLOGICAL STRATEGY

Let us summarize the general point concerning the deontological strategy for human action.

Exercising reason in moral willing expresses our human nature. This is the main point. Unlike the utilitarian strategy with which we began, happiness is not considered by the deontologist to be the goal of human conduct. On the contrary, the goal of human conduct is the worthiness to be happy, and that is affirmed by engaging in moral willing whenever the possibility arises. By so doing, we engage in a kind of conduct that distinguishes us from the rest of the brute animals for whom happiness is the sole and exclusive goal for action. Human realization is made possible by moral willing. Thus, the goal or purpose of action is morality, not happiness; though in Kant's view, the moral person deserves to be happy (but may or may not be due to circumstances beyond one's control).

Kant expresses this theme over and over again in his writing. Below, two other citations are listed from the discussion of the categorical imperative which resound this point.

> *Everything in nature works according to laws. Rational beings alone have the faculty of acting according to our conception of laws, that is, according to principles, that is, have a will. . . .*

> *Man, and generally any rational being, exists as an end-in-itself, not merely as a means to be arbitrarily used . . . as a thing. . . . (Rational beings are persons.)*

94

Kant's deontological theory supposes that "persons" are those creatures who are capable of exercising reason for duty's sake. This rational activity, obeying a law—the Moral Law—that we impose upon ourselves, which Kant calls autonomy, underscores the essential difference between humans and other earthly creatures. It is in the exercise of this activity that we express, affirm, and come to clearly recognize our essential nature—the answer to the question: "Who am I?"

NOTE

[1] This chapter draws heavily on Immanuel Kant's "The Categorical Imperative," in *Fundamental Principles of the Metaphysic of Morals* (originally published in 1785), trans. L.W. Beck, New York: Liberal Arts Press, 1959.

Chapter 8

Utilitarian Strategies[1]

A. UTILITARIAN MOTIVATIONS: CONSEQUENTIAL

We continue to reflect upon the problem of determining the rightness of conduct in terms of intentions or motivations for action. We investigate various strategies that offer us criteria for drawing the distinction between what does or does not count as "right." Stated differently, we try to determine under what conditions conduct falls beneath the threshold of permissibility—the line in the air I am referring to as the *harm principle* defined as *harmful wrongdoing*. Conduct that falls *below* the level of this line is to be regarded as immoral or impermissible, and so worthy of constraint. Our continuing debates will be to decide what actions fall below the level of the line demarcating the harm principle.

In the last chapter, we pursued the deontological strategy articulated by Kant. The right thing to do, according to Kant, is expressed in a maxim for action that is capable of being universalized, and hence a moral law, an imperative to act that is "categorical" or exceptionless. The right thing to do is never assessed by reference to anticipated consequences as a result of our actions. When we do the right thing, we do it because it *ought* to be done, irrespective of the consequences that follow. For Kant, this means that human animals are different from all the other creatures on the earth; we alone subject ourselves to rules that we impose upon ourselves, and this self-legislation is the defining moment of our moral nature. All the other animals, in his estimation, act from instinct and not moral deliberation. When we impose a universalizable rule on ourselves, we exhibit autonomous willing; we do what we ought to do despite the fact that we may feel inclined not to do so, perhaps because of the unpleasant consequences we fear as a result of complying. For Kant, goodness is the result of obeying the moral law.

We do what we ought, and what we ought to do is what is prescribed in a universalizable maxim, a rule for action that anyone in the same general circumstance ought to do.

Now, we shall contrast the deontological strategy with that of the utilitarian. Attention will be given to John Stuart Mill's exegesis of the principle of utility with respect to human conduct. The deontologist insists that the ultimate criteria of right and wrong is whether or not an action is in accord with duty. Duty is expressed in the exercise of reason, that is, in rational activity. Through the exercise of reason, we determine the right conduct by following a rule. For the deontologist that rule is expressed in terms of a moral law, or autonomous willing. A maxim or rule for action proves to be a moral law when it successfully passes the test of universalizability. If a maxim can be universalized, and thus proves to be a moral law, then such an action proves to be in accord with duty and therefore is determined to be right.

The utilitarian, on the other hand, insists that the ultimate criteria of right and wrong is understood in terms of good and bad *consequences*. That is, right and wrong conduct are relative determinations with regard to the happiness that can be anticipated. The ultimate test for the utilitarian for the rightness of conduct is the effect or consequence of an action or rule on the welfare of society. Thus, from the utilitarian point of view, distinguishing right from wrong conduct involves a large measure of means/ends reasoning. The deontologist regards this strategy as morally intolerable because the anticipation of good consequences places humans alongside all the other animals that are regarded to be consequentialists— they are motivated by instinct toward goal-oriented behavior.

The utilitarian must determine the proper meaning of happiness because it is the goal of all action. Happiness must be properly understood in terms of the overall social welfare, determined within the context of consequences, measured in terms of the greatest good produced for the greatest number of people. By contrast, the deontologist assesses happiness differently. Not happiness *per se* but rather the worthiness to be happy is central to deontologist's project. Willing in accordance with the moral law, binding oneself to a self-imposed principle, is the mark of *virtue* and indicates the merit or worthiness of being happy. The deontologist's project is to isolate a purely formal determination of the will. From it, the deontologist believes that some sort of categorical imperative can be gleaned. The specific content is placed within the formal structure of the maxim, and the maxim in which it is expressed is tested to see if it can be universalized. If so, it proves to be a moral law, and the recommended action is judged to be "right." Consistently willing in this fashion is the mark of *virtue*. If, instead, the maxim will not permit of unambiguous universalization, the rule proves to be merely subjective, is a case of heteronomy, and is not deemed to be "moral." Thus, choosing Pepsi over Dr. Pepper, from Kant's point of view, is an amoral decision. It is not immoral; it is just that with regard to so many material decisions we are called upon to make, the issue of morality never arises. The utilitarian, however, finds this procedure to be much ado about nothing.

The utilitarian envisages persons to be rational creatures and sees the exercise of reason in conduct as a definitive mark of our humanity. But the need to understand a human meaning exclusively in terms of how persons are to be distinguished from other animals is found to be perverse. Like other animals, humans pursue happiness. The deontologist finds the utilitarian view to equate happiness with pleasure and sees this strategy as no different from the swine whose lifelong pursuit consists in rolling in the mud. But this conception of happiness is inadequate for humans who have a higher, more exalted platform of happiness. Thus, the utilitarian denies that the pursuit of human happiness is to be equated with pleasure. The utilitarian is not merely a hedonist. For, while the utilitarian will agree that happiness should be pleasurable, the pursuit of pleasure alone is no guarantee to human happiness.

From the perspective of extreme hedonism only pleasant experiences are valuable in themselves. Everything else we value, such as health, money, education, and so on, are only a means to that end of pleasure. The utilitarian, like Mill, confronts that argument with a challenge. Are any pleasures better than any others? And if so, how would we compare pleasant experiences so as to distinguish between them?

Some hold the position that pleasures differ basically only in intensity and duration. This means that any two pleasures may be compared in these terms. Two pleasures are deemed equally valuable unless they differ in intensity or duration. In order to assess the claims of each pleasure, a sort of calculus is devised. In terms of this calculus, each pleasure is rated in terms of comparative intensities and comparative durations. The standards may vary from person to person so that, for example, one pleasure may be much more intense than it is for another but of much briefer duration, or vice versa. The individual then assesses the relative merits and determines, overall, where the greatest pleasure lies. This is the initial basis of choice in conduct.

In order to escape the predicament of the extreme hedonist that Mill is insistent upon, he must make sense of the claim that there are "higher quality" pleasures and that these pleasures are more valuable than others. In making this distinction, Mill hopes to escape the charge that persons are no different and hence no better than beasts.

Happiness is the utilitarian criterion for distinguishing between right and wrong. But in order to understand Mill's resolution to the problem of distinguishing higher from lower or base pleasures, we must first turn to consider another distinction. Is the happiness criterion to be applied to actions or to systems of rules (= moral codes)?

> *Act Utilitarianism:* Happiness is the criterion for distinguishing between right and wrong. Happiness is assessed in terms of particular actions to which it is applied. If the anticipated happiness from performing an action is comparatively greater than other specific options available, then that action is deemed the right thing to do.

> *Rule Utilitarianism:* Happiness is the criterion for distinguishing between right and wrong. Happiness is assessed in terms of the system of rules or moral codes to which it is applied. If the anticipated happiness by appealing to one set of codes is comparatively greater than another set of rules, then the conduct in conformity with that first set of rules is deemed the right thing to do.

Mill advocates "rule utilitarianism," unlike his predecessor, Jeremy Bentham, who was a proponent of "act utilitarianism." In Mill's estimation, the "right" act would be the one that would be allowed by a moral code or set of rules that would be welfare maximizing in the agent's society. For Bentham, each "act"—not the rule—would be the focus of determining right and wrong.

Mill came to be recognized as the proponent of the Utility or Greatest Happiness Principle. That principle holds that actions are right in proportion as they tend to promote happiness, wrong as they tend to promote the reverse. "Happiness" becomes partially equated with "pleasure" and the "absence of pain." "Unhappiness" is largely announced in terms of the "presence of pain" and the "privation of pleasure."

The deontologist objects to pleasure as the central criterion for assessing the relative merits of conduct since the rightness of action is judged by the same means employed by swine who evidently enjoy that same strategy. Mill addresses this objection directly. He insists that a beast's pleasures do not satisfy a human being's conception of happiness. This is because human beings have capacities far more elevated than mere animal appetites. Still, we are saddled with the difficulty of distinguishing between two pleasures. Mill appeals to the general sentiment to adjudicate between conflicting ideas concerning pleasure.

Of two pleasures, he declares, if there is one to which all or almost all who have the experience of both give a decided preference, then *that* is the most desirable pleasure. For Mill, it is an unquestionable fact that those who are acquainted with any two competing pleasures do give a marked preference to that manner of existence which employs their higher faculties. And thus, since a being of higher faculties requires more to make him happy than other brute animals, the pursuit of happiness will not reduce us to the status of swine and other brutes. Objectors still find this argument questionable or unacceptable. They often point out that it is in the form of a restricted *ad populum* argument. The masses are often pleased by the grossest of pleasures and one ought not appeal to them in order to determine the rightness of conduct. And if Mill is appealing to the authority of the "higher critics"—those who enjoy privilege in a society—one is reminded that in different societies, the opinions of people of privilege differ.

Mill's argument, however, is to appeal to competent judges who have had a wide range of experience since he is convinced that individual happiness stands in indissoluble association with the good of the whole. Happiness, he insists, is desirable, and the only thing desirable. All other things are desirable only to that end. Mill believes that the sole evidence it is possible to produce that anything is desirable is the fact that people do indeed desire it. Mill points out that no reason can be given why the general happiness is desirable except that each person desires his/her own happiness—thus the happiness of the whole is a cumulative consequence of every person's natural pursuit of his/her own happiness.

From this utilitarian perspective, happiness is thus a good. Each person's happiness is a good to that person and the general happiness, therefore, is a good to the aggregate of all persons. But, how shall the utilitarian meet the objection that virtuous conduct might not be chosen when it fails to produce the desired happiness? If happiness is what we desire most and is that which we desire exclusively, then how shall we deal with the objection that sometimes what is clearly the "right" thing to do will be avoided when it may fail to produce happiness? Take the case of someone who promises to repay a loan in order to borrow money and then, afterwards, refuses to repay as promised because it would make him decidedly less happy? The (rule) utilitarian would quickly point out that happiness is not to be assessed merely with regard to an individual's judgment on a single action because an individual stands in an indissoluble relation to the whole social order. The utility principle appeals to a standard of the greatest happiness for the greatest number and, like the deontologist, would surely insist that promise-keeping is clearly in the interest of the happiness of the greatest number of persons. The "greatest number of persons" naturally applies to the individual in question who is presently refusing to repay a debt on a solemn promise; it is in that individual's interest to regard a solemn promise as binding because, invariably, this individual's happiness will require that others keep their promises to him/her.

The utilitarian seeks to show, then, not only that people desire happiness, but that they never desire anything else. Happiness is the sole criterion for distinguishing between right and wrong. The deontologist may further challenge, why be virtuous? Mill's response is to insist that virtue is to be desired disinterestedly for its own sake. Why? Because, in his estimation, it does produce a higher pleasure and brings together both individual happiness and the happiness of the whole.

The error the deontologist makes in criticizing the utilitarian is assuming that the latter equates happiness with pleasure. An individual does experience pleasure when that person is happy. But the pursuit of pleasure, without qualification, is no guarantee to happiness. All happiness is pleasurable, the utilitarian claims, but not all pleasure provides the same degree of happiness. Human beings, because they are capable of higher pleasures, according to Mill, will not find a satisfactory happiness through the pursuit of brute pleasures. The deontologist understands human identity to be distinguishable from other brute creatures. The utilitarian agrees. But the utilitarian sees the possibility of this distinction without giving up the goal-directed pursuit of happiness.

B. TESTING STRATEGIES FOR ACTION: THE HYPOTHETICAL CASE OF "DOWN IN THE JUNGLE"

In order to debate these apparently inconsistent strategies, the deontological and the utilitarian, we turn to consider a hypothetical situation. Following the lead of author Bernard Williams, the scenario may be entitled "Down in the Jungle." The details are adapted to suit our particular purposes. This exercise draws out in extreme the differing stances and commitments of both of these strategies when tested by a difficult and troubling problem about the right thing to do. The reader is challenged to discover whether his/her moral intuitions are deontological or utilitarian, or some third strategy.

> You find yourself walking in a jungle and hear the tribal drums beating. You enter a clearing and see a chieftain and his men preparing to execute ten persons who are tied hand and foot and lined up against a wall. Your presence is noted by the chief, who stops the process, and places you in the following predicament: You are offered the "special of the day." You may pick up a weapon and kill any one of the ten persons tied hand and foot against the wall, and then you and the remaining nine persons will go free. Or, you may turn around and walk away; no harm will come to you, but in an instant all ten persons will be killed. It's your choice. And you will not be able to determine whether the ten persons awaiting execution are innocent victims or mass murderers. In both cases, no harm will come to you whether you pick up the weapon and kill one, or refuse and walk away. What's the right decision given only these two choices?

In order to think deeply about this challenge, the reader must be reminded that there are only two possible alternatives in this exercise. Either the killing of one person is agreed to, leaving the other nine to go free, or no one is chosen and all ten persons will be killed. Inquiry about the circumstances that led to this situation is not permitted. Perhaps these ten persons are vicious killers themselves. Or, perhaps, they are innocent persons rounded up for the amusement of the chief and his men. The decision must be reached without any information concerning their predicament—all things being equal. (And no third alternative may be given.)

The task is to try to reconcile two distinct strategies concerning conduct. Let us try to distinguish these two alternatives:

Deontological Strategy: The right thing to do is to turn and walk away. Why? You have no idea what circumstances prompted this execution. But what you do know is that you were not a party to it nor ought you to interfere. The maxim for action here would be incapable of universalizability. Since it is clear that to kill someone without a good reason could never be justified, it is clearly a violation of the principle of harm to others. The world contains evil only to the degree that each one of us knowingly commits evil acts. To kill someone without a good reason is to kill someone unjustifiably and therefore must be an evil act. Since you have no good reason to kill anyone there, the only right conduct open to you is to turn and leave. You will not commit an evil voluntarily.

Utilitarian Strategy: The right thing to do is to pick up the gun and kill one person. Why? Despite the fact that the details of this situation are unknown, saving even one life produces clearly the greater good for the greater number of persons. And if you were at all unclear as to what to do, simply ask the persons standing against the wall. What would they recommend that you do? They are one and all shouting for you to pick up the gun and shoot. They know very well that if you turn and walk away they will all be dead in the next instant; their chances for living are 0%. If you shoot, each person stands a ninety percent chance of walking away alive and free. The obviously greater good for the greater number of persons is to pick up the gun and kill one, and this is what the utilitarian recommends we do.

In this scenario, the conundrum is to determine whether it is better to commit an evil knowingly, in order to minimize a greater evil (all things being equal) and produce the greater good for the greater number of people, or whether to refuse to subscribe to the permissibility of justifying the means by the ends and refuse to commit an evil voluntarily.

In order to get clearer on our own choices, let's complicate the matter slightly: in scenario #2, the jungle situation is the same, but now the arrangement the chief offers requires that you kill five persons on the line, and the other five will be let go. In scenario #3, you must kill nine and the tenth will go free. How do these changes affect your strategy? If you hold the view that human life

103

has a value that cannot be stated in material terms, and that saving a life or lives outweighs the evil which you otherwise have to commit—recall that all 10 will be killed instantly upon your refusal to participate further—then you ought to pick up the weapon in *all* scenarios #1, #2, and #3.

Some persons believe that given only the two alternatives, they would, in scenario #1, pick up the weapon and kill one person. But, many who tend to opt for that strategy express increasing reluctance to pick up the weapon in scenario #2, because the amount of evil they are forced to enact seems increasingly discomforting, indeed, unbearable. Many people who take the utilitarian stance in scenarios #1 and #2, however, refuse to elect the same strategy in #3. Can these positions be maintained within the utilitarian framework? The challenge is to discover whether or not your positions are ethically *consistent*. It is not always easy to see how. If life is considered inviolate, then it would seem that the chance to save even a single life—all other things being equal—should compel the utilitarian to kill one, five, nine, perhaps even thousands, to save even a few lives which would otherwise be hopelessly sacrificed. But, at some point, the individual recognizes that the amount of killing required in the name of decency seems utterly indecent, or at least indecent for one to do by oneself.

> The deontologist can take pride in the refusal to commit an evil voluntarily. But, how would you, the deontologist, react if you found yourself on the line awaiting an execution (unjust or not). Would you recommend that the person being addressed by the chief not commit an evil knowingly? Or would you be begging and screaming for that person to pick up the weapon and do some shooting, since otherwise you will surely be dead in the next instant? The utilitarian reminds the deontologist that we live in an imperfect world where, perhaps, it is better to commit lesser evils than permit greater evils to be perpetrated.

This hypothetical scenario also permits us to raise a different kind of question. Should our assessment of human conduct be made from the perspective of:

(i) the agent or actor who initiates the action; or

(ii) the victim or patient to whom the action is directed?

The deontologist seems to have the strongest argument when judging the role of the person who must decide whether or not to commit an unjustified killing(s). But, from the perspective of the victim standing against the wall, the issue of unjustifiable evil might well count as preciously little when the alternative is certain death. After all, don't we commonly speak as if every person has a right to life? Animal instinct alone guarantees our natural drive toward self-preservation. Can we blame anyone on the line for wanting to save his/her life at almost any cost? In the case of the utilitarian, the strategy is more comparably shared by agent and victim. For the utilitarian agent, the principle of acting to maximize the greatest good for the greatest number seems to endorse killing one or more of those who would, otherwise, surely die. As for the utilitarian victim, the answer seems clear that every person would recommend that the agent pick up the gun and commence firing.

What is the right thing to do and why? What conduct is impermissible? What strategy is impermissible and why?

NOTE

[1] This chapter draws heavily on J.S. Mill's *Utilitarianism, Liberty, and Representative Government,* New York: Dent and Sons, 1931 (originally published in 1861).

Name_____ TA _____

Section #_____

1) Define the "Categorical Imperative." What does categorical mean in this context?

2) How can we distinguish between "mere maxims" which are subjective, and "moral laws" which are objective?

Name_____ TA _____

Section #_____

3) For Kant (the deontologist), is it ever permissible to lie? Why or why not?

4) Describe the difference between "heteronomy" and "autonomy."

Name_____ TA _____

Section # _____

5) Describe the utilitarian moral position.

6) Describe the difference between a deontologist and a utilitarian: state specifically how important consequences are for each.

Name_____ TA _____

Section #_____

7) Is the theory of Rational Self Interest closer to a deontological or a utilitarian perspective? Why?

Chapter 9

The Command Strategy: Morality and Religion[1]

A. MOTIVATIONS BY COMMAND: SCRIPTURE AND/OR REVELATION

In contrast to deontological and utilitarian strategies for action, some have argued that a different kind of strategy is both possible and necessary for right conduct. These persons suggest that religion alone prevents morality from simply being an arbitrary agreement among persons in different societies and different times as to what exactly is right and wrong. The command theorist insists that only God, the supreme power and creator of the universe, creates morality. God creates morality by willing or *commanding*. The right thing to do is determined by consulting scripture or by appeal to divine revelation. All other strategies are, ultimately, theories of convenience or culturally endorsed efforts to attain standards in a community, but are always the efforts of imperfect and sinful creatures.

According to a usage still common in America, the term "morality" is inextricably linked to the idea of religion. Supposedly religion teaches morality and morality means the difference between right and wrong. The consequence, accordingly, is that religion is necessary for morality. Religious organizations try to capitalize on this point under names such as the "Moral Majority." The nominal selection attempts to underscore that those who know "moral" teachings know the difference between right and wrong. Religion is thus seen to be the indispensable key to right conduct. Without religion one cannot be moral because one cannot know the difference between right and wrong.

All of this suggests that the word "morality" has an approbative force in our society. To be recognized as a moral person is to be recognized as being deserving of accolade. Those who are not religious are seen to be immoral, and those who are not moral are considered base, wicked, or otherwise nefarious.

Since we have come to see that human identity is fundamentally moral—a term whose meaning we are exploring in our ethical investigations—it is important to determine if formal or traditional religion is necessary for the attainment of morality and for the realization of human meaning. Or if it is not, we must attempt to become clear what role, if any, religion plays in developing our moral nature.

B. DOES MORALITY DEPEND UPON RELIGION?

Does morality depend upon religion? This question might mean at least two different things. And we shall begin by following John Arthur's article entitled "Does Morality Depend Upon Religion?" First, the question can mean "Is religion necessary for people to do what is right?" The question asks if religion provides an incentive to right conduct. Second, the question might mean "Is religion necessary for determining the difference between right and wrong?" The second question asks whether revelation alone can provide moral knowledge.

Let us consider whether religion is necessary in order for people to do what is right. Some thinkers have supposed that religion is necessary for morality, that without religion there would be no reason for people to restrain themselves in circumstances in which it was not convenient or desirable to do so. In those situations, persons restrained themselves only because there was some incentive to do so either in the form of God's reward or damnation, on the one hand, or for the fulfillment of God's plan, on the other.

Religion provides an answer to the question "Why be moral?" Why do what seems morally right when it is clearly not in our self(ish) interest to do so? The answer religion proposes is that if God rewards eternal happiness to those who do the right thing—duty—and punishes those who do not, then that seems to be a good reason for doing the "right" thing.

Other proponents of the incentive thesis have suggested that the reason we do the right thing, that is, engage in moral behaviors is that it is God's plan for man. By our moral conduct, we realize His goals. To live a moral life is to live in harmony with a larger, divinely created order. Thus, the answer to the interrogative "Why be moral?" in this second response is also in terms of an incentive. But the incentive is understood in terms of realizing the divine plan, God's project, rather than the promise of reward and the fear of hell.

The question of whether religion is necessary for morality has been interpreted to mean not only whether religion is necessary for people to do the right thing, but also whether religion is necessary for determining the difference between right and wrong. Religious thinkers have often tried to point out the ultimate futility of man-made laws. Laws made by humans are ultimately arbitrary, they are agreed-upon conventions. If there were no divinely-authored laws, there would be no real guidance to distinguish between the conflicting claims of different peoples.

Those who envisage religion to be necessary for morality, in this second sense, by and large subscribe to what we may call a command theory of morality. *God creates morality by commanding it.* Through commandments, humans discover the difference between right and wrong. All human authorship of legal codes is fundamentally capricious and can be neither ultimately binding nor ultimately instructive about what is truly right.

Thus, some religious proponents argue that religion is necessary for morality because without God's commandment there could be no right and wrong. God creates morality by commanding or desiring that His creatures follow His will. In this interpretation, religion is necessary for everyone and without it, morality would collapse since we could not know what is right. In this view, revelation alone, either through scripture or divine grace, provides moral knowledge. Morality—knowing what is right—has no meaning other than to follow God's commandments.

Thus, some argue that religion is necessary for morality. Without religion, morality would collapse, either because there would be a lack of incentive to do the right thing (= problem 1), or because of our inability to know what is right (= problem 2).

C. CAN ONE BE "RIGHTLY" COMMANDED TO DO AN "IMMORAL" ACT?

Traditional defenses of the necessity of religion for morality lead to challenges and objections from those who do not hold these views. The thrust of the objections is to show that in order to do the "right" thing, religion is in no way necessary. Religion may be useful and may have extremely salutary effects, but it is no guarantee for making decent and thoughtful persons.

The deontologist claims that the meaning of "right" is decided by an appeal to a principle, a maxim for action capable of being universalized. The utilitarian claims that "right" is decided by a calculation determining the likelihood of one course of action producing greater benefit for a greater number of persons. In terms of the defense of traditional religion, what is the meaning of "right?" The answer is: "Whatever God commands." Thus, if God approves something, it is right by definition. A problem arises. If God "approved of" or "commanded" the torture of an innocent infant (i.e., the story of Abraham and Isaac), would that make such an act right?

In no way are we entering here into scriptural interpretation. Those matters are best left for the clergy and those trained in matters of theology. Our problem does not require that we debate the details or interpretations of the Abraham story. Our problem is the question as to whether an act is moral because God or anyone else *commanded* it. Is that adequate? Could the meaning of morality rest on a command theory?

In the Abraham story, God commands Abraham to sacrifice his son. It so happens, according to the story, that God seems only to be testing Abraham, testing his faith. But, sure enough, God commands Abraham to make a sacrifice of his son; he is commanded to what is tantamount to torturing his son. Proponents of traditional religion have held the position that the meaning of "right" is extensionally identical to whatever God commands. Thus, our question is whether an act is moral because God, or any other authority for that matter, commands it. Those who wish to object claim that the answer is unequivocally "no." This issue calls for further comment.

If God is "moral," then surely God would want His creatures to behave morally. But, does the morality of our behavior usher forth from the fact that:

(i) God said or commanded it (= command theory of morality); or

(ii) The principle in the action meets the conditions for morality.

If a rule for action is said to be moral not in principle but because God commanded it, can moral decisions be anything but arbitrary? This problem can be stated differently. Suppose God commands some action. Now, either God has a reason that explains why this conduct is right or He does not. If God has no reason, then the command is strictly arbitrary. The consequence is that morality becomes some strangely terrible game like a grown-up "Simon says." Why do something or other? If there is no reason, then all conduct is ultimately arbitrary. On the other hand, if God has good reasons why such conduct is commanded, then the rightness of that conduct does not consist, first and foremost, in God's having commanded it, but rather in the reason(s) for that command. In that case, by understanding God's reasons, God's wisdom, morality ceases to be arbitrary. But then, the rightness of action is not secured by God's command but rather by a reason or reasons that prompt that command. In any case, the command theory seems dispensable, either because it fails to be informative, or because it renders God an arbitrary and capricious deity who does not know why He commands the things He does.

D. WHY DO THE "RIGHT" THING EVEN WHEN IT DOES NOT SEEM TO BE IN OUR SELF-INTEREST?

The view we have been examining supposes a Judeo-Christian-Islamic ethic that underlies socially permissible conduct. Of course, in other nations, different traditions underlie social practices. Our focus has been on moral issues and the manner in which we discover the difference between right and wrong and how we are motivated to act in accordance with that understanding. This examination has sought to focus exclusively on conduct in recent and current American society.

In order to challenge such views, it will be useful to call upon a different analysis that emerges from a very different tradition. Our purpose in such an enterprise is not to malign our traditions. The intention is to offer another fruitful vision that reminds us of how different our social mentality might have been if historical circumstances were radically different. I turn to a well-known example from Western literature, Plato's dialogue entitled the *Republic.* The main character, Socrates, discusses the ideal state, its nature and the kind of conduct that would be exhibited by its ideal citizens. Among the many issues that the dialogue explores is the question "Why be moral?" The question asks about the conditions that motivate us to do the "right" thing when it is apparently not in our self-interest. The answer proposed is unlike the ones we have considered earlier.

So far, we have proposed that one is impelled to do the "right" thing by an incentive theory of conduct. Either the promise of reward or the fear of hell are sufficient conditions to motivate our doing the "right" thing. As for the distinction between right and wrong, the earlier thesis proclaimed that it is only by virtue of God's commandments that we are even able to distinguish between the two, all other criteria would be merely arbitrary. Plato offers us a different resolution, more or less four hundred years before the birth of Christ.

The *Republic,* in Book II of its ten books, offers us the myth of Gyges. The underlying question is "Why do the right thing if it is apparently not in your self-interest?" and, more pointedly, "Why do the right thing if you could be certain that you would not be caught and punished for doing the wrong thing?" Here's how the story unfolds:

> A man named Gyges finds a ring. He puts it on and continues his daily routines. One day he notices the strangest thing. When he turns the ring so that the stone, usually pointing outward on his finger, turns inwards, lo and behold, he becomes invisible. Gyges is stunned. He tries it over and over again. Sure enough, the same amazing result occurs. He can become invisible at will. By turning the ring so that the stone points inside his hand, he vanishes; by turning the stone outward again, he reappears. After trying this over and over again, he becomes convinced that its operation is foolproof.

With this newly acquired power, Gyges gets greedy. He realizes that so long as he can become invisible at will, he is capable of doing whatever he wants with impunity. He then conceives a fiendish plot. He seduces the Queen with his amazing power, and gains her acquiescence to kill the King. Of course, this is no problem for Gyges. He turns the ring, becomes invisible, steals into the King's chambers and murders him. Then, he proclaims himself King and marries the Queen. By virtue of the ability to become invisible at will, he is capable of doing whatever he pleases.

This myth puts into question Socrates' own theory that a good man, a moral person, is a happy person. Why? Because here we have the situation showing that a person acts morally only to avoid being caught, to avoid punishment. Persons are moral only to avoid punishment. The case of Gyges suggests that if a person could be sure that he would never be caught and face punishment, then he would engage in the most barbaric, ruthless, and objectionable conduct when it pleased him. Thus, it seems to be a fear of retribution which constrains our behavior. Why be moral? The answer to be gleaned from the Gyges case seems to be that moral conduct is desirable only because it is less dangerous and involves less suffering. BUT, if there were no punishment, there would be no reason to constrain conduct. In this view, persons are self-interested and selfish and the only reason that people act morally is out of fear of reprisal.

Socrates' response offers us an alternative defense of why we ought to do the "right" thing. In this case, it is not by appeal to divine intervention, whether by reward or punishment. Socrates' response advances two distinct arguments. In the dialogue entitled the *Meno,* Socrates insists that no one commits an evil voluntarily. Why? Because, Socrates argues, the result of committing an evil is to cause harm to others and to oneself. Now, no one intentionally attempts to cause harm to himself or herself. The things people do are calculated to produce good and thereby happiness rather than evil and if any unhappiness follows it does so from iniquitous actions. Thus, by the *Meno's* argument, no one commits an evil voluntarily. Everyone desires the good but often mistakes what is good for what is not.

In the *Republic* the argument is different. Socrates' response is that Gyges would not be a happy man, though he indeed might gain acquisition of many things. Happiness is a result of being in balance and establishing accord with the components that constitute our personality. Socrates' argument is that when we are engaged in action naturally suited to us—what he calls "doing one's own"—there is justice or harmony within us. This experience of accord or balance Socrates describes as happiness. He insists that there is no way one can commit injustice—which Socrates defines as non-harmonious, or imbalanced action—and still retain that internal accord which is a concomitant of happiness.

Thus, "Why be moral?" or why do the "right" thing even when it is apparently not in our best interest? Socrates' answer is that failing to do so will interfere with our natural balance and thus our fundamental happiness. Those who engage in immoral conduct are deeply unhappy. We do the right thing because, among other things, it makes us feel happy.

The theory Socrates advances in the *Republic* is not the only challenge to the defense of traditional religion in terms of incentives for constraining behavior. It offers an alternative view to that traditional and familiar defense of Judeo-Christian-Islamic morality. With this in mind, it is fitting that we begin to think hard about our answer to the question: "Why be moral?" Why do the "right" thing, even if we are sure that we would not be caught and punished for doing the "wrong" thing?

It should also be clear that this Socratic response to the proponents of traditional command strategies is not an argument against self-interested motivations to action. The theory of self-interest that we have considered insists only that our choices are motivated by what we believe to be in our self-interest whether or not it turns out to be. The Socratic thesis is that it is in everyone's interest to be happy and acting in a balanced and harmonious fashion will promote that interest. We do the "right" thing, not because someone else tells us to, whether or not with the incentive of a reward; we do the right thing without coercion. The right thing proves to be action that preserves harmony and balance, and thereby the happiness of the individual and group. For the Socratic thesis empowers us by enhancing our self-interested motivations with the wisdom or enlightenment of recognizing we are part of an interconnected world.

NOTE

1 This chapter draws heavily on John Arthur's "Does Morality Rest Upon Religion?" in *Morality and Moral Controversies*, Englewood, New Jersey: Prentice-Hall, ed. by John Arthur. 1981.

Chapter 10

The Morality of Punishment—
A Deontological or
Retributive Defense[1]

A. THE PROBLEM OF PUNISHMENT: WHY THE INSTITUTION OF PUNISHMENT NEEDS A MORAL DEFENSE

We have begun to explore the question "Who am I?" directly and indirectly. We have reflected on our self-interested motivations in action and our identity in context of the harm principle. We have wondered about ourselves in terms of our life choices and in terms of what conduct is impermissible and deserving of constraint. We have discussed our identity in terms of personhood and rights and have considered immoral conduct which deprives a person of a right by depriving him of his very nature. Thus far, our sense of self-identity has been illuminated by an understanding of those fundamental rights, the deprivation of which threatens to rob us of what we ultimately are. The idea of immoral conduct can point the way to delineate our moral nature.

We raised questions about and will seek provisional judgments upon a wide range of social practices. We will later address problems concerning the morality of killing in the debate over abortion, infanticide, euthanasia, suicide, capital punishment, and animal rights; and we will examine questions of sexual behavior and morality in issues of rape, monogamous marriage, adultery, pornography, sodomy, sexism and racism. In all cases where it may seem clear that conduct is impermissible, it remains for us to decide what we ought to do in response to them. This naturally leads us to a consideration of the practice of punishment.

Punishment presents more difficulties than one might first suspect. This tends to strike many of us by surprise because the supposition that "wrongs" should be "made right," that punishment is somehow a fitting response to iniquitous conduct and evil deeds, is deeply ingrained in the social practices of our Western civilization. Why must we justify the practice of punishment? The simple answer is that since punishment involves just the sort of harm to others that characterizes the clearly objectionable offense of harming itself, we must defend the permissibility of the State (or anyone else) to engage in the very practices deemed abhorrent and objectionable in the first place.

Why must we justify the practice of punishment? As Martin Perlmutter presents the case in his article, "Punishment and Desert," the argument about the permissibility of punishment might be stated as follows:

(1) Punishment is a form of harm or deprivation. If there is no "harming," then there is no punishment.

(2) Thus, in depriving someone, we harm them, and this means that we make that person worse off than he or she was before.

(3) But, it seems that we have a *prima facie* obligation not to make others worse off.

(4) Therefore, the practice of punishment needs a justification for which the apparent obligation not to make others worse off can be overridden.

Thus, the point of the argument is that punishment involves harmful conduct that was deemed objectionable, or immoral. But that harmful conduct that is now being addressed seemed to cry out for some kind of retribution in the name of justice. Since the initial conduct was objectionable precisely because it caused an inexcusable or unjustifiable harm to others and thus deprived another of his or her domain and hence his or her essential nature, the defense of punishment requires that we explain why harmful conduct is now justified in our retribution. Stated differently, if certain conduct is judged to be immoral because it was inexcusably harmful, why can we respond to that detestable action with practices that, too, are harmful? If we are to produce a successful argument on behalf of the permissibility of punishment, we must show that ordinary prohibitions against harming can be overridden. When can such prohibitions be overridden? When addressing cases of wrongful harming, the harmfulness of punishment may be excused. To justify the punishments of harmful wrongdoers, then, we must be prepared to show that the harming of punishment addresses the wrongdoing of the offenders, and by this appeal we override the objections against punishment as harming.

Two essential features of punishment must be discerned before we can proceed. This is required since an appraisal of punishment must focus upon conditions that sufficiently identify its nature. First, punishment must inflict *harm*. That is, unless we cause pain and suffering by a kind of deprivation, then there is no punishment. Granted, many societies accept different forms of harm as permissible. Some older motion pictures depicted earlier judicial remedies of sentencing convicted criminals to "hard labor" and invariably picture the convicts in striped uniforms (with matching cap) working on rock piles with sledgehammers. In the United States, we no longer find this sort of punishment permissible, but instead try to impress the criminal with the importance of freedom by merely restricting his/her freedom through highly structured containment—a big adult "time out." Of course, there are other nations that permit practices of punishment which we find unacceptable. In Saudi Arabia, for example, a person convicted of theft might lose a finger or an entire limb—literally "an eye for an eye, a tooth for a tooth" mentality of justice. There was a case in Singapore where an American teenager found guilty of vandalism was punished by caning—receiving ten lashes or so with a cane. In the United States we have come to regard such punishments as both cruel and unusual. But, of course, we have not come to conclude that punishment is inappropriate, only that it must not be corporal.

Secondly, punishment not only requires the inflicting of harm or suffering by means of deprivation, it also requires wrongdoing. Imposing harm is not by itself punishment unless it is connected with a past wrongdoing. When we hear on a sports broadcast that one hockey team "punished" the opponent the night before, images of violence and fighting appear in our imagination, but this is "punishing" in a poetic or metaphorical sense and not the one meant here. The same is true when we hear the meteorologist say that a coastal town took a terrible punishment from powerful winds in a hurricane. Again, damage and harm were inflicted but wholly without a sense of wrongdoing. In order to count as punishment there must be an event that gives a clear sense that the punishment is in response to an unjustifiable wrongdoing.

This last scenario naturally prompts our attention to another key issue in understanding the institutionalization of punishment. This requires that we consider restrictions on who can punish whom.

The legitimate domain of punishment is restricted, within our society at least, to special relationships.

(a) A state can punish its citizens.

(b) Parents can punish children.

(c) Teachers can punish students.

Generally, these relationships are not reversible. Only by special permission can a citizen sue, and subsequently "punish" by restricted means, a government or state. Ordinarily, children are unable to punish their parents. Recent cases where children have taken their parents to court over improprieties, abuse, or to obtain rights to permanent separation, are recent exceptions to the long-established general rule. Teachers can punish students, but there are many more restrictions on this conduct than a parent's capacity to punish one of his/her children.

Thus, in order to evaluate more clearly the permissibility of punishment we must keep in mind that certain conditions must be met in order to consider conduct that counts as punishment. The conduct must inflict harm through some kind of deprivation. The harm must be linked to past wrongdoing on account of which it is meted out. And finally, punishment requires not mere harm and wrongdoing, but enforcement by virtue of special relationships.

B. CONTRASTING DEONTOLOGICAL AND UTILITARIAN DEFENSES OF PUNISHMENT

Let us distinguish two different strategies toward punishment. The first we might call deontological or retributive, while the second strategy we might call utilitarian.

(a) *Strategy 1: Deontological or Retributive.* This strategy looks to the past to justify the practice of harming others—punishment—to see that one is treated as one treated others, to see that one gets what one deserves.

(b) *Strategy 2: Utilitarian.* This strategy looks to the future to justify the practice of harming others, to see if the long-term good outweighs the bad.

Both strategies offer a defense of the permissibility of punishment, that is, of harming others. Both agree that the apparent obligation not to make others worse off can be overridden. But both accept certain types of conduct for very different reasons.

The utilitarian insists that punishment is permissible and desirable only where it can be clearly shown that the greatest good for the greatest number of people will likely be the consequence of such a practice. Where consequences cannot be clearly drawn, punishment would not be clearly defensible. The utilitarian is future-oriented and punishes insofar as the probability of maximizing the good for the many is enhanced.

The deontologist or retributivist opposes utilitarian grounds for the permissibility of punishment. The deontologist's critique is, first of all, to insist that morality must not rest on strategies whereby the essential condition of acceptability is "future-consequences." The objection is that punishment is treated like every other action in that its permissibility is a function dependent entirely upon future consequences. Hence, every action becomes a moral issue and this seems absurd. The deontologist objects that this strategy blurs the important distinction between the choice of, for example, (i) a bottle of Dr. Pepper as opposed to Pepsi, or (ii) killing someone.

The deontologist (or retributivist) also opposes the utilitarian strategy on the grounds of the kind of character it promotes. The defense of punishment by appeal to probable future consequences reduces us to the status of mere calculating and manipulative animals. If it could be shown that the greatest civil good for a riot-torn sector of the country might likely be achieved by public execution of the opposition leaders—even if they were innocent of charges of heinous conduct—then, according to the utilitarian point of view, such punishment might be acceptable, or even desirable. The deontologist opposes a practice whereby one might be compelled to punish others without good reason, if one judged such conduct to be conducive to promote the greatest good for the greatest number of people.

The deontologist or retributivist wants to insist that our fundamental identity is moral and thus our conduct is constrained by principles of which we are conscious and which we impose upon ourselves. To do the "right" thing is never determined by an appeal to consequences. This is because the deontological strategy envisages persons to be ends-in-themselves as opposed to means to some end. To adopt a utilitarian strategy is to accept visions of persons as means to ends and thus view persons as objects to be manipulated to achieve those ends. The deontologist regards that strategy as despicable, for no one is entitled to a moral contradiction: One cannot reduce persons to things in the process of attempting to enhance their moral status as agents and subjects.

C. A DEONTOLOGICAL **DEFENSE** OF PUNISHMENT

The deontological or retributivist strategy has had many adherents. But, as Perlmutter points out, none has served so prominent a place in discussions over the last two centuries as has the philosopher G.W.F. Hegel. The cornerstone of the retributivist defense might be stated as follows:

> *In punishment, the offender is honored as a rational being, since the punishment is looked upon as his right.*

If the offender deserves to be punished in view of his past wrongdoing, then if we do not punish him, we should have some reason for not treating him as he deserves. Thus, in punishing for past wrongdoing we respect the rights of another by giving that person his due, his just deserts. This means, from the retributivist point of view, that persons have a right to be punished because they have a right to get what they deserve.

Let us try to understand this strategy better by arguing from analogy. As Perlmutter suggested, let us consider the idea of awarding a prize to the winner of some competition. If it is agreed that a prize be offered for the winner of some contest, and we are the appointed judges, then it is required of us to give that award to the winner, since this is what the winner deserves. If we refuse to give the prize to the winner, it would be incumbent upon us to explain why we did not give the winner what the winner deserved. To refuse to give someone their due is illegitimate for we failed to give that person their just deserts. So also for punishment. If we fail to punish another whose wrongdoing merits that conduct, then we would be failing to give this person his due, his just deserts. In that case, too, it would be incumbent upon us to explain why we did not give that person what he deserved. To understand how the treatment must be meted out to both winner and villain, we must come to see that justice requires fairness. And fairness requires that we honor the agent by giving him his due.

The idea that punishment is a right might surely first strike us as strange. We are accustomed to view rights as those dimensions of human moral identity which underscore and secure our interests. Since pain and suffering hardly seem to be in our interest, we might at first suppose that punishment is hardly a right, that under certain conditions we have a right to be harmed. Nevertheless, the retributivist view comes to envisage punishment as something of a derivative right that follows from the respect for the person. Respect for persons requires that we honor those persons by treating them as they deserve. If punishment is one's due, then the retributivist theory of moral agency requires it.

NOTE

[1] This chapter draws heavily on Martin Perlmutter's "Punishment and Desert" in *Morality and Moral Controversies*, ed. John Arthur, Englewood, New Jersey: Prentice-Hall, 1981.

Name_____ TA _____

Section #_____

1) How does a "command theorist" decide right from wrong?

2) For the purposes of this class: can a command theorist justifiably tell non-believers what to do (proscribe conduct) on the basis of their own beliefs? Why or why not?

Name_____ TA _____

Section #_____

3) What are the 2 essential features of "punishment"?

Name_____ TA _____

Section #_____

4) What are 3 types of relationships where punishment is seen as permissible?

5) Why do we need a moral defense of punishment?

Name_____ TA _____

Section #_____

6) What is the difference between a deontological and a utilitarian defense of punishment?

Chapter 11

The Morality of Punishment— A Utilitarian Defense[1]

A. WHY THE INSTITUTION OF PUNISHMENT NEEDS A MORAL DEFENSE

We addressed the problem of providing a defense for the institution of punishment, but we found ourselves with a problem when we examined the difficulties of deciding what to do as a response to immoral conduct. We granted that immoral conduct, minimally, causes harm to others and such conduct thereby deprives another of an essential right by depriving another of his or her rightful domain. Further, we granted that to deprive others of their rightful domain is to deprive them of their essential nature, and that was the fundamental character of immoral practices. Now, having granted that, it becomes incumbent upon us to decide what actions, if any, ought to be taken against those who enact such harmful behavior.

We found ourselves faced with defending the propriety of punishment. For if punishment inflicts harm and must do so in order to count as punishment and harming others in ways we ordinarily regard as impermissible, then a moral defense of punishment seemed in order. This was so because we agreed that conduct that harms another, without good reason, is unacceptable. We ordinarily arrest and bring to trial those who are accused of causing just this sort of harm. But if harming others is *prima facie* impermissible, then why should we institutionalize those very practices that we found objectionable in the first place? The institution of punishment needs a moral defense in which the injunction *not* to inflict harm upon others can be overridden in those special cases where persons have already caused harm to others. Stated differently, punishment can be accepted as a defensible practice if and when we can show that the institutionalized infliction of harm is *justifiable*.

We began by distinguishing between the deontological or retributive strategy, on the one hand, and the utilitarian, on the other. We focused predominately upon the deontological/retributive argument. Now we shall offer a stronger defense of the utilitarian argument. The reader may then find it easier to embrace one or the other or propose some third alternative. To do so thoughtfully, the reader should master a succinct defense for both positions and then, if appropriate, formulate objections and offer a third position.

B. THE COMPATIBILITY OF DEONTOLOGICAL AND UTILITARIAN DEFENSES OF PUNISHMENT

John Rawls, in his classic article, "Two Concepts of Rules," sets out to provide a utilitarian defense of punishment. We shall follow his strategy in an outline. Rawls begins by setting out and then trying to distinguish the logical differences between justifying a practice, on the one hand, and justifying a particular action falling under it, on the other. In order to demonstrate the strategic importance of this distinction, Rawls sets out two conceptions of rules. Rawls proceeds, as did Perlmutter, to distinguish between the retributive and utilitarian perspectives.

The retributivist argues that it is morally fitting that a person who does wrong should suffer in proportion to his wrongdoing. The justification for punishing a criminal follows from his proven guilt and the severity of the punishment should reflect the depravity of his act. The retributivist thus concludes that the state of affairs where a wrongdoer suffers punishment is morally better than the state of affairs where he does not and this is irrespective of any other consequences which might arise as a result of instituting such punishment.

The utilitarian argues that bygones are bygones and only future consequences are material to present decisions. Hence, Rawls points out that punishment, for the utilitarian, is justifiable only by reference to the probable consequences of maintaining it as one of the devices of the social order. Only if punishment can be shown to promote effectively the interests of society is it justifiable.

Rawls's strategy is to argue that in order to justify a practice as a system of rules, the utilitarian arguments are appropriate. But, when one is trying to justify a particular action that falls under those rules, it is the retributive arguments that are appropriate.

Rawls presents a scenario, and tries to contrast the two separate issues that are raised in this question. He believes that his distinction shows that there are two separate questions being asked, and depending upon the construct, two separate answers are being called for.

Scenario: A child asks a parent: Why was 'F' put in jail?

Question 1a: Why was 'F' put in jail yesterday?

Question 2a: Why do people put other people in jail?

In this first case, the child's question could be interpreted to mean at least two very different things. Interpretation 1a wants to know why 'F' was put into jail. Thus, the child would be asking to justify a particular action. But interpretation 2a wants to know why it is supposed permissible to put anyone into a jail and thus invites us to justify a practice as a system of rules.

Scenario: The parent answers the child's question:

Answer 1b: Because 'F' robbed the bank and was duly tried and found guilty.

Answer 2b: To protect good people from bad; to stop people from doing things which make it difficult to go to bed at night and sleep in peace.

The parent's reply in 1b is a retributive answer. The parent's response attempts to justify the particular action taken against 'F' by citing the specific conduct that was alleged and noting both the trial and the finding of the jury. The parent's reply in 2b is different and is a utilitarian answer. The parent's response attempts to justify a practice that reflects a system of rules. The overall interests of society are supposed to be promoted when people can sleep in peace, quite independently of deciding whether 'F' was or was not guilty of this particular offense.

By the proposed analysis, we distinguish between two conceptions of rules and thus two different kinds of questions about the permissibility of punishment.

Question 1a and Answer 1b: Why is this particular person being punished?

Question 2a and Answer 2b: Why do we have the practice or institution of punishment?

This analysis naturally leads to the recognition of the appropriateness of two different kinds of defense of punishment. Question 1a and Answer 1b: The defense of particular acts of punishment is Retributive. The retributive defense of punishment is past-looking. We determine that some particular person, 'F', broke the law by engaging in a particular kind of conduct that violated those legal codes. The law, the judge, and the jury, all look back to that event, and when the accused is found guilty, a punishment is visited upon that person for what that person did.

Question 2a and Answer 2b: The defense of the practice or institution of punishment is Utilitarian. The utilitarian defense of punishment is future-looking by an ideal legislator as part of a system of laws to be applied impartially from case to case. The legislator—not the judge and jury—attempts to propose such penalties independently of addressing any specific case.

Rawls's two conceptions of rules propose two distinct strategies for thinking about punishment. Reflecting the two distinct interpretations of the kinds of questions a child in the scenario might ask a parent, offered as 1a and 2a, Rawls is led to distinguish the two different offices to which those kinds of questions apply.

> Question 1a: The Retributivist strategy for justifying a particular action of punishment is addressed to the Judge.

> Question 2a: The Utilitarian strategy for justifying a practice or institution of punishment is addressed to the Legislator.

It is not as if these strategies are mutually exclusive because they are inconsistent. Rawls's argument offers us a view that makes both approaches acceptable, and succeeds in achieving this effect by insisting that they address different offices. When we want to justify a particular punishment visited upon a particular person, we must seek the appropriate retributivist argument. When we wish to justify a practice, that is, the institution of punishment, we must seek out the suitable utilitarian arguments.

In either case, we gain clarity in this controversy by inquiring how each stands with regard to a system of rules which make up the law. We discover that what counts as a "good" argument is different in both domains. Thus, following Rawls, we reconcile these two views by the time-honored device of making them apply to different situations.

NOTE

[1] This chapter draws heavily on John Rawls's "Two Concepts of Rules," in *The Philosophical Review*, Vol. 64, 1955, pp. 3–13.

Name_____ TA _____

Section #_____

1) Which governmental position utilizes a deontological (retributivist) strategy when applying punishment? Which position utilizes a utilitarian strategy?

2) Give an example of when we (as a country) punish people for deontological reasons. Give an example of when we punish people for utilitarian reasons.

Name_____ TA _____

Section #_____

3) Which justification for punishment do you find most convincing? Why?

SECTION II

The Morality of Killing

Chapter 12

Introduction: *The Morality of Killing*

A. PERSONS, HARMS, AND THE RIGHT-TO-LIFE

One aspect of Section I of the text has been to gain a deeper insight into self-identity. Our efforts began with an exploration of the doctrines of *rational self-interest* in order to grasp the motivations for our actions, and *alienation* in order to grasp our ontological status. These approaches, of course, were not the only ones we could have adopted, but these helped us to venture a preliminary answer to the important question: Who am I? They offer one way, among many, to begin to see general patterns to our behavior and offer an explanation of why we might be motivated to adopt these patterns. The kind of discourse that this approach has unfolded in attempt to answer the question "Who am I?" is one that claims to be the same for each and every one of us. The personal answer to the question of self-identity, curiously enough, is one that we all share. It is *generality* which marks the decisive feature of this philosophical exploration into self-identity.

Discussions of the *harm principle* opened another vista in which we hoped to gain insight into our nature. We considered the idea of being a "person" to be a creature who has "rights." And we wondered about our moral nature in terms of conduct which deprived us of a right by harming us unjustly and thus deprived us of our very nature. This approach offered us the chance to delineate what "immoral" conduct might be: any behavior that violates the harm principle . . . that *harms others* unjustly. We left open for debate the question of whether harms to self and impersonal harms should also count as immoral actions and why.

Next, we continued to examine methodologies by turning to consider three different strategies for action. Rational self-interest might find expression by appeal (i) merely to principles, independent of the consequences of our action [*deontological*], (ii) exclusively with regard to the anticipated consequences of our action [*utilitarian*], or (iii) exclusively by an appeal to the commands of an ultimate and divine authority [*command*]. These strategies did not pretend to exhaust all possibilities but offered the readers a chance to reflect upon, and perhaps discover, the peculiar features of his or her own self-identity so far as it found expression in life-strategies.

Finally, in Section I, we reflected deeply on our identity by asking about what action, if any, was appropriate in response to the violation of the harm principle. The answer we investigated was the idea of *punishment*. We noticed that there is more than one way to defend the institution of punishment. The reason we needed a defense was simply because we were confronted by the familiar question: "Do two wrongs make a right?" If the harming of others unjustly is impermissible and harming in general is to be avoided since it makes persons worse off than they were before, why should the state (or anyone else) be permitted to retaliate by administering harmful actions? Or, in other words, what justifies harming in the form of institutional punishment that failed to justify it in the original case. After all, isn't harming harmful wherever and whenever it is present? By offering some defenses for the permissibility of punishment we invited the reader to think deeply about what makes a meaningful life. Justifying the permissibility of punishment advances an idea of *respect* for persons and claims that we are prepared to take bold and constraining measures to make possible a *dignified* life in the presence of conduct deemed to be unjust. And these ideals of a meaningful life are a significant part of our sense of self-identity.

In Section II, we begin with the idea that a meaningful life requires respect and dignity. Indeed, we often hear people claim that *life is sacred*. But when such things are said they seem to prove quite misleading upon further investigation. Such people who declare that "life is sacred" are usually undisturbed by the killing of a cow or a turnip and may be elated by the killing of a pesky insect or rodent. What such people usually mean is that "*human* life is sacred." And this formula invites us to consider what it means to assert that (i) life is *sacred,* and (ii) *human* life is sacred. To say that human life is sacred shall mean for our discussion that it is always wrong to take human life *unjustly.* And in our discussions we will have to determine if and when the taking of human life is unjust. Thus, we are not declaring that all human killing is impermissible but only that we must be prepared to show how and when killing can be defended or excused. Secondly, we must come to understand our own self-identity as part of a species—homo sapien sapiens—and formulate a coherent and convincing answer as to why our species or simply, "human life" deserves special protections and why other non-human animal life and vegetative life do not seem to merit that same respect. In the process we will try to reach a conclusion as to whether our common practices toward other animals and plants are justified.

The idea that human life is sacred is the idea that such life is special and deserves to be protected from harm. In the next series of chapters we shall try to formulate a strategy that informs us if and when human beings can be killed, not unjustly. Stated differently, *we want to determine if and when cases of human killing violate the harm principle.* If a person is a domain expressed in rights, central among which is the right-to-life, under what conditions, if any, can a person be deprived of the right-to-life defensibly.

We will investigate this problem of the meaning of persons, rights, and harm, beginning with an examination of the idea of animal rights and the permissibility of killing non-human animals. We then turn to consider the issues of abortion, infanticide, euthanasia and suicide, and capital punishment.

We begin our discussion and debate with the problem of animal rights and the permissibility of killing non-human animals. Judging by the way we in fact behave, our society finds the killing of non-human animals, ordinarily, to be permissible and where regulated against by law, to prescribe punishments modest in both degree and severity. Since this is how we do behave, it behooves us to ask why. What justifications can we offer to defend our common practices?

Many persons express that it seems clear to them what is right and wrong when it comes to the abortion debate: the permissibility of killing the *human* fetus. But many of these same persons are initially unsure about the permissibility of killing non-human animals and how to justify the practices in which they engage. How can we account for the clarity in one case and obscurity in the other? Part of the reason may be that we tend to approach issues involving killing as if they could (and should?) be addressed separately, as if they were not connected. We tend to be clear, at least to ourselves, about right and wrong when it comes to abortion, but so much less clear when pressed to defend our practices permitting the killing of non-human animals. We fail to consider what principles we invoke with their far-reaching implications over the many domains in which we permit killing. Indeed, central to the approach offered here, it will be argued that when we get clearer about the principles we in fact espouse, as revealed by the abortion controversy, we will see that those same principles have implications for other questions about killing.

Our task is to discover our positions, to investigate the reasons that support our positions, to jettison reasons that are unsuitable to support our positions, and to change our positions if we cannot adequately defend them. Then, having cleaned our intellectual and emotionally filled house of ideas, our business is to find good and compelling reasons to serve as our principles to guide us about the permissibility of killing and by applying those principles to each of our problems—non-human animal killing, abortion, infanticide, euthanasia, suicide, and capital punishment—to see if we can provide a consistent, judicious, and defensible account of the morality of killing.

When this work is complete, when we have come to establish some positions about if and when the killing of human life can be justified, we then must turn again from human animals to consider the case for non-human animals, and even vegetative life. How do the justifications for our positions concerning human life guide our understanding concerning the lives of other animals? Can our common behavior be defended? The reader must keep in mind that every time someone chomps down on two all *beef* patties, special sauce, on a sesame-seed bun, that someone is an accomplice in a killing. In this case, the killing of a cow. Is this killing permissible? Why? We must be prepared to defend our practices and to recognize that the principles operative in this case have significant implications for the morality of killing.

Our discussion concerning human killing begins with the abortion debate. We will consider the United States legal framing of this issue: whether the fetus counts as a person. If it does, we must be prepared to explain our position. And even if it does, we must ask under what conditions, if any, may the fetus be deprived of the right to life, defensibly. Whatever positions the reader arrives at with regard to aborting the fetus, there will clearly be implications for the case of the newborn. Our next topic is to determine whether severely defective newborns—a baby born without a brain or with a terminal illness—may be deprived of the right-to-life not unjustly. From the case of the terminally ill or severely defective newborn, we turn to consider the permissibility of killing terminally ill adults, and the problem of euthanasia in general: aged and debilitated grandparents or patients suffering from the final stages of cancer, AIDS, or other devastating illness. If these terminally ill patients ask to be relieved of their sufferings, on what grounds, if any, shall we deny their requests? The recent debates about the work of Dr. Kevorkian and his "suicide machines" will enter into the discussion. If human life is so sacred that it merits respect, dignity, and protection, are there any conditions under which the quality of that life falls beneath a certain minimal threshold and thereby justifies termination in the name of respect and dignity?

B. THE IDEA OF INFORMAL FALLACIES

In this second section, our conversation becomes more technical and more specific. This is a natural consequence of focusing upon a series of specific moral questions and the decisions which accompany them.

Unlike formal logic presented in symbolic form, arguments concerning moral issues are commonly presented and debated in everyday language. Our everyday language often occludes the structure of our argument by diverting our attention from that structure. This may take place by the use of rhetorical devices, difficult or ambiguous vocabulary, or even by altering the inflection of the voice.

The point of every argument is to persuade the listener to accept a certain point of view, expressed as the conclusion of an argument. On the most cursory reflection, however, it becomes obvious that persuasion may be extracted for reasons which we ought not to countenance. This means that not every reason ought to persuade us of some position or other. Stated differently, some consideration of what should count as acceptable forms of persuasion is in order.

How can we be alerted to fallacies in reasoning? Can we assemble some list of informal errors in our reasoning which extract persuasion but ought not to? The predicament, unfortunately, is that although there are a few sound patterns of reasoning, there are innumerable ways to make mistakes. Let's look at this matter more closely.

Suppose I ask you for directions from one town into another. Suppose I stipulate that you are located in a certain town A, at a certain intersection, let's say, streets 'D' and 'E'. And suppose I ask you to formulate various strategies to travel to a nearby town B. and find your way to the intersection of streets 'F' and 'G'. The only additional constraint I place upon your formulations is that you must use only paved roads, and observe all traffic laws. Now, granting this scenario, let us contrast two different kinds of questions:

(1) How many ways are there to travel from the intersection of streets 'D' and 'E' in town A to the intersection of streets 'F' and 'G' in town B?

(2) How many ways are there to get lost?

Although there are a finite number of ways to travel from one town to another, obeying the traffic laws and staying on paved roads, there are an infinite number of ways to become confused and get lost. By analogy, although there are a finite number of ways to argue persuasively or soundly from one set of premises to a desired conclusion, there are an infinite number of ways to confound an argument. Alas, there is no organized way to set out all the ways in which one can make mistakes!

Having made this problem clear, our situation is still not hopeless. We can make a preliminary start by alerting the reader to certain kinds of fallacies in reasoning. The errors which we shall consider make no "formal" mistakes; the arguments are unsound because of "informal" problems. And the reader should be reminded that these few pitfalls which we shall consider are in no way exhaustive. But we start such a consideration because in order to constructively debate all the difficult moral issues which now lie before us it is imperative to be on guard for arguments which attempt to gain our assent for reasons which deserve to be dismissed out of hand. We must be on the lookout for arguments which try to persuade us of a conclusion by appealing to reasons irrelevant to the argument before us.

The informal fallacies which we will now consider might best be called "fallacies of relevance." This means that an argument attempts to persuade us of a certain conclusion by appealing to reasons irrelevant to the conclusion which the argument seeks to secure. If we keep in mind that the purpose of a philosophical argument is to gain the assent of the listener/reader by persuading him or her of a particular conclusion, then the minimal issue before us is to decide whether or not the reasons offered are relevant to the desired conclusion.

C. FALLACIES OF RELEVANCE

Informal Fallacies: The following informal fallacies are appropriately called "fallacies of relevance."

(1) *Argumentum ad Baculum* (appeal to force)

(2) *Argumentum ad Hominem* (against the man)

(3) *Argumentum ad Ignorantiam* (from ignorance)

(4) *Argumentum ad Misericordiam* (appeal to pity)

(5) *Argumentum ad Populum* (appeal to the many)

(6) *Argumentum ad Verecundiam* (appeal to authority)

(7) *Accident*

(8) *Converse Accident* (hasty generalization)

(9) *False Cause (post hoc ergo propter hoc)*

(10) *Petitio Principii* (circular definition)

(11) *Complex Question* (two questions at once)

Each of these eleven fallacies of relevance will be considered by definition and by example. After each technical name, an example or two is offered to help make concrete the abstract idea of the informal fallacy.

There are, of course, many illustrations of each of these fallacies of relevance and the reader is encouraged to formulate a list of examples. These examples can be produced by advancing hypothetical possibilities generated from routine stories in newspapers and magazines. These periodicals are chock full of examples of fallacious reasoning.

(1) *ad BACULUM:* We try to persuade someone to accept a desired conclusion by somehow threatening them.

    (a) "Gentlemen, I am sure that if you think it over you will see that my suggestion has real merit. It is only a suggestion, of course, and not an order. As I mentioned at our last conference, I am planning to reorganize the whole business. I still hope it will not be necessary to curtail the operations of your department."

    (b) "It is too my turn to pitch today. After all, it is my ball."

(2) *ad HOMINEM* (abusive/genetic fallacy): We try to persuade someone to accept a desired conclusion—against a conclusion advanced by another person on the grounds that there is something unacceptable about the other person, independent of the issue being argued.

    (a) "I wouldn't believe John's claim that Wonder bread is nutritionally superior to other breads on the market. You know he's a Communist, don't you?"

(3) *ad IGNORANTIAM* (from ignorance): We try to persuade someone to accept a desired conclusion on the basis of what we don't know.

    (a) "There must be ghosts, since no one has ever proven that there aren't any."

    (b) "There is no proof that the secretary leaked the news to the papers, so he cannot have done it."

(4) *ad MISERICORDIAM* (appeal to pity): We try to persuade someone to accept a desired conclusion by irrelevantly attempting to get their pity.

    (a) "My client is the sole support of his aged parents. If he is sent to prison it will break their hearts, and they will be left homeless and penniless. You surely cannot find it in your hearts to reach any other verdict than *not guilty.*"

    (b) "I appeal to you not for Thomas Kidd, but I appeal to you for the long line—the long, long line reaching back through the ages and forward to the years to come—the long line of despoiled and downtrodden people of the earth. I appeal to you for those men who rise in the morning before daylight comes and who go home at night when the light has faded from the sky and give their life, their strength, their toil to make others rich and great. I appeal to you in the name of those women who are offering up their lives to this modern god of gold, and I appeal to you in the name of those little children, the living and the unborn."

(5) *ad POPULUM* (to the many or gallery): We try to persuade someone to accept a desired conclusion on the grounds that many people evidently agree.

    (a) "You ought to drink Pepsi. It's the beverage of the 'New Generation'."

    (b) The Ford Escort is the best car on the market. It must be since it is the best-selling car in the entire world.

(6) *ad VERECUNDIAM* (appeal to authority): We try to persuade someone to accept a desired conclusion by appealing to an authority whose expertise is unconnected to the desired conclusion.

    (a) Supply-side economics is superior to every other economic strategy. After all, Einstein himself said so.

(7) *ACCIDENT:* We try to persuade someone to accept a desired conclusion when although agreeing with a general principle, the accidental circumstances render the general rule inapplicable.

    (a) Anyone who deliberately strikes another person should be punished. Therefore the middleweight boxing champion should be severely punished for he assaults all of his opponents.

(8) *CONVERSE ACCIDENT* (hasty generalization): We try to persuade someone to accept a desired conclusion which generalizes a claim best restricted to individual cases.

    (a) Everyone should use the new medicine called "No-Cold" when flu strikes. It worked for me!

(9) *FALSE CAUSE:* We try to persuade someone to accept a desired conclusion which states that an event A causes event B on the mere grounds that whenever event B takes place, event A tends to precede it.

    (a) Every time we drive past the church, the church bells begin to ring; therefore our driving past the church causes the bells to ring.

(b) Isn't it true that students who get all A's study hard? So if you want me to study hard, Professor, the best way to do it is to give me A's in all my courses.

(10) *PETITIO PRINCIPII* (begging the question or circular definition): We try to persuade someone to accept a desired conclusion by circular reasoning.

(a) God exists because the Bible tells us so, and we know that what the Bible tells us must be true because it is the revealed word of God.

(11) *COMPLEX QUESTION:* We try to persuade someone to accept a desired conclusion by confusing the issue by asking two questions at once (although it seems like a single question).

(a) Have you stopped beating your wife?

(b) Was it through stupidity or through deliberate dishonesty that the Administration has hopelessly botched its foreign policy? In either case, unless you are in favor of stupidity or dishonesty, you should vote against the incumbents.

Chapter 13

The Killing of Non-Human Animals: Do (Non-Human) Animals Have Rights? Do They Have the Right-to-Life?[1]

A. ANIMALS: HUMAN AND NON-HUMAN AND THE PROSCRIPTIVE APPROACH

Do animals have rights? Do any of them have the right-to-life? Do all of them? What good reasons can we provide to shed light on the serious questions: Is the killing of a non-human animal ever immoral? Is it always immoral? Does the answer lie somewhere in between? And most importantly, what criteria should guide our moral deliberations on this matter? What is it about any living creature—as we regard human animals—that earns it the right to be treated with such protection and respect that if its life is taken unjustly then the creature who took that life unjustly is liable to have visited upon it our harshest punishments? Do any of the non-human animals measure up that standard?

So many of us eat animals for our food. So many of us wear clothing that is made from animals. In both cases we must acknowledge that we are complicit in the killing of them. Just as members of a gang who commit a robbery in which someone is killed in its commission are all held liable for the murder, so also everyone who eats meat or wears leather belts and shoes is part of the conspiracy in the killing of the animal. The getaway driver may have remained in the car throughout the course of the robbery, never stepped inside the store where the robbery took place, and perhaps never agreed to or decided to use the

147

firearm in this case, but nevertheless, the law regards that even that person is responsible for the murder. So also, by analogy, is the case with all meat-eaters and animal-clothes-wearers. It is as if we shot the bullet into the cow's brain or slit its throat from ear to ear, pulled the skin off of its still warm body, disembowled and butchered it. Here, then, is the stark reality of our diet and our fashions. Are these practices morally defensible?

It is our objective to raise the questions, and urge the readers, to think about their feelings on these matters, to reflect on them and come to terms with how we behave, and hopefully, come to grips with why we find our behavior acceptable, or why we need to modify or change it entirely. I very much urge you to discover what seems right to you, what feels right to you. But we must be prepared to do something more, namely, to supply reasons to defend our choices. On the one hand, we must see if we can supply reasons to explain our own feelings, but on the other, we must see if we can supply reasons to guide others or guide ourselves in our view of other's choices. You might be revolted by the idea of eating "veal" on the grounds that a newborn calf, a mere one hour old, is taken from its mother and placed in a box so small that it can neither stand up nor turn around, and confined within it, it must remain for 18–20 weeks until it is killed for its tender meat. And deeply disturbing it is. But being disturbed, revolted, and outraged are not good reasons to determine whether conduct is right or wrong— the upset must, through reflection, lead to the formulation of reasons to justify our positions.

In keeping with our proscriptive strategy, the question that you must answer goes far beyond that question of your feelings and even reasons to explain what you think is right *for you*. If John or Mary claims that they want to eat beef burgers, veal, pork chops, roast chicken, tuna and lobster, do we have any good reasons to tell them that they must not do so? Here we have a very different question. The vegetarian might be repulsed at the thought of eating chicken in the full knowledge that by doing so they have become an accomplice in its killing. The vegetarian might offer a different kind of answer, however, for why they refused to eat chicken. They might claim that the process of food production is so unsafe—never mind for the moment its cruelty—as to place in jeopardy their own health and well-being. In these two justifications, the vegetarians offers very different reasons to explain their gastronomic choices. When each of you comes to terms with the reasons that explain your feelings and reasons to guide your own choices of food consumption, are these sufficient to urge the constraint of the conduct of others? Are the killing, eating, and wearing of animals violations of the harm principle? If they are, then those acts would be immoral and worthy of constraint by advocating liberty-limiting principles.

B. ANIMALS: HUMAN AND NON-HUMAN

By "animals" I am here using the term in contrast to "humans," though I recognize this distinction to be, at once, both a commonplace and a disservice. I say disservice because "human" is a shorthand for "human animal" and thus the question "Do animals have rights?" must also include human animals and thus must be answered affirmatively: YES. But judging by the way our society has been accustomed to behave—though this seems to be changing given the new laws and enforcement that attempt to protect animals from abuse—the answer to that question is NO because humans are regarded as different from animals (although they are, indeed, part of the same kingdom—we are neither minerals nor vegetables), and animals are regarded to fall below the human threshold and consequently below the threshold of those who are entitled to rights.

Humans are, of course, animals. We tend to use the word "human" to refer to creatures we believe are a higher order of life than those creatures we designate by the term "animal." Judging by the way we behave, we regard humans—at least some of them—as having rights, whereas we, as a society, behave as if the other animals have none. So, for the purpose of introducing an argument defending the claim that animals (i.e., other than humans) have rights, we examine Tom Regan's thoughtful and provocative article "The Case for Animal Rights." Problems with this may be fruitfully criticized.

No adequate account of our behavior toward animals, however, can fail to distinguish the peculiarities of our attitudes and treatment of different kinds of animals. We seem to have a range of distinct attitudes and behaviors in regard to the following groups of non-human animals: (1) *pets*, (2) *zoo animals*, (3) *circus animals*, (4) *farm animals*, and (5) *animals in the wild*. And if we took the time to examine these attitudes, we might find them broadly irrational, inconsistent, and indefensible. Nevertheless, we hold and operate upon those attitudes.

C. INADEQUATE ARGUMENTS FOR ANIMAL RIGHTS

The question of whether or not animals have rights is a question about the moral status of animals. If we concur that animals have no moral status then we are forced to conclude that we have *no direct duties* to them. To say we have *direct duties* to some other creature—for example other persons—means that we have obligations to them, that we can harm them unjustly by our actions, and if we do harm them unjustly we risk deserved punishment; thus if we have *direct duties* to other creatures, we must treat them with the respect and protection we demand for ourselves. On the contrary, to say that we have *no direct duties* towards animals is to claim that we owe them nothing, that is, we have no obligations to them and that we can do no wrong towards them. However, we might instead claim that although animals have no moral status we can have *indirect duties* to them. To say that we have only indirect duties to animals is to claim that we can do wrong acts that *involve* animals but not to them; we would then have duties *regarding* them though none to them. Let's see if this important distinction can be clarified by an illustration.

> Suppose your neighbor kicks your dog. Has your neighbor done something wrong, and if so, precisely what? If one has no direct duties to animals then one has no direct duties to this (or any) dog. Your neighbor who kicks the dog has not wronged the dog any more than someone's smashing a windshield of a car has wronged the car. If I have at most indirect duties to the dog then I have not wronged the dog but perhaps I have wronged X, the owner of that dog, either by upsetting you or by damaging your property. But, in both cases, your neighbor no more wrongs your dog than wrongs your car and its windshield. At most, in the second case, your neighbor's duties involving your dog are indirect duties to you.

How might such a view be justified? After all, when your neighbor kicks your dog, the animal seems to be caused pain and hence harmed, so how is it that our society tends to reason that the dog has not been wronged (since a wrong can be done only to a creature that has rights)? It might be argued that animals do not feel pain and thus this dog does not feel pain when kicked, though no rational person would hold such a view. Or it might be argued that although the animal feels pain only human pain matters, but no rational person would hold such a view either, since pain is pain wherever it occurs. And if causing of pain is wrong, all other things being equal, then causing pain to your dog must also be wrong. Thus, the reasonable argument seems to be that your neighbor's kicking the dog is wrong because of the pain that action has caused. And if one judges the act to cause pain and the causing of pain to be a bad thing, then the wrongness of the act seems to be a violation of a direct duty. But the way our society tends to behave, we have no direct duties to animals and can argue, at most, that the act is wrong because it harms your property. Let's pursue further the indirect duties argument.

Proponents of the indirect duties argument towards animals tend to be proponents of what we may call *contractarianism*. Risking oversimplification, we can say that this view holds that morality can be expressed as a kind of contract. The contract specifies a set of rules that individuals agree to abide by. There is *direct* coverage of the terms of the contract for all those who understand and accept them for these individuals have rights created, recognized, and protected in the contract. Those who understand and accept the terms of the contract are directly covered and can specify coverage for those who lack the ability either to understand morality or to sign the contract themselves but who are loved and cherished by those who can. In this way, young children unable to understand or sign for moral principles expressed in such contracts are nevertheless covered by them, namely, through their parents.

The case for animals begins like the case for children. Since animals are not able to understand or sign contracts, they have no rights *directly*. At most, they have protection and coverage because of the sentiments of those who can understand and sign, and love and cherish them. Simply, we love our dog or our cat or our bird or baby seals, whales, dolphins, gorillas, spotted owls and so on. And these animals enjoy protection, if they enjoy it at all, because of the sentimental interests of people who care about them. But according to contractarianism, we have no duty directly to a pet dog or any other animal and not even the duty not to cause it pain and suffering. Our duty not to hurt animals is at most a duty we have to other people who care what happens to them. And if animals are not cared for by many people, like laboratory animals, such as rats, or farm animals then those animals enjoy less and less protection. This point helps to make clearer that we have no direct duties towards animals but at most *indirect* duties towards them which consist in our duties to those who have sentimental interests in certain animals.

The contractarian approach sets a formidable problem for those attempting to argue for animal rights. In order to defend animal rights, we must successfully challenge the theory of contractarianism. The argument against it attempts to show its inadequacy as a moral theory for human beings, nonetheless animals. Consider this: on the contract theory, morality amounts to a set of rules that people agree to abide by. Who makes the rules? People in a country, in a city, in a town. What people? The people who control the politics of that town, city, or country. In short, the contract theory turns out to be justified by the principle that *might makes right,* a most dubious moral principle, indeed. Where enough people come together, state a cause and are prepared to enforce its provisions, there will be the morally right course of action. For minorities not represented or for those disenfranchised from the provisions of the contract, suffering may ensue. If the theory of contractarianism has such flaws and thereby so little to recommend it as a moral theory guiding our treatment of fellow humans, there can be nothing more to recommend it as a theory of how to treat our fellow animals. In Regan's argument the theory for *indirect duties* to animals depends upon a successful defense of contractarian theories; the flaw that Regan detects undermines the theory that we have, at best, only indirect duties to animals. Thus, we may have indirect duties to animals but that practice cannot be adequately defended morally by appealing to contractarianism. Indeed, Regan believes that we have direct duties to animals and thereby must call upon another argument entirely. In order to get to that argument, he proceeds to undermine two other arguments: (i) the Cruelty-Kindness defense, and (ii) Utilitarianism.

If we can make sense of *direct duties* to animals, another theoretical frame is required. The first of the two theories he considers might be called the cruelty-kindness theory: we have a direct duty to be kind to animals and a direct duty not to be cruel. Although the terms have a nice ring to them, Regan argues against their theoretical adequacy as part of a sufficient account of right action. Although it is surely a good thing to be kind towards animals, it is possible to act kindly while holding unjust theories. For example, a racist might act generously to a group while at the same time holding hateful feelings toward others. The racist's acts of kindness might well be positively rooted in injustice. Thus, kindness as a disposition in no way guarantees that one is behaving from a foundation that is morally worthy.

So also for avoiding cruelty. Cruel acts are ones in which a display is made either in showing a lack of sympathy or by conveying enjoyment in the face of another's suffering. No one could rationally argue that indiscriminate cruelty was a good thing, indeed, it is a tragic human failing. But the issue is whether the avoidance of cruelty guarantees good action and for this no guarantee is secured through the strategy of avoiding cruelty. Thus Regan concludes that, of course, let us be for kindness and against cruelty, but this will not offer us an adequate theory for deciding right from wrong action.

Another possible theory for defending animal rights as direct duties to animals is some form of *utilitarianism*. Why? The utilitarian, in Regan's analysis, accepts two central principles: (i) Equality: everyone's interests count, and each one's interest has equal weight, thus whether male or female, white or black, Indian or Chinese, short or tall, fat or thin, each one's expressed interests matter equally; and (ii) the principle of Utility: the act that is right is the one that will bring about the best balance between the satisfactions and frustrations for everyone involved. The action is right so far as it maximizes the satisfactions for the most people and minimizes their frustrations. For the utilitarian, this is where my duty lies.

The persuasive ingredient in the utilitarian defense is *its egalitarian* emphasis; the interests of women and minorities, should not count less than anyone else's interests. But, Regan argues, the egalitarian emphasis is offset by the emphasis on *interests* rather than with the *individual* who has those interests. The utilitarian is concerned with satisfying an individual's interests rather than the individual whose interests they are. This means that from a utilitarian standpoint, neither an individual nor an animal as such has any value in its own right; only feelings or interests have a value. By analogy, Regan argues, let's say we have some cups with liquid in them, some more sweet and some more bitter and let's say we declare that sweeter is better. We could then evaluate the contents of each cup, and judge which is better. But no cup is better than any other, only the liquid in the cup is better (or worse). For the utilitarian, just like the cups, no creature has a value as an individual, and thus has no equal value. On the contrary, only our feelings of satisfaction (or frustration) have value, positive and negative. Thus, we perform a kind of calculus, adding up in each situation the positive and negative consequences that we suppose an act will bring. Then the right thing to do is the one which is assessed to likely produce the greatest satisfaction of interests, with the least frustration of interests.

The trouble with utilitarianism is that such a theory commits us to the view that we should be required to perform an obviously immoral act if it could be shown that many more individual interests will be satisfied by performing that act than by not acting. Consider the following example.

> Let's say Jim has an Aunt Bea. She is an old, cranky, sour person though not incapacitated. She has willed that upon her death, Jim will inherit a great amount of money, though she refuses to give him any of it until her passing. Now let's say Jim has an opportunity to make the investment of a lifetime and this investment will likely produce an even greater amount of money. In order to avoid a huge tax bite, Jim plans to donate a large part of his profits to a children's hospital, with the very happy consequence that many children and their parents will benefit. And let's say that Jim knows that this opportunity will be lost if he does not get the money soon and further that Jim knows a good deal about the shady past of a doctor with an interest in just this investment who can be counted on to cooperate in bringing about the untimely end of Aunt Bea. And let's add that there is very little chance of being caught and that, as for Jim's guilt-ridden conscience, Jim expects to get by very well on a tropical beach south of the border that has no extradition treaty with the United States.

Now, let's say that Aunt Bea is killed and the rest of the story turns out as hoped. Has anything immoral been done? Well, from the utilitarian point of view, with the many children whose health has been repaired and the grief and anxiety of their parents relieved, Aunt Bea's misfortune seems like a small price to pay. That is, if the right thing to do proves to be the production of the greatest satisfaction and the least frustration for the most persons that an act will affect, then killing Aunt Bea might even prove to be the right thing to do (and not merely "not wrong")!

The point is that utilitarian arguments consistently run into just this challenge. If the happiness of the greatest number of people can be secured by committing a terrible act of injustice against one person, or just a few, then utilitarianism seems committed to the position that such an act would be what duty required, that is, the moral thing to do. Again, the utilitarian theory seems inadequate as a moral theory for humans; how will it prove more adequate for guiding our treatment of our fellow animals?

D. DEFENDING ANIMAL RIGHTS: THE THEORY OF INHERENT VALUE

Regan, then, turns to consider what he regards as a positive alternative, a theory that might be called *Inherent Value*. He wants to place value, not on the liquid in the cups, but on the cups themselves: we need to consider a theory that defends the view that we ourselves or some other creature, has inherent value, that we are not merely receptacles and containers for feelings or interests. Regan's theory of inherent value requires that each individual who has this value has it *equally*, regardless of sex, race, religion, or any other accidental feature of existence. By this he means that the genius and the learning-impaired, the Olympic racer and the physically-disadvantaged, the wealthy and the impoverished, the saintly and the criminal, each possess the *same* inherent value. This value is in no way dependent upon one's usefulness, and in this important sense challenges the utilitarian argument. Thus, on Regan's theory, to act immorally is to perform actions that fail to respect another's independent value, for such an act would violate that in which each individual is inviolate.

Regan's theory of *Inherent Value* is at once a *Rights View*. This theory holds all forms of social, racial, sexual, and religious discrimination to be morally intolerable. It thereby challenges contractarianism in principle since it makes impossible the defense of such practices by a select group of individuals that might make and enforce such a contract. It also challenges utilitarianism since it refuses to accept that ends could justify means, that good achieved through evil means could be acceptable. In both cases, the *rights* of others would be violated in the process of promoting morality and Regan regards this contradiction as intolerable.

Regan cautions, however, that if such a rights view were to be shown to be applicable only to humans, then he would have to look elsewhere for a satisfactory defense of animal rights. But, he believes, efforts to limit such an account to only humans would be rationally defective. He grants that many other animals lack many abilities that humans possess; they cannot read, do higher mathematics, build a bookcase, or cook. But he is quick to point out that this is also true of many humans and, judging by the way we behave and the way in which our legal system works, these humans are not judged to have less inherent value, less of a right to be treated with respect, than do others. The granting of basic rights by the theory of inherent value is awarded in terms of similarities that we all share rather than on the differences that distinguish each one of us from the other. Regan believes the fundamental ingredient of similarity to be that:

> . . . we are each of us the experiencing subject of a life, a conscious creature having an individual welfare that has importance to us whatever our usefulness to others. We want and prefer things, believe and feel things, recall and expect things. And all these dimensions of our life, including our pleasure and pain, our enjoyment and suffering, our satisfaction and frustration, our continued existence or untimely death, all make a difference to the quality of our life as lived, as experienced, by us as individuals. As the same is true of those animals that concern us (the ones that are eaten and trapped, for example) they too must be viewed as the experiencing subjects of a life, with inherent value of its own.

Having stated his position, Regan anticipates some criticism. To those who might argue that the theory of inherent value applies only to human beings, he challenges by asserting that they are guilty of speciesism and commit the same mistake of the racist and the sexist. Those who would argue that the theory applies only to humans—on religious grounds—that only humans have immortal souls (other animals do not) have the unhappy predicament of resting one controversial moral issue on an even more controversial issue of who does or does not have an immortal soul; Regan thus dismisses that objection.

Or, it may be objected that the argument concerning inherent value is not adequate. For while it might be argued that animals have inherent value it might further be challenged that they have less inherent value than humans and hence are not entitled to equal treatment. What could rationally justify this appraisal? It might be objected that other animals lack reason or autonomy or intellect. But even if we grant that assertion, how do we reach the conclusion that animals are entitled to less respect? Some humans, Regan argues, have extreme mental impairment and others suffer from extreme forms of mental disorder. But these deficiencies do not seem to be regarded as sufficient to rationally sustain the view that those persons have less inherent value. For Regan's view is that *"inherent value belongs equally to those who are the experiencing subjects of a life."* And when we reflect upon the possibility that inherent value may belong to rocks and rivers, trees and glaciers, he only concludes that we do not know and may never know. But, as he sees it, we do not need to answer these questions in order to make the case for animal rights any more than we need to insist that we need to know everyone who is eligible to vote in the Presidential election in order to know if one person is.

The case for animal rights comes to this. We must ask whether the animals in our culture that are routinely eaten, hunted, and used in our laboratories are like us in being subjects of a life. The answer to this question, according to Regan, is YES. And so we must recognize that many, many animals are subjects of a life, have inherent value, and are entitled to be treated with respect. And since, judging by current behavior in our society, our conduct is in violation of this minimum threshold of respect we must change our behavior and change our habits and change our laws to reflect our illuminated understanding. This is what we are morally required to do. We have *direct duties* to any and all animals that experience themselves as the subject of a life for, like us, they have a right not to be harmed, certainly not to be tortured, and especially not to be killed unjustly.

E. OBJECTIONS TO REGAN'S DEFENSE OF ANIMAL RIGHTS

Before taking up specific criticisms of Regan's argument, it is worth emphasizing that although we may have the intuition that non-human animals, at least some of them, are entitled to respect not presently received, it is another thing entirely to defend that intuition with reasons. For while we may have the deep-seated feeling that the systematic mistreatment of animals is unjust, this is very different from formulating an argument that defends adequately our feelings and that shows us what the injustice is, its nature and limits. So, while we might feel inclined to recommend a more careful and respectful attitude towards animals, we might not be convinced of Regan's defense. Let us not feel forced to throw out the baby with the bathwater; perhaps we must reject Regan's argument but we must still wonder whether animals have rights, which rights in particular and by virtue of what reasons.

What is most central to Regan's defense of animal rights is his defense of the principle of inherent value, that all human life has the *same* worth, that here we have a moral reason to answer the question: What is it about any living creature that earns it the right-to-life, that identifies it as a "person" and extends to it the protection and respect that reveals its special worth? We might want to challenge and refine these lines of thought when we explore those advanced by Michael Tooley or James Rachels, namely, that the value of life is a function of its quality, and that when the quality of life falls below a certain defineable threshold, then the demands for maintaining and valuing that life are properly undermined. A baby born without a brain or with a hopeless and terminal illness (as Tooley argues in his discussion of infanticide), can be directly released from its hopeless misery—killed not unjustly—because the quality of this life has fallen below a minimum threshold demanding protection. The permissibility of practicing active euthanasia, Rachels argues, may be more effective in achieving the end of terminal suffering—the policy that motivates the permissibility of passive euthanasia—when illness has diminished human life to the status of the merely vegetative. For Rachels (and Tooley), all human life does not have the same inherent value. Indeed, the right-to-life that we grant to humans in general may, in some cases, be deprived not unjustly. And if we accept that claim, then perhaps Regan's argument collapses since the defense of animal rights is grounded on the extended claim of inherent value. For now the objection could be that given diminished self-consciousness, lack of autonomy, and the dimunition of other mental functions—the robust *qualities* of human life that form the basis of inherent value—the conditions for establishing inherent value are now missing. It is this lack of certain *qualities* of life that Tooley identifies with the self-consciousness criterion. It is the basis for excluding many or most non-human animals from having a serious right-to-life and at once makes infanticide, and certain cases of euthanasia, permissible within the domain of human animals.

Regan regards being a "subject of experiences" a sufficient condition for qualifying as an animal with rights among which is the right-to-life. Tooley's condition requires a much more sophisticated sense of subjectivity. This distinction merits our reflection. Tooley's position seems to commit him to the view that animals can have rights without being entitled to the right-to-life. He argues against those who hold that without the right-to-life, no animal is entitled to any right whatsoever. He argues that animals show clearly their desire not to be tortured and holds that animals have the right not to be tortured since a creature has a right to something whenever that creature desires something and it would be wrong not to grant that thing to it. But Tooley's argument seems to preclude granting the right-to-life to many animals that Regan believes are entitled to that right, for Tooley's argument is something like this: a creature has a right to something when it is at least capable of desiring that thing; and since most other animals do not seem to be conscious of their own mortality, they have no right-to-life. Only those creatures who have attained a self-consciousness of their mortality, that they will die some day, desire to be living as long as possible with no interventions that bring their lives to a close prematurely, are so entitled. Most other animals—dogs, cats, and rats, and human fetuses, and even newborn babies, but perhaps not mature gorillas and dolphins—have not attained that level of self-consciousness, and so have not attained a level of quality in their lives to entitle them to the right-to-life.

The difficulty of the argument is that we require a reason for granting a right to something. If we say that all and only Republicans, or Democrats, may enter a certain room, we have established who has a right to enter but we have *not* provided a reason as to WHY they have a right to enter. If we say that humans, or other animals, have a right to something we must be prepared to offer a reason, and specifically one that compels us to grant the right to that particular thing. Tooley's self-consciousness criterion offers the reason that the consciousness of one's own mortality, that one does not wish one's life to end prematurely though it will indeed end some day, is sufficient to entitle one to the right not to have one's life ended prematurely. To end this life prematurely is to deprive it of that to which it has a right unjustly—the right-to-life. But where there is no consciousness then there is no compelling reason to recognize a right to it. For Regan, on the other hand, to be a subject of experience is sufficient to entitle that creature not to have its subjectivity ended prematurely. Is this a compelling reason to entitle such creatures to the right-to-life?

NOTE

[1] This chapter draws heavily on Tom Regan's "The Case for Animal Rights," in *Animal Rights and Human Obligations*, eds. Tom Regan and Peter Singer, Englewood, New Jersey: Prentice-Hall, 1989.

Name_____ TA _____

Section #_____

1) Which of the fallacies listed in chapter 12 do you think is used most commonly? Give an example of its use.

Name_____ TA _____

Section #_____

2) What is the difference between a "human" and a
   "person"?

3) Can an animal be a "person"? Why or why not?

Name_____ TA _____

Section #_____

4) Explain the difference between "direct" and "indirect duties." Give an example of someone/something which you have a direct duty to, and an example of someone/something which you have an indirect duty to.

5) Describe the "contractarian" position on animal killing.

Name_____ TA _____

Section #_____

6) Explain Regan's argument against "contractarianism."
   What theory does he offer instead?

Chapter 14

Abortion and the
Meaning of the Right-to-Life[1]

A. WHAT IS THE ABORTION QUESTION?
THE PROSCRIPTIVE APPROACH

Throughout our discussions we have been distinguishing between two strategies or approaches—prescriptive and proscriptive—and consistently adopting the proscriptive approach. While readers are invited, and urged, to discover their feelings and reasons that guide their own choices of conduct, and to scrutinize them, *our* question is whether or not those *reasons* are sufficiently compelling to recommend liberty-limiting principles for others, and ourselves. The female reader is urged to consider what she would elect to do should she become pregnant and wonder whether abortion is morally permissible. The male reader is urged to consider what he would recommend to the female who informs him that she is pregnant by him—should she decide to ask, since lawful abortion in our country does not require it. But this is not *our* question. Our question is this: If Mary should say that she is pregnant and wants to abort, do we have any good and compelling reasons to offer why she must not? Would the specific circumstances surrounding the pregnancy— whether it was the result of sexual assault, the mother's health to continue to term, the use or not of birth control measures, her readiness for parenting, economic concerns—be of sufficient import to appropriately affect her decision. If abortion violates the harm principle, and thus is immoral, we must be prepared to argue why and how this is so. What, then, could count as good and compelling reasons to stand in Mary's way? This is our proscriptive approach.

B. PERSONS, DOMAINS, AND THE RIGHT-TO-LIFE

In Section II, we return to our discussion of the harm principle in Section I but this time we examine the principle by tracing out a series of problems concerning the meaning of our identity, and possible conditions that undermine it. Here we begin with the view that persons are domains expressed by rights. We accept the idea that to deprive another unjustly of a right is to deprive another of his or her rightful domain. To deprive another of his or her rightful domain is to deprive another of his or her essential nature. And to deprive another of his or her essential nature is to be deprived of the very essence of what one is. This, we agreed, was the meaning of immoral conduct. Stated differently, immoral conduct is a violation of the harm principle.

Section II begins by viewing persons by supposing that the right-to-life is the fundamental domain of the human being. We explore under what conditions, if any, an individual may forfeit that right. We examine abortion, infanticide, euthanasia, suicide, and capital punishment, having first entered into the context of this discussion by an examination of [non-human] animal rights and the permissibility of animal killing. The purpose of this organization is to help the reader think deeply about the justifications given for our familiar conduct and the defenses we commonly hear regarding the acceptability of our practices.

We begin by asking whether questions concerning the morality of killing, that is, questions formulated in terms of the right-to-life, are biological or moral. That is, we wonder what distinctions have been found to be relevant, and ought to be relevant, to decide questions concerning the right-to-life. The general position embraced is that questions concerning the right-to-life are moral, not biological, questions. Accordingly, they cannot properly be decided by appeal to biological data.

This might be all well and good, but a serious objection naturally presents itself. Questions pertaining to the right-to-life may properly be moral and not biological in nature. But conduct concerning issues of the right-to-life take place within our social organization, and to that extent, grievances are settled by an appeal to law. This means that although issues might cry out for certain kinds of approaches under the law, the biological determinants may play a role far greater than moral theory requires or should even allow, and this naturally leads us to certain confusions and complications.

The problem is difficult, but not inscrutable. The crux of the matter is that the law is not nor does it pretend to be a fundamentally moral institution, even if magistrates claim that popular ideals of morality continually shape the law. The law is a compromise among conflicting claims. Despite other kinds of appeals, our conception of "law" is directed to try to balance divergent views if the civil order is to be preserved. The difficulty for our purposes is that the law may not be suitable to guide our investigations of moral conduct and, indeed, may mislead us. Of course, our debate of these pressing and disturbing issues must always consider the guidance, or lack of it, that current law avails.

C. SETTING THE PROBLEM OF ABORTION IN THE CONTEXT OF PROBLEMS OF KILLING

In order to investigate the question whether or not abortion is permissible, we first inquire about what sort of answer we are seeking. We ask, in short, what could count as an answer? Then, we turn to a hypothetical situation—entitled *Welcome to the Planet Zeldar!*—intended to constructively provoke us to consider what kind of response would count as a *moral* answer to this moral question.

Next, we focus on the legacy of our cultural reception to this problem in the context of the legal debate: *Roe v. Wade*, the Supreme Court decision of 1973. In the following chapters, we continue our examination of arguments concerning the permissibility of abortion, introduced by Judith Jarvis Thomson, and the permissibility of abortion in relation to infanticide, discussed by Michael Tooley.

The abortion issue has proven to be profoundly difficult. What we hope to accomplish is to arrive at a clearer perception of the difficulties inherent in the problem. Our approach is neither to encourage nor recommend abortion any more than we should encourage or recommend pornography or specific sexual practices. Indeed, we have a predilection to preserve and encourage the life of persons in general. But, from the proscriptive approach, our question here is only whether abortion is impermissible for Sally who requests it. It is impermissible if we determine it is wrong and wrong if we determine that it causes harm *unjustly*. Thus, we must determine *if* it causes harm to others, or ourself, and if so, just what sort of harm, and whether the harm is indefensible. At every event, our focus is to determine whether the grounds that any of you find convincing to reach the conclusion that abortion is always wrong or sometimes wrong are sufficient to stand in Sally's way and tell her that the abortion she requests is immoral and that you are prepared to advocate liberty-limiting principles to constrain her.

We will define our problem by asserting that a creature who has a serious right-to-life is to be called a *person*. In terms of our legal system, we hold that the unjustified killing of a person represents, perhaps, the most serious crime anyone can commit. But our laws are usually phrased in terms of "human life," not that of "persons." Let's be clear about the difference. "Human" is a biological term; "person" is a moral term. We are searching for moral reasons to defend moral positions and decisions, not biological ones. It might be that all human beings should count as persons—the way our laws do—but maybe not, maybe this position turns out to be morally indefensible. It might be that under certain conditions, humans are persons and when those conditions are not met, then we might well have cases where humans were not persons. For example, we might reach the conclusion that humans who become vegetatively comatose should no longer be regarded as "persons," but we are entitled to reach such a conclusion only when we become very clear about what it means to be a "person," the defining marks of personhood. Conversely, it might be that some non-human animals should count as "persons," and in such cases it becomes increasingly apparent that we need to become clearer about who counts as a person and why. In our culture, anyone convicted of a premeditated act of killing a person—murder in the first-degree—runs the serious risk of losing his or her own life either by execution or by a lifetime of incarceration.

Thus, if we identify a creature as a "person" we recognize that that creature has a *serious right-to-life,* and if that right is deprived unjustly, then whoever has deprived that right unjustly runs the risk of very serious punishment. The focus of Section II in our deliberations, is to wonder *how* to identify persons. We will wonder if animals, other than human animals, qualify as "persons," and if so by what reason(s). And in the process, having granted that adult humans have a serious right-to-life, we must think deeply about what good reasons we have to defend our practice, and whether or not the fetus, the newborn, and the terminally ill can be deprived of the right-to-life not unjustly.

D. MORAL ANSWERS TO MORAL QUESTIONS: WELCOME TO THE PLANET ZELDAR!

What counts as a *moral* answer to a moral question? We have begun by defining a *person* as a creature with a serious right-to-life. Now our problem is to determine the kind of answer for which we are searching. If we say that adult humans are creatures with a serious right-to-life we must recognize that we have answered only part of the question, namely, at least one group that should be counted among those constituting the class of persons. Are there others that belong in this group? How shall we answer this question?

In order to determine what creatures belong in the class of persons we must determine by what reason(s) membership is gained into this class. If adult humans are members, why is this so? Once we know the answer to this question we can then ask if other creatures also have the same characteristic(s) and thus would be entitled to membership in the class of persons. To help make this approach clearer, let us consider the following hypothetical example.

Let's say that we board an intergalactic rocket ship heading off to another planetary system. Welcome to the planet Zeldar! We arrive at the planet Zeldar and we discover creatures on Zeldar that in no way resemble any creatures we have ever found on Earth. Moreover, on Zeldar we discover that there is no human DNA nor is there any DNA that matches any creatures on the Earth. Now let us try to meet the challenge of answering the question of whether any of the creatures on Zeldar have a serious right-to-life. Even if we could not communicate with any of them, by virtue of what characteristic(s) would a creature be entitled to be counted in the class of persons?

This hypothetical example should help us become immediately clear about the inadequacy of identifying *persons* in terms of adult human animals. When we become clear as to *why* adult humans are entitled to the *right*-to-life, and hence are persons, we will then be in possession of a *moral* reason. We can then ask whether or not any of the creatures on Zeldar satisfy that condition. If any do, then they are entitled to be included in the class of persons. If any non-human animals satisfy that condition or conditions, then they, too, have a serious right-to-life and are entitled to be included in the class of persons; and this means that if anyone deprives them of that right unjustly then that individual should run the risk of losing his or her own life, or the harshest punishments we visit upon such perpetrators.

When we have determined by virtue of what characteristic(s) or condition(s) adult human-animals have the right-to-life, we will then be in a position to answer the question as to which creatures on Zeldar, or non-human animals on the Earth, are also *persons,* that is, creatures with a serious right-to-life. And when we have that answer, we finally have a *moral* reason for guiding our moral decision-making in the question of whether or not the fetus is a person, and thus whether or not abortion is impermissible.

E. THE SUPREME COURT DECISION: *ROE V. WADE*

In the case of abortion—the termination of a fetus—is the issue of the right-to-life of a fetus a matter that will be resolved by appeal to biological arguments? It seems that the answer is "no," although a simple response will not adequately reflect the complexity of the issue. In order to come to grips with the problem, we turn first to the 1973 Supreme Court decision to exhibit the legal verdict and the reasons that the Court offered for our guidance. This discussion will not in itself be adequate to formulate a cogent response to the challenge of determining whether abortion is permissible conduct and under what conditions. But it will help us to understand the peculiar circumstance in which the issue is currently being debated.

In 1973, in the case *Roe v. Wade,* the United States Supreme Court found by a five to four decision that abortion was permissible upon a woman's demand when the pregnancy had not passed the second trimester, or 24 weeks. The grounds on which the Court opined, in order to establish permissible conduct, was the number of weeks a pregnancy normally takes before the fetus attains viability, that is, the capacity to respire and ingest on its own, outside the mother's womb. At that stage, the fetus was determined to be a person and thereby had rights guaranteed by the Constitution, like all other persons. Before that time, the fetus was not to be recognized as a person, and thereby not to be accorded the right-to-life as are persons. After twenty-four weeks, on account of viability, the fetus is to be recognized as a person. Unless the mother's life is in imminent danger, the mother may not abort, that is, terminate the pregnancy, after that time without risking prosecution for "wrongful death."

The majority decision was written by Justice Blackmun. The argument outlines the reasons why Texas law had determined abortions to be illegal. Three reasons were offered. First of all, abortions were deemed illegal in order to discourage sexual conduct out of wedlock. Second, abortions were declared illegal due to risks from the medical procedure to the mother who often became seriously ill or died after such procedures were administered. Third, abortions were made illegal out of duty to protect the prenatal life, that is, the fetus, who was unable to demand its own right-to-life.

Blackmun's opinion raises a series of objections to the arguments advanced on behalf of Texas law. First, he notes that the Texas laws opposing abortion were not motivated to protect prenatal life so much as the mother's life. The medical procedure for abortion had not been safe and there had been many deaths due to complications following the procedure. However, not all medical procedures are safe for women. Thus, the argument on behalf of medical risks is no longer binding. Second, because the woman would not be prosecuted for self-abortion, and the medical risks are much greater from the self-administered procedure, making abortion permissible is in the interest of the woman's health. Finally, the Texas law proceeded as if the prenatal fetus is a "person" but it provided no good reason for it.

The majority opinion found that the 14th Amendment, guaranteeing the rights of persons, applies postnatally. Although Texas asserts that "life"—that is, "personhood"—begins at conception, the judiciary cannot make a biological conclusion. The Court also recognizes that different religious organizations and groups of conscience have maintained divergent opinions on the issue. The Court recognizes those discrepancies and offers a compromise between conflicting claims.

The Court observed that the position "life does not begin until live birth" has a long history of support. The ancient Stoics held such a view, as do certain groups of Jews, large segments of the Protestant community, and many organized groups of conscience. The long history of these traditions does not constitute a sufficient argument for the Court's position, but does suggest that there is widescale disagreement by thoughtful and responsible groups constituting a very great number of persons. The Court would try to achieve a compromise among these differing opinions. Apart from "live-birth," the Court found that the condition of viability, attained at more or less 24–28 weeks of pregnancy, would provide the same minimal condition. Therefore, the Court decided that the State may not interfere with a woman's right to abort before the end of the second trimester. Each State may set the exact limit, not less than 24 weeks of pregnancy and not later than 28 weeks. After that time, the State is obliged to interfere with requested abortions, unless unusual medical problems concerning the well-being of the mother or the fetus present special risk.

What the Court's decision affirmed was that the issue of the permissibility of abortion, before the twenty-fourth week, was to be decided by the expectant mother. Thus, the issue became reduced to the question of the right of the mother to decide what happens in and to her body, before the end of the second trimester. Because an expectant mother is not required to submit to questions of an administrative body, because she may receive an abortion upon demand, the abortion issue, because of the ruling, became an issue of a woman's rights to determine what happens to her, by her consent. This is the conclusion that the Court adopted. It is a legal remedy to a conflict among claims. We must inquire further in order to determine whether, by our moral assessments, that decision is defensible.

Granting the Court's decision, we must pass beyond the requirement of finding a compromise between conflicting claims. We must decide, first of all, whether biological grounds are the basis for determining "moral" rights. We must determine whether biological grounds for the right-to-life permit distinctions between quantity and quality. That is, if the prospective or present quality of life is unacceptable, can this count as a sufficient reason for a "person" to be terminated?

The reader should also be made wary about setting 24 weeks as *morally* instructive, or some even suggest 10-weeks when there might be a heartbeat or 12-weeks when there might be signs first of electrical activity in the brain. Why? We must be cautious because, by themselves, biological markers are not moral markers. My dog Fido, in utero, had a heartbeat at some point, and electrical activity in his brain; he has both of those functions now as he runs around outside. But we do not customarily regard him to have a serious right-to-life. Biological reasons are no substitute for moral reasons. Biological functions—gestational development—must be followed in our moral debates by arguments as to why these biological markers are *morally* relevant. If we are to argue, on the slippery slope, that these are beginning stages that lead to human life today, and the personhood we attach to it postnatally, we must be prepared to show that we *must* treat the potential as if it's the actual, and not simply that we *may*. Of course, treating life with care and respect is always a good thing, but our arguments must show more than beneficence, that is, they must show that we have a moral requirement, a duty to do so. We cannot simply wish it, implore it, but moreover show why we must treat the potential as if it's the actual when there are so many examples in life when there is no duty to do so. When a student turns in part of an unfinished assignment, when a less than minimum payment is provided on our loan, it is gracious of the instructor or banker to accept part of what is required to fulfill responsibilities, but where is the requirement, the reasonable demand that the instructor must take the early part of the assignment, or the less than required payment *as if* it fulfills the whole requirement?

F. THE CONSERVATIVE ANTI-ABORTION ARGUMENT

Some philosophers have supposed that the first and most central question which must be answered concerning abortion is whether or not the fetus is a person. Furthermore, the onus has been to show by virtue of what reasons we reach a reasonable position on the status of the fetus as a person. Thus, the familiar anti-abortion argument tends to proceed by supposing that the fetus is a person, and abortion deprives that person of the right-to-life without any reasonable justification.

Argument 1: Abortion is Impermissible.

1. (Assumption) Persons have the right to life.

2. (Assumption) The fetus is a person from the moment of conception.

3. To abort the fetus is to kill the fetus, without any reasonable justification.

4. Therefore, abortion is impermissible. An abortion ought not be performed.

Objections against Argument 1 can be raised. The initial objection is to insist that no good reasons have been provided as to why we must accept the position that "the fetus is a person." Opponents of Argument 1 will grant, of course, that the fetus is a living thing. At the moment of conception when the cell undergoes mitosis and begins a cycle of replication, the fetus is undoubtedly a living organism. But some opponents of Argument 1 contend that to claim the fetus is a living thing, to which no one can object, is a far cry from claiming that the fetus is a *person* and is entitled to protection under a broad set of rights that we extend to persons.

170

Some objectors try to point out gross inconsistencies in our policies concerning the morality of killing. Cows are living things, for example, and most people find permissible their killing without the slightest demand for justification. For surely it will be agreed that humans do not require the ingestion of cows—hamburgers, steaks, and so on—for survival. Among those who oppose abortion as unjustified killing, there is little opposition to the permissibility of killing animals. This means, minimally, that the same people who oppose abortion clearly do not object to killing living things. Thus, the argument must show, and not simply assert, that the fetus, as an undoubtedly living thing, is also a person. The opponents of Argument 1 tend to argue that anti-abortionists who endorse this reasoning offer no good reasons for defense of the crucial assumption that the fetus is a person, but merely assert it.

Problem 1: Is the fetus a person? We will surely grant that the fetus is a living thing. But since not all living things—cows, birds, fish, and so on—are "persons," we must determine how to distinguish among living things in order to isolate persons who have among other rights, the right-to-life.

The right-to-life does not mean a recommendation to avoid harming and killing animals without extraordinary reason. One who violates another's right-to-life unjustly is subject within our legal systems to the loss of his or her own life for that conduct, or the most serious penalties short of that. Perhaps some will grant that the killing of innocent animals is a terrible thing. But in terms of our legal system, the way we behave tends to minimize the severity of that conduct, even when we intentionally harm other animals. If we intentionally run over a groundhog which has found its way onto the public highway—or a dog for that matter—we are liable for very little, though these laws are currently changing. If these animals had the right-to-life, then a person who killed any of these animals would be liable to face capital punishment. Thus, regardless of how we stand on the issue of capital punishment, for the time being, legally speaking, the meaning of the right-to-life in our society is understood in terms of the possibility of forfeiting one's own right-to-life by engaging in conduct that deprives another animal of that fundamental right. In our social organization, the only animal which has that right so protected is the human animal.

Is the fetus a *person*? This question may be stated differently. Indeed, it might be raising two questions at once. First, to inquire about the identity and meaning of a "person" and so investigate the conditions under which an individual living thing does or does not qualify for personhood and for protection in terms of such rights. Second, the question might be whether a multicelled fetus is more entitled to certain rights than a fully grown domestic pet like a dog or cat, or a fully grown primate like a gorilla or chimpanzee. We shall return to this line of thought in the next chapter. But here we ought to identify the reasons we shall propose to defend. We must be prepared to identify the meaning of a person, and defend that identification by appeal to reasons—not storytelling. And we must be ready to defend such arguments by showing further why other animals are not entitled to those same rights.

Our debate takes place not in a court of law but rather in a court of reason—a rational court—in which positions are to be argued in terms of the reasons advanced to support a view.

If you had absolute faith in the prophecy of Tarot Cards, your astrologer and horoscope, the Magic 8 Ball, or your religion as a faithful believer, we should all be able to understand why you would lead your life through such instruments of guidance. But, if you regard that these testimonies of faith should be sufficient to authorize liberty-limiting principles for others, you are sadly mistaken. To allow one person's faithful beliefs—without recourse to any evidence but blind and devout faith—to dictate the limits of *other's* conduct is entirely unacceptable. Recitation of sacred stories—or what may be called scripture thumping for every religious tradition—is inadmissible in this court. The recitation of religious assumptions and beliefs may be sufficient to guide one's own conduct but is an insufficient ground in this court of reason to compel others. To see the merit of this approach, each reader can reflect on the kind of stubborn and indignant attitude each of us tends to feel when confronted by others who try to insist that we accept their points of view based upon their own brands of religious assumptions and doctrines, especially when their interpretations are not our own. However, the reader is not to be discouraged from consulting his or her own religious traditions and utilizing the wisdom of those sacred stories in the effort to strengthen reasoning in this debate. But to authorize liberty-limiting principles to constrain others, to stand in the way of others, we must be prepared to offer more than simply to recite the tenets of our faith, tenets to which others may not subscribe. To be sure that readers have grasped this point consider only how *you* would feel, if you were a person of great "faith," and you were demeaned by a person of a different faith for failing to behave according to their standards and scriptures. Appeals to faith are good enough to justify the limits of your own behavior, but without clarifying the reasoning behind religious commands and edicts, they are not sufficient to authorize liberty-limiting constraints over others.

NOTE

[1] This chapter draws heavily on Judith Jarvis Thomson's "A Defense of Abortion" in *Philosophy and Public Affairs*, Vol. I, no. 1, 1971, pp. 47–66.

Chapter 15

Abortion and Personhood[1]

A. THE STRONG ARGUMENT AGAINST ABORTION

In order to investigate the issue of abortion more deeply, we turn to set out and then challenge the most conservative viewpoints on this issue. We direct our attention to those who hold that abortion is not permissible under any circumstances whatsoever, that it is a violation of the harm principle in each and every instance. If we can show that, in at least some circumstances, abortion ought not be impermissible, that the harm it causes can be excused or defended under at least some circumstances, then it will have been demonstrated that the most extreme and conservative anti-abortionist argument is untenable. From there, our strategy will be to wonder under what other conditions abortion is not impermissible, if any, and why. But let us be very clear from the outset of this new chapter that we are not interested in recommending abortion as wise or desirable, or even unwise and undesirable but nevertheless permissible—we are not recommending or prescribing anything. Our only focus is to answer the question: If some woman who is pregnant requests an abortion is it ever permissible to stand in her way, deny it to her, and declare that such conduct is immoral? Do the specific circumstances concerning the pregnancy affect our moral deliberations on the question of abortion's permissibility? If abortion is morally wrong in any or every circumstance, what good reasons can we present to justify the advocation of liberty-limiting principles?

In order to do justice to the strongest opponents to abortive practices, we shall grant an argument that needs not be granted. But, in following an article by Judith Jarvis Thomson, "In Defense of Abortion," we shall grant without argument, for the sake of this chapter alone, the conservative claim that personhood is established at the moment of conception. Hence, we will grant out of hand—without argument—that the fetus is a *person* at conception, when the sperm unites with the egg and the combined cell replicates. Since most parties who argue for the permissibility of abortion do not want to grant the claim that the fetus is a *person* (and some even tend to argue that the fetus cannot be shown in any conclusive sense to be a person, although it is most certainly a living human animal), we begin here by granting the anti-abortionist the strongest case. How does the argument go from there? The point is that at conception the fetus is, biologically speaking and in terms of DNA evidence, a living human organism. But the moral question is this: When is any living creature a "person," a moral agent worthy of protection and respect. Now we insist on moral reasons, not biological ones.

If the most conservative argument is surmountable even though the fetus is granted personhood, then that argument proves to be inconclusive. This is Judith Jarvis Thomson's strategy. Thomson tries to show that even if one grants that the fetus is a person at conception, abortion still ought to be permissible in the case of rape and in the case of the mother's life in danger, and perhaps in other instances as well. Her claim is, however, that the argument for the permissibility of abortion in the case of rape is different in important ways from the argument for the permissibility of abortion when the mother's life is in danger. We must consider these arguments as critically and cautiously as possible. We must accept no position—for either side of the argument—until good reasons have been supplied. And we must be ready to raise objections to both sides of the issue if we hope to achieve clarity in our thinking and conduct.

The standard anti-abortionist argument, having granted that the fetus is a person at the moment of conception, might go as follows:

Argument 2: Abortion is Impermissible.

1. Every person has a right-to-life.

2. Thus, the fetus has a right-to-life. (Granting the assumption that the fetus is a person.)

3. No doubt, the mother has a right to decide what happens in and to her body. But surely, a person's right-to-life is stronger than the mother's right to decide what happens in and to her body.

4. Therefore, the fetus may not be killed. An abortion may not be performed.

This argument challenges us to determine under what conditions, if any, one may forfeit the right-to-life, that is, be deprived of the right-to-life without being so deprived unjustly. The objections to be raised initially are two-fold. That in the case of (i) rape and (ii) when the mother's life is in danger, the fetus may be aborted not unjustly, even if we grant

174

that the fetus is a person and persons have the right-to-life. I proceed with an argument by analogy, following Professor Thomson.

B. REFUTING THE STRONG ARGUMENT AGAINST ABORTION

Let us imagine the following scenario. One day assailants come to your door and render you unconscious. You are then taken to another location, that so happens to be a medical care unit. You awaken to find yourself frightened, confused, and in considerable discomfort. A doctor rushes to your side and offers the following explanation and consolation.

You have been kidnapped. You have been taken, without your consent, and against your will, to the bedside of a violinist. A very famous violinist, you are assured. And now you are told the whole sordid tale. You see, this famous violinist is very ill, and is suffering from kidney failure. But you, of all the people in the whole region, were discovered to have the same rare blood type as the famous violinist. The violinist's life was in the gravest danger, and needed assistance. The violinist, however, could not count on your willingness to help, and so at the violinist's request, you were kidnapped, and brought to his bedside. You now find yourself presently lying back-to-back with this famous violinist. Your kidneys are aiding his failing ones. If you unplug him, he will die.

Now, of course, this is a very troubling circumstance. You did not ask to become involved in this scenario. This scenario begins with a violation of the *Volenti* maxim. You were kidnapped—taken without your consent and against your will. You might surely grant, in the name of benevolence, that it would be a wonderful thing to help save someone's life. But—and this is the crucial point—if you decided that this whole situation was too much for you, that you did not want to stay, that you were indignant that someone would take you against your will and without your consent, and moreover that you did not know the health risks that were now posed to you, and thereby demanded to be released, is there any reasonable moral ground on which the case could be made that you must stay, that you are required to stay? Even if it be acknowledged that by unplugging yourself from this famous violinist, the violinist will die, ought anyone stand in your way to prevent you from acting on your decision to unplug and leave? Thomson takes it that the clear and unambiguous answer must be NO.

In this scenario, you are not simply confronted by the challenge that failing to offer your services will result in the death of this famous violinist. You are challenged by the charge that if you unplug the violinist, that act will directly result in the violinist's death. Your decision to withhold the use of your kidneys from the violinist, prior to being connected, would have been a case of refraining to provide extraordinary means to save the life of another and thus simply "let-one-die" or "allow nature to take its course and bring an end to a sick person." But now, already connected, your act of unplugging will directly kill. When we take up the distinction between active and passive euthanasia in two chapters—the distinction between "directly-killing" vs. "letting-one-die"—we will return to this example. Let us imagine the scenario was just a bit different, that you were medically hooked up to the violinist and you had agreed to help for 9 months (!) but, at the end of this time period things had changed. The violinist was not fully recovered and still in danger of death upon disconnection, but now you discover that you are not feeling well and the doctor informs you that you will likely die as a result of this assist on the violinist's kidneys! BUT, the argument against your disconnection seems to remain the same: you still must not disconnect yourself because to do so will directly kill the violinist (= murder!) while doing nothing and allowing the process to continue you will simply die, and directly killing is always worse than letting one die! How might this argument clarify your moral inclinations on the right thing to do?

In general, the argument by analogy attempts to make the point that in the case of rape, abortion is permissible, even if we grant that the fetus is a person and has the right-to-life. Here's how the analogy works; what do you think about this argument? Because the pregnant woman neither agreed nor consented to take on the responsibility of the fetus, the fetus has no right to remain—whether or not the fetus is capable of voicing that right, or someone voices this argument on behalf of the fetus. Of course, the fetus is "innocent" but Thomson's argument is that this no more entitles the fetus to remain against the woman's wishes. And, according to Thomson, no one else should succeed in persuading us to intervene against the woman's request, on behalf of the fetus because the fetus—this other person—did not receive consent to enter that womb in the first place.

It would be very kind of you to be willing to remain to aid the violinist. Indeed, it would be an act of supreme beneficence. But, if you are told that you must stay in bed for nine months, or the rest of your life for that matter, to help this violinist, and you did not want to, then by what good reason(s) should anyone feel entitled to interfere with your decision to unplug yourself and leave, even if the violinist will certainly die by your actions? The reason that your conduct would be permissible, Thomson's argument goes, is that you did not give consent to the activity in the first place. The fetus, even if we grant it the status of being a person, has been harmed by the abortion since abortion is an act of killing; but the killing is not unjust since the fetus had no right to be in that womb in the first place. The *Volenti* maxim, according to Thomson's argument, absolves the pregnant woman from the blame of moral wrongdoing.

On Thomson's account, the woman who is the victim of rape and who becomes pregnant and is then told that she must carry the pregnancy to term because the fetus is a person and persons have rights, including the right-to-life, has every right to object to such harassment. If she chooses to carry the fetus to term, she has behaved like the Good Samaritan by going above and beyond any call of duty. But if she refuses to do so and wants the consequence of rape to be abrogated, then, Thomson argues, no party has any reasonable claim to interfere and insist that she must do otherwise. Without consent, the fetus has no standing, no right to remain. Just as the rape itself is wrong because the rapist failed to gain consent and it is the failure to gain consent that undermines another person's rights, the fetus too, however innocent, still does not have the *right* to remain, unless by consent.

Let's return to the case of the famous violinist, this time altering the scenario somewhat. Our purpose is to formulate an argument by analogy concerning the right to abort the fetus, even if the fetus is a person, if and when the *mother's life is in danger.*

> In the new case, you have not been kidnapped, but rather answered an advertisement appealing for someone with the right blood type to help the ailing violinist. By your own consent, you agreed to assist the failing kidneys of the dying violinist. The doctors informed you that this process would have to continue for nine months and that your health should not be in danger. However, after several weeks the doctors inform you that your own health has unexpectedly deteriorated, and that your own life now seems to be in danger by continuing with this process but that you must not unplug from him or else the violinist will surely die. Unfortunately for you, it is likely that after nine months your body will probably become so debilitated that you will die. Still, you must not unplug the violinist because the violinist will certainly die if unplugged while in your case it is merely probable that you will die if you continue. What shall we say about this argument by analogy?

How can we judge a situation in which a woman becomes pregnant by consent and subsequently learns that her own life is in grave danger if she carries the pregnancy to term? If she aborts, the fetus—which we have granted by this argument is a person—will surely die. If she does not abort and continues the pregnancy to term, it is extremely likely that she will die. In this case, we have two persons. Both have the right-to-life and both have the right to save their own life. How shall we decide? That is, by virtue of what good reasons is one more entitled to live than the other? In this case, we are not forced to choose one or the other. For Thomson, we are only asked what seems to be the right advice to give to the expectant mother, and further, what measures, if any, ought to be taken to interfere with her decision if it somehow violates the harm principle. For *our* proscriptive approach, we ask a slightly different question:

If the mother asks to have the pregnancy terminated to save her own life, do we have any good reasons to stand in her way, tell her that she must not abort, and approve liberty-limiting principles if she tries to go forward with her plan. This proscriptive approach shows us a very different side of the matter. We are not asked to recommend on our feelings, our religious beliefs, the advice from the Magic 8 Ball or the Tarot Cards should they instruct us that abortion is impermissible—because she may not share our religious beliefs or our faith in certain instruments of prophecy and guidance, and we would be indignant if someone were to force their testimonies of faith or prophecy upon us; we are asked only what *good reasons* do we have to stand in the way of this woman who wants to save her own life. Now, the problem here is not merely to decide on the morality of abortion but moreover on the limits, if any, for someone to fight for and preserve their own life. If the right-to-life means anything, it would seem to mean that—life being sacred and worthy of protection and respect—everyone has the right to fight for their own life. To deny the woman who requests it the right to abort in *this* situation is to deny her the right to fight for her own life.

Does the right-to-life of the fetus supervene that same right of the mother? If so, why? Does wisdom dictate that we shall place the greater right with the mother who is alive, the patient who is under the care of the physician and engaged in the world? Or shall we insist that the fetus ought to be defended since it cannot defend itself? And if so, on what grounds? If the mother wishes to carry to term and take the risk of dying in order to save the fetus, she is welcome to make that choice. But if she should decide to fight for her own life, is there any good reason to refuse her that choice? Shall we say that since the mother has enjoyed fifteen or twenty or thirty years of life, then she ought to step aside for the fetus—this other person? Is that a good reason?

> How compelling would it be to you to find yourself attached to the ailing violinist, by your own consent, and with the assurances from the doctors that your health would not be impaired, and that your danger would last only a few months. And then, how different the circumstance would be—would it not?—to learn that, unexpectedly, your body took a serious turn for the worse. The doctors notify you that should you continue, it now appears likely that you will die, but you still must not unplug yourself from the violinist, because if you do that the violinist will certainly die. Ought not you be able to say "Hold on here. Remove me at once." Ought not you be able to save your own life? Is not the right-to-life the sort of moral domain to which you are entitled no less than others? Don't you have a right to save your own life? Don't you have an obligation to save your own life, or otherwise, we seem to have made suicide not merely permissible but benevolently required? Would not such a position prove too much?

Moreover, suppose the woman's situation is that she already has three children, and she is a single mother. If she carries to term with the likelihood of dying, she now must consider who will take care of the three children she already has. Would the reality of these contingencies—the specific circumstances—affect moral deliberations? Do such situations suggest that moral decisions cannot be made in a vacuum but rather always in the context of the particular circumstances in which we find ourselves?

We are considering Thomson's argument for the permissibility of abortion and wondering if it would be both wrong to stand in the way of a woman who had been raped or one whose pregnancy placed her life in imminent danger to interfere with her request for an abortion, should she demand one. If the pregnant woman wished to carry to term the fetus which resulted from rape or which endangered her health, she is surely entitled to make such a difficult decision. But is she any less entitled to decide to abort in these circumstances because in the one case she did not consent to that pregnancy and in the other she attempts to save her own life from the physical dangers of carrying that pregnancy to term? In the case of the mother's life being in danger by carrying the fetus to term, it may be insisted that if the right-to-life means anything it must mean that the mother has a right, no less than anyone else, to fight for her own life, even if it means that another must die, not unjustly, in the process.

Against the most conservative position that insists that if we shall grant that the fetus is a person, abortion is always impermissible, Thomson believes she has argued successfully that abortion can be defended as permissible in the case of rape and the mother's life being in danger. This means that if we accept Thomson's arguments, the extreme anti-abortion position is untenable, that is, it cannot be adequately defended. We must now go on to consider how Thomson's arguments might work in cases which are open to even more widespread objection. Those cases include the permissibility of abortion when (a) pregnancy results following consensual intercourse when birth control measures are employed for the purpose of avoiding pregnancy, and (b) pregnancy results following consensual intercourse when no preventive birth control measures are employed. How do these circumstances affect the argument?

The general problem in the case of pregnancy as a consequence of rape is that the argument justifying the permissibility of abortion claims that where the fetus has not been invited, where there is no consent, then the fetus does not have a right to remain in the woman's womb, even if the fetus is a person at the moment of conception. This is a violation of the *Volenti* maxim. But can this maxim be reasonably extended to cases where intercourse is consensual but pregnancy is *not* consented to? If this argument is judged to be successful, then abortion might very well be justifiable by the same argument in the case of consensual intercourse where birth control methods are employed. Is conception a sufficient ground to defend the right of the fetus to remain? If the use of birth control methods are intended to avoid pregnancy, then clearly the fetus has not been invited to remain. How does the argument go?

Again, let us argue by analogy, following the example of Professor Thomson.

> Let us suppose a burglar passes by your house and finds an open window. The burglar enters the house without your permission. You return home later to find that a burglar is sitting in your living room watching television. The burglar has committed a "break in and entry." Incensed, you demand that the burglar leave immediately or you shall call the police. The burglar then replies that he has no intention of leaving nor do you have a right to force him out. Although you did not explicitly invite him in, you did leave your window open and that, for the burglar, amounts to the very same thing. Even if uninvited, he now has made entry and you have no right now to eject him. How would you respond?

> Or, let us complicate this scenario just a bit. Let's say that it is the dead of winter and it is a bitterly cold and snowy day and furthermore, the burglar has no coat. When you order him out of your house the burglar might become seriously ill and die due to exposure. Are you responsible for his well-being and fate even if you believe that he may freeze to death? Are you obliged to let him stay in your home?

> The likely response would be to pick up the phone and call the police. The result would be entirely appropriate. The police would come, hear the scenario, and would immediately determine that the uninvited burglar had no right to remain (indeed, because he had no right to enter in the first place) and they would approve of your right to insist that he leave or they would assist you by escorting the burglar out if he refused.

If this argument by analogy proves to be instructive, it does so by making the point that where there is no consent, the fetus, even if it is a person, has no right to remain—it is a violation of the *Volenti* maxim, and mitigates the charge of harmful wrongdoing. To those who object by insisting that anyone who engages in intercourse naturally runs the risk of pregnancy, Thomson's response is that the fetus has no more right to remain in the womb than a burglar has the right to remain in someone's living room on the grounds that the window is slightly ajar. Of course, anyone who leaves his or her windows ajar runs the risk of a burglar's entry but the burglar who gains entry without permission *has no right to remain* simply because he has succeeded in gaining entry. The point is that he did not gain entry legitimately, by permission. The argument suggests that consent, here as elsewhere, seems to be necessary to justify a practice. Our enduring problem is to determine whether or not it is sufficient as well.

And let us add one more factor to this scenario. Suppose that the windows around your apartment or house have "burglar bars," that is, metal bars installed to make unwanted entry even more difficult. And suppose because of a defect in one of the bars, a burglar nevertheless was able to gain access. Would the burglar have any right to remain in your house? Again, Thomson believes the answer is clearly "no." In this case, the burglar bars are analogous to birth-control measures; they are employed to prevent unwanted entry. Are their uses sufficient to secure the claim that the burglar or fetus has no right to remain, should it nevertheless gain entry?

In the case where no birth control protection is employed, but conception is not desired, the argument becomes more strained, but even then, Thomson wonders, whether the conclusion would be different. For the objector naturally insists that throwing out the burglar is not consigning him to his death. Still, if one returned home on a very cold night to find a burglar inside who demanded to remain because it was so cold and he feared freezing to death, the homeowner would be under no legal requirement to permit him to remain. We are still challenged to decide whether the homeowner would be under any moral compulsion to act differently. Can the consequences that follow for the burglar constitute a sufficient moral ground for the homeowner to be forced to provide shelter at the burglar's demand? Thus, analogously, our problem is to determine, even in the case where no preventative birth control measures are taken—when consensual intercourse occurs on the spur of an unprepared moment, and where conception is unintended and expressly unwanted—whether the fetus, even if it is a person, would still have a right to remain. Would aborting this fetus deprive it of the right-to-life not unjustly?

There is an important legal issue to reflect upon here that may help the reader think again about this matter. In 1964 in Queens, New York, in broad daylight, a woman named Kitty Genovese was walking down the street when she was attacked by a knife-wielding assailant. More than three dozen witnesses watched this horrendous act from their apartments and not a single person even picked up the telephone and called the police to report a stabbing in progress. In full view of so many persons, Kitty Genovese was stabbed many, many times and no one even notified the police. Afterwards, eye witnesses claimed that they were frightened by the possibility of reprisals if they volunteered information. But there was not even one anonymous call to the police. And in this situation, not a single person who witnessed this heinous act was brought up on any charge. What all this means is that by our law, no one is (really) required to do anything at all to save the life of another.

And certainly no one is required to place themselves in any danger whatsoever to save the life of another. Why do we treat the abortion question so differently? On what grounds do we require the mother to behave differently from all other citizens?

Anti-abortionists have argued that state regulations against abortion discourage sexual conduct out-of-wedlock. The most conservative factions argue against the permissibility of abortion on the grounds that it tends to promote sexual intercourse between persons who have not made lifelong commitments, and such conduct is deemed both irresponsible and unacceptable. Could the wish to socially regulate sexual intercourse be a sufficient condition to interfere with a woman's demand for abortion (prior to the sixth month of pregnancy, 24–28 weeks)? Thomson's point is that it is difficult to see how this position can be adequately defended.

Many persons hold widely varying views about what constitutes appropriate sexual conduct. These would be cases of what we have termed *impersonal harms*. Those people who hold strong and restrictive views should certainly follow their consciences and constrain their conduct in accord with the guidelines for decency that they have adopted. But on what grounds—by what reasons—can one person's guidelines be compelling for other persons? There are already an extensive number of laws that regulate sexual behavior in public places. Later, in Section III, we shall debate whether the *private* consensual practices of adults ought to be free from state regulation, except in cases where wrongful harm to others can be demonstratively shown. We are still challenged by the arguments concerning the impermissibility of conduct that results in impersonal harms.

Thomson's argument suggests that the policy to refuse permission to abort on the grounds that such permission would sanction and encourage sexual intercourse out-of-wedlock seems uncompelling. The permissibility of abortive practice cannot be defended by appeal to the desirability to regulate sexual practices, one way or the other. That concern alone is irrelevant to the abortion question, though some thinkers have not merely supplied that argument but have created the strong impression that it was this matter which motivated them to speak out about abortion. Thus, Thomson's argument is that the question of the permissibility of abortion ought to be severed completely from the question of the desirability of prevailing courtship practices. Are Thomson's argument persuasive?

NOTE

[1] This chapter draws heavily on Judith Jarvis Thomson's "A Defense of Abortion" in *Philosophy and Public Affairs,* Vol. I, no. 1, 1971, pp. 47–66.

Name_____ TA _____

Section #_____

1) What is "the law"? Is the law a moral institution?

2) What question does the example of "Planet Zeldar" ask us about personhood?

Name_____ TA _____

Section #_____

3) Summarize the 1973 *Roe v. Wade* Supreme Court Case.

4) Until what point during pregnancy is abortion allowed under *Roe v. Wade?*

Name_____ TA _____

Section #_____

5) If one were to take the position that a fetus should be counted as a person: what do we do if the interests of the fetus conflict with the interests of the mother? Whose interests come first?

Chapter 16

Abortion and Infanticide[1]

A. FETUS, PERSONS, AND THE CASE AGAINST ABORTION

Our investigation on the permissibility of abortion helped us propose a provisional answer to the question of self-identity. "I am a *person*." A person is a domain expressed in *rights,* chief among which is the right-to-life. To understand the meaning of the "right-to-life" is to understand the moral meaning of our essential human nature. The provisional answer we advanced is that the "right-to-life" is the "right not to be killed unjustly." Thus, at least human life is sacred to the degree that we regard humans as "persons."

We have set out the view that persons are creatures who are entitled to live free from unjust harms. Without good reasons, the liberty to pursue interests should not be restricted but persons can and must be called to account for killing another person when it is not prompted by circumstances overriding the duty to respect a life. Persons who kill other persons unjustly run the risk of being forced to forfeit their own lives as a consequence of their conduct.

But if persons are creatures with the right-to-life, it still is not clear how "to recognize one when we see one." Many cases of personhood seem clear at first, but as soon as we inquire about the distinguishing mark, the essential criterion of it, we find ourselves somewhat at a loss. Questions about the fetus, newborn babies with the most serious congenital defects, terminally ill persons, those who kill other persons unjustly, and a wide range of sophisticated animals, such as the primates, force us to wonder about how to distinguish a person and by virtue of what criteria. For in doing so, we will be assured as to whether or not such a being is deprived of its fundamental nature unjustly and hence, treated immorally.

Judging by the way we behave, adult humans are recognized as persons. But this is only to acknowledge who is included as members of a group. To say that adult humans are to be extended various rights, especially the right-to-life, in no way answers the core question: Why? This core question must be answered and we shall now consider another possible reply. Our first moral reply was proposed by Regan who argued, in effect, that a person is a subject of a life who desires things and has essential value whether or not it has a usefulness to others; as such, many non-human animals seem to qualify for "personhood" and hence the right-to-life.

We raised the question as to whether the fetus is a person; we examined the strong anti-abortion argument by accepting without argument that the fetus *is* a person at the moment of conception and we considered what consequences followed concerning the permissibility of abortion. Now, we will raise the question of the status of the fetus again, this time entertaining the argument that the fetus is *not* a person.

In an earlier discussion, we noted that the position of our Supreme Court affirmed that until more or less the twenty-fourth week of pregnancy, the fetus does not count as a person—the expressions they used was "human life" but the moral sense was "person." Thus, until the fetus attains a stage of development where its capacity to be *viable* can be realized—that it can respire and ingest on its own outside the mother—it may be treated as another living thing while not being accorded the right-to-life that is accorded to other persons. The wisdom of the Court offers a biological solution to a moral question, identifying a *person* as a human organism at least twenty-four weeks old and thus granting it rights when it is capable of sustaining life independent of the womb. This suggests that moral rights are not granted to creatures whose capacities are merely potential. Let us consider this matter more closely.

Those who argue that the fetus deserves the right-to-life, that the fetus is a person at the moment of conception, have accepted the argument that we ought to treat the *potential* as the *actual*. This means that since the fetus may eventually be expected to grow up, mature, and subsequently develop into a moral agent, we may grant the fetus some basic rights while it is only potential. Further, we—our society—have a vested interest in protecting the lives of future citizens (and taxpayers!). Does this argument make any sense and, if so, why? We are trying to focus on whether or not abortion is *impermissible*.

Let us suppose that you make plans to build a house and you enter into negotiations with a builder. Let us say that the plan calls for a substantial amount of wood and it is agreed that all the woodwork will be done in golden oak. And finally, let it be agreed that you will pay a substantial sum—say, $50,000 extra—for the wood from many select oak trees and you pay that huge sum to the builder who agrees to have the lumber delivered tomorrow. Sure enough, a large truck arrives the next morning, as agreed, but rather than finding long beds of great oaks, instead you find many, many acorns.

It would be fair to guess that you would be furious. You would feel cheated, and would challenge the builder as a fraud for having promised the golden oak from many oak trees while instead having delivered only many acorns. And, as a sign of your anger, you probably would have called your lawyer to start proceedings for a lawsuit regarding the fraud just perpetrated.

What was the fraud? The builder attempted to equate the potential with the actual. He asked you to treat the potential oak tree—the acorn—as if it were an actual, fully-grown and developed oak tree. Naturally, your payment of $50,000 for the acorns is ridiculous. The potential is not the actual, nor ought it to be regarded and treated as if it were the actual.

Should the argument that the fetus is a person and ought to be treated as one be open to the same sort of objections. The fetus is, it may be objected, potentially a person. But, like the acorns it only has capacities that sometime in the distant future shall qualify it for personhood. It would be kind and generous to extend care and respect to a creature whose own development provides no good reason to merit that distinction. But would extending such treatment to it be necessary? The objection to insisting that the fetus is a person is to try to make the point that a fetus is merely potentially a person, as the acorn is potentially an oak. A person would no more find it reasonable to pay $50,000 for many acorns when expecting fully grown trees, than they would treat a fetus as an adult moral agent. The argument, then, is that the potential is not the actual and ought not be treated as such. To be persuaded by it, we then have a strong objection against the argument in which we granted the fetus person-status at conception. Is this a compelling argument?

On another front, the argument advanced by the Supreme Court risks the charge of the so-called "slippery slope." As soon as the Court determines that at some arbitrarily determined mark of the number of weeks of a pregnancy—let's say twenty-four weeks—we shall begin to treat the fetus as a person, such a ruling runs the risk of objecting that the Court is caught on a slippery slope. Why? In some cases it can surely be argued that the fetus is viable at twenty-one weeks and thus, in that particular case, it would be wrong to permit abortion on the court's grounds after that time. In another case, it might be that the particular fetus is not viable at thirty weeks and thus abortion ought to be permitted but must be refused because of the grounds set as guidelines. In general, every attempt to draw a reasonably precise line of demarcation for personhood in terms of fetal development—biological reasons—runs the risk of being an arbitrary judgment. Thus, some have argued that in the name of consistency, it is better to argue either that the fetus is a person at conception, or personhood is established only postnatally. Any other assessment, some argue, places our judgment on a slippery slope that undermines respect for the consistency of such judgments.

In the case of the rape victim who finds herself pregnant and then demands an abortion, we wondered if there were any good reasons why we ought to stop her from having her request fulfilled. For, should we accept that argument, abortion deprives the fetus of nothing to which it has a right, even if we shall grant that the fetus is a person at the moment of conception and thus, has a right-to-life. Aborting in this case is, of course, an act of killing, but the argument is that it is not an act of killing unjustly.

The case of abortion for the pregnant woman whose ill health places her life in imminent danger if she carries the fetus to term, again, asked us to consider that her request to abort should be honored. To be persuaded in this case is to reflect the view that each person does not have an equal right-to-life. If we are to be persuaded by the argument, we must come to see that the mother has every right to save her own life. The mother's right claims priority over the fetus as she tries—if she decides—to fight for her own life. Let us try to clarify this point by appeal to another argument by analogy.

> Let's say that two homeless persons are found outside on a terribly cold day. It so happens that Smith owns a winter coat but Jones has temporarily wrestled the coat from Smith. Smith then calls upon us for help in regaining possession of the coat without which he will surely die. There is no problem deciding who is entitled to the coat. Smith is the owner of the coat and not merely the man who lacks possession of it at present. Smith, like the mother, has a right to that coat or a right to protect his own life and no one ought to tell him that although he is the owner but not the possessor of the coat, he has less a right to the coat. The mother is the owner, the fetus the tenant. The mother has a right to preserve her own life. The right-to-life ought to be accorded first to the living and viable in this sort of situation if the mother wishes to continue to live.

Let's try this circumstance again, by a slightly different analogy. Each of these accounts offers us another test to better articulate the relation between mother and fetus, with regard to resolving a conflict in regard to the right-to-life.

> Suppose we have two brothers, one a few years older than the other. Let us imagine two different cases. In the first case, the older boy is given a box of chocolates with the instructions that he share the

chocolates with his brother. The chocolates are given to him to share and thus both of them have a right to the chocolates. In the second case, the chocolates are given only to the older boy, without any instructions, who refuses to share them with his younger brother.

The argument for the permissibility of abortion rests on showing that the scenario is more like the second case than the first. In the first case, someone is being deprived of that to which they have an equal right. In the second case someone is also being deprived, but not unjustly, since he did not have a right to what he was deprived of in the first place. Do these analogies lend clarity, or where have they fallen short?

In the case of consensual intercourse without the use of birth control, the analogy we drew involved the burglar entering our home through an open window. Are you partially responsible and thereby blameworthy for the burglar's "breaking and entering?" This claim seems to be uncompelling. By analogy, the woman who becomes pregnant, but did not wish to, is refused a request for abortion on the grounds that the fetus has a right to which it nevertheless has not been deprived seems no less weak.

In the case of pregnancy resulting after the use of birth control, the circumstance seems even more absurd.

Suppose you place bars around the windows of your house to prevent burglars from entering. But, due to a defect in those bars, a burglar gets in. Ought you to be responsible for the break-in, despite the fact that extraordinary measures were taken to avoid unauthorized entrance? The answer surely seems to be no. You took exceptional precautions to avoid certain consequences. Are you now responsible for an unwanted and unanticipated consequence? Or, stated differently by this argument by analogy, does the fetus have a right to that from which it has not been deprived? Thomson's argument suggested that you were not. Is she right about this?

To the question of whether anyone is obliged to make large sacrifices to sustain the life of another who has no right to demand them, the answer was clearly no. We have neither "Good Samaritan laws," nor even "minimally decent Samaritan laws," with the only possible exception being the case of abortion. This point is strikingly made, so Thomson argues, in the case of Kitty Genovese. The case shows that no one is legally required to save sustain the life of another, and certainly not put themselves in harms way to do so. So why is it that such stringent efforts are insisted upon with regard to pregnant mothers?

We turn now to deepen our investigation by adopting a new starting point and proceed to ask how our position on abortion applies to defective newborns. The case we turn to is the one concerning the permissibility of infanticide.

B. ABORTION: MORAL VS. BIOLOGICAL ARGUMENTS

We begin by raising, again, the question as to what would count as a morally relevant argument for the permissibility of terminating the fetus—that is, abortion—or the permissibility of terminating the newborn—that is, infanticide. We begin this way because it is instructive to consider the irrelevance of various biological arguments. The fact that the fetus has little hands or a beating heart or electrical activity in the brain are powerful emotional pleas to restrain inclinations to termination. But are those kinds of argument relevant to instruct others concerning the very difficult judgments that they have to make? The mother, or mother and father, who decides against terminating a fetus or a terminally ill newborn should not be interfered with. But we are asking under what conditions, if any, is it appropriate to interfere with the mother, or mother and father, who wants to terminate the life of the fetus or the severely defective newborn? We are asking only when liberty-limiting principles may be applied to restrict conduct.

Let us proceed by asking a question not raised often enough in the debate over abortion and infanticide. Under what conditions, if any, is it permissible to terminate the life of a crocodile, a dog or cat, or perhaps a primate like a gorilla? Let us forget about the abortion/infanticide issues for humans for one moment and ask about the appropriateness of our harmful conduct to these other creatures. With regard to the morality of killing, do any of these animals have the right-to-life that we insist human animals do? If not, why not?

This is a troubling question that often underscores how capricious and ill-thought-out our strongest views are concerning the permissibility of killing. Some people are so very sure that the killing of the fetus is a serious offense: it is murder or "unjustified killing." In most states, the penalty for that crime may be death for the killer, that is, the unjustified killing may be punished by forfeiting the right-to-life. If other animals had the right-to-life, then an unjustified killing ought to be treated as an equally serious and egregious offense. The killer would then run the risk of forfeiting his/her own right-to-life. Our social organization and its legal structure do not affirm this attitude. Thus, it is all the more significant for us to understand why humans enjoy rights that the other animals do not. We behave as if *human* life is sacred; why do we not behave so towards other animals?

The right-to-life is not a biological award. It is not by virtue of having a certain kind of DNA or cell structure or a certain size of brain or a particular heart rate, that any thoughtful person comes to recognize that humans have the right-to-life. To affirm that humans have the right-to-life is to treat humans with a kind of respect and dignity, recognizing their moral nature, their self-conscious capacities, and their ability to restrain conduct when they nevertheless feel inclined to act otherwise. Thus, the right-to-life is a moral right, not a biological one. And to extend to other creatures such rights, we must be prepared to offer moral arguments to justify this conduct.

To all those who argue that the fetus is a person when there are signs of little hands, or a heart beat, or brain activity, the response we now offer is that these biological concerns are entirely beside the point. For the countless number of other animals walking the earth with little feet and little hands, with a self-sustaining heartbeat, brain activities, and the countless creatures that swim in the water and fly through the air, not one of them do we generally recognize as having the right-to-life. The biological arguments upon which we decide the permissibility of moral rights are irrelevant. What makes us so sure that humans—even a fetus—has the right-to-life, but other animals do not?

C. THE MORAL ARGUMENT: THE SELF-CONSCIOUSNESS CRITERION

Michael Tooley, in his article, "Abortion and Infanticide," challenges us to be clear about what a "right" is and under what conditions moral rights are to be affirmed. Tooley defines right as follows:

> Rights: *An individual has a right to something whenever it is the case that, if he wants that thing, it would be wrong for others to deprive him of it.*

Thus, the presence of a "right" is indicated when others attempt to interfere with the realization of someone's desire when it would be wrong to do so. To deprive another of a desire without some overriding reason is to violate someone's nature, hence that person's rights.

Tooley asks whether or not a creature can have rights if it lacks the right-to-life. The argument has often been made that creatures who have the right-to-life also have other rights. But a creature who lacks the right-to-life lacks rights altogether. Tooley objects to this traditional view.

The case of the kitten seems clear. We do not attribute to the newborn kitten the right-to-life, nor to the mature cat. But Tooley thinks that we do extend to the kitten and cat other rights, for instance, the right not to be tortured. We know very well that the kitten does not want to be harmed. The kitten shrieks when it is harmed. It actively attempts to avoid further discomfort. A creature like the newborn kitten has a right to something—in this case, the right not to be tortured—whenever it is the case that if the kitten wants that something, it would be wrong for others to deprive the kitten of it.

Unlike kittens, human beings are regarded as having the right-to-life. But the term "human being" is a biological term, not a moral one. So let us carefully distinguish the term "human being" from "person" and regard "person" as a moral term. All "persons" have the right-to-life. Now, what do biological or physiological characteristics have to do with the moral question of whether or not an organism is a person? The immediate answer seems to be "nothing."

If the right-to-life is attributed to persons, then what properties must some organism have in order to be a "person," that is, to have a serious right-to-life? Here, Tooley offers us a moral argument for defending the granting of a moral right. The criterion he offers might best be called the "self-consciousness" requirement.

> The Self-Consciousness Requirement: *An organism possesses a serious right to life only if it possesses the concept of a self as a continuing subject of experiences and other mental states, and believes that it itself is such a continuing entity.*

According to Tooley's self-consciousness requirement, a creature is a "person" only if it possesses a certain kind of self-consciousness. This is the foundation of a moral argument. Moral rights are extended to creatures that are conscious of what it would mean to be deprived of those rights. Where there is no self-consciousness (so far as we can determine?), then there can be no reasonable argument for extending rights to those creatures.

Creatures who are not merely self-conscious, but are conscious of their own finitude, their own mortality, are creatures that would have a right to it—a right-to-life. Since neither the fetus nor the newborn have this sort of self-consciousness then neither could have nor be protected by the right-to-life. Let us reflect more deeply upon this criterion and what it means.

Why is it, on Tooley's criteria, that a newborn kitten has certain rights but not the right-to-life? As Tooley understands it, the newborn kitten, and even the fully mature adult cat, has no consciousness of its own mortality and, thereby, no *right* to be protected against interference with its existence. The developed human has a right-to-life because such a creature is self-conscious in this requisite sort of way. Developed human beings view themselves as a continuing subject of experiences and are conscious of the desire to continue experiencing in terms of a *future*. The human fetus, or even the newborn, does not have this consciousness and, thereby, is not entitled to these rights. This does not mean, according to Tooley, that we ought to harm the fetus or newborn babies. On the contrary, what the moral argument succeeds in instructing is that *if* it should be deemed necessary to terminate the fetus or the newborn infant, permissibility would be justified on the grounds that no rights had been deprived *unjustly*.

By Tooley's criterion, the newborn has no right to be better protected, from a *moral* standpoint, than the newborn kitten or fully mature cat, or even the newborn giraffe that is capable of standing up and walking within hours of birth, although it is clear that the newborn kitten or giraffe is far more self-conscious and capable of independence than is the newborn baby. And even more so, if we consider the fully mature cat or giraffe. But both cases fail to meet the self-consciousness criterion—according to Tooley who relies on what zoologists and their psychological associates relate—and therefore neither conforms to the moral requirements for the right-to-life. Clearly, Tooley disagrees with Regan who regarded *the experience of being a subject of a life* as *sufficient* grounds to earn the right-to-life.

Tooley's demand for a moral argument allocating moral rights directly challenges the conventional wisdom of someone like Judith Jarvis Thomson as well as Regan. In order to understand how, let us test the self-consciousness criterion in order to see how it applies to other proposed resolutions.

In the case of abortion, the Supreme Court and many others have tried to argue that after twenty-four or twenty-eight weeks of pregnancy, or following others, at the end of ten or twelve weeks, or according to still others, right up until the time of live birth, abortion may be permissible. In every case, Tooley's argument points out the arbitrary character of the slippery slope justification. By Tooley's assessment, abortion may never be desirable, but is permissible right up until delivery. Why? Because the fetus lacks the self-consciousness that entitles it to the right-to-life. Abortion would be killing a living organism but not a "person." The importance of the self-consciousness criterion, as Tooley sees it, is that it provides a moral argument—even if it is an emotionally difficult one in terms of our common suppositions—for both the permissibility of abortion *and* infanticide.

Infanticide is the practice of killing an infant, of terminating the life of a severely defective newborn. By the conventional legal wisdom, viability is the criterion for determining when there exists a living human being who, according to the Court, has access to the rights guaranteed by the Fourteenth Amendment. According to the Court's decision in *Roe v. Wade,* rights apply only after viability and thus certainly postnatally. A creature is understood to be viable when it is capable of respiring on its own and is capable of ingesting/digesting, also on its own accord, outside of the mother's body. Tooley has made clear the ambiguity inherent in such a definition as the basis for allocating moral rights. If it is claimed that only viable creatures are entitled to the full panoply of rights, then all the medically ill and older citizens, who are sustained by iron lungs and/or intravenous feeding would, *ex hypothesi,* have forfeited (or be in danger of forfeiting) their right-to-life and all other rights that go along with it. What Tooley's argument claims to show is that viability—which the Court regarded as central—is the wrong place to locate the core of a theory about moral rights. And what it exhibits further is that the self-consciousness of those persons, viable or not, is the essential point in morally determining who ought to have rights.

Now we must return to an earlier question. Why don't animals belonging to species other than *homo sapiens* have the right-to-life? If we apply Tooley's criterion, the general answer would be that wherever we shall find an organism that possesses the concept of a self as the continuing subject of experiences, and believes that it itself is such a continuing entity, there we will have isolated a person. That organism would have a serious right-to-life, be it a human animal or non-human animal.

Many interesting cases present themselves from the animal kingdom who seem to fulfill Tooley's criterion of being a "person" and hence deserving of those rights we tend to extend only to human beings. In a California preserve, there is a well-known primate, a gorilla, by the name of Koko. Koko is unusual because she has been taught American Sign Language. According to animal psychologists who work with her, Koko is capable of speaking more than two thousand words in sign language. We are immediately struck by the self-conscious capacities of Koko.

Not long ago, Koko developed a friendship with another animal, a little cat. The cat was killed in an accident. When Koko learned of her friend's fate, Koko gave the sign of "frowning-sad." Koko then described the situation in sign-language as "sleep-cat." There seems to be little doubt that Koko understood her friend's mortality. Koko was conscious that her friend the cat had died. And if, following Tooley, we agreed that an organism would have a serious right-to-life only if it possesses the concept of a self as a continuing subject of experiences and so on, then Koko clearly would seem to qualify as having that serious right-to-life. This means, by Tooley's criterion, Koko clearly seems to qualify as a "person." A creature has a right to something, according to Tooley, whenever it is the case that if she wants that thing, it would be wrong for others to deprive her of it. Clearly, Koko's consciousness of mortality would entitle her to the right-to-life on Tooley's conditions. Are his conditions sound? Are they persuasive?.

If we accept this argument, the conclusion is of staggering importance. It shows that there is a serious error engendered in supposing that "person" is a term coextensive with "human being" or definable in terms of human genetic structure. To grant Koko the status of personhood is to refuse a biological definition for moral rights. The biological arguments are irrelevant in establishing the province of moral rights. Only moral arguments will do. In Tooley's assessment it is not the potential but the actual status of self-consciousness which serves as the basis for the permissibility of being extended rights, among them the right-to-life.

The conclusion that Tooley draws is that if the meaning of "person" is to be equated with self-conscious entities, and if other animals will fulfill this condition, then evidently our everyday treatment of other animals may be morally indefensible. In these cases, we may in fact be murdering countless innocent *persons*. The stark lesson with which Tooley's assessment challenges us is that our moral approach to understanding abortion has been overly myopic. We need to ask under what conditions the termination of other animals is permissible and by virtue of what grounds. Only then will we be able to have a clearer understanding of moral conduct with regard to the right-to-life.

Tooley wants to be able to say to a mother and father who have learned that their newborn child is terminally ill or is suffering from so severe a defect that it will not only be unable to attain a fully adult life but also will suffer terribly, the termination of such a defective newborn is morally permissible. The killing of such extraordinary infants is, of course, a case of harming, but since the killing is not unjust, it is not a case of wrongful harm. Emphasizing the self-consciousness criterion, Tooley is clear that not only is the fetus not self-conscious but neither is the newborn. Thus, the mother and father who consult teams of doctors to save their seriously defective newborns and who then learn that the situation is hopeless may take solace in the fact that termination is permissible because their baby is not yet a creature who meets the conditions of a "person." The killing proves to be not unjust because it does not deprive a right, no less a right unjustly.

> No newborn will meet the self-consciousness criterion. Consider the case, announced some years ago in a New York newspaper, *The Daily News*. Not more than two weeks after giving birth to her first child, a fifteen year old was invited to the birthday party of one of her friends—a Sweet Sixteen party. She tried to get a babysitter but was unable to find one. The fifteen year old wanted to go to the party very badly and, in a moment of desperation, bundled up the baby, and quietly slipped the newborn down the incinerator chute as she set off for the party.

On Tooley's criterion, we would have no good grounds for being morally appalled, because we had agreed that the newborn baby did not have the right-to-life because it had not yet attained the required self-consciousness. Tooley believed the criterion set forth would be wide enough to make meaningful and defensible the termination of severely defective newborns, terminally ill infants. But, in the process, he seems to have left the opening so wide that, as this other scenario shows, we would be helpless to respond critically to a case which ought not to be tolerated, which seems morally unacceptable.

Tooley's argument, despite the weakness that has been noted, succeeds in emphasizing that biological arguments miss the critical locus for the proper debate of the issue. He makes his point even clearer when he presses the question: Is the right-to-life exclusively an issue of the "continued existence of a biological organism?" He challenges our commonly held notions by appealing to the case of *brain-substitution.*

> Let us imagine the following situation. You have been brought into the laboratory of a talented, but evil, surgeon who operates on you. Let us say that he has perfected a technique for removing from your brain every sense impression, memory, and experience that you ever had. Without harming a physical molecule of your body, including your brain, he then substitutes for your sensations, memories, and experiences the sensations, memories, and experiences of someone else. In brief, he has substituted all your mental states with someone else's mental states, leaving your body and physical constitution absolutely intact. Now, would you say that you had been killed, that you had ceased to exist?

Naturally, this question requires some struggle, but many are convinced of Tooley's point that, indeed, if all of our experiences are wiped out, like the data on a computer disk, then we would cease to exist. Tooley's point is that the right-to-life is not a matter just of the continued biological existence, but is a *right of a subject who has experiences and other mental states to continue to exist.* The brain-substitution analogy forces us to consider further whether the right-to-life is a biological issue to be supplanted by biological arguments or whether it is a moral issue that requires moral arguments.

NOTE

[1] This chapter draws heavily on Michael Tooley's "Abortion and Infanticide," in *Philosophy and Public Affairs,* Vol. I, no. 1, 1972.

Chapter 17

Infanticide, Euthanasia, Suicide[1]

A. FROM INFANTICIDE TO EUTHANASIA: SHALL WE HONOR THE OTHER'S REQUEST TO BE RELEASED FROM TERMINAL SUFFERING?

We have supposed that human beings are persons and persons are creatures who are entitled to the right-to-life. The problem presented by severely ill and defective newborns bears close resemblance not merely to problems concerning the termination of the fetus, but also to problems concerning euthanasia, or the termination of the terminally ill, the elderly as well as young. Under what conditions, if any, is it permissible to honor someone's request to be terminated? Under what conditions, if any, is it morally acceptable to permit an individual to take his/her own life? Do euthanasia and/or suicide deprive a person of a right unjustly?

The problem of euthanasia or "mercy-killing" has several aspects which are not always connected in terms of their consequences. For instance, the problem of dealing with a terminally ill patient requires different strategies when dealing with the elderly still capable of making rational decisions or with newborns in critical condition. The newborn is not in a position to request termination and so that request must be made by a third party. In this important respect consists its complication. In the case an elderly person who has, for example, a severely progressed and terminal cancer, who requests to be put out of his/her misery, the assistance of another might be required to accomplish that end. This scenario calls for consideration of the role of third persons— often the doctor or nurse—in carrying out the wishes of a terminally ill adult, or in the case of a terminally ill child, the parents. These are a few of the complications that attend our reflections on euthanasia.

Our focus shall not be whether such conduct is wise or desirable. We are not concerned to recommend such practices in any case. Our focus will be on those who request to be freed from terminal misery. If an elderly person makes such a request while clearly in his or her right mind, under what conditions, if any, shall we determine that the request is permissible? Our concern will also reflect the difficulty of parents who have a terminally ill child. But our most general examination will be directed to the question of whether it is impermissible to end one's life when certain conditions undermine what we may call a minimal threshold of quality or decency. Ought persons to have the right to live and die with dignity? After a general consideration of these issues, we will have to return to address the permissibility of suicide, because this is the issue which fundamentally underlies our discussion.

B. ACTIVE VS. PASSIVE EUTHANASIA

Discussions of the permissibility of mercy-killing must include understanding the distinction between active and passive euthanasia. According to the law and the American Medical Association, passive euthanasia is permissible while active euthanasia is not. Is this distinction defensible? Does it lead to reasonable guidelines for conduct?

As James Rachels points out in his article "Passive and Active Euthanasia," there are problems inherent in the distinction and troubling consequences for policy that follows from it. By "passive euthanasia" we mean the withholding of extraordinary medical treatment that permits patients to die of their own accord, that allows nature to take its course in bringing a life to an end. By "active euthanasia" we mean taking direct action in lethal and immediate forms to bring about the patient's death.

Active euthanasia is considered unacceptable because the third-party who assists the death fulfills the role of a premeditated murderer—the only exceptional difference is that the victim has consented, indeed requested to be delivered from hopeless suffering. By contrast, persons who administer the lethal injection or medication to themselves are actors in suicide, and this too violates law. In the one case, the third-party stands liable to be charged with harm to others; in the other case, the individual stands charged with harm to (him/her) self. The arguments against the permissibility of premeditated murder and against suicide are supposed to be clear and insurmountable. Thus, what makes active euthanasia impermissible entails the very same reasoning that makes murder and suicide unacceptable.

We must now consider whether cases of terminally ill persons mitigate the otherwise familiar arguments against euthanasia. If we suppose that the arguments against it are formidable, we must decide whether specific issues override reasonable objections. If those restrictions can be overridden then euthanasia, though harmful, will not be unjust.

The familiar argument with regard to euthanasia is that directly killing, or active euthanasia, is always worse than simply letting someone die, or passive euthanasia. Direct killing is identified with murder and is thus unacceptable as a case of wrongful harm. Letting someone die, on the other hand, is merely supposed to allow nature to take its course and is considered to be a tolerable practice. Such has been the fate of peoples everywhere throughout the ages. This is the strategy we have generally adopted concerning "merciful" remedies to end a life of terrible suffering. But does it fulfill the demands of being merciful? Let us consider this argument by analogy.

> Let us imagine two persons, Smith and Jones, who both have six-year-old nephews. In both cases, Smith and Jones are next in line to inherit a fortune bequeathed to the respective nephews. If something should happen to the nephews, both Smith and Jones would inherit the fortunes. Now let us suppose that both Smith and Jones have dastardly intentions to get hold of these fortunes and both plot to bring the life of their young nephews to an abrupt end. Further, both plan to employ the same strategy to drown the little tykes during the evening bath.

> That night both Smith and Jones put their plans into action. Smith draws the bath for his young nephew and when the boy steps into the bath, Smith pushes his head under the water and holds it until that young life is no more. Jones has the very same intention, but his plan is unexpectedly altered. When his nephew steps into the bath, the boy slips on the soap, hits his head on the edge of the bath, and is knocked unconscious. When his nephew falls beneath the water, Jones simply stands back and does nothing. This young man, like Smith's nephew, came to the same tragic end; both boys died.

From a moral point of view, shall we say that there was really a substantial difference between the conduct of Smith and Jones? True, Smith *directly killed* his nephew while Jones merely *let die* the young boy. Rachels thinks that most would be inclined to judge that both uncles acted abhorrently and that neither's conduct was superior from a moral standpoint. By virtue of this analogy, can we make sense of the argument that directly killing is always worse than letting someone die? Or has the case been made, by analogy, that in certain situations, direct killing is no worse than letting someone die? If we reach the latter conclusion then either we shall be forced to deem passive euthanasia to be as unacceptable as active euthanasia, or we will have to grant that in some situations, active euthanasia is no worse than passive euthanasia and may not only be acceptable but perhaps also preferable in carefully distinguished circumstances.

In order to think this matter through more deeply, we must consider the idea of suffering in more detail. The intention is to become clearer about what promotes acceptable strategies concerning mercy.

We noted that animals can have rights *even if* they do not fulfill condition(s) entitling them to the right-to-life. The example Tooley advanced concerned a kitten: animals have the right "not to suffer." If a person is suffering from a terminal illness, does that person have the right to request an end to excruciating suffering from which there shall never be a future relief? According to current policy, the answer is NO, since active euthanasia is considered murder. Murder is unjustified killing. Would the killing in this case, at the request of a terminally ill patient, be justified? The answer to this difficult and troubling question depends upon our response to the additional question of whether, in the name of mercy, we have an overriding obligation that militates against the charge of murder.

We argued that the torture of animals was impermissible because animals do not wish to suffer, and yet they seem to have a right to merciful treatment. If a deer is hit by a car and found by a state trooper on the roadside, it is common for the trooper to put the suffering animal out of its misery by using a service revolver. The animal is killed because it is suffering, and ending that suffering appears as a merciful act. How, then, can it be that animals have a right not to suffer while humans are somehow required to endure terrible discomforts? The problem is that in the case of euthanasia we have a conflict of duties. On the one hand, we feel compelled to alleviate suffering as well as needless or hopeless agony. On the other hand, we oppose the conduct of premeditated killing, for that seems wholly unjust. How shall we decide between these conflicting duties?

If our conduct is motivated by mercy, how does it apply in the following case where passive euthanasia is permitted, but not active euthanasia.

Let's say that you have a wonderful grandmother who has been kind to you all your life. She took care of you when you were a baby in your parents' absence, and she cared for you many times as you grew into adulthood. She always brought you treats, gave you presents at holiday time, and sent you little notes that expressed her love for you. Grandma is now almost ninety years old. She has lived a full, productive, and happy life. Alas, she is a victim of both Alzheimer's disease, a malady that we used to call senility, and suffers from an advanced state of cancer. Your wonderful grandmother is becoming increasingly ill, confused, disoriented, and is in terrible discomfort. She knows only too well that she is losing her "right-mind," that she will continue to fail in health, that her sufferings will only become worse, and that she will soon fail to recognize her family and friends whom she has loved for so long.

As time marches on, grandma takes turn after turn for the worse. She is now in a miserable state and is failing fast. In a moment of lucidity, your grandmother tells the whole family of her awful suffering, her clear understanding that this is the end and begs all her loved ones to please put her out of this misery. The doctors concur that she has only the shortest time left to live and that her suffering will become worse and worse and her senility will increase until not one of her dearest family is recognizable to her. Given this scenario, is there any reason you—or someone you designate such as a medical professional—should fail to grant your beloved grandmother this final request?

The argument, by analogy, is that in some cases, active euthanasia is not merely permissible, but in comparison with passive euthanasia that forces our grandmothers to protract their sufferings needlessly, the "direct killing" or active euthanasia seems more merciful and thus more desirable, if that be the final wish of those grandmothers.

The argument here is not that active euthanasia is a commendable practice. The problem is to determine if it is morally impermissible. In circumstances like the one concerning the aged grandmother above, active euthanasia seems not merely acceptable but, in the name of mercy, more desirable than passive euthanasia. Those who have, or who've ever had, a family pet, a loved dog, a cat, pet gerbil or hamster, who reach an age or state of sickness where it must be "put down" or "put to sleep," have made a decision which was surely wrenching and deeply troubling. And yet, the wisdom of that choice to avoid the protracted suffering of that animal, when it was clear that it was dying, was obvious. So, should we be able to see the wisdom of such a course of action in the case of persons in certain situations where circumstances seem utterly hopeless and the person suffering asks to have their terminal suffering to end? More importantly for our proscriptive approach, if someone requests that we intervene and bring to an end—by active euthanasia— their terminal, hopeless suffering, are there any good reasons to deny them what they desire?

C. EUTHANASIA AND SUICIDE

In order to pursue this matter even further, we pursue it to its roots: the permissibility of suicide. Is the person who takes his/her own life acting immorally?

Later we will take up an argument concerning the impermissibility of suicide. That discussion will emerge in the context of Kant's discussion of "Duties Toward the Body in Respect of Sexual Impulse." There, Kant argues that persons are subjects and agents and not fundamentally bodies, properties or mere things. Human moral agency and, hence, human identity is to be affirmed in conduct that distinguishes us from the other brute animals. Sex and other bodily activities are engaged in by all animals and so do not distinguish us nor properly affirm our human moral dignity.

Kant's argument about the fundamental identity of persons leads to the view that if persons are agents and not property, then slavery is impermissible because it reduces persons to the status of property. That argument then advances the consequence that suicide is as impermissible as slavery because both make the unacceptable error of regarding persons as property and reduce persons to the status of mere objects or things, that can be used as one pleases. What is wrong with slavery and suicide, according to Kant's deontological arguments, is that it condones, or makes permissible, just this unacceptable abuse of persons.

In the case of slavery one person acts toward others as if it were justifiable to treat persons as mere things. Kant rejects the permissibility of suicide on the grounds that if a person cannot be a thing for another person, then a person cannot properly be a thing for himself either. If a person is not a property, then one cannot justifiably do with oneself as one pleases. This same reasoning leads Kant to find practices like masturbation and sodomy utterly unacceptable, since persons are not property and cannot do with themselves as they please. Thus, persons have duties towards themselves, as well as towards others, if they are to affirm their moral nature and their fundamental human identity.

Even if we grant Kant's argument—which we will not—we would still be saddled with resolving problems concerning the permissibility of suicide in more complicated cases. The situation of the victims of Nazi atrocities, during the Second World War, suggests that suicide may be a permissible, perhaps even a desirable, practice under certain extraordinary circumstances. To understand why, we must reflect upon the difference between biological and moral arguments for the right-to-life that we have already considered.

The position that the right-to-life is a moral issue and requires a moral, not a biological defense, underscores that the phenomenon of personhood demands a minimal threshold of quality in order for life to be worth preserving. The example of the brain-substitution case raised the question of whether the right-to-life is simply a continuation of a biological organism or rather requires also the continuation of a consciousness with experiences it recognizes as its own. Without those experiences, as the brain-substitution case tries to force us to see, the threshold of personhood has itself been violated, and discussion of protecting rights seem no longer compelling.

The victims in Nazi Germany, it might be argued, had every right to insist upon a minimum level of dignity that had been systematically denied. To instruct those victims that suicide was impermissible would be to commit the informal fallacy of accident. That fallacy is committed whenever we grant a general principle and try to apply it to circumstances where the accidental features of those circumstances render the general principle inapplicable. This is not to say that we ought to recommend suicide to the victims of the Nazi atrocities, or to other victims in similar circumstances. The point is that, in these situations, we need to consider whether the choice of suicide has merit to be considered as a meaningful response to the otherwise impossible condition of being reduced to the mere property of others. The atrocity consisted, first of all, in the Nazi attitude that regarded certain persons as if they were mere things, producing an almost unimaginable horror for its victims. In this case, we can consider whether suicide seems to be justifiable in the face of hopelessness and unmitigated tyranny. The case, then, offers the challenge that suicide is not absolutely impermissible from a moral point of view, but that under certain circumstances individuals may take their own life, or request others to assist their suicide.

For those who find this argument persuasive, we are now challenged by its implications for our thinking about euthanasia. For if suicide seems permissible, even desirable, in confrontation with the most loathsome scenarios, then it would seem that euthanasia must be permissible for persons confronting the most loathsome terminal diseases. If the taking of one's own life, or the request for another's assistance to achieve that end, seems defensible in the most dire situations, then arguments in support of the permissibility of active euthanasia seem to be given additional support in these most dreadful cases.

We acknowledged that "passive euthanasia" is deemed acceptable by the American Medical Association and by law. But if the grounds for distinguishing between "passive" and "active" euthanasia collapse in the name of mercy itself, then one of two consequences would seem to follow. Either the criticism of active euthanasia must be extended to passive euthanasia and make both unacceptable, or both passive and active euthanasia must be considered acceptable (in certain circumstances) and active euthanasia may, at times, be determined to be preferable. For if the policy is motivated by mercy, active euthanasia surely seems to be, at times, more merciful. Do these considerations lead us to such provisional conclusions?

NOTE

[1] This chapter draws heavily on James Rachel's "Active and Passive Euthanasia" in the *New England Journal of Medicine*, Vol. 292, no. 2, January 9, 1975, pp. 396–406.

Section II: Week 10: Ch 16–17

Name_____ TA _____

Section #_____

1) What problems might arise if we decide to treat the "potential" as the "actual" in the case of abortion?

2) Describe Michael Tooley's argument for how we should decide to grant creatures moral rights.

Name_____ TA _____

Section #_____

3) What consequences does Tooley's argument have for the question of "infanticide"?

4) Describe the difference between active and passive euthanasia. Give an example of each.

Name_____ TA _____

Section #_____

5) Is it morally right for someone to stand idly by and watch a person die when they could save that person's life? Do we need "Good Samaritan" laws?

SECTION III

Sexual Morality

Chapter 18

Introduction: Sexual Morality

A. RE-FRAMING THE HARM PRINCIPLE

In Section I, we set out a descriptive theory of *how* human animals are inclined to behave and *why*. We began by considering the doctrine of rational self-interest as a motivation to actions, and advanced the doctrine of alienation to provide a wider context in which our own identity might find a purposeful expression for this self-interested behavior.

Next, we advanced normative concerns—the harm principle—that sought to further challenge us concerning our self-identity and our relation to others. If individuals are motivated to maximize their own self-interests, we must be prepared to promote liberties, to promote freedoms, so that each person can achieve the specific ingredients that fulfill their happiness. But, we also saw in the formulation of the harm principle that promoting freedom also has its limits whenever the exercise of liberty wrongfully set-back the interests of others; promotions of these freedoms are intolerable because they are immoral. The exercise of freedom and liberty are not always good things; they have their limits.

Our discussions of the harm principle began by accepting the impermissibility of harm to others. Harm to others meant a *wrongful set-back to the interests* of another and we offered the view that when another is deprived of that to which he/she has a right, then the treatment of this other has been wrong. But when we proceeded to consider the issues of harm to self and impersonal harm, the cases were not so clear. This was principally because of the objections set by the *Volenti* maxim.

B. TESTING THE *VOLENTI* MAXIM: IS CONSENT NECESSARY *AND* SUFFICIENT?

The *Volenti* maxim maintains that where there is consent there can be no wrongdoing, and thus no unjust harm. When persons consent to conduct and suffer harm, those persons have had their interests set back but they have not been *wronged*. The essence of the harm principle consists in the *wrongful* setback of interests. Once one accepts the force of the *Volenti* maxim, it is difficult to judge that harms to oneself are ever wrong and thereby impermissible. And by the same argument, if one cannot show *directly* harm to others, and the wrongfulness of harm to self is dismissed because there can be no wrong when there is consent, then it seems that one cannot hold that *impersonal harms* are wrong (for the same reasons). Is this reasoning flawed? If we still come away from these discussions feeling that certain conduct, though consensual, is still "wrong," then we must acknowledge that, perhaps, there are limits to the application of the *Volenti* maxim—that consent while necessary is *not* sufficient—and there needs to be some other considerations about what makes conduct wrong even when adults consent. Accordingly, in the development of the discussion of the harm principle, we introduced "free-floating evils" to introduce some ways of trying to make sense about how conduct might still be regarded as wrong even where adults consent.

In Section III, we take up questions concerning sexual morality. We recognize that sexual behavior has long been a source of both interest and anxiety in our culture. We wonder whether or not sexual conduct ought to be constrained and, if so, how and why. The arguments concerning restrictions to sexual behavior vary considerably and we will examine a host of them, in different contexts.

The thesis that we shall debate concerns the status of the *Volenti* maxim. For it is on this principle that our positions on harms to self and impersonal harms rest. Shall we assent to the claim that where there is (adult) consent, there is no wrongdoing (although there may be harm)? Shall we accept the recommendation that where there is consent there is no sexual conduct that deserves to be judged impermissible? To test this principle, we advance the thesis, to accept or reject, that with regard to sexual morality: *Consent is both necessary and sufficient to justify adult sexual practices engaged in private.* And we note that the argument centers not on the part of the thesis that asserts that consent is *necessary* to justify the permissibility of practices but rather that it is also *sufficient*. The obstacle to this thesis is the objection that, although consent is certainly necessary, it is *not* sufficient to justify some practices. And if we remain convinced that some conduct is still wrong although adults freely consent to engage in it, then we must search for some other meaning of its wrongfulness.

We begin this examination of the *Volenti* maxim by reflecting on arguments concerning the wrongness of rape. We begin here because the core of arguments concerning the wrongness of rape always include a focus on the issue of consent. Because there is *no* consent, rape is wrong. Thus, we have the clear case for the backbone of our thesis that consent is *necessary* to justify adult sexual practices.

But this analysis may not be adequate. In order to consider the arguments, we introduce a feminist critique of the wrongness of rape. This feminist critique seeks to show that the wrongness of rape extends well beyond its obvious criminality. While it is true that in rape a person is treated in a harmful way, without consent, this analysis is basically true of all kinds of assault. And so, we try to understand the wrongness of rape that extends beyond its obvious criminality.

We will consider the Victorian and then the Freudian background to our cultural orientation, and then challenge those conceptual orientations of our conduct. We will consider the idea of intimacy and the limits of morally acceptable behavior that have been operative throughout the past century. We will then consider what is a standard or accepted model of courtship today, and then take another look at the question of the wrongness of rape. We will consider an argument that claims our forms of accepted courtship are themselves, perhaps, modeled on rape.

The peculiar nature of rape rests on the peculiar nature of sexual intercourse. Not only is sexual intercourse allowable in our society, but within certain contexts it is considered a sacred act. However, without consent, the very same *physical* act of sexual intercourse is transformed from sacred to criminal. And this peculiar circumstance deserves our thoughtful reflection since it underscores the importance of understanding *motivations* when we try to determine the permissibility of conduct.

Our discussions of sexual morality and the *Volenti* maxim continue with a two-part investigation of the institution of monogamous marriage and the question of the wrongness of adultery. In the first part, we wonder about the nature of a marriage contract. Unlike other contracts in the English language, the marriage contract is the only one that cannot be broken by the parties alone that make it. The contract is vested within the institution of the State and we wonder what interests the State has in this contract. We offer the thesis, connected with the idea of parenting, that the marriage license make permissible (and sanctified) sexual intercourse. And not only does a license make sexual intercourse permissible, it also makes it *exclusive*. Since so many marriages fail—statistics suggest that as many as 50% of all new marriages in the United States end in divorce—we question the institution itself and its condition of sexual exclusivity. In the context of sexual morality, we will look at the connections among love, intimacy, and exclusivity.

In the second part of this investigation, we will consider arguments concerning the wrongness of adultery. First, we will consider the familiar arguments that adultery involves various forms of deception, whether to one's spouse, one's partner, or oneself. Since the marriage contract requires monogamy, adultery belies the exclusivity and the special intimacy that the contract seeks to secure. But what if both partners agree to accept extramarital sexual liaisons? In such a case, the arguments concerning deception seem to no longer have a standing. In open marriages, where is the violation of the harm principle? Nevertheless, by the nature of the marriage contract, any adulterous behavior violates those provisions. Thus, the claim that "adultery is wrong" turns out, ultimately, to be a declaration that marriage can be defended as a *moral* institution (i.e., worthwhile, sacred, and deserving of protection). The wrongness of adultery seems to rest on arguments concerning the rightness of exclusively monogamous marriage. Can such arguments be formulated in terms of the harm principle?

Our next topic in the debate over the *Volenti* maxim arises in the context of pornography and obscenity. We begin by defining pornography as any visual, literary, or audible media whose main or exclusive purpose is to sexually stimulate the viewer, reader, or listener. We then wonder under what conditions, if any, such conduct violates the harm principle. Some persons claim that although consent is necessary to justify adult sexual practices engaged in private, it is *not* sufficient. Those who raise this objection want to censor what they identify as both pornographic and obscene. For our debate, "obscene" will mean anything that causes so great an offense to a community that regulation or other restriction is permissible. And we will wonder whether pornography deserves to be identified with obscenity.

For our discussion, we will not consider the objections that concern pornography and minors, nor will we consider any media in which pornography is connected with other criminal conduct that violates the harm principle. In short, we advance no arguments that seek to undermine these clear and obvious harms to others. Our debate is focused entirely on the issue of consenting adults who participate in the production of pornographic materials and consenting adults who view, read, or listen to them. Do we have good reasons to deny these adults these exercises of their freedom? Does the promotion, production, and consumption of pornography violate the harm principle and so is immoral?

We consider many arguments as to why pornography causes harm and the reader must weigh the force of these arguments, not only to discover which, if any, are persuasive but also to discern how their persuasiveness may guide us on the question of the *Volenti* maxim itself. We begin with the report of the Meese Commission, undertaken during the presidency of Ronald Reagan. The central argument of the Meese Commission states that pornography is immoral irrespective of causing direct harm to anyone in particular. The commission found pornography to be debasing and degrading, to foster an atmosphere of disrespect and insensitivity, and other harmful attitudes in a community, and thereby deserving of suppression. There is no doubt that the moral sentiment of a community may, through the electoral process, lead to legislation restricting pornography. But then, we must raise difficult and penetrating questions about the imposition of liberty-limiting principles.

What if the moral sentiment of a community declared that African Americans or Hispanics or Vietnamese or some other ethnic group were not entitled to certain rights that were extended to others in the community? And what if the grounds that were advanced to defend such legislation, or the call for legislation, insisted that certain groups of people were base and unworthy of these rights? Most of us would be horrified to hear such hateful declarations. American legal history is replete with examples of just these sorts of hate-filled legal statutes, for instance, the legalization of slavery. Arguments that African Americans—blacks imported to America on slave ships—were no different from brute animals and were undeserving of the respect extended to Caucasians now seem utterly obscene to most of us, but were tolerated as adequate judgments in our past. Indeed, it may well be argued that such views are still, unfortunately, far too widely held. Nonetheless, when a community declares certain practices to be inherently immoral *without further argument,* we are left in a very unpleasant dilemma. On the one hand, we want to recognize that communities have a right to remove from their midst behavior that is deeply offensive; and on the other hand, we are all too conscious of the unacceptable extremes to which such offended emotions may extend.

Once we get past, without argument, the assertion that pornography is an *impersonal harm,* we go on to consider very interesting arguments concerning the need for liberty-limiting restrictions on some other kinds of sexual behavior. These objections are directed either to the charge of *harm to self or impersonal harm.* And we must consider these objections when assessing whether the *Volenti* maxim justifies the permissibility of such conduct.

But, first of all, there are the arguments that pornography is not an impersonal harm, but rather causes harm to others in terms of inciting some to violent behavior, such as rape. We must consider this argument because if true, we should be required by our own commitment to the harm principle, to recommend the suppression of pornography. Next, we consider various kinds of harmfulness in the form of antisocial attitudes and behavior: that pornography encourages or fosters demystification and undermining of the special intimacy of private sexual relations, that it promotes self-indulgent, infantile, and masturbatory predilections rather than mature social interactions, that it develops tyrannical attitudes by desensitizing the viewers/readers/listeners and thereby undermines the power of shame that is required for civil polity, and so on. We are not debating the question of whether the pursuit of pornography is either wise or desirable; we are only debating the question of whether the pursuit of pornography is impermissible. It is impermissible if it *causes* harm to others. But if we cannot conclusively demonstrate this, can we still show that it is unacceptable even when there is consent? Or do we conclude that the *Volenti* maxim is indeed a successful litmus test for the boundaries of liberty-limiting principles?

The argument that consent is both necessary and sufficient to justify adult sexual practices engaged in private is significantly challenged in our review of the 1986 Supreme Court case, *Bowers v. Hardwick*. This is the so-called "Sodomy" case. The Supreme Court argued, in effect, that although consent is necessary to justify sodomy, it still is *not* sufficient.

The legal conclusion held that the people of Georgia have a legitimate right to suppress what they consider to be obscene and immoral conduct and sodomy fell under that rule. Even though the sexual practice under debate was fully consensual and performed in privacy, still the behavior, by law, could be repressed.

The case of *Bowers v. Hardwick* is very unusual since it is difficult to understand how a complaint could be made regarding a *private* act to which both parties willfully *consented*. Michael Hardwick, the defendant, received a citation and was summoned to appear in court on charges of consuming alcohol (a beer) in a public park in downtown Atlanta. A city statute made such consumption illegal. He failed to appear and, as is customary, a bench warrant was issued for his arrest. The arresting officer went to his apartment and knocked on the door. The person who answered was not Michael Hardwick. The officer then asked where he could find Michael Hardwick and he was directed to a room. As he reached the door, the officer found himself visually confronted by Michael Hardwick engaged in an act of oral intercourse with another adult male. He was arrested for the outstanding warrant and further charged with violating the State of Georgia's criminal statute of "crimes against nature." According to that statute, even a first offense is punishable by up to twenty years in prison.

As it so happened, the grand jury refused to hand down an indictment on the crimes against nature statute. But Hardwick was incensed and challenged the constitutionality of the statute in District Court. The case was dismissed because the Court claimed he did not have a standing. He appealed that ruling to the Federal Appeals Court where it was agreed that the statute was unconstitutional. The State of Georgia appealed the ruling of the Federal Court; the Supreme Court agreed to hear the case and decided by a vote of 5–4 to overturn the Federal Court ruling. The Supreme Court decided that the State of Georgia had a legitimate right to suppress such conduct, that although consent is necessary to justify sodomy, it is *not* sufficient to justify it. Have the Court's arguments offered us good reasons to abandon the *Volenti* maxim?

Our next step is to contrast the Supreme Court's decision in *Bowers v. Hardwick* (1986) with the more recent *Lawrence and Garner v. State of Texas* (2003). In this remarkable case, again, we had adults accused of engaging in private and consensual acts that violated the crimes against nature statute of the state of Texas. The result this time, however, was that by a 5–4 decision the Court reversed its position in *Bowers v. Hardwick* and declared that the pivotal issue is properly a matter of the right to privacy. We will consider how the Court accepted different arguments to advocate their majority decision more than fifteen years later.

Finally, we turn to consider sexism and racism to complete our introductory investigation of sexual morality. We try to compare and contrast these two objectionable practices. These cases both share the ingredient of wrongdoing in the form of harm to others. Both practices assign unequal distributions of benefits and burdens with regard to gender or race—factors that can rightfully be argued are inappropriate to such allocations. Persons who are victims of sexism or racism are deprived of equitable benefits because of their gender or their race. But the phenomenon of why sexism has proven to be more difficult to see than racism merits our attention. We must investigate why.

Chapter 19

The Wrongness of Rape: A Feminist Critique[1]

A. RAPE AS A VIOLATION OF THE HARM PRINCIPLE

We begin our examination of sexual morality by considering rape. We may hold that rape is wrong without agreeing why it is wrong. We grant that rape is a violation of the harm principle; rape is a violation of the principle of wrongful harm to others. And we begin with the case of rape because it shows clearly that *consent is necessary* for the permissibility of adult sexual intercourse. As our investigations continue, we will see if it is also sufficient to justify *any* adult practices.

Rape is surely not like other cases of assault even though it clearly is a kind of assault. Psychologists point out that rape is not primarily an issue about sex, though it involves sex; rape is an issue of power and control expressing anger and violence toward the victim. But in order to understand why rape was not always identified as a crime, and until recently it has not been in public focus, we must examine the phenomenon of rape in the context of our cultural taboos and sexual habits. For although rape is a violent act, it is also a sexual act since it is an act of sexual intercourse.

The act of rape as an act of sexual intercourse is unlike other kinds of physical assault in that sexual intercourse is widely practiced, enjoyed, and within acceptable contexts, it is regarded as a special and sacred act. This means that a significant difference between an unacceptable sexual assault, rape, and sexual intercourse is principally one thing: consent. And this "consent," is no small thing, of course; it transforms completely the context of an individual's motivation. The wrongness of rape consists, in part, in the violation of the harm principle. But at the same time, the arguments we shall pursue show the soundness and force of the *Volenti* maxim—that where there is consent, there is no wrongdoing.

There was a time not so very long ago when rape was not considered to be a crime. In some societies, for instance, women were regarded as not fully human—and so not fully persons—and so like slaves, were not considered to have rights that could be violated in the first place, even by conduct such as rape. In other contexts, women were regarded to cause uncontrollable sexual excitement in males, relieving men of responsibility for conduct, even rape, on that account. By still other accounts, women were considered to be asexual and not interested in engaging in sexual intercourse—unless they were nymphomaniacs and thus abnormal—and so there could be no violation of the female domain.

Rape occurs whenever one person is unwilling to engage in sexual intercourse and is coerced against her/his will. We must recognize that "rape" names a kind of conduct that can be perpetrated against women or men, but here we shall restrict ourselves to the female victim. The reason for this is not because rape committed against men, especially within the homosexual community, is not considered grievous, but rather because the focus here is directed to an examination of inequities within our society, the uneven distribution of benefits and burdens in social organization. The widescale phenomenon of double-standard treatment for females prompts this more focused strategy. "Rape" will be restricted to mean non-consensual intercourse rather than other kinds of non-consensual sexual conduct that, in legal terms, is treated as sexual and deviant-sexual *assault*.

B. THE WRONGNESS OF RAPE AS A CRIMINAL ACT

If rape is wrong, then by our present hypothesis it deprives a woman of a right through deprivation of an essential domain and in this sense causes harm to others. The Other, by being deprived of an essential domain, is thereby deprived of her essential nature. To be deprived of one's essential nature is to be deprived of who one is, of one's fundamental identity, and is to be treated immorally. Does this sort of account go far enough to explain the wrongness of rape?

It has been argued by Frye and Shafer in "The Criminality of Rape" that the wrongness of rape is to be accounted for in terms of deprivation of rights. Frye/Shafer argue that:

(i) Rape involves the use of a person without her consent in the performance of an act which is against her own best interest, and

222

(ii) Rape is a social means of reinforcing the status of women as kinds of entities who lack, and ought to lack, the full privileges of personhood, namely, the freedom to move as they will through what is rightfully their own domain.

Thus, Frye/Shafer provide one way of understanding what is wrong about rape. The crime is not merely one of sexual misuse. Rape violates a woman's essential nature. Thus, rape is wrong because it treats another immorally. Rape is immoral because by depriving another of her rightful domain, it deprives another of her essential nature.

Pamela Foa, in her article "What's Wrong with Rape" calls into question the thesis advanced by Frye and Shafer. Foa accepts their thesis but insists that it does not go far enough to account for the pernicious character of this violation. Her point of departure grants the thesis about assault, but shows that this thesis may be true of any kind of assault directed against women and does not address the specific injurious character of rape. In short, Foa insists that the wrongness of rape goes far beyond its criminality which is the limit of Frye/Shafer's argument.

Foa is in agreement with Frye/Shafer on the first condition that rape involves the use of a person without her consent and not in her own best interest. Although Foa also agrees with the second condition, that rape reinforces an unjustifiable lower status of women, she points out that there are other cases in which rape is also considered wrong and objectionable where it clearly involves what we commonly regard as unequals. In the case of (i) the rape of children (minors), (ii) the pet dog, and (iii) the rape of the mentally impaired, Foa argues that while we immediately find the conduct wrong few would argue children, animals, or the mentally impaired would be considered equals. Thus, Foa's point is that the unjustifiable reinforcement of a second-class status for women is not sufficient to account for the wrongness of rape because we can easily agree that rape is wrong even when it happens to persons we ordinarily grant are unequal.

Rape is also not like other cases of assault and in this respect the argument by Frye/Shafer did not go far enough. Foa tries to show that the wrongness of rape goes beyond a criminal act, beyond the failure to gain consent. Her argument consists of, first, comparing, and then contrasting, two victims of assault:

(i) the victim of the "mad slasher," and

(ii) the victim of rape

Both are victims of a physical assault but do not receive equal kinds of consequences.

The victim of the mad slasher, on the one hand, tends to be any person who is standing in the path of a psychopath who slashes whomever he comes across. The victims receive sympathy from the community since they were unfairly harmed. But the victims of rape, on the other hand, fare differently. The rape victim tends to be considered demeaned by the rape, and is sometimes ostracized from the community, as if she were now dirtied. The victim of rape is also often accused of provoking, initiating, or enjoying the attack. It is unlikely that the victims of the mad slasher would be judged as culpable for their attack.

Thus, Foa's initial response to Frye/Shafer is to agree with the stated thesis, but to insist that the thesis does not go far enough to account for the wrongness of rape. Rape harms persons and reinforces the status of women as second-class citizens. But these conditions merely point to the criminality of rape and fail to distinguish it from other kinds of assault because other kinds of assaults against women are designed to reinforce their status as second-class citizens who cannot go wherever they choose whenever they want, like males. Foa's contribution is to indicate that the wrongness of rape is due not merely to its reinforcement of second-class status of women because rape is clearly seen as wrong between unequals; rape is no mere case of assault because the victim is often treated as if she were the perpetrator or guilty party which is not the case for victims of violent assault such as the mad slasher.

C. THE WRONGNESS OF RAPE GOES BEYOND ITS CRIMINALITY

If the wrongness of rape goes beyond its criminality, then we are obliged to detail that account. The thrust of Foa's argument is that the wrongness of rape pervades the American courting behavior. She means that the basic model for heterosexual dating is fundamentally rapacious. We now turn to explore this thesis. If Foa is right, we must rethink the acceptable rules for social and sexual interaction in order to rectify this unacceptable conduct. To make sense of her claim, we must first consider inherited socially permissible practices in our contemporary conduct. This requires a consideration of the links among sex, intimacy, and pleasure.

A succinct version of the Victorian view of sexual conduct is provided by Basch, who points to two prevailing ideals in the late nineteenth century:

(i) Sex without intimacy was wrong.

(ii) Women who experienced sexual pleasure were nymphomaniacs.

American attitudes at the turn of this century varied in different parts of the country, but shared certain common features with regard to sexual conduct. Sexual intimacy was deemed appropriate only in marriage. Hence, sexual activity was permissible but only when it was legally certified by marriage. Without marriage that affirmed intimacy, sex was widely held to be shameful.

Further, if Basch is right, male and female experience, with respect to sexual enjoyment, was supposed to be entirely asymmetrical. Men were considered to be brute animals who eagerly pursued and enjoyed sex, while women, on the other hand, were delicate creatures who did not naturally enjoy sex. Women assented to sex as part of marital duty but not because it was desirable. If women did find pleasure in sexual acts, they were deemed nymphomaniacs, and to that extent, abnormal, and suffering from an illness.

The Victorian mentality was challenged and effectively transformed during the early part of the twentieth century. The change in social venue was effected by several influences, but most substantially by the work of Sigmund Freud in the first-quarter of the twentieth century. The Victorian picture envisaged men as sexual creatures. By contrast, women and children were supposed to be asexual. Sexual interests, expressed by females, were symptomatic of perverse and promiscuous tendencies; by and large, such interests were regarded as signs of dire sickness. Freud's pioneering studies in psychoanalysis revealed the startling claim that both women and children are sexual creatures.

Freud's prolific studies advanced the thesis that, contrary to what had become a commonplace, women were capable of sexual arousal and healthy women enjoyed sexual relations. Even more startling was the thesis advanced by Freud that children, too, were capable of sexual arousal and even at the most tender ages enjoyed sexual gratification. Today, we take these claims for granted. Healthy males and females are generally regarded to be sexually interested and capable of deriving pleasure from sexual activities. Children, as well, are understood to enjoy sexual gratifications of all sorts. But it is important to grasp that these views were not always accepted and at the turn of the twentieth century were largely repudiated.

In the early 1950s, Freud's findings about the sexual inclination of women and children were substantiated by the research of Masters and Johnson. In their studies on human sexual response, Masters and Johnson agreed with Freud's assessment that women were capable of sexual enjoyment and argued further that women have the full capacity for sexual pleasure. This included orgasmic pleasure as well.

Pamela Foa, in her article "What's Wrong with Rape," acknowledges the historical transformation of social/sexual attitudes and applies this information to our understanding of rape. In her estimation, women's sexuality has been used as yet another defense of rape. Now, men could be absolved from blame for committing rape by a new argument, built upon old foundations. The new argument may be outlined as follows:

(i) Women find pleasure in sexual activity.

(ii) Rape involves sexual activity.

(iii) Therefore, since every sexual act must be pleasurable to some degree, the victim of rape must be enjoying herself to some degree, and hence at some level enjoying herself. Thus, there is no crime committed when the so-called victim is enjoying the act—that is, no harm has been done.

(iv) And therefore, since the victim of rape is enjoying herself, to whatever degree, and that act is part of a non-intimate and/or non-private experience the enjoyment is shameful.

The argument formulated is, of course, very troubling. The woman who is forced to submit to the demands of her attacker is now being harassed for her complaint. The rapist, or the defense counsel on his behalf, attempts to argue that rather than seeing rape as a heinous act of assault, it is now to be seen as an act of charity because the woman must be receiving pleasure. Since Freud showed that women derive pleasure from sexual activity, the defense counsel may say, then this sexual act must provide pleasure, not suffering. Thus, no harm has been engendered in the act of rape. Since the rape victim must be gaining some sexual satisfaction from the intercourse—despite her unwillingness to consent at the outset—the decisive character of the sexual experience is enjoyment.

Foa's argument, no doubt, is not the only way to account for the most recent dismissals of rape. But to whatever degree that it mirrors contemporary sentiment, to that extent it still reflects the persistence of a reactionary mentality. The reactionary view takes special instruction from a certain kind of reading of the Genesis story of the Bible. The sexual nature of women, since the time of Eve, has been a cause for humiliation. Women, on this reading, are fundamentally to blame for all the world's sexual problems, just as in Greek mythology Pandora's box—the nature of women—is ultimately responsible for sexual trouble. This view, in the tradition of the Bible or the Greek mythology, places sexual blame on the feminine character, rather than on the attacker. The persistent result is to relieve males of blameworthiness. It is the female, so the argument goes, who is really and already to blame.

If it is supposed to be immoral to engage in sexual activity without intimacy, and rape involves sex without that intimacy, then to acknowledge being a rape victim is to be forced to acknowledge one's own immorality. The persuasiveness of this argument consists in appealing to a common social reaction to rape victims. Traditionally such women have been ostracized. If Foa is right, males will tend to avoid sexual pursuit of a rape victim. The female will find herself substantially isolated within her own community. The victim of the mad slasher, or any other kind of physical assault, will not usually suffer comparable consequences. Thus, the rape victim is seen not merely as a victim of assault, but as a survivor of a social transgression. Certainly for this sort of reason, Foa's thesis must strike us as particularly compelling. The argument of

Frye/Shafer, identifying the criminality of rape, does not go far enough to account for the wrongness of rape.

D. THE "ACCEPTABLE" MODEL OF COURTSHIP: RAPE

The hypothesis advanced by Foa that the wrongness of rape consists, ultimately, in the fact that American sexual conduct is fundamentally modeled on rape, can finally be explored. Foa advances a thesis of sexual socialization. Her argument is that the courting behavior of our grandparents, parents, and in large measure, the latest generations are modeled on a pattern that is virtually indistinguishable from rape. How is this so?

According to Foa, boys and girls have long been socialized differently. Although this is no doubt changing, girls are still advised to be chaste and to rebuff the advances made by males. A premium is placed on refusing the importunities of males and remaining a virgin until marriage. Girls are thus counseled regarding what to expect from boys; the boys' strategy will be to urge or beg with troublesome persistence for the girl to accede to their sexual desires.

Thus, girls have long been tutored to always say "no" to male overtures, whether or not they are, in fact, interested. Thus, according to Foa, girls become so accustomed to this mode of behavior that they continue to say "no" even when they are genuinely interested. The result, according to Foa's analysis, is that females are taught to discount their real feelings. The justification for this strategy seems clear enough. Giving in to the feelings that incline one to say "yes" is to be immoral.

For the female the presupposition is that sexual intercourse is immoral except where exclusive intimacy is established. And perhaps even then there is a lingering ambivalence about the propriety of intercourse. The female is taught to habitually refuse male advances that she has been assured will be frequent. She is not to consult her feelings because any inclination to give in to these feelings is to promulgate immoral conduct.

Males, on the other hand, have been socialized differently. First, sexual conduct is not only deemed acceptable, but is touted as highly desirable. Boys are advised to pursue girls with the utmost perseverance as a sign of masculinity. Achieving acquiescence from females is a sign of male success, a sign of sexual conquest and is prized highly by males.

Boys know about the strategy unilaterally adopted by females and know that the girls have been told to say "no" regardless of what is said or done. Since girls have been told to say "no" even if they are interested, the females' verbal protests are basically meaningless. The males therefore learn not to pay attention at all to what the female says since she does not seem to know what are her own genuine feelings in the first place.

Thus, the girls who have been told to reject sexual advances made by males learn that acquiescence to those advances is immoral. Boys who have been told to sexually pursue the girls learn that sexual success is a mark of male excellence and, since a girl will say "no" to all importunities, they ought not pay any attention to what she says at all.

If Foa's thesis is sound, then the socialized behavior of boys and girls always places the female in the situation of saying "no." Sex take place in a curious and ambivalent context in which "no" changes to "yes" only at the very last minute. Social agreements of a sexual nature are not clear decisions. On Foa's analysis, the man's advance to the woman's habitual "no" places him in a situation which bears resemblance to rape. In the case of rape, her "no" never changes to "yes." But, according to Foa's analysis, the male is sure that she will never really say "yes" to any sexual intimacy even if she wants to say "yes." Thus, according to Foa, the socially adopted and accepted model for dating that leads to sexual intercourse is preciously close to rape, so close to it that it is structurally indistinguishable.

So, what's wrong with rape? Is it a criminal act? Yes, of course. But is this a sufficient explanation of its wrongness? Is it a symbol of symptomatic ill treatment of women? Yes. But is this enough? Is rape wrong because it is emblematic of a model of male sexuality that our social organization has accepted? If so, then the wrongness of rape would mean that we must recognize that the unacceptability of rape is itself an expression of the very pattern of social/sexual conduct that our society endorses and promulgates.

NOTE

[1] This chapter draws heavily on Pamela Foa's "What's Wrong with Rape" in *Feminism and Philosophy,* Mary Vetterling-Braggin, Frederick A. Elliston, and Jane English, eds. Rowman and Littlefield, 1981, pp. 347–359.

Section III: Week 12: Ch 18–19

Name_____ TA _____

Section #_____

1) Describe the difference between "necessary conditions" and "sufficient conditions." Do you think "consent" is necessary or sufficient to make actions permissible?

2) Describe the 3 justifications the book lists which have been used to allow rape in the past: even as recently as in 19th century England.

Name_____ TA _____

Section #_____

3) Pamela Foa argues that the wrongness of rape is *not* fully captured by its use in holding women as "second-class" citizens. What is her argument?

Name_____ TA _____

Section #_____

4) Do you find that the "Victorian view" that women do not (normally) enjoy sex is still held today? What harm might this view cause?

5) Describe the new (post-Freudian) argument which is sometimes used to defend rape.

Name_____ TA _____

Section #_____

6) Do you agree that modern courtship is modeled on rape?
   Give an example to support your position.

Chapter 20

Marriage and Monogamy[1]

A. WHY THE CONTRACT: MARRIAGE = MONOGAMY?

Marriage is the only contractual agreement, in the English language at least, that cannot be abrogated by the parties who enter into it. That is, the marriage contract is vested in a third-party, namely, the State, whose permission must be secured in order to dissolve the contract. With other contracts, if the parties involved mutually consent to dissolve the previous agreements, they may do so. But not so for marriage. And so we wonder why it is that the State takes so great an interest in marriage that it should approve both the entering into and the disbanding of that contract.

What does the State believe its interests to be? An obvious response might be that the institution of marriage is closely related to the institution of parenting. Thus, the State might insist that in order to protect the interests of its youngest citizens—children—the marriage contract is suitably regulated by an agency concerned with the well-being of the community at large.

With the exception of the last few of generations, the sexual behavior of persons in America has been regulated by the institution of marriage. Sexual intercourse was largely supposed to be impermissible before marriage and desirable after it. Married couples joined the rank of decent citizens who were naturally expected to take part in the production of the next generation. Understood in this sense, marriage is more immediately connected with the permissibility of certain kinds of sexual conduct. From the State's point of view marriage is legalized intercourse.

Let us take another brief look at this matter. When a person obtains a license to drive a car, we know very well what that person is entitled

233

to do. Within stated restrictions, that person is permitted to operate a motor vehicle on public roads and highways. When a person obtains a hunting license, that person, too, is entitled to engage in certain kinds of conduct (of course, subject to certain restrictions). So also for those who obtain a license in cosmetology, in architecture, in medicine, in automotive repair, and in every other practice legislated by the state. But when one obtains a marriage license, in what sort of conduct is that person entitled to engage? The marriage license has traditionally served to permit the parties so licensed to engage in sexual intercourse. Marriage is legalized intercourse.

Our point of departure is to consider the need to establish social controls over sexual conduct. Thus, we begin our analysis of marriage and monogamy by reflecting upon our inherited ideologies concerning sexual practices.

B. REFLECTIONS ON THE JUDEO-CHRISTIAN TRADITIONS CONCERNING MARRIAGE AND MONOGAMY

Among the many stories that have deeply influenced our social organization and our "moral" teachings, the biblical tales of the so-called Old and New Testaments have played a prominent part. Like the stories from Greek mythology, the biblical stories have influenced countless writers, artists, and statesmen. No analysis of our social behavior can neglect consideration of these stories and the impact they have on our present way of thinking. We will look at two biblical stories from the perspective of an outsider who does not believe them to be exclusive and sacred since our interest focuses only on the social attitudes projected by the details of those stories.

The two stories focused upon are from the Bible. The first is the creation story from Genesis. The second is the New Testament story of the birth of Christ. In both cases, a new religious and, thereby, social epoch is announced by means of a miraculous event in which there is an astonishing sexual reversal in nature. Both stories are patriarchal, that is, they seem to be the product of male authorship, and give a special prominent role to males in the account of nature.

One aspect of the Genesis story concerns the origins of human beings. Our focus is upon the birth of Eve. God creates Adam. Adam is lonely and God responds to Adam's desolate condition by miraculously creating Eve. According to the story, God took one of Adam's ribs and from it fashioned Eve. The story is of interest to us because it suggests that for the only time in the history of human beings, woman is born from man. This suggests that the beginning of a new tradition is coincidentally announced by reversing the natural order of birth. It is from women, of course, that all of us have come. But, in the beginning, woman came from man. Thus, all human beings ultimately owe their existence to Adam, that is, to a male origin.

In the second story, a new tradition is announced, in the New Testament, by the birth of Christ. In this story, Mary becomes pregnant without engaging in intercourse. The two startling revelations prove to be that:

(i) God is male [the divine child is Jesus not Josephine] and

(ii) sexual intercourse is somehow defective.

Let us reflect upon this story more closely.

For the person who stands outside the Biblical tradition, the story of the virgin birth sounds remarkable indeed. But suppose the story included a virgin birth, but rather than Mary being the pregnant virgin, suppose it was Joseph? The response to such a situation might well be "unbelievable" and simply would not do. The tale of Christ's birth is miraculous precisely because it is unbelievable. If this story can be taken seriously—that is, miracles happen—one should be equally willing to take seriously that the story went that it was Joseph, not Mary, who became miraculously pregnant. If one believes in the possibility of such miraculous interventions in our everyday lives, then one should be prepared to entertain the possibility that Joseph, and not Mary, became pregnant. The point is, however, that this is not how the story reaches us, and if we take the position of people outside of our traditions, that is, people who do not believe these sacred stories, they might wonder who benefits by telling the story *this* way—that virgin Mary becomes pregnant with a male child by God almighty?

From the perspective of the storyteller, human beings are born to women, but that the perfect being—God—is not the result of sexual intercourse. Thus, there seems something defective about intercourse. The perfection of the deity and human intercourse are somehow incompatible. And secondly, the story informs us that God is male. From the point of view of a nonbeliever, the obvious inference might be that the inspiration of this tale comes from men who wish to assert their primacy, their superiority, and their special right to authority.

There can be little doubt that the Old and New Testaments have exercised substantial effects on our traditional "moral" teachings. Whether one holds these stories to be sacred or not, the stories are patriarchal in tone. They seem to favor males and announce new traditions by the inversion of the natural order of things in terms of the mechanics of sexual progeneration. Males are seen to be the origins of all things and, in the latter story, man is clearly God. In both stories, the natural and usual course of sexual conduct is somehow reversed.

C. KANT'S THESIS: SEXUAL PRACTICES
ARE PERMISSIBLE ONLY WITHIN
MONOGAMOUS MARRIAGE

In the last quarter of the eighteenth century, Immanuel Kant, a professor of philosophy at the University of Konigsberg, wrote many essays on ethics, one of which was entitled "Duties toward the Body in Respect of Sexual Impulse."

Kant's approach is extremely conservative with regard to sexuality. He himself was a religious man and belonged to an order of Christians known as Pietists. It is noteworthy that Kant offers a philosophical defense of a position on sexual behavior without resorting to quoting scripture. In this important sense, he offers the most conservative thinkers a way in which to defend traditional views on sexual practices and he does so by employing a rational argument, not a theological one.

Kant identifies sexual conduct as a kind of appetite. Like eating and drinking, sexual activity, taken by itself, is nothing but appetite. The consequence, according to Kant, is that the Other is reduced to a mere object. In Kant's estimation, this works both ways: the man reduces the woman to the status of a mere object, and the woman reduces the man to the status of a mere object. This objectification is the natural result of all appetite which views the desired end as an object of gratification. Since an object is a thing, and a thing can be used by anyone as he or she pleases then sexual activity reduces persons to things. Moral relationships, however, take place between persons (or agents), not things. And thus, for Kant, sexual relations are troubling from the outset as obstacles to moral life.

Kant's argument rests on the view that human beings are what we have been calling "persons." For Kant, "persons" are moral agents. Moral agents are beings who are unlike other animals insofar as they can restrain themselves—they can self-legislate, that is, impose principles upon themselves for no other reason than to affirm their moral nature. Unlike all other animals that act in accordance with instinct, persons can affirm their moral nature by refusing to give in to mere instinct and appetite. Following animal appetite and instinct or refusing to succumb to that brute nature and thereby affirming our moral nature, is the choice we make in asserting our moral agency. Sexual activity, in itself, only indicates our brute nature and thus is both unacceptable and not truly human conduct. Let us examine this argument more closely.

From Kant's point of view, although consent is necessary to make sexual conduct permissible, it is not sufficient. Kant holds that certain activities are morally impermissible even if the adults involved give consent. Among them Kant includes: (i) prostitution, (ii) sex for pleasure, and (iii) sodomy. For Kant, sex by its very nature of objectification reduces persons to the status of mere objects and are thereby robbed of their rightful status as moral agents.

Stated differently, Kant holds that persons are essentially subjects and agents. Sexual activity, in general, makes one into an object of gratification for another, and the other is rendered an object for one's own gratification. But human dignity consists in the affirmation of moral agency that distinguishes us from all other brute animals. Sex does not so distinguish us. Thus, in general, without certain overriding constraints, sexual activity is to be avoided because it debases human moral integrity.

The prohibitions against sexual practices are, of course, not absolute. Kant recognizes that sexual activity is an essential ingredient for the perpetuation of the species and, as such, is indispensable. Without sex we would not be here, nor would Kant have lived to write his essay. Thus, he finds himself with a problem: if sexual intercourse is essential for species survival, but our moral agency is affirmed by those activities that distinguish us from the other animals, then under what condition(s) is sexual activity permissible? Whatever the condition(s) might be, the result must be the same. Sexual practices must be permissible but the deleterious effects of "sex by itself" must be overridden by measures that safeguard, and promote, our moral nature.

The solution that Kant proposes is that sexual intercourse is permissible only in monogamous marriage. The reason he offers is that only in the case of monogamous marriage does one have the right to dispose over the Other person as a whole and, hence, as a person—subject and moral agent—and not a mere thing. Thus, sex is permissible only when individuals become committed to each other as life-long moral companions, moral agents. Moreover, although Kant supposes that sexuality by its very nature is an appetite that reduces another to an object or thing, sex can be deemed permissible in the context of marriage. Without marriage, sexual activity proves to be base. Persons are reduced to the status of mere animals, using each other for the purpose of mere gratification. Monogamous marriage is a means to affirm our moral integrity.

D. PERSONS VS. THINGS: ARGUMENTS AGAINST SLAVERY, SUICIDE, MASTURBATION

Kant expands upon this argument when he applies it to the impermissibility of (a) slavery, (b) suicide, (c) masturbation, and (d) incest.

His reasoning is as follows: Persons are not properties or things that can be disposed over as one pleases. Thus, man cannot dispose over himself because he is not a thing. Hence, man is not his own property. He is a subject in which ownership can be vested and, therefore, he cannot own himself as if he were an object or property. He cannot simultaneously be both the owner and the owned.

On Kant's account, therefore, slavery is impermissible for it reduces other human beings to the status of things. This not only mistreats other moral agents, but also it shows the slave owner has failed to recognize the meaning of his moral agency. Kant regards slavery to be morally impermissible.

The case of suicide follows the same line of thought. Not only is it impermissible to reduce other persons to the status of mere things but also it is impermissible for a person to reduce himself to the status of a mere thing. Suicide attempts just that objectification. Because persons are neither properties nor things, they may not do with themselves as they please. Suicide is emblematic of one's attempt to dispose over oneself as one pleases, as if one could be both owner and owned. But, as Kant has argued, persons are subjects, not objects, and may not do with themselves as they please without undermining their very nature.

The case of masturbation is resolved in the same fashion as slavery and suicide. Like suicide, persons are not entitled to do to themselves as they please. Masturbation, in Kant's estimation, reduces one to an object of self-gratification. This conduct Kant declares impermissible. In another essay Kant goes so far as to say that masturbation is a greater evil than suicide.

E. THE IMPERMISSIBILITY OF INCEST

The treatment Kant offers of incest also follows the general guidelines offered in his analysis of sexual activity. He distinguishes between two kinds of incest: (i) between parents and children, and (ii) between brothers and sisters. Kant regards incest to be morally impermissible, absolutely prohibited in the case of parents and children, and relatively prohibited in the case of brother and sisters. In both cases, he seeks to determine moral grounds for justifying his position.

Kant rules out incest committed between parents and children absolutely and unconditionally. His reasoning is as follows. In sexual intercourse, each person engages in the greatest degree of intimacy and, therefore, the sexual union is between equals. But the relation between parents and children requires respect in the form of submission of the child to the parents and is thus fundamentally unequal. Hence, incest between parents and children is forbidden by nature because it undermines the respect that is required in and for that relation.

The case is not quite the same for sexual conduct between brothers and sisters. Kant recognizes that although the state prohibits this sort of incest, "in the beginning" there must have been brother/sister incest, otherwise, the flourishing of the human population would have been impossible. But in Kant's view, nature has implanted within us a natural opposition to incest. This is because, as Kant understands it, nature intended us to combine with other races so as to prevent too great a sameness in one society. Too close a connection, too intimate an acquaintance, according to him, produces sexual indifference and repugnance.

NOTE

[1] This chapter draws heavily on Immanuel Kant's "Duties toward the Body in Respect of Sexual Impulse," in *Lectures on Ethics,* trans. L. Infield, Harper and Row, 1963, pp. 162–168.

Chapter 21

Is Adultery Immoral?[1]

A. IS ADULTERY ALWAYS IMPERMISSIBLE?

Prohibitions against adultery have a long history and appear in many traditions. The prohibitions arise as a direct consequence of the fact that the social institution of marriage has been, by definition, monogamous. Extramarital sexual practices—adultery—are thereby impermissible because such adulterous conduct violates the agreement of marriage and thus constitutes a breach of contract. But this initial assessment of the wrongness of adultery does not seem adequate to understand the social complexities of it.

When questions are raised about the wrongness of adultery, the familiar response seems to be that it is wrong because it is fundamentally deceptive. The fact that adultery represents a breach of contract and is a violation of it is usually considered an important but not the most heinous part of the offensive behavior. Because the marriage agreement makes sexual exclusivity a requirement, adulterous practices necessarily involve deception of all kinds and it is deception which is deemed the unacceptable evil.

But let us imagine a circumstance in which a married couple, by mutual consent, engage in extramarital sexual conduct. In this case, adultery is taking place, but there is apparently no deception involved. Still, it may be objected, that adultery is wrong. Why? If one insists that the wrongness of adultery, in this case, consists in a violation of the marriage contract, we now find ourselves confronted by a more perplexing and wide-ranging challenge. Adultery is wrong because it violates the marriage contract. The marriage contract requires monogamy. We must now be prepared to show that monogamous marriage is a morally desirable institution. Hence, the wrongness of adultery rests ultimately on a defense of the moral desirability of marriage.

The case of adultery offers us a clear view of how an act can both violate and not violate the harm principle. If and when one of the partners in a marriage is adulterous without the other's knowledge, the other has been treated deceptively and thus harmed wrongfully. In many cases, adultery proves to be a harm to others and thus is morally impermissible. But in the case where both persons in a marriage consent to partake in extramarital sexual activities it seems that there is no deception and no wrongdoing—though, of course, there may be unanticipated harm. From a moral standpoint, one and the same action seems to both impermissible and permissible. Let us think more deeply about marriage = monogamy and the transgression of adultery.

B. ARGUMENTS FOR THE IMPERMISSIBILITY OF ADULTERY

There are several standard arguments for the immorality of adultery. Richard Wasserstrom, in his article, "Is Adultery Immoral?" states that adultery includes:

(i) breach of promise

(ii) deception and lying

(iii) deception, but not lying

(iv) active and passive deception

(v) deception via intimacy

Arguments that attempt to point out what is wrong with adultery insist that it entails a breach of contract. Thus, adultery is wrong in just the sense that any other breach of contract is wrong. To break a contract is to not uphold one's "word" which is itself an indispensable condition of interaction among persons in a civilized society. Persons who break contracts cannot be trusted because they are unwilling to "live up" to their own declarations and promises. What is wrong with adultery is the failure to maintain the provisions of one's contractual agreements.

Others have objected that "breach of contract" presents one evil entailed in adultery but does not adequately account for its immorality because breach of contract alone does not distinguish it from other kinds of abrogation of contractual arrangements. The deception and lying involved in adultery specifically account for its particular evil. Invariably those who engage in adultery must resort to deceptive practices and lie in order to continue the subterfuge.

Others point out that there may be deception in adultery without lying. The spouse involved in the adultery can simply say nothing at all about the extramarital affair but this is deception nonetheless.

Others try to reconcile various forms of these arguments and suggest that the immorality of adultery consists in deception that is both active and passive. In some cases, the adulterous spouse must fabricate tales to mislead the other spouse; in other cases, simply refraining from discussion accomplishes deception. In both cases, it is agreed that deception takes place and it is that element that constitutes the immorality of the conduct.

Still others insist that the account of deception is inadequate, although it is granted that deception takes place. The deception involved in the work of a "con-man" is also objectionable, but it is not the same kind of deception. The argument here is that adultery involves a deception vis-à-vis intimacy itself. Let us examine this last hypothesis in greater detail.

Wasserstrom argues that traditional American socialization insists upon a connection between sex and intimacy. The degree of intimacy felt is communicated by the degree of sexual involvement. If only a little intimacy existed, sexual rapport might be restricted to hand holding or to a kiss on the cheek. In the event of greater intimacy, so was the degree of sexual activity. Intercourse is reserved as an expression of the most intimate feelings. Thus, Wasserstrom's analysis proceeds upon the premise that in order to understand sexual activity and ideas concerning intimacy, we must reflect upon its cultural setting. It follows that such ideas would not be found in all societies, and perhaps not even in our own today. Wasserstrom focuses upon the social culture of the 1940s, 1950s, and the early 1960s.

Wasserstrom's argument attempts to answer the simple question: Why is some sex better than other sex? Wasserstrom's response is two-fold:

(i) sexual intimacy communicated the degree of one's feelings,

(ii) those feelings were linked to exclusivity.

Thus, Wassertrom's analysis leads him to the conclusion that adultery is wrong because it involves an intimate deception to both the spouse and the third-party. The argument insists that if the culture in which sexual relations take place operates on the presumption that the degree of intimacy that persons feel parallels sexual intimacy, then marriage proves to be a public declaration of the strongest and most exclusive feelings. The spouse left out of the extramarital encounter is deceived regarding the promise of exclusive intimacy. And the third-party in the adulterous relation is also led to believe that sex equals emotional intimacy, but almost always (and certainly in the early stages of adulterous relations) the married partner continues to share intimacies with his/her spouse.

C. OBJECTIONS TO THE TRADITIONAL ARGUMENTS AGAINST ADULTERY

Objections can be raised to the analysis given above. Wasserstrom himself also advances objections since he is quick to acknowledge that today's youth differ from the more traditional culture in which he grew up. In that traditional pattern of socialization, sexual intimacy was supposed to communicate the degree of one's affection and those feelings were linked to exclusivity.

Two initial strategies present themselves for objecting to that traditional culture: It may be argued plausibly that:

  (i) sex should be separated from love and affection, and

 (ii) love should be separated from exclusivity.

The first proposal is that while the earlier culture tied together sex-love-affection, there is no reason why they should necessarily be so connected. As Wasserstrom notes, if today we consider sex to be an intense, exciting, sensuous activity, why must sex be restricted to a traditional framework? The first proposal is that such restrictions are not necessary which thus leads to different sexual/social conduct.

The second proposal is that an inextricable connection between love and exclusivity is perhaps unnecessary. If it were necessary for love to be tied to exclusivity then we would be called to wonder how parents can "love" several children. Can parents love several children? Most parents can answer "yes" without hesitation. If this is so, then why can't adults have several lovers? Judging by the widespread proliferation of adultery in our present society, it seems not merely possible but increasingly desirable to separate love from exclusivity. Marriage requires sexual exclusivity for a lifetime. Is it not likely that people will find at least a few special persons in a lifetime with whom they may share an intimate, energetic, and intense sexual communication? Should the social culture restrict, by making illegal and impermissible, this sort of conduct? And if so, by virtue of what reasons? The second proposal rests on the plausibility that no sufficient reason could be given to insist upon the traditional restriction.

Suppose, then, asks Wasserstrom that we could succeed in separating from any required connection: (i) sex and love, and (ii) love and exclusivity. And suppose that we are confronted by a challenge brought by the case of a couple who has an "open-marriage," that is, an agreement in advance for the permissibility of extramarital sex hence no deception would be incurred by extramarital sexual activity. And suppose one or both spouses engages in intercourse outside the confines of the marriage. Is adultery here immoral?

Although one might first be tempted to say "no," Wasserstrom argues that upon reflection this response will not do. The very concepts of marriage and adultery are incompatible because marriage means monogamy. Thus, the very structure of our socialization is rigidly outlined by the cultural equation that marriage equals monogamy. Within that structure, there is no way to permissibly have extramarital sex without violating the institution of marriage.

This interesting conclusion naturally presents us with a clearer focus on our problem. In order to more deeply understand and more wisely assess the nature of adultery we must turn to investigate the nature of marriage.

D. TRADITIONAL VIEWS
ON MARRIAGE = MONOGAMY

Are there necessary conditions for marriage? Wasserstrom examines this question by reflecting on practices in America and elsewhere, although the cross-cultural sketch is neither detailed nor very extensive. He shows that although there are general guidelines for marriage, there are palatable exceptions to every "rule" and thus no hard and fast requirements. This conclusion makes it all the more obvious that marriage is an arbitrary social institution that deserves our critical scrutiny. Is marriage a morally desirable institution? Let us follow the argument more closely.

Some thinkers have proposed that at least three necessary and perhaps sufficient conditions can be isolated for marriage. First, there is usually a formal ceremony of some kind which states mutual obligations. Second, the parties involved must have the capacity to engage in sexual intercourse. Third, the parties must be willing to have intercourse only with each other.

Objections naturally arise to the statement of these conditions. As Wasserstrom observes, we can surely imagine persons to be "married" in cases where those conditions are not met. For instance, couples who live together for more than seven years are recognized by many states to be married according to "common-law." In this instance there is no formal ceremony. Couples who lack the capacity or interest for intercourse are still accepted as being "married," hence the usual second condition seems open to exceptions. And marriages of state or convenience involve neither love nor the willingness to have intercourse, and yet such cases are recognized as being "marriages." These objections make the point that there seem to be no necessary conditions for marriage.

If it be further objected that all marriages must be sexually exclusive and that constitutes a necessary condition, it may be noted that other societies permit polygamy. Thus sexual exclusivity is not necessary for marriage although it indicates its existence. Sexual exclusivity is not a universally necessary condition for marriage, but it is widely prevalent. What conclusions can we draw concerning exclusivity?

The demand for sexual exclusivity is a fundamental part of the social organization in our community. Its design is to establish a certain kind of life pattern, and to reinforce that pattern. The social injunction, according to Wasserstrom, seems to be: Get married and stay married.

If this analysis is sound, then the expression "Adultery is wrong" means that the prohibition on extramarital sex is a way of helping to maintain the institution of marriage and the nuclear family. This implies that the social objection to adultery is merely instrumental. The value of its prohibition consists in its usefulness in maintaining the institution of marriage. And if this assessment of the consequences of the foregoing argument is sound, the proper focus for answering the question of what is wrong with adultery consists in determining whether marriage is a morally desirable institution.

E. SOME REFLECTIONS ON MONOGAMOUS MARRIAGE AND THE NUCLEAR FAMILY

If we take seriously the above analysis, where does the argument proceed from here? How would we even begin to think about proposing a critique of the institution of marriage? The suitable critique would have to force us to consider at least some alternative vision of the social order.

A critique of the traditional or nuclear family and thus the institution of marriage was presented in the writings of an early Greek philosopher, Plato. Plato was born in the last quarter of the fifth century B.C.E. and died around the middle of the fourth century B.C.E. He was a student of the famous Socrates. Plato presents a critique of the traditional social order in a dialogue entitled the *Republic*.

Socrates, the main interlocutor in the dialogue, wonders about the ideal state as an ideal social organization and how it might be brought about. Conscious that certain social practices produced unsatisfactory results for the Athenians, he wonders what to do and why.

One point which occupies his attention is familiar in our own social organization. If some person is chief executive officer (CEO) of a powerful and wealthy company, or is a senator or governor in one of our states, that CEO, senator, or governor might try to maintain influence by passing the power of command to one of his/her children or other relatives. We might agree that the most able persons should direct commerce or society but because every parent is always concerned about the welfare of his/her children, that concern might override his/her concern for finding the most competent CEO, senator, or governor. The consequence is invariably that persons who inherit wealth and power are ill-suited or at least not best suited for the task and everyone in the community suffers as a result.

The solution put forth by Socrates was to radically alter the traditional connection between parenting and childrearing by means of a most unusual upheaval in social organization. Here's how it works. Since not everyone is as competent as every other person, the most efficient work environment would have persons engage in the tasks to which they are most competent, most naturally suited. Not everyone is competent to raise children. Thus, the argument goes, the community would benefit if only those most competent in childrearing would actually raise the children, and so on.

In order to facilitate this plan, children would be removed from their natural parents at birth and placed in the communal care of a state-supported staff who would watch over and train the children. The most competent children would then be promoted, step-by-step, to the most difficult tasks and each child would be progressively guided to those tasks for which the child exhibited a natural talent. Because no one would know whose child is whose, the community would conjointly take a caring interest in all the children. And no child would ever find him/herself in a position of authority by virtue of mere inheritance and thus the favoritism in the social order would be eliminated. Neither women nor men would any longer be forced to remain in marriages because of children. Marriage and parenting would be socially separated.

For those readers who wonder how we would explain the situation to the first generation of children placed in such a new social environment, Socrates offered an answer to his compatriots. Socrates suggests that we tell the young children that they were spawned in the earth from seeds. When his associates reacted by insisting that no one would believe such an unbelievable tale, he agrees with them, but adds that in a few generations they'll believe it, no matter how ridiculous it presently sounds. For those who do not believe in the literal truth of the Old and New Testaments, the situation seems parallel.

The case before us is surely not exhaustive. If concerns about the morality of adultery force us to see that objections to such practices arise because of the nature of the institution of marriage, we must take a careful look at whether or not monogamous marriage is a morally desirable institution. No examination of marriage can seriously take place without beginning to list features in our current social organization that are clearly undesirable. Then we may proceed to consider a different scenario, let's say the one offered by Plato, to show how some of those deficiencies might be rectified. Every reader will notice, however, that correcting problems always seems to come at a price. Yes, we may eliminate problems from one social organization but create new ones in the process. And then there is always the difficulty of determining how we would institute those changes even if we believed the benefits would outweigh the burdens.

The important exercise is for each of us to think seriously about these issues. Without careful and detailed reflection, we will all be relegated to repeat the problems and inequities of the past. Without careful thought, we will not be able to constructively change the future.

NOTE

[1] This chapter draws heavily on Richard Wasserstrom's "Is Adultery Immoral?" in *Morality and Moral Controversies,* ed. John Arthur, Englewood, New Jersey: Prentice Hall, 1977, pp. 108–120.

Section III: Week 13: Ch 20–21

Name_____ TA _____

Section #_____

1) Does the Bible favor "male patriarchy"? How is the devaluing of sex tied to the devaluing of women?

Section III: Week 13: Ch 20–21

Name_____ TA _____

Section #_____

2) Describe Kant's problem with sexual activity.

3) Does monogamous marriage make sexual conduct permissible for Kant? How so?

Name_____ TA _____

Section # _____

4) Do you think that the immorality of adultery rests entirely in the fact that it is a "breach of contract"? Why or why not?

5) Describe the 3 traits which people have said are necessary for marriage. Do you think a successful marriage requires all 3 of these? Is there a trait missing?

Name_____ TA _____

Section #_____

6) Give Socrates' (Plato's) solution to the problem of marriage from *The Republic*.

Chapter 22

Pornography and Obscenity[1]

A. THE PROBLEM OF PORNOGRAPHY

Mention of the word "pornography" is usually enough to generate controversy in most company and many tend to respond adversely to it. The word "pornography" suggests to some obscene conduct. Here the word "obscene" serves to connote immorality or at least socially undesirable behavior.

In order to determine whether pornography constitutes impermissible conduct, we must first determine its nature more clearly. Only then will we be able to render a judgment about it. Accordingly, we shall set out to define the province of "pornography" broadly enough to include what many persons find either of questionable moral value or entirely lacking in it. Then, we shall proceed to pronounce judgment on its permissibility, investigating not whether it is suitable for recommendation but only whether consenting adults who produce it and consume it are behaving impermissibly. Does pornography violate the harm principle, does it harm wrongfully?

The general strategy we shall adopt, then, in this: we will not set out to determine whether the pursuit of such conduct is either wise or desirable. Our strategy here is concerned exclusively with determining whether pornography is something that must be restricted. We are interested to judge whether pornography ought to be censored or otherwise regulated by law. Stated differently, we set out to determine whether adult consent is a sufficient condition to justify pornography, its creators, actors, and audience. Consent is a necessary condition for sexual activity in general. Our problem is to test again in this case whether it is also sufficient.

In the language of "harms," the issue is a question of *impersonal harms*, and occasionally, harms to self. We shall not debate questions concerning pornography and minors, nor shall we consider cases in which adult participation is not fully consensual—such activities are already proscribed by law. We are concerned, however, about allegations that the community is somehow endangered by consensual adult participation in pornography and whether the character of the individual who participates is somehow damaged, and damaging further others with whom he/she interacts. Our problem: Where's the *wrongful* harm? And is the charged violation impermissible, and therefore immoral?

B. DEFINING PORNOGRAPHY

So much confusion has entered into discussion and debate about pornography because people understand the term "differently." There are some who regard any displays at all of nudity to be pornographic, and here, "pornographic" means "obscene." A community certainly has a right to try to repress any conduct that it regards as offensive and objectionable; to identify any conduct as "obscene" means it is regarded as worthy of suppression. Our approach is to get clear about how we will use the term "pornographic" and then explore in what ways it does or does not count as "obscene."

Let us define "pornography" as any graphic, literary, or audible means of expression whose sole or overwhelming purpose is sexual arousal. By defining pornography in this way we avoid the endless controversies of whether *this* sexual display or *that* counts as "pornography." The motivation of the pornographer is to sexually stimulate an audience. The central problem for our investigation is to determine not whether such stimulation is wise or desirable but rather whether we ought to constrain interest in pornography ourselves and authorize constraint over others. In order to justify constraint, we must be able to show precisely what sort of wrongful harm is perpetrated, acknowledging in advance that all kinds of harm result from adult activities without directly wronging anyone. Thus, we must investigate whether we can show that harm causes individuals to be deprived of their rights, and thus their rightful domain. The focus must be on the wrongfulness of the conduct, and for this we must be prepared to invoke and argue persuasively for the guidance of the harm principle if pornography merits censorship.

In the discussions about rape, marriage and monogamy, and adultery, we focused upon the question of consent and thereby tested the *Volenti* maxim. We argued that consent was a necessary condition for making sexual activities permissible; failure to obtain consent renders sexual activities impermissible. The lingering question was to determine if consent was also a sufficient condition to justify conduct. The proponents of censoring pornographic materials constitute one group that believes that although consent is necessary to make conduct permissible, it is not sufficient to justify practices. Like rape, marriage/monogamy, and adultery, the discussion about pornography requires that we come to a decision about whether or not the sexual impulse must be regulated and under what conditions.

Stated differently, those who advocate the censorship of pornography do not accept the force of the *Volenti* maxim. The *Volenti* maxim insists that where there is consent there can be no wrongdoing. But, of course, there can be harm. The advocates of censorship insist that the community and individuals themselves are caused various impersonal harms and those harms demonstrate that pornography is objectionable and therefore impermissible. The state, therefore, has a vested interest in protecting citizens by "enforcing morality." And what this means for our exploration of the harm principle is that if we come to regard pornography as "wrong" even though it does not undermine the *Volenti* maxim, then the wrongness of pornography might be argued for more clearly by identifying it with some free-floating evil. And if this is to be successful, we must find a way to become clearer yet about the meanings of "free-floating evils."

In his article, "Pornography and Obscenity," Fred Berger begins by defining "pornography" more broadly:

> *Any art or literature which explicitly depicts sexual activity or arousal in a manner having little or no artistic or literary value.*

This definition is separated into two parts. In the first part, Berger specifies that pornography conveys sexual activity or arousal as its "sole, exclusive, or overwhelming purpose." In the second part, Berger acknowledges that medical and scientific texts, although having neither artistic nor literary value would not, of course, be at issue. Thus, by definition, Berger proposes that the problem confronting us is whether media whose main purpose is sexual arousal be subject to control.

Our primary strategy will be to determine whether such conduct deprives others, or ourselves, of our rightful domain. This is another way of asking whether such practices cause wrongful harm to others and hence violate the harm principle. If a case can be made unambiguously for wrongful harm, then we may conclude that persons have been deprived of their rightful domain. In that case, control may be an appropriate option in the form of imposing liberty-limiting principles. If harm cannot be clearly shown, an attempt to authorize control would not be justifiable.

C. CONSERVATIVE ARGUMENTS AGAINST THE PERMISSIBILITY OF PORNOGRAPHY: PORNOGRAPHY *CAUSES* HARM

Let us follow Berger's essay and begin by presenting the most conservative arguments against pornography. The reason for this approach is to isolate the strongest arguments against its permissibility in order to understand what conceptual hurdles will have to be overcome if the argument can be made that pornography should escape regulation. We are not debating whether pornography is a good thing, is wise or desirable; we are only debating whether or not it is impermissible, if adults choose to participate in its production or consumption, are they behaving immorally? Conservative approaches tend to identify pornography as immoral and recommend control in the form of censorship.

Argument 1: Pornography is itself immoral or evil, irrespective of the consequences that flow from it.

This is the conclusion of the Presidential Commission Report on Pornography and Obscenity produced in the 1980s. This commission was chaired by Edwin Meese, the former U.S. Attorney General. The claim is that certain kinds of conduct are recognized by name to be immoral without further argument and are thereby suitable for repression.

Argument 2: Pornography is immoral because most citizens in a community deem it so and, therefore it should be repressed.

This argument consists in the attempt to show that irrespective of the moral issue *per se*, pornography is something most people in a community find abhorrent and disgusting and necessary to repress. This part of the argument bears close resemblance to an informal fallacy we discussed, the *argumentum ad populum* or fallacious appeal to the masses. Those who champion this argument hold that moral decisions are not like other kinds of decisions. Popular consensus, in this view, may not only be useful in pointing out widespread moral views, but repugnance felt by a sufficient number of persons is supposed to be sufficient to guide practice. Objectors point out that, in the 1950s and earlier, pre-civil rights legislation, if a sufficient number of persons in a community found it morally permissible to insist that blacks ride at the rear of a bus or be denied entrance to a restaurant, that was sufficient to justify the practice.

Argument 3: Pornography promotes or leads to certain kinds of socially harmful attitudes or behavior.

This, too, was a central doctrine of the Meese Commission report. This argument suggests that pornography be seen as preliminary to some sort of violent crime. And because it is agreed that violent crime constitutes grievous anti-social conduct deserving of repression and restriction—clear violations of the harm principle—then pornography, too, as the source and cause of that violent conduct, ought to be subject to control.

The first two arguments seem undeserving of our serious consideration. Without further clarity and consideration, objecting to a practice and recommending its external control seem mindless. If pornography is evil, we must specify the evil it commits and address that description. It is entirely insufficient to rule it out without further specification. The second argument fares no better. The fact that large portions of a population find certain practices abhorrent is certainly a good enough reason for those persons to refrain from that conduct. But, the appeal *ad populum* ought to be rejected as sufficient grounds to claim a conduct evil and serve as sufficient reason for others to constrain conduct.

The third argument poses a serious concern and we turn to examine it further. The argument that "pornography causes harm" presents a serious challenge. As acknowledged earlier, if we can make unambiguous sense of this charge, the issue of social control becomes appropriate to the discussion. For then we will have made clear that there is an evil committed as well as its specific nature.

Argument 3a: Pornography causes harm because it provides incitement to rape.

The structure of this kind of argument is clear. Pornography arouses sexual desire because that is its purpose. That sexual desire often seeks an outlet in anti-social forms, such as rape. The question for us is not whether the argument is clear. The question is whether the argument is true.

The Meese Commission report sought to argue that pornography incites men to commit violent sex crimes. There are several problems with this thesis. First of all, pornography is read and viewed by many, many more people who do not commit violent crimes, judging by reports about how widespread are the consumers of the pornography industry. Thousands of people attended showings of the movie *Deep Throat* and the *Devil in Miss Jones,* among other movies, at public theaters in the 1970s when pornographic movies first became available at major public theaters. Thousands of people choose to view sexually explicit material in the privacy of their own homes, presumably for sexual arousal, without committing violent crimes. If so many can view these sorts of materials without exhibiting objectionable anti-social behavior, then can we conclude that pornographic materials *cause* such offensive conduct? Clearly, that answer is "no."

Suppose the argument is further restricted. Suppose the research could show that a certain, small group of men who do commit violent sexual crimes, viewed violent, sexually oriented materials immediately prior to their sexual assaults. What will then have been shown? The problem is to determine whether the explicit and violent sexual materials could be held causally responsible. Such a case would be as indefensible as blaming liquor companies for manufacturing alcoholic intoxicants in a case where a drunk driver killed a pedestrian, especially given the fact that millions of people consume alcohol without committing a crime. Can sexually explicit and violent materials be justifiably blamed for assaults committed by those who use pornography prior to those assaults, any more than the liquor companies that produce alcohol products?

The problem with the Meese report also consists in a failure to clearly distinguish the violent from the merely sexually explicit. If it is argued that the most violent sexual crimes seem to be committed by those who view the most violent sexual pornography, some comparable study should have investigated the likelihood of aggravated criminal assault after viewing any kind of violent materials. For it may be that viewing violent materials stimulates violent acts quite independently of sexual conduct. Thus the commission, in the name of consistency, ought to have equally recommended controls and restrictions for violent cowboy movies, war movies, and every "creature-feature" that panders to violent tendencies.

Argument 3b: Pornography causes harm because it alters basic sex-attitudes, the result of which is anti-social behavior.

This is the general argument advanced by George Steiner in "Night Words." Steiner begins by presuming that sexual relations are private. This, of course, is corroborated by legal codes that restrict most sexual conduct from public places. Most other acts, unlike sexual acts, are not disallowed in public places. Thus, the pornographers destroy the intimacy made possible by this privacy.

Steiner's complaint seems to be in part that the new pornographers do our imagining for us, thereby robbing us of the moments of privacy in which our private lives are worked out. The argument bears resemblance to Wasserstrom's discussion of sex and intimacy. In Wasserstrom's argument, the traditional morality identifies sexual activity as appropriate only in that case where there is a special intimacy. The meaning of that "special" intimacy is exclusivity. Here, we may interpret part of the meaning of exclusivity as also constituted by a demand for privacy.

Suppose we grant Steiner his claim. What follows? If we can show that an important private realm of our private lives is somehow compromised, at best we might conclude that participation in such conduct is undesirable. But we are not interested, first and foremost, in determining what conduct is wise or desirable. We merely wish to know if an offense is perpetrated that merits regulation. If someone shall object to Steiner's analysis, insisting that reading or viewing such materials has in his/her estimation salutary effects on his/her personal life, do we have any good reason, by Steiner's argument, to interfere?

Suppose a woman argues, as does Wendy McElroy in her book *XXX: A Woman's Right to Pornography* (1997), that in order to explore sexual possibilities now that the world has sexually-transmittable diseases that could kill you and that experimenting with men you do not know could lead to assault and even death, pornography offers a safe outlet for such exploration. In such a case, the woman is exploring new ways to think about sexual activities, and to gain a sense about which possibilities she might be interested to pursue when she finds the right partner. By Steiner's argument, the pursuit of pornographic materials could only be an impediment to meaningful relations, but this position seems seriously challenged by arguments by McElroy and others.

Argument 3c: Pornography causes harm by depersonalizing sex, reducing it to mere animal activity thereby debasing it.

This sort of argument finds adherents from those like Kant in his "Duties Toward the Body in Regard of Sexual Impulse" and from contemporaries like Irving Kristol.

For Kant, pornography would be judged to be immoral—or at least amoral—since it encourages sexual pleasure for its own sake. The pursuit of sexual gratification is accepted in Kant's estimation only within the context of monogamous marriage, for only in that case do we engage the Other as a whole person. By itself alone, sexual conduct is debasing.

Irving Kristol's argument is different but reaches the same conclusion. He insists that viewing pornographic materials encourages a preference for masturbation over mature adult relations. The consequence of such a predilection is to lead to increasingly infantile behavior. Infantile behavior is auto-erotic, self-gratifying, and this Kristol believes, is dangerous to society.

The argument seems to be as follows: Infantile behavior is a way of characterizing conduct in persons who lack maturity. Infantile behavior is not only directed to immediate gratification but sees itself as means and ends to that satisfaction. As Freud put it, civilization means discontent. As long as we live with others, it is not possible to have the immediate gratification we always desire and thus we must transcend the infantile desire for it. Adult life is thus exhibited by showing strategies for deferred gratification. Further, adult or mature persons recognize the presence of others. Infantile behavior fails to develop strategies with others except to secure satisfaction. Kristol understands the importance persons place on sexual satisfaction. His argument insists that viewers and readers of pornography are driven away from mature adult relations that are characterized by communication and sharing. The pursuit of pornography is the pursuit of selfish and infantile gratification. Individuals achieve sexual satisfactions on their own and are led into increasingly anti-social conduct.

Suppose we embrace Kristol's argument, that certain socially immature and undesirable attitudes are fostered by pornography. Could this be a good enough reason to legislate against it, as opposed to alert those of potential set-backs? If we grant that socially unsuitable habits are endorsed or facilitated by pornography, would this be a sufficient reason to censor such materials? If it could be shown that this was the result for every viewer and reader, that would be one thing. But since the many persons who view and read pornography are not led to this end, what shall be the sufficient ground to justify restriction and regulation?

Argument 3d: Pornography causes harm by breaking down the feelings of shame that we associate with sex. The political consequences are dangerous insofar as they foster increasingly tyrannical attitudes in citizens.

This argument has been advanced by Walter Berns. Order in a social organization requires respect for authority. One important way in which that respect is established is through fostering "shame" and guilt. If someone commits a crime, we publish his/her name in a newspaper, we place him/her on trial, and we empower our social organizations with the authority to punish him/her for misconduct. An important element in aiding the social enforcement of legal codes is shame.

With regard to sexual conduct, we attempt to bridle our animal propensities. We restrict sexual conduct to private places, in part, to emphasize that the conduct is shameful in public. Social attitudes are inculcated in many different domains of social practice. Berns's argument is that the shame essential for protecting love is the very same promoter of self-restraint. This ability to be shamed thereby functions as a means to secure self-restraint, an essential ingredient for a democratic polity.

The personality of those who have not learned self-restraint is tyrannical. Indeed, in Berns's estimation, tyranny is the natural and inevitable mode of government for those who are shameless and self-indulgent and who have carried liberty beyond any restraint.

Berns's argument is difficult to embrace. The political implications that seem so clear to Berns are not so clear to his critics. There are many kinds of activities that tend to foster tyrannical behavior. One might, at best, advance the argument that certain kinds of conduct tend to foster questionable or even objectionable attitudes. But this is hardly a suitable argument that such conduct requires regulation. Some things may not be good for us and yet are insufficient to count as violations of harmful wrongdoing.

Argument 3e: Pornography causes harm by encouraging desensitized social attitudes in persons that lead to a loss of empathy with others and encourages violence and anti-social acts.

This argument has been advanced by Ernest van den Haag. It suggests that certain kinds of conduct lead to an imbalanced personality. Violent conduct is seen as a natural consequence.

The watching or reading of pornographic materials, in Van den Haag's opinion, de-individualizes and de-humanizes sexual acts. It achieves this effect by displaying persons, probably not emotionally involved, engaging in sexual acts. Further, the viewer or reader is also a participant, as voyeur, in intimate practices with those he/she surely does not know. In this sense, sexual conduct becomes understood as de-individualized or de-humanized. We come to view others as mere objects. Violence is a natural consequence when we come to regard others persons as "things."

Van den Haag's argument is interesting but will it supply the grounds for justifying censorship? If such an argument were sufficient, then we must be prepared to censor any materials that present attitudes that are deemed socially objectionable. Anything that de-sensitizes us to persons around us seems both unwise and undesirable. How are such offenses wrongful?

The conservative arguments may be summarized, according to Berger, in terms of two general commitments. First, pornography is stark. It tends to remove warmth and those feelings that are supposed to be central to adult sexual relations. Secondly, pornography undermines our understanding of privacy/intimacy by effectively estranging us from others.

If pornography, according to our general strategy, is to be deemed immoral, it must succeed in depriving persons of their rightful domain unjustly. This means that those who charge certain conduct with immorality must demonstrate that those practices are not merely insulting, and thereby deeply offensive to some, but show that a measurable and definable harm has been perpetrated wrongfully.

The conservative arguments have tried to demonstrate that a definable harm has been committed, and that harm is wrongful although it is nevertheless consensual. The critical arguments seek to show that in human adult sexual relations, at least a minimum of sensitivity and empathy is sacrificed through pornography, and an essential part of our private and intimate conduct is destroyed by pornography as well. In the latter case, all kinds of anti-social conduct may be fostered. Suppose we grant *all* of these arguments that suggest the dangers and disadvantages that pornography may visit upon us, would these arguments be sufficient to justify censorship? Is adult consent still sufficient to justify a practice. The practice may strike us as undesirable and generally unwise but is that alone enough to defend the recommendation for social control and regulation? And if the reader comes to regard that pornography does violate the harm principle and so merits censorship, granting that we are addressing the world of adult consenters, what is the specific reason that this harming counts as *wrongful*?

D. LIBERAL OBJECTIONS TO THE CONSERVATIVE ARGUMENTS

Now we turn to a more extensive challenge to these conservative arguments that attempt to identify what is unacceptable behavior in pornography as a way of recommending social regulation and control. Following Berger, we proceed to set out, and critically assess, the presuppositions of these arguments.

The conservative view supposes that sex is normal and proper only within the context of deep commitment and shared responsibility. This means that mature adult sexual relations require both restraint and repression of desires for pure pleasure. From this perspective, the conservative view comes to understand "beautiful love" to be non-physical. And sexual practices are seen to be permissible only where there is a special intimacy that finds expression in exclusivity.

Berger and Wasserstrom adopt a common strategy: to put forth a view of social practices prevalent years ago and to challenge it in the context of today's society where those views are widely rejected.

The Radical Critique: The conservative arguments are entirely out of touch with current conduct. The entire facade of sexual attitudes in our society represents a sham and is an unnecessary form of social control. The picture the conservative paints and addresses is rather unrealistic and romanticized. The fact, the radical critique says, is that sex tends to be routinized, dull, unfulfilling, and a source of neurosis, precisely because of these inculcated conservative sexual restraints.

Those restraints include: (i) with whom to have sex, (ii) when to have sex, (iii) where to have sex, (iv) how often to have sex, and so on. There were taboos, stated and unstated, that regulated the permissible sexual conduct. The preoccupation with restraints projected a view of sex that was riddled with guilt. Indeed, the web of guilt and shame tends to destroy sexual enjoyment, not promote it.

Thus, the radical critique led to a solution that consisted in a recommendation for a radical revision of attitudes concerning sexual activity: Treat sex as a physical act. Sex is animal coupling. To insist upon making more of sex invites dishonesty and neurosis. As Berger observes, this is the position that conservatives fear the most. From the conservative view, our social organization persists because of a powerful repression over individual conduct. The radical critique, in the name of honesty, demands that the repression be abandoned. The conservative fears that removal of repression will lead to political anarchy where no one follows any recognized authority or guidelines.

The conservative response objects that by removing repression by social institutions and taboos, the result is de-humanization. Pornography, from the conservative perspective, reduces persons to objects or things by reducing them to mere sources of pleasure. Without emotional commitment, persons are reduced to mere instruments to a desired end and thus are treated as means to ends. To be regarded as a means to pleasure is to be regarded as a means in general. The conservative argument holds, by formulators like Kant, that persons are ends-in-themselves and must never be reduced to the status of a means.

The counter objection is to show that the conservative goes too far in drawing conclusions from otherwise interesting points. If business people are permitted to make profits in business, must they come to see others merely as sources of profit? By analogy, if one no longer thinks of sex in terms of shame and guilt, must one come to lose shame and guilt at harming others?

The counter objection can be pressed even more forcefully. Suppose we agree that, with Kant, sexual conduct by nature is appetite. In that appetite each person becomes an object of gratification for the Other. Can we thereby never have relations with others in which we accept the Other as a subject? Granted that we are not only bodies, that we are persons and subjects, what good reasons are there why we cannot also enjoy the Other, by consent, as a body, as an object? Isn't it possible to have sexual relations where the delight consists in sharing bodily pleasures without losing sense of each other's agency? Isn't such marvelous appreciation of each other and communication with each other one way of understanding the meaning of having "great sex?" The conservative position, so stated, can be accused of bad faith. Granted, we are more than bodies and hence subjects among other things. But aren't we also bodies and hence objects? Isn't to be loved and accepted also to be loved and accepted for the bodies that we are?

Perhaps current social attitudes toward sex are in need of greater liberation. For it may be argued that shame, guilt, and duty are not necessary aspects of fully human sex, though they may prove desirable. Pornography might prove to be one way of moving the social organization to a more open and freer attitude towards sex. It might even prove to be of therapeutic value in breaking down emotional barriers to produce more open communication in some cases. Perhaps pornography might have a positive value.

But our strategy in approaching this issue was not to determine whether pornography represents wise or desirable practice. Our focus was to address those conservative arguments that complain that pornography is immoral and ought to be subjected to social control. Before we stand in the way of others and harass them for making choices that are opposed by other groups, we had better have better reasons than that conduct is revolting and aberrant to us. For those feelings are sufficient to guide a person to avoid those activities that are regarded to be revolting and disgusting for themselves. But the feelings of offense and disgust are not sufficient by themselves to justify standing in the way of others and recommending liberty-limiting principles. We must be prepared to document specific harm—violations of the harm principle—for which pornography, and not the individual's misjudgment, is to blame, and moreover to show how it is wrongful. Have any of the arguments demonstrated that the pornography is to blame for specific harm any more than a TV program ought to be found culpable for an individual's motivation to commit a bank robbery? Shall we blame a TV program or the bank robbers when they rob the bank? We blame individuals for inexcusable conduct. We shall, in general, hold the individual blameworthy for his/her conduct. For the theory of morality we are unfolding regards persons as moral agents, regards them as free to make choices and to exercise constraint over inclinations, to unfold their self-interests with due reflection and self-control, and to respect their right to discover their own way in the world. Thus, our theory thereby also holds individuals responsible for their conduct and thus blameworthy for unacceptable behavior—behavior that is harmful and wrongful. But we are first of all consenters. And who knows better than each and every one of us what is or is not in our best interest?

NOTE

[1] This chapter draws heavily on Fred Berger's "Pornography and Obscenity," in *Social Theory and Practice,* Vol. 4, no. 2, spring 1977, pp. 1983–2009.

Chapter 23

The Supreme Court on Sodomy

A. SUMMARIZING THE HARM PRINCIPLE AND *VOLENTI* MAXIM IN CASES OF SEXUAL MORALITY

In the discussion that addressed the immorality of rape, we reached the provisional conclusion that, among adults, consent was necessary to make sexual activity permissible. We have struggled to understand better what role consent plays in broader issues concerning the permissibility and thus the morality of sexual practices. In each new discussion we tested, directly or indirectly, the *Volenti* maxim: Where there is consent, there can be no wrongdoing. And by testing this ideal of consent, we gain deeper understandings into our self-identity. In this discussion, we will test again whether it makes sense to say that no one knows better than each of us what is in our own best interest. Adult choices—consent—seems to be both necessary and sufficient to justify adult sexual practices, engaged in private. But, those who are unpersuaded by this argument must become clear how to make sense of *wrongdoing*—to make sense of specific free-floating evils—when the offensive behavior is nevertheless consensual.

In the discussions of marriage and monogamy, we examined Kant's claim that consent, although necessary for sexual conduct, is not sufficient. The argument Kant offered is that without the marriage contract, sexual conduct is debasing and humiliating because it otherwise reduces persons to objects of appetite and thus things. Because persons are subjects and agents, and by Kant's argument sex reduces persons to mere things, then consent, although necessary, is not sufficient to justify that sexual activity.

Kant's argument is not popularly enjoined by many people today. That is because the presumptions that underlie Kant's view concerning ideas of intimacy and the demand for exclusivity, no longer play the central roles that they played for him and his society. If we reject Kant's argument making consent necessary but not sufficient because we reject his insistence upon the sacredness of those presumptions, then we have affirmed that consent seems to be both necessary and sufficient to justify adult practices, pending further argument. That is, we would then have accepted the *Volenti* maxim over and against Kant's objections.

In the discussion of adultery, we again examined the claim that consent is both necessary and sufficient to make permissible the conduct between consenting adults in private. This time we wondered whether extramarital sexual practices could ever be justified and if in what sense adultery is wrong. We granted that in cases involving active or passive deception, adultery seemed wrong because it represented not merely a breach of contract but also a deception to one's spouse and perhaps to the third-party in the matters of intimacy and exclusivity.

The difficult problem presented itself in the case of open marriage, when persons mutually agree to engage in and perhaps sustain extramarital sexual liaisons. In this case, if adultery is wrong it could not be because there is either active or passive deception. We came to the conclusion that if adultery is wrong in that case—since there is no harm to others—it could only be because the nature of the marriage agreement is by definition monogamous and thereby rules out of hand against extramarital sex.

This conclusion forced us to acknowledge that the wrongness of adultery in the case of this strongest objection, could be defended only by showing that marriage itself was a morally desirable institution, but even so, adultery would be merely an impersonal harm. The wrongness of adultery, then, would be inextricably tied to the breach of the marriage contract—not because it harmed others—and, hence, adultery would be wrong because it vitiates the monogamous demand of the institution of marriage. We were unable, however, to provide that argument and merely considered one alternative model, replete with its own problems. Thus, the conclusion we came to was that in the case of adultery, consent, although necessary to justify a practice is apparently insufficient. The insistence that consent is insufficient was bolstered by noting that even in an open marriage where there is mutual consent adultery still seems wrong. But, again, its wrongness would rest upon a morally unequivocal defense of the present institution of marriage and this we were unable to provide. Only with that argument could we say that adultery was always impermissible and, thus, immoral in general. Without that argument, we again found ourselves with the apparent conclusion that consent is both necessary and sufficient to justify the permissibility of a practice. Where there is consent in conduct among adults the question of immorality cannot properly arise. Thus, the *Volenti* maxim, again, seemed to have strong support. And again, for those who are unpersuaded by these provisional conclusions, the challenge is to produce arguments that show how, despite adult consent, harmful wrongness rests on some free-floating evil that can be specified, and that is not merely offensive to someone's religious beliefs, culture, or personal tastes.

In the case of adultery and then again with regard to pornography, no effort was made to recommend such conduct. In no way did we enter into a discussion of whether such practices were wise or desirable. Our problem was to determine only whether we ought to interfere or recommend that the state interfere with the practices of consenting adults with specific regard to pursuing graphic, literal, or audible media whose sole or overwhelming purpose was to sexually stimulate the viewers, readers, or hearers.

In the case of pornography, we again tackled the question of whether consent is necessary and sufficient to justify the practices among persons who engage in such visual, literary, or audible displays or among its viewers, readers, and listeners. Again, our challenge was to determine if consent was sufficient to justify such practices because we have continued to insist that it is certainly necessary.

The arguments suggesting that pornography merits social control and regulation all sought to declare that pornography perpetrates harm, and did so wrongfully. Those who hold that pornography is an evil irrespective of its consequences were challenged to account for the alleged harm. Those who provided no reason, or appealed to various religious scriptures were dismissed for failure to state a claim. Those who insisted that such conduct reduces others to the status of mere objects or things deserved a serious reply, for they suggested that the consequence of such a view was to subject persons to abuses and disrespect of all kinds. But, at most, this claimed impersonal harms and/or harm to self. The first response was to counter the objection by noting that, although we are not merely bodies, we are, indeed, also bodies. Those who engage in pornography with full adult consent ordinarily hold different assumptions about the permissibility of sexual conduct, a different view of their identity as bodies, and find the kinds of explicit sexual conduct involved in pornography acceptable. Those views generally do not suppose that sexual activity must be restricted to relations of the greatest intimacy nor do they regard exclusivity as being fundamental to sexual relations. Unless we are ready to propose additional reasons, we will have to take seriously the desires of pornographic performers to engage in their chosen activities and their viewers, readers, listeners to exercise their discretion in consuming pornography. Without dismissing the claim that, perhaps, impersonal harms are engendered, the harm of imposing liberty-limiting principles seems to outweigh greatly the deleterious effects.

A series of additional challenges was advanced against the permissibility of pornographic endeavors. Each of these arguments attempted to show, again, the harm that issued forth from such conduct. Among those objections was the insistence that pornography led to infantile and non-mature behavior among adults; that pornography fostered tyrannical dispositions in its viewers, readers, and listeners; and that most especially, pornography leads to a host of anti-social behaviors: Pornography causes sexual violence. In that chapter it was objected that none of the arguments was sufficient to establish their case, even though it was agreed that pornography might have specifically inspired a wide variety of anti-social attitudes and behaviors while not causing harm directly to others.

The counter-argument that was advanced challenged those objectors to show causal connection rather than, at best, occasional connection. If the perpetrators of violent sex crimes viewed violent pornographic materials just prior to their crimes, it remains for us to determine whether we should rightly conclude that the pornographic materials caused the conduct and, thereby, relieve the criminal himself of blame. Or, instead, whether we should conclude that criminal intentions might be motivated to criminal actions for any number of conditions immediately antecedent to criminal conduct. Its not that pornography *caused* the violent sex crime but rather that the criminal did, and would have done so with or without the pornographic preliminary. Ought the person who watches a war movie, perhaps of the *Rambo* style, and then proceeds to commit a violent act be relieved of the responsibility of his/her conduct by appealing to the movie viewed just prior to the objectionable action? Shall we excuse the drunk driver from the damage caused on the grounds that watching a TV program that advertised beer caused him to drink? That conclusion applies to the pornography argument *mutatis mutandis*.

To those who argue that pornography fosters anti-social attitudes, it is sufficient to object that it does not produce this effect in all viewers, readers, or listeners. Thus, the causal charge is discredited. True, pornography may produce undesirable social attitudes in some people, and so might the consumption of alcohol, or even the watching of professional football. Does pornography produce more objectionable attitudes than watching a violent hockey game or a violent movie about gangland wars? Or science fiction, or horror movies? Are we prepared to remove the accurate accounts of widespread violence from the TV news and documentary cinema because acknowledging such behavior indirectly fosters more of the same? Or must we rather come to see that individuals must be held responsible and blameable for the conduct in which they engage and are therefore entitled to watch, read, or listen to what they please and suffer the appropriate consequences for their anti-social conduct? We suggested that this latter course seems less objectionable, in the absence of direct harm to others. This strategy of toleration seems less objectionable than depriving persons of the liberty to choose their own sources of private pleasure.

Finally, it may be argued that pornography degrades women and contributes to the oppression of women and thus merits censorship. To this claim it might well be objected that discrimination against women did not come into being with the advent of pornography in the 19th and 20th centuries, nor is it likely to be reversed by its censorship. Further, it should be noted that in countries where pornography has never been publicly tolerated—such as Iran and Saudi Arabia, for examples—we see no signs of enlightened treatment and egalitarianism towards women. Thus pornography does not cause discrimination against women, although some might argue that it contributes toward that end, and comparable discrimination (and worse) is evidenced against women even where pornography is forbidden by law. The simple claim that pornography causes wrongful harm seems not to have been proven.

To adopt this stance is to give additional support to the strategy that consent is a necessary and sufficient condition to justify adult practices when harm to others cannot be clearly defined and demonstrated.

Pornography may not present us with practices wise or desirable. Yet, to interfere with those adults who choose to engage in them freely, we must provide demonstrations of the harm being committed, that someone in particular has had his/her interests set back wrongfully. If minors are involved, we do indeed have laws to constrain that conduct. If adults participate without consent, we have laws that include sexual assault, kidnapping, coercion, and so on, that can be brought to bear. But among consenting adults, even if such conduct shall strike us as unwise, does not our commitment to the exercise of personal freedom—*to maximize self-interest by refraining from imposing liberty-limiting principles whenever possible*—require that adults make decisions about their own choices of conduct without interference from others? Let each of us decide, in cases that do not cause harm unambiguously wrongful to others, what is in our own best interest. And let each person make his/her own mistakes, to enjoy or suffer the consequences of them.

B. THE SUPREME COURT DECISIONS ON SODOMY

In 1986, the Supreme Court voted narrowly to uphold the rights of states to restrict private, consensual sexual activities. This was the decision in *Bowers v. Hardwick,* which we shall examine in detail shortly. That decision stood in place some seventeen years—until a more recent decision in *Lawrence and Garner v. Texas* superceded and overturned it, 26 June 2003. The main thrust of the narrowly voted decision to overturn *Bowers v. Hardwick* was to insist that consensual sexual activities conducted in private were matters protected by rights to privacy.

As we shall discuss, although the Georgia state statute criminalizing "sodomy" was rewritten in 1968 to cover *both* homosexual and heterosexual sodomy, the Supreme Court held, in its majority decision written by Justice White, that the Constitution did not guarantee the right to "homosexual" sodomy. In a footnote to that opinion, Justice White writes that no decision was being made concerning "heterosexual" sodomy although the language of the Georgia statute extended to both. While it is usual for the majority decision to begin by citing the particular statute being addressed, there is no formal statement of it in the majority decision. Thus, it was difficult to avoid the conclusion that the Court's decision was directed against homosexuals, since Hardwick was an avowed homosexual, even though the statute was changed in 1968 to cover "sodomy" regardless of whether it was practiced by homosexuals or heterosexuals.

Lawrence and Garner v. Texas

What follows here is the "summary" of the Supreme Court decision in 2003:

> Responding to a reported weapons disturbance in a private residence, Houston police entered petitioner Lawrence's apartment and saw him and another adult man, petitioner Garner, engaging in a private, consensual sexual act. Petitioners were arrested and convicted of deviate sexual intercourse in violation of a Texas statute forbidding two persons of the same sex to engage in certain intimate sexual conduct. In affirming, the State Court of Appeals held, *inter alia,* that the statute was not unconstitutional under the Due Process Clause of the Fourteenth Amendment. The court considered *Bowers v. Hardwick,* 478 U.S. 186, controlling on that point.
>
> Held: The Texas statute making it a crime for two persons of the same sex to engage in certain intimate sexual conduct violates the Due Process Clause. Pp. 3–18.
>
> (a) Resolution of this case depends on whether petitioners were free as adults to engage in private conduct in the exercise of their liberty under the Due Process Clause. For this inquiry the Court deems it necessary to reconsider its *Bowers* holding. The Bowers Court's initial substantive statement—"The issue presented is whether the Federal Constitution confers a fundamental right upon homosexuals to engage in sodomy . . . ," 478 U.S., at 190—discloses the Court's failure to appreciate the extent of the liberty at stake. To say that the issue in *Bowers* was simply the right to engage in certain sexual conduct demeans the claim the individual put forward, just as it would demean a married couple were it said that marriage is just about the right to have sexual intercourse. Although the laws involved in *Bowers* and here purport to do not more than pro-

hibit a particular sexual act, their penalties and purposes have more far-reaching consequences, touching upon the most private human conduct, sexual behavior, and in the most private of places, the home. They seek to control a personal relationship that, whether or not entitled to formal recognition in the law, is within the liberty of persons to choose without being punished as criminals. The liberty protected by the Constitution allows homosexual persons the right to choose to enter upon relationships in the confines of their homes and their own private lives and still retain their dignity as free persons. Pp. 3–6.

(b) Having misapprehended the liberty claim presented to it, the Bowers Court stated that proscriptions against sodomy have ancient roots. 478 U.S., at 192. It should be noted, however, that there is no longstanding history in this country of laws directed at homosexual conduct as a distinct matter. Early American sodomy laws were not directed at homosexuals as such but instead sought to prohibit nonprocreative sexual activity more generally, whether between men and women or men and men. Moreover, early sodomy laws seem not to have been enforced against consenting adults acting in private. Instead, sodomy prosecutions often involved predatory acts against those who could not or did not consent: relations between men and minor girls or boys, between adults involving force, between adults implicating disparity in status, or between men and animals. The longstanding criminal prohibition of homosexual sodomy upon which *Bowers* placed such reliance is as consistent with a general condemnation of nonprocreative sex as it is with an established tradition of prosecuting acts because of their homosexual character. Far from possessing "ancient roots," ibid., American laws targeting same-sex couples did not develop until the last third of the 20th century. Even now, only nine States have singled out same-sex relations for criminal prosecution. Thus, the historical grounds relied upon in *Bowers* are more complex than the majority opinion and the concurring opinion by Chief Justice Burger there indicated. They are not without doubt and, at the very least, are overstated. The Bowers Court was, of course, making the broader point that for centuries there have been powerful voices to condemn homosexual conduct as immoral, but this Court's obligation is to define the liberty of all, not to mandate its own moral code, *Planned Parenthood of Southeastern Pa. v. Casey*, 505 U.S. 833, 850. The Nation's laws and traditions in the past half century are most relevant here. They show an emerging awareness that liberty gives substantial protection to adult persons in deciding how to conduct their private lives in matters pertaining to sex. See *County of Sacramento v. Lewis*, 523 U.S. 833, 857. Pp. 6–12.

(c) *Bowers'* deficiencies became even more apparent in the years following its announcement. The 25 States with laws prohibiting the conduct referenced in *Bowers* are reduced now to 13, of which

4 enforce their laws only against homosexual conduct. In those States, including Texas, that still proscribe sodomy (whether for same-sex or heterosexual conduct), there is a pattern of nonenforcement with respect to consenting adults acting in private. Casey, supra, at 851—which confirmed that the Due Process Clause protects personal decisions relating to marriage, procreation, contraception, family relationships, child rearing, and education—and *Romer v. Evans,* 517 U.S. 620, 624—which struck down class-based legislation directed at homosexuals—cast *Bowers'* holding into even more doubt. The stigma the Texas criminal statute imposes, moreover, is not trivial. Although the offense is but a minor misdemeanor, it remains a criminal offense with all that imports for the dignity of the persons charged, including notation of convictions on their records and on job application forms, and registration as sex offenders under state law. Where a case's foundations have sustained serious erosion, criticism from other sources is of greater significance. In the United States, criticism of *Bowers* has been substantial and continuing, disapproving of its reasoning in all respects, not just as to its historical assumptions. And, to the extent *Bowers* relied on values shared with a wider civilization, the case's reasoning and holding have been rejected by the European Court of Human Rights, and that other nations have taken action consistent with an affirmation of the protected right of homosexual adults to engage in intimate, consensual conduct. There has been no showing that in this country the governmental interest in circumscribing personal choice is somehow more legitimate or urgent. Stare decisis is not an inexorable command. *Payne v. Tennessee,* 501 U.S. 808, 828. *Bowers'* holding has not induced detrimental reliance of the sort that could counsel against overturning it once there are compelling reasons to do so. Casey, supra, at 855–856. *Bowers* causes uncertainty, for the precedents before and after it contradicts its central holding. Pp. 12–17.

(d) *Bowers'* rationale does not withstand careful analysis. In his dissenting opinion in *Bowers* Justice Stevens concluded that (1) the fact a State's governing majority has traditionally viewed a particular practice as immoral is not a sufficient reason for upholding a law prohibiting the practice, and (2) individual decisions concerning the intimacies of physical relationships, even when not intended to produce offspring, are a form of "liberty" protected by due process. That analysis should have controlled *Bowers,* and it controls here. *Bowers* was not correct when it was decided, is not correct today, and is hereby overruled. This case does not involve minors, persons who might be injured or coerced, those who might not easily refuse consent, or public conduct or prostitution. It does involve two adults who, with full and mutual consent, engaged in sexual practices common to a homosexual lifestyle. Petitioners' right to liberty under the Due Process Clause gives them the full right to engage in private conduct without government intervention. Casey, supra, at 847. The Texas statute furthers no legitimate state interest which can justify its intrusion into the individual's personal and private life. Pp. 17–18.

41 S. W. 3d 349, reversed and remanded.

Kennedy, J., delivered the opinion of the Court, in which Stevens, Souter, Ginsburg, and Breyer, J.J., joined. O'Connor, J., filed an opinion concurring in the judgment. Scalia, J., filed a dissenting opinion, in which Rehnquist, C. J., and Thomas, J., joined. Thomas, J., filed a dissenting opinion.

In 2003 Justice Kennedy, writing for the 5–4 majority, explained that *Bowers v. Hardwick* held that the due process clause of the federal Constitution's 14th Amendment neither conferred a fundamental right for homosexuals to engage in consensual sodomy, nor did it invalidate the state of Georgia's statute that criminalizes acts of consensual sodomy—regardless of whether the participants were of the same sex—even when the acts occurred in the privacy of home.

When the Supreme Court finally heard the Texas case, they decided just that, the Texas statute was unconstitutional. They *reversed* the ruling in *Bowers* and maintained that states do *not* have a legitimate right to restrict the consensual and private sexual choices of adults. While the *Bowers v. Hardwick* ruling focused on the question of whether the Constitution granted homosexuals the right to engage in consensual sodomy, *Lawrence v. Texas* focused on the issue of under what conditions consenting adults have a right to privacy about the most intimate decisions in their lives.

Writing for the majority, Justice Kennedy argued that the Texas statute violated the two men's right to liberty and privacy protected by the due process clause of the federal Constitution's 14th Amendment. The Texas statute sought to control a personal relationship that, the Supreme Court now held, was properly within the liberty for them to choose without being punished as criminals. Furthermore, the decision of *Bowers v. Hardwick* was overruled also for two other reasons: (i) There is an emerging recognition that liberty gave a substantial protection to adults to determine how to conduct their sexual lives in private, and (ii) To the extent that *Bowers v. Hardwick* relied on values shared by a wider civilization, the reasoning of that decision had been rejected by various courts outside of the United States. In short, within the changing culture of the United States, reflected also by decisions made in courts throughout the western world, a new consensus has developed affirming the rights of adults to pursue consensual sexual relations in private, free from governmental interference.

We will now turn to consider the *Bowers v. Hardwick* decision of 1986 and the legal climate in which it was made. Since that decision set precedence for almost two decades, it is illuminating to consider in detail what it held and how it argued that while consent is necessary to justify adult sexual practices conducted in private, such consent is *not* sufficient to justify a practice. It was precisely that principle that the Court reversed in 2003.

Michael Hardwick was arrested in Atlanta, Georgia for having an open container of alcohol— a beer—in a public place for which alcoholic beverages were proscribed by law. Answering the ticket required a court appearance that he did not make. Consequently, a bench warrant was issued for his arrest. It took almost two years for his name to come to the top of the list and an arresting officer went to Hardwick's listed address and knocked at the door. Hardwick's roommate answered and when the officer asked for Michael Hardwick, the roommate pointed to a room down the hallway. The officer went to the open door to find Michael Hardwick engaged in an act of oral intercourse with another male. Hardwick was arrested on the outstanding warrant, and charges were presented to the grand jury for indictment of a violation against Georgia's crimes against nature statute. But, as it happened, the grand jury refused to indict, probably because of the remarkable circumstance in which Hardwick was with another adult in private. But, Hardwick was incensed and through his legal counsel sought to have the constitutionality of the Georgia law challenged. At the District Court, his challenge was dismissed because he lacked standing—he was not in fact arrested for violating the statute. And so, the next legal challenge was at the Federal Court of Appeals that did find in Hardwick's favor by a vote of 2–1 that the Georgia statute was unconstitutional. As is usual, when a state's law is ruled unconstitutional the Attorney General of that state, in defending the laws passed by the people of that state, appeals to the Supreme Court. Attorney General Bowers appealed to the Supreme Court and they issued a Writ of Certiorari; this means that they agreed to hear the case.

After hearing the arguments, the justices declared on 30 June 1986 that, by a vote of 5-4, they were reversing the decision of the Federal Appeals Court and finding for the State of Georgia. In effect they held that the state of Georgia had the right to pass and enforce laws that restricted certain kinds of sexual activity even if it were to take place in private between consenting adults. The opinion of the majority was written by Justice White who offered four principal reasons for the decision: (1) the constitution does not provide a right to engage in homosexual sodomy, (2) there has been a long tradition of Biblical, Roman, English, and American law that have found such practices to be unacceptable, (3) not every conduct engaged in private is immune from prosecution, and (4) the popular sentiment of the peoples of a state is sufficient to justify a practice.

Justice Blackmun writing for the minority criticized the reasoning in the majority opinion. He pointed out that the state statute was directed equally to homosexual and heterosexual conduct but the majority opinion focused too narrowly by only addressing homosexual conduct. And most importantly, Blackmun argued that the majority opinion missed the main point—the right to privacy, the right to be left alone. This was the heart of the legal issue that the majority opinion failed to respect and honor.

It seems clear that while the constitution does not identify a right to engage in homosexual sodomy, it also does not provide a right for heterosexual sodomy. Judging by the Court's revising its decision in such matters in *Lawrence and Garner vs the State of Texas*, the importance of the right to privacy won out finally. While there has been a long tradition of Biblical, Roman, English, and American law that regarded sodomy as unacceptable, there is also such a long tradition that endorsed the permissibility of slavery. Legal precedence may be a good argument in the Courts but it seems to prove too much in moral debates. While it seems true that not all conduct conducted in private is immune from prosecution—gambling, assault, and so on—a good argument needs to show where is the wrongful harm in the case of consensual sodomy. Finally, the argument that the popular sentiment of the peoples of a state may be sufficient to justify a law, it offers morally dubious grounds to accept a general principle. If the popular sentiment of the majority were morally sufficient alone, then we are left to suppose that in the south when slavery was legal and supported overwhelmingly by the general populations, then that practice too was morally sound. No person of good conscience could hold such a position.

Name_____ TA _____

Section #_____

1) Give the books' definition of "pornography." How does this differ from the definition of pornography given by Fred Berger?

2) Which of the arguments against pornography given by the book do you find the most convincing? Why?

Name_____ TA _____

Section #_____

3) Describe the "radical critique" of conservative arguments against pornography. Do you find this critique compelling? Why or why not?

4) What was the result of the 1986 Supreme Court case *Bowers v. Hardwick*?

Name _____ TA _____

Section # _____

5) What was the result of the 2003 Supreme Court case *Lawrence and Garner v. Texas*? What reason did the majority give for their decision?

6) How do these two cases show different points of view on the sufficiency of consent for moral action?

Chapter 24

Sexism and Racism[1]

A. SEXISM AND RACISM: AN OVERVIEW OF HARM TO OTHERS

There can be no doubt that both sexism and racism constitute objectionable social practices. In both cases, benefits and burdens are not equitably distributed. The victims of sexism, women in general or those who constitute minorities in terms of sexual roles like homosexuals and lesbians, and the victims of racism, generally the minorities in any country, are discriminated against so as to assume a disproportionate amount of burden for the very modest benefit they receive. In both cases, the victims of sexism and racism are systematically discriminated against for no other reason than that their gender, sexual role, or race is different from—and thus supposed to be inferior to—those who are in positions of authority and power. In both practices, we have clear and unambiguous harm to others. Persons are caused to have their interests set back wrongfully; they are deprived of those domains to which they have a right unjustly. Accordingly, both practices may be regarded as immoral on the grounds that both violate the harm principle.

As we discussed earlier, no thoughtful analysis of the social predicaments in America can neglect to identify stories like those emanating from the Bible that play prominent roles in our socialization. The disposition of those stories has shaped our social attitudes. Those attitudes help us to understand better our cultural context, replete with its inequities. The Biblical stories we addressed earlier deserve mention here because they help to underscore the predominance of paternalism.

Paternalism, or male-dominated social organization, indicates the kind of inequities that we may anticipate a social analysis would reveal.

The Adam and Eve story of the so-called Old Testament declares that all human progeneration is ultimately founded on male generation rather than on female procreation which is part of the usual natural order. The order of nature is reversed in the process of announcing the rise of a new social order. In that new social order, the male, not female, stands in a privileged position.

So also for the virgin-birth story of Christ in the so-called New Testament. The usual and natural order of procreation is disturbed for one and only one time in the history of the universe, according to that received tradition. In that case, God is born in human form. Human sexual intercourse is apparently defective and is unable to generate the divine. And God is male. Again, by virtue of the story, males continue to enjoy a privileged position within the context of the meaningfulness of the story. In both of these central stories, sexual inversions announce the beginning of a new tradition. Both are paternal and, to that extent, offer a justification for the appropriateness of a certain distribution of benefits and burdens. Males deserve a larger share of the benefits and a smaller share of the burdens, because, somehow, God favors males. In the final analysis this is the consequence of paternalism.

Whenever we isolate culturally preferred stories, whether in our American tradition, or any other tradition, it is suggested that we ask "who paid for them to be told" over and over again? This question means who might benefit most from the telling of such stories? From the standpoint of a non-believer, we can ask who benefits from telling this story? Who is disadvantaged? If we can take a look from the distance, we can see benefits and burdens as consequences of these narratives. Our critical attitude towards biblical stories should be the same constructive one we bring to the sacred stories of every other tradition. By refusing to accept the inviolability of these stories—at first, at least—we enjoy the privilege of doubt. This privilege allows us to gain a constructive and critical distance in order to assess our own special stories and those of others. The result will either be a change of attitude toward those stories, or a deepening of our conviction and belief in them. In either case, such a scrutiny proves to be a manner of great respect. If the sacredness of the stories can withstand our scrutiny, then our belief will be strengthened in a thoughtful way. If our traditional beliefs are shaken, then perhaps we will attain another stance that leads to a transformed respect for these accounts of our nature and the order in the cosmos. By asking "who paid for these stories to be told?" we ask in whose interests would be the telling of them, the fostering of them, and the publicity of them. Who might likely benefit by subscription to these stories? Those groups who would benefit disproportionately would likely be saddled with a lesser portion of burdens. In the case of the biblical stories, the paternalistic attitudes favor males over females, and have been interpreted to favor Caucasians over other races.

In both the cases of sexism and racism, the victims have not consented to the disequitable distribution of benefits and burdens. This is surely one way of understanding what is wrong with sexist and racist conduct. But, this analysis does not expose the pernicious features of such behavior. For a deeper understanding of how such conduct is perpetrated, we must examine the social realities more closely.

B. SEXISM AND RACISM: THE SOCIAL REALITIES

Following Richard Wasserstrom's insightful article "Racism and Sexism," we turn to examine three questions:

(1) What are the social realities with regard to racism and sexism?

(2) What is an adequate explanation of how things got this way?

(3) What is the ideal of a non-racist and non-sexist society?

When persons are asked, and they have been often, what is wrong with racism or sexism, the familiar response is to say that certain insignificant social factors such as skin color or gender are the basis for discrimination. Apparently irrelevant characteristics serve as the basis for the unequal distribution of benefits and burdens. Thus, the familiar response is that racism and sexism are wrong because characteristics not deserving to be the basis of rewards and punishment, in fact, systematically facilitate the distribution of just those rewards and punishments.

Thus, racism and sexism occur when an irrelevant characteristic, such as race or sex, is utilized to systematically allocate social benefits and burdens. The defect, then, consists in the choice of irrelevant criteria that results in a treatment of individuals both arbitrary and capricious.

The persuasiveness of Wasserstrom's article consists in its point of departure. For Wasserstrom observes that, for whatever else we say to the contrary, race or 'skin color,' and sex or 'gender,' are very *significant* social categories. Despite the familiar response that skin color and sex are not fundamentally important, the way we, in fact, behave underscores the significance of these social categories. Race and sex make substantial differences in the way we regard others, despite protestations to the contrary.

One way to see this point more clearly would be to consider the difference between:

skin color vs. eye color

Except in the remarkable cases of those like fashion models, eye color is rarely the basis of discrimination. That is because eye color is not a significant social category. Benefits and burdens are not distributed, ordinarily, on the basis of specific eye color. But, the situation is very different with regard to skin color. Individuals are treated differently by virtue of skin color and that makes the point that skin color is an important social category.

It is also important to consider that race and gender are categories created by our society. All animals engage in various patterns of conduct that isolate certain members of their community. Our groups have selected skin color and gender as peculiarly significant. It does not have to be that way, but an examination of the social realities reveals that indeed, for us, it is that way. Thus, an analysis of racism and sexism must begin with the social realities, or what is the case with regard to our behavior.

In the cases of racism and sexism, we noted that both subject individuals to discrimination. Although the familiar analysis has been that the wrongness of such conduct is illuminated by observing that it is on the basis of unimportant characteristics that unfair allocation of rewards and punishment takes place, we have now considered the defect in that analysis. Race and sex are important social categories. In this sense, both racism and sexism share the same structure of discrimination. But racism and sexism are also not alike and attention to the distinction proves fruitful for our understanding.

The object of racism is always denigrated, never elevated. For the racist, there is no approval for the object of disdain. Every individual of the hated race is somehow deficient, no matter how distinguished some of those members may seem to be. If blacks are the objects of derision, then even the most distinguished black doctors, lawyers, teachers, athletes, and all other roles that the majority hold estimable, are somehow to be written off as defective. If the objects of racism consist of Asian peoples, or religious minorities, again, the same sort of analysis applies. The objects of racism are always debased.

In contrast, as Wasserstrom points out, sexism is a more insidious evil than racism precisely because it is more difficult to see. The sexist, like the racist, unfairly distributes benefits and burdens. And in this sense, the object of sexism is denigrated. But, while the object of sexism is relegated to the status of a second-class citizen, the object of sexism is also elevated to an extraordinary height and held up to tremendous accolade. This is clearest in the case of women who are treated by husbands with the greatest of respect and appreciation, within some domains, and at once treated as though they were incapable, incompetent, and of lower worth in other domains. The woman in such a situation is put up on a pedestal by her adoring husband, on the one hand, and cast into the role of second-class citizen, on the other, when she attempts to assume the wide range of roles that he selects for himself.

In this sense, racism and sexism are asymmetrical social phenomena. Both involve the denigration of persons and the consequential reduction to the status of second-class citizenry. But, unlike racism where the hated person is always relegated to denigration, the object of sexism is at once elevated to a pedestal while also being subjected to systematic mistreatment. It is for this reason that it is more difficult to see the injustice of sexism because it surely seems to the sexist that the woman is not being disdained in the manner that the object of racism indeed is.

This point might be made even clearer if we consider the difference between two public declarations. In the first case, a Caucasian publicly declares:

(i) "I am a racist."

And let us contrast this public declaration with one of a different sort in which the same Caucasian declares:

(ii) "I am a male chauvinist pig."

Despite the recent public resurgence of racist epithets, it seems more unlikely in a mixed and public company to hear someone announce the first claim, that he is a racist, than to hear that same person announce he is a male chauvinist pig, though this too has become politically incorrect and has fallen increasingly into disfavor. But, why? If Wasserstrom's suspicion is sound, our social organization is much clearer today about the wrongness of racism than it is about the wrongness of sexist behavior. There is nothing kind or forgiving in racist conduct, and thus that behavior strikes us more clearly as irredeemably wrong. But, in the second case, the male who declares himself to be a male chauvinist pig might well see himself as a male who identifies with traditional male-gender roles, who likes or even loves women and regards his appreciation of them with respect. At the same time, it is likely that this same person does not sympathize with the desire of women to become part of the work force or have equal benefits in the workplace. And yet, unlike the object of racism, the object of sexism is also accorded accolade and respect. This example is useful if it helps us to understand more clearly why sexism is more difficult to see than racism. And if such systematic and ill-grounded mistreatment is equally applicable to sexism and racism, then the greater the difficulty to see the sexism, the more insidious the evil.

Secondly, we turn to consider briefly how we got here in the first place, how our social attitudes developed over the last century. An explanation of the social realities can be divided into an examination of sexist, and then racist attitudes.

An explanation of sexist attitudes focuses upon the different ways in which men and women are socialized. Men and women are both instructed about their natures and differences. In Wasserstrom's appraisal, men and women are taught to see men and women differently.

Men are:

   (i)   independent

  (ii) capable

 (iii) powerful

Women are:

   (i)   dependent

  (ii) limited in abilities

 (iii) passive

If Wasserstrom has soundly detected patterns of socialization, all persons in our social organization come to see men in a serious and potent light, while women are seen to be inferior. An important consequence of such differences in socialized roles is that men and women would come to measure their success in different terms. Men would measure their success in terms of occupation, property, acquisition of material goods, money, authority in the work setting. Women would tend to measure their success largely in terms of activities within the family, marriage, "wifely tasks" such as domestic affairs, housework, child care, emotional welfare of husband and children. The woman's status in society tends to reflect her husband's vocation.

For whatever advantages this social arrangement provides, there can be little doubt that the distribution of benefits and burdens is disequitable. If acquisition of material goods is regarded as a benefit, then in a society where benefits are equitably distributed, men and women would have equal opportunity to it. This is clearly not the case. If child rearing and housecleaning are generally agreed to be disagreeable tasks, then, if women are socialized to accept the larger burden without substantial compensations, again the distribution would be unfair.

In our society, the economic status of women is clearly worse off than men, with comparable circumstances. In general:

(a) Women are worse off than men.

(b) There is no ostensible pay for work done at home.

(c) There are only comparatively smaller numbers of women in the workforce who enjoy high prestige and salary jobs.

(d) There is, in comparison with men, a conspicuous absence of women from positions of authority in major political and economic institutions.

In these senses, our society exhibits sexist behavior. This means that the ordinary allocations of rewards and punishment, in terms of desirable acquisitions and tasks, is inequitable.

The same sort of conclusion can be reached with regard to race relations, though the specific scenario is different. In the decades since the passage of the first civil rights legislation, conduct in public has been affected. However our attitudes, by and large, retain their racist stamps, there have been important restrictions placed on public practices. In order to see the progress, however far we have yet to go, let us turn to consider the circumstance prior to the civil rights legislation of 1964.

In the late 1950s and early 1960s, certain common behavior was interrupted by civil rights activists. We can consider racially segregated bathrooms.

Why were bathrooms segregated racially? Especially in the South, public racist conduct was, in general, more extreme, pronounced, and public than elsewhere in the United States. Blacks, and other minorities, were prevented from eating in certain restaurants, were required by law to sit in the backs of buses and other public transportation, and at the filling or gas station were invariably required to use bathrooms set aside for them. It would be an understatement of substantial proportions to say that those bathrooms were almost certainly in worse condition than those reserved for white people. Why were such measures imposed?

There is only one way to understand these practices and that is to recognize that the predominantly white population viewed the African-Americans as basically dirty animals, not fully worthy or deserving of first-class human status. The attitude was not merely one that distinguished blacks, and other minorities, as different; the attitude declared these minorities less worthy as human beings. No decent person could hold such a view. And yet, these objectionable and aberrant attitudes were institutionalized in America and flaunted in the South.

By our current social practices (including this period decades ago) bathrooms are also sexually segregated—one for males and another for females. One way of more clearly understanding the difference between racism and sexism is to understand the very different motivations for these practices. Bathrooms were racially segregated because it was supposed that blacks and other minorities were dirty and that white people might become infected by the diseases which these dirt-ridden people carried.

Bathrooms are segregated sexually for very different reasons. In order to heighten the heterosexual disposition, we have isolated men and women in places where genitals are exposed in public places. In order to strengthen heterosexual attitudes, the genitalia of opposite sexes are kept mysterious. And bathroom behavior, that might strike us as unseemly, is restricted to persons of the same gender. Thus, bathrooms were segregated racially and sexually to intensify the consciousness of differences. But, in the case of racial segregation, the difference was supposed to be one that proved a lesser or lower value of those segregated persons. In the case of sexual segregation, the consciousness of difference is designed to heighten interest and desire.

In 1954, the Supreme Court handed down a landmark decision in the case of *Brown v. The Board of Education.* In that decision, the Court found that the policy of "separate but equal" was unconstitutional. In part, it was impossible to produce separate but equal education; in part, the very idea was rejected as a vision of equality and freedom, in a land that had become known as a "melting pot." Since then, many attempts have been made to secure greater equality, including forced busing of children to schools in order to achieve integrated communities. It is clear that this attempted resolution has not achieved the desired success. Despite the fact that racist attitudes persist and indeed loom large in various parts of our nation, it is also clear that progress has been made from absolutely intolerable conditions. Benefits and burdens are clearly not equitably distributed, despite the progress.

C. THE NON-SEXIST, NON-RACIST MODEL: THE ASSIMILATIONIST IDEAL

Thirdly, we turn to consider the ideal of a non-racist and non-sexist society. What would it look like? What features would characterize it most clearly?

Wasserstrom introduced what he called the assimilationist ideal. A non-racist society would be one in which the race of an ideal individual would be the functional equivalent of eye color of individuals in our society today. This means that because eye color determines no basic political or economic rights, and determines no important institutional benefits and burdens, skin color or race in a non-racist society would serve comparably.

How such a circumstance could be brought about, we leave to the social worker and politician, for implementing social programs is more suitably delegated to their expertise. The questions concerning instrumental implementation are beyond the scope of our inquiry here.

The assimilationist ideal for sex presents a different challenge. It seems clear that the assimilationist ideal presents a valuable model for a social organization that claims the importance of equality and equitable distribution of benefits and burdens. But the social implications of non-sexist society require that we rethink the heterosexual primacy of our organization. Why?

If a non-sexist society would regard gender distinction as no more significant than eye color in today's society, then laws that require persons who are getting married to be of different sexes would clearly be sexist laws. Non-sexist society could not insist that heterosexual conduct was superior to homosexual or bisexual practices. We would then be compelled to radically alter our practices concerning the family and marriage. It is clear by recent Court cases, and by legislation in many of our states that have made gay marriage legal, that we are moving towards non-sexist society. It will, of course, take much time to change people's attitudes, but the changes in the laws points to the new direction to be developed in the hearts of people everywhere.

D. AN ARGUMENT AGAINST RACISM: BEHIND THE VEIL

Since racism is so pernicious an evil, and so widespread still in our day and age, one more illustration will be added to help readers address the issue squarely. The illustration I turn to was advanced by a philosopher named John Rawls. He calls it "Behind the Veil" and I adapt his hypothetical case here:

> Let us imagine that we are seated in front of a stage. On that stage every person who has ever lived, or who will ever live, walks across. As they do, we are permitted, in this illustration, to assign rights. In short, we are called upon to distribute benefits and burdens. And we may distribute them however we please. If there is some group, or some individuals, who fall into your disfavor, you may deny them rights, let's say voting rights, or the right to consent over sexual conduct, or what have you. If some persons strike your fancy, you may award them greater benefits, and no burdens. In this scenario, you will assign benefits and burdens to your heart's pleasure. You may discriminate against all those you hate, and heap rewards on those you esteem.

> But, of course, there is a little catch to the story. Enter "Behind the Veil." It is easy to assign rewards and burdens from our current social circumstance. This is one of the issues that blinds us to the reprehensible character of discriminatory practices. If we are benefiting, it is easy to bolster our good fortune by maligning other groups. But, in this illustration, this privilege is suspended.

> In our illustration, while you watch each person who has ever lived, or who ever will live, walk across the stage, the one piece of information that you do *not* know is *who you are behind the veil*. And when you are finished delegating advantage and oppression to those who stand before you, only then shall we lift up the veil and discover *your* identity on the other side. Perhaps you will find that you belong to one of those groups who enjoy tremendous benefit and little burden. But it is equally likely that you will find yourself a member of the group from which voting rights and sexual rights have been deprived and in which heaps of burden replace the heaps of benefit.

> Not knowing their identity behind the veil, would anyone risk finding themselves without rights? If you did not know how you would

fit into some social order and yet had to reasonably assign rights, rewards and hardships, would any right minded person risk casting themselves into slavery or worse when they had the choice to delegate rights differently?

Rawls's illustration "Behind the Veil" surely suggests that the answer to this question would be "no." Racist and sexist behavior are engaged in by persons who already enjoy a privileged position in that social order. But Rawls's illustration makes the point that such conduct is defenseless. More than that, no one would recommend such disequity if they risked being a member of the maligned group deprived of simple and basic privileges. The racist and sexist hold their offensive attitudes because of the incidental fact that they are presently in a position of advantage. But no persons, Rawls challenges us to consider, would reasonably expose groups to systematic oppression if they realized that they may be members of just that group.

NOTE

[1] This chapter draws heavily on Richard Wasserstrom's "Racism, Sexism, and Preferential Treatment: An Approach to the Topics," in *UCLA Law Review,* Vol. 24, 1977, pp. 581–622.

Name_____ TA _____

Section #_____

1) What is the common feature of racism and sexism? What makes them different (aside from the type of person involved)?

2) Describe the ideal society which Wasserstrom describes as "assimilationist."

Name_____ TA _____

Section #_____

3) Describe John Rawls thought experiment in which we should make decisions "behind the veil."

SECTION IV

Readings

Grounds for Coercion

Joel Feinberg

1. THE PRESUMPTIVE CASE FOR LIBERTY

Whatever else we believe about freedom, most of us believe it is something to be praised, or so luminously a Thing of Value that it is beyond praise. What is it that makes freedom a good thing? Some say that freedom is good in itself quite apart from its consequences. On the other hand, James Fitzjames Stephen wrote that ". . . the question whether liberty is a good or a bad thing appears as irrational as the question whether fire is a good or a bad thing."[1] Freedom, according to Stephen, is good (when it is good) only because of what it does, not because of what it is.

It would be impossible to demonstrate that freedom is good for its own sake, and indeed, this proposition is far from self-evident. Still, Stephen's analogy to fire seems an injustice to freedom. Fire has no constant and virtually invariant effects that tend to make it, on balance, a good thing whenever and wherever it occurs, and bad only when its subsequent remoter effects are so evil as to counterbalance its direct and immediate ones. Thus, a fire in one's bed while one is sleeping is dreadful because its effects are evil, but a fire under the pot on the stove is splendid because it makes possible a hot cup of coffee when one wants it. The direct effect of fire in these and all other cases is to oxidize material objects and raise the temperature in its immediate environment; but *these* effects, from the point of view of human interests, and considered just in themselves, are neither good nor bad.

Freedom has seemed to most writers quite different in this respect. When a free man violates his neighbor's interests, then his freedom, having been put to bad use, was, on balance, a bad thing, but unlike the fire in the bed, it was not an unalloyed evil. Whatever the harmful consequences of freedom in a given case, there is always a direct effect on the person of its possessor which must be counted a positive good. Coercion may prevent great evils, and be wholly justified on that account, but it always has its price. Coercion may be on balance a great gain, but its direct effects always, or nearly always, constitute a definite loss. If this is true, there is always a *presumption* in favor of freedom, even though it can in some cases be overridden by more powerful reasons on the other side.

The presumption in favor of freedom is usually said to rest on freedom's essential role in the development of traits of intellect and character which constitute the good of individuals and are centrally important means to the progress of societies. One consensus argument, attributable with minor variations to Von Humboldt, Mill, Hobhouse, and many others, goes roughly as follows. The highest good for man is neither enjoyment, nor passive contentment, but rather a dynamic process of growth and self-realization. This can be called "happiness" if we mean by that term what the Greeks did, namely, "the exercise of vital powers along lines of excellence in a life affording them scope."[2] The highest social good is then the greatest possible amount of individual self-realization and (assuming that different persons are inclined by their natures in different ways) the resultant diversity and fullness of life. Self-realization consists in the actualization of certain uniquely human potentialities, the bringing to full development of certain powers and abilities. This in turn requires constant practice in making difficult choices among alternative hypotheses, policies, and actions—and the more difficult the better. John Stuart Mill explained why:

> The human faculties of perception, judgment, discriminative feeling, mental activity, and even moral preference are exercised only in making a choice. He who does anything because it is the custom makes no choice. He gains no practice either in discerning or in desiring what is best. The mental and moral, like the muscular, powers are improved only by being used.[3]

In short, one does not realize what is best in oneself when social pressures to conform to custom lead one mindlessly along. Even more clearly, one's growth will be stunted when one is given no choice in the first place, either because of being kept in ignorance or because one is terrorized by the wielders of bayonets.

Freedom to decide on one's own while fully informed of the facts thus tends to promote the good of the person who exercises it, even if it permits him to make foolish or dangerous mistakes. Mill added to this argument the citation of numerous social benefits that redound indirectly but uniformly to those who grant freedom as well as those who exercise it. We all profit from the fruits of genius, he maintained, and genius, since it often involves doggedness and eccentricity, is likely to flourish only where coercive pressures toward conformity are absent. Moreover, social progress is more likely to occur where there is free criticism of prevailing ways and adventurous experiments in living. Finally, true understanding of human nature requires freedom, since without liberty there will be little diversity, and without diversity *all* aspects of the human condition will be ascribed to fixed nature rather than to the workings of a particular culture.

Such are the grounds for holding that there is always a presumption in favor of freedom, that whenever we are faced with an option between forcing a person to do something and letting him decide on his own whether or not to do it, other things being equal, we should always opt for the latter. If a strong general presumption for freedom has been established, the burden of proof rests on the shoulders of the advocate of coercion, and the philosopher's task will be to state the conditions under which the presumption can be overridden.

2. THE ANARCHISTIC PRINCIPLE

It will be instructive to see why certain very simple statements of the conditions for justified social and political coercion are unsatisfactory. The first of these, which might with propriety be called "anarchistic," insists that society and the state should grant to every citizen "complete liberty to do whatever he wishes." In this view, no coercive power exercised by state or society is ever justified. What then of the coercion imposed by one individual or group on another? If every man is free to do whatever he wishes, it follows that all men are free to inflict blows on John Doe, to hold noisy parties under his window every night, and to help themselves to his possessions. How can it then be true that John Doe is free at the same time to come and go as he pleases, to sleep at night, and to enjoy exclusive use of his possessions?

There is no *logical* inconsistency in holding both that Doe is dispositionally free to do something and that someone else, Roe, is dispositionally free to prevent him from doing that thing. (I am considering these judgments only when made from the sociological, not the juridical, perspective.) Consider the statements that Doe is free to go to Chicago and Roe is free to keep Doe from going anywhere. It would be something of an oversimplification, but useful for our present purposes, to regard these statements as equivalent to the following hypotheticals: (1) If Doe chooses to go to Chicago, he will in fact go to Chicago, and (2) If Roe chooses to have Doe stay at home, Doe will in fact stay at home. There are conceivable circumstances in which both of these statements would be true. One set of facts that would make them both true would be those obtaining when Roe has the power to prevent Doe from leaving home, but does not choose to exercise that power, and no other obstacle stands in Doe's way. Thus, (1) is true because if, in these circumstances, Doe chooses to go to Chicago, there is nothing to stop him; (2) is true because if (contrary to fact) Roe were to choose to keep Doe at home, Doe would be kept at home. For any Doe and any Roe, whether or not (1) and (2) are true together depends upon what the facts happen to be. The conjunction of (1) and (2), therefore, cannot be logically contradictory.

There is no logical barrier to its being true that *everyone* is free (from coercion) to do whatever he may choose. One can conceive of logically possible worlds in which this would be the case. But in order for it to be true of our actual world, there would have to be a disappearance of conflict between choices: As soon as two men attempt to acquire what only one can have, or one man desires something that can be acquired only by frustrating the desires of someone else, then one man's freedom is possible only at the cost of another man's constraint. The anarchistic principle, in short, would be workable only in a world in which human desires and choices, through a miracle of preestablished harmony, could never conflict. In our own world, where conflict and rivalry are ineradicable facts, "complete liberty for all" on the anarchist formula would mean greater freedom for the strong than the weak, and no very stable freedoms for anyone.

Given that the important desires of men can and usually do conflict, one person will be free to act on a desire only to the extent that others are unfree to act on conflicting desires; if the state is to guarantee to all men the freedom to do one certain kind of thing, then, in all likelihood, it must make all men unfree to prevent others from doing that sort of thing. "As against the coercion applicable by individual to individual," wrote Bentham, "no liberty can be given to one man but in proportion as it is taken away from another. All coercive laws, therefore, and in particular all laws creative of liberty, are as far as they go abrogative of liberty."[4] But if prohibitive laws destroy a liberty for every liberty they confer or protect, while the anarchistic principle would neither add nor subtract liberties from the natural situation of men, don't they yield precisely the same net totals of liberty and constraint, differing merely in the manner of distribution? This conclusion is yet another trap we can fall into by interpreting usefully loose talk about "amounts" of freedom in a precise quantitative way.

Most civilized societies have prohibitive laws or other social devices to prevent individuals from inflicting blows on the faces of other individuals. There is sometimes a great deal of pleasure to be derived from bopping someone in the nose, but most of us think that this pleasure is worth sacrificing for the greater good of security from physical attack by others. Suppose, however, that some rugged individualist complains that our law infringes on his freedom, making it virtually impossible for him to enjoy the thrill of smashing noses, and just because of the scruples of a lot of weak-kneed, lily-livered sissies. "Since the days of the frontier," he might say, "there hasn't been any real freedom in this country." We should no doubt try to explain to him that the interest people have in the physical integrity of their noses is *more important* than their aggressive interests, and therefore more worthy of protection.

Now suppose that we had quite different rules, and that more people were free to hit others in the nose, and correspondingly fewer were free to enjoy the full beauty and utility of their own unbloodied probosces. Would this new arrangement have a greater or smaller "amount" of freedom in it, on balance? Perhaps it is least misleading to say that there would be not "less" freedom but freedom of a morally inferior kind. Most societies have recognized that there are some relatively permanent desires present in all men that must be singled out, given precedence, and made legally sacrosanct. When these interests are so recognized and protected by law, they come to be called *rights*. Selection of those interests important enough to be protected in this way is made in accordance with the settled value judgments of the community by application of some standard other than that of "simple freedom" itself, which is quite insufficient. To receive "complete liberty" from society and its government would be to incur other constraints from private individuals, and almost all who have thought about this exchange consider it a bad trade.

3. THE FORMALISTIC PRINCIPLE

The second unsatisfactory principle of freedom distribution does not have such obvious failings. In fact, many have spoken as if it were a self-evident truth. Society, it says, should grant to every person "full liberty to do what he pleases providing only that he does not interfere with the like liberty of another."[5] This principle is the right answer to the wrong question. It insists that liberty should be distributed impartially, and that no individual take exception to the general prohibitive laws. But if it is taken as an answer to our question—when is political or social coercion justified?—it is entirely formal and empty, and consistent with any system of legal constraints that is not arbitrary. A general rule permitting nose bopping would satisfy it just as well as one prohibiting it; the anarchistic principle conforms to it, as well as a principle prohibiting all aggressive behavior. The principle employs a sound maxim of justice, insisting as it does on nondiscriminatory legislation and impartial enforcement, but it provides no guide to the proper *content* of the law. Its inadequacy as a substantive principle of freedom distribution was well appreciated by L. T. Hobhouse, who wrote, "My right to keep my neighbor awake by playing the piano all night is not satisfactorily counterbalanced by his right to keep a dog which howls all the time the piano is being played."[6] Each party in this example would use his freedom to the detriment of the other under a law which recognizes a "like liberty" for the other party to do the same if he can. That the law is nondiscriminatory would be small consolation to either party if it permitted his interests to be seriously harmed.

4. THE CONCEPT OF HARM

If social and political coercion is a harm-causing evil, then one way to justify it is to show that it is necessary for the prevention of even greater evils. That is the generating insight of the "harm to others principle" (henceforth called simply "the harm principle") which permits society to restrict the liberty of some persons in order to prevent harm to others. Two versions of this principle can be distinguished. The first would justify restriction of one person's liberty to prevent injury to other specific individuals, and can therefore be called "the private harm principle." The second can be invoked to justify coercion on the distinct ground that it is necessary to prevent impairment of institutional practices and regulatory systems that are in the public interest; thus it can be called "the public harm principle." That the private harm principle (whose chief advocate was J. S. Mill) states at least one of the acceptable grounds for coercion is virtually beyond controversy. Hardly anyone would deny the state the right to make criminal such directly injurious conduct as willful homicide, assault and battery, and robbery. Mill often wrote as if prevention of private harm is the *sole* valid ground for state coercion, but this must not have been his considered intention. He would not have wiped from the books such crimes as tax evasion, smuggling, and contempt of court, which need not injure any specific individuals, except insofar as they weaken public institutions in whose health we all have a stake. I shall assume that Mill held both the public and private versions of the harm principle.

In its simplest formulations, the harm principle is still a long way from being a precise guide to the ideal legislator, especially in those difficult cases where harms of different orders, magnitudes, and probabilities must be balanced against one another. Even when made fully explicit and qualified in appropriate ways, however, the unsupplemented harm principle cannot be fairly assessed until it is known precisely what is meant by "harm."

(i) Harm as the Invasion of an Interest

It has become common, especially in legal writings, to take the object of harm always to be an *interest*. The *Restatement of the Law of Torts* gives one sense of the term "interest" when it defines it as "anything which is the object of human desire,"[7] but this seems much too broad to be useful for our present purposes. A person is often said to "have an interest" in something he does not presently desire. A dose of medicine may be "in a man's interest" even when he is struggling and kicking

299

to avoid it. In this sense, an object of an interest is "what is truly good for a person whether he desires it or not." Even interest defined in this second way may be indirectly but necessarily related to desires. The only way to argue that X is in Doe's interest even though Doe does not want X may be to show that X would effectively integrate Doe's total set of desires leading to a greater net balance of desire-fulfillment in the long run. If most of Doe's acknowledged important desires cannot be satisfied so long as he is ill, and he cannot become well unless he takes the medicine, then taking the medicine is in Doe's interest in this desire-related sense.

Legal writers classify interests in various ways. One of the more common lists "Interests of Personality," "Interests of Property," "Interest in Reputation," "Interest in Domestic Relations," and "Interest in Privacy," among others. A humanly inflicted harm is conceived as the violation of one of a person's interests, an injury to something in which he has a genuine stake. In the lawyer's usage, an interest is something a person always possesses in some condition, something that can grow and flourish or diminish and decay, but which can rarely be totally lost. Other persons can be said to promote or hinder an individual's interest in bodily health, or in the avoidance of damaging or offensive physical contacts, or in the safety and security of his person, his family, his friends, and his property. One advantage of this mode of speaking is that it permits us to appraise harms by distinguishing between more and less important interests, and between those interests which are, and those which are not, worthy of legal recognition and/or protection.

(ii) Harm vs. Hurt: The Role of Knowledge

Is it true that "what a person doesn't know can't *harm* him"? For most cases, this maxim certainly does *not* apply, and it is one of the merits of the "interest" analysis of harm that it explains why. Typically, having one's interests violated is one thing, and knowing that one's interests have been violated is another. The rich man is harmed at the time his home is burgled, even though he may not discover the harm for months; similarly, a soldier is harmed the moment he is wounded, though in the heat of the battle he may not discover even his serious wounds for some time. The law does not permit a burglar to plead "He will never miss it" even when that plea is true, for the crime of burglary consists in inflicting a forbidden harm, whether or not it will be discovered or will hurt. It is true that not all harms *hurt*, partly because not all harms ever come to be noticed. There may well be a relatively narrow and precise sense of "harm" in ordinary usage such that "being harmed" can be contrasted with being hurt (as well as with "being shocked" and "being offended"). However, if harm is understood as the violation of an interest, and all men have an interest in not being hurt, it follows that hurt is one species of harm. Hence, even though not all harms *hurt*, all hurts do harm (or more accurately, are themselves harm), and the harm principle could conceivably be used to justify coercion when it is necessary to prevent hurts, even when the hurts do not lead to any *further* harm.

There are some special cases where the maxim "What a person doesn't know can't *hurt* him" seems quite sound. In these cases, knowledge of some fact, such as the adulterous infidelities of one's spouse, is itself hurtful; indeed, the whole hurt consists in the knowledge and is inseparable from it. Here knowledge is both a necessary and sufficient condition of a hurt: What the cuckolded husband doesn't know "can't hurt him." That is not to say that he cannot be *harmed* unless he is hurt.

An undetected adultery damages one of the victim's "interests in domestic relations," just as an unknown libelous publication can damage his interest in a good reputation, or an undetected trespass on his land can damage his interest in "the exclusive enjoyment and control" of that land. In all these cases, violation of the interest in question is itself a harm even though no *further* harm may result to any other interests.

The distinction between hurt and (generic) harm raises one additional question. We must include in the category of "hurts" not only physical pains but also forms of mental distress. Our question is whether, in applying the harm principle, we should permit coercion designed to prevent mental distress when the distress is not likely to be followed by hurt or harm of any other kind. Some forms of mental distress (e.g., "hurt feelings") can be ruled out simply on the ground that they are too minor or trivial to warrant interference. Others are so severe that they can lead to mental breakdowns. In such cases, however, it is the consequential harm to mental health and not the mere fact of distress that clearly warrants interference on the ground of harmfulness. Thus, a convenient criterion for determining whether a hurt is sufficiently harmful to justify preventive coercion on that ground suggests itself: The hurt is serious enough if and only if it is either a symptom of a prior or concurrent harm of another order (as a pain in an arm may be the result and sign of a broken bone), or is in itself the cause of a consequential harm (e.g., mental breakdown) of another order.

(iii) Harm vs. Offense

The relation of offensiveness to harmfulness can be treated in much the same way as that of hurtfulness to harmfulness. The following points can be made of both:

1. Some harms do not offend (as some do not hurt).

2. All offenses (like all hurts) are harms, inasmuch as all men have an interest in not being offended or hurt.

3. Some offenses (like some hurts) are symptoms or consequences of prior or concurrent harms.

4. Some offenses (like some hurts) are causes of subsequent harms: in the case of extreme hurt, harm to health; in the case of extreme offense, harm from provoked ill will or violence. These subsequent harms are harms of a different order, i.e., violations of interests other than the interest in not being hurt or offended.

5. Some offenses, like some hurts, are "harmless," i.e., do not lead to any *further* harm (violations of any interests other than the interest in not being hurt or offended).

6. Although offense and hurt are in themselves harms, they are harms of a relatively trivial kind (unless they are of sufficient magnitude to violate interests in health and peace).

Partly because of points 5 and 6, many writers use the word "harm" in a sense that is much narrower than "the invasion of any interest." In this narrower sense, harm is distinguished from and even contrasted with "mere offense." Some distinguish "harm to one's interests" from "offense to one's feelings" (as if there were no interest in unoffended feelings). This is a permissible, even useful, way of talking, if we agree that offensiveness as such is strictly speaking a kind of harm, but harm of such a trivial kind that it cannot by itself ever counterbalance the direct and immediate harm caused by coercion. One should appreciate how radical the harm principle is when interpreted in the strict and narrow way that excludes mere offensiveness as a relevant sort of harm. Both the British Wolfenden Report and the American Model Penal Code, for example, recognize "harmless" offensiveness as a ground for preventive coercion in some circumstances (see Chapter 3). For clarity and convenience only, I shall stipulate then that "offensiveness as such" is a proposed ground for coercion distinct from harm of the sort required by the harm principle (narrowly interpreted), so that "the offense principle" can be treated as an independent principle in its own right.

Offensive behavior is such, in virtue of its capacity to induce in others any of a large miscellany of mental states, that have little in common except that they are unpleasant, uncomfortable, or disliked. These states do not necessarily "hurt," as do sorrow and distress. Rather the relation between them and hurt is analogous to that between physical unpleasantness and pain, for there is also a great miscellany of unpleasant but not painful bodily states—itches, shocks, and discomforts—that have little in common except that they don't hurt but are nevertheless universally disliked. Among the main sorts of "harmless but disliked" *mental* states are irritating sensations (e.g., bad smells, cacophony, clashing colors), disgust, shocked moral sensibilities, and shameful embarrassment.

(iv) Harm vs. Nonbenefit

When the harm principle is unsupplemented by any other accepted ground for coercion, it decrees that state power may not be used against one person to *benefit* another, but only to prevent harm to another. One way of coercing citizens is to force them to pay taxes in support of various state activities. A partisan of the harm principle might be expected to cast a suspicious eye on all such schemes of involuntary support. Indeed, he might argue that taxing some to educate others is to coerce some merely to benefit others, or that taxing some to provide libraries, museums, theatres, or concert halls for others is to coerce some merely to amuse, inspire, or edify others, and is therefore unjustified.[8] On the other hand, an advocate of the harm principle could with consistency *deny* the foregoing propositions if he had a different way of construing the harm-nonbenefit distinction.

One muddled way of basing the distinction between harms and mere nonbenefits is to make it correspond to that between acting and omitting to act to another's detriment.[9] That will not do for the obvious reason that it is possible to harm or to benefit another either by action or omission. In other words, both actions and omissions can be the *cause* of changes in another's condition for better or worse. If we judge that Doe's failure to save the drowning swimmer Roe was the cause of Roe's death, then we can label Doe's omission the mere "withholding of a benefit" only if we judge the loss of life itself, in the circumstances, to be the loss of a benefit rather than the incurring of a harm. If, on the other hand, loss of one's life, like loss of one's health, fortune, or loved ones, is itself a harm, then anything that causes such a loss, whether it be act, omission, or fortuitous event, causes a harm.

Another unsatisfactory way of basing the harm-nonbenefit distinction is to hold that being without something good is a mere nonbenefit, whereas being in possession of something evil is a harm. It would follow from such a view that not learning truths is not having a good and hence not being benefited, whereas being told lies is to be in possession of something bad, and is therefore to be harmed. Thus it would follow that education is a mere-benefit and its lack no harm. But surely this will not do. To be effectively deprived of all food is clearly to be harmed as much as to be given poisoned food; the upshot in each case is death. Similarly, to have hardly any knowledge of the world is to be handicapped so severely as to be harmed, though perhaps not as severely as to have imposed on one a systematic set of falsehoods. In either case the result is damage to one's vital interests. Harm, therefore, is no more linked to "positive" possessions than it is to "positive" actions. It can consist in a lack as well as a presence, just as it can be caused by an omission as well as an action.

More promising correlations, at first sight, are those between harms and unmet *needs* and between benefits and unneeded goods. We harm a man when we deny or deprive him of something he needs; we fail to benefit him (merely) when we deny or deprive him of some good he does not need. An unneeded good is something a person wants which is not necessary for his welfare, something he can do without. To receive something one wants but does not need is to benefit or profit, but not to the point where loss of the gain would be a harm. Thus, if I have an annual salary of one hundred thousand dollars, and my employer gives me a fifty thousand dollar raise, I benefit substantially from his largesse. If he fails to give me a raise, I am not so benefited, but surely not harmed either (given my needs). If he reduces me to five thousand or fires me, however, he not merely fails to benefit me, he causes me harm by withholding money I *need*. These examples suggest that a statesman or legislator who is committed to an unsupplemented harm principle must have means for distinguishing authentic human needs from mere wants, and that his problem is little different in principle from that of the ordinary householder who must often distinguish between "luxuries" and "necessities" when he plans his household budget.

The problem is more complex, however, than these homey examples suggest. The "unmet need" analysis of harm would imply, for example, that a rich man is not harmed by a minor larceny, a conclusion we have already rejected. Still another distinction can be helpful at this point: that between *being in a harmful condition* (whatever its cause or origin) and undergoing *a change in one's condition in a harmful direction*. To deprive even a rich man of money is to damage his interests, that is, to change his condition for the worse, even though not yet to the state of actual injury. Thus, it is to "harm" him in one sense, but not in another. At best, the "unmet need" criterion is a test for determining when a damaged interest has reached the threshold of "actual injury," rather than a weathervane indicator of harmful directions. Let us stipulate at this point, for the sake of clarity and convenience, that the harm principle be interpreted in such a way that changes in the condition of a protectable interest in harmful directions, even short of the stage of "actual injury" (unmet need), count as a kind of harm, the prevention of which, in some circumstances, may justify coercion. However, when harms have to be ranked and balanced in a given application of the harm principle, an actually injurious condition should outweigh a mere change in a harmful direction.

5. LINES OF ATTACK ON MILL

Arguments against Mill's unsupplemented harm principle (his claim that the private and public harm principles state the *only* grounds for justified interference with liberty) have been mainly of two different kinds.[10] Many have argued that the harm principle justifies too much social and political interference in the affairs of individuals. Others allow that the prevention of individual and social harm is always a ground for interference, but insist that it is by no means the only ground.

(i) "No Man Is an Island"

Mill maintained in *On Liberty* that social interference is never justified in those of a man's affairs that concern himself only. But no man's affairs have effects on himself alone. There are a thousand subtle and indirect ways in which every individual act, no matter how private and solitary, affects others. It would therefore seem that society has a right, on Mill's own principles, to interfere in every department of human life. Mill anticipated this objection and took certain steps to disarm it. Let it be allowed that no human conduct is entirely, exclusively, and to the last degree self-regarding. Still, Mill insisted, we can distinguish between actions that are plainly other-regarding and those that are "directly," "chiefly," or "primarily" self-regarding. There will be a twilight area of cases difficult to classify, but that is true of many other workable distinctions, including that between night and day.

It is essential to Mill's theory that we make a distinction between two different kinds of consequences of human actions: the consequences *directly* affecting the interests of others, and those of primarily self-regarding behavior which only *indirectly* or *remotely* affect the interests of others. "No person ought to be punished simply for being drunk," Mill wrote, "but a soldier or policeman should be punished for being drunk on duty."[11] A drunk policeman directly harms the interests of others. His conduct gives opportunities to criminals and thus creates grave risk of harm to other citizens. It brings the police into disrepute, and makes the work of his colleagues more dangerous. Finally, it may lead to loss of the policeman's job, with serious consequences for his wife and children.

Consider, on the other hand, a hard working bachelor who habitually spends his evening hours drinking himself into a stupor, which he then sleeps off, rising fresh in the morning to put in another hard day's work. His drinking does not *directly* affect others in any of the ways of the drunk policeman's conduct. He has no family; he drinks alone and sets no direct example; he is not prevented from discharging any of his public duties; he creates no substantial risk of harm to the interests of other individuals. Although even his private conduct will have some effects on the interests of others, these are precisely the sorts of effects Mill would call "indirect" and "remote." First, in spending his evenings the way he does, our solitary tippler is *not* doing any number of other things that might be of greater utility to others. In not earning and spending more money, he is failing to stimulate the economy (except for the liquor industry) as much as he might. Second, he fails to spend his evening time improving his talents and making himself a better person. Perhaps he has a considerable native talent for painting or poetry, and his wastefulness is depriving the world of some valuable art. Third, he may make those of his colleagues who like him sad on his behalf. Finally, to those who know of his habits, he is a "bad example."[12] All of these "indirect harms" together, Mill maintained, do not outweigh the direct and serious harm that would result from social or legal coercion.

Mill's critics have never been entirely satisfied by this. Many have pointed out that Mill is concerned not only with political coercion and legal punishment but also with purely social coercion—moral pressure, social avoidance, ostracism. No responsible critic would wish the state to punish the solitary tippler, but social coercion is another matter. We can't prevent people from disapproving of an individual for his self-regarding faults or from expressing that disapproval to others, without undue restriction on *their* freedom. Such expressions, in Mill's view, are inevitably coercive, constituting a "milder form of punishment." Hence "social punishment" of individuals for conduct that directly concerns only themselves— the argument concludes—is both inevitable and, according to Mill's own principles, proper.

Mill anticipated this objection, too, and tried to cope with it by making a distinction between types of social responses. We cannot help but lower in our estimation a person with serious self-regarding faults. We will think ill of him, judge him to be at fault, and make him the inevitable and proper object of our disapproval, distaste, even contempt. We may warn others about him, avoid his company, and withhold gratuitous benefits from him— "not to the oppression of his individuality but in the exercise of ours."[13] Mill concedes that all of these social responses can function as "penalties"—but they are suffered "only insofar as they are the natural and, as it were, the spontaneous consequences of the faults themselves, not because they are purposely inflicted on him for the sake of punishment."[14] Other responses, on the other hand, add something to the "natural penalties"—pointed snubbing, economic reprisals, gossip campaigns, and so on. The added penalties, according to Mill, are precisely the ones that are never justified as responses to merely self-regarding flaws—"if he displeases us, we may express our distaste; and we may stand aloof from a person as well as from a thing that displeases us, but we shall not therefore feel called on to make his life uncomfortable."[15]

(ii) Other Proposed Grounds for Coercion

The distinction between self-regarding and other-regarding behavior, as Mill intended it to be understood, does seem at least roughly serviceable, and unlikely to invite massive social interference in private affairs. I think most critics of Mill would grant that, but reject the harm principle on the opposite ground that it doesn't permit enough interference. These writers would allow at least one, and as many as five or more, additional valid grounds for coercion. Each of these proposed grounds is stated in a principle listed below. One might hold that restriction of one person's liberty can be justified:

1. To prevent harm to others, either

    a. injury to individual persons *(The Private Harm Principle),* or

    b. impairment of institutional practices that are in the public interest *(The Public Harm Principle);*

2. To prevent offense to others *(The Offense Principle);*

3. To prevent harm to self *(Legal Paternalism);*

4. To prevent or punish sin, i.e., to "enforce morality as such" *(Legal Moralism);*

5. To benefit the self *(Extreme Paternalism);*

6. To benefit others *(The Welfare Principle).*

The liberty-limiting principles on this list are best understood as stating neither necessary nor sufficient conditions for justified coercion, but rather specifications of the *kinds* of reasons that are always relevant or acceptable in support of proposed coercion, even though in a given case they may not be conclusively. Each principle states that interference might be permissible *if* (but not *only if*) a certain condition is satisfied. Hence the principles are not mutually exclusive; it is possible to hold two or more of them at once, even all of them together, and it is possible to deny all of them. Moreover, the principles cannot be construed as stating sufficient conditions for legitimate interference with liberty, for even though the principle is satisfied in a given case, the general presumption against coercion might not be outweighed. The harm principle, for example, does not justify state interference to prevent a tiny bit of inconsequential harm. Prevention of minor harm always counts in favor of proposals (as in a legislature) to restrict liberty, but in a given instance it might not count *enough* to outweigh the general presumption against interference, or it might be outweighed by the prospect of practical difficulties in enforcing the law, excessive costs, and forfeitures of privacy. A liberty-limiting principle states considerations that are always good reasons for coercion, though neither exclusively nor, in every case, decisively good reasons.

It will not be possible to examine each principle in detail here, and offer "proofs" and "refutations." The best way to defend one's selection of principles is to show to which positions they commit one on such issues as censorship of literature, "morals offenses," and compulsory social security programs. General principles arise in the course of deliberations over particular problems, especially in the efforts to defend one's judgments by showing that they are consistent with what has gone before. If a principle commits one to an antecedently unacceptable judgment, then one has to modify or supplement the principle in a way that does the least damage to the harmony of one's particular and general opinions taken as a group. On the other hand, when a solid, well-entrenched principle entails a change in a particular judgment, the overriding claims of consistency may require that the judgment be adjusted. This sort of dialectic is similar to the reasonings that are prevalent in law courts. When similar cases are decided in opposite ways, it is incumbent on the court to distinguish them in some respect that will reconcile the separate decisions with each other and with the common rule applied to each. Every effort is made to render current decisions consistent with past ones unless the precedents seem so disruptive of the overall internal harmony of the law that they must, reluctantly, be revised or abandoned. In social and political philosophy every person is on his own, and the counterparts to "past decisions" are the most confident judgments one makes in ordinary normative discourse. The philosophical task is to extract from these "given" judgments the principles that render them consistent, adjusting and modifying where necessary in order to convert the whole body of opinions into an intelligible, coherent system. There is no a priori way of refuting another's political opinions, but if our opponents are rational men committed to the ideal of consistency, we can always hope to show them that a given judg-ment is inconsistent with one of their own acknowledged principles. Then some-thing will have to give.

NOTES

[1] James Fitzjames Stephen, *Liberty, Equality, Fraternity* (London: 1873), p. 48.

[2] See Edith Hamilton, *The Greek Way* (New York: W.W. Norton & Company, Inc., 1942), pp. 35 ff.

[3] John Stuart Mill, *On Liberty* (New York: Liberal Arts Press, 1956), p. 71.

[4] Jeremy Bentham, "Anarchical Fallacies," in *The Works of Jeremy Bentham*, Vol. 2, ed. John Bowring (Edinburgh, 1843).

[5] L. T. Hobhouse, *The Elements of Social Justice* (London: George Allen & Unwin Ltd., 1922), p. 60. Hobhouse rejects this formula, and I have adapted his argu-ment against it in the text.

[6] L. T. Hobhouse, *Liberalism* (New York: Holt, Rinehart and Winston, Inc. 1911), pp. 63–64.

[7] *Restatement of the Law of Torts* (St. Paul: American Law Institute, 1939), p. 1.

[8] Cf. Stephen, *Liberty, Equality, Fraternity*, p. 16.

[9] See, for example, James Barr Ames, "Law and Morals," *Harvard Law Review*, XXII (1908), pp. 97–113, and Lord Macaulay, "Notes on the Indian Penal Code," *Works* (London: Longmans, Green & Co. Ltd., 1866), Vol. VII, p. 497.

[10] Cf. H. L. A. Hart, *Law, Liberty, And Morality* (Stanford: Stanford University Press, 1963), p. 5.

[11] Mill, *On Liberty*, pp. 99–100.

[12] Mill has a ready rejoinder to this last point: If the conduct in question is supposed to be greatly harmful to the actor himself, "the example, on the whole must be more salutory" than harmful socially, since it is a warning lesson, rather than an allur-ing model, to others. See Mill, *On Liberty*, p. 101.

[13] Mill, *On Liberty*, p. 94.

[14] Mill, *On Liberty*, p. 95.

[15] Mill, *On Liberty*, p. 96.

Hard Cases for the Harm Principle

Joel Feinberg

1. MORALS OFFENSES AND LEGAL MORALISM

Immoral conduct is no trivial thing, and we should hardly expect societies to tolerate it; yet if men are *forced* to refrain from immorality, their own choices will play very little role in what they do, so that they can hardly develop critical judgment and moral traits of a genuinely praiseworthy kind. Thus legal enforcement of morality seems to pose a dilemma. The problem does not arise if we assume that all immoral conduct is socially harmful, for immoral conduct will then be prohibited by law not just to punish sin or to "force men to be moral," but rather to prevent harm to others. If, however, there are forms of immorality that do not necessarily cause harm, "the problem of the enforcement of morality" becomes especially acute.

The central problem cases are those criminal actions generally called "morals offenses." Offenses against morality and decency have long constituted a category of crimes (as distinct from offenses against the person, offenses against property, and so on). These have included mainly sex offenses, such as adultery, fornication, sodomy, incest, and prostitution, but also a miscellany of nonsexual offenses, including cruelty to animals, desecration of the flag or other venerated symbols, and mistreatment of corpses. In a useful article,[1] Louis B. Schwartz maintains that what sets these crimes off as a class is not their special relation to morality (murder is also an offense against morality, but it is not a "morals offense") but the lack of an essential connection between them and social harm. In particular, their suppression is not required by the public security. Some morals offenses may harm the perpetrators themselves, but the risk of harm of this sort has usually been consented to in advance by the actors. Offense to other parties, when it occurs, is usually a consequence of perpetration of the offenses *in public*, and can be prevented by statutes against "open lewdness," or "solicitation" in public places. That still leaves "morals offenses" committed by consenting adults in private. Should they really be crimes?

In addition to the general presumption against coercion, other arguments against legislation prohibiting private and harmless sexual practices are drawn from the harm principle itself; laws governing private affairs are extremely awkward and expensive to enforce, and have side effects that are invariably harmful. Laws against homosexuality, for example, can only be occasionally and randomly enforced, and this leads to the inequities of selective enforcement and opportunities for blackmail and private vengeance. Moreover, "the pursuit of homosexuals involves policemen in degrading entrapment practices, and diverts attention and effort"[2] from more serious (harmful) crimes of aggression, fraud, and corruption.

These considerations have led some to argue against statutes that prohibit private immorality, but, not surprisingly, it has encouraged others to abandon their exclusive reliance on the harm and/or offense principles, at least in the case of morals offenses. The alternative principle of "legal moralism" has several forms. In its more moderate version it is commonly associated with the views of Patrick Devlin,[3] whose theory, as I understand it, is really an application of the public harm principle. The proper aim of criminal law, he agrees, is the prevention of harm, not merely to individuals, but also (and primarily) to society itself. A shared moral code, Devlin argues, is a necessary condition for the very existence of a community. Shared moral convictions function as "invisible bonds" tying individuals together into an orderly society. Moreover, the fundamental unifying morality (to switch the metaphor) is a kind of "seamless web";[4] to damage it at one point is to weaken it throughout. Hence, society has as much right to protect its moral code by legal coercion as it does to protect its equally indispensable political institutions. The law cannot tolerate politically revolutionary activity, nor can it accept activity that rips assunder its moral fabric. "The suppression of vice is as much the law's business as the suppression of subversive activities; it is no more possible to define a sphere of private morality than it is to define one of private subversive activity."[5]

H.L.A. Hart finds it plausible that some shared morality is necessary to the existence of a community, but criticizes Devlin's further contention "that a society is identical with its morality as that is at any given moment of its history, so that a change in its morality is tantamount to the destruction of a society."[6] Indeed, a moral critic might admit that we can't exist as a society without some morality, while insisting that we can perfectly well exist without *this* morality (if we put a better one in its place). Devlin seems to reply that the shared morality *can* be changed even though protected by law, and, when it does change, the emergent reformed morality in turn deserves *its* legal protection.[7] The law then functions to make moral reform difficult, but there is no preventing change where reforming zeal is fierce enough. How does one bring about a change in prevailing moral beliefs when they are enshrined in law? Presumably by advocating conduct which is in fact illegal, by putting into public practice what one preaches, and by demonstrating one's sincerity by marching proudly off to jail for one's convictions:

> there is . . . a natural respect for opinions that are sincerely held. When such opinions accumulate enough weight, the law must either yield or it is broken. In a democratic society . . . there will be a strong tendency for it to yield—not to abandon all defenses so as to let in the horde, but to give ground to those who are prepared to fight for something that they prize. To fight may be to suffer. A

willingness to suffer is the most convincing proof of sincerity. Without the law there would be no proof. The law is the anvil on which the hammer strikes.[8]

In this remarkable passage, Devlin has discovered another argument for enforcing "morality as such," and incidentally for principled civil disobedience as the main technique for initiating and regulating moral change. A similar argument, deriving from Samuel Johnson and applying mainly to changes in religious doctrine, was well known to Mill. According to this theory, religious innovators deserve to be persecuted, for persecution allows them to prove their mettle and demonstrate their disinterested good faith, while their teachings, insofar as they are true, cannot be hurt, since truth will always triumph in the end. Mill held this method of testing truth, whether in science, religion, or morality, to be both uneconomical and ungenerous.[9] But if self-sacrificing civil disobedience is *not* the most efficient and humane remedy for the moral reformer, what instruments of moral change are available to him? This question is not only difficult to answer in its own right, it is also the rock that sinks Devlin's favorite analogy between "harmless" immorality and political subversion.

Consider the nature of subversion. Most modern law-governed countries have a constitution, a set of duly constituted authorities, and a body of statutes created and enforced by these authorities. The ways of changing these things will be well known, orderly, and permitted by the constitution. For example, constitutions are amended, legislators are elected, and new legislation is introduced. On the other hand, it is easy to conceive of various sorts of unpermitted and disorderly change—through assassination and violent revolution, or bribery and subornation, or the use of legitimately won power to extort and intimidate. Only these illegitimate methods of change can be called "subversion." But here the analogy between positive law and positive morality begins to break down. There is no "moral constitution," no well-known and orderly way of introducing moral legislation to duly constituted moral legislators, no clear convention of majority rule. Moral subversion, if there is such a thing, must consist in the employment of disallowed techniques of change instead of the officially permitted "constitutional" ones. It consists not simply of change as such, but of illegitimate change. Insofar as the notion of legitimately induced moral change remains obscure, illegitimate moral change is no better. Still, there is enough content to both notions to preserve some analogy to the political case. A citizen works *legitimately* to change public moral beliefs when he openly and forthrightly expresses his own dissent, when he attempts to argue, persuade, and offer reasons, and when he lives according to his own convictions with persuasive quiet and dignity, neither harming others nor offering counterpersuasive offense to tender sensibilities. A citizen attempts to change mores by *illegitimate* means when he abandons argument and example for force and fraud. If this is the basis of the distinction between legitimate and illegitimate techniques of moral change, then the use of state power to affect moral belief *one way or the other*, when harmfulness is not involved, is a clear example of illegitimacy. Government enforcement of the conventional code is not to be called "moral subversion," of course, because it is used on behalf of the status quo; but whether conservative or innovative, it is equally in defiance of our "moral constitution" (if anything is).

The second version of legal moralism is the pure version, not some other principle in disguise. Enforcement of morality as such and the attendant punishment of sin are not justified as means to some further social aim (such as preservation of social cohesiveness) but are ends in themselves. Perhaps J. F. Stephen was expressing this pure moralism when he wrote that "there are acts of wickedness so gross and outrageous that . . . [protection of others apart], they must be prevented at any cost to the offender and punished if they occur with exemplary severity."[10] From his examples it is clear that Stephen had in mind the very acts that are called "morals offenses" in the law.

It is sometimes said in support of pure legal moralism that the world as a whole would be a better place without morally ugly, even "harmlessly immoral," conduct, and that our actual universe is intrinsically worse for having such conduct in it. The threat of punishment, the argument continues, deters such conduct. Actual instances of punishment not only back up the threat, and thus help keep future moral weeds out of the universe's garden, they also erase past evils from the universe's temporal record by "nullifying" them, or making it as if they never were. Thus punishment, it is said, contributes to the intrinsic value of the universe in two ways: by canceling out past sins and preventing future ones.[11]

There is some plausibility in this view when it is applied to ordinary harmful crimes, especially those involving duplicity or cruelty, which really do seem to "set the universe out of joint." It is natural enough to think of repentance, apology, or forgiveness as "setting things straight," and of punishment as a kind of "payment" or a wiping clean of the moral slate. But in cases where it is natural to resort to such analogies, there is not only a rule infraction, there is also a victim— some person or society of persons who have been harmed. Where there is no *victim*—and especially where there is no profit at the expense of another—"setting things straight" has no clear intuitive content.

Punishment may yet play its role in discouraging harmless private immoralities for the sake of "the universe's moral record." But if fear of punishment is to keep people from illicit intercourse (or from desecrating flags, or mistreating corpses) in the privacy of their own rooms, then morality shall have to be enforced with a fearsome efficiency that shows no respect for individual privacy. If private immoralities are to be deterred by threat of punishment, the detecting authorities must be able to look into the hidden chambers and locked rooms of anyone's private domicile. When we put this massive forfeiture of privacy into the balance along with the usual costs of coercion—loss of spontaneity, stunting of rational powers, anxiety, hypocrisy, and the rest—the price of securing mere outward conformity to the community's moral standards (for that is all that can be achieved by the penal law) is exorbitant.

Perhaps the most interesting of the nonsexual morals offenses, and the most challenging case for application of liberty-limiting principles, is cruelty to animals. Suppose that John Doe is an intelligent, sensitive person with one very severe neurotic trait—he loves to see living things suffer pain. Fortunately, he never has occasion to torture human beings (he would genuinely regret that), for he can always find an animal for the purpose. For a period he locks himself in his room every night, draws the blind, and then beats and tortures a dog to death. The sounds of shrieks and moans, which are music to his ears, are nuisances to his neighbors, and when his landlady discovers what he has been doing she is so shocked she has to be hospitalized. Distressed that he has caused harm to human beings, Doe leaves the rooming house, buys a five hundred acre ranch, and moves into a house in the remote, unpopulated center of his own property. There, in the perfect privacy of his own home, he spends every evening maiming, torturing, and beating to death his own animals.

What are we to say of Doe's bizarre behavior? We have three alternatives. First we can say that it is perfectly permissible since it consists simply in a man's destruction of his own property. How a man disposes in private of his own property is no concern of anyone else providing he causes no nuisance such as loud noises and evil smells. Second, we can say that this behavior is patently immoral even though it causes no harm to the interests of anyone other than the actor; further, since it obviously should *not* be permitted by the law, this is a case where the harm principle is inadequate and must be supplemented by legal moralism. Third, we can extend the harm principle to animals, and argue that the law can interfere with the private enjoyment of property not to enforce "morality as such," but rather to prevent harm to the animals. The third alternative is the most inviting, but not without its difficulties. We *must* control animal movements, exploit animal labor, and, in many cases, deliberately slaughter animals. All these forms of treatment would be "harm" if inflicted on human beings, but cannot be allowed to count as harm to animals if the harm principle is to be extended to them in a realistic way. The best compromise is to recognize one supreme interest of animals, namely the interest in freedom from cruelly or wantonly inflicted pain, and to count as "harm" all and only invasions of *that* interest.

2. OBSCENITY AND THE OFFENSE PRINCIPLE

Up to this point we have considered the harm and offense principles together in order to determine whether between them they are sufficient to regulate conventional immoralities, or whether they need help from a further independent principle, legal moralism. Morals offenses were treated as essentially private so that the offense principle could not be stretched to apply to them. Obscene literature and pornographic displays would appear to be quite different in this respect. Both are materials deliberately published for the eyes of others, and their existence can bring partisans of the unsupplemented harm principle into direct conflict with those who endorse *both* the harm and offense principles.

In its untechnical, prelegal sense, the word "obscenity" refers to material dealing with nudity, sex, or excretion in an offensive manner. Such material becomes obscene in the legal sense when, because of its offensiveness or for some other reason [this question had best be left open in the definition], it is or ought to be without legal protection. The legal definition then incorporates the everyday sense, and essential to both is the requirement that the material be *offensive*. An item may offend one person and not another. "Obscenity," if it is to avoid this subjective relativity, must involve an interpersonal objective sense of "offensive." Material must be offensive by prevailing community standards that are public and well known, or be such that it is apt to offend virtually everyone.

Not all material that is generally offensive need also be harmful in any sense recognized by the harm principle. It is partly an empirical question whether reading or witnessing obscene material causes social harm; reliable evidence, even of a statistical kind, of causal connections between obscenity and antisocial behavior

313

is extremely hard to find.[12] In the absence of clear and decisive evidence of harmfulness, the American Civil Liberties Union insists that the offensiveness of obscene material cannot be a sufficient ground for its repression:

> . . . the question in a case involving obscenity, just as in every case involving an attempted restriction upon free speech, is whether the words or pictures are used in such circumstances and are of such a nature as to create a clear and present danger that they will bring about a substantial evil that the state has a right to prevent. . . . We believe that under the current state of knowledge, there is grossly insufficient evidence to show that obscenity brings about *any* substantive evil.[13]

The A.C.L.U. argument employs *only* the harm principle among liberty-limiting principles, and treats literature, drama, and painting as forms of expression subject to the same rules as expressions of opinion. In respect to both types of expression, "every act of deciding what should be barred carries with it a danger to the community."[14] The suppression itself is an evil to the author who is squelched. The power to censor and punish involves risks that socially valuable material will be repressed along with the "filth." The overall effect of suppression, the A.C.L.U. concludes, is almost certainly to discourage nonconformist and eccentric expression generally. In order to override these serious risks, there must be in a given case an even more clear and present danger that the obscene material, if not squelched, will cause even greater harm; such countervailing evidence is never forthcoming. (If such evidence were to accumulate, the A.C.L.U. would be perfectly willing to change its position on obscenity.)

The A.C.L.U. stand on obscenity seems clearly to be the position dictated by the unsupplemented harm principle and its corollary, the clear and present danger test. Is there any reason at this point to introduce the offense principle into the discussion? Unhappily, we may be forced to if we are to do justice to all of our particular intuitions in the most harmonious way. Consider an example suggested by Professor Schwartz. By the provisions of the new Model Penal Code, he writes, "a rich homosexual may not use a billboard on Times Square to promulgate to the general populace the techniques and pleasures of sodomy."[15] If the notion of "harm" is restricted to its narrow sense, that is, contrasted with "offense," it will be hard to reconstruct a rationale for this prohibition based on the harm principle. There is unlikely to be evidence that a lurid and obscene public poster in Times Square would create a clear and present danger of injury to those who fail to avert their eyes in time as they come blinking out of the subway stations. Yet it will be surpassingly difficult for even the most dedicated liberal to advocate freedom of expression in a case of this kind. Hence, if we are to justify coercion in this case, we will likely be driven, however reluctantly, to the offense principle.

There is good reason to be "reluctant" to embrace the offense principle until driven to it by an example like the above. People take perfectly genuine offense at many socially useful or harmless activities, from commercial advertisements to inane chatter. Moreover, widespread irrational prejudices can lead people to be disgusted, shocked, even morally repelled by perfectly innocent activities, and we should be loath to permit their groundless repugnance to override the innocence. The offense principle, therefore, must be formulated very precisely and applied in accordance with carefully formulated standards so as not to open the door to wholesale and intuitively unwarranted repression. At the very least we should require that the prohibited conduct or material be of the sort apt to offend almost everybody, and not just some shifting majority or special interest group.

It is instructive to note that a strictly drawn offense principle would not only justify prohibition of conduct and pictured conduct that is in its inherent character repellent, but also conduct and pictured conduct that is inoffensive in itself but offensive in inappropriate circumstances. I have in mind so-called indecencies such as public nudity. One can imagine an advocate of the unsupplemented harm principle arguing against the public nudity prohibition on the grounds that the sight of a naked body does no one any harm, and the state has no right to impose standards of dress or undress on private citizens. How one chooses to dress, after all, is a form of self-expression. If we do not permit the state to bar clashing colors or bizarre hair styles, by what right does it prohibit total undress? Perhaps the sight of naked people could at first lead to riots or other forms of antisocial behavior, but that is precisely the sort of contingency for which we have police. If we don't take away a person's right of free speech for the reason that its exercise may lead others to misbehave, we cannot in consistency deny his right to dress or undress as he chooses for the same reason.

There may be no answering this challenge on its own ground, but the offense principle provides a ready rationale for the nudity prohibition. The sight of nude bodies in public places is for almost everyone acutely *embarrassing*. Part of the explanation no doubt rests on the fact that nudity has an irresistible power to draw the eye and focus the thoughts on matters that are normally repressed. The conflict between these attracting and repressing forces is exciting, upsetting, and anxiety-producing. In some persons it will create at best a kind of painful turmoil, and at worst that experience of exposure to oneself of "peculiarly sensitive, intimate, vulnerable aspects of the self"[16] which is called *shame*. "One's feeling is involuntarily exposed openly in one's face; one is uncovered . . . taken by surprise . . . made a fool of."[17] The result is not mere "offense," but a kind of psychic jolt that in many normal people can be a painful wound. Even those of us who are better able to control our feelings might well resent the nuisance of having to do so.

If we are to accept the offense principle as a supplement to the harm principle, we must accept two corollaries which stand in relation to it similarly to the way in which the clear and present danger test stands to the harm principle. The first, the *standard of universality*, has already been touched upon. For the offensiveness (disgust, embarrassment, outraged sensibilities, or shame) to be sufficient to warrant coercion, it should be the reaction that could be expected from almost any person chosen at random from the nation as a whole, regardless of sect, faction, race, age, or sex. The second is the *standard of reasonable avoidability*. No one has a right to protection from the state against offensive experiences if he can effectively avoid those experiences with no unreasonable effort or inconvenience. If a nude person enters a public bus and takes a seat near the front, there may be no effective way for other patrons to avoid intensely shameful embarrassment (or other insupportable feelings) short of leaving the bus, which would be an unreasonable inconvenience. Similarly, obscene remarks over a loudspeaker, homosexual billboards in Times Square, and pornographic handbills thrust into the hands of passing pedestrians all fail to be reasonably avoidable.

On the other hand, the offense principle, properly qualified, can give no warrant to the suppression of *books* on the grounds of obscenity. When printed words hide decorously behind covers of books sitting passively on bookstore shelves, their offensiveness is easily avoided. The contrary view is no doubt encouraged by the common comparison of obscenity with "smut," "filth," or "dirt." This in turn suggests an analogy to nuisance law, which governs cases where certain activities create loud noises or terrible odors offensive to neighbors, and "the courts must weigh the gravity of the nuisance [substitute "offense"] to the neighbors against the social utility [substitute "redeeming social value"] of the defendant's conduct."[18] There is, however, one vitiating disanalogy in this comparison. In the case of "dirty books" the offense is easily avoidable. There is nothing like the evil smell of rancid garbage oozing right out through the covers of a book. When an "obscene" book sits on a shelf, who is there to be offended? Those who want to read it for the sake of erotic stimulation presumably will not be offended (or else they wouldn't read it), and those who choose not to read it will have no experience by which to be offended. If its covers are too decorous, some innocents may browse through it by mistake and be offended by what they find, but they need only close the book to escape the offense. Even this offense, minimal as it is, could be completely avoided by prior consultation of trusted book reviewers. I conclude that there are no sufficient grounds derived either from the harm or offense principles for suppressing obscene literature, unless that ground be the protection of children; but I can think of no reason why restrictions on sales to children cannot work as well for printed materials as they do for cigarettes and whiskey.

3. LEGAL PATERNALISM*

The liberty-limiting principle called legal paternalism justifies state coercion to protect individuals from self-inflicted harm, or, in its extreme version, to guide them, whether they like it or not, toward their own good. Parents can be expected to justify interference in the lives of their children (e.g., telling them what they must eat and when they must sleep) on the ground that "daddy knows best." Legal paternalism seems to imply that, since the state often perceives the interests of individual citizens better than do the citizens themselves, it stands as a permanent guardian of those interests *in loco parentis*. Put this bluntly, paternalism seems a preposterous doctrine. If adults are treated as children they will come in time to be like children. Deprived of the right to choose for themselves, they will soon lose the power of rational judgment and decision. Even children, after a certain point, had better not be "treated as children," or they will never acquire the outlook and capability of responsible adults.

Yet if we reject paternalism entirely, and deny that a person's own good is ever a valid ground for coercing him, we seem to fly in the face both of common sense and long-established customs and laws. In the criminal law, for example, a prospective victim's freely granted consent is no defense to the charge of mayhem or homicide. The state simply refuses to permit anyone to agree to his own disablement or killing. The law of contracts similarly refuses to recognize as valid contracts to sell oneself into slavery, or to become a mistress, or a second wife. Any ordinary citizen is legally justified in using reasonable force to prevent another from mutilating himself or committing suicide. No one is allowed to purchase certain

316

drugs even for therapeutic purposes without a physician's prescription (doctor knows best). The use of other drugs, such as heroin, for mere pleasure is not permitted under any circumstances. It is hard to find any convincing rationale for all such restrictions apart from the argument that beatings, mutilations, death, concubinage, slavery, and bigamy are always bad for a person whether he or she knows it or not, and that antibiotics are too dangerous for any nonexpert, and narcotics for anyone at all, to take on his own initiative.

The trick is stopping short once one undertakes this path, unless we wish to ban whiskey, cigarettes, and fried foods, which tend to be bad for people, too. We must somehow reconcile our general repugnance for paternalism with the apparent necessity, or at least reasonableness, of some paternalistic regulations. The way to do this is to find mediating maxims or standards of application for the paternalistic principle which restrict its use in a way analogous to that in which the universality and reasonable avoidance tests delimit the offense principle. Let us begin by rejecting the views that the protection of a person from himself is *always* a valid ground for interference and that it is *never* a valid ground. It follows that it is a valid ground only under certain conditions, which we must now try to state.

It will be useful to make some preliminary distinctions. The first is between those cases in which a person directly produces harm to himself (where the harm is the certain and desired end of his conduct), and those cases in which a person simply creates a risk of harm to himself in the course of activities directed toward other ends. The man who knowingly swallows a lethal dose of arsenic will certainly die, and death must be imputed as his goal. Another man is offended by the sight of his left hand, so he grasps an ax in his right hand and chops his left hand off. He does not thereby "endanger" his interest in the physical integrity of his limbs, or "risk" the loss of his hand; he brings about the loss directly and deliberately. On the other hand, to smoke cigarettes or to drive at excessive speeds is not to harm oneself directly, but rather to increase beyond a normal level the probability that harm to oneself will result.

The second distinction is that between reasonable and unreasonable risks. There is no form of activity (or inactivity, for that matter) that does not involve some risks. On some occasions we have a choice between more and less risky actions, and prudence dictates that we take the less risky course. However, what is called "prudence" is not always reasonable. Sometimes it is more reasonable to assume a great risk for a great gain than to play it safe and forfeit a unique opportunity. Thus, it is not necessarily more reasonable for a coronary patient to increase his life expectancy by living a life of quiet inactivity than to continue working hard at his career in the hope of achieving something important, even at the risk of a sudden fatal heart attack. Although there is no simple mathematical formula to guide one in making such decisions or for judging them "reasonable" or "unreasonable," there are some decisions that are manifestly unreasonable. It is unreasonable to drive at sixty miles an hour through a twenty mile an hour zone in order to arrive at a party on time, but it may be reasonable to drive fifty miles an hour to get a pregnant wife to the maternity ward. It is foolish to resist an armed robber in an effort to protect one's wallet, but it may be worth a desperate lunge to protect one's very life.

All of these cases involve a number of distinct considerations. If there is time to deliberate one should consider: (1) the degree of probability that harm to oneself will result from a given course of action, (2) the seriousness of the harm being risked, i.e., "the value or importance of that which is exposed to the risk," (3) the degree of probability that the goal inclining one to shoulder the risk will in fact result from the course of action, (4) the value or importance of achieving that goal, that is, just how worthwhile it is to one (this is the intimately personal factor, requiring a decision about one's own preferences, that makes it so difficult for the outsider to judge the reasonableness of a risk), and (5) the necessity of the risk, that is, the availability or absence of alternative, less risky, means to the desired goal.[19]

Certain judgments about the reasonableness of risk assumptions are quite uncontroversial. We can say, for example, that the greater are considerations 1 and 2, the less reasonable the risk, and the greater are considerations 3, 4, and 5, the more reasonable the risk. But in a given difficult case, even where questions of "probability" are meaningful and beyond dispute, and where all the relevant facts are known, the risk decision may defy objective assessment because of its component personal value judgments. In any case, if the state is to be given the right to prevent a person from risking harm to himself (and only himself), it must not be on the ground that the prohibited action is risky, or even extremely risky, but rather that the risk is extreme and, in respect to its objectively assessable components, manifestly unreasonable. There are sometimes very good reasons for regarding even a person's judgment of personal worthwhileness (consideration 4) to be "manifestly unreasonable," but it remains to be seen whether (or when) that kind of unreasonableness can be sufficient grounds for interference.

The third and final distinction is between fully voluntary and not fully voluntary assumptions of a risk. One assumes a risk in a fully voluntary way when one shoulders it while informed of all relevant facts and contingencies, and in the absence of all coercive pressure or compulsion. To whatever extent there is neurotic compulsion, misinformation, excitement or impetuousness, clouded judgment (as, e.g., from alcohol), or immature or defective faculties of reasoning, the choice falls short of perfect voluntariness.[20] Voluntariness, then, is a matter of degree. One's "choice" is *completely involuntary* when it is no choice at all, properly speaking—when one lacks all muscular control of one's movements, or is knocked down or sent reeling by a blow or an explosion—or when, through ignorance, one chooses something other than what one means to choose, as when one thinks the arsenic powder is table salt and sprinkles it on one's scrambled eggs. Most harmful choices, as most choices generally, fall somewhere between the extremes of perfect voluntariness and complete involuntariness.

The central thesis of Mill and other individualists about paternalism is that the fully voluntary choice or consent (to another's doing) of a mature and rational human being concerning matters that directly affect only his own interests is so precious that no one else (especially the state) has a right to interfere with it simply for the person's "own good." No doubt this thesis was also meant to apply to almost-but-not-quite fully voluntary choices as well, and probably even to some substantially nonvoluntary ones (e.g., a neurotic person's choice of a wife who will satisfy his neurotic needs, but only at the price of great unhappiness, eventual divorce, and exacerbated guilt). However, it is not probable that the individualist thesis was meant to apply to choices near the bottom of the voluntariness scale, and Mill himself left no doubt that he did not intend it to apply to completely involuntary "choices." Neither should we expect antipaternalistic individualism to deny protection to a person from his own nonvoluntary choices, for insofar as the choices are not voluntary they are just as alien to him as the choices of someone else.

Thus Mill would permit the state to protect a man from his own ignorance, at least in circumstances that create a strong presumption that his uninformed or misinformed choice would not correspond to his eventual enlightened one.

> If either a public officer or anyone else saw a person attempting to cross a bridge which had been ascertained to be unsafe, and there were no time to warn him of his danger, they might seize him and turn him back, without any real infringement of his liberty; for liberty consists in doing what one desires, and he does not desire to fall into the river.[21]

Of course, for all the public officer may know, the man on the bridge does desire to fall into the river, or to take the risk of falling for other purposes. Then, Mill argues, if the person is fully warned of the danger and wishes to proceed anyway, that is his business alone, despite the advance presumption that most people do not wish to run such risks. Hence the officer was justified, Mill would argue, in his original interference.

On other occasions a person may need to be protected from some other condition that may render his informed choice substantially less than voluntary. He may be "a child, or delirious, or in some state of excitement or absorption incompatible with the full use of the reflecting faculty."[22] Mill would not permit any such person to cross an objectively unsafe bridge. On the other hand, there is no reason why a child, or an excited person, or a drunkard, or a mentally ill person should not be allowed to proceed on his way home across a perfectly safe thoroughfare. Even substantially nonvoluntary choices deserve protection unless there is good reason to judge them dangerous.

For all we can know, the behavior of a drunk or an emotionally upset person would be exactly the same even if he were sober and calm. But when the behavior seems patently self-damaging and is of a sort in which most calm and normal persons would not engage, then there are strong grounds, if only of a statistical sort, for inferring the opposite; these grounds, on Mill's principle, would justify interference. It may be that there is no kind of action of which it can be said, "No mentally competent adult in a calm, attentive mood, fully informed, and so on, would ever choose (or consent to) that." Nevertheless, there are some actions that create a powerful presumption that an actor in his right mind would not choose them. The point of calling this hypothesis a "presumption" is to require that it be completely overridden before legal permission be given to a person who has already been interfered with to go on as before. For example, if a policeman (or anyone else) sees John Doe about to chop off his hand with an ax, he is perfectly justified in using force to prevent him, because of the presumption that no one could voluntarily choose to do such a thing. The presumption, however, should always be taken as rebuttable in principle; it will be up to Doe to prove before an official tribunal that he is calm, competent, and free, and still wishes to chop off his hand. Perhaps this is too great a burden to expect Doe himself to "prove," but the tribunal should require that the presumption against voluntariness be overturned by evidence from some source or other. The existence of the presumption should require that an objective determination be made, whether by the usual adversary procedures of law courts, or simply by a collective investigation by the tribunal into the available facts. The greater the presumption to be overridden, the more elaborate and fastidious should be the legal paraphernalia required, and the stricter the standards of evidence. The point of the procedure would not be to evaluate the wisdom or worthiness of a person's choice, but rather to determine whether the choice really is his.

This seems to lead us to a form of paternalism so weak and innocuous that it could be accepted even by Mill, namely, that the state has the right to prevent self-regarding harmful conduct only when it is substantially nonvoluntary, or when temporary intervention is necessary to establish whether it is voluntary or not. A strong presumption that no normal person would voluntarily choose or consent to the kind of conduct in question should be a proper ground for detaining the person until the voluntary character of his choice can be established. We can use the phrase "the standard of voluntariness" as a label for considerations that mediate application of the principle that a person can be protected from his own folly.

Consider a typical hard case for the application of the voluntariness standard, the problem of harmful drugs. Suppose that Richard Roe requests a prescription of drug X from Dr. Doe, and the following discussion ensues:

> DR. DOE: I cannot prescribe drug X to you because it will do you physical harm.

> MR. ROE: But you are mistaken. It will not cause me physical harm.

In a case like this, the state, of course, backs the doctor, since it deems medical questions to be technical matters subject to expert opinions. If a layman disagrees with a physician on a question of medical fact, the layman is presumed wrong, and if he nevertheless chooses to act on his factually mistaken belief, his action will be substantially less than fully voluntary. That is, the action of *ingesting a substance which will in fact harm him* is not the action he voluntarily chooses to do (because he does not believe that it is harmful). Hence the state intervenes to protect him not from his own free and voluntary choices, but from his own ignorance.

Suppose however that the exchange goes as follows:

> DR. DOE: I cannot prescribe drug X to you because it will do you physical harm.

> MR. ROE: Exactly. That's just what I want. I want to harm myself.

In this case Roe is properly apprised of the facts; he suffers from no delusions or misconceptions. Yet his choice is so odd that there exists a reasonable presumption that he has been deprived of the "full use of his reflecting faculty." It is because we know that the overwhelming majority of choices to inflict injury for its own sake on oneself are not fully voluntary that we are entitled to presume that the present choice is not fully voluntary. If no further evidence of derangement, illness, severe depression, or unsettling excitation can be discovered, however, and the patient can convince an objective panel that his choice is voluntary (unlikely event!), then our "voluntariness standard" would permit no further state constraint.

Now consider the third possibility:

DR. DOE: I cannot prescribe drug X to you because it is very likely to do you physical harm.

MR. ROE: I don't care if it causes me physical harm. I'll get a lot of pleasure first, so much pleasure, in fact, that it is well worth running the risk of physical harm. If I must pay a price for my pleasure I am willing to do so.

This is perhaps the most troublesome case. Roe's choice is not patently irrational on its face. A well thought-out philosophical hedonism may be one of his profoundest convictions, involving a fundamental decision of principle to commit himself to the intensely pleasurable, even if brief, life. If no third-party interests are directly involved, the state can hardly be permitted to declare his philosophical convictions unsound or "sick" and prevent him from practicing them, without assuming powers that it will inevitably misuse.

On the other hand, this case may be quite similar to the preceding one, depending on what the exact facts are. If the drug is known to give only an hour's mild euphoria and then cause an immediate, violently painful death, then the risks appear so unreasonable as to create a powerful presumption of nonvoluntariness. The desire to commit suicide must always be presumed to be both nonvoluntary and harmful to others until shown otherwise. (Of course, in some cases it can be shown otherwise.) Alternatively, drug X may be harmful in the way nicotine is now known to be harmful; twenty or thirty years of heavy use may create a grave risk of lung cancer or heart disease. Using the drug for pleasure when the risks are of this kind may be to run unreasonable risks, but that is no strong evidence of nonvoluntariness. Many perfectly normal, rational persons voluntarily choose to run precisely these risks for whatever pleasures they find in smoking. To assure itself that such practices are truly voluntary, the state should continually confront smokers with the ugly medical facts so that there is no escaping the knowledge of the exact medical risks to health. Constant reminders of the hazards should be at every hand, with no softening of the gory details. The state might even be justified in using its taxing, regulatory, and persuasive powers to make smoking (and similar drug usage) more difficult or less attractive; but to prohibit it outright would be to tell the voluntary risk-taker that his informed judgments of what is worthwhile are less reasonable than those of the state, and therefore he may not act on them. This is paternalism of the strong kind, unmediated by the voluntariness standard. As a principle of public policy it has an acrid moral flavor, and creates serious risks of governmental tyranny.

4. COLLECTIVE GOODS AND COLLECTIVE ACTION

Despite the presumptive case for liberty, there seem to be numerous examples in which the modern state has no choice but to force (usually by compulsory taxation) both willing and unwilling citizens to support public projects that are clearly in the public interest. In many of these cases those who do not benefit directly from a public service are made to pay as much in its support as those who do, or even more. Thus nondrivers are taxed to support highways and nonparents to support schools. This has the appearance of injustice, and the justification of unhappy necessity. Often the alternative to mandatory taxation—a system of purely voluntary support requiring only users to pay fees—is subject to a fatal defect that forces us to choose between universal compulsory support for the public facility or no facility at all.

Consider, for example, public municipal parks. Suppose the town of Metropolis decides to create a large public park with gardens, woods, trails, and playgrounds. John Doe appreciates living in an attractive community but has no direct personal need for such a park, since he already has a ten acre yard with gardens, picnic tables, tennis courts, and the like. Why, he asks, should he be forced to support something he doesn't need and doesn't want strongly enough to pay for? Suppose, however, that the city charges only those who wish to use the park, and that this group constitutes 90 percent of the population. The richest 10 percent opt out, thus raising the average costs to the remainder. That rise, in turn, forces some of the 90 percent to withdraw, thus raising the cost to the others, forcing still more to drop out, and so on. This process will continue until either a very expensive equilibrium is reached, or, what is more likely, the whole project collapses (as in the case of some voluntary public medical and insurance plans).

It is avoidance of this characteristic escalation effect, rather than paternalism, that provides the rationale for compulsory social security and medicare programs. Here it is important to apply the various principles of liberty distribution not to individual cases, such as the compulsory taxation of John Doe, but to rules and general financing schemes. Compulsory rather than voluntary schemes are justified when the social good in question cannot be secured in any other way. Whether compulsion on this ground accords with the harm principle depends on whether loss of the good would be classified as a social harm or the mere withholding of a benefit. Where the good is security, medical care, or education, there is little doubt that its loss would properly be called a "harm" to those who incur it.

In cases of the sort we have been considering, some people who don't want a given public service are forced to pay for it because there is no other practical way of supporting it, and its loss would be a harm to those who do want it. In a more interesting and troublesome kind of case, *all* of the members of a community or group want some good which is in fact in the interests of each individual equally, and yet it is in no individual's interest to contribute toward the goal unless all are *made* to do so. This paradoxical state of affairs has attracted considerable attention from economists who have noticed its similarity to the condition of a company in an industry that enjoys "perfect competition." So long as the price of a manufactured product on the free market exceeds the marginal cost of production, it will be in the interest of each company to increase its output and thus maximize its profit. But the consequence of increased output will be lower prices, so in the end all companies will be worse off for "maximizing profits" than they might otherwise have been. If any single firm, anticipating this unhappy result, were to restrict its own output unilaterally, it would be in still more trouble, for its restriction of output in a large industry would not prevent the fall of prices, and it would suffer lower sales in addition to lower prices. It is in the interest of each firm that *all the others* restrict output, but, in a purely competitive situation, none of the others dare do that. Where there is no coercion, we have the paradoxical result that it is "rational" for each firm to pursue policies that will destroy its interests in the end. It is more rational still to prefer general coercion.

Problems like that raised by "perfect competition" tend to occur wherever large organizations have come into existence to advance the interests of their members. A great many such organizations, from consumer societies and labor unions to (as many have claimed) the political state itself, exist primarily to advance some common interest in virtue of which the members can be supposed to have banded together in the first place. Now, some of the collective aims to which large organizations are devoted have a very special character. They are directed at goods which, if they are made available to any one member of the group, cannot feasibly be withheld from any other member. Examples of such generalized and indivisible goods are supported prices for companies in the same industry in a not-so-competitive market, the power of collective bargaining for members of a union, and certain goods provided for its citizens by the state, such as police protection, courts of law, armies, navies, and public health agencies. Perhaps it would be technically possible to "sell" these goods only to those willing to pay for them, but it would hardly be "feasible." It is not clear, for example, how an organization, private or public, could eliminate air pollution only for those willing to pay. Nonpayers would breathe the expensively purified air, and there would be no way of preventing this "freeloading" short of banishment or capital punishment. In such cases, it is in each member's interest to let the others pay the bill and then share in consumption of the indivisible benefit; since each member knows that every member knows this as well as he, each has reason to think that he may be taken advantage of if he voluntarily pays his share. Yet if each member, following his own self-interest, refuses to pay, the collective good for which they are united cannot be achieved. Voluntarily submitting to a coercion understood by each to apply to all seems the only way out.

It is in virtue of such considerations that compulsory taxation, at least in support of collective goods and indivisible services of an essential kind, can be justified by the harm principle. That principle would not justify compulsory taxation in support of benefits to private groups, or even of public benefits of the sort whose loss would not constitute a serious harm, but that does not mean that the friends of public libraries, museums, and parks need be driven to embrace the welfare principle. When persons and groups are deprived of what they *need*, they are harmed; it may not be implausible to insist that the country as a whole, in this and future generations (including people who have no present desire for culture, history, nature, or beauty), *needs* large national parks, wilderness areas, enormous libraries, museums, atomic accelerators for physical research, huge telescopes, and so on. To argue that we need these things is to claim that we cannot in the end get along very well without them. That is the kind of case that must be made if we are to justify compulsion, on liberal principles, to the reluctant taxpayer.

NOTES

* This section reprinted from my "Legal Paternalism" in Volume I, no. 1 of the *Canadian Journal of Philosophy* (1971), by permission of the Canadian Association for Publishing in Philosophy.

[1] Louis B. Schwartz, "Morals, Offenses and the Model Penal Code," *Columbia Law Review*, LXIII (1963), 669 ff.

[2] Schwartz, "Morals, Offenses and the Model Penal Code," 671.

3 Patrick Devlin, *The Enforcement of Morals* (London: Oxford University Press, 1965).

4 The phrase is not Devlin's but that of his critic, H.L.A. Hart, in *Law, Liberty, and Morality* (Stanford: Stanford University Press, 1963), p. 51. In his rejoinder to Hart, Devlin writes: "Seamlessness presses the simile rather hard but apart from that, I should say that for most people morality is a web of beliefs rather than a number of unconnected ones." Devlin, *The Enforcement of Morals,* p. 115.

5 Devlin, *The Enforcement of Morals,* pp. 13–14.

6 Hart, *Law, Liberty, and Morality,* p. 51.

7 Devlin, *The Enforcement of Morals,* pp. 115 ff.

8 Devlin, *The Enforcement of Morals,* p. 116.

9 John Stuart Mill, *On Liberty* (New York: Liberal Arts Press, 1956) pp. 33–34.

10 James Fitzjames Stephen, *Liberty, Equality, Fraternity* (London: 1873), p. 163.

11 Cf. C. D. Broad, "Certain Features in Moore's Ethical Doctrines," in P. A. Schilpp *The Philosophy of G. E. Moore* (Evanston, Ill.: Northwestern University Press, 1942), pp. 48 ff.

12 There have been some studies made, but the results have been inconclusive. See the *Report of the Federal Commission on Obscenity and Pornography* (New York: Bantam Books, 1970), pp. 169–308.

13 *Obscenity and Censorship* (Pamphlet published by the American Civil Liberties Union, New York, March, 1963), p. 7.

14 *Obscenity and Censorship,* p. 4.

15 Schwartz, "Morals, Offenses and the Model Penal Code," 680.

16 Helen Merrill Lynd, *On Shame and the Search for Identity* (New York: Science Editions, Inc., 1961), p. 33.

17 Lynd, *On Shame and the Search for Identity,* p. 32.

18 William L. Prosser, *Handbook of the Law of Torts* (St. Paul: West Publishing Co., 1955), p. 411.

19 The distinctions in this paragraph have been borrowed from Henry T. Terry's "Negligence," *Harvard Law Review,* XXIX (1915), pp. 40–50.

20 My usage of the term "voluntary" differs from that of Aristotle in his famous analysis in Book III of the *Nicomachean Ethics,* but corresponds closely to what Aristotle called "deliberate choice."

21 Mill, *On Liberty,* p. 117.

22 Mill, *On Liberty,* p. 117.

from *Transition from the Common Rational Knowledge of Morality to the Philosophical*

Immanuel Kant

Nothing can possibly be conceived in the world, or even out of it, which can be called good without qualification, except a good *will*. Intelligence, wit, judgment, and the other *talents* of the mind, however they may be named, or courage, resolution, perseverance, as qualities of temperament, are undoubtedly good and desirable in many respects; but these gifts of nature may also become extremely bad and mischievous if the will which is to make use of them, and which, therefore, constitutes what is called *character*, is not good. It is the same with the *gifts of fortune*. Power, riches, honor, even health, and the general well-being and contentment with one's condition which is called *happiness*, inspire pride, and often presumption, if there is not a good will to correct the influence of these on the mind, and with this also to rectify the whole principle of acting, and adapt it to its end. The sight of a being who is not adorned with a single feature of a pure and good will, enjoying unbroken prosperity, can never give pleasure to an impartial rational spectator. Thus a good will appears to constitute the indispensable condition even of being worthy of happiness.

There are even some qualities which are of service to this good will itself, and may facilitate its action, yet which have no intrinsic unconditional value, but always presuppose a good will, and this qualifies the esteem that we justly have for them, and does not permit us to regard them as absolutely good. Moderation in the affections and passions, self-control, and calm deliberation are not only good in many respects, but even seem to constitute part of the intrinsic worth of the person; but they are far from deserving to be called good without qualification, although these have been so unconditionally praised by the ancients. For without the principles of a good will, they may become extremely bad; and the coolness of a villain not only makes him far more dangerous, but also directly makes him more abominable in our eyes than he would have been without it.

A good will is good not because of what it performs or effects, not by its aptness for the attainment of some proposed end, but simply by virtue of the volition—that is, it is good in itself, and considered by itself is to be esteemed much higher than all that can be brought about by it in favor of any inclination, nay, even of the sum-total of all inclinations. Even if it should happen that, owing to special disfavor of fortune, or the niggardly provision of a stepmotherly nature, this will should wholly lack power to accomplish its purpose, if with its greatest efforts it should yet achieve nothing, and there should remain only the good will (not, to be sure, a mere wish, but the summoning of all means in our power), then, like a jewel, it would still shine by its own light, as a thing which has its whole value in itself. Its usefulness or fruitlessness can neither add to nor take away anything from this value. It would be, as it were, only the setting to enable us to handle it the more conveniently in common commerce, or to attract to it the attention of those who are not yet connoisseurs, but not to recommend it to true connoisseurs, or to determine its value.

• • •

To be beneficent when we can is a duty; and besides this, there are many minds so sympathetically constituted that, without any other motive of sanity or self-interest, they find a pleasure in spreading joy around them, and can take delight in the satisfaction of others so far as it is their own work. But I maintain that in such a case an action of this kind, however proper, however amiable it may be, has nevertheless no true moral worth, but is on a level with other inclinations, for example, the inclination to honor, which, if it is happily directed to that which is in fact of public utility and accordant with duty, and consequently honorable, deserves praise and encouragement, but not esteem. For the maxim lacks the moral import, namely, that such actions be done *from duty*, not from inclination. Put the case that the mind of that philanthropist was clouded by sorrow of his own, extinguishing all sympathy with the lot of others, and that while he still has the power to benefit others in distress, he is not touched by their trouble because he is absorbed with his own; and now suppose that he tears himself out of this dead insensibility and performs the action without any inclination to it, but simply from duty, then . . . has his action its genuine moral worth. . . .

It is just in this that the moral worth of the character is brought out which is incomparable the highest of all, namely, that he is beneficent, not from inclination, but from duty. . . .

• • •

The second[1] proposition is: That an action done from duty derives its moral worth *not from the purpose* which is to be attained by it, but from the maxim by which it is determined, and therefore does not depend on the realization of the object of the action, but merely on the *principle of volition* by which the action has taken place, without regard to any object of desire. It is clear from what precedes that the purposes which we may have in view in our actions, or their effects regarded as ends and springs of the will, cannot give to actions any unconditional or moral worth. In what, then, can their worth lie if it is not to consist in the will and in reference to its expected effect? It cannot lie anywhere but in the *principle of the will* without regard to the ends which can be attained by the action.

The third proposition, which is a consequence of the two preceding, I would express thus: *Duty is the necessity of acting from respect for the law.* I may have *inclination* for an object as the effect of my proposed action, but I cannot have respect for it just for this reason that it is an effect and not an energy of will. Similarly, I cannot have respect for inclination, whether my own or another's; I can at most, if my own, approve it; if another's, sometimes even love it, that is, look on it as favorable to my own interest. It is only what is connected with my will as a principle, by no means as an effect—what does not subserve my inclination, but overpowers it, or at least in case of choice excludes it from its calculation—in other words, simply the law of itself, which can be an object of respect, and hence a command. Now an action done from duty must wholly exclude the influence of inclination, and with it every object of the will, so that nothing remains which can determine the will except objectively the *law*, and subjectively *pure respect* for this practical law, and consequently the maxim² that I should follow this law even to the thwarting of all my inclinations.

Thus the moral worth of an action does not lie in the effect expected from it, nor in any principle of action which requires to borrow its motive from this expected effect. For all these effects—agreeableness of one's condition, and even the promotion of the happiness of others—could have been also brought about by other causes, so that for this there would have been no need of the will of a rational being; whereas it is in this alone that the supreme and unconditional good can be found. The pre-eminent good which we call moral can therefore consist in nothing else than *the conception of law* in itself, *which certainly is only possible in a rational being*, in so far as this conception, and not the expected effect, determines the will. This is a good which is already present in the person who acts accordingly, and we have not to wait for it to appear first in the result.

But what sort of law can that be the conception of which must determine the will, even without paying any regard to the effect expected from it, in order that this will may be called good absolutely and without qualification? As I have deprived the will of every impulse which could arise to it from obedience to any law, there remains nothing but the universal conforming of its actions to law in general, which alone is to serve the will as a principle, that is, I am never to act otherwise than so *that I could also will that my maxim should become a universal law.* Here, now, it is the simple conformity to law in general, without assuming any particular law applicable to certain actions, that serves the will as its principle, and must so serve it if duty is not to be a vain delusion and a chimerical notion. The common reason of men in its practical judgments perfectly coincides with this, and always has in view the principle here suggested. Let the question be, for example: May I when in distress make a promise with the intention not to keep it? I readily distinguish here between the two significations which the question may have: whether it is prudent or whether it is right to make a false promise? The former may undoubtedly often be the case. I see clearly indeed that it is not enough to extricate myself from a present difficulty by means of this subterfuge, but it must be well considered whether there may not hereafter spring from this lie much greater inconvenience than that from which I now free myself, and as, with all my supposed *cunning*, the consequences cannot be so easily foreseen but that credit once lost may be much more injurious to me than any mischief which I seek to avoid at present, it should be considered whether it would not be more *prudent* to act herein according to a universal maxim, and to make it a habit to promise nothing except with the intention of keeping it. But it is soon clear to me that such a maxim will still only be based on the fear of consequences. Now it is a wholly different thing to be truthful from duty, and to be so from apprehension of injurious consequences. In the first case, the very notion of the action already implies a law for me; in the second case, I must first look about elsewhere to see what results may be combined with it which would affect myself. For to deviate from the principle of duty is beyond all doubt wicked, but to be unfaithful to my maxim of prudence may often be very advantageous to me, although to abide by it is certainly safer. The shortest way, however, and an unerring one, to discover the answer to this question whether a lying promise is consistent with duty, is to ask myself, Should I be content that my maxim (to extricate myself from difficulty by a false promise) should hold good as a universal law, for myself as well as for others; and should I be able to say to myself, "Every one may make a deceitful promise when he finds himself in a difficulty from which he cannot otherwise extricate himself"? Then I presently become aware that, while I can will the lie, I can by no means will that lying should be a universal law. For with such a law there would be no promises at all, since it would be in vain to allege my intention in regard to my future actions to those who would not believe this allegation, or if they over-hastily did so, would pay me back in my own coin. Hence my maxim, so soon as it should be made a universal law, would necessarily destroy itself.

I do not, therefore, need any far-reaching penetration to discern what I have to do in order that my will may be morally good. Inexperienced in the course of the world, incapable of being prepared for all its contingencies, I only ask myself: Canst thou also will that thy maxim should be a universal law? If not, then it must be rejected, and that not because of a disadvantage accruing from it to myself or even to others, but because it can not enter as a principle into a possible universal legislation, and reason extorts from me immediate respect for such legislation. I do not indeed as yet *discern* on what this respect is based (this the philosopher may inquire), but at least I understand this—that it is an estimation of the worth which far outweighs all worth of what is recommended by inclination, and that the necessity of acting from pure respect for the practical law is what constitutes duty, to which every other motive must give place because it is the condition of a will being good *in itself*, and the worth of such a will is above everything.

Thus, then, without quitting the moral knowledge of common human reason, we have arrived at its principle. And although, no doubt, common men do not conceive it in such an abstract and universal form, yet they always have it really before their eyes and use it as the standard of their decision. Here it would be easy to show how, with this compass in hand, men are well able to distinguish, in every case that occurs, what is good, what bad, conformably to duty or inconsistent with it.

• • •

Now all *imperatives* command either *hypothetically* or *categorically*. The former represent the practical necessity of a possible action as means to something else that is willed (or at least which one might possibly will). The categorical imperative would be that which represented an action as necessary of itself without reference to another end, that is, as objectively necessary. . . .

• • •

If now the action is good only as a means *to something else*, then the imperative is hypothetical; if it is conceived as good in *itself* and consequently as being necessarily the principle of a will which of itself conforms to reason, then it is *categorical*. . . .

• • •

Accordingly the hypothetical imperative only says that the action is good for some purpose, *possible* or *actual*. In the first case it is a *problematical*, in the second an *assertorial* practical principle. The categorical imperative which declares an action to be objectively necessary in itself without reference to any purpose, that is, without any other end is valid as an *apodictic* (practical) principle.

• • •

Everything in nature works according to laws. Rational beings alone have the faculty of acting according to *the conception* of laws—that is, according to principles, that is, have a *will*. . . .

When I conceive a hypothetical imperative, in general I do not know beforehand what it will contain until I am given the condition. But when I conceive a categorical imperative, I know at once what it contains. For as the imperative contains besides the law only the necessity that the maxims[3] shall conform to this law, while the law contains no conditions restricting it, there remains nothing but the general statement that the maxim of the action should conform to a universal law, and it is this conformity alone that the imperative properly represents as necessary.

There is therefore but one categorical imperative, namely, this: Act *only on that maxim whereby thou canst at the same time will that it should become a universal law.*

Now if all imperatives of duty can be deduced from this one imperative as from their principle, then, although it should remain undecided whether what is called duty is not merely a vain notion, yet at least we shall be able to show what we understand by it and what this notion means.

We will now enumerate a few duties, adopting the usual division of them into duties to ourselves and to others, and into perfect and imperfect duties.

1. A man reduced to despair by a series of misfortunes feels wearied of life, but is still so far in possession of his reason that he can ask himself whether it would not be contrary to his duty to himself to take his own life. Now he inquires whether the maxim of his action could become a universal law of nature. His maxim is: From self-love I adopt it as a principle to shorten my life when its longer duration is likely to bring more evil than satisfaction. It is asked then simply whether this principle founded on self-love can become a universal law of nature. Now we see at once that a system of nature of which it should be a law to destroy life by means of the very feeling whose special nature it is to impel to the improvement of life would contradict itself, and therefore could not exist as a system of nature; hence that maxim cannot possibly exist as a universal law of nature, and consequently would be wholly inconsistent with the supreme principle of all duty.

2. Another finds himself forced by necessity to borrow money. He knows that he will not be able to repay it, but sees also that nothing will be lent to him unless he promises stoutly to repay it in a definite time. He desires to make this promise, but he has still so much conscience as to ask himself: Is it not unlawful and inconsistent with duty to get out of a difficulty in this way? Suppose, however, that he resolves to do so, then the maxim of his action would be expressed thus: When I think myself in want of money, I will borrow money and promise to repay it, although I know that I never can do so. Now this principle of self-love or of one's own advantage may perhaps be consistent with my whole future welfare; but the question now is, Is it right? I change then the suggestion of self-love into a universal law, and state the question thus: How would it be if my maxim were a universal law? Then I see at once that it could never hold as a universal law of nature, but would necessarily contradict itself. For supposing it to be a universal law that everyone when he thinks himself in a difficulty should be able to promise whatever he pleases, with the purpose of not keeping his promise, the promise itself would become impossible, as well as the end that one might have in view in it, since no one would consider that anything was promised to him, but would ridicule all such statements as vain pretenses.

3. A third finds in himself a talent which with the help of some culture might make him a useful man in many respects. But he finds himself in comfortable circumstances and prefers to indulge in pleasure rather than to take pains in enlarging and improving his happy natural capacities. He asks, however, whether his maxim of neglect of his natural gifts, besides agreeing with his inclination to indulgence, agrees also with what is called duty. He sees then that a system of nature could indeed subsist with such a universal law, although men (like the South Sea islanders) should let their talents rest and resolve to devote their lives merely to idleness, amusement, and propagation of their species—in a word, to enjoyment; but he cannot possibly *will* that this should be a universal law of nature, or be implanted in us as such by a natural instinct. For, as a rational being, he necessarily wills that his faculties be developed, since they serve him, and have been given him, for all sorts of possible purposes.

4. A fourth, who is in prosperity, while he sees that others have to contend with great wretchedness and that he could help them, thinks: "What concern is it of mine? Let everyone be as happy as Heaven pleases, or as he can make himself; I will take nothing from him nor even envy him, only I do not wish to contribute anything to his welfare or to his assistance in distress!" Now no doubt, if such a mode of thinking were a universal law, the human race might very well subsist, and doubtless even better than in a state in which everyone talks of sympathy and good-will, or even

takes care occasionally to put it into practice, but, on the other side, also cheats when he can, betrays the rights of men, or otherwise violates them. But although it is possible that a universal law of nature might exist in accordance with that maxim, it is impossible to *will* that such a principle should have the universal validity of a law of nature. For a will which resolved this would contradict itself, inasmuch as many cases might occur in which one would have need of the love and sympathy of others, and in which, by such a law of nature, sprung from his own will, he would deprive himself of all hope of the aid he desires.

These are a few of the many actual duties, or at least what we regard as such, which obviously fall into two classes on the one principle that we have laid down. We must be *able to will* that a maxim of our action should be a universal law. This is the canon of the moral appreciation of the action generally. Some actions are of such a character that their maxim cannot without contradiction be even *concealed* as a universal law of nature, far from it being possible that we should *will* that it *should* be so. In others, this intrinsic impossibility is not found, but still it is impossible to will that their maxim should be raised to the universality of a law of nature, since such a will would contradict itself. . . .

• • •

The will is conceived as a faculty of determining oneself to action *in accordance with the conception of certain laws*. And such a facility can be found only in rational beings. . . .

• • •

Now I say: man and generally any rational being *exists* as an end in himself, *not merely as a means* to be arbitrarily used by this or that will, but in all his actions, whether the concern himself or other rational beings, must be always regarded at the same time as an end. All objects of the inclinations have only a conditional worth; for if the inclinations and the wants founded on them did not exist, then their object would be without value. . . .

Thus the worth of any object which is *to be acquired* by our action is always conditional. Beings whose existence depends not on our will but on nature's, have nevertheless, if they are nonrational beings, only a relative value as means, and are therefore called *things*; rational beings, on the contrary, are called *persons*, because their very nature points them out as ends in themselves, that is, as something which must not be used merely as means, and so far therefore restricts freedom of action (and is an object of respect). These, therefore, are not merely subjective ends whose existence has a worth *for us* as an effect of our action, but *objective ends*, that is, things whose existence is an end in itself—an end, moreover, for which no other can be substituted, which they should subserve *merely* as means, for otherwise nothing whatever would possess *absolute worth*. . . .

• • •

Accordingly the practical imperative will be as follows: *So act as to treat humanity, whether in thine own person or in that of any other, in every case as an end withal, never as means only.* We will now inquire whether this can be practically carried out.

To abide by the previous examples:

First, under the head of necessary duty to oneself: He who contemplates suicide should ask himself whether his action can be consistent with the idea of humanity *as an end in itself*. If he destroys himself in order to escape from painful circumstances, he uses a person merely as *a mean* to maintain a tolerable condition up to the end of life. But a man is not a thing, that is to say, something which can be used merely as means, but must in all his actions be always considered as an end in himself. I cannot, therefore, dispose in any way of a man in my own person so as to mutilate him, to damage or kill him. . . .

• • •

Secondly, as regards necessary duties, or those of strict obligation, towards others: He who is thinking of making a lying promise to others will see at once that he would be using another man *merely as a mean*, without the latter containing at the same time the end in himself. For he whom I propose by such a promise to use for my own purposes cannot possibly assent to my mode of acting towards him, and therefore cannot himself contain the end of this action. . . .

NOTES

[1] The first proposition is that to have moral worth an action must be done from duty.

[2] A *maxim* is the subjective principle of volition. The objective principle (i.e., that which would also serve subjectively as a practical principle to all rational beings if reason had full power over the faculty of desire) is the practical *law*.

[3] A *maxim* is a subjective principle of action, and must be distinguished from the *objective principle*, namely practical law. The former contains the practical rule set by reason according to the conditions of the subject (often its ignorance or its inclinations), so that it is the principle on which the subject acts; but the law is the objective principle valid for every rational being, and is the principle which it *ought to act*—that is an imperative.

from *Utilitarianism*

John Stuart Mill

The creed which accepts as the foundation of morals, Utility, or the Greatest Happiness Principle, holds that actions are right in proportion as they tend to promote happiness, wrong as they tend to produce the reverse of happiness. By happiness is intended pleasure, and the absence of pain; by unhappiness, pain, and the privation of pleasure.

Now, such a theory of life excites in many minds, and among them in some of the most estimable in feeling and purpose, inveterate dislike. To suppose that life has (as they express it) no higher end than pleasure—no better and nobler object of desire and pursuit—they designate as utterly mean and grovelling; as a doctrine worthy only of swine, to whom the followed of Epicurus were, at a very early period, contemptuously likened;

When thus attacked, the Epicureans have always answered, that it is not they, but their accusers, who represent human nature in a degrading light; since the accusation supposes human beings to be capable of no pleasures except those of which swine are capable. The comparison of the Epicurean life to that of beasts is felt as degrading, precisely because a beast's pleasures do not satisfy a human being's conceptions of happiness. Human beings have faculties more elevated than the animal appetites, and when once made conscious of them, do not regard anything as happiness which does not include their gratification.

It is quite compatible with the principle of utility to recognise the fact, that some *kinds* of pleasure are more desirable and more valuable than others. It would be absurd that while, in estimating all other things, quality is considered as well as quantity, the estimation of pleasures should be supposed to depend on quantity alone.

If I am asked, what I mean by difference of quality in pleasures, or what makes one pleasure more valuable than another, merely as a pleasure, except its being greater in amount, there is but one possible answer. Of two pleasures, if there be one to which all or almost all who have experience of both give a decided preference, irrespective of any feeling of moral obligation to prefer it, that is the more desirable pleasure. If one of the two is, by those who are competently acquainted with both placed so far above the other that they prefer it, even though knowing it to be attended with a greater amount of discontent, and would not resign it for any quantity of the other pleasure which their nature is capable of, we are justified in ascribing to the preferred enjoyment a superiority in quality, so far outweighing quantity as to render it, in comparison, of small account.

Now it is an unquestionable fact that those who are equally acquainted with, and equally capable of appreciating and enjoying, both, do give most marked preference to the manner of existence which employs their higher faculties. Few human creatures would consent to be changed into any of the lower animals, for a promise of the fullest allowance of a beast's pleasures; no intelligent human being would consent to be a fool, no instructed person would be an ignoramus, no person of feeling and conscience would be selfish and base, even though they should be persuaded that the fool, the dunce, or the rascal is better satisfied with his lot than they are with theirs.

A being of higher faculties requires more to make him happy, is capable probably of more acute suffering, and certainly accessible to it at more points, than one of an inferior type; but in spite of these liabilities, he can never really wish to sink into what he feels to be a lower grade of existence.

It is better to be a human being dissatisfied than a pig satisfied; better to be Socrates dissatisfied than a fool satisfied. And if the fool, or the pig, are of a different opinion, it is because they only know their own side of the question. The other party to the comparison knows both sides.

From this verdict of the only competent judges, I apprehend there can be no appeal. On a quest on which is the best worth having of two pleasures, or which of two modes of existence is the most grateful to the feelings, apart from its moral attributes and from its consequences, the judgment of those who are qualified by knowledge of both, or, if they differ, that of the majority among them, must be admitted as final. And there needs be the less hesitation to accept this judgment respecting the quality of pleasures, since there is no other tribunal to be referred to even on the question of quantity. What means are there of determining which is the acutest of two pains, or the intensest of two pleasurable sensations, except the general suffrage of those who are familiar with both? Neither pains nor pleasures are homogeneous, and pain is always heterogeneous with pleasure. What is there to decide whether a particular pleasure is worth purchasing at the cost of a particular pain, except the feelings and judgment of the experienced? When, therefore, those feelings and judgment declare the pleasures derived from the higher faculties to be preferable *in kind*, apart from the question of intensity, to those of which the animal nature, disjoined from the higher faculties, is susceptible, they are entitled on this subject to the same regard.

I must again repeat, what the assailants of utilitarianism seldom have the justice to acknowledge, that the happiness which forms the utilitarian standard of what is right in conduct, is not the agent's own happiness, but that of all concerned. As between his own happiness and that of others, utilitarianism requires him to be as strictly impartial as a disinterested and benevolent spectator. In the golden rule of Jesus of Nazareth, we read the complete spirit of the ethics of utility. To do as you would be done by, and to love your neighbour as yourself, constitute the ideal perfection of utilitarian morality. As the means of making the nearest approach to this ideal, utility would enjoin, first, that laws and social arrangements should place the happiness, or (as speaking practically it may be called) the interest, of every individual, as nearly as possible in harmony with the interest of the whole;

and secondly, that education and opinion, which have so vast a power over human character, should so use that power as to establish in the mind of every individual an indissoluble association between his own happiness and the good of the whole; especially between his own happiness and the practice of such modes of conduct, negative and positive, as regard for the universal happiness prescribes; so that not only he may be unable to conceive the possibility of happiness to himself, consistently with conduct opposed to the general good, but also that a direct impulse to promote the general good may be in every individual one of the habitual motives of action, and the sentiments connected therewith may fill a large and, prominent place in every human being's sentient existence.

The objectors to utilitarianism cannot always be charged with representing it in a discreditable light. On the contrary, those among them who entertain anything like a just idea of its disinterested character, sometimes find fault with its standard as being too high for humanity. They say it is exacting too much to require that people shall always act from the inducement of promoting the general interests of society. But this is to mistake the very meaning of a standard of morals, and confound the rule of action with the motive of it. It is the business of ethics to tell us what are our duties, or by what test we may know them; but no system of ethics requires that the sole motive of all we do shall be a feeling of duty; on the contrary, ninety-nine hundredths of all our actions are done from other motives, and rightly so done, if the rule of duty does not condemn them. It is a misapprehension of the utilitarian mode of thought, to conceive it as implying that people should fix their minds upon so wide a generality as the world, or society at large. The great majority of good actions are intended not for the benefit of the world, but for that of individuals, of which the good of the world is made up; and the thoughts of the most virtuous man need not on these occasions travel beyond the particular persons concerned, except so far as is necessary to assure himself that in benefiting them he is not violating the rights, that is, the legitimate and authorised expectations, of any one else.

Indeed—of things which people forbear to do from moral considerations, though the consequences in the particular case might be beneficial—it would be unworthy of an intelligent agent not to be consciously aware that the action is of a class which, if practised generally, would be generally injurious, and that this is the ground of the obligation to abstain from it. The amount of regard for the public interest implied in this recognition, is no greater than is demanded by every system of morals, for they all enjoin to abstain from whatever is manifestly pernicious to society.

It has already been remarked, that questions of ultimate ends do not admit of proof, in the ordinary acceptation of the term. To be incapable of proof by reasoning is common to all first principles; to the first premises of our knowledge, as well as to those of our conduct. But the former, being matters of fact, may be the subject of a direct appeal to the faculties which judge of fact—namely, our senses, and our internal consciousness. Can an appeal be made to the same faculties on questions of practical ends? Or by what other faculty is cognisance taken of them?

Questions about ends are, in other words, questions what things are desirable. The utilitarian doctrine is, that happiness is desirable, and the only thing desirable, as an end; all other things being only desirable as means to that end. What ought to be required of this doctrine—what conditions is it requisite that the doctrine should fulfil—to make good its claim to be believed?

The only proof capable of being given that an object is visible, is that people actually see it. The only proof that a sound is audible, is that people hear it: and so of the other sources of our experience. In like manner, I apprehend, the sole evidence it is possible to produce that anything is desirable, is that people do actually desire it. If the end which the utilitarian doctrine proposes to itself were not, in theory and in practice, acknowledged to be an end, nothing could ever convince any person that it was so. No reason can be given why the general happiness is desirable, except that each person, so far as he believes it to be attainable, desires his own happiness. This, however, being a fact, we have not only all the proof which the case admits of, but all which it is possible to require, that happiness is a good: that each person's happiness is a good to that person, and the general happiness, therefore, a good to the aggregate of all persons. Happiness has made out its title as one of the ends of conduct, and consequently one of the criteria of morality.

But it has not, by this alone, proved itself to be the sole criterion. To do that, it would seem, by the same rule, necessary to show, not only that people desire happiness, but that they never desire anything else. Now it is palpable that they do desire things which, in common language, are decidedly distinguished from happiness. They desire, for example, virtue, and the absence of vice, no less really than pleasure and the absence of pain. The desire of virtue is not as universal, but it is as authentic a fact, as the desire of happiness. And hence the opponents of the utilitarian standard deem that they have a right to infer that there are other ends of human action besides happiness, and that happiness is not the standard of approbation and disapprobation.

But does the utilitarian doctrine deny that people desire virtue, or maintain that virtue is not a thing to be desired? The very reverse. It maintains not only that virtue is to be desired, but that it is to be desired disinterestedly, for itself. Whatever may be the opinion of utilitarian moralists as to the original conditions by which virtue is made virtue; however they may believe (as they do) that actions and dispositions are only virtuous because they promote another end than virtue; yet this being granted, and it having been decided, from considerations of this description, what is virtuous, they not only place virtue at the very head of the things which are good as means to the ultimate end, but they also recognise as a psychological fact the possibility of its being, to the individual, a good in itself, without looking to any end beyond it; and hold, that the mind is not in a right state, not in a state conformable to Utility, not in the state most conducive to the general happiness, unless it does love virtue in this manner—as a thing desirable in itself, even although, in the individual instance, it should not produce those other desirable consequences which it tends to produce, and on account of which it is held to be virtue. This opinion is not, in the smallest degree, a departure from the Happiness principle.

Virtue, according to the utilitarian conception, is a good of this description. There was no original desire of it, or motive to it, save its conduciveness to pleasure, and especially to protection from pain. But through the association thus formed, it may be felt a good in itself, and desired as such with as great intensity as any other good; and with this difference between it and the love of money, of power, or of fame, that all of these may, and often do, render the individual noxious to the other members of the society to which he belongs, whereas there is nothing which makes him so much a blessing to them as the cultivation of the disinterested love of virtue.

And consequently, the utilitarian standard, while it tolerates and approves those other acquired desires, up to the point beyond which they would be more injurious to the general happiness than promotive of it, enjoins and requires the cultivation of the love of virtue up to the greatest strength possible, as being above all things important to the general happiness.

Does Morality Depend upon Religion?

John Arthur

The question I discuss in this paper was famously captured by a character in Dostoyevsky's novel *The Brothers Karamazov*: "Without God" said Ivan, "everything is permitted." I want to argue that this is wrong: there is in fact no important sense in which morality depends on religion. Yet, I will also argue, there do remain important other respects in which the two are related. In the concluding section I extend the discussion of the origins of morality beyond religion by considering the nature of conscience, the ways morality is "social," and the implications of these ideas for moral education. First, however, I want to say something about the subjects: just what are we referring to when we speak of morality and of religion?

1. MORALITY AND RELIGION

A useful way to approach the first question—the nature of morality—is to ask what it would mean for a society to exist without a social moral code. How would such people think and behave? What would that society look like? First, it seems clear that such people would never feel guilt or resentment. For example, the notions that I ought to remember my parents' anniversary, that he has a moral responsibility to help care for his children after the divorce, that she has a right to equal pay for equal work, and that discrimination on the basis of race is unfair would be absent in such a society. Notions of duty, rights, and obligations would not be present, except perhaps in the legal sense; concepts of justice and fairness would also be foreign to these people. In short, people would have no tendency to evaluate or criticize the behavior of others, nor to feel remorse about their own behavior. Children would not be taught to be ashamed when they steal or hurt others, nor would they be allowed to complain when others treat them badly. (People might, however, feel regret at a decision that didn't turn out as they had hoped; but that would only be because their expectations were frustrated, not because they feel guilty.)

Such a society lacks a moral code. What, then, of religion? Is it possible that people lacking a morality would nonetheless have religious beliefs? It seems clear that it is possible. Suppose every day these same people file into their place of worship to pay homage to God (they may believe in many gods or in one all-powerful creator of heaven and earth). Often they can be heard praying to God for help in dealing with their problems and thanking Him for their good fortune. Frequently they give sacrifices to God, sometimes in the form of money spent to build beautiful temples and churches, other times by performing actions they believe God would approve such as helping those in need. These practices might also be institutionalized, in the sense that certain people are assigned important leadership roles. Specific texts might also be taken as authoritative, indicating the ways God has acted in history and His role in their lives or the lives of their ancestors.

To have a moral code, then, is to tend to evaluate (perhaps without even expressing it) the behavior of others and to feel guilt at certain actions when we perform them. Religion, on the other hand, involves beliefs in supernatural power(s) that created and perhaps also control nature, the tendency to worship and pray to those supernatural forces or beings, and the presence of organizational structures and authoritative texts. The practices of morality and religion are thus importantly different. One involves our attitudes toward various forms of behavior (lying and killing, for example), typically expressed using the notions of rules, rights, and obligations. The other, religion, typically involves prayer, worship, beliefs about the supernatural, institutional forms, and authoritative texts.

We come, then, to the central question: What is the connection, if any, between a society's moral code and its religious practices and beliefs? Many people have felt that morality is in some way dependent on religion or religious truths. But what sort of "dependence" might there be? In what follows I distinguish various ways in which one might claim that religion is necessary for morality, arguing against those who claim morality depends in some way on religion. I will also suggest, however, some other important ways in which the two are related, concluding with a brief discussion of conscience and moral education.

2. RELIGIOUS MOTIVATION AND GUIDANCE

One possible role which religion might play in morality relates to motives people have. Religion, it is often said, is necessary so that people will *do* right. Typically, the argument begins with the important point that doing what is right often has costs: refusing to shoplift or cheat can mean people go without some good or fail a test; returning a billfold means they don't get the contents. Religion is therefore said to be necessary in that it provides motivation to do the right thing. God rewards those who follow His commands by providing for them a place in heaven or by insuring that they prosper and are happy on earth. He also punishes those who violate the moral law. Others emphasize less self-interested ways in which religious motives may encourage people to act rightly. Since God is the creator of the universe and has ordained that His plan should be followed, they point out, it is important to live one's life in accord with this divinely ordained plan. Only by living a moral life, it is said, can people live in harmony with the larger, divinely created order.

The first claim, then, is that religion is necessary to provide moral motivation. The problem with that argument, however, is that religious motives are far from the only ones people have. For most of us, a decision to do the right thing (if that is our decision) is made for a variety of reasons: "What if I get caught? What if somebody sees me—what will he or she think? How will I feel afterwards? Will I regret it?" Or maybe the thought of cheating just doesn't arise. We were raised to

340

be a decent person, and that's what we are—period. Behaving fairly and treating others well is more important than whatever we might gain from stealing or cheating, let alone seriously harming another person. So it seems clear that many motives for doing the right thing have nothing whatsoever to do with religion. Most of us, in fact, do worry about getting caught, being blamed, and being looked down on by others. We also may do what is right just because it's right, or because we don't want to hurt others or embarrass family and friends. To say that we need religion to act morally is mistaken; indeed it seems to me that many of us, when it really gets down to it, don't give much of a thought to religion when making moral decisions. All those other reasons are the ones which we tend to consider, or else we just don't consider cheating and stealing at all. So far, then, there seems to be no reason to suppose that people can't be moral yet irreligious at the same time.

A second argument that is available for those who think religion is necessary to morality, however, focuses on moral guidance and knowledge rather than on people's motives. However much people may want to do the right thing, according to this view, we cannot ever know for certain what is right without the guidance of religious teaching. Human understanding is simply inadequate to this difficult and controversial task; morality involves immensely complex problems, and so we must consult religious revelation for help.

Again, however, this argument fails. First, consider how much we would need to know about religion and revelation in order for religion to provide moral guidance. Besides being sure that there is a God, we'd also have to think about which of the many religions is true. How can anybody be sure his or her religion is the right one? But even if we assume the Judeo-Christian God is the real one, we still need to find out just what it is He wants us to do, which means we must think about revelation.

Revelation comes in at least two forms, and not even all Christians agree on which is the best way to understand revelation. Some hold that revelation occurs when God tells us what He wants by providing us with His words: The Ten Commandments are an example. Many even believe, as evangelist Billy Graham once said, that the entire Bible was written by God using thirty-nine secretaries. Others, however, doubt that the "word of God" refers literally to the words God has spoken, but believe instead that the Bible is an historical document, written by human beings, of the events or occasions in which God revealed Himself. It is an especially important document, of course, but nothing more than that. So on this second view, revelation is not understood as statements made by God but rather as His acts such as leading His people from Egypt, testing Job, and sending His son as an example of the ideal life. The Bible is not itself revelation; it's the historical account of revelatory actions.

If we are to use revelation as a moral guide, then, we must first know what is to count as revelation—words given us by God, historical events, or both? But even supposing that we could somehow answer those questions, the problems of relying on revelation are still not over since we still must interpret that revelation. Some feel, for example, that the Bible justifies various forms of killing, including war and capital punishment, on the basis of such statements as "An eye for an eye." Others, emphasizing such sayings as "Judge not lest ye be judged" and "Thou shalt not kill," believe the Bible demands absolute pacifism. How are we to know which interpretation is correct? It is likely, of course, that the answer people give to such religious questions will be influenced in part at least by their own moral beliefs: if capital punishment is thought to be unjust, for example, then an interpreter will seek to read the Bible in a way that is consistent with that moral truth. That is not, however, a happy conclusion for those wishing to rest morality on revelation, for it means that their understanding of what God has revealed is itself dependent on their prior moral views. Rather than revelation serving as a guide for morality, morality is serving as a guide for how we interpret revelation.

So my general conclusion is that far from providing a short-cut to moral understanding, looking to revelation for guidance often creates more questions and problems. It seems wiser under the circumstances to address complex moral problems like abortion, capital punishment, and affirmative action directly, considering the pros and cons of each side, rather than to seek answers through the much more controversial and difficult route of revelation.

3. THE DIVINE COMMAND THEORY

It may seem, however, that we have still not really gotten to the heart of the matter. Even if religion is not necessary for moral motivation or guidance, it is often claimed, religion is necessary in another more fundamental sense. According to this view, religion is necessary for morality because without God there could be no right or wrong. God, in other words, provides the foundation or bedrock on which morality is grounded. This idea was expressed by Bishop R. C. Mortimer:

> God made us and all the world. Because of that He has an absolute claim on our obedience. . . . From [this] it follows that a thing is not right simply because we think it is. It is right because God commands it.[1]

What Bishop Mortimer has in mind can be seen by comparing moral rules with legal ones. Legal statutes, we know, are created by legislatures; if the state assembly of New York had not passed a law limiting the speed people can travel, then there would be no such legal obligation. Without the statutory enactments, such a law simply would not exist. Mortimer's view, *the divine command theory*, would mean that God has the same sort of relation to moral law as the legislature has to statutes it enacts: without God's commands there would be no moral rules, just as without a legislature there would be no statutes.

Defenders of the divine command theory often add to this a further claim, that only by assuming God sits at the foundation of morality can we explain the objective difference between right and wrong. This point was forcefully argued by F. C. Copleston in a 1948 British Broadcasting Corporation radio debate with Bertrand Russell.

Copleston: . . .The validity of such an interpretation of man's conduct depends on the recognition of God's existence, obviously. . . . Let's take a look at the Commandant of the [Nazi] concentration camp at Belsen. That appears to you as undesirable and evil and to me too. To Adolph Hitler we suppose it appeared as something good and desirable. I suppose you'd have to admit that for Hitler it was good and for you it is evil.

Russell: No, I shouldn't go so far as that. I mean, I think people can make mistakes in that as they can in other things. If you have jaundice you see things yellow that are not yellow. You're making a mistake.

Copleston: Yes, one can make mistakes, but can you make a mistake if it's simply a question of reference to a feeling or emotion? Surely Hitler would be the only possible judge of what appealed to his emotions.

Russell: . . . You can say various things about that; among others, that if that sort of thing makes that sort of appeal to Hitler's emotions, then Hitler makes quite a different appeal to my emotions.

Copleston: Granted. But there's no objective criterion outside feeling then for condemning the conduct of the Commandant of Belsen, in your view. . . . The human being's idea of the content of the moral law depends certainly to a large extent on education and environment, and a man has to use his reason in assessing the validity of the actual moral ideas of his social group. But the possibility of criticizing the accepted moral code presupposes that there is an objective standard, that there is an ideal moral order, which imposes itself . . . It implies the existence of a real foundation of God.[2]

Against those who, like Bertrand Russell, seek to ground morality in feelings and attitudes, Copleston argues that there must be a more solid foundation if we are to be able to claim truly that the Nazis were evil. God, according to Copleston, is able to provide the objective basis for the distinction, which we all know to exist, between right and wrong. Without divine commands at the root of human obligations, we would have no real reason for condemning the behavior of anybody, even Nazis. Morality, Copleston thinks, would then be nothing more than an expression of personal feeling.

To begin assessing the divine command theory, let's first consider this last point. Is it really true that only the commands of God can provide an objective basis for moral judgments? Certainly many philosophers have felt that morality rests on its own perfectly sound footing, be it reason, human nature, or natural sentiments. It seems wrong to conclude, automatically, that morality cannot rest on anything but religion. And it is also possible that morality doesn't have any foundation or basis at all, so that its claims should be ignored in favor of whatever serves our own self-interest.

In addition to these problems with Copleston's argument, the divine command theory faces other problems as well. First, we would need to say much more about the relationship between morality and divine commands. Certainly the expressions "is commanded by God" and "is morally required" do not *mean* the same thing. People and even whole societies can use moral concepts without understanding them to make any reference to God. And while it is true that God (or any other moral being for that matter) would tend to want others to do the right thing, this hardly shows that being right and being commanded by God are the same thing. Parents want their children to do the right thing, too, but that doesn't mean parents, or anybody else, can make a thing right just by commanding it!

I think that, in fact, theists should reject the divine command theory. One reason is what it implies. Suppose we were to grant (just for the sake of argument) that the divine command theory is correct, so that actions are right just because they are commanded by God. The same, of course, can be said about those deeds that we believe are wrong. If God hadn't commanded us not to do them, they would not be wrong.

But now notice this consequence of the divine command theory. Since God is all-powerful, and since right is determined solely by His commands, is it not possible that He might change the rules and make what we now think of as wrong into right? It would seem that according to the divine command theory the answer is "yes": it is theoretically possible that tomorrow God would decree that virtues such as kindness and courage have become vices while actions that show cruelty and cowardice will henceforth be the right actions. (Recall the analogy with a legislature and the power it has to change law.) So now rather than it being right for people to help each other out and prevent innocent people from suffering unnecessarily, it would be right (God having changed His mind) to create as much pain among innocent children as we possibly can! To adopt the divine command theory therefore commits its advocate to the seemingly absurd position that even the greatest atrocities might be not only acceptable but morally required if God were to command them.

Plato made a similar point in the dialogue *Euthyphro*. Socrates is asking Euthyphro what it is that makes the virtue of holiness a virtue, just as we have been asking what makes kindness and courage virtues. Euthyphro has suggested that holiness is just whatever all the gods love.

Socrates: Well, then, Euthyphro, what do we say about holiness? Is it not loved by all the gods, according to your definition?

Euthyphro: Yes.

Socrates: Because it is holy, or for some other reason?

Euthyphro: No, because it is holy.

Socrates: Then it is loved by the gods because it is holy: it is not holy because it is loved by them?

Euthyphro: It seems so.

Socrates: . . .Then holiness is not what is pleasing to the gods, and what is pleasing to the gods is not holy as you say, Euthyphro. They are different things.

Euthyphro: And why, Socrates?

Socrates: Because we are agreed that the gods love holiness because it is holy: and that it is not holy because they love it.[3]

This raises an interesting question: Why, having claimed at first that virtues are merely what is loved (or commanded) by the gods, would Euthyphro so quickly contradict this and agree that the gods love holiness *because* it's holy, rather than the reverse? One likely possibility is that Euthyphro believes that whenever the gods love something they do so with good reason, not without justification and arbitrarily. To deny this, and say that it is merely the gods' love that makes holiness a virtue, would mean that the gods have no basis for their attitudes, that they are arbitrary in what they love. Yet—and this is the crucial point—it's far from clear that a religious person would want to say that God is arbitrary in that way. If we say that it is simply God's loving something that makes it right, then what sense would it make to say God wants us to do right? All that could mean, it seems, is that God wants us to do what He wants us to do; He would have no reason for wanting it. Similarly "God is good" would mean little more than "God does what He pleases." The divine command theory therefore leads us to the results that God is morally arbitrary, and that His wishing us to do good or even God's being just mean nothing more than that God does what He does and wants whatever He wants. Religious people who reject that consequence would also, I am suggesting, have reason to reject the divine command theory itself, seeking a different understanding of morality.

This now raises another problem, however. If God approves kindness because it is a virtue and hates the Nazis because they were evil, then it seems that God discovers morality rather than inventing it. So haven't we then identified a limitation on God's power, since He now, being a good God, must love kindness and command us not to be cruel? Without the divine command theory, in other words, what is left of God's omnipotence?

But why, we may ask, is such a limitation on God unacceptable? It is not at all clear that God really can do anything at all. Can God, for example, destroy Himself? Or make a rock so heavy that He cannot lift it? Or create a universe which was never created by Him? Many have thought that God cannot do these things, but also that His inability to do them does not constitute a serious limitation on His power since these are things that cannot be done at all: to do them would violate the laws of logic. Christianity's most influential theologian, Thomas Aquinas, wrote in this regard that "whatever implies contradiction does not come within the scope of divine omnipotence, because it cannot have the aspect of possibility. Hence it is more appropriate to say that such things cannot be done than that God cannot do them."[4]

How, then, ought we to understand God's relationship to morality if we reject the divine command theory? Can religious people consistently maintain their faith in God the Creator and yet deny that what is right is right because He commands it? I think the answer to this is "yes." Making cruelty good is not like making a universe that wasn't made, of course. It's a moral limit on God rather than a logical one. But why suppose that God's limits are only logical?

One final point about this. Even if we agree that God loves justice or kindness because of their nature, not arbitrarily, there still remains a sense in which God could change morality even having rejected the divine command theory. That's because if we assume, plausibly I think, that morality depends in part on how we reason, what we desire and need, and the circumstances in which we find ourselves, then morality will still be under God's control since God could have constructed us or our environment very differently. Suppose, for instance, that he created us so that we couldn't be hurt by others or didn't care about freedom. Or perhaps our natural environment were created differently, so that all we have to do is ask and anything we want is given to us. If God had created either nature or us that way, then it seems likely our morality might also be different in important ways from the one we now think correct. In that sense, then, morality depends on God whether or not one supports the divine command theory.

4. ON DEWEY'S THOUGHT THAT "MORALITY IS SOCIAL"

I have argued here that religion is not necessary in providing moral motivation or guidance, and against the divine command theory's claim that God is necessary for there to be morality at all. In this last section, I want first to look briefly at how religion and morality sometimes *do* influence each other. Then I will consider the development of moral conscience and the important ways in which morality might correctly be thought to be "social."

Nothing I have said so far means that morality and religion are independent of each other. But in what ways are they related, assuming I am correct in claiming morality does not *depend* on religion? First, of course, we should note the historical influence religions have had on the development of morality as well as on politics and law. Many of the important leaders of the abolitionist and civil rights movements were religious leaders, as are many current members of the pro-life movement. The relationship is not, however, one-sided: morality has also influenced religion, as the current debate within the Catholic church over the role of women, abortion, and other social issues shows. In reality, then, it seems clear that the practices of morality and religion have historically each exerted an influence on the other.

But just as the two have shaped each other historically, so, too, do they interact at the personal level. I have already suggested how people's understanding of revelation, for instance, is often shaped by morality as they seek the best interpretations of revealed texts. Whether trying to understand a work of art, a legal statute, or a religious text, interpreters regularly seek to understand them in the best light—to make them as good as they can be, which requires that they bring moral judgment to the task of religious interpretation and understanding.

The relationship can go the other direction as well, however, as people's moral views are shaped by their religious training and beliefs. These relationships between morality and religion are often complex, hidden even from ourselves, but it does seem clear that our views on important moral issues, from sexual morality and war to welfare and capital punishment, are often influenced by our religious outlook. So not only are religious and moral practices and understandings historically linked, but for many religious people the relationship extends to the personal level—to their understanding of moral obligations as well as their sense of who they are and their vision of who they wish to be.

Morality, then, is influenced by religion (as is religion by morality), but morality's social character extends deeper even than that, I want to argue. First, of course, we possess a socially acquired language within which we think about our various choices and the alternatives we ought to follow, including whether a possible course of action is the right thing to do. Second, morality is social in that it governs relationships among people, defining our responsibilities to others and theirs to us. Morality provides the standards we rely on in gauging our interactions with family, lovers, friends, fellow citizens, and even strangers. Third, morality is social in the sense that we are, in fact, subject to criticism by others for our actions. We discuss with others what we should do, and often hear from them concerning whether our decisions were acceptable. Blame and praise are a central feature of morality.

While not disputing any of this, John Dewey has stressed another, less obvious aspect of morality's social character. Consider then the following comments regarding the origins of morality and conscience in an article he titled "Morality Is Social":

> In language and imagination we rehearse the responses of others just as we dramatically enact other consequences. We foreknow how others will act, and the foreknowledge is the beginning of judgment passed on action. We know *with* them; there is conscience. An assembly is formed within our breast which discusses and appraises proposed and performed acts. The community without becomes a forum and tribunal within, a judgment-seat of charges, assessments and exculpations. Our thoughts of our own actions are saturated with the ideas that others entertain about them. . . . Explicit recognition of this fact is a prerequisite of improvement in moral education. . . . Reflection is morally indispensable.[5]

So Dewey's thought is that to consider matters from the moral point of view means we must think beyond ourselves, by which he means imagining how we as well as others might respond to various choices now being contemplated. To consider a decision from the *moral* perspective, says Dewey, requires that we envision an "assembly of others" that is "formed within our breast." That means, in turn, that morality and conscience cannot be sharply distinguished from our nature as social beings since conscience invariably brings with it, or constitutes, the perspective of the other. "Is this right?" and "What would this look like were I to have to defend it to others?" are not separable questions.[6]

It is important not to confuse Dewey's point here, however. He is *not* saying that what is right is finally to be determined by the reactions of actually existing other people, or even by the reaction of society as a whole. What is right or fair can never be finally decided by a vote, but instead might not meet the approval of any specific others. But what then might Dewey mean in speaking of such an "assembly of others" as the basis of morality? The answer is that rather than actual people or groups, the assembly Dewey envisions is hypothetical or "ideal." The "community without" is thus transformed into a "forum and tribunal within, a judgment seat of charges, assessments and exculpations." So it is through the powers of our imagination that we can meet our moral responsibilities and exercise moral judgment, using these powers to determine what morality requires by imagining the reaction of Dewey's "assembly of others."

Morality is therefore *inherently* social, in a variety of ways. It depends on socially learned language, is learned from interactions with others, and governs our interactions with others in society. But it also demands, as Dewey put it, that we know "with" others, envisioning for ourselves what their points of view would require along with our own. Conscience demands we occupy the positions of others.

Viewed in this light, God would play a role in a religious person's moral reflection and conscience since it is unlikely a religious person would wish to exclude God from the "forum and tribunal" that constitutes conscience. Rather, for the religious person conscience would almost certainly include the imagined reaction of God along with the reactions of others who might be affected by the action. Other people are also important, however, since it is often an open question just what God's reaction would be; revelation's meaning, as I have argued, is subject to interpretation. So it seems that for a religious person morality and God's will cannot be separated, though the connection between them is not the one envisioned by defenders of the divine command theory.

Which leads to my final point, about moral education. If Dewey is correct, then it seems clear there is an important sense in which morality not only can be taught but must be. Besides early moral training, moral thinking depends on our ability to imagine others' reactions and to imaginatively put ourselves into their shoes. "What would somebody (including, perhaps, God) think if this got out?" expresses more than a concern with being embarrassed or punished; it is also the voice of conscience and indeed of morality itself. But that would mean, thinking of education, that listening to others, reading about what others think and do, and reflecting within ourselves about our actions and whether we could defend them to others are part of the practice of morality itself. Morality cannot exist without the broader, social perspective introduced by others, and this social nature ties it, in that way, with education and with public discussion, both actual and imagined. "Private" moral reflection taking place independent of the social world would be no moral reflection at all. It follows that moral *education,* in the form of both studying others' moral ideas and subjecting our own to discussion and criticism, is not only possible, but essential.

NOTES

[1] R.C. Mortimer, *Christian Ethics* (London: Hutchinson's University Library, 1950) pp. 7–8.

[2] This debate was broadcast on the "Third Program" of the British Broadcasting Corporation in 1948.

[3] Plato, *Euthyphro*, trans. H.N. Fowler (Cambridge, MA: Harvard University Press, 1947).

[4] Thomas Aquinas, *Summa Theologica*, Part I, Q. 25, Art. 3.

[5] John Dewey, "Morality Is Social" in *The Moral Writings of John Dewey*, rev. ed., ed. James Gouinlock (Amherst, NY: Prometheus Books, 1994) pp. 182–4.

[6] Obligations to animals raise an interesting problem for this conception of morality. Is it wrong to torture animals only because other *people* could be expected to disapprove? Or is it that the animal itself would disapprove? Or, perhaps, duties to animals rest on sympathy and compassion while human moral relations are more like Dewey describes, resting on morality's inherently social nature and on the dictates of conscience viewed as an assembly of others?

Punishment and Desert

Martin Perlmutter

'Shall we receive good at the hand of God, and shall we not receive evil?' In all this Job did not sin with his lips.

Job 2:10

Punishment is a form of harm or deprivation: in punishing somebody, we are making that person worse off than he was before. And since it seems that we have a *prima facie* obligation not to make others worse off, the practice of punishment needs a justification in virtue of which that *prima facie* obligation is overridden. Why are we entitled to harm persons when we punish them?

There are two general answers to this question. The first looks to the future and to the overall consequences of inflicting the harm; it maintains that one is entitled to make a person worse off if the consequences of doing so outweigh the harm done. Inflicting harm is justified when the harm done is part of a larger chain in which that harm results in yet greater good. The good produced by the harm might be the rehabilitation of the offender, the protection of others from the offender, or the deterrence of other future offenders. This answer is utilitarian; it looks to future goods, which outweigh the present harm, as the justification of the present harm. The second looks to the past and to the past deeds of the offender; it maintains that one is entitled to make a person worse off if that person's past deeds are such that he deserves to be punished. Just as it is fitting to reward someone who does well with some goods, whether those be a trophy, a better job, or a salary increase, so it is appropriate to deprive someone who does poorly of those same goods. On some occasions, a person deserves to be punished when the punishment has nothing to do with the future consequences of the harm inflicted. Of course, it would be nice if good consequences proceeded from the punishment, just as it would be nice if good consequences proceeded from giving the trophy to the winner rather than to the loser, but good consequences, like rehabilitation, protection, or deterrence, are not in any way integral to punishment. This answer is the retributive view of punishment; it looks to past deeds in virtue of which the harm is deserved as justification of the harm.[1]

In this paper I will argue that the focus of punishment, like the focus of many other moral notions, is the past: it is thus a retributive concept. Just as the concepts "praise," "blame," and, more importantly, "desert" have a backward focus, so too "punishment" looks to the past. The justification of punishment is another matter, for punishment might be both retributive and indefensible. I will maintain that there can be no forward-looking defense of punishment, though the moral acceptability of punishing an individual does on occasion rest on forward-looking considerations. The justification of punishment, if there is one, is to be found in the notion of desert, another backward-looking concept. As a postscript, I will make some general comments about treating somebody as a person. In doing so, I will try to make sense of the seemingly absurd Hegelian view that "in punishment the offender is honored as a rational being, since the punishment is looked on as his right. . . ."

1. THE CONCEPT OF PUNISHMENT

Before we ask questions about the justification of punishment, we should be clear about what punishment is. Otherwise, we would not know whether or not it is punishment that we are justifying. So, for example, justifying the reform or rehabilitation of an offender might not be a difficult task, but it would be a justification of punishment only if punishment were essentially a reformative or rehabilitative notion.

There are two features of punishment that are essential to it. First, punishment is inflicting harm; nothing can count as punishment unless it is a deprivation or causes pain or suffering to the person on whom it is inflicted. This is not quite right since a person might prefer his punishment to the alternatives available to him; on occasion, a drunkard might prefer a warm cell with a mattress to the cold outside and a child might rather be banished to his room than continue to play with his friends. The intention in punishing, however, is to do harm; in punishing somebody, we intend to make the person worse off than he would be without the punishment.[2] So, punishment must involve pain or other consequences normally considered unpleasant.

Not every case of making a person worse off, however, is an instance of punishment. Confining a person who has an infectious disease, hitting somebody just for the fun of it, and taxing the wealthy might well be instances of harming persons, but they are not cases of punishment, even if they were deprivations that we were justified in imposing. For a deprivation to be a punishment, it has to be associated with past wrongdoing. A heavily taxed wealthy person would be overstating his case if he complained that he was being punished for being wealthy, for there is no presumption of any past wrongdoing in his case.

Second, then, a person may be punished if and only if there is some presumption of past wrongdoing. Again, this is a conceptual requirement; it is part of the meaning of "punishment." Imposing harm is not punishment unless the imposition of the harm is connected with a supposed past wrongdoing. There need not be any actual wrongdoing. A mother might punish her daughter for sexual behavior which she mistakenly perceives to be wrong; a country might punish antiwar activists for activities that are morally correct; and a teacher might punish a student for persisting in his correct answer to a question. Each of these would be an instance of punishment because the harm inflicted is a response to past behavior that is perceived to be wrong. Of course, it might be morally unacceptable to punish a person who has done nothing wrong. But the harm inflicted in such a case is still a punishment, though it might have been wrong to inflict it. And we are presently concerned with understanding what is involved in punishment and not with justifying the imposition of harm.[3]

Some persons have maintained that there is a conceptual link between wrongdoing and punishment. It may be claimed that the explication of the concept of wrongdoing itself must contain a reference to punishment; that is, an act is an instance of wrongdoing if and only if the agent is subject to punishment for performing it. In legal contexts, a natural home for the discussion of punishment, such a view has had some currency. An act is a legal offense just in case there is a sanction that attaches to performing it: a rule of law requires that a person perform or forbear from performing some act and promises harm in case of noncompliance. As a more general thesis, however, it is false: wrongdoing or offense cannot have liability to punishment in its explication, for there are many offenses that do not subject the offender to any penalty. Punishment, however, does require reference to wrongdoing.

The imposition of harm and past wrongdoing are closely related. The harm imposed is in virtue of the past wrongdoing; the person deserves to suffer because he committed an offense. It is appropriate that the person suffer harm or deprivation because of the person's past deeds; had the person not done wrong, he would not have deserved the suffering. This is central to punishment. In much the same way that doing well sometimes entitles a person to an increase in goods, so doing poorly occasionally makes it acceptable to deprive a person of goods.[4]

The legitimate domain of punishment is restricted to special relationships. A state can legitimately punish its citizens; it is within a parent's province to punish his or her child: and a teacher has the authority to punish his or her students. Not everyone, however, is entitled to punish, even in response to past wrongdoing. As a general rule, a citizen cannot punish the state, a child cannot punish a parent, and a student cannot punish a teacher. Were a father to search out the person who molested his daughter and kill him, he would be acting illegitimately, even if the harm inflicted is identical with the punishment that would be inflicted by the appropriate authority.

Although blame is similar to punishment in many ways—in blaming a person, we are causing that person a limited sort of harm in virtue of a past wrongdoing—blame is more general than punishment in this way.[5] The legitimate domain of blame is not restricted to special relationships. While it may be morally unacceptable to blame somebody, though he is blameworthy, that unacceptability is in virtue of considerations of the future. On occasion, the bad consequences of blaming make blaming unacceptable. It might be unacceptable to blame somebody for past deeds if that person is on his deathbed; it might be silly for you to blame somebody if doing so would upset you a great deal; and there might be no point to blaming somebody who would enjoy the loss of your esteem. In each of these cases, it might be morally unacceptable or imprudent to blame him, even though he is blameworthy. But it is not a question of authority; blame, unlike punishment, is not restricted to special relationships. Each of these three cases would be a paradigmatic instance of blaming, just as a morally unacceptable case of telling the truth would be a para-digmatic instance of truth-telling. The father who searched out and killed his daughter's molester, however, would not be a paradigmatic instance of punishing.

Both punishment and blame have past wrongdoing as their focus. Even if it were true that inflicting harm on an individual needs past wrongdoing as its justification, and that is not true, it would have little to do with an explication of punishment. For punishing is inflicting harm in virtue of past wrongdoing, just as blaming has a past misdeed as its focus. And whether or not the practice of punishment is morally acceptable, that is what the practice is.

2. A UTILITARIAN CRITIQUE OF PUNISHMENT

A utilitarian might focus on the analogy of punishment to blame to argue that though punishment has a backward focus, the moral acceptability of inflicting the harm must derive from the future consequences of the harm inflicted. If it is morally unacceptable to express blame to a person on his deathbed, though the person is blameworthy, then blameworthiness is not sufficient for the moral acceptability of blaming. And it is forward-looking considerations that make expressing the blame morally unacceptable; that is, since nothing good will be accomplished by expressing the blame and somebody will be worse off for it, the blame should not be expressed. Similarly, in punishment, past wrongdoing is not sufficient for the moral acceptability of inflicting the harm. Even if inflicting harm requires past wrongdoing for it to be punishment, it requires good consequences for it to be morally acceptable. As a result, in a utilitarian view, it is the consequences of inflicting harm that determine whether or not it is morally acceptable to inflict the harm, though it is backward-looking considerations that determine whether or not it is punishment. Just as taxing the wealthy might be a morally acceptable way of harming the wealthy only if the consequences justify it, so too fining a traffic offender is morally acceptable only if the consequences justify it. Of course, taxing the wealthy is not based on past wrongdoing, so it is not punishment, whereas fining the traffic offender is punishment. But whether or not inflicting harm is punishment is only a detail and does not speak to the moral acceptability of inflicting it.

This utilitarian view is general and not restricted to punishment. According to it, one should always do what has the best consequences. What has already happened is relevant only insofar as the future is concerned. The fact that a person has committed an offense might be a reason for inflicting harm on the person, but only in virtue of the future benefits of the harm. Thus, a past offense might serve as evidence for future offenses and future offenses are to be avoided, so it might be best to protect his future victims by imprisoning him. Or, it might be best to discourage future offenders by inflicting harm on him for this offense. But unless there is a justification in the future, it would be morally unacceptable to inflict the harm. For if there were no such future benefits, then, all things considered, in punishing one is increasing the amount of suffering in the world and that is morally unacceptable.

This utilitarian challenge might require abandoning the practice of punishment. If punishment involves intending to make a person worse off because of past wrongdoing, then the only utilitarian defense of punishment could be deterrence. For reform of the offender or protection of society from the offender's future offenses does not involve intentionally making the offender worse off any more than curing a person of an infectious disease involves that intention. Were we able to cure a person of a disease without inconveniencing the victim, one would surely do so. Similarly, if reform were the aim of punishment, punishment would not necessarily involve making the offender worse off, even temporarily. The same holds true for societal protection as an aim of punishment; it too does not necessarily involve making a person worse off. Deterrence fares a little better, but even it does not require actually inflicting the harm as opposed to merely appearing to others to inflict the harm.

An example might help. Suppose my son lies to me and suppose also that I am persuaded that I have no evidence that sending him to his room will do any more good than not sending him to his room. I might still think that he deserves to be punished for what he did and send him to his room, thereby inflicting harm on him for what he did. A utilitarian might claim that I should not have done it for no good will result from my harming my son in this way. And he might be right. But if he is right, it is not because he has a different theory of punishment which yields a different result in this case. Rather, it is because punishment is not justified; it is because, on his view, I am never entitled to inflict harm unless a greater good will result. The utilitarian is giving a critique of punishment, not an alternative theory of punishment.

Punishment is a response to one's past wrongdoing much as reward is a response to one's having done well. Someone might contend that it is morally unacceptable to award the prize to the winner if there is somebody who could use it a lot more and if, all things considered, more good will be accomplished by giving the prize to the person in need. And he might be right. But that is no more an alternative theory of reward than a utilitarian's is an alternative theory of punishment. Punishment is a retributive notion; the person deserves to be deprived because he committed an offense. Punishment, then, necessarily involves deprivation, whereas reform and protection do not. What is operative in punishment is desert for past wrongdoing, not the future gains of the deprivation.

Even if the utilitarian does not provide an alternative theory of punishment, he might be right in his critique of punishment. My punishing my son for lying might be morally unacceptable, because reform, protection, or deterrence are not gained by it. It might be morally unacceptable to do anything whose foreseeable consequences involve more harm than good. And if it is, then the practice of punishment ought to be abandoned.

3. A CRITIQUE OF UTILITARIANISM

The appropriate response to this challenge is the denial of the contention that it is morally unacceptable ever to choose an action whose foreseeable consequences involve more harm than its alternatives. That utilitarian contention, though plausible, conflicts with many of our ordinary intuitions about morality.

There are a variety of reasons why the utilitarian contention is false, even if we ignore issues about what is foreseeable, what constitutes harm, and whether or not the consequences are quantifiable in a way that allows for the application of the utilitarian contention. First, it does not take into account the fact that a person is morally entitled to take his own interests more seriously than the interests of others. Thus, it is morally acceptable for me to keep my two kidneys rather than donate one of them to a person in need, though that course of action does involve more foreseeable harm than the alternative. And I am surely morally entitled to keep my only kidney even though more good consequences would result from my donating it to a philanthropist in need. Second, the utilitarian contention puts every action into a moral sphere. Although it might be imprudent to do something whose foreseeable consequences involve more harm than good, it is not morally unacceptable to do so. Thus, if I choose pumpkin pie rather than apple pie, realizing that I have an allergy to pumpkins, I may be acting imprudently, but not in a morally unacceptable way. Third, there is a logical problem with the utilitarian position. Suppose I use the utilitarian contention in order to decide that the morally acceptable thing to do is not to vote—there are no foreseeable harmful consequences of my not voting and by not voting I will get the added pleasure of being able to take a nap. If everyone were to reason the same way, they would all be acting morally and would all abstain from voting. The result of that, however, would be harmful, presumably a breakdown in democratic institutions, even though my not voting has no harmful consequences. This seems wrong; how can everyone's doing the morally right thing have as a consequence everyone's being worse off? But that does seem to be a result of the utilitarian contention.

Most important for our purposes, however, the utilitarian contention ignores the fact that many of our moral concepts are backward-looking. Most often, we are morally required to do things because of what happened in the past. It is that which makes social contract theories appealing; we are obligated to behave in accordance with an implicit contract, something which we already tacitly agreed to do. More simply, though, we are required to keep a promise because we made it, we are required to award the prize to the winner because he won the race, and we are required to repay a debt because we borrowed the money. Frequently, it is the past and not the future which determines the moral acceptability of an action. Of course, keeping a promise has consequences for the practice of promise-keeping and the fact that a promise was made also has consequences since the promise created expectations. But what makes it right to keep a promise is the past fact that a promise was made. So, the well-known example of a secret promise to a dying man to deliver a hoard of money, which he entrusts to me, to his already rich son is relevant. It is the promise, and not the consequences, which makes it right to give his son the money.

The utilitarian is correct in recognizing that, on occasion, we are morally required to look to the future and that the future sometimes affects what it is morally acceptable to do, even in the case of backward-looking concepts. Thus, though a promise was made, perhaps to meet somebody for lunch, it would be morally unacceptable to do so if it would result in somebody's death, because of the need to rush somebody to the hospital. But in cases such as this, it is not *merely* minimizing harm or maximizing benefit that is operative. Rather, a rational person would not expect the promise to be kept to him in a case such as this. The commitment involved in promises does not create an obligation in such a case.

It would be a mistake to think, however, that merely weighing benefits and harms is what is operative here. For if that were true, the fact that I would benefit more than the person would suffer by my not keeping the promise should be enough to show that I should not keep the promise. A utilitarian might respond that there are harmful consequences to the institution of promise-keeping and that when these harmful consequences are taken into account, keeping the promise will ordinarily be the morally correct action. But the damage done to the institution of promise-keeping would not be damaging an institution that a utilitarian should consider worth keeping, if that institution required me to do something that would not maximize benefits. For, on utilitarian assumptions, there is only questionable utility in an institution that required behavior which, other things being equal, resulted in more harm than good.

So, even though the utilitarian contention about maximizing benefits and minimizing harm has some plausibility, it does not conform to our everyday moral intuitions about what is morally acceptable. Of course, a utilitarian might urge that it is unreasonable to take the past as seriously as we do and that it is immoral to take our own interests more seriously than we take other person's interests. But until we become persuaded by such urgings, and it is not clear that we should become persuaded by them, we should continue to take our everyday moral notions seriously and reject the utilitarian contention. Using these moral notions, we must conclude that the past plays a large role in justifying moral behavior.

4. PUNISHMENT AND DESERT

The notion of desert is central to punishment. What a person deserves is most often determined by what he has done. Does a person ever deserve to have harm inflicted on him for what he has done? The answer seems straightforward. On occasion, when a person knowingly and intentionally does wrong, he should be punished for what he did. In much the same way as a person occasionally deserves to be blamed, deserves the loss of another's esteem, a person occasionally deserves to have harm inflicted upon him.

A view which emphasizes deterrence as the rationale for inflicting the harm would also require such a notion of desert. Otherwise, it would be morally unacceptable to harm somebody merely to deter others. Presumably, on this view, in doing wrong, a person made it acceptable to have harm inflicted on himself, thereby, deterring others. That is, he deserves the harm: Punishment is morally acceptable.

More generally, if desert has any place in moral discourse, and clearly it does, then there are lots of things that people deserve. For example, the winner of the race deserves the prize. In giving the winner the prize, however, we are harming others. Suppose that one of the losers contended that he had counted on winning, that he could really use the prize, and that he was harmed in not getting the prize. All of these contentions might be true, but none of them are at all relevant for determining desert in this case. If he is in fact harmed by not getting the prize, then he deserves to be harmed. In fact, any system that uses desert as a criterion for distributing goods has as a consequence that persons on occasion deserve to be harmed, since not getting the good is most often a harm.

The fact that a person deserves to be harmed should not seem at all strange. It is merely an extension of any system of desert. Regardless of our criteria of worthiness, if the most worthy person gets the job, somebody is being harmed for their not being the most worthy, for not getting the job is in fact a harm. Punishment is merely another instance of deserving to be harmed.

We are now in a position to understand the Hegelian view that "in punishment the offender is honored as a rational being, since the punishment is looked on as his right." If the offender deserves to be punished in virtue of his past wrongdoing, then if we do not punish him, then we should have some reason for not treating him as he deserves. If we are in no way excusing what he did but merely exempting him from the harm, then we are not dealing with him as he deserves. In choosing to do wrong and in realizing the consequences of what he did, he brought the punishment upon himself. In punishing him, we are respecting his choice. The punishment is his due in much the same way as the prize is the due of the winner. If we refused the winner the prize merely because we did not want him to benefit, then we would be acting illegitimately by not giving him his desert. So too with punishment. In punishment we are honoring the integrity of the agent by giving him his due.

The right to be punished is a strange sort of right. Rights are generally associated with what is in one's interest, so we must say that it is in the offender's interest to be punished. Pain or suffering is undesirable, however, so people will ordinarily not claim their right to be punished. Nevertheless, persons do have an interest in being treated as persons, as genuine members of the moral community. Such treatment requires that one's choices are honored and that one is dealt with in a manner appropriate to those choices. The right to be punished, then, is derivative on the right to be treated as a person. Just as persons deserve to be rewarded, so too persons deserve to be punished. Both rewarding and punishing are instances of respecting the rights of persons.

On occasion, it is more appropriate to use a therapy model than the model of honoring the integrity of human beings. Wrongdoing is occasionally pathological and should be dealt with much as one deals with other pathological conditions. If the agent was himself a victim of the wrongdoing, then it is appropriate to treat him as a victim in the way that a therapy model does. So, one might treat the person for this illness much as one would treat a person for a cancer. In treating a person in this way, however, one is treating him as a victim, not as an agent, one is not respecting his choices, and one is not honoring him as a human being. Most often, the therapy model is inappropriate. When it is inappropriate, the person as a moral agent has a right to be punished, not treated. It is demeaning to have our choices be treated as if they were something over which we have no control! And although it is difficult to isolate reasons why it is in our interest to be treated as a person, as an autonomous moral agent, we ordinarily do want our choices to be respected as emanating from us, rather than to be dealt with as symptoms of an ailment over which we have no control.

The deathbed example is a difficult case. Should we punish a person on his deathbed for a past wrongdoing? And if we choose not to punish him, we are no longer dealing with him in a way appropriate to persons as autonomous moral agents? After all, is it not because we respect him as a person that we might be inclined to refuse to inflict harm on him? The answer to these questions depends on how a person on his deathbed is viewed. If the only interest, or the overwhelming interest, that we associate with a dying person is a peaceful death, then we should not punish him. A dying person would require special treatment in virtue of that dominant interest. If he wants a promise to be made, even an unreasonable promise, it might be best to make it, later to break it. If he is blameworthy, it might be unacceptable to blame him. It might even be acceptable to lie to him about his prospects for survival. But insofar as we are entitled to do all these things, we are compromising his status as a full-fledged member of the moral community. If the pressing interest to die comfortably and untroubled overrides his generally more important interest to be treated as a person, then our ordinary moral discourse fails. It is not, however, because we respect him as a person that we are willing to do these things. Rather, it is because his situation is so dire that it demands that his immediate needs be met. Issues of desert are overwhelmed by issues of immediate need.

Most often, however, it is desert that determines the moral acceptability of behavior. Occasionally, what one deserves is for harm to be inflicted. On those occasions, one deserves to be punished; it is one's right as a person.

NOTES

[1] These two general answers do get a bit more complex. For the utilitarian might go on to maintain that inflicting harm can only be punishment if it is in virtue of a past deed that the harm is inflicted. Taking from the wealthy to feed starving children might be a morally acceptable way of harming the wealthy, but it is a conceptual mistake to view it as a punishment. Inflicting harm to prevent yet greater harm or to produce beneficial consequences might be morally acceptable, but it is not *punishment* unless it is backward-looking enough so that it is inflicted in virtue of some past action. And the retributivist might not want to be saddled with punishing a person when no possible earthly benefit will derive from it. It seems severe to inflict harm on another in those cases when absolutely nothing will be gained from it, except perhaps a balancing of the moral scales. So, punishment may become a bit backward-looking for the utilitarian and a bit forward-looking for the retributivist.

Thus, both views, when modified, seem to agree that both backward-looking and forward-looking considerations are relevant for determining the moral acceptability of punishment. Yet, the focus of the two views is different. For the retributivist thinks that it is the past wrongdoing which makes inflicting harm morally acceptable, whereas the utilitarian maintains that inflicting harm can be made morally acceptable only by considering the future consequences of the harm. Thus, the retributivist is not committed to the view that inflicting the harm is morally acceptable only if doing so produces better consequences than not inflicting it, for he believes that the justification lies in the past.

[2] Again, this will not do. A judge might realize that the drunken defendant prefers the warm cell, yet punish him by sentencing him to a night in jail. Presumably, a night in jail is normally considered less pleasant than not spending a night in jail even if it is not so in every case. In legal contexts, the penalty must be determined by what is normally considered harmful or unpleasant.

[3] In the Ten Commandments, God is said to visit the inequity of the fathers upon the children to the third and fourth generation. In doing so, God is punishing the father; He is causing the father harm for his past wrongdoing, presumably because it is the father's interest that his children not suffer. But if the children are not even presumed guilty of any wrongdoing, then He is punishing them only in an attenuated sense. In much the same way, children may be harmed by the imprisonment of their father. But they are not being punished, except in some derivative sense. There is some

question about whether it is morally acceptable to cause children harm when they have done nothing wrong. So, Ezekiel seems to renounce the view that children suffer at the hands of God for the misdeeds of the fathers (Ezekiel: 18).

4 Webster's confirms this explication of punishment. The main entry for "punish" is "to afflict with pain, loss, or suffering for a crime or fault"; and the law entry for "punishment" is "a penalty inflicted by a court of justice on a convicted offender as a past retribution. . . ." Harm, wrongdoing, and desert are thus all part of what is involved in punishment.

5 For our purposes, there are three features associated with blame that need to be distinguished. First, there is blameworthiness. Blameworthiness is wholly backward-looking, focusing exclusively on the agent and his past deeds. Blameworthiness is analogous to responsibility, another backward-looking concept. Second, there is blaming, whether or not we ever express the disapproval or indignation to anybody. We might hold a person accountable for his past misdeeds, without ever engaging in any verbal rebuke. Third, there is expressing the blame, typically to the blameworthy person. On occasion, it is morally unacceptable to express blame, though blame is appropriate. The deathbed case might be such a case. Clearly, the fact that a man is dying does not affect his blameworthiness, for it has nothing whatever to do with his being accountable for his past misdeeds.

Two Concepts of Rules

John Rawls

In this paper I want to show the importance of the distinction between justifying a practice[1] and justifying a particular action falling under it, and I want to explain the logical basis of this distinction and how it is possible to miss its significance. While the distinction has frequently been made,[2] and is now becoming commonplace, there remains the task of explaining the tendency either to overlook it altogether, or to fail to appreciate its importance.

To show the importance of the distinction I am going to defend utilitarianism against those objections which have traditionally been made against it in connection with punishment. I hope to show that if one uses the distinction in question then one can state utilitarianism in a way which makes it a much better explication of our considered moral judgments than these traditional objections would seem to admit.[3] Thus the importance of the distinction is shown by the way it strengthens the utilitarian view regardless of whether that view is completely defensible or not.

To explain how the significance of the distinction may be overlooked, I am going to discuss two conceptions of rules. One of these conceptions conceals the importance of distinguishing between the justification of a rule or practice and the justification of a particular action falling under it. The other conception makes it clear why this distinction must be made and what is its logical basis.

The subject of punishment, in the sense of attaching legal penalties to the violation of legal rules, has always been a troubling moral question.[4] The trouble about it has not been that people disagree as to whether or not punishment is justifiable. Most people have held that, freed from certain abuses, it is an acceptable institution. Only a few have rejected punishment entirely, which is rather surprising when one considers all that can be said against it. The difficulty is with the justification of punishment: Various arguments for it have been given by moral philosophers, but so far none of them has won any sort of general acceptance; no justification is without those who detest it. I hope to show that the use of the aforementioned distinction enables one to state the utilitarian view in a way which allows for the sound points of its critics.

For our purposes we may say that there are two justifications of punishment. What we may call the retributive view is that punishment is justified on the grounds that wrongdoing merits punishment. It is morally fitting that a person who does wrong should suffer in proportion to his wrongdoing. That a criminal should be punished follows from his guilt, and the severity of the appropriate punishment depends on the depravity of his act. The state of affairs where a wrongdoer suffers punishment is morally better than the state of affairs where he does not; and it is better irrespective of any of the consequences of punishing him.

What we may call the utilitarian view holds that on the principle that bygones are bygones and that only future consequences are material to present decisions, punishment is justifiable only by reference to the probable consequences of maintaining it as one of the devices of the social order. Wrongs committed in the past are, as such, not relevant considerations for deciding what to do. If punishment can be shown to promote effectively the interest of society it is justifiable, otherwise it is not.

I have stated these two competing views very roughly to make one feel the conflict between them: One feels the force of *both* arguments and one wonders how they can be reconciled. From my introductory remarks it is obvious that the resolution which I am going to propose is that in this case one must distinguish between justifying a practice as a system of rules to be applied and enforced, and justifying a particular action which falls under these rules; utilitarian arguments are appropriate with regard to questions about practices, while retributive arguments fit the application of particular rules to particular cases.

We might try to get clear about this distinction by imagining how a father might answer the question of his son. Suppose the son asks, "Why was F put in jail yesterday?" The father answers, "Because he robbed the bank at B. He was duly tried and found guilty. That's why he was put in jail yesterday." But suppose the son had asked a different question, namely, "Why do people put other people in jail?" Then the father might answer, "To protect good people from bad people" or "To stop people from doing things that would make it uneasy for all of us; for otherwise we wouldn't be able to go to bed at night and sleep in peace." There are two very different questions here. One question emphasizes the proper name: it asks why F was punished rather than someone else, or it asks what he was punished for. The other question asks why we have the institution of punishment: why do people punish one another rather than, say, always forgiving one another?

Thus the father says in effect that a particular man is punished, rather than some other man, because he is guilty, and he is guilty because he broke the law (past tense). In his case the law looks back, the judge looks back, the jury looks back, and a penalty is visited upon him for something he did. That a man is to be published, and what his punishment is to be, is settled by its being shown that he broke the law and that the law assigns that penalty for the violation of it.

On the other hand we have the institution of punishment itself, and recommend and accept various changes in it, because it is thought by the (ideal) legislator and by those to whom the law applies that, as a part of a system of law impartially applied from case to case arising under it, it will have the consequence, in the long run, of furthering the interests of society.

One can say, then that the judge and the legislator stand in different positions and look in different directions: one to the past, the other to the future. The justification of what the judge does, *qua* judge, sounds like the retributive view; the justification of what the (ideal) legislator does, *qua* legislator, sounds like the utilitarian view. Thus both views have a point (this is as it should be since intelligent and sensitive persons have been on both sides of the argument); and one's initial confusion disappears once one sees that these views apply to persons holding different offices with different duties, and situated differently with respect to the system of rules that make up the criminal law.[5]

One might say, however, that the utilitarian view is more fundamental since it applies to a more fundamental office, for the judge carries out the legislator's will so far as he can determine it. Once the legislator decides to have laws and to assign penalties for their violation (as things are there must be both the law and the penalty) an institution is set up which involves a retributive conception of particular cases. It is part of the concept of the criminal law as a system of rules that the application and enforcement of these rules in particular cases should be justifiable by arguments of a retributive character. The decision whether or not to use law rather than some other mechanism of social control, and the decision as to what laws to have and what penalties to assign, may be settled by utilitarian arguments; but if one decides to have laws then one has decided on something whose working in particular cases is retributive in form.[6]

The answer, then, to the confusion engendered by the two views of punishment is quite simple: one distinguishes two offices, that of the judge and that of the legislator, and one distinguishes their different stations with respect to the system of rules which make up the law; and then one notes that the different sorts of considerations which would usually be offered as reasons for what is done under the cover of these offices can be paired off with the competing justifications of punishment. One reconciles the two views by the time-honored device of making them apply to different situations.

But can it really be this simple? Well, this answer allows for the apparent intent of each side. Does a person who advocates the retributive view necessarily advocate, as an *institution*, legal machinery whose essential purpose is to set up and preserve a correspondence between moral turpitude and suffering? Surely not.[7] What retributionists have rightly insisted upon is that no man can be punished unless he is guilty, that is, unless he has broken the law. Their fundamental criticism of the utilitarian account is that, as they interpret it, it sanctions an innocent person's being punished (if one may call it that) for the benefit of society.

On the other hand, utilitarians agree that punishment is to be inflicted only for the violation of law. They regard this much as understood from the concept of punishment itself.[8] The point of the utilitarian account concerns the institution as a system of rules: Utilitarianism seeks to limit its use by declaring it justifiable only if it can be shown to foster effectively the good of society. Historically it is a protest against the indiscriminate and ineffective use of the criminal law.[9] It seeks to dissuade us from assigning to penal institutions the improper, if not sacrilegious, task of matching suffering with moral turpitude. Like others, utilitarians want penal institutions designed so that, as far as humanly possible, only those who break the law run afoul of it. They hold that no official should have discretionary power to inflict penalties whenever he thinks it for the benefit of society; for on utilitarian grounds an institution granting such power could not be justified.[10]

The suggested way of reconciling the retributive and the utilitarian justifications of punishment seems to account for what both sides have wanted to say. There are, however, two further questions which arise, and I shall devote the remainder of this section to them.

First, will not a difference of opinion as to the proper criterion of just law make the proposed reconciliation unacceptable to retributionists? Will they not question whether, if the utilitarian principle is used as the criterion, it follows that those who have broken the law are guilty in a way which satisfies their demand that those punished deserve to be punished? To answer this difficulty, suppose that the rules of the criminal law are justified on utilitarian grounds (it is only for laws that meet his criterion that the utilitarian can be held responsible). Then it follows that the actions which the criminal law specifies as offenses are such that, if they are tolerated, terror and alarm would spread in society. Consequently, retributionists can only deny that those who are punished deserve to be punished if they deny that such actions are wrong. This they will not want to do.

The second question is whether utilitarianism doesn't justify too much. One pictures it as an engine of justification which, if consistently adopted, could be used to justify cruel and arbitrary institutions. Retributionists may be supposed to concede the utilitarians *intend* to reform the law and to make it more humane; that utilitarians do not wish to justify any such thing as punishment of the innocent; and that utilitarians may appeal to the fact that punishment presupposes guilt in the sense that by punishment one understands an institution attaching penalties to the infraction of legal rules, and therefore that it is logically absurd to suppose that utilitarians in justifying punishment might also have justified punishment (if we may call it that) of the innocent. The real question, however, is whether the utilitarian, in justifying *punishment*, hasn't used arguments which commit him to accepting the infliction of suffering on innocent persons if it is for the good of society (whether or not one calls this punishment). More generally, isn't the utilitarian committed in principle to accepting many practices which he, as a morally sensitive person, wouldn't want to accept? Retributionists are inclined to hold that there is no way to stop the utilitarian principle from justifying too much except by adding to it a principle which distributes certain rights to individuals. Then the amended criterion is not the greatest benefit of society *simpliciter*, but the greatest benefit of society subject to the constraint that no one's rights may be violated. Now while I think that the classical utilitarians proposed a criterion of this more complicated sort, I do not want to argue that point here.[11] What I want to show is that there is *another* way of preventing the utilitarian principle from justifying too much, or at least of making it much less likely to do so; namely, by stating utilitarianism in a way which accounts for the distinction between the justification of an institution and the justification of a particular action falling under it.

I begin by defining the institution of punishment as follows: a person is said to suffer punishment whenever he is legally deprived of some of the normal rights of a citizen on the ground that he has violated a rule of law, the violation having been established by trial according to the due process of law, provided that the deprivation is carried out by the recognized legal authorities of the state, that the rule of law clearly specifies both the offense and the attached penalty, that the courts construe statutes strictly, and that the statute was on the books prior to the time of the offense.[12] This definition specifies what I shall understand by punishment. The question is whether utilitarian arguments may be found to justify institutions widely different from this and such as one would find cruel and arbitrary.

The question is best answered, I think, by taking up a particular accusation. Consider the following from Carritt:

> . . . the utilitarian must hold that we are justified in inflicting pain always and only to prevent worse pain or bring about greater happiness. This, then, is all we need to consider in so-called punishment, which must be purely preventive. But if some kind of very cruel crime becomes common, and none of the criminals can be caught, it might be highly expedient, as an example, to hang an innocent man, if a charge against him could be so framed that he were universally thought guilty; indeed this would only fail to be an ideal instance of utilitarian "punishment" because the victim himself would not have been so likely as a real felon to commit such a crime in the future; in all other respects it would be perfectly deterrent and therefore felicific.[13]

Carritt is trying to show that there are occasions when a utilitarian argument would justify taking an action which would be generally condemned; and thus that utilitarianism justifies too much. But the failure of Carritt's argument lies in the fact that he makes no distinction between the justification of the general system of rules which constitutes penal institutions and the justification of particular applications of these rules to particular cases by the various officials whose job it is to administer them. This becomes perfectly clear when one asks who the "we" are of whom Carritt speaks. Who is this who has a sort of absolute authority on particular occasions to decide that an innocent man shall be "punished" if everyone can be convinced that he is guilty? Is this person the legislator, or the judge, or the body of private citizens, or what? It is utterly crucial to know who is to decide such matters, and by what authority, for all of this must be written into the rules of the institution. Until one knows these things, one doesn't know what the institution is whose justification is being challenged; and as the utilitarian principle applies to the institution, one doesn't know whether it is justifiable on utilitarian grounds or not.

Once this is understood it is clear what the countermove to Carritt's argument is. One must describe more carefully what the *institution* is which his example suggests, and then ask oneself whether or not it is likely that having this institution would be for the benefit of society in the long run. One must not content oneself with the vague thought that, when it's a question of *this* case, it would be a good thing if *somebody* did something even if an innocent person were to suffer.

Try to imagine, then, an institution (which we may call "telishment") which is such that officials set up by it have authority to arrange a trial for the condemnation of an innocent man whenever they are of the opinion that doing so would be in the best interests of society. The discretion of officials is limited, however, by the rule that they may not condemn an innocent man to undergo such an ordeal unless there is, at the time, a wave of offenses similar to that with which they charge him and telish him for. We may imagine that the officials having the discretionary authority are the judges of the higher courts in consultation with the chief of police, the minister of justice, and a committee of the legislature.

Once one realizes that one is involved in setting up an *institution*, one sees that the hazards are very great. For example, what check is there on the officials? How is one to tell whether or not their actions are authorized? How is one to limit the risks involved in allowing such systematic deception? How is one to avoid giving anything short of complete discretion to the authorities to telish anyone they like? In addition to these considerations, it is obvious that people will come to have a very different attitude towards their penal system when telishment is adjoined to it. They will be uncertain as to whether a convicted man has been punished to telished. They will wonder whether or not they should feel sorry for him. They will wonder whether the same fate won't at any time fall on them. If one pictures how such an institution would actually work, and the enormous risks involved in it, it seems clear that it would serve no useful purpose. A utilitarian justification for this institution is most unlikely.

It happens, in general, that as one drops off the defining features of punishment one ends up with an institution whose utilitarian justification is highly doubtful. One reason for this is that punishment works like a kind of price system: by altering the prices one has to pay for the performance of actions it supplies a motive for avoiding some actions and doing others. The defining features are essential if punishment is to work in this way; so that an institution which lacks these features, e.g., an institution which is set up to "punish" the innocent, is likely to have about as much point as a price system (if one may call it that) where the prices of things change at random from day to day and one learns the price of something after one has agreed to buy it.[14] If one is careful to apply the utilitarian principle to the institution which is to authorize particular actions, then there is *less* danger of its justifying too much. Carritt's example gains plausibility by its indefiniteness and by its concentration on the particular case. His argument will only hold if it can be shown that there are utilitarian arguments which justify an institution whose publicly ascertainable offices and powers are such as to permit officials to exercise that kind of discretion in particular cases. But the requirement of having to build the arbitrary features of the particular decision into the institutional practice makes the justification much less likely to go through.

NOTES

From John Rawls, "Two Concepts of Rules," *The Philosophical Review*, Vol. 64 (1955), pp. 3–13. Reprinted with the permission of the author and *The Philosophical Review*. This is a revision of a paper given at the Harvard Philosophy Club on April 30, 1954.

[1] I use the word "practice" throughout as a sort of technical term meaning any form of activity specified by a system of rules which defines offices, roles, moves, penalties, defenses, and so on, and which gives the activity its structure. As examples one may think of games and rituals, trials and parliaments.

[2] The distinction is central to Hume's discussion of justice in *A Treatise of Human Nature*, bk. III, pt. 11, esp. secs. 2–4. It is clearly stated by John Austin in the second lecture of *Lectures on Jurisprudence* (4th ed.: London, 1873). I, 116ff. (1st ed., 1832). Also it may be argued that J. S. Mill took it for granted in *Utilitarianism*; on this point cf. J. O. Urmson, "The Interpretation of the Moral Philosophy of

J. S. Mill," *Philosophical Quarterly*, vol. III (1953). In addition to the arguments given by Urmson there are several clear statements of the distinction in *A System of Logic* (8th ed.; London, 1872), bk. VI, ch. xii, pars. 2, 3, 7. The distinction is fundamental to J. D. Mabbott's important paper, "Punishment," *Mind*, n.s., vol. XLVIII (April, 1939). More recently the distinction has been stated with particular emphasis by S. F. Toulmin in *The Place of Reason in Ethics* (Cambridge, 1950), see esp. ch. xi, where it plays a major part of his account of moral reasoning. Toulmin doesn't explain the basis of the distinction, nor how one might overlook its importance, as I try to in this paper, as I in my review of his book (*Philosophical Review*, vol. LX [October, 1951]), as some of my criticisms show, I failed to understand the force of it. See also II D. Aiken, "The Levels of Moral Discourse," *Ethics*, vol. LXII (1952), A. M. Quinton, "Punishment," *Analysis*, vol. XIV (June, 1954), and P. H. Nowell-Smith, *Ethics* (London, 1954), pp. 2, 6, 239, 271–273.

3 On the concept of explication see the author's paper, *Philosophical Review*, vol. LX (April, 1951).

4 While this paper was being revised, Quinton's appeared; footnote 2 supra. There are several respects in which my remarks are similar to his. Yet as I consider some further questions and rely on somewhat different arguments, I have retained the discussion of punishment and promises together as two test cases for utilitarianism.

5 Note the fact that different sorts of arguments are suited to different offices. One way of taking the differences between ethical theories is to regard them as accounts of the reasons expected in different offices.

6 In this connection see Mabbott, *op. cit.*, pp. 163–164.

7 On this point see Sir David Ross, *The Right and the Good* (Oxford, 1930), pp. 57–60.

8 See Hobbes's definition of punishment in *Leviathan*, ch. xxviii; and Bentham's definition in *The Principles of Morals and Legislation*, ch. xii, par. 36, ch. xv, par. 28, and in *The Rationale of Punishment* (London, 1830), bk. I, ch. i. They could agree with Bradley that: "Punishment is punishment only when it is deserved. We pay the penalty, because we owe it, and for no other reason; and if punishment is inflicted for any other reason whatever than because it is merited by wrong, it is a gross immorality, a crying injustice, an abominable crime, and not what it pretends to be." *Ethical Studies* (2nd ed.; Oxford, 1927), pp. 26–26. Certainly by definition it isn't what it pretends to be. The innocent can only be punished by mistake; deliberate "punishment" of the innocent necessarily involves fraud.

9 Cf. Leon Radzinowicz, *A History of English Criminal Law: The Movement for Reform 1750–1833* (London, 1948), esp. ch. xi on Bentham.

10 Bentham discusses how corresponding to a punitory provision of a criminal law there is another provision which stands to it as an antagonist and which needs a name as much as the punitory. He calls it, as one might expect, the *anaetiosostic*, and of it he says: "The punishment of guilt is the object of the former one; the preservation of innocence that of the latter." In the same connection he asserts that it is never thought fit to give the judge the option of deciding whether a thief (that is, a person whom he believes to be a thief, for the judge's belief is what the question

must always turn upon) should hang or not, and so the law writes the provision. "The judge shall not cause a thief to be hanged unless he have been duly convicted and sentenced in course of law" (*The Limits of Jurisprudence Defined*, ed. C. W. Everett [New York, 1940], pp. 238–239).

[11] By the classical utilitarians I understand Hobbes, Hume, Bentham, J. S. Mill, and Sidgwick.

[12] All these features of punishment are mentioned by Hobbes; cf. *Leviathan*, ch. xxviii.

[13] *Ethical and Political Thinking* (Oxford, 1947), p. 65.

[14] The analogy with the price system suggests an answer to the question how utilitarian considerations insure that punishment is proportional to the offense. It is interesting to note that Sir David Ross, after making the distinction between justifying a penal law and justifying a particular application of it, and after stating that utilitarian considerations have a large place in determining the former, still holds back from accepting the utilitarian justification of punishment on the grounds that justice requires that punishment be proportional to the offense, and that utilitarianism is unable to account for this. Cf. *The Right and the Good*, pp. 61–62. I do not claim that utilitarianism can account for this requirement as Sir David might wish, but it happens, nevertheless, that if utilitarian considerations are followed penalties will be proportional to offenses in this sense; the order of offenses according to seriousness can be paired off with the order of penalties according to severity. Also the absolute level of penalties will be as low as possible. This follows from the assumption that people are rational (i.e., that they are able to take into account the "prices" the state puts on actions), the utilitarian rule that a penal system should provide a motive for preferring the less serious offense, and the principle that punishment as such is an evil. All this was carefully worked out by Bentham in *The Principles of Morals and Legislation*, chs. xiii–xv.

The Case for Animal Rights

Tom Regan

How to proceed? We begin by asking how the moral status of animals has been understood by thinkers who deny that animals have rights. Then we test the mettle of their ideas by seeing how well they stand up under the heat of fair criticism. If we start our thinking in this way, we soon find that some people believe that we have no duties directly to animals, that we owe nothing to them, that we can do nothing that wrongs them. Rather, we can do wrong acts that involve animals, and so we have duties regarding them, though none to them. Such views may be called *indirect duty views.* By way of illustration: suppose your neighbor kicks your dog. Then your neighbor has done something wrong. But not to your dog. The wrong that has been done is a wrong to you. After all, it is wrong to upset people, and your neighbor's kicking your dog upsets you. So you are the one who is wronged, not your dog. Or again: by kicking your dog your neighbor damages your property. And since it is wrong to damage another person's property, your neighbor has done something wrong—to you, of course, not to your dog. Your neighbor no more wrongs your dog than your car would be wronged if the windshield were smashed. Your neighbor's duties involving your dog are indirect duties to you. More generally, all of our duties regarding animals are indirect duties to one another—to humanity.

How could someone try to justify such a view? Someone might say that your dog doesn't feel anything and so isn't hurt by your neighbor's kick, doesn't care about the pain since none is felt, is as unaware of anything as is your windshield. Someone might say this, but no rational person will, since, among other considerations, such a view will commit anyone who holds it to the position that no human beings feel pain either—that human beings also don't care about what happens to them. A second possibility is that though both humans and your dog are hurt when kicked, it is only human pain that matters. But, again, no rational person can believe this. Pain is pain wherever it occurs. If your neighbor's causing you pain is wrong because of the pain that is caused, we cannot rationally ignore or dismiss the moral relevance of the pain that your dog feels.

Philosophers who hold indirect duty views—and many still do— have come to understand that they must avoid the two defects just noted: that is, both the view that animals don't feel anything as well as the idea that only human pain can be morally relevant. Among such thinkers the sort of view now favored is one or another form of what is called *contractarianism*.

Here, very crudely, is the root idea: morality consists of a set of rules that individuals voluntarily agree to abide by, as we do when we sign a contract (hence the name contractarianism). Those who understand and accept the terms of the contract are covered directly; they have rights created and recognized by, and protected in, the contract. And these contractors can also have protection spelled out for others who, though they lack the ability to understand morality and so cannot sign the contract themselves, are loved or cherished by those who can. Thus young children, for example, are unable to sign contracts and lack rights. But they are protected by the contract nonetheless because of the sentimental interests of others, most notably their parents. So we have, then, duties involving these children, duties regarding them, but no duties to them. Our duties in their case are indirect duties to other human beings, usually their parents.

As for animals, since they cannot understand contracts, they obviously cannot sign; and since they cannot sign, they have no rights. Like children, however, some animals are the object of the sentimental interest of others. You, for example, love your dog or cat. So those animals that enough people care about (companion animals, whales, baby seals, the American bald eagle), though they lack rights themselves, will be protected because of the sentimental interests of people. I have, then, according to contractarianism, no duty directly to your dog or any other animal, not even the duty not to cause them pain or suffering; my duty not to hurt them is a duty I have to those people who care about what happens to them. As for other animals, where no or little sentimental interest is present—in the case of farm animals, for example, or laboratory rats—what duties we have grow weaker and weaker, perhaps to the vanishing point. The pain and death they endure, though real, are not wrong if no one cares about them.

When it comes to the moral status of animals, contractarianism could be a hard view to refute if it were an adequate theoretical approach to the moral status of human beings. It is not adequate in this latter respect, however, which makes the question of its adequacy in the former case, regarding animals, utterly moot. For consider: morality, according to the (crude) contractarian position before us, consists of rules that people agree to abide by. What people? Well, enough to make a difference—enough, that is, *collectively* to have the power to enforce the rules that are drawn up in the contract. That is very well and good for the signatories but not so good for anyone who is not asked to sign. And there is nothing in contractarianism of the sort we are discussing that guarantees or requires that everyone will have a chance to participate equally in framing rules of morality. The result is that this approach to ethics could sanction the most blatant forms of social, economic, moral, and political injustice, ranging from a repressive caste system to systematic racial or sexual discrimination. Might, according to this theory, does make right. Let those who are the victims of injustice suffer as they will. It matters not so long as no one else—no contractor, or too few of them—cares about it. Such a theory takes one's moral breath away . . . as if, for example, there would be nothing wrong with apartheid in South Africa if few white South Africans were upset by it. A theory with so little to recommend it at the level of the ethics of our treatment of our fellow humans cannot have anything more to recommend it when it comes to the ethics of how we treat our fellow animals.

The version of contractarianism just examined is, as I have noted, a crude variety, and in fairness to those of a contractarian persuasion, it must be noted that much more refined, subtle, and ingenious varieties are possible. For example, John Rawls, in his *A Theory of Justice*, sets forth a version of contractarianism that forces contractors to ignore the accidental features of being a human being—for example, whether one is white or black, male or female, a genius or of modest intellect. Only by ignoring such features, Rawls believes, can we ensure that the principles of justice that contractors would agree upon are not based on bias or prejudice. Despite the improvement a view such as Rawls's represents over the cruder forms of contractarianism, it remains deficient: it systematically denies that we have direct duties to those human beings who do not have a sense of justice—young children, for instance, and many mentally retarded humans. And yet it seems reasonably certain that, were we to torture a young child or a retarded elder, we would be doing something that wronged him or her, not something that would be wrong if (and only if) other humans with a sense of justice were upset. And since this is true in the case of these humans, we cannot rationally deny the same in the case of animals.

Indirect duty views, then, including the best among them, fail to command our rational assent. Whatever ethical theory we should accept rationally, therefore, it must at least recognize that we have some duties directly to animals, just as we have some duties directly to each other. The next two theories I'll sketch attempt to meet this requirement.

The first I call the cruelty-kindness view. Simply stated, this says that we have a direct duty to be kind to animals and a direct duty not to be cruel to them. Despite the familiar, reassuring ring of these ideas, I do not believe that this view offers an adequate theory. To make this clearer, consider kindness. A kind person acts from a certain type of motive compassion or concern, for example. And that is a virtue. But there is no guarantee that a kind act is a right act. If I am a generous racist, for example, I will be inclined to act kindly towards members of my own race, favoring their interests above those of others. My kindness would be real and, so far as it goes, good. But I trust it is too obvious to require argument that my kind acts may not be above moral reproach—may, in fact, be positively wrong because rooted in injustice. So kindness, notwithstanding its status as a virtue to be encouraged, simply will not carry the weight of a theory of right action.

Cruelty fares no better. People or their acts are cruel if they display either a lack of sympathy for or, worse, the presence of enjoyment in another's suffering. Cruelty in all its guises is a bad thing, a tragic human failing. But just as a person's being motivated by kindness does not guarantee that he or she does what is right, so the absence of cruelty does not ensure that he or she avoids doing what is wrong. Many people who perform abortions, for example, are not cruel, sadistic people. But that fact alone does not settle the terribly difficult question of the morality of abortion. The case is no different when we examine the ethics of our treatment of animals. So, yes, let us be for kindness and against cruelty. But let us not suppose that being for the one and against the other answers questions about moral right and wrong.

Some people think that the theory we are looking for is *utilitarianism*. A utilitarian accepts two moral principles. The first is that of equality: everyone's interests count, and similar interests must be counted as having similar weight or importance. White or black, American or Iranian, human or animal—everyone's pain or frustration matters, and matters just as much as the equivalent pain or frustration of anyone else. The second principle a utilitarian accepts is that of utility: Do the act that will bring about the best balance between satisfaction and frustration for everyone affected by the outcome.

As a utilitarian, then, here is how I am to approach the task of deciding what I morally ought to do: I must ask who will be affected if I choose to do one thing rather than another, how much each individual will be affected, and where the best results are most likely to lie—which option, in other words, is most likely to bring about the best results, the best balance between satisfaction and frustration. That option, whatever it may be, is the one I ought to choose. That is where my moral duty lies.

The great appeal of utilitarianism rests with its uncompromising *egalitarianism*: Everyone's interests count and count as much as the like interests of everyone else. The kind of odious discrimination that some forms of contractarianism can justify—discrimination based on race or sex, for example—seems disallowed in principle by utilitarianism, as is speciesism, systematic discrimination based on species membership.

The equality we find in utilitarianism, however, is not the sort an advocate of animal or human rights should have in mind. Utilitarianism has no room for the equal rights of different individuals because it has no room for their equal inherent value or worth. What has value for the utilitarian is the satisfaction of an individual's interests, not the individual whose interests they are. A universe in which you satisfy your desire for water, food, and warmth is, other things being equal, better than a universe in which these desires are frustrated. And the same is true in the case of an animal with similar desires. But neither you nor the animal have any value in your own right. Only your feelings do.

Here is an analogy to help make the philosophical point clearer: a cup contains different liquids, sometimes sweet, sometimes bitter, sometimes a mixture of the two. What has value are the liquids: the sweeter the better, the bitterer the worse. The cup, the container, has no value. It is what goes into it, not what they go into, that has value. For the utilitarian, you and I are like the cup; we have no value as individuals and thus no equal value. What has value is what goes into us, what we serve as receptacles for; our feelings of satisfaction have positive value, our feelings of frustration negative value.

Serious problems arise for utilitarianism when we remind ourselves that it enjoins us to bring about the best consequences. What does this mean? It doesn't mean the best consequences for me alone, or for my family or friends, or any other person taken individually. No, what we must do is, roughly, as follows: we must add up (somehow!) the separate satisfactions and frustrations of everyone likely to be affected by our choice, the satisfactions in one column, the frustrations in the other. We must total each column for each of the options before us. That is what it means to say the theory is aggregative. And then we must choose that option which is most likely to bring about the best balance of totalled satisfactions over totalled frustrations. Whatever act would lead to this outcome is the one we ought morally to perform—it is where our moral duty lies. And that act quite clearly might not be the same one that would bring about the best results for me personally, or for my family or friends, or for a lab animal. The best aggregated consequences for everyone concerned are not necessarily the best for each individual.

That utilitarianism is an aggregative theory—different individuals' satisfactions or frustrations are added, or summed, or totalled—is the key objection to this theory. My Aunt Bea is old, inactive, a cranky, sour person, though not physically ill. She prefers to go on living. She is also rather rich. I could make a fortune if I could get my hands on her money, money she intends to give me in any event, after she dies, but which she refuses to give me now. In order to avoid a huge tax bite, I plan to donate a handsome sum of my profits to a local children's hospital. Many, many children will benefit from my generosity, and much joy will be brought to their parents, relatives, and friends. If I don't get the money rather soon, all these ambitions will come to naught. The once-in-a-lifetime opportunity to make a real killing will be gone. Why, then, not kill my Aunt Bea? Oh, of course I *might* get caught. But I'm no fool and, besides, her doctor can be counted on to cooperate (he has an eye for the same investment and I happen to know a good deal about his shady past). The deed can be done . . . professionally, shall we say. There is very little chance of getting caught. And as for my conscience being guiltridden, I am a resourceful sort of fellow and will take more than sufficient comfort—as I lie on the beach at Acapulco—in contemplating the joy and health I have brought to so many others.

Suppose Aunt Bea is killed and the rest of the story comes out as told. Would I have done anything wrong? Anything immoral? One would have thought that I had. Not according to utilitarianism. Since what I have done has brought about the best balance between totalled satisfaction and frustration for all those affected by the outcome, my action is not wrong. Indeed, in killing Aunt Bea the physician and I did what duty required.

This same kind of argument can be repeated in all sorts of cases, illustrating, time after time, how the utilitarian's position leads to results that impartial people find morally callous. It is wrong to kill my Aunt Bea in the name of bringing about the best results for others. A good end does not justify an evil means. Any adequate moral theory will have to explain why this is so. Utilitarianism fails in this respect and so cannot be the theory we seek.

What to do? Where to begin anew? The place to begin, I think, is with the utilitarian's view of the value of the individual—or, rather, the lack of value. In its place, suppose we consider that you and I, for example, do have value as individuals— what we'll call *inherent value*. To say we have such value is to say that we are something more than, something different from, mere receptacles. Moreover, to ensure that we do not pave the way for such injustices as slavery or sexual discrimination, we must believe that all who have inherent value have it equally, regardless of their sex, race, religion, birthplace, and so on. Similarly to be discarded as irrelevant are one's talents or skills, intelligence and wealth, personality or pathology, whether one is loved and admired or despised and loathed. The genius and the retarded child, the prince and the pauper, the brain surgeon and the fruit vendor, Mother Teresa and the most unscrupulous used-car salesman—all have inherent value, all possess it equally, and all have an equal right to be treated with respect, to be treated in ways that do not reduce them to the status of things, as if they existed as resources for others. My value as an individual is independent of my usefulness to you. Yours is not dependent on your usefulness to me. For either of us to treat the other in ways that fail to show respect for the other's independent value is to act immorally, to violate the individual's rights.

Some of the rational virtues of this view—what I call the *rights view*—should be evident. Unlike (crude) contractarianism, for example, the rights view in *principle* denies the moral tolerability of any and all forms of racial, sexual, or social discrimination; and unlike utilitarianism, the view in *principle* denies that we can justify good results by using evil means that violate an individual's rights—denies, for example, that it could be moral to kill my Aunt Bea to harvest beneficial consequences for others. That would be to sanction the disrespectful treatment of the individual in the name of the social good, something the rights view will not—categorically will not—ever allow.

The rights view, I believe, is rationally the most satisfactory moral theory. It surpasses all other theories in the degree to which it illuminates and explains the foundation of our duties to one another—the domain of human morality. On this score it has the best reasons, the best arguments, on its side. Of course, if it were possible to show that only human beings are included within its scope, then a person like myself, who believes in animal rights, would be obliged to look elsewhere.

But attempts to limit its scope to humans only can be shown to be rationally defective. Animals, it is true, lack many of the abilities humans possess. The can't read, do higher mathematics, build a bookcase, or make *baba ghanoush*. Neither can many human beings, however, and yet we don't (and shouldn't) say that they (these humans) therefore have less inherent value, less of a right to be treated with respect, than do others. It is the *similarities* between those human beings who most clearly, most noncontroversially have such value (the people reading this, for example), not our differences, that matter most. And the really crucial, the basic similarity is simply this: We are each of us the experiencing subject of a life, a conscious creature having an individual welfare that has importance to us whatever our usefulness to others. We want and prefer things, believe and feel things, recall and expect things. And all these dimensions of our life, including our pleasure and pain, our enjoyment and suffering, our satisfaction and frustration, our continued existence or our untimely death—all make a difference to the quality of our life as lived, as experienced, by us as individuals. As the same is true of those animals that concern us (the ones that are eaten and trapped, for example), they too must be viewed as the experiencing subjects of a life, with inherent value of their own.

Some there are who resist the idea that animals have inherent value. "Only humans have such value," they profess. How might this narrow view be defended? Shall we say that only humans have the requisite intelligence, or autonomy, or reason? But there are many, many humans who fail to meet these standards and yet are reasonably viewed as having value above and beyond their usefulness to others. Shall we claim that only humans belong to the right species, the species *Homo sapiens*? But this is blatant speciesism. Will it be said, then, that all—and only—humans have immortal souls? Then our opponents have their work cut out for them. I am myself not ill-disposed to the proposition that there are immortal souls. Personally, I profoundly hope I have one. But I would not want to rest my position on a controversial ethical issue on the even more controversial question about who or what has an immortal soul. That is to dig one's hole deeper, not to climb out. Rationally, it is better to resolve moral issues without making more controversial assumptions than are needed. The question of who has inherent value is such a question, one that is resolved more rationally without the introduction of the idea of immortal souls than by its use.

Well, perhaps some will say that animals have some inherent value, only less than we have. Once again, however, attempts to defend this view can be shown to lack rational justification. What could be the basis of our having more inherent value than animals? Their lack of reason, or autonomy, or intellect? Only if we are willing to make the same judgment in the case of humans who are similarly deficient. But it is not true that such humans—the retarded child, for example, or the mentally deranged—have less inherent value than you or I. Neither, then, can we rationally sustain the view that animals like them in being the experiencing subjects of a life have less inherent value. *All* who have inherent value have it *equally*, whether they be human animals or not.

Inherent value, then, belongs equally to those who are the experiencing subjects of a life. Whether it belongs to others—to rocks and rivers, trees and glaciers, for example—we do not know and may never know. But neither do we need to know, if we are to make the case for animal rights. We do not need to know, for example, how many people are eligible to vote in the next presidential election before we can know whether I am. Similarly, we do not need to know how many individuals have inherent value before we can know that some do. When it comes to the case for animal rights, then, what we need to know is whether the animals that, in our culture, are routinely eaten, hunted, and used in our laboratories, for example, are like us in being subjects of a life. And we do know this. We do know that many—literally, billions and billions—of these animals are the subjects of a life in the sense explained and so have inherent value if we do. And since, in order to arrive at the best theory of our duties to one another, we must recognize our equal inherent value as individuals, reason—not sentiment, not emotion—reason compels us to recognize the equal inherent value of these animals and, with this, their equal right to be treated with respect.

That, very roughly, is the shape and feel of the case for animal rights. Most of the details of the supporting argument are missing. They are to be found in the book that bears the same title as this essay.[1] Here, the details go begging, and I must, in closing, limit myself to two final points.

The first is how the theory that underlies the case for animal rights shows that the animal rights movement is a part of, not antagonistic to, the human rights movement. The theory that rationally grounds the rights of animals also grounds the rights of humans. Thus those involved in the animal rights movement are partners in the struggle to secure respect for human rights—the rights of women, for example, or minorities, or workers. The animal rights movement is cut from the same moral cloth as these.

Second, having set out the broad outlines of the rights view, I can now say why its implications for farming and science, among other fields, are both clear and uncompromising. In the case of the use of animals in science, the rights view is categorically abolitionist. Lab animals are not our tasters; we are not their kings. Because these animals are treated routinely, systematically as if their value were reducible to their usefulness to others, they are routinely, systematically treated with a lack of respect, and thus are their rights routinely, systematically violated. This is just as true when they are used in trivial, duplicative, unnecessary or unwise research as it is when they are used in studies that hold out real promise of human benefits. We can't justify harming or killing a human being (my Aunt Bea, for example) just for these sorts of reason. Neither can we do so even in the case of so lowly a creature as a laboratory rat. It is not just refinement or reduction that is called for, not just larger, cleaner cages, not just more generous use of anesthesia or the elimination of multiple surgery, not just tidying up the system. It is complete replacement. The best we can do when it comes to using animals in science is—not to use them. That is where our duty lies, according to the rights view.

As for commercial animal agriculture, the rights view takes a similar abolitionist position. The fundamental moral wrong here is not that animals are kept in stressful close confinement or in isolation, or that their pain and suffering, their needs and preferences are ignored or discounted. All these *are* wrong, of course, but they are not the fundamental wrong. They are symptoms and effects of the deeper, systematic wrong that allows these animals to be viewed and treated as lacking independent value, as resources for us—as, indeed, a renewable resource. Giving farm animals more space, more natural environments, more companions does not right the fundamental wrong, any more than giving lab animals more anesthesia or bigger, cleaner cages would right the fundamental wrong in their case. Nothing less than the total dissolution of commercial animal agriculture will do this, just as, for similar reasons I won't develop at length here, morality requires nothing less than the total elimination of hunting and trapping for commercial and sporting ends. The rights view's implications, then, as I have said, are clear and uncompromising.

NOTE

[1] *The Case for Animal Rights* (Berkeley: University of California Press, 1983).

Supreme Court Decision

Roe vs. Wade

Appeal from the United States District Court for the Northern District of Texas

No. 70–18. Argued December 13, 1971—Reargued October 11, 1972—Decided January 22, 1973

A pregnant single woman (Roe) brought a class action challenging the constitutionality of the Texas criminal abortion laws, which proscribe procuring or attempting an abortion except on medical advice for the purpose of saving the mother's life. A licensed physician (Hallford), who had two state abortion prosecutions pending against him, was permitted to intervene. A childless married couple (the Does), the wife not being pregnant, separately attacked the laws, basing alleged injury on the future possibilities of contraceptive failure, pregnancy, unpreparedness for parenthood, and impairment of the wife's health. A three-judge District Court, which consolidated the actions, held that Roe and Hallford, and members of their classes, had standing to sue and presented justifiable controversies. Ruling that declaratory, though not injunctive, relief was warranted, the court declared the abortion statutes void as vague and overbroadly infringing those plaintiffs' Ninth and Fourteenth Amendment rights. The court ruled the Does' complaint not justifiable. Appellants directly appealed to this Court on the injunctive rulings, and appellee cross-appealed from the District Court's grant of declaratory relief to Roe and Hallford.
Held:

1. While 28 U. S. C. §1253 authorizes no direct appeal to this Court from the grant or denial of declaratory relief alone, review is not foreclosed when the case is properly before the Court on appeal from specific denial of injunctive relief and the arguments as to both injunctive and declaratory relief are necessarily identical. P. 123.

2. Roe has standing to sue; the Does and Hallford do not. Pp. 123–129.

   (a) Contrary to appellee's contention, the natural termination of Roe's pregnancy did not moot her suit. Litigation involving pregnancy, which is "capable of repetition, yet evading review," is an exception to the usual federal rule that an actual controversy must exist at review stages and not simply when the action is initiated. Pp. 124–125.

(b) The District Court correctly refused injunctive, but erred in granting declaratory, relief to Hallford, who alleged no federally protected right not assertable as a defense against the good-faith state prosecutions pending against him. *Samuels v. Mackell*, 401 U. S. 66. Pp. 125–127.

(c) The Does' complaint, based as it is on contingencies, any one or more of which may not occur, is too speculative to present an actual case or controversy. Pp. 127–129.

3. State criminal abortion laws, like those involved here, that except from criminality only a life-saving procedure on the mother's behalf without regard to the stage of her pregnancy and other interests involved violate the Due Process Clause of the Fourteenth Amendment, which protects against state action the right to privacy, including a woman's qualified right to terminate her pregnancy. Though the State cannot override that right, it has legitimate interests in protecting both the pregnant woman's health and the potentiality of human life, each of which interests grows and reaches a "compelling" point at various stages of the woman's approach to term. Pp. 147–164.

(a) For the stage prior to approximately the end of the first trimester, the abortion decision and its effectuation must be left to the medical judgment of the pregnant woman's attending physician. Pp. 163, 164.

(b) For the stage subsequent to approximately the end of the first trimester, the State, in promoting its interest in the health of the mother, may, if it chooses, regulate the abortion procedure in ways that are reasonably related to maternal health. Pp. 163, 164.

(c) For the stage subsequent to viability the State, in promoting its interest in the potentiality of human life, may, if it chooses, regulate, and even proscribe, abortion except where necessary, in appropriate medical judgment, for the preservation of the life or health of the mother. Pp. 163–164; 164–165.

4. The State may define the term "physician" to mean only a physician currently licensed by the State, and may proscribe any abortion by a person who is not a physician as so defined. P. 165.

5. It is unnecessary to decide the injunctive relief issue since the Texas authorities will doubtless fully recognize the Court's ruling that the Texas criminal abortion statutes are unconstitutional. P. 166.

314 F. Supp. 1217, affirmed in part and reversed in part.

BLACKMUN, J., delivered the opinion of the Court, in which BURGER, C. J., and DOUGLAS, BRENNAN, STEWART, MARSHALL, and POWELL, JJ., joined. BURGER, C. J., post, p. 207, DOUGLAS, J., post, p. 209, and STEWART, J., post, p. 167, filed concurring opinions. WHITE, J., filed a dissenting opinion, in which REHNQUIST, J., joined, post, p. 221. REHNQUIST, J., filed a dissenting opinion, post, p. 171.

Sarah Weddington reargued the cause for appellants. With her on the briefs were *Roy Lucas, Fred Bruner, Roy L. Merrill, Jr.,* and *Norman Dorsen.*

Robert C. Flowers, Assistant Attorney General of Texas, argued the cause for appellee on the reargument. *Jay Floyd,* Assistant Attorney General, argued the cause for appellee on the original argument. With them on the brief were *Crawford C.*

Martin, Attorney General, *Nols White*, First Assistant Attorney General, *Alfred Walker*, Executive Assistant Attorney General, *Henry Wade*, and *John B. Tolle*.*

MR. JUSTICE BLACKMUN delivered the opinion of the Court.

This Texas federal appeal and its Georgia companion, *Doe v. Bolton, post,* p. 179, present constitutional challenges to state criminal abortion legislation. The Texas statutes under attack here are typical of those that have been in effect in many States for approximately a century. The Georgia statutes, in contrast, have a modern cast and are a legislative product that, to an extent at least, obviously reflects the influences of recent attitudinal change, of advancing medical knowledge and techniques, and of new thinking about an old issue.

We forthwith acknowledge our awareness of the sensitive and emotional nature of the abortion controversy, of the vigorous opposing views, even among physicians, and of the deep and seemingly absolute convictions that the subject inspires. One's philosophy, one's experiences, one's exposure to the raw edges of human existence, one's religious training, one's attitudes toward life and family and their values, and the moral standards one establishes and seeks to observe, are all likely to influence and to color one's thinking and conclusions about abortion.

In addition, population growth, pollution, poverty, and racial overtones tend to complicate and not to simplify the problem.

Our task, of course, is to resolve the issue by constitutional measurement, free of emotion and of predilection. We seek earnestly to do this, and, because we do, we have inquired into, and in this opinion place some emphasis upon, medical and medical-legal history and what that history reveals about man's attitudes toward the abortion procedure over the centuries. We bear in mind, too, Mr. Justice Holmes' admonition in his now vindicated dissent in *Lochner v. New York*, 198 U. S. 45, 76 (1905):

> "[The Constitution] is made for people of fundamentally differing views, and the accident of our finding certain opinions natural and familiar or novel and even shocking ought not to conclude our judgment upon the question whether statutes embodying them conflict with the Constitution of the United States."

I

The Texas statutes that concern us here are Arts. 1191–1194 and 1196 of the State's Penal Code.[1] These make it a crime to "procure an abortion," as therein defined, or to attempt one, except with respect to "an abortion procured or attempted by medical advice for the purpose of saving the life of the mother." Similar statutes are in existence in a majority of the States.[2]

Texas first enacted a criminal abortion statute in 1854. Texas Laws 1854, c. 49, § 1, set forth in 3 H. Gammel, Laws of Texas 1502 (1898). This was soon modified into language that has remained substantially unchanged to the present time. See Texas Penal Code of 1857, c. 7 Arts. 531–536; G. Paschal Laws of Texas, Arts. 2192–2197 (1866); Texas Rev. Stat., c. 8, Arts. 536–541 (1879); Texas Rev. Crim. Stat., Arts. 1071–1076 (1911). The final article in each of these compilations provided the same exception, as does the present Article 1196, for an abortion by "medical advice for the purpose of saving the life of the mother."[3]

II

Jane Roe,[4] a single woman who was residing in Dallas County, Texas, instituted this federal action in March 1970 against the District Attorney of the county. She sought a declaratory judgment that the Texas criminal abortion statutes were unconstitutional on their face, and an injunction restraining the defendant from enforcing the statutes.

Roe alleged that she was unmarried and pregnant; that she wished to terminate her pregnancy by an abortion "performed by a competent, licensed physician, under safe, clinical conditions"; that she was unable to get a "legal" abortion in Texas because her life did not appear to be threatened by the continuation of her pregnancy; and that she could not afford to travel to another jurisdiction in order to secure a legal abortion under safe conditions. She claimed that the Texas statutes were unconstitutionally vague and that they abridged her right of personal privacy, protected by the First, Fourth, Fifth, Ninth, and Fourteenth Amendments. By an amendment to her complaint Roe purported to sue "on behalf of herself and all other women" similarly situated.

James Hubert Hallford, a licensed physician, sought and was granted leave to intervene in Roe's action. In his complaint he alleged that he had been arrested previously for violations of the Texas abortion statutes and that two such prosecutions were pending against him. He described conditions of patients who came to him seeking abortions, and he claimed that for many cases he, as a physician, was unable to determine whether they fell within or outside the exception recognized by Article 1196. He alleged that, as a consequence, the statutes were vague and uncertain, in violation of the Fourteenth Amendment, and that they violated his own and his patients' rights to privacy in the doctor-patient relationship and his own right to practice medicine, rights he claimed were guaranteed by the First, Fourth, Fifth, Ninth, and Fourteenth Amendments.

John and Mary Doe,[5] a married couple, filed a companion complaint to that of Roe. They also named the District Attorney as defendant, claimed like constitutional deprivations, and sought declaratory and injunctive relief. The Does alleged that they were a childless couple; that Mrs. Doe was suffering from a "neural-chemical" disorder; that her physician had "advised her to avoid pregnancy until such time as her condition has materially improved" (although a pregnancy at the present time would not present "a serious risk" to her life); that, pursuant to medical advice, she had discontinued use of birth control pills; and that if she should become pregnant, she would want to terminate the pregnancy by an abortion performed by a competent, licensed physician under safe, clinical conditions. By an amendment to their complaint, the Does purported to sue "on behalf of themselves and all couples similarly situated."

The two actions were consolidated and heard together by a duly convened three-judge district court. The suits thus presented the situations of the pregnant single woman, the childless couple, with the wife not pregnant, and the licensed practicing physician, all joining in the attack on the Texas criminal abortion statutes. Upon the filing of affidavits, motions were made for dismissal and for summary judgment.

The court held that Roe and members of her class, and Dr. Hallford, had standing to sue and presented justifiable controversies, but that the Does had failed to allege facts sufficient to state a present controversy and did not have standing. It concluded that, with respect to the requests for a declaratory judgment, abstention was not warranted. On the merits, the District Court held that the "fundamental right of single women and married persons to choose whether to have children is protected by the Ninth Amendment, through the Fourteenth Amendment," and that the Texas criminal abortion statutes were void on their face because they were both unconstitutionally vague and constituted an overbroad infringement of the plaintiffs' Ninth Amendment rights. The court then held that abstention was warranted with respect to the requests for an injunction. It therefore dismissed the Does' complaint, declared the abortion statutes void, and dismissed the application for injunctive relief. 314 F. Supp. 1217, 1225 (ND Tex. 1970).

The plaintiffs Roe and Doe and the intervener Hallford, pursuant to 28 U. S. C. § 1253, have appealed to this Court from that part of the District Court's judgment denying the injunction. The defendant District Attorney has purported to cross-appeal, pursuant to the same statute, from the court's grant of declaratory relief to Roe and Hallford. Both sides also have taken protective appeals to the United States Court of Appeals for the Fifth Circuit. That court ordered the appeals held in abeyance pending decision here. We postponed decision on jurisdiction to the hearing on the merits. 402 U. S. 941 (1971).

III

It might have been preferable if the defendant, pursuant to our Rule 20, had presented to us a petition for certiorari before judgment in the Court of Appeals with respect to the granting of the plaintiffs' prayer for declaratory relief. Our decisions in *Mitchell* v. *Donovan*, 398 U. S. 427 (1970), and *Gunn* v. *University Committee*, 399 U. S. 383 (1970), are to the effect that § 1253 does not authorize an appeal to this Court from the grant or denial of declaratory relief alone. We conclude, nevertheless, that those decisions do not foreclose our review of both the injunctive and the declaratory aspects of a case of this kind when it is properly here, as this one is, on appeal under § 1253 from specific denial of injunctive relief, and the arguments as to both aspects are necessarily identical. See *Carter* v. *Jury Comm'n*, 396 U. S. 320 (1970); *Florida Lime Growers* v. *Jacobsen*, 362 U. S. 73, 80–81 (1960). It would be destructive of time and energy for all concerned were we to rule otherwise. Cf. *Doe* v. *Bolton, post,* p. 179.

IV

We are next confronted with issues of justifiability, standing, and abstention. Have Roe and the Does established that "personal stake in the outcome of the controversy," *Baker* v. *Carr,* 369 U. S. 186, 204 (1962), that insures that "the dispute sought to be adjudicated will be presented in an adversary context and in a form historically viewed as capable of judicial resolution," *Flast* v. *Cohen,* 392 U. S. 83, 101 (1968), and *Sierra Club* v. *Morton,* 405 U. S. 727, 732 (1972)? And what effect did the pendency of criminal abortion charges against Dr. Hallford in state court have upon the propriety of the federal court's granting relief to him as a plaintiff-intervenor?

A. *Jane Roe.* Despite the use of the pseudonym, no suggestion is made that Roe is a fictitious person. For purposes of her case, we accept as true, and as established, her existence; her pregnant state, as of the inception of her suit in March 1970 and as late as May 21 of that year when she filed an alias affidavit with the District Court; and her inability to obtain a legal abortion in Texas.

Viewing Roe's case as of the time of its filing and thereafter until as late as May, there can be little dispute that it then presented a case or controversy and that, wholly apart from the class aspects, she, as a pregnant single woman thwarted by the Texas criminal abortion laws, had standing to challenge those statutes. *Abele* v. *Markle,* 452 F. 2d 1121, 1125 (CA2 1971); *Crossen* v. *Breckenridge,* 446 F. 2d 833, 838–839 (CA6 1971); *Poe* v. *Menghini,* 339 F. Supp. 986, 990–991 (Kan. 1972). See *Truaz* v. *Raich,* 239 U. S. 33 (1915). Indeed, we do not read the appellee's brief as really asserting anything to the contrary. The "logical nexus between the status asserted and the claim sought to be adjudicated," *Flast* v. *Cohen,* 392 U. S., at 102, and the necessary degree of contentiousness, *Golden* v. *Zwickler,* 394 U. S. 103 (1969), are both present.

The appellee notes, however, that the record does not disclose that Roe was pregnant at the time of the District Court hearing on May 22, 1970,[6] or on the following June 17 when the court's opinion and judgment were filed. And he suggests that Roe's case must now be moot because she and all other members of her class are no longer subject to any 1970 pregnancy.

The usual rule in federal cases is that an actual controversy must exist at stages of appellate or certiorari review, and not simply at the date the action is initiated. *United States* v. *Munsingwear, Inc.,* 340 U. S. 36 (1950); *Golden* v. *Zwickler, supra; SEC* v. *Medical Committee for Human Rights,* 404 U. S. 403 (1972).

But when, as here, pregnancy is a significant fact in the litigation, the normal 266-day human gestation period is so short that the pregnancy will come to term before the usual appellate process is complete. If that termination makes a case moot, pregnancy litigation seldom will survive much beyond the trial stage, and appellate review will be effectively denied. Our law should not be that rigid. Pregnancy often comes more than once to the same woman, and in the general population, if man is to survive, it will always be with us. Pregnancy provides a classic justification for a conclusion of nonmootness. It truly could be "capable of repetition, yet evading review." *Southern Pacific Terminal Co.* v. *ICC,* 219 U. S. 498, 515 (1911). See *Moore* v. *Ogilvie,* 394 U. S. 814, 816 (1969); *Carroll* v. *Princess Anne,* 393 U. S. 175, 178–179 (1968); *United States* v. *W. T. Grant Co.,* 345 U. S. 629, 632–633 (1953).

We, therefore, agree with the District Court that Jane Roe had standing to undertake this litigation, that she presented a justifiable controversy, and that the termination of her 1970 pregnancy has not rendered her case moot.

B. *Dr. Hallford.* The doctor's position is different. He entered Roe's litigation as a plaintiff-intervenor, alleging in his complaint that he:

> [I]n the past has been arrested for violating the Texas Abortion Laws and at the present time stands charged by indictment with violating said laws in the Criminal District Court of Dallas County, Texas to-wit: (1) The State of Texas vs. James H. Hallford, No.

C-69-5307-IH, and (2) The State of Texas vs. James H. Hallford, No. C 69-2524-H. In both cases the defendant is charged with abortion. . . .

In his application for leave to intervene, the doctor made like representations as to the abortion charges pending in the state court. These representations were also repeated in the affidavit he executed and filed in support of his motion for summary judgment.

Dr. Hallford is, therefore, in the position of seeking, in a federal court, declaratory and injunctive relief with respect to the same statutes under which he stands charged in criminal prosecutions simultaneously pending in state court. Although he stated that he has been arrested in the past for violating the State's abortion laws, he makes no allegation of any substantial and immediate threat to any federally protected right that cannot be asserted in his defense against the state prosecutions. Neither is there any allegation of harassment or bad-faith prosecution. In order to escape the rule articulated in the cases cited in the next paragraph of this opinion that, absent harassment and bad faith, a defendant in a pending state criminal case cannot affirmatively challenge in federal court the statutes under which the State is prosecuting him, Dr. Hallford seeks to distinguish his status as a present state defendant from his status as a "potential future defendant" and to assert only the latter for standing purposes here.

We see no merit in that distinction. Our decision in *Samuels v. Mackell,* 401 U. S. 66 (1971), compels the conclusion that the District Court erred when it granted declaratory relief to Dr. Hallford instead of refraining from so doing. The court, of course, was correct in refusing to grant injunctive relief to the doctor. The reasons supportive of that action, however, are those expressed in *Samuels v. Mackell, supra,* and in *Younger v. Harris,* 401 U. S. 37 (1971); *Boyle v. Landry,* 401 U. S. 77 (1971); *Perez v. Ledesma,* 401 U. S. 82 (1971); and *Byrne v. Karalezis,* 401 U. S. 216 (1971). See also *Dombrowski v. Pfister,* 380 U. S. 479 (1965). We note, in passing, that *Younger* and its companion cases were decided after the three-judge District Court decision in this case.

Dr. Hallford's complaint in intervention, therefore, is to be dismissed.[7] He is remitted to his defenses in the state criminal proceedings against him. We reverse the judgment of the District Court insofar as it granted Dr. Hallford relief and failed to dismiss his complaint in intervention.

C. *The Does.* In view of our ruling as to Roe's standing in her case, the issue of the Does' standing in their case has little significance. The claims they assert are essentially the same as those of Roe, and they attack the same statutes. Nevertheless, we briefly note the Does' posture.

Their pleadings present them as a childless married couple, the woman not being pregnant, who have no desire to have children at this time because of their having received medical advice that Mrs. Doe should avoid pregnancy, and for "other highly personal reasons." But they "fear . . . they may face the prospect of becoming parents." And if pregnancy ensues, they "would want to terminate" it by an abortion. They assert an inability to obtain an abortion legally in Texas and, consequently, the prospect of obtaining an illegal abortion there or of going outside Texas to some place where the procedure could be obtained legally and competently.

We thus have as plaintiffs a married couple who have, as their asserted imme-diate and present injury, only an alleged "detrimental effect upon [their] marital happiness" because they are forced to "the choice of refraining from normal sex-ual relations or of endangering Mary Doe's health through a possible pregnancy." Their claim is that sometime in the future Mrs. Doe might become pregnant because of possible failure of contraceptive measures, and at that time in the future she might want an abortion that might then be illegal under the Texas statutes.

This very phrasing of the Does' position reveals its speculative character. Their alleged injury rests on possible future contraceptive failure, possible future preg-nancy, possible future unpreparedness for parenthood, and possible future impair-ment of health. Any one or more of these several possibilities may not take place and all may not combine. In the Does' estimation, these possibilities might have some real or imagined impact upon their marital happiness. But we are not prepared to say that the bare allegation of so indirect an injury is sufficient to present an actual case or controversy. *Younger v. Harris,* 401 U. S., at 41–42; *Golden v. Zwickler,* 394 U. S., at 109–110; *Abele v. Markle,* 452 F. 2d, at 1124–1125; *Crossen v. Breckenridge,* 446 F. 2d, at 839. The Does' claim falls far short of those resolved otherwise in the cases that the Does urge upon us, namely, *Investment Co. Institute v. Camp,* 401 U. S. 617 (1971); *Data Processing Service v. Camp,* 397 U. S. 150 (1970); and *Epperson v. Arkansas,* 393 U. S. 97 (1968). See also *Truax v. Raich,* 239 U. S. 33 (1915).

The Does therefore are not appropriate plaintiffs in this litigation. Their com-plaint was properly dismissed by the District Court, and we affirm that dismissal.

V

The principal thrust of appellant's attack on the Texas statutes is that they improp-erly invade a right, said to be possessed by the pregnant woman, to choose to ter-minate her pregnancy. Appellant would discover this right in the concept of personal "liberty" embodied in the Fourteenth Amendment's Due Process Clause; or in personal, marital, familial, and sexual privacy said to be protected by the Bill of Rights or its penumbras, see *Griswold v. Connecticut,* 381 U. S. 479 (1965); *Eisenstadt v. Baird,* 405 U. S. 438 (1972); *id.,* at 460 (WHITE, J., concurring in result); or among those rights reserved to the people by the Ninth Amendment, *Griswold v. Connecticut,* 381 U. S., at 486 (Goldberg, J., concurring). Before ad-dressing this claim, we feel it desirable briefly to survey, in several aspects, the his-tory of abortion, for such insight as that history may afford us, and then to examine the state purposes and interests behind the criminal abortion laws.

VI

It perhaps is not generally appreciated that the restrictive criminal abortion laws in effect in a majority of States today are of relatively recent vintage. Those laws, generally proscribing abortion or its attempt at any time during pregnancy except when necessary to preserve the pregnant woman's life, are not of ancient or even of common-law origin. Instead, they derive from statutory changes effected, for the most part, in the latter half of the 19th century.

1. *Ancient attitudes*. These are not capable of precise determination. We are told that at the time of the Persian Empire abortifacients were known and that criminal abortions were severely punished.[8] We are also told, however, that abortion was practiced in Greek times as well as in the Roman Era,[9] and that "it was resorted to without scruple."[10] The Ephesian, Soranos, often described as the greatest of the ancient gynecologists, appears to have been generally opposed to Rome's prevailing free-abortion practices. He found it necessary to think first of the life of the mother, and he resorted to abortion when, upon this standard, he felt the procedure advisable.[11] Greek and Roman law afforded little protection to the unborn. If abortion was prosecuted in some places, it seems to have been based on a concept of a violation of the father's right to his offspring. Ancient religion did not bar abortion.[12]

2. *The Hippocratic Oath*. What then of the famous Oath that has stood so long as the ethical guide of the medical profession and that bears the name of the great Greek (460(?)–377(?) B.C.), who has been described as the Father of Medicine, the "wisest and the greatest practitioner of his art," and the "most important and most complete medical personality of antiquity," who dominated the medical schools of his time, and who typified the sum of the medical knowledge of the past?[13] The Oath varies somewhat according to the particular translation, but in any translation the content is clear: "I will give no deadly medicine to anyone if asked, nor suggest any such counsel; and in like manner I will not give to a woman a pessary to produce abortion,"[14] or "I will neither give a deadly drug to anybody if asked for it, nor will I make a suggestion to this effect. Similarly, I will not give to a woman an abortive remedy."[15]

Although the Oath is not mentioned in any of the principal briefs in this case or in *Doe v. Bolton, post,* p. 179, it represents the apex of the development of strict ethical concepts in medicine, and its influence endures to this day. Why did not the authority of Hippocrates dissuade abortion practice in his time and that of Rome? The late Dr. Edelstein provides us with a theory:[16] The Oath was not uncontested even in Hippocrates' day; only the Pythagorean school of philosophers frowned upon the related act of suicide. Most Greek thinkers, on the other hand, commended abortion, at least prior to viability. See Plato, Republic, V, 461; Aristotle, Politics, VII, 1335b 25. For the Pythagoreans, however, it was a matter of dogma. For them the embryo was animate from the moment of conception, and abortion meant destruction of a living being. The abortion clause of the Oath, therefore, "echoes Pythagorean doctrines," and "[i]n no other stratum of Greek opinion were such views held or proposed in the same spirit of uncompromising austerity."[17]

Dr. Edelstein then concludes that the Oath originated in a group representing only a small segment of Greek opinion and that it certainly was not accepted by all ancient physicians. He points out that medical writings down to Galen (A. D. 130–200) "give evidence of the violation of almost every one of its injunctions."[18] But with the end of antiquity a decided change took place. Resistance against suicide and against abortion became common. The Oath came to be popular. The emerging teachings of Christianity were in agreement with the Pythagorean ethic. The Oath "became the nucleus of all medical ethics" and "was applauded as the embodiment of truth." Thus, suggests Dr. Edelstein, it is "a Pythagorean manifesto and not the expression of an absolute standard of medical conduct."[19]

This, it seems to us, is a satisfactory and acceptable explanation of the Hippocratic Oath's apparent rigidity.

It enables us to understand, in historical context, a long accepted and revered statement of medical ethics.

3. *The common law.* It is undisputed that at common law, abortion performed *before* "quickening"— the first recognizable movement of the fetus in utero, appearing usually from the 16th to the 18th week of pregnancy[20]—was not an indictable offense.[21] The absence of a common-law crime for pre-quickening abortion appears to have developed from a confluence of earlier philosophical, theological, and civil and canon law concepts of when life begins. These disciplines variously approached the question in terms of the point at which the embryo or fetus became "formed" or recognizably human, or in terms of when a "person" came into being, that is, infused with a "soul" or "animated." A loose consensus evolved in early English law that these events occurred at some point between conception and live birth.[22] This was "mediate animation." Although Christian theology and the canon law came to fix the point of animation at 40 days for a male and 80 days for a female, a view that persisted until the 19th century, there was otherwise little agreement about the precise time of formation or animation. There was agreement, however, that prior to this point the fetus was to be regarded as part of the mother, and its destruction, therefore, was not homicide. Due to continued uncertainty about the precise time when animation occurred, to the lack of any empirical basis for the 40-80-day view, and perhaps to Aquinas' definition of movement as one of the two first principles of life, Bracton focused upon quickening as the critical point. The significance of quickening was echoed by later common-law scholars and found its way into the received common law in this country.

Whether abortion of a *quick* fetus was a felony at common law, or even a lesser crime, is still disputed. Bracton, writing early in the 13th century, thought it homicide.[23] But the later and predominant view, following the great common-law scholars, has been that it was, at most, a lesser offense. In a frequently cited passage, Coke took the position that abortion of a woman "quick with childe" is "a great misprision, and no murder."[24] Blackstone followed, saying that while abortion after quickening had once been considered manslaughter (though not murder), "modern law" took a less severe view.[25] A recent review of the common-law precedents argues, however, that those precedents contradict Coke and that even post-quickening abortion was never established as a common-law crime.[26] This is of some importance because while most American courts ruled, in holding or dictum, that abortion of an unquickened fetus was not criminal under their received common law,[27] others followed Coke in stating that abortion of a quick fetus was a "misprision," a term they translated to mean "misdemeanor."[28] That their reliance on Coke on this aspect of the law was uncritical and, apparently in all the reported cases, dictum (due probably to the paucity of common-law prosecutions for post-quickening abortion), makes it now appear doubtful that abortion was ever firmly established as a common-law crime even with respect to the destruction of a quick fetus.

4. *The English statutory law.* England's first criminal abortion statute, Lord Ellenborough's Act, 43 Geo. 3, c. 58, came in 1803. It made abortion of a quick fetus, § 1, a capital crime, but in § 2 it provided lesser penalties for the felony of abortion

before quickening, and thus preserved the "quickening" distinction. This contrast was continued in the general revision of 1828, 9 Geo. 4, c. 31, § 13. It disappeared, however, together with the death penalty, in 1837, 7 Will. 4 & 1 Vict., c. 85. § 6, and did not reappear in the Offenses Against the Person Act of 1861. 24 & 25 Vict., c. 100, § 59, that formed the core of English anti-abortion law until the liberalizing reforms of 1967. In 1929, the Infant Life (Preservation) Act 19 & 20 Geo. 5, c. 34, came into being. Its emphasis was upon the destruction of "the life of a child capable of being born alive." It made a willful act performed with the necessary intent a felony. It contained a proviso that one was not to be found guilty of the offense "unless it is proved that the act which caused the death of the child was not done in good faith for the purpose only of preserving the life of the mother."

A seemingly notable development in the English law was the case of *Rex* v. *Bourne*, [1939] 1 K. B. 687. This case apparently answered in the affirmative the question whether an abortion necessary to preserve the life of the pregnant woman was excepted from the criminal penalties of the 1861 Act. In his instructions to the jury, Judge Macnaghten referred to the 1929 Act, and observed that that Act related to "the case where a child is killed by a wilful act at the time when it is being delivered in the ordinary course of nature." *Id.*, at 691. He concluded that the 1861 Act's use of the word "unlawfully," imported the same meaning expressed by the specific proviso in the 1929 Act, even though there was no mention of preserving the mother's life in the 1861 Act. He then construed the phrase "preserving the life of the mother" broadly, that is, "in a reasonable sense," to include a serious and permanent threat to the mother's *health,* and instructed the jury to acquit Dr. Bourne if it found he had acted in a good-faith belief that the abortion was necessary for this purpose. *Id.*, at 693–694. The jury did acquit.

Recently, Parliament enacted a new abortion law. This is the Abortion Act of 1967, 15 & 16 Eliz. 2, c. 87. The Act permits a licensed physician to perform an abortion where two other licensed physicians agree (a) "that the continuance of the pregnancy would involve risk to the life of the pregnant woman, or of injury to the physical or mental health of the pregnant woman or any existing children of her family, greater than if the pregnancy were terminated," or (b) "that there is a substantial risk that if the child were born it would suffer from such physical or mental abnormalities as to be seriously handicapped." The Act also provides that, in making this determination, "account may be taken of the pregnant woman's actual or reasonably foreseeable environment." It also permits a physician, without the concurrence of others, to terminate a pregnancy where he is of the good-faith opinion that the abortion "is immediately necessary to save the life or to prevent grave permanent injury to the physical or mental health of the pregnant woman."

5. *The American law.* In this country, the law in effect in all but a few States until mid-19th century was the pre-existing English common law. Connecticut, the first State to enact abortion legislation, adopted in 1821 that part of Lord Ellenborough's Act that related to a woman "quick with child."[29] The death penalty was not imposed. Abortion before quickening was made a crime in that State only in 1860.[30] In 1828, New York enacted legislation[31] that, in two respects, was to serve as a model for early anti-abortion statutes. First, while barring destruction of an unquickened fetus as well as a quick fetus, it made the former only a misdemeanor, but the latter second-degree manslaughter. Second, it incorporated a con-

cept of therapeutic abortion by providing that an abortion was excused if it "shall have been necessary to preserve the life of such mother, or shall have been advised by two physicians to be necessary for such purpose." By 1840, when Texas had received the common law,[32] only eight American States had statutes dealing with abortion.[33] It was not until after the War Between the States that legislation began generally to replace the common law. Most of these initial statutes dealt severely with abortion after quickening but were lenient with it before quickening. Most punished attempts equally with completed abortions. While many statutes included the exception for an abortion thought by one or more physicians to be necessary to save the mother's life, that provision soon disappeared and the typical law required that the procedure actually be necessary for that purpose.

Gradually, in the middle and late 19th century the quickening distinction disappeared from the statutory law of most States and the degree of the offense and the penalties were increased. By the end of the 1950s, a large majority of the jurisdictions banned abortion, however and whenever performed, unless done to save or preserve the life of the mother.[34] The exceptions, Alabama and the District of Columbia, permitted abortion to preserve the mother's health.[35] Three States permitted abortions that were not "unlawfully" performed or that were not "without lawful justification," leaving interpretation of those standards to the courts.[36] In the past several years, however, a trend toward liberalization of abortion statutes has resulted in adoption, by about one-third of the States, of less stringent laws, most of them patterned after the ALI Model Penal Code, §230.3,[37] set forth as Appendix B to the opinion in *Doe v. Bolton, post,* p. 205.

It is thus apparent that at common law, at the time of the adoption of our Constitution, and throughout the major portion of the 19th century, abortion was viewed with less disfavor than under most American statutes currently in effect. Phrasing it another way, a woman enjoyed a substantially broader right to terminate a pregnancy than she does in most States today. At least with respect to the early stage of pregnancy, and very possibly without such a limitation, the opportunity to make this choice was present in this country well into the 19th century. Even later, the law continued for some time to treat less punitively an abortion procured in early pregnancy.

6. *The position of the American Medical Association.* The anti-abortion mood prevalent in this country in the late 19th century was shared by the medical profession. Indeed, the attitude of the profession may have played a significant role in the enactment of stringent criminal abortion legislation during that period.

An AMA Committee on Criminal Abortion was appointed in May 1857. It presented its report, 12 Trans. of the Am. Med. Assn. 73–78 (1859), to the Twelfth Annual Meeting. That report observed that the Committee had been appointed to investigate criminal abortion "with a view to its general suppression." It deplored abortion and its frequency and it listed three causes of "this general demoralization":

> The first of these causes is a wide-spread popular ignorance of the true character of the crime—a belief, even among mothers themselves, that the foetus is not alive till after the period of quickening.

> The second of the agents alluded to is the fact that the profession themselves are frequently supposed careless of foetal life. . . .

The third reason of the frightful extent of this crime is found in the grave defects of our laws, both common and statute, as regards the independent and actual existence of the child before birth, as a living being. These errors, which are sufficient in most instances to prevent conviction, are based, and only based, upon mistaken and exploded medical dogmas. With strange inconsistency, the law fully acknowledges the foetus in utero and its inherent rights, for civil purposes; while personally and as criminally affected, it fails to recognize it, and to its life as yet denies all protection. *Id.,* at 75–76.

The Committee then offered, and the Association adopted, resolutions protesting "against such unwarrantable destruction of human life," calling upon state legislatures to revise their abortion laws, and requesting the cooperation of state medical societies "in pressing the subject." *Id.,* at 28, 78.

In 1871 a long and vivid report was submitted by the Committee on Criminal Abortion. It ended with the observation, "We had to deal with human life. In a matter of less importance we could entertain no compromise. An honest judge on the bench would call things by their proper names. We could do no less." 22 Trans. of the Am. Med. Assn. 258 (1871). It proffered resolutions, adopted by the Association, *id.,* at 38–39, recommending, among other things, that it "be unlawful and unprofessional for any physician to induce abortion or premature labor, without the concurrent opinion of at least one respectable consulting physician, and then always with a view to the safety of the child— if that be possible," and calling "the attention of the clergy of all denominations to the perverted views of morality entertained by a large class of females—aye, and men also, on this important question."

Except for periodic condemnation of the criminal abortionist, no further formal AMA action took place until 1967. In that year, the Committee on Human Reproduction urged the adoption of a stated policy of opposition to induced abortion, except when there is "documented medical evidence" of a threat to the health or life of the mother, or that the child "may be born with incapacitating physical deformity or mental deficiency," or that a pregnancy "resulting from legally established statutory or forcible rape or incest may constitute a threat to the mental or physical health of the patient," two other physicians "chosen because of their recognized professional competence have examined the patient and have concurred in writing," and the procedure "is performed in a hospital accredited by the Joint Commission on Accreditation of Hospitals." The providing of medical information by physicians to state legislatures in their consideration of legislation regarding therapeutic abortion was "to be considered consistent with the principles of ethics of the American Medical Association." This recommendation was adopted by the House of Delegates. Proceedings of the AMA House of Delegates 40–51 (June 1967).

In 1970, after the introduction of a variety of proposed resolutions, and of a report from its Board of Trustees, a reference committee noted "polarization of the medical profession on this controversial issue"; division among those who had testified; a difference of opinion among AMA councils and committees; "the remarkable shift in testimony" in six months, felt to be influenced "by the rapid changes in state laws and by the judicial decisions which tend to make abortion more freely available"; and a feeling "that this trend will continue." On June 25, 1970, the House of Delegates adopted preambles and most of the resolutions proposed by the reference committee. The preambles emphasized "the best interests of the patient," "sound clinical judgment," and "informed patient consent," in contrast to "mere acquiescence to the patient's demand." The resolutions asserted that abortion is a medical procedure that should be performed by a licensed physician in an accredited hospital only after consultation with two other physicians and in conformity with state law, and that no party to the procedure should be required to violate personally held moral principles.[38] Proceedings of the AMA House of Delegates 220 (June 1970). The AMA Judicial Council rendered a complementary opinion.[39]

7. *The position of the American Public Health Association.* In October 1970, the Executive Board of the APHA adopted Standards for Abortion Services. These were five in number:

a. Rapid and simple abortion referral must be readily available through state and local public health departments, medical societies, or other nonprofit organizations.

b. An important function of counseling should be to simplify and expedite the provision of abortion services; it should not delay the obtaining of these services.

c. Psychiatric consultation should not be mandatory. As in the case of other specialized medical services, psychiatric consultation should be sought for definite indications and not on a routine basis.

d. A wide range of individuals from appropriately trained, sympathetic volunteers to highly skilled physicians may qualify as abortion counselors.

e. Contraception and/or sterilization should be discussed with each abortion patient. Recommended Standards for Abortion Services, 61 Am. J. Pub. Health 396 (1971).

Among factors pertinent to life and health risks associated with abortion were three that "are recognized as important":

a. the skill of the physician,

b. the environment in which the abortion is performed, and above all

c. the duration of pregnancy, as determined by uterine size and confirmed by menstrual history. *Id.,* at 397.

It was said that "a well-equipped hospital" offers more protection "to cope with unforeseen difficulties than an office or clinic without such resources. . . . The factor of gestational age is of overriding importance." Thus, it was recommended that abortions in the second trimester and early abortions in the presence of existing medical complications be performed in hospitals as inpatient procedures. For pregnancies in the first trimester, abortion in the hospital with or without overnight stay "is probably the safest practice." An abortion in an extramural facility, however, is an acceptable alternative "provided arrangements exist in advance to admit patients promptly if unforeseen complications develop." Standards for an abortion facility were listed. It was said that at present abortions should be performed by physicians or osteopaths who are licensed to practice and who have "adequate training." *Id.*, at 398.

8. *The position of the American Bar Association.* At its meeting in February 1972 the ABA House of Delegates approved, with 17 opposing votes, the Uniform Abortion Act that had been drafted and approved the preceding August by the Conference of Commissioners on Uniform State Laws. 58 A. B. A. J. 380 (1972). We set forth the Act in full in the margin.[40] The Conference has appended an enlightening Prefatory Note.[41]

VII

Three reasons have been advanced to explain historically the enactment of criminal abortion laws in the 19th century and to justify their continued existence.

It has been argued occasionally that these laws were the product of a Victorian social concern to discourage illicit sexual conduct. Texas, however, does not advance this justification in the present case, and it appears that no court or commentator has taken the argument seriously.[42] The appellants and *amici* contend, moreover, that this is not a proper state purpose at all and suggest that, if it were, the Texas statutes are overbroad in protecting it since the law fails to distinguish between married and unwed mothers.

A second reason is concerned with abortion as a medical procedure. When most criminal abortion laws were first enacted, the procedure was a hazardous one for the woman.[43] This was particularly true prior to the development of antisepsis. Antiseptic techniques, of course, were based on discoveries by Lister, Pasteur, and others first announced in 1867, but were not generally accepted and employed until about the turn of the century. Abortion mortality was high. Even after 1900, and perhaps until as late as the development of antibiotics in the 1940s, standard modern techniques such as dilation and curettage were not nearly so safe as they are today. Thus, it has been argued that a State's real concern in enacting a criminal abortion law was to protect the pregnant woman, that is, to restrain her from submitting to a procedure that placed her life in serious jeopardy.

Modern medical techniques have altered this situation. Appellants and various *amici* refer to medical data indicating that abortion in early pregnancy that is prior to the end of the first trimester although not without its risk is now relatively safe. Mortality rates for women undergoing early abortions, where the procedure is legal, appear to be as low as or lower than the rates for normal childbirth.[44] Consequently any interest of the State in protecting the woman from an inherently hazardous procedure except when it would be equally dangerous for her to forgo it has largely disappeared. Of course, important state interests in the areas of health and medical standards do remain. The State has a legitimate interest in seeing to it that abortion, like any other medical procedure, is performed under circumstances that insure maximum safety for the patient. This interest obviously extends at least to the performing physician and his staff, to the facilities involved, to the availability of after-care, and to adequate provision for any complication or emergency that might arise. The prevalence of high mortality rates at illegal "abortion mills" strengthens, rather than weakens, the State's interest in regulating the conditions under which abortions are performed. Moreover, the risk to the woman increases as her pregnancy continues. Thus, the State retains a definite interest in protecting the woman's own health and safety when an abortion is proposed at a late stage of pregnancy.

The third reason is the State's interest—some phrase it in terms of duty—in protecting prenatal life. Some of the argument for this justification rests on the theory that a new human life is present from the moment of conception.[45] The State's interest and general obligation to protect life then extends, it is argued, to prenatal life. Only when the life of the pregnant mother herself is at stake, balanced against the life she carries within her, should the interest of the embryo or fetus not prevail. Logically, of course, a legitimate state interest in this area need not stand or fall on acceptance of the belief that life begins at conception or at some other point prior to live birth. In assessing the State's interest, recognition may be given to the less rigid claim that as long as at least *potential* life is involved, the State may assert interests beyond the protection of the pregnant woman alone.

Parties challenging state abortion laws have sharply disputed in some courts the contention that a purpose of these laws, when enacted was to protect prenatal life.[46] Pointing to the absence of legislative history to support the contention they claim that most state laws were designed solely to protect the woman. Because medical advances have lessened this concerns at least with respect to abortion in early pregnancy, they argue that with respect to such abortions the laws can no longer be justified by any state interest. There is some scholarly support for this view of original purpose.[47] The few state courts called upon to interpret their laws in the late 19th and early 20th centuries did focus on the State's interest in protecting the woman's health rather than in preserving the embryo and fetus.[48] Proponents of this view point out that in many States including Texas,[49] by statute or judicial interpretation, the pregnant woman herself could not be prosecuted for self-abortion or for cooperating in an abortion performed upon her by another.[50] They claim that adoption of the "quickening" distinction through received common law and state statutes tacitly recognizes the greater health hazards inherent in late abortion and impliedly repudiates the theory that life begins at conception.

It is with these interests, and the weight to be attached to them, that this case is concerned.

VIII

The Constitution does not explicitly mention any right of privacy. In a line of decisions, however, going back perhaps as far as *Union Pacific R. Co. v. Botsford,* 141 U. S. 250, 251 (1891), the Court has recognized that a right of personal privacy, or a guarantee of certain areas or zones of privacy, does exist under the Constitution. In varying contexts, the Court or individual Justices have, indeed, found at least the roots of that right in the First Amendment, *Stanley* v. *Georgia,* 394 U. S. 557, 564 (1969); in the Fourth and Fifth Amendments, *Terry* v. *Ohio,* 392 U. S. 1, 8–9 (1968), *Katz* v. *United States,* 389 U. S. 347, 350 (1967), *Boyd* v. *United States,* 116 U. S. 616 (1886), see *Olmstead* v. *United States,* 277 U. S. 438, 478 (1928) (Brandeis, J., dissenting); in the penumbras of the Bill of Rights, *Griswold* v. *Connecticut,* 381 U. S., at 484485; in the Ninth Amendment, *id.,* at 486 (Goldberg, J., concurring); or in the concept of liberty guaranteed by the first section of the Fourteenth Amendment, see *Meyer* v. *Nebraska,* 262 U. S. 390, 399 (1923). These decisions make it clear that only personal rights that can be deemed "fundamental" or "implicit in the concept of ordered liberty," *Palko* v. *Connecticut,* 302 U. S. 319, 325 (1937), are included in this guarantee of personal privacy. They also make it clear that the right has some extension to activities relating to marriage, *Loving* v. *Virginia,* 388 U. S. 1, 12 (1967); procreation, *Skinner* v. *Oklahoma,* 316 U. S. 535, 541–542 (1942); contraception, *Eisenstadt* v. *Baird,* 405 U. S., at 453–454; *id.,* at 460, 463–465 (WHITE, J., concurring in result); family relationships, *Prince* v. *Massachusetts,* 321 U. S. 158, 166 (1944); and child rearing and education, *Pierce* v. *Society of Sisters,* 268 U. S. 510, 535 (1925), *Meyer* v. *Nebraska, supra.*

This right of privacy, whether it be founded in the Fourteenth Amendment's concept of personal liberty and restrictions upon state action, as we feel it is, or, as the District Court determined, in the Ninth Amendment's reservation of rights to the people, is broad enough to encompass a woman's decision whether or not to terminate her pregnancy. The detriment that the State would impose upon the pregnant woman by denying this choice altogether is apparent. Specific and direct harm medically diagnosable even in early pregnancy may be involved. Maternity, or additional offspring, may force upon the woman a distressful life and future. Psychological harm may be imminent. Mental and physical health may be taxed by child care. There is also the distress, for all concerned, associated with the unwanted child, and there is the problem of bringing a child into a family already unable, psychologically and otherwise, to care for it. In other cases, as in this one, the additional difficulties and continuing stigma of unwed motherhood may be involved. All these are factors the woman and her responsible physician necessarily will consider in consultation.

On the basis of elements such as these, appellant and some *amici* argue that the woman's right is absolute and that she is entitled to terminate her pregnancy at whatever time in whatever way, and for whatever reason she alone chooses. With this we do not agree. Appellant's arguments that Texas either has no valid interest at all in regulating the abortion decision, or no interest strong enough to support any limitation upon the woman's sole determination, are unpersuasive. The Court's decisions recognizing a right of privacy also acknowledge that some state regulation in areas protected by that right is appropriate. As noted above, a State may properly assert important interests in safeguarding health, in maintaining medical standards and in protecting potential life. At some point in pregnancy, these respective interests become sufficiently compelling to sustain regulation of the factors that govern the abortion decision. The privacy right involved, therefore, cannot be said to be absolute. In fact, it is not clear to us that the claim asserted by some *amici* that one has an unlimited right to do with one's body as one pleases bears a close relationship to the right of privacy previously articulated in the Court's decisions. The Court has refused to recognize an unlimited right of this kind in the past.

Jacobson v. *Massachusetts,* 197 U. S. 11 (1905) (vaccination); *Buck* v. *Bell,* 274 U. S. 200 (1927) (sterilization).

We, therefore, conclude that the right of personal privacy includes the abortion decision, but that this right is not unqualified and must be considered against important state interests in regulation.

We note that those federal and state courts that have recently considered abortion law challenges have reached the same conclusion. A majority, in addition to the District Court in the present case, have held state laws unconstitutional, at least in part, because of vagueness or because of overbreadth and abridgment of rights. *Abele* v. *Markle,* 342 F. Supp. 800 (Conn. 1972), appeal docketed, No. 72–56; *Abele* v. *Markle,* 351 F. Supp. 224 (Conn. 1972), appeal docketed, No. 72–730; *Doe* v. *Bolton,* 319 F. Supp. 1048 (ND Ga. 1970), appeal decided today, *post,* p. 179; *Doe* v. *Scott,* 321 F. Supp. 1385 (ND Ill. 1971), appeal docketed, No. 70–105; *Poe* v. *Menghini,* 339 F. Supp. 986 (Kan. 1972); *YWCA* v. *Bugler,* 342 F. Supp. 1048 (NJ 1972); *Babbitz* v. *McCann,* 310 F. Supp. 293 (ED Wis. 1970), appeal dismissed, 400 U. S. 1 (1970); *People* v. *Belous,* 71 Cal. 2d 954, 458 P. 2d 194 (1969), cert. denied, 397 U. S. 915 (1970); *State* v. *Barquet,* 262 So. 2d 431 (Fla. 1972).

Others have sustained state statutes. *Crosses* v. *Attorney General,* 344 F. Supp. 587 (ED Ky. 1972), appeal docketed, No. 72–256; *Rosen* v. *Louisiana State Board of Medical Examiners,* 318 F. Supp. 1217 (ED La. 1970), appeal docketed, No. 70–42; *Corkey* v. *Edwards,* 322 F. Supp. 1248 (WDNC 1971), appeal docketed, No. 71–92; *Steinberg* v. *Brown,* 321 F. Supp. 741 (ND Ohio 1970); *Doe* v. *Rampton* (Utah 1971), appeal docketed, No. 71–5666; *Cheaney* v. *State,* —Ind.—, 285 N. E. 2d 265 (1972); *Spears* v. *State,* 257 So. 2d 876 (Miss. 1972); *State* v. *Munson,* 86 S. D. 663, 201 N. W. 2d 123 (1972), appeal docketed, No. 72–631.

Although the results are divided, most of these courts have agreed that the right of privacy, however based, is broad enough to cover the abortion decision; that the right, nonetheless, is not absolute and is subject to some limitations; and that at some point the state interests as to protection of health, medical standards, and prenatal life, become dominant. We agree with this approach.

Where certain "fundamental rights" are involved, the Court has held that regulation limiting these rights may be justified only by a "compelling state interest," K*ramer* v. *Union Free School District,* 395 U. S. 621, 627 (1969); *Shapiro* v. *Thompson,* 394 U. S. 618, 634 (1969), *Sherbert* v. *Verner,* 374 U. S. 398, 406 (1963), and that legislative enactments must be narrowly drawn to express only the legitimate state interests at stake. *Griswold* v. *Connecticut,* 381 U. S., at 485; *Aptheker* v. *Secretary of State,* 378 U. S. 500, 508 (1964); *Cantwell* v. *Connecticut,* 310 U. S. 296, 307408 (1940); see *Eisenstadt* v. *Baird,* 405 U. S., at 460, 463–464 (WHITE, J., concurring in result).

In the recent abortion cases, cited above, courts have recognized these principles. Those striking down state laws have generally scrutinized the State's interests in protecting health and potential life, and have concluded that neither interest justified broad limitations on the reasons for which a physician and his pregnant patient might decide that she should have an abortion in the early stages of pregnancy. Courts sustaining state laws have held that the State's determinations to protect health or prenatal life are dominant and constitutionally justifiable.

IX

The District Court held that the appellee failed to meet his burden of demonstrating that the Texas statute's infringement upon Roe's rights was necessary to support a compelling state interest, and that, although the appellee presented "several compelling justifications for state presence in the area of abortions," the statutes outstripped these justifications and swept "far beyond any areas of compelling state interest." 314 F. Supp., at 1222–1223. Appellant and appellee both contest that holding. Appellant, as has been indicated, claims an absolute right that bars any state imposition of criminal penalties in the area. Appellee argues that the State's determination to recognize and protect prenatal life from and after conception constitutes a compelling state interest. As noted above, we do not agree fully with either formulation.

A. The appellee and certain *amici* argue that the fetus is a "person" within the language and meaning of the Fourteenth Amendment. In support of this, they outline at length and in detail the well-known facts of fetal development. If this suggestion of personhood is established, the appellant's case, of course, collapses, for the fetus' right to life would then be guaranteed specifically by the Amendment. The appellant conceded as much on reargument.[51] On the other hand, the appellee conceded on reargument[52] that no case could be cited that holds that a fetus is a person within the meaning of the Fourteenth Amendment.

The Constitution does not define "person" in so many words. Section 1 of the Fourteenth Amendment contains three references to "person." The first, in defining "citizens," speaks of "persons born or naturalized in the United States." The word also appears both in the Due Process Clause and in the Equal Protection Clause. "Person" is used in other places in the Constitution: in the listing of qualifications for Representatives and Senators, Art. I, §2, cl. 2, and §3, cl. 3; in the Apportionment Clause, Art. I, § 2, cl. 3;[53] in the Migration and Importation provision, Art. I, § 9, cl. 1; in the Emolument Clause, Art. I, § 9, cl. 8; in the Electors provisions, Art. II, g 1, cl. 2, and the superseded cl. 3; in the provision outlining qualifications for the office of President, Art. II, § 1, cl. 5; in the Extradition provisions, Art. IV, § 2, cl. 2, and the superseded Fugitive Slave Clause 3; and in the Fifth, Twelfth, and Twenty-second Amendments, as well as in §§ 2 and 3 of the Fourteenth Amendment. But in nearly all these instances, the use of the word is such that it has application only postnatally. None indicates, with any assurance, that it has any possible prenatal application.[54]

All this, together with our observation, supra, that throughout the major portion of the 19th century prevailing legal abortion practices were far freer than they are today, persuades us that the word "person," as used in the Fourteenth Amendment, does not include the unborn.[55] This is in accord with the results reached in those few cases where the issue has been squarely presented. *McGarvey v. Magee-Womens Hospital*, 340 F. Supp. 751 (WD Pa. 1972); *Byrn v. New York City Health & Hospitals Corp.*, 31 N. or. 2d 194, 286 N. E. 2d 887 (1972), appeal docketed, No. 72–434; *Abele v. Markle*, 351 F. Supp. 224 (Conn. 1972), appeal docketed, No. 72-730. Cf. *Cheaney v. State*, —Ind., at—, 285 N. E. 2d, at 270; *Montana v. Rogers*, 278 F. 2d 68, 72 (CA7 1960), aff'd *sub nom. Montana v. Kennedy*, 366 U. S. 308 (1961); *Reeler v. Superior Court*, 2 Cal. 3d 619, 470 P. 2d 617 (1970); *State v. Dickinson*, 28 Ohio St. 2d 65, 275 N. E. 2d 599 (1971). Indeed, our decision in *United States* v. *Vuitch*, 402 U. S. 62 (1971), inferentially is to the same effect, for we there would not have indulged in statutory interpretation favorable to abortion in specified circumstances if the necessary consequence was the termination of life entitled to Fourteenth Amendment protection.

This conclusion, however, does not of itself fully answer the contentions raised by Texas, and we pass on to other considerations.

B. The pregnant woman cannot be isolated in her privacy. She carries an embryo and, later, a fetus, if one accepts the medical definitions of the developing young in the human uterus. See Dorland's Illustrated Medical Dictionary 478–479, 547 (24th ed. 1965). The situation therefore is inherently different from marital intimacy, or bedroom possession of obscene material, or marriage, or procreation, or education, with which *Eisenstadt* and *Griswold, Stanley, Loving, Skinner,* and *Pierce* and *Meyer* were respectively concerned. As we have intimated above, it is reasonable and appropriate for a State to decide that at some point in time another interest, that of health of the mother or that of potential human life, becomes significantly involved. The woman's privacy is no longer sole and any right of privacy she possesses must be measured accordingly.

Texas urges that, apart from the Fourteenth Amendment, life begins at conception and is present throughout pregnancy, and that, therefore, the State has a compelling interest in protecting that life from and after conception. We need not resolve the difficult question of when life begins. When those trained in the respective disciplines of medicine, philosophy, and theology are unable to arrive at any consensus, the judiciary, at this point in the development of man's knowledge, is not in a position to speculate as to the answer.

It should be sufficient to note briefly the wide divergence of thinking on this most sensitive and difficult question. There has always been strong support for the view that life does not begin until live birth. This was the belief of the Stoics.[56] It appears to be the predominant, though not the unanimous, attitude of the Jewish faith.[57] It may be taken to represent also the position of a large segment of the Protestant community, insofar as that can be ascertained; organized groups that have taken a formal position on the abortion issue have generally regarded abortion as a matter for the conscience of the individual and her family.[58] As we have noted, the common law found greater significance in quickening. Physicians and their scientific colleagues have regarded that event with less interest and have tended to focus either upon conception, upon live birth, or upon the interim point at which the fetus becomes "viable," that is, potentially able to live outside the mother's womb, albeit with artificial aid.[59] Stability is usually placed at about seven months (28 weeks) but may occur earlier, even at 24 weeks. The Aristotelian theory of "mediate animation," that held sway throughout the Middle Ages and the Renaissance in Europe, continued to be official Roman Catholic dogma until the 19th century, despite opposition to this "ensoulment" theory from those in the Church who would recognize the existence of life from the moment of conception.[60] The latter is now, of course, the official belief of the Catholic Church. As one brief *amicus* discloses, this is a view strongly held by many non-Catholics as well, and by many physicians. Substantial problems for precise definition of this view are posed, however, by new embryological data that purport to indicate that conception is a "process" over time, rather than an event, and by new medical techniques such as menstrual extraction, the "morning-after" pill, implantation of embryos, artificial insemination, and even artificial wombs.[61]

In areas other than criminal abortion, the law has been reluctant to endorse any theory that life, as we recognize it, begins before live birth or to accord legal rights to the unborn except in narrowly defined situations and except when the rights are contingent upon live birth. For example, the traditional rule of tort law denied recovery for prenatal injuries even though the child was born alive.[62] That rule has been changed in almost every jurisdiction. In most States, recovery is said to be permitted only if the fetus was viable, or at least quick, when the injuries were sustained, though few courts have squarely so held.[63] In a recent development, generally opposed by the commentators, some States permit the parents of a stillborn child to maintain an action for wrongful death because of prenatal injuries.[64] Such an action, however, would appear to be one to vindicate the parents' interest and is thus consistent with the view that the fetus, at most, represents only the potentiality of life. Similarly, unborn children have been recognized as acquiring rights or interests by way of inheritance or other devolution of property, and have been represented by guardians *ad litem*.[65] Perfection of the interests involved, again, has generally been contingent upon live birth. In short, the unborn have never been recognized in the law as persons in the whole sense.

X

In view of all this, we do not agree that, by adopting one theory of life, Texas may override the rights of the pregnant woman that are at stake. We repeat, however, that the State does have an important and legitimate interest in preserving and protecting the health of the pregnant woman, whether she be a resident of the State or a nonresident who seeks medical consultation and treatment there, and that it has still *another* important and legitimate interest in protecting the potentiality of human life. These interests are separate and distinct. Each grows in substantiality as the woman approaches term and, at a point during pregnancy, each becomes "compelling."

With respect to the State's important and legitimate interest in the health of the mother, the "compelling" point, in the light of present medical knowledge, is at approximately the end of the first trimester. This is so because of the now-established medical fact that until the end of the first trimester mortality in abortion may be less than mortality in normal childbirth. It follows that, from and after this point, a State may regulate the abortion procedure to the extent that the regulation reasonably relates to the preservation and protection of maternal health. Examples of permissible state regulation in this area are requirements as to the qualifications of the person who is to perform the abortion; as to the licensure of that person; as to the facility in which the procedure is to be performed, that is, whether it must be a hospital or may be a clinic or some other place of less-than-hospital status; as to the licensing of the facility; and the like.

This means, on the other hand, that, for the period of pregnancy prior to this "compelling" point, the attending physician, in consultation with his patient, is free to determine, without regulation by the State, that, in his medical judgment, the patient's pregnancy should be terminated. If that decision is reached, the judgment may be effectuated by an abortion free of interference by the State.

With respect to the State's important and legitimate interest in potential life, the "compelling" point is at viability. This is so because the fetus then presumably has the capability of meaningful life outside the mother's womb. State regulation protective of fetal life after viability thus has both logical and biological justifications. If the State is interested in protecting fetal life after viability, it may go so far as to proscribe abortion during that period, except when it is necessary to preserve the life or health of the mother.

Measured against these standards, Art. 1196 of the Texas Penal Code, in restricting legal abortions to those "procured or attempted by medical advice for the purpose of saving the life of the mother," sweeps too broadly. The statute makes no distinction between abortions performed early in pregnancy and those performed later, and it limits to a single reason, "saving" the mother's life, the legal justification for the procedure. The statute, therefore, cannot survive the constitutional attack made upon it here.

This conclusion makes it unnecessary for us to consider the additional challenge to the Texas statute asserted on grounds of vagueness. See *United States* v. *Vuitch,* 402 U. S., at 67–72.

XI

To summarize and to repeat:

1. A state criminal abortion statute of the current Texas type, that excepts from criminality only a *lifesaving* procedure on behalf of the mother, without regard to pregnancy stage and without recognition of the other interests involved, is violative of the Due Process Clause of the Fourteenth Amendment.

(a) For the stage prior to approximately the end of the first trimester, the abortion decision and its effectuation must be left to the medical judgment of the pregnant woman's attending physician.

(b) For the stage subsequent to approximately the end of the first trimester, the State, in promoting its interest in the health of the mother, may, if it chooses, regulate the abortion procedure in ways that are reasonably related to maternal health.

(c) For the stage subsequent to viability, the State in promoting its interest in the potentiality of human life may, if it chooses, regulate, and even proscribe, abortion except where it is necessary, in appropriate medical judgment, for the preservation of the life or health of the mother.

2. The State may define the term "physician," as it has been employed in the preceding paragraphs of this Part XI of this opinion, to mean only a physician currently licensed by the State, and may proscribe any abortion by a person who is not a physician as so defined.

In *Doe* v. *Bolton, post,* p. 179, procedural requirements contained in one of the modern abortion statutes are considered. That opinion and this one, of course, are to be read together.[66]

This holding, we feel, is consistent with the relative weights of the respective interests involved, with the lessons and examples of medical and legal history, with the lenity of the common law, and with the demands of the profound problems of the present day. The decision leaves the State free to place increasing restrictions on abortion as the period of pregnancy lengthens, so long as those restrictions are tailored to the recognized state interests. The decision vindicates the right of the physician to administer medical treatment according to his professional judgment up to the points where important state interests provide compelling justifications for intervention. Up to those points, the abortion decision in all its aspects is inherently, and primarily, a medical decision, and basic responsibility for it must rest with the physician. If an individual practitioner abuses the privilege of exercising proper medical judgment, the usual remedies, judicial and intra-professional, are available.

XII

Our conclusion that Art. 1196 is unconstitutional means, of course, that the Texas abortion statutes, as a unit, must fall. The exception of Art. 1196 cannot be struck down separately, for then the State would be left with a statute proscribing all abortion procedures no matter how medically urgent the case.

Although the District Court granted appellant Roe declaratory relief, it stopped short of issuing an injunction against enforcement of the Texas statutes. The Court has recognized that different considerations enter into a federal court's decision as to declaratory relief, on the one hand, and injunctive relief, on the other. *Zwickler* v. *Koota,* 389 U. S. 241, 252–255 (1967); *Dombrowski* v. *Pfister,* 380 U. S. 479 (1965). We are not dealing with a statute that, on its face, appears to abridge free expression, an area of particular concern under *Dombrowski* and refined in *Younger* v. *Harris,* 401 U. S., at 50.

We find it unnecessary to decide whether the District Court erred in withholding injunctive relief, for we assume the Texas prosecutorial authorities will give full credence to this decision that the present criminal abortion statutes of that State are unconstitutional.

The judgment of the District Court as to intervener Hallford is reversed, and Dr. Hallford's complaint in intervention is dismissed. In all other respects, the judgment of the District Court is affirmed. Costs are allowed to the appellee.

It is so ordered.

Mr. Justice Stewart, concurring.

In 1963, this Court, in *Ferguson* v. *Skrupa,* 372 U. S. 726, purported to sound the death knell for the doctrine of substantive due process, a doctrine under which many state laws had in the past been held to violate the Fourteenth Amendment. As Mr. Justice Black's opinion for the Court in *Skrupa* put it: "We have returned to the original constitutional proposition that courts do not substitute their social and economic beliefs for the judgment of legislative bodies, who are elected to pass laws." *Id.,* at 730.[1]

Barely two years later, in *Griswold* v. *Connecticut,* 381 U. S. 479, the Court held a Connecticut birth control law unconstitutional. In view of what had been so recently said in *Skrupa,* the Court's opinion in *Griswold* understandably did its best to avoid reliance on the Due Process Clause of the Fourteenth Amendment as the ground for decision. Yet, the Connecticut law did not violate any provision of the Bill of Rights, nor any other specific provision of the Constitution.[2] So it was clear to me then, and it is equally clear to me now, that the *Griswold* decision can be rationally understood only as a holding that the Connecticut statute substantively invaded the "liberty" that is protected by the Due Process Clause of the Fourteenth Amendment.[3] As so understood, *Griswold* stands as one in a long line of *pre-Skrupa* cases decided under the doctrine of substantive due process, and I now accept it as such.

"In a Constitution for a free people, there can be no doubt that the meaning of 'liberty' must be broad indeed." *Board of Regents* v. *Roth.*, 408 U. S. 564, 572. The Constitution nowhere mentions a specific right of personal choice in matters of marriage and family life, but the "liberty" protected by the Due Process Clause of the Fourteenth Amendment covers more than those freedoms explicitly named in the Bill of Rights. See *Schware* v. *Board of Bar Examiners,* 353 U. S. 232, 238239; *Pierce* v. *Society of Sisters,* 268 U. S. 510, 534–535; *Meyer* v. *Nebraska,* 262 U. S. 390, 399–400. Cf. *Shapiro* v. *Thompson,* 394 U. S. 618, 629–630; *United States* v. *Guest,* 383 U. S. 745, 757–758; *Carrington* v. *Rash,* 380 U. S. 89, 96; *Aptheker* v. *Secretary of State,* 378 U. S. 500, 505; *Kent* v. *Dulles,* 357 U. S. 116, 127; *Bolting* v. *Sharpe,* 347 U. S. 497, 499–500; *Truaz* v. *Raich,* 239 U. S. 33, 41.

As Mr. Justice Harlan once wrote: "[T]he full scope of the liberty guaranteed by the Due Process Clause cannot be found in or limited by the precise terms of the specific guarantees elsewhere provided in the Constitution. This 'liberty' is not a series of isolated points pricked out in terms of the taking of property; the freedom of speech, press, and religion; the right to keep and bear arms; the freedom from unreasonable searches and seizures; and so on. It is a rational continuum which, broadly speaking, includes a freedom from all substantial arbitrary impositions and purposeless restraints . . . and which also recognizes, what a reasonable and sensitive judgment must, that certain interests require particularly careful scrutiny of the state needs asserted to justify their abridgment." *Poe* v. *Ullman,* 367 U. S. 497, 543 (opinion dissenting from dismissal of appeal) (citations omitted). In the words of Mr. Justice Frankfurter, "Great concepts like . . . 'liberty' . . . were purposely left to gather meaning from experience. For they relate to the whole domain of social and economic fact, and the statesmen who founded this Nation knew too well that only a stagnant society remains unchanged." *National Mutual Ins. Co.* v. *Tidewater Transfer Co.,* 337 U. S. 582, 646 (dissenting opinion).

Several decisions of this Court make clear that freedom of personal choice in matters of marriage and family life is one of the liberties protected by the Due Process Clause of the Fourteenth Amendment. *Loving* v. *Virginia,* 388 U. S. 1, 12; *Griswold* v. *Connecticut, supra; Pierce* v. *Society of Sisters, supra; Meyer* v. *Nebraska, supra.* See also *Prince* v. *Massachusetts,* 321 U. S. 158, 166; *Skinner* v. *Oklahoma,* 316 U. S. 535, 541. As recently as last Term, in *Eisenstadt* v. *Baird,* 405 U. S. 438, 453, we recognized "the right of the *individual,* married or single, to be free from unwarranted governmental intrusion into matters so fundamentally affecting a person as the decision whether to bear or beget a child." That right necessarily includes the right of a woman to decide whether or not to terminate her pregnancy. "Certainly the interests of a woman in giving of her physical and emotional self during pregnancy and the interests that will be affected throughout her life by the birth and raising of a child are of a far greater degree of significance and personal intimacy than the right to send a child to private school protected in *Pierce* v. *Society of Sisters,* 268 U. S. 510 (1925), or the right to teach a foreign language protected in *Meyer* v. *Nebraska,* 262 U. S. 390 (1923)." *Abele* v. *Markle,* 351 F. Supp. 224, 227 (Conn. 1972).

Clearly, therefore, the Court today is correct in holding that the right asserted by Jane Roe is embraced within the personal liberty protected by the Due Process Clause of the Fourteenth Amendment.

It is evident that the Texas abortion statute infringes that right directly. Indeed, it is difficult to imagine a more complete abridgment of a constitutional freedom than that worked by the inflexible criminal statute now in force in Texas. The question then becomes whether the state interests advanced to justify this abridgment can survive the "particularly careful scrutiny" that the Fourteenth Amendment here requires.

The asserted state interests are protection of the health and safety of the pregnant woman, and protection of the potential future human life within her. These are legitimate objectives, amply sufficient to permit a State to regulate abortions as it does other surgical procedures, and perhaps sufficient to permit a State to regulate abortions more stringently or even to prohibit them in the late stages of pregnancy. But such legislation is not before us, and I think the Court today has thoroughly demonstrated that these state interests cannot constitutionally support the broad abridgment of personal liberty worked by the existing Texas law. Accordingly, I join the Court's opinion holding that that law is invalid under the Due Process Clause of the Fourteenth Amendment.

MR. JUSTICE REHNQUIST, dissenting.

The Court's opinion brings to the decision of this troubling question both extensive historical fact and a wealth of legal scholarship. While the opinion thus commands my respect, I find myself nonetheless in fundamental disagreement with those parts of it that invalidate the Texas statute in question, and therefore dissent.

I

The Court's opinion decides that a State may impose virtually no restriction on the performance of abortions during the first trimester of pregnancy. Our previous decisions indicate that a necessary predicate for such an opinion is a plaintiff who was in her first trimester of pregnancy at some time during the pendency of her lawsuit. While a party may vindicate his own constitutional rights, he may not seek vindication for the rights of others. *Moose Lodge* v. *Irvis*, 407 U. S. 163 (1972); *Sierra Clubs* v. *Morton*, 405 U. S. 727 (1972) . The Court's statement of facts in this case makes clear, however, that the record in no way indicates the presence of such a plaintiff. We know only that plaintiff Roe at the time of filing her complaint was a pregnant woman; for aught that appears in this record, she may have been in her *last* trimester of pregnancy as of the date the complaint was filed.

Nothing in the Court's opinion indicates that Texas might not constitutionally apply its proscription of abortion as written to a woman in that stage of pregnancy. Nonetheless, the Court uses her complaint against the Texas statute as a fulcrum for deciding that States may impose virtually no restrictions on medical abortions performed during the *first* trimester of pregnancy. In deciding such a hypothetical lawsuit, the Court departs from the longstanding admonition that it should never "formulate a rule of constitutional law broader than is required by the precise facts to which it is to be applied." *Liverpool, New York & Philadelphia S. S. Co.* v. *Commissioners of Emigration*, 113 U. S. 33, 39 (1885). See also *Ashwander* v. *TVA,* 297 U. S. 288, 345 (1936) (Brandeis, J., concurring).

II

Even if there were a plaintiff in this case capable of litigating the issue which the Court decides, I would reach a conclusion opposite to that reached by the Court. I have difficulty in concluding, as the Court does, that the right of "privacy" is involved in this case. Texas, by the statute here challenged, bars the performance of a medical abortion by a licensed physician on a plaintiff such as Roe. A transaction resulting in an operation such as this is not "private" in the ordinary usage of that word. Nor is the "privacy" that the Court finds here even a distant relative of the freedom from searches and seizures protected by the Fourth Amendment to the Constitution, which the Court has referred to as embodying a right to privacy. *Katz v. United States*, 389 U. S. 347 (1967).

If the Court means by the term "privacy" no more than that the claim of a person to be free from unwanted state regulation of consensual transactions may be a form of "liberty" protected by the Fourteenth Amendment, there is no doubt that similar claims have been upheld in our earlier decisions on the basis of that liberty. I agree with the statement of MR. JUSTICE STEWART in his concurring opinion that the "liberty," against deprivation of which without due process the Fourteenth Amendment protects, embraces more than the rights found in the Bill of Rights. But that liberty is not guaranteed absolutely against deprivation, only against deprivation without due process of law. The test traditionally applied in the area of social and economic legislation is whether or not a law such as that challenged has a rational relation to a valid state objective. *Williamson v. Lee Optical Co.*, 348 U. S. 483, 491 (1955). The Due Process Clause of the Fourteenth Amendment undoubtedly does place a limit, albeit a broad one, on legislative power to enact laws such as this. If the Texas statute were to prohibit an abortion even where the mother's life is in jeopardy, I have little doubt that such a statute would lack a rational relation to a valid state objective under the test stated in *Williamson, supra*. But the Court's sweeping invalidation of any restrictions on abortion during the first trimester is impossible to justify under that standard, and the conscious weighing of competing factors that the Court's opinion apparently substitutes for the established test is far more appropriate to a legislative judgment than to a judicial one.

The Court eschews the history of the Fourteenth Amendment in its reliance on the "compelling state interest" test. See *Wever v. Aetna Casualty & Surety Co.*, 406 U. S. 164, 179 (1972) (dissenting opinion). But the Court adds a new wrinkle to this test by transposing it from the legal considerations associated with the Equal Protection Clause of the Fourteenth Amendment to this case arising under the Due Process Clause of the Fourteenth Amendment. Unless I misapprehend the consequences of this transplanting of the "compelling state interest test," the Court's opinion will accomplish the seemingly impossible feat of leaving this area of the law more confused than it found it.

While the Court's opinion quotes from the dissent of Mr. Justice Holmes in *Lochner v. New York*, 198 U. S. 45, 74 (1905), the result it reaches is more closely attuned to the majority opinion of Mr. Justice Peckham in that case. As in *Lochner* and similar cases applying substantive due process standards to economic and social welfare legislation, the adoption of the compelling state interest standard will inevitably require this Court to examine the legislative policies and pass on the wisdom of these policies in the very process of deciding whether a particular state interest put forward may or may not be "compelling." The decision here to break pregnancy into three distinct terms and to outline the permissible restrictions the State may impose in each one, for example, partakes more of judicial legislation than it does of a determination of the intent of the drafters of the Fourteenth Amendment.

The fact that a majority of the States reflecting, after all, the majority sentiment in those States, have had restrictions on abortions for at least a century is a strong indication, it seems to me, that the asserted right to an abortion is not "so rooted in the traditions and conscience of our people as to be ranked as fundamental," *Snyder* v. *Massachusetts,* 291 U. S. 97, 105 (1934). Even today, when society's views on abortion are changing, the very existence of the debate is evidence that the "right" to an abortion is not so universally accepted as the appellant would have us believe.

To reach its result, the Court necessarily has had to find within the scope of the Fourteenth Amendment a right that was apparently completely unknown to the drafters of the Amendment. As early as 1821, the first state law dealing directly with abortion was enacted by the Connecticut Legislature. Conn. Stat., Tit. 22, §§ 14, 16. By the time of the adoption of the Fourteenth Amendment in 1868, there were at least 36 laws enacted by state or territorial legislatures limiting abortion.[1] While many States have amended or updated their laws, 21 of the laws on the books in 1868 remain in effect today.[2] Indeed, the Texas statute struck down today was, as the majority notes, first enacted in 1857 and "has remained substantially unchanged to the present time." *Ante,* at 119.

There apparently was no question concerning the validity of this provision or of any of the other state statutes when the Fourteenth Amendment was adopted. The only conclusion possible from this history is that the drafters did not intend to have the Fourteenth Amendment withdraw from the States the power to legislate with respect to this matter.

III

Even if one were to agree that the case that the Court decides were here, and that the enunciation of the substantive constitutional law in the Court's opinion were proper, the actual disposition of the case by the Court is still difficult to justify. The Texas statute is struck down *in toto,* even though the Court apparently concedes that at later periods of pregnancy Texas might impose these selfsame statutory limitations on abortion. My understanding of past practice is that a statute found to be invalid as applied to a particular plaintiff, but not unconstitutional as a whole, is not simply "struck down" but is, instead, declared unconstitutional as applied to the fact situation before the Court. *Yick Wo* v. *Hopkins,* 118 U. S. 356 (1886); *Street* v. *New York,* 394 U. S. 576 (1969).

For all of the foregoing reasons, I respectfully dissent.

NOTES

[1] "Article 1191. Abortion

"If any person shall designedly administer to a pregnant woman or knowingly procure to be administered with her consent any drug or medicine, or shall use towards her any violence or means whatever externally or internally applied, and thereby procure an abortion, he shall be confined in the penitentiary not less than two nor more than five years; if it be done without her consent, the punishment shall be doubled. By 'abortion' is meant that the life of the fetus or embryo shall be destroyed in the woman's womb or that a premature birth thereof be caused.

"Art. 1192. Furnishing the means

"Whoever furnishes the means for procuring an abortion knowing the purpose intended is guilty as an accomplice.

"Art. 1193. Attempt at abortion

"If the means used shall fail to produce an abortion, the offender is nevertheless guilty of an attempt to produce abortion, provided it be shown that such means were calculated to produce that result, and shall be fined not less than one hundred nor more than one thousand dollars.

"Art. 1194. Murder in producing abortion

"If the death of the mother is occasioned by an abortion so produced or by an attempt to effect the same it is murder."

"Art. 1196. By medical advice

"Nothing in this chapter applies to an abortion procured or attempted by medical advice for the purpose of saving the life of the mother."

The foregoing Articles, together with Art. 1195, compose Chapter 9 of Title 15 of the Penal Code. Article 1195 not attacked here, reads:

"Art. 1195. Destroying unborn child

"Whoever shall during parturition of the mother destroy the vitality or life in a child in a state of being born and before actual birth, which child would otherwise have been born alive, shall be confined in the penitentiary for life or for not less than five years."

---

2 Ariz. Rev. Stat. Ann. §13–211 (1956); Conn. Pub. Act No. 1 (May 1972 special session) (in 4 Conn. Leg. Serv. 677 (1972)), and Conn. Gen. Stat. Rev. §§53–29, 53–30 (1968) (or unborn child); Idaho Code § 18–601 (1948); Ill. Rev. Stat., c. 38, § 23–1 (1971); Ind. Code § 35–1–58–1 (1971); Iowa Code § 701.1 (1971); Ky. Rev. Stat. §436.020 (1962); La. Rev. Stat. §37:1285 (6) (1964) (loss of medical license) (but see § 14:87 (Supp. 1972) containing no exception for the life of the mother under the criminal statute); Me. Rev. Stat. Ann., Tit. 17, §51 (1964); Mass. Gen. Laws Ann., c. 272, § 19 (1970) (using the term "unlawfully," construed to exclude an abortion to save the mother's life, Rudish v. Bd. of Registration, 356 Mass. 98, 248 N. E. 2d 264 (1969)); Mich. Comp. Laws § 750.14 (1948); Minn. Stat. § 617.18 (1971); Mo. Rev. Stat. §559.100 (1969); Mont. Rev. Codes Ann. §94–401 (1969); Neb. Rev. Stat. §28–405 (1964); Nev. Rev. Stat. §200.220 (1967); N. H. Rev. Stat. Ann. §585:13 (1955); N. J. Stat. Ann. §2A:87–1 (1969) ("without lawful justification"); N. D. Cent. Code §§ 12–2501, 12–2542 (1960); Ohio Rev. Code Ann. § 2901.16 (1953); Okla. Stat. Ann., Tit. 21, § 861 (1972–1973 Supp.); Pa. Stat. Ann., Tit. 18, §§ 4718, 4719 (1963) ("unlawful"); R. I. Gen. Laws Ann. § 1141 (1969); S. D. Comp. Laws Ann. §22–17–1 (1967); Tenn. Code Ann. §§ 39–301, 39–302 (1956); Utah Code Ann. §§ 76–2–1, 76–2–2 (1953); Vt. Stat. Ann., Tit. 13, § 101 (1958); W. Va. Code Ann. § 61–2–8 (1966); Wis. Stat. § 940.04 (1969); Wyo. Stat. Ann. §§ 6–77, 6–78 (1957) .

³ Long ago, a suggestion was made that the Texas statutes were unconstitutionally vague because of definitional deficiencies. The Texas Court of Criminal Appeals disposed of that suggestion peremptorily, saying only,

"It is also insisted in the motion in arrest of judgment that the statute is unconstitutional and void in that it does not sufficiently define or describe the offense of abortion. We do not concur in respect to this question." *Jackson* v. *State, 55* Tex. Cr. R. 79, S9, 115 S. W. 262, 268 (1908).

The same court recently has held again that the State's abortion statutes are not unconstitutionally vague or overbroad. *Thompson* v. *State* (Ct. Crim. App. Tex. 1971), appeal docketed, No. 71–1200. The court held that "the State of Texas has a compelling interest to protect fetal life"; that Art. 1191 "is designed to protect fetal life"; that the Texas homicide statutes, particularly Art. 1205 of the Penal Code, are intended to protect a person "in existence by actual birth" and thereby implicitly recognize other human life that is not "in existence by actual birth"; that the definition of human life is for the legislature and not the courts; that Art. 1196 "is more definite than the District of Columbia statute upheld in *[United States* v. *] Vuitch"* (402 U. S. 62); and that the Texas statute "is not vague and indefinite or overbroad." A physician's abortion conviction was affirmed.

In *Thompson*, n. 2, the court observed that any issue as to the burden of proof under the exemption of Art . 1196 "is not before us." But see *Feeders* v. *State.* 172 Tex. Cr. R. 162, 1691–69, 354 S. W. 2d 161, 166–167 (1962). Cf. *United States* v. *Vuitch*, 402 U. S. 62, 69–71 (1971).

⁴ The name is a pseudonym.

⁵ These names are pseudonyms.

⁶ The appellee twice states in his brief that the hearing before the District Court was held on July 22, 1970. Brief for Appellee 13. The docket entries, App. 2, and the transcript, App. 76, reveal this to be an error. The July date appears to be the time of the reporter's transcription. See App. 77.

⁷ We need not consider what different result, if any, would follow if Dr. Hallford's intervention were on behalf of a class. His complaint in intervention does not purport to assert a class suit and makes no reference to any class apart from an allegation that he "and others similarly situated" must necessarily guess at the meaning of Art. 1196. His application for leave to intervene goes somewhat further, for it asserts that plaintiff Roe does not adequately protect the interest of the doctor "and the class of people who are physicians . . . [and] the class of people who are . . . patients. . . ."

The leave application, however, is not the complaint. Despite the District Court's statement to the contrary, 314 F. Supp., at 1225, we fail to perceive the essentials of a class suit in the Hallford complaint.

⁸ A. Castiglioni, A History of Medicine 84 (2d ed. 1947), E. Krumbhaar, translator and editor (hereinafter Castiglioni).

⁹ J. Ricci, The Genealogy of Gynaecology 52, 84, 113, 149 (2d ed. 1950) (hereinafter Ricci); L. Lader, Abortion 75–77 (1966) (hereinafter Lader); K. Niswander, Medical Abortion Practices in the United States, in Abortion and the Law 37, 38–40 (D. Smith ed. 1967); G. Williams, The Sanctity of Life and the Criminal Law 148 (1957)

(hereinafter Williams); J. Noonan, An Almost Absolute Value in History, in The Morality of Abortion 1, 3–7 (J. Noonan ed. 1970) (hereinafter Noonan); Quay, Justifiable Abortion—Medical and Legal Foundations (pt. 2), 49 Geo. L. J. 395, 406–422 (1961) (hereinafter Quay).

[10] L. Edelstein, The Hippocratic Oath 10 (1943) (hereinafter Edelstein) But see Castiglioni 227.

[11] Edelstein 12; Ricci 113–114, 118–119; Noonan 5.

[12] Edelstein 13–14

[13] Castiglioni 148.

[14] *Id.,* at 154

[15] Edelstein 3.

[16] *Id.,* at 12, 15–18.

[17] *Id.,* at 18; Lader 76.

[18] Edelstein 63

[19] *Id.,* at 64.

[20] Dorland's Illustrated Medical Dictionary 1261 (24th ed. 1965).

[21] E. Coke, Institutes III *50; 1 W. Hawkins, Pleas of the Crown, c. 31, § 16 (4th ed. 1762); 1 W. Blackstone, Commentaries "129-130; M. Hale, Pleas of the Crown 433 (1st Amer. ed. 1847). For discussions of the role of the quickening concept in English common law, see Lader 78; Noonan 22S–226; Means, The Law of New York Concerning Abortion and the Status of the Foetus, 1664–1968: A Case of Cessation of Constitutionality (pt. 1), 14 N. Y. L. F. 411, 418–428 (1968) (hereinafter Means I); Stern, Abortion: Reform and the Law, 59 J. Crim. L. C. & P. S. 84 (1968) (hereinafter Stern); Quay 430–432; Williams 152.

[22] Early philosophers believed that the embryo or fetus did not become formed and begin to live until at least 40 days after conception for a male, and 80 to 90 days for a female. See, for example, Aristotle, Hist. Anim. 7.3.583b; Gen. Anim. 2.3.736, 2.5.741; Hippocrates, Lib. de Nat. Puer. No. 10. Aristotle's thinking derived from his three-stage theory of life: vegetable, animal, rational. The vegetable stage was reached at conception, the animal at "animation," and the rational soon after live birth. This theory, together with the 40/80 day view, came to be accepted by early Christian thinkers.

The theological debate was reflected in the writings of St. Augustine, who made a distinction between *embryo inanimatus,* not yet endowed with a soul, and *embryo animatus.* He may have drawn upon Exodus 21:22. At one point, however, he expressed the view that human powers cannot determine the point during fetal development at which the critical change occurs. See Augustine, De Origine Animae 4.4 (Pub. Law 44.527). See also W. Reany, The Creation of the Human Soul, c. 2 and 83-86 (1932); Huser, The Crime of Abortion in Canon Law 15 (Catholic Univ. of America, Canon Law Studies No. 162, Washington, D. C., 1949).

Galen, in three treatises related to embryology, accepted the thinking of Aristotle and his followers. Quay 426–427. Later, Augustine on abortion was incorporated by Gratian into the Decretum, published about 1140. Decretum Magistri Gratiani 232.2.7 to 232.2.10, in 1 Corpus Juris Canonici 1122, 1123 (A. Friedburg, 2d ed. 1879). This Decretal and the Decretals that followed were recognized as the definitive body of canon law until the new Code of 1917.

For discussions of the canon-law treatment, see Means I, pp. 411–412; Noonan 20–26; Quay 426–430; see also J. Noonan, Contraception: A History of Its Treatment by the Catholic Theologians and Canonists 18–29 (1965).

23 Bracton took the position that abortion by blow or poison was homicide "if the foetus be already formed and animated, and particularly if it be animated." 2 II. Bracton, De Legibus et Consuetudinibus Angliae 279 (T. Twiss ed. 1879), or, as a later translation puts it, "if the foetus is already formed or quickened, especially if it is quickened," 2 H. Bracton, On the Laws and Customs of England 341 (S. Thorne ed. 1968). See Quay 431; see also 2 Fleta 60–61 (Book 1, c. 23) (Selden Society ed. 1955).

24 E. Coke, Institutes III *50.

25 W. Blackstone, Commentaries *129–130.

26 Means, The Phoenix of Abortional Freedom: Is a Penumbral or Ninth-Amendment Right About to Arise from the Nineteenth-Century Legislative Ashes of a Fourteenth-Century Common-Law Liberty?, 17 N. Y. L. F. 335 (1971) (hereinafter Means II). The author examines the two principal precedents cited marginally by Coke, both contrary to his dictum, and traces the treatment of these and other cases by earlier commentators. He concludes that Coke, who himself participated as an advocate in an abortion ease in 1601, may have intentionally misstated the law. The author even suggests a reason: Coke's strong feelings against abortion, coupled with his determination to assert common-law (secular) jurisdiction to assess penalties for an offense that traditionally had been an exclusively ecclesiastical or canon-law crime. See also Lader 78–79, who notes that some scholars doubt that the common law ever was applied to abortion; that the English ecclesiastical courts seem to have lost interest in the problem after 1527; and that the preamble to the English legislation of 1803, 43 Geo. 3, c. 58, §1, referred to in the text, *infra,* at 136, states that "no adequate means have been hitherto provided for the prevention and punishment of such offenses."

27 *Commonwealth v. Bangs,* 9 Mass. 387, 388 (1812); *Commonwealth v. Parker,* 50 Mass. (9 Metc.) 263, 265–266 (1845); *State v. Cooper,* 22 N. J. L. 52, 58 (1849); *Abrams v. Foshee,* 3 Iowa 274, 278-280 (1856); *Smith v. Gaffard,* 31 Ala. 45, 51 (1857); *Mitchell v. Commonwealth,* 78 Ky. 204, 210 (1879); *Eggart v. State,* 40 Fla. 527, 532, 25 So. 144, 145 (1898); *State v. Alcorn,* 7 Idaho 599, 606, G4 P. 1014, 1016 (1901); *Edwards v. State,* 79 Neb. 251, 252, 112 N. W. 611, 612 (1907); *Gray v. State,* 77 Tex. Cr. R. 221, 224, 178 S. W. 337, 338 (1915); *Miller v. Bennett,* 190 Va. 162, 169, 56 S. E. 2d 217, 221 (1949). *Contra, Mills v. Commonwealth,* 13 Pa. 631, 633 (1850); *State v. Slagle,* 83 N. C. 630, 632 (1880).

[28] See *Smith* v. *State,* 33 Me. 48, 55 (1851); *Evans* v. *People,* 49 N. Y. 86, 88 (1872); *Lamb* v. *State,* 67 Md. 524, 533, 10 A. 208 (1887) .

[29] Conn. Stat., Tit . 20, § 14 (1821) .

[30] Conn. Pub. Acts, c. 71, §1 (1860).

[31] N. Y. Rev. Stat., pt. 4, c. 1, Tit. 2, Art. 1, §9, p. 661, and Tit. 6, §21, p. 694 (1829).

[32] Act of Jan. 20, 1840, § 1, set forth in 2 H. Gammel, Laws of Texas 177–178 (1898); see *Grigsby* v. *Reib,* 105 Tex. 597, 600, 153 S. W. 1124, 1125 (1913).

[33] The early statutes are discussed in Quay 435–438. See also Lader 85–88; Stern 85–86; and Means II 375–376.

[34] Criminal abortion statutes in effect in the States as of 1961, together with historical statutory development and important judicial interpretations of the state statutes, are cited and quoted in Quay 447–520. See Comment, A Survey of the Present Statutory and Case Law on Abortion: The Contradictions and the Problems, 1972 U. Ill. L. F. 177, 179, classifying the abortion statutes and listing 25 States as permitting abortion only if necessary to save or preserve the mother's life.

[35] Ala. Code, Tit. 14, § 9 (1958); D. C. Code Ann. § 22–201 (1967).

[36] Mass. Gen. Laws Ann., c. 272, § 19 (1970); N. J. Stat. Ann. §2A:87-1 (1969); Pa. Stat. Ann., Tit. 18, §§4718, 4719 (1963).

[37] Fourteen States have adopted some form of the ALI statute. See Ark. Stat. Ann. §§ 41–303 to 41–310 (Supp. 1971); Calif. Health & Safety Code §§ 25950–25955.5 (Supp. 1972); Colo. Rev. Stat. Ann. §§40–2–50 to 40–2–53 (Cum. Supp. 1967); Del. Code Ann., Tit. 24, §§ 1790–1793 (Supp. 1972); Florida Law of Apr. 13, 1972, c. 72–196, 1972 Fla. Sess. Law Serv., pp. 380–382; Ga. Code §§ 26–1201 to 26–1203 (1972); Kan. Stat. Ann. § 21–3407 (Supp. 1971); Md. Ann. Code, Art. 43, §§137–139 (1971); Miss. Code Ann. § 2223 (Supp. 1972); N. M. Stat. Ann. §§ 40A-5–1 to 40A-5–3 (1972); N. C. Gen. Stat. § 14–45.1 (Supp. 1971); Ore. Rev. Stat. §§ 435.405 to 435.495 (1971); S. C. Code Ann. §§ 1682 to 16–89 (1962 and Supp. 1971); Va. Code Ann. §§ 18.1–62 to 18.1–62.3 (Supp. 1972). Mr. Justice Clark described some of these States as having "led the way." Religion, Morality, and Abortion: A Constitutional Appraisal, 2 Loyola U. (L. A.) L. Rev. 1, 11 (1969).

By the end of 1970, four other States had repealed criminal penalties for abortions performed in early pregnancy by a licensed physician, subject to stated procedural and health requirements. Alaska Stat. §11.15.060 (1970); Haw. Rev. Stat. §453–16 (Supp. 1971); N. Y. Penal Code § 125.05, subd. 3 (Supp. 1972–1973); Wash. Rev. Code §§ 9.02.060 to 9.02.080 (Supp. 1972). The precise status of criminal abortion laws in some States is made unclear by recent decisions in state and federal courts striking down existing state laws, in whole or in part.

[38] "Whereas, Abortion, like any other medical procedure, should not be performed when contrary to the best interests of the patient since good medical practice requires due consideration for the patient's welfare and not mere acquiescence to the patient's demand; and

"Whereas, The standards of sound clinical judgment, which, together with informed patient consent should be determinative according to the merits of each individual case; therefore be it

"RESOLVED, That abortion is a medical procedure and should be performed only by a duly licensed physician and surgeon in an accredited hospital acting only after consultation with two other physicians chosen because of their professional competency and in conformance with standards of good medical practice and the Medical Practice Act of his State; and be it further

"RESOLVED, That no physician or other professional personnel shall be compelled to perform any act which violates his good medical judgment. Neither physician, hospital, nor hospital personnel shall be required to perform any act violative of personally-held moral principles. In these circumstances good medical practice requires only that the physician or other professional personnel withdraw from the case so long as the withdrawal is consistent with good medical practice." Proceedings of the AMA House of Delegates 220 (June 1970).

[39] "The Principles of Medical Ethics of the AMA do not prohibit a physician from performing an abortion that is performed in accordance with good medical practice and under circumstances that do not violate the laws of the community in which he practices.

"In the matter of abortions, as of any other medical procedure, the Judicial Council becomes involved whenever there is alleged violation of the Principles of Medical Ethics as established by the House of Delegates."

[40] UNIFORM ABORTION ACT

"SECTION 1. [Abortion Defined; When Authorized.]

"(a) 'Abortion' means the termination of human pregnancy with an intention other than to produce a live birth or to remove a dead fetus.

"(b) An abortion may be performed in this state only if it is performed:

"(1) by a physician licensed to practice medicine [or osteopathy] in this state or by a physician practicing medicine [or osteopathy] in the employ of the government of the United States or of this state, [and the abortion is performed [in the physician's office or in a medical clinic, or] in a hospital approved by the [Department of Health] or operated by the United States, this state, or any department, agency, or political subdivision of either;] or by a female upon herself upon the advice of the physician; and "(2) within [20] weeks after the commencement of the pregnancy [or after [20] weeks only if the physician has reasonable cause to believe (i) there is a substantial risk that continuance of the pregnancy would endanger the life of the mother or would gravely impair the physical or mental health of the mother, (ii) that the child would be born with grave physical or mental defect, or (iii) that the pregnancy resulted from rape or incest, or illicit intercourse with a girl under the age of 16 years].

"SECTION 2. [Penalty.] Any person who performs or procures an abortion other than authorized by this Act is guilty of a [felony] and, upon conviction thereof, may be sentenced to pay a fine not exceeding [$1,000] or to imprisonment [in the state penitentiary] not exceeding [5 years], or both.

"SECTION 3. [Uniformity of Interpretation.] This Act shall be construed to effectuate its general purpose to make uniform the law with respect to the subject of this Act among those states which enact it.

"SECTION 4. [Short Title.] This Act may be cited as the Uniform Abortion Act.

"SECTION 5. *[Severability.]* If any provision of this Act or the application thereof to any person or circumstance is held invalid, the invalidity does not affect other provisions or applications of this Act which can be given effect without the invalid provision or application, and to this end the provisions of this Act are severable.

"SECTION 6. *[Repeal.]* The following acts and parts of acts are repealed:

"(1)

"(2)

"(3)

"SECTION 7. *[Time of Taking Effect.]* This Act shall take effect. . . ."

[41] "This Act is based largely upon the New York abortion act following a review of the more recent laws on abortion in several states and upon recognition of a more liberal trend in laws on this subject. Recognition was given also to the several decisions in state and federal courts which show a further trend toward liberalization of abortion laws, especially during the first trimester of pregnancy.

"Recognizing that a number of problems appeared in New York, a shorter time period for 'unlimited' abortions was advisable. The time period was bracketed to permit the various states to insert a figure more in keeping with the different conditions that might exist among the states. Likewise, the language limiting the place or places in which abortions may be performed was also bracketed to account for different conditions among the states. In addition, limitations on abortions after the initial 'unlimited' period were placed in brackets so that individual states may adopt all or any of these reasons, or place further restrictions upon abortions after the initial period.

"This Act does not contain any provision relating to medical review committees or prohibitions against sanctions imposed upon medical personnel refusing to participate in abortions because of religious or other similar reasons, or the like. Such provisions, while related, do not directly pertain to when, where, or by whom abortions may be performed; however, the Act is not drafted to exclude such a provision by a state wishing to enact the same."

[42] See, for example, *YWCA* v. *Kidder,* 342 F. Supp. 1048, 1074 (N. J. 1972); *Abele* v. *Markle,* 342 F. Supp. 800, 805–806 (Conn. 1972) (Newman, J., concurring in result), appeal docketed, No. 72–56; *Walsingham* v. *State,* 250 So. 2d 857, 863 (Irvin, J., concurring) (Fla. 1971); *State* v. *Gedicke,* 43 N. J. L. 86, 90 (1881); Means II 381–382.

[43] See C. Haagensen & W. Lloyd, A Hundred Years of Medicine 19 (1943) .

[44] Potts, Postconceptive Control of Fertility, 8 Int'l J. of G. & O. 957, 967 (1970) (England and Wales); Abortion Mortality, 20 Morbidity and Mortality) 208, 209 (June 12, 1971) (U. S. Dept. of HEW, Public Health Service) (New York City); Tietze, United States: Therapeutic Abortions. 1963–196S, 59 Studies in Family Planning 5, 7 (1970); Tietze, Mortality with Contraception and Induced Abortion, 45 Studies in Family Planning 6 (1969) (Japan, Czechoslovakia, Hungary); Tietze & Lehfeldt, Legal Abortion in Eastern Europe, 175 J. A. M. A. 1149, 1152 (April 1961). Other sources are discussed in Lader 17–23.

45 See Brief of *Amicus* National Right to Life Committee; R. Drinan, The Inviolability of the Right to Be Born, in Abortion and the Law 107 (D. Smith ed. 1967); Louisell, Abortion, The Practice of Medicine and the Due Process of Law, 16 U. C. L. A. L. Rev. 233 (1969); Noonan 1.

46 See, e.g. *Abele* v. *Markle,* 342 F. Supp. 800 (Conn. 1972), appeal docketed, No. 72–56.

47 See discussions in Means I and Means II.

48 See, e.g. *State v. Murphy,* 27 N. J. L. 112, 114 (1858).

49 *Watson* v. *State,* 9 Tex. App. 237, 244–245 (1880); *Moore* v. *State,* 37 Tex. Cr. R. 552, 561, 40 S. W. 287, 290 (1897); *Shaw* v. *State,* 73 Tex. Cr. R. 337, 339, 165 S. W. 930, 931 (1914); *Fondren* v. *State.* 74 Tex. Cr. R. 552, 557, 169 S. W. 411, 414 (1914); *Gray* v. *State,* 77 Tex. Cr. R. 221, 229, 17S S. W. 337, 341 (1915). There is no immunity in Texas for the father who is not married to the mother. *Hammett* v. *State,* 84 Tex. Cr. R. 635, 209 S. W. 661 (1919); *Thompson* v. *State* (Ct. Crim. App. Tex. 1971), appeal docketed, No. 71–1200

50 See *Smith* v. *State,* 33 Me., at 55; *In re Vince,* 2 N. J. 443, 450, 67 A. 2d 141, 144 (1949). A short discussion of the modern law on this issue is contained in the Comment to the ALI's Model Penal Code § 207.11, at 158 and nn. 35–37 (Tent. Draft No. 9, 1959).

51 Tr. of Oral Rearg. 20–21.

52 Tr. of Oral Rearg. 24.

53 We are not aware that in the taking of any census under this clause, a fetus has ever been counted.

54 When Texas urges that a fetus is entitled to Fourteenth Amendment protection as a person, it faces a dilemma. Neither in Texas nor in any other State are all abortions prohibited. Despite broad proscription, an exception always exists. The exception contained in Art. 1196, for an abortion procured or attempted by medical advice for the purpose of saving the life of the mother, is typical. But if the fetus is a person who is not to be deprived of life without due process of law, and if the mother's condition is the sole determinant, does not the Texas exception appear to be out of line with the Amendment's command?

There are other inconsistencies between Fourteenth Amendment status and the typical abortion statute. It has already been pointed out, n. 49, *supra,* that in Texas the woman is not a principal or an accomplice with respect to an abortion upon her. If the fetus is a person, why is the woman not a principal or an accomplice? Further, the penalty for criminal abortion specified by Art. 1195 is significantly less than the maximum penalty for murder prescribed by Art. 1257 of the Texas Penal Code. If the fetus is a person, may the penalties be different?

55 Cf. the Wisconsin abortion statute, defining "unborn child" to mean "a human being from the time of conception until it is born alive," Wis. Stat. § 940.04 (6) (1969), and the new Connecticut statute, Pub. Act No. 1 (May 1972 special session), declaring it to be the public policy of the State and the legislative intent "to protect and preserve human life from the moment of conception."

[56] Edelstein 16.

[57] Lader 97–99; D. Feldman, Birth Control in Jewish Law 251 294 (1968). For a stricter view, see I. Jakobovits, Jewish Views on Abortion, in Abortion and the Law 124 (D. Smith ed. 1967).

[58] Amicus Brief for the American Ethical Union et al. For the position of the National Council of Churches and of other denominations, see Lader 99–101.

[59] L. Hellman & J. Pritchard, Williams Obstetrics 493 (14th ed. 1971); Dorland's Illustrated Medical Dictionary 1689 (24th ed. 1965).

[60] For discussions of the development of the Roman Catholic position, see D. Callahan, Abortion: Law, Choice, and Morality 409447 (1970); Noonan 1.

[61] See Brodie, The New Biology and the Prenatal Child, 9 J. Family L. 391, 397 (1970); Gorney, The New Biology and the Future of Man, 15 U. C. L. A. L. Rev. 273 (1968); Note, Criminal Law—Abortion—The "Morning-After Pill" and Other Pre-Implantation Birth-Control Methods and the Law, 46 Ore. L. Rev. 211 (1967); G. Taylor, The Biological Time Bomb 32 (1968); A. Rosenfeld, The Second Genesis 138-139 (1969); Smith, Through a Test Tube Darkly: Artificial Insemination and the Law, 67 Mich. L. Rev. 127 (1968); Note, Artificial Insemination and the Law, 196S U. 111. L. F. 203.

[62] W. Prosser, The Law of Torts 335-338 (4th ed. 1971); 2 F. Harper & F. James, The Law of Torts 1028–1031 (1956); Note, 63 Harv. L. Rev. 173 (1949).

[63] See cases cited in Prosser, *supra*, n. 63, at 336–338; Annotation, Action for Death of Unborn Child, 15 A. L. R. 3d 992 (1967).

[64] *Prosser, supra, n. 63*, at 338; Note, The Law and the Unborn Child: The Legal and Logical Inconsistencies, 46 Notre Dame Law. 349, 354–360 (1971).

[65] Louisell, Abortion, The Practice of Medicine and the Due Process of Law, 16 U. C. L. A. L. Rev. 233, 235–238 (1969); Note, 56 Iowa L. Rev. 994, 999–1000 (1971); Note, The Law and the Unborn Child, 46 Notre Dame Law. 349, 351–354 (1971).

[66] Neither in this opinion nor in *Doe v. Bolton. post,* p. 179, do we discuss the father's rights, if any exist in the constitutional context in the abortion decision. No paternal right has been asserted in either of the cases, and the Texas and the Georgia statutes on their face take no cognizance of the father. We are aware that some statutes recognize the father under certain circumstances. North Carolina, for example, NT, C, Gen. Stat. § 1445.1 (Supp. 1971), requires written permission for the abortion from the husband when the woman is a married minor, that is, when she is less than 18 years of age, 41 N. C. A. G. 489 (1971); if the woman is an unmarried minor, written permission from the parents is required. We need not now decide whether provisions of this kind are constitutional.

* * *

[1] Only Mr. Justice Harlan failed to join the Court's opinion, 372 U. S., at 733.

[2] There is no constitutional right of privacy, as such. "[The Fourth] Amendment protects individual privacy against certain kinds of governmental intrusion, but its protections go further, and often have nothing to do with privacy at all. Other

provisions of the Constitution protect personal privacy from other forms of governmental invasion. But the protection of a person's *general* right to privacy—his right to be let alone by other people—is, like the protection of his property and of his very life, left largely to the law of the individual States." *Katz v. United States*, 389 U. S. 347, 350–351 (footnotes omitted).

[3] This was also clear to Mr. Justice Black, 381 U. S., at 507 (dissenting opinion); to Mr. Justice Harlan, 381 U. S., at 499 (opinion concurring in the judgment); and to Mr. Justice White, 381 U. S., at 502 (opinion concurring in the judgment). See also Mr. Justice Harlan's thorough and thoughtful opinion dissenting from dismissal of the appeal in *Poe v. Ullman*, 367 U. S. 497, 522.

* * *

[1] Jurisdictions having enacted abortion laws prior to the adoption of the Fourteenth Amendment in 1868:

1. Alabama—Ala. Acts, c. 6, §2 (1840).
2. Arizona—Howell Code, c. 10, § 45 (1865).
3. Arkansas—Ark. Rev. Stat., c. 44, div. III, Art. II, § 6 (1838).
4. California—Cal. Sess. Laws, c. 99, §45, p. 233 (1849–1850).
5. Colorado (Terr.)—Colo. Gen. Laws of Terr. of Colo., 1st Sess. §42, pp. 296–297 (1861).
6. Connecticut—Conn. Stat., Tit. 20, §§ 14, 16 (1821). By 1868, this statute had been replaced by another abortion law. Conn. Pub. Acts, c. 71, §§ 1, 2, p. 65 (1860).
7. Florida—Fla. Acts 1st Sess., c. 1637, subc. 3, §§ 10, 11, subc. 8, §§9, 10, 11 (1868), as amended, now Fla. Stat. Ann. §§782.09, 782.10, 797.01, 797.02, 782.16 (1965).
8. Georgia—Ga. Pen. Code, 4th Div., § 20 (1833).
9. Kingdom of Hawaii—Hawaii Pen. Code, c. 12, §§ 1, 2, 3 (1850).
10. Idaho (Terr.)—Idaho (Terr.) Laws, Crimes and Punishments §§ 33, 34, 42, pp. 441, 443 (1863).
11. Illinois—Ill. Rev. Criminal Code §§ 40, 41, 46, pp. 130, 131 (1827). By 1868, this statute had been replaced by a subsequent enactment. Ill. Pub. Laws §§ 1, 2, 3, p. 89 (1867).
12. Indiana—Ind. Rev. Stat. §§ 1, 3, p. 29A (1S38). By 1868 this statute had been superseded by a subsequent enactment. Ind. Laws, c. IXXXI, §2 (1859).
13. Iowa (Terr.)—Iowa (Terr.) Stat., 1st Legis., 1st Sess., § 18, p. 145 (1838). By 1868, this statute had been superseded by a subsequent enactment. Iowa (Terr.) Rev. Stat., c. 49, §§ 10, 13 (1843).
14. Kansas (Terr.)—Kan. (Terr.) Stat., c. 48, §§ 9, 10, 39 (1855). By 1868, this statute had been superseded by a subsequent enactment. Kan. (Terr.) Laws, c. 28, §§ 9, 10, 37 (1859).
15. Louisiana—La. Rev. Stat., Crimes and Offenses § 24, p. 138 (1856).
16. Maine—Me. Rev. Stat., c. 160, §§ 11, 12, 13, 14 (1840).
17. Maryland—Md. Laws, c. 179, § 2, p. 315 (1868).
18. Massachusetts—Mass. Acts & Resolves, c. 27 (1845).
19. Michigan—Mich. Rev. Stat., c. 153, §§32,- 33, 34, p. 662 (1846).

20. Minnesota (Terr.)—Minn. (Terr.) Rev. Stat., c. 100, §.§ 10, 11, p. 493 (1851).

21. Mississippi—Miss. Code, c. 64, §§8, 9, p. 958 (1848).

22. Missouri—Mo. Rev. Stat., Art. II, §§ 9, 10, 36, pp. 168, 172 (1835).

23. Montana (Terr.)—Mont. (Terr.) Laws, Criminal Practice Acts § 41, p. 184 (1864).

24. Nevada (Terr.)—Nev. (Terr.) Laws, c. 28, §42, p. 63 (1861).

25. New Hampshire—N. H. Laws, c. 743, § 1, p. 708 (1848).

26. New Jersey—N. J. Laws, p. 266 (1849).

27. New York—N. Y. Rev. Stat., pt. 4, c. 1, Tit. 2, §§8, 9, pp. 12-13 (1828). By 1868, this statute had been superseded. N. Y. Laws, c. 260, §§ 1–6, pp. 285–286 (1845); N. Y. Laws, c. 22, § 1, p. 19 (1846).

28. Ohio—Ohio Gen. Stat. §§ 111 (1), 112 (2), p. 252 (1841).

29. Oregon—Ore. Gen. Laws, Crim. Code, c. 43, § 509, p. 528 (1845–1864).

30. Pennsylvania—Pa. Laws No. 374, §§ 87, 88, 89 (1860).

31. Texas—Tex. Gen. Stat. Dig., c. VII, Arts. 531–536, p. 524 (Oldham & White 1859).

32. Vermont—Vt. Acts No. 33, § 1 (1846). By 1868, this statute had been amended. Vt. Acts No. 57, §§ 1, 3 (1867).

33. Virginia—Va. Acts, Tit. II, c. 3, §9, p. 96 (1848).

34. Washington (Terr.)—Wash. (Terr.) Stats., e. II, §§37, 38, p. 81 (1854).

35. West Virginia—See Acts., Tit. II, c. 3, § 9, p. 96 (1848); W. Va. Const., Art. XI, par. 8 (1863).

36. Wisconsin—Wis. Rev. Stat., c. 133, §§ 10, 11 (1849). By 1868, this statute had been superseded. Wis. Rev. Stat., c. 164, §§ 10, 11; c. 169, §§ 58, 59 (1858).

[2] Abortion laws in effect in 1868 and still applicable as of August 1970:

1. Arizona (1865).
2. Connecticut (1860).
3. Florida (1868).
4. Idaho (1863).
5. Indiana (1838).
6. Iowa (1843).
7. Maine (1840).
8. Massachusetts (1845).
9. Michigan (1846).
10. Minnesota (1851).
11. Missouri (1835).
12. Montana (1864).
13. Nevada (1861).
14. New Hampshire (1848).
15. New Jersey (1849).
16. Ohio (1841).
17. Pennsylvania (1860).
18. Texas (1859).
19. Vermont (1867).
20. West Virginia (1863).
21. Wisconsin (1858).

* Briefs of *amici curiae* were filed by *Gary K. Nelson*, Attorney General of Arizona, *Robert K. Killian*, Attorney General of Connecticut, *Ed W. Hancock*, Attorney General of Kentucky, *Clarence A. H. Meyer*, Attorney General of Nebraska, and *Vernon B. Romney*, Attorney General of Utah; by *Joseph P. Witherspoon, Jr.*, for the Association of Texas Diocesan Attorneys; by *Charles E. Rice* for Americans United for Life; by *Eugene J. McMahon* for Women for the Unborn et al.; by *Carol Ryan* for the American College of Obstetricians and Gynecologists et al.; by *Dennis J. Horan, Jerome A. Frazel, Jr., Thomas M. Crisham*, and *Dolores V. Horan* for Certain Physicians, Professors and Fellows of the American College of Obstetrics and Gynecology; by *Harriet F. Pilpel, Nancy F. Wechsler*, and *Frederic S. Nathan* for Planned Parenthood Federation of America, Inc., et al.; by *Alan F. Charles* for the National Legal Program on Health Problems of the Poor et al.; by *Marttie L. Thompson* for State Communities Aid Assn.; by *Alfred L. Scanlan, Martin J. Flynn*, and *Robert M. Byrn* for the National Right to Life Committee; by *Helen L. Buttenwieser* for the American Ethical Union et al.; by *Norma G. Zarky* for the American Association of University Women et al.; by *Nancy Stearns* for New Women Lawyers et al.; by the California Committee to Legalize Abortion et al.; and by *Robert E. Dunne* for Robert L. Sassone.

A Defense of Abortion

Judith Jarvis Thomson

Most opposition to abortion relies on the promise that the fetus is a human being, a person, from the moment of conception. The premise is argued for, but, as I think, not well. Take, for example, the most common argument. We are asked to notice that the development of a human being from conception through birth into childhood is continuous; then it is said that to draw a line, to choose a point in this development and say "before this point the thing is not a person, after this point it is a person" is to make an arbitrary choice, a choice for which in the nature of things not good reason can be given. It is concluded that the fetus is, or anyway that we had better say it is, a person from the moment of conception. But this conclusion does not follow. Similar things might be said about the development of an acorn into an oak tree, and it does not follow that acorns are oak trees, or that we had better say they are. Arguments of this form are sometimes called "slippery slope arguments"—the phrase is perhaps self-explanatory—and it is dismaying that opponents of abortion rely on them so heavily and uncritically.

I am inclined to agree, however, that the prospects for "drawing a line" in the development of the fetus look dim. I am inclined to think also that we shall probably have to agree that the fetus has already become a human person well before birth. Indeed, it comes as a surprise when one first learns how early in its life it begins to acquire human characteristics. By the tenth week, for example, it already has a face, arms and legs, fingers and toes; it has internal organs, and brain activity is detectable.[1] On the other hand, I think that the premise is false, that the fetus is not a person from the moment of conception. A newly fertilized ovum, a newly implanted clump of cells, is no more a person than an acorn is an oak tree. But I shall not discuss any of this. For it seems to me to be of great interest to ask what happens if, for the sake of argument, we allow the premise. How, precisely, are we supposed to get from there to the conclusion that abortion is morally impermissible? Opponents of abortion commonly spend most of their time establishing that the fetus is a person, and hardly any time explaining the step from there to the impermissibility of abortion. Perhaps they think the step too simple and obvious to require much comment. Or perhaps instead they are simply being economical in argument. Many of those who defend abortion rely on the premise that the fetus is not a person, but only a bit of tissue that will become a person at birth:

415

and why pay out more arguments than you have to? Whatever the explanation, I suggest that the step they take is neither easy nor obvious, that it calls for closer examination than it is commonly given, and that when we do give it this closer examination we shall feel inclined to reject it.

I propose then, that we grant that the fetus is a person from the moment of conception. How does the argument go from here? Something like this, I take it. Every person has a right to life. So the fetus has a right to life. No doubt the mother has a right to decide what shall happen in and to her body; everyone would grant that. But surely a person's right to life is stronger and more stringent than the mother's right to decide what happens in and to her body, and so outweighs it. So the fetus may not be killed; an abortion may not be performed.

It sound plausible. But now let me ask you to imagine this. You wake up in the morning and find yourself back to back in bed with an unconscious violinist. A famous unconscious violinist. He has been found to have a fatal kidney ailment, and the Society of Music Lovers has canvassed all the available medical records and found that you alone have the right blood type to help. They have therefore kidnapped you, and last night the violinist's circulatory system was plugged into yours, so that your kidneys can be used to extract poisons from his blood as well as your own. The director of the hospital now tells you, "Look, we're sorry the Society of Music Lovers did this to you—we would never have permitted it if we had known. But still, they did it, and the violinist now is plugged into you. To unplug you would be to kill him. But never mind, its only for nine months. By then he will have recovered from his ailment, and can safely be unplugged from you." Is it morally incumbent on you to accede to this situation? No doubt it would be very nice of you if you did, a great kindness. But do you *have* to accede to it? What if it were not nine months, but nine years? Or longer still? What if the director of the hospital says, "Tough luck, I agree, but you've now got to stay in bed, with the violinist plugged into you, for the rest of your life. Because remember this. All persons have a right to life, and violinists are persons. Granted you have a right to decide what happens in and to your body, but a person's right to life outweighs your right to decide what happens in and to your body. So you cannot ever be unplugged from him." I imagine you would regard this as outrageous, which suggests that something really is wrong with that plausible-sounding argument I mentioned a moment ago.

In this case, of course, you were kidnapped; you didn't volunteer for the operation that plugged the violinist into your kidneys. Can those who oppose abortion on the ground I mentioned make an exception for a pregnancy due to rape? Certainly. They can say that persons have a right to life only if they didn't come into existence because of rape; or they can say that all persons have a right to life, but that some have less of a right to life than others, in particular, that those who come into existence because of rape have less. But these statements have a rather unpleasant sound. Surely the question of whether you have a right to life at all, or how much of it you have, shouldn't turn on the question of whether or not you are the product of a rape. And in fact the people who oppose abortion on the ground I mentioned do not make this distinction, and hence do not make an exception in case of rape.

Nor do they make an exception for a case in which the mother has to spend the nine months of her pregnancy in bed. They would agree that would be a great pity, and hard on the mother; but all the same, all persons have a right to life, the fetus is a person, and so on. I suspect, in fact, that they would not make an exception for a case in which, miraculously enough, the pregnancy went on for nine years, or even the rest of the mother's life.

Some won't even make an exception for a case in which continuation of the pregnancy is likely to shorten the mother's life; they regard abortion as impermissible even to save the mother's life. Such cases are nowadays very rare, and many opponents of abortion do not accept this extreme view. All the same, it is a good place to begin: a number of points of interest come out in respect to it.

1. THE EXTREME ANTI-ABORTION VIEW

Let us call the view that abortion is impermissible even to save the mother's life "the extreme view." I want to suggest first that it does not issue from the argument I mentioned earlier without the addition of some fairly powerful premises. Suppose a woman has become pregnant, and now learns that she has a cardiac condition such that she will die if she carries the baby to term. What may be done for her? The fetus, being a person, has a right to life, but as the mother is a person too, so has she a right to life. Presumably they have an equal right to life. How is it supposed to come out that an abortion may not be performed? If mother and child have an equal right to life, shouldn't we perhaps flip a coin? Or should we add to the mother's right to life her right to decide what happens in and to her body, which everybody seems to be ready to grant—the sum of her rights now outweighing the fetus' right to life?

The most familiar argument here is the following. We are told that performing the abortion would be directly killing[2] the child, whereas doing nothing would not be killing the mother, but only letting her die. Moreover, in killing the child, one would be killing an innocent person, for the child has committed no crime, and is not aiming at his mother's death. And then there are a variety of ways in which this might be continued. (1) But as directly killing an innocent person is always and absolutely impermissible, an abortion may not be performed. Or, (2) as directly killing an innocent person is murder, and murder is always and absolutely impermissible, an abortion may not be performed.[3] Or, (3) as one's duty to refrain from directly killing an innocent person is more stringent than one's duty to keep a person from dying, an abortion may not be performed. Or, (4) if one's only options are directly killing an innocent person or letting a person die, one must prefer letting the person die, and thus an abortion may not be performed.[4]

Some people seem to have thought that these are not further premises which must be added if the conclusion is to be reached, but that they follow from the very fact that an innocent person has a right to life.[5] But this seems to me to be a mistake, and perhaps the simplest way to show this is to bring out that while we must certainly grant that innocent persons have a right to life, the theses in (1) through (4) are all false. Take (2), for example. If directly killing an innocent person is murder, and thus is impermissible, then the mother's directly killing the innocent person inside her is murder, and thus is impermissible. But it cannot seriously be thought to be murder if the mother performs an abortion on herself to save her life. It cannot seriously be said that she *must* refrain, that she *must* sit passively by and wait for her death. Let us look again at the case of you and the violinist. There you are, in bed with the violinist, and the director of the hospital says to you, "It's all most distressing, and I deeply sympathize, but you see this is putting an additional strain on your kidneys, and you'll be dead within the month. But you *have* to stay where you are all the same. Because unplugging you would be directly killing an innocent violinist, and that's murder, and that's impermissible." If anything in the world is true, it is that you do not commit murder, you do not do what is impermissible, if you reach around to your back and unplug yourself from that violinist to save your life.

The main focus of attention in writings on abortion has been on what a third party may or may not do in answer to a request from a woman for an abortion. This is in a way understandable. Things being as they are, there isn't much a woman can safely do to abort herself. So the question asked is what a third party may do, and what the mother may do, if it is mentioned at all, is deduced, almost as an afterthought, from what it is concluded that third parties may do. But it seems to me that to treat the matter in this way is to refuse to grant to the mother that very status of person which is so firmly insisted on for the fetus. For we cannot simply read off what a person may do from what a third party may do. Suppose you find yourself trapped in a tiny house with a growing child. I mean a very tiny house, and a rapidly growing child—you are already up against the wall of the house and in a few minutes you'll be crushed to death. The child on the other hand won't be crushed to death; if nothing is done to stop him from growing he'll be hurt, but in the end he'll simply burst open the house and walk out a free man. Now I could well understand it if a bystander were to say, "There's nothing we can do for you. We cannot choose between your life and his, we cannot be the ones to decide who is to live, we cannot intervene." But it cannot be concluded that you too can do nothing, that you cannot attack it to save your life. However innocent the child may be, you do not have to wait passively while it crushes you to death. Perhaps a pregnant woman is vaguely felt to have the status of house, to which we don't allow the right to self-defense. But if the woman houses the child, it should be remembered that she is a person who houses it.

I should perhaps stop to say explicitly that I am not claiming that people have a right to do anything whatever to save their lives. I think, rather, that there are drastic limits to the right of self-defense. If someone threatens you with death unless you torture someone else to death, I think you have not the right, even to save your life, to do so. But the case under consideration here is very different. In our case there are only two people involved, one whose life is threatened, and one who threatens it. Both are innocent: the one who is threatened is not threatened because of any fault, the one who threatens does not threaten because of any fault. For this reason we may feel that we bystanders cannot intervene. But the person threatened can.

In sum, a woman surely can defend her life against the threat to it posed by the unborn child, even if doing so involves its death. And this shows not merely that the theses in (1) through (4) are false; it shows also that the extreme view of abortion is false, and so we need not canvass any other possible ways of arriving at it from the argument I mentioned at the outset.

2. INTERVENTION OF OTHERS

The extreme view could of course be weakened to say that while abortion is permissible to save the mother's life, it may not be performed by a third party, but only by the mother herself. But this cannot be right either. For what we have to keep in mind is that the mother and the unborn child are not like two tenants in a small house which has, by an unfortunate mistake, been rented to both: the mother *owns* the house. The fact that she does adds to the offensiveness of deducing that the mother can do nothing from the supposition that third parties can do nothing. But it does more than this: it casts a bright light on the supposition that third parties can do nothing. Certainly it lets us see that a third party who says "I cannot choose between you" is fooling himself if he thinks this is impartiality. If Jones has found and fastened on a certain coat, which he needs to keep him from freezing, but which Smith also needs to keep him from freezing, then it is not impartiality that says "I cannot choose between you" when Smith owns the coat. Women have said again and again, "This body is *my* body!" and they have reason to feel angry, reason to feel that it has been like shouting into the wind. Smith, after all, is hardly likely to bless us if we say to him, "Of course it's your coat, anybody would grant that it is. But no one may choose between you and Jones who is to have it."

We should really ask what it is that says "no one may choose" in the face of the fact that the body that houses the child is the mother's body. It may be simply a failure to appreciate this fact. But it may be something more interesting, namely the sense that one has a right to refuse to lay hands on people, even where it would be just and fair to do so, even where justice seems to require that somebody do so. Thus justice might call for somebody to get Smith's coat back from Jones, and yet you have a right to refuse to be the one to lay hands on Jones, a right to refuse to do physical violence to him. This, I think, must be granted. But then what should be said is not "no one may choose," but only "*I* cannot choose," and indeed not even this, but "*I* will *not act*," leaving it open that somebody else can or should, and in particular that anyone in a position of authority, with the job of securing people's rights, both can and should. So this is no difficulty, I have not been arguing that any given third party must accede to the mother's request that he perform an abortion to save her life, but only that he may.

I suppose that in some views of human life the mother's body is only on loan to her, the loan not being one which gives her any prior claim to it. One who held this view might well think it impartiality to say "I cannot choose." But I shall simply ignore this possibility. My own view is that if a human being has any just, prior claim to anything at all, he has a just, prior claim to his own body. And perhaps this needn't be argued for here anyway, since, as I mentioned, the arguments against abortion we are looking at do grant that the woman has a right to decide what happens in and to her body.

But although they do grant it, I have tried to show that they do not take seriously what is done in granting it. I suggest the same thing will reappear even more clearly when we turn away from cases in which the mother's life is at stake, and attend, as I propose we now do, to the vastly more common cases in which a woman wants an abortion for some less weighty reason than preserving her own life.

3. THE RIGHT TO LIFE

Where the mother's life is not at stake, the argument I mentioned at the outset seems to have a much stronger pull. "Everyone has a right to life, so the unborn person has a right to life." And isn't the child's right to life weightier than anything other than the mother's own right to life, which she might put forward as ground for an abortion?

This argument treats the right to life as if it were unproblematic. It is not, and this seems to me to be precisely the source of the mistake.

For we should now, at long last, ask what it comes to, to have a right to life. In some views having a right to life includes having a right to be given at least the bare minimum one needs for continued life. But suppose that what in fact is the bare minimum a man needs for continued life is something he has no right at all to be given? If I am sick unto death, and the only thing that will save my life is the touch of Henry Fonda's cool hand on my fevered brow, then all the same, I have no right to be given the touch of Henry Fonda's cool hand on my fevered brow. It would be frightfully nice of him to fly in from the West Coast to provide it. It would be less nice, though no doubt well meant, if my friends flew out to the West Coast and carried Henry Fonda back with them. But I have no right at all against anybody that he should do this for me. Or again, to return to the story I told earlier, the fact that for continued life that violinist needs the continued use of your kidneys does not establish that he has a right to be given the continued use of your kidneys. He certainly has no right against you that you should give him continued use of your kidneys. for nobody has any right to use your kidneys unless you give him such a right; and nobody has the right against you that you shall give him this right—if you do allow him to go on using your kidneys, this is a kindness on your part, and not something he can claim from you as his due. Nor has he any right against anybody else that *they* should give him continued use of your kidneys. Certainly he had no right against the Society of Music Lovers that they should plug him into you in the first place. And if you now start to unplug yourself, having learned that you will otherwise have to spend nine years in bed with him, there is nobody in the world who must try to prevent you, in order to see to it that he is given something he has a right to be given.

Some people are rather stricter about the right to life. In their view, it does not include the right to be given anything, but amounts to, and only to, the right not to be killed by anybody. But here a related difficulty arises. If everybody is to refrain from killing that violinist, then everybody must refrain from doing a great many different sorts of things. Everybody must refrain from slitting his throat, everybody must refrain from shooting him—and everybody must refrain from unplugging you from him. But does he have a right against everybody that they shall refrain from unplugging you from him? To refrain from doing this is to allow him to continue to use your kidneys. It could be argued that he has a right against us that we should allow him to continue to use your kidneys. That is, while he had no right against us that we should give him the use of your kidneys, it might be argued that he anyway has a right against us that we shall not now intervene and deprive him of the use of your kidneys. I shall come back to third-party interventions later. But certainly the violinist has no right against you that *you* shall allow him to continue to use your kidneys. As I said, if you do allow him to use them, it is a kindness on your part, and not something you owe him.

The difficulty I point to here is not peculiar to the right to life. It reappears in connection with all the other natural rights; and it is something which an adequate account of rights must deal with. For present purposes it is enough just to draw attention to it. But I should stress that I am not arguing that people do not have a right to life—quite to the contrary, it seems to me that the primary control we must place on the acceptability of an account of rights is that it should turn out in that account to be a truth that all persons have a right to life. I am arguing only that having a right to life does not guarantee having either a right to be given the use of or a right to be allowed continued use of another person's body—even if one needs it for life itself. So the right to life will not serve the opponents of abortion in the very simple and clear way in which they seem to have thought it would.

4. THE RIGHT TO USE THE MOTHER'S BODY

There is another way to bring out the difficulty. In the most ordinary sort of case, to deprive someone of what he has a right to is to treat him unjustly. Suppose a boy and his small brother are jointly given a box of chocolates for Christmas. If the older boy takes the box and refuses to give his brother any of the chocolates, he is unjust to him, for the brother has been given a right to half of them. But suppose that, having learned that otherwise it means nine years in bed with that violinist, you unplug yourself from him. You surely are not being unjust to him for you gave him no right to use your kidneys, and no one else can have given him any such right. But we have to notice that in unplugging yourself, you are killing him; and violinists, like everybody else, have a right to life, and thus in the view we were considering just now, the right not to be killed. So here you do what he supposedly has a right you shall not do, but you do not act unjustly to him in doing it.

The emendation which may be made at this point is this: the right to life consists not in the right not to be killed, but rather in the right not to be killed unjustly. This runs a risk of circularity, but never mind; it would enable us to square the fact that the violinist has a right to life with the fact that you do not act unjustly toward him in unplugging yourself, thereby killing him. For if you do not kill him unjustly, you do not violate his right to life, and so it is no wonder you do him no injustice.

But if this emendation is accepted, the gap in the argument against abortion stares us plainly in the face; it is by no means enough to show that the fetus is a person, and to remind us that all persons have a right to life—we need to be shown also that killing the fetus violates its right to life, i.e., that abortion is unjust killing. And is it?

I suppose we may take it as a datum that in a case of pregnancy due to rape the mother has not given the unborn person a right to the use of her body for food and shelter. Indeed, in what pregnancy could it be supposed that the mother has given the unborn person such a right? It is not as if there were unborn persons drifting about the world, to whom a woman who wants a child says "I invite you in."

But it might be argued that there are other ways one can have acquired a right to the use of another person's body than by having been invited to use it by that person. Suppose a woman voluntarily indulges in intercourse, knowing of the chance it will issue in pregnancy, and then she does become pregnant; is she not in part responsible for the presence, in fact the very existence, of the unborn person inside her? No doubt she did not invite it in. But doesn't her partial responsibility for its being there itself give it a right to the use of her body? If so, then her aborting it would be more like the boy's taking away the chocolates, and less like your unplugging yourself from the violinist—doing so would be depriving it of what it does have a right to, and thus would be doing it an injustice.

And then, too, it might be asked whether or not she can kill it even to save her own life: If she voluntarily called it into existence, how can she now kill it, even in self-defense?

The first thing to be said about this is that it is something new. Opponents of abortion have been so concerned to make out the independence of the fetus, in order to establish that it has a right to life, just as its mother does, that they have tended to overlook the possible support they might gain from making out that the fetus is *dependent* on the mother, in order to establish that she has a special kind of responsibility for it, a responsibility that gives it rights against her which are not possessed by any independent person—such as an ailing violinist who is a stranger to her.

On the other hand, this argument would give the unborn person a right to its mother's body only if her pregnancy resulted from a voluntary act, undertaken in full knowledge of the chance a pregnancy might result from it. It would leave out entirely the unborn person whose existence is due to rape. Pending the availability of some further argument, then, we would be left with the conclusion that unborn persons whose existence is due to rape have no right to the use of their mothers' bodies, and thus that aborting them is not depriving them of anything they have a right to and hence is not unjust killing.

And we should also notice that it is not at all plain that this argument really does go even as far as it purports to. For there are cases and cases, and the details make a difference. If the room is stuffy, and I therefore open a window to air it, and a burglar climbs in, it would be absurd to say, "Ah, now he can stay, she's given him a right to the use of her house—for she is partially responsible for his presence there, having voluntarily done what enabled him to get in, in full knowledge that there are such things as burglars, and that burglars burgle." It would be still more absurd to say this if I had had bars installed outside my windows, precisely to prevent burglars from getting in, and a burglar got in only because of a defect in the bars. It remains equally absurd if we imagine it is not a burglar who climbs in, but an innocent person who blunders or falls in. Again, suppose it were like this: people-seeds drift about in the air like pollen, and if you open your windows, one may drift in and take root in your carpets or upholstery. You don't want children, so you fix up your windows with fine mesh screens, the very best you can buy. As can happen, however, and on very, very rare occasions does happen, one of the screens is defective; and a seed drifts in and takes root. Does the person-plant who now develops have a right to the use of your house? Surely not—despite the fact that you voluntarily opened your windows, you knowingly kept carpets and upholstered furniture, and you know that screens were sometimes defective. Someone may argue that you are responsible for its rooting, that it does have a right to your house, because after all you *could* have lived out your life with bare floors and furniture, or with sealed windows and doors. But this won't do—for by the same token, anyone can avoid a pregnancy due to rape by having a hysterectomy, or anyway by never leaving home without a (reliable!) army.

It seems to me that the argument we are looking at can establish at most that there are *some* cases in which the unborn person has a right to the use of its mother's body, and therefore *some* cases in which abortion is unjust killing. There is room for much discussion and argument as to precisely which, if any. But I think we should sidestep this issue and leave it open, for at any rate the argument certainly does not establish that all abortion is unjust killing.

5. DECENCY AND INJUSTICE

There is room for yet another argument here, however. We surely must all grant that there may be cases in which it would be morally indecent to detach a person from your body at the cost of his life. Suppose you learn that what the violinist needs is not nine years of your life, but only one hour: all you need do to save his life is to spend one hour in that bed with him. Suppose also that letting him use your kidneys for that one hour would not affect your health in the slightest. Admittedly you were kidnapped. Admittedly you did not give anyone permission to plug him into you. Nevertheless it seems to me plain you *ought* to allow him to use your kidneys for that hour—it would be indecent to refuse.

Again, suppose pregnancy lasted only an hour, and constituted no threat to life or health. And suppose that a woman becomes pregnant as a result of rape. Admittedly she did not voluntarily do anything to bring about the existence of a child. Admittedly she die nothing at all which would give the unborn person a right to the use of her body. All the same it might well be said, as in the newly emended violinist story, that she *ought* to allow it to remain for that hour—that it would be indecent in her to refuse.

Now some people are inclined to use the term "right" in such a way that it follows from the fact that you ought to allow a person to use your body for the hour he needs, that he has a right to use your body for the hour he needs, even though he has not been given the right by any person or act. They may say that it follows also that if you refuse, you act unjustly toward him. This use of the term is perhaps so common that it cannot be called wrong; nevertheless it seems to me to be an unfortunate loosening of what we would do better to keep a tight rein on. Suppose that box of chocolates I mentioned earlier had not been given to both boys jointly, but was given only to the older boy. There he sits, stolidly eating his way through the box, his small brother watching enviously. Here we are likely to say "You ought not to be so mean. You ought to give your brother some of those chocolates." My own view is that it just does not follow from the truth of this that the brother has any right to any of the chocolates. If the boy refuses to give his brother any, he is greedy, stingy, callous—but not unjust. I suppose that the people I have in mind will say it does follow that the brother has a right to some of the chocolates, and thus that the boy does act unjustly if he refuses to give his brother any. But the effect of saying this is to obscure what we should keep distinct, namely the difference between the boy's refusal in this case and the boy's refusal in the earlier case, in which the box was given to both boys jointly, and in which the small brother thus had what was from any point of view clear title to half.

A further objection to so using the term "right," that from the fact that A ought to do a thing for B, it follows that B has a right against A that A do it for him, is that it is going to make the question of whether or not a man has a right to a thing turn on how easy it is to provide him with it; and this seems not merely unfortunate, but morally unacceptable. Take the case of Henry Fonda again. I said earlier that I had no right to the touch of his cool hand on my fevered brow, even though I needed it to save my life. I said it would be frightfully nice of him to fly in from the West Coast to provide me with it, but that I had no right against him that he should do so. But suppose he isn't on the West Coast. Suppose he has only to walk across the room, place a hand briefly on my brow—and lo, my life is saved. Then surely he ought to do it, it would be indecent to refuse. It is to be said "Ah, well, it follows that in this case she has a right to the touch of his hand on her brow, and so it would be an injustice in him to refuse"? So that I have a right to it when it is easy for him to provide it, though no right when it's hard? It's rather a shocking idea that anyone's rights should fade away and disappear as it gets harder and harder to accord them to him.

So my own view is that even though you ought to let the violinist use your kidneys for the one hour he needs, we should not conclude that he has a right to do so—we would say that if you refuse, you are, like the boy who owns all the chocolates and will give none away, self-centered and callous, indecent in fact, but not unjust. And similarly, that even supposing a case in which a woman pregnant due to rape ought to allow the unborn person to use her body for the hour he needs, we should not conclude that he has a right to do so; we should conclude that she is self-centered, callous, indecent, but not unjust, if she refuses. The complaints are no less grave; they are just different. However, there is no need to insist on this point. If anyone does wish to deduce "he has a right" from "you ought," then all the same he must surely grant that there are cases in which it is not morally required of you that you allow that violinist to use your kidneys, and in which he does not have a right to use them, and in which you do not do him an injustice if you refuse. And so also for mother and unborn child. Except in such cases as the unborn person has a right to demand it—and we were leaving open the possibility that there may be such cases—nobody is morally *required* to make large sacrifices, of health, of all other interests and concerns, of all other duties and commitments, for nine years, or even for nine months, in order to keep another person alive.

6. GOOD SAMARITANISM AND DUTY

We have in fact to distinguish between two kinds of Samaritan: the Good Samaritan and what we might call the Minimally Decent Samaritan. The story of the Good Samaritan, you will remember, goes like this:

> A certain man went down from Jerusalem to Jericho, and fell among thieves, which stripped him of his raiment, and wounded him, and departed, leaving him half dead.

> And by chance there came down a certain priest that way; and when he saw him, he passed by on the other side.

> And likewise a Levite, when he was at the place, came and looked on him, and passed by on the other side.

> But a certain Samaritan, as he journeyed, came where he was; and when he saw him he had compassion on him.

And went to him, and bound up his wounds, pouring in oil and wine, and set him on his own beast, and brought him to an inn, and took care of him.

And on the morrow, when he departed, he took out two pence, and gave them to the host, and said unto him, "Take care of him; and whatsoever thou spendest more, when I come again, I will repay thee."

(Luke 10:30–35)

The Good Samaritan went out of his way, at some cost to himself, to help one in need of it. We are not told what the options were, that is, whether or not the priest and the Levite could have helped by doing less than the Good Samaritan did, but assuming they could have, then the fact they did nothing at all shows they were not even Minimally Decent Samaritans, not because they were not Samaritans, but because they were not even minimally decent.

These things are a matter of degree, of course, but there is a difference, and it come out perhaps most clearly in the story of Kitty Genovese, who, as you will remember, was murdered while thirty-eight people watched or listened, and did nothing at all to help her. A Good Samaritan would have rushed out to give direct assistance against the murderer. Or perhaps we had better allow that it would have been a Splendid Samaritan who did this, on the ground that it would have involved a risk of death for himself. But the thirty-eight not only did not do this, they did not even trouble to pick up a phone to call the police. Minimally Decent Samaritanism would call for doing at least that, and their not having done it was monstrous.

After telling the story of the Good Samaritan, Jesus said "Go, and do thou likewise." Perhaps he meant that we are morally required to act as the Good Samaritan did. Perhaps he was urging people to do more than is morally required of them. At all events it seems plain that it was not morally required of any of the thirty-eight that he rush out to give direct assistance at the risk of his own life, and that it is not morally required of anyone that he give long stretches of his life—nine years or nine months—to sustaining the life of a person who has no special right (we are leaving open the possibility of this) to demand it.

Indeed, with one rather striking class of exceptions, no one in any country in the world is *legally* required to do anywhere near as much as this for anyone else. The class of exceptions is obvious. My main concern here is not the state of the law in respect to abortion, but it is worth drawing attention to the fact that in no state in this country is any man compelled by law to be even a Minimally Decent Samaritan to any person; there is no law under which charges could be brought against the thirty-eight who stood by while Kitty Genovese died. By contrast, in most states in this country women are compelled by law to be not merely Minimally Decent Samaritans, but Good Samaritans to unborn persons inside them. This doesn't by itself settle anything one way or the other, because it may well be argued that there should be laws in this country—as there are in many European countries—compelling at least Minimally Decent Samaritanism.[6] But it does show that there is a gross injustice in the existing state of the law. And it shows also that the groups currently working against liberalization of abortion laws, in fact working toward having it declared unconstitutional for a state to permit abortion, had better start working for the adoption of Good Samaritan laws generally, or earn the charge that they are acting in bad faith.

I should think, myself, that Minimally Decent Samaritan laws would be one thing. Good Samaritan laws quite another, and in fact highly improper. But we are not here concerned with the law. What we should ask is not whether anybody should be compelled by law to be a Good Samaritan, but whether we must accede to a situation in which somebody is being compelled—by nature, perhaps—to be a Good Samaritan. We have, in other words, to look now at third-party interventions. I have been arguing that no person is morally required to make large sacrifices to sustain the life of another who has no right to demand them, and this even where the sacrifices do not include life itself; we are not morally required to be Good Samaritans or anyway Very Good Samaritans to one another. But what if a man cannot extricate himself from such a situation? What if he appeals to us to extricate him? It seems to me plain that there are cases in which we can, cases in which a Good Samaritan would extricate him. There you are, you were kidnapped, and nine years in bed with that violinist lie ahead of you. You have your own life to lead. You are sorry, but you simply cannot see giving up so much of your life to the sustaining of his. You cannot extricate yourself, and ask us to do so. I should have thought that—in light of his having no right to the use of your body—it was obvious that we do not have to accede to your being forced to give up so much. We can do what you ask. There is no injustice to the violinist in our doing so.

7. MATERNAL RESPONSIBILITY

Following the lead of the opponents of abortion, I have throughout been speaking of the fetus merely as a person, and what I have been asking is whether or not the argument we began with, which proceeds only from the fetus being a person, really does establish its conclusion. I have argued that it does not.

But of course there are arguments and arguments, and it may be said that I have simply fastened on the wrong one. It may be said that what is important is not merely the fact that the fetus is a person, but that it is a person for whom the woman has a special kind of responsibility issuing from the fact that she is its mother. And it might be argued that all my analogies are therefore irrelevant—for you do not have that special kind of responsibility for that violinist, Henry Fonda does not have that special kind of responsibility for me. And our attention might be drawn to the fact that men and women both *are* compelled by law to provide support for their children.

I have in effect dealt (briefly) with this argument in Section 4 above; but a (still briefer) recapitulation now may be in order. Surely we do not have any such "special responsibility" for a person unless we have assumed it, explicitly or implicitly. If a set of parents do not try to prevent pregnancy, do not obtain an abortion, and then at the time of birth of the child do not put it out for adoption, but rather take it home with them, then they have assumed responsibility for it, they have given it rights, and they cannot *now* withdraw support from it at the cost of its life because they now find it difficult to go on providing for it. But if they have taken all responsible precautions against having a child, they do not simply by virtue of their biological relationship to the child who comes into existence have a special responsibility for it. They may wish to assume responsibility for it, or they may not wish to. And I am suggesting that if assuming responsibility for it would require large sacrifices, then they may refuse. A Good Samaritan would not refuse— or anyway, a Splendid Samaritan, if the sacrifices that had to be made were enormous. But then so would a Good Samaritan assume responsibility for that violinist; so would Henry Fonda, if he is a Good Samaritan, fly in from the West Coast and assume responsibility for me.

8. TWO OBJECTIONS

My argument will be found unsatisfactory on two counts by many of those who want to regard abortion as morally permissible. First, while I do argue that abortion is not impermissible, I do not argue that it is always permissible. There may well be cases in which carrying the child to term requires only Minimally Decent Samaritanism of the mother, and this is a standard we must not fall below. I am inclined to think it a merit of my account precisely that it does *not* give a general yes or a general no. It allows for and supports our sense that, for example, a sick and desperately frightened fourteen-year-old schoolgirl, pregnant due to rape, may *of course* choose abortion, and that any law which rules this out is an insane law. And it also allows for and supports our sense that in other cases resort to abortion is even positively indecent. It would be indecent in the woman to request an abortion, and indecent in a doctor to perform it, if she is in her seventh month, and wants the abortion just to avoid the nuisance of postponing a trip abroad. The very fact that the arguments I have been drawing attention to treat all cases of abortion, or even all cases of abortion in which the mother's life is not at stake, as morally on a par ought to have made them suspect at the outset.

Secondly, while I am arguing for the permissibility of abortion in some cases, I am not arguing for the right to secure the death of the unborn child. It is easy to confuse these two things in that up to a certain point in the life of the fetus it is not able to survive outside the mother's body; hence removing it from her body guarantees its death. But they are importantly different. I have argued that you are not morally required to spend nine months in bed, sustaining the life of that violinist; but to say this is by no means to say that if, when you unplug yourself, there is a miracle and he survives, you then have a right to turn round and slit his throat. You may detach yourself even if this costs him his life; you have no right to be guaranteed his death, by some other means, if unplugging yourself does not kill him. There are some people who will feel dissatisfied by this feature of my argument. A woman may be utterly devastated by the thought of a child, a bit of herself, put out for adoption and never seen or heard of again. She may therefore want not merely that the child be detached from her, but more, that it die. Some opponents of abortion are inclined to regard this as beneath contempt—thereby showing insensitivity to what is surely a powerful source of despair. All the same, I agree that the desire for the child's death is not one which anybody may gratify, should it turn out to be possible to detach the child alive.

At this place, however, it should be remembered that we have only been pretending throughout that the fetus is a human being from the moment of conception. A very early abortion is surely not the killing of a person, and so is not dealt with by anything I have said here.

NOTES

[1] Daniel Callahan, *Abortion: Law, Choice and Morality* (New York, 1970), p. 373. This book gives a fascinating survey of the available information on abortion. The Jewish tradition is surveyed in David M. Feldman, *Birth Control in Jewish Law* (New York, 1968), Part 5, the Catholic tradition in John T. Noonan, Jr., "An Almost Absolute Value in History," in *The Morality of Abortion*, ed. John T. Noonan, Jr. (Cambridge, Mass., 1970).

[2] The term "direct" in the arguments I refer to is a technical one. Roughly, what is meant by "direct killing" is either killing as an end in itself, or killing as a means to some end, for example, the end of saving someone else's life. See note 5 below, for an example of its use.

[3] Cf. *Encyclical Letter of Pope Pius XI on Christian Marriage*, St. Paul Editions (Boston, n.d.), p. 32: "However much we may pity the mother whose health and even life is gravely imperiled in the performance of the duty allotted to her by nature, nevertheless what could ever by a sufficient reason for excusing in any way the direct murder of the innocent? This is precisely what we are dealing with here." Noonan (*The Morality of Abortion*, p. 43) reads this as follows: "What cause can ever avail to excuse in any way the direct killing of the innocent? For it is a question of that."

[4] The thesis in (3) is in an interesting way weaker than those in (1), (2), and they rule out abortion even in cases in which both mother and child will die if the abortion is not performed. By contrast, one who held the view expressed in (3) could consistently say that one needn't prefer letting two persons die to killing one.

[5] Cf. the following passage from Pius XII, *Address to the Italian Catholic Society of Midwives*: "The baby in the maternal breast has the right to life immediately from God.—Hence there is no man, no human authority, no science, no medical, eugenic, social, economic or moral 'indication' which can establish or grant a valid judicial ground for a direct deliberate disposition of an innocent human life that is a disposition which looks to its destruction either as an end or as a means to another end perhaps in itself not illicit.—The baby, still not born, is a man in the same degree and for the same reason as the mother" (quoted in Noonan, *The Morality of Abortion*, P. 45).

[6] For a discussion of the difficulties involved, and a survey of the European experience with such laws, see *The Good Samaritan and the Law*, ed. James M. Ratcliffe (New York, 1966).

Abortion and Infanticide

Michael Tooley

This essay deals with the question of the morality of abortion and infanticide. The fundamental ethical objection traditionally advanced against these practices rests on the contention that human fetuses and infants have a right to life. It is this claim which will be the focus of attention here. The basic issue to be discussed, then, is what properties a thing must possess in order to have a serious right to life. My approach will be to set out and defend a basic moral principle specifying a condition an organism must satisfy if it is to have a serious right to life. It will be seen that this condition is not satisfied by human fetuses and infants, and thus that they do not have a right to life. So unless there are other substantial objections to abortion and infanticide, one is forced to conclude that these practices are morally acceptable ones. In contrast, it may turn out that our treatment of adult members of other species—cats, dogs, polar bears—is morally indefensible. For it is quite possible that such animals do possess properties that endow them with a right to life.

1. ABORTION AND INFANTICIDE

One reason the question of the morality of infanticide is worth examining is that it seems very difficult to formulate a completely satisfactory liberal position on abortion without coming to grips with the infanticide issue. The problem the liberal encounters is essentially that of specifying a cutoff point which is not arbitrary: at what stage in the development of human being does it cease to be morally permissible to destroy it? It is important to be clear about the difficulty here. The conservative's objection is not that since there is a continuous line of development from a zygote to a newborn baby, one must conclude that if it is seriously wrong to destroy a newborn baby it is also seriously wrong to destroy a zygote or any intermediate stage in the development of a human being. His point is rather that if one says it is wrong to destroy a newborn baby but not a zygote or some intermediate stage in the development of a human being, one should be prepared to point to a *morally relevant* difference between a newborn baby and the earlier stage in the development of a human being.

Precisely the same difficulty can, of course, be raised for a person who holds that infanticide is morally permissible. The conservative will ask what morally relevant differences there are between an adult human being and a newborn baby. What makes it morally permissible to destroy a baby, but wrong to kill an adult? So the challenge remains. But I will argue that in this case there is an extremely plausible answer.

Reflecting on the morality of infanticide forces one to face up to this challenge. In the case of abortion a number of events—quickening or viability, for instance—might be taken as cutoff points, and it is easy to overlook the fact that none of these events involves any morally significant change in the developing human. In contrast, if one is going to defend infanticide, one has to get very clear about what makes something a person, what gives something a right to life.

One of the interesting ways in which the abortion issue differs from most other moral issues is that the plausible positions on abortion appear to be extreme positions. For if a human fetus is a person, one is inclined to say that, in general, one would be justified in killing it only to save the life of the mother.[1] Such is the extreme conservative position.[2] On the other hand, if the fetus is not a person, how can it be seriously wrong to destroy it? Why would one need to point to special circumstances to justify such action? The upshot is that there is no room for a moderate position on the issue of abortion such as one finds, for example, in the Model Penal Code recommendations.[3]

Aside from the light it may shed on the abortion question, the issue of infanticide is both interesting and important in its own right. The theoretical interest has been mentioned: it forces one to face up to the question of what makes something a person. The practical importance need not be labored. Most people would prefer to raise children who do not suffer from gross deformities or from severe physical, emotional, or intellectual handicaps. If it could be shown that there is no moral objection to infanticide the happiness of society could be significantly and justifiably increased.

Infanticide is also of interest because of the strong emotions it arouses. The typical reaction to infanticide is like the reaction to incest or cannibalism, or the reaction of previous generations to masturbation or oral sex. The response, rather than appealing to carefully formulated moral principles, is primarily visceral. When philosophers themselves respond in this way, offering no arguments, and dismissing infanticide out of hand, it is reasonable to suspect that one is dealing with a taboo rather than with a rational prohibition.[4] I shall attempt to show that this is in fact the case.

2. TERMINOLOGY: "PERSON" VERSUS "HUMAN BEING"

How is the term "person" to be interpreted? I shall treat the concept of a person as a purely moral concept, free of all descriptive content. Specifically, in my usage the sentence "X is a person" will be synonymous with the sentence "X has a (serious) moral right to life."

This usage diverges slightly from what is perhaps the more common way of interpreting the term "person" when it is employed as a purely moral term, where to say that X is a person is to say that X has rights. If everything that had rights had a right to life, these interpretations would be extensionally equivalent. But I am inclined to think that it does not follow from acceptable moral principles that whatever has any rights at all has a right to life. My reason is this. Given the choice between being killed and being tortured for an hour, most adult humans would surely choose the latter. So it seems plausible to say it is worse to kill an adult human being than it is to torture him for an hour. In contrast, it seems to me that while it is not seriously wrong to kill a newborn kitten, it is seriously wrong to torture one for an hour. This *suggests* that newborn kittens may have a right not to be tortured without having a serious right to life. For it seems to be true that an individual has a right to something whenever it is the case that, if he wants that thing, it would be wrong for others to deprive him of it. Then if it is wrong to inflict a certain sensation upon a kitten if it doesn't want to experience that sensation, it will follow that the kitten has a right not to have sensation inflicted upon it.[5] I shall return to this example later. My point here is merely that it provides some reason for holding that it does not follow from acceptable moral principles that if something has any rights at all, it has a serious right to life.

There has been a tendency in recent discussions of abortion to use expressions such as "person" and "human being" interchangeably. B. A. Brody, for example, refers to the difficulty of determining "whether destroying the fetus constitutes the taking of a human life," and suggests it is very plausible that "the taking of a human life is an action that has had bad consequences for him whose life is being taken."[6] When Brody refers to something as a human life he apparently construes this as entailing that the thing is a person. For if every living organism belonging to the species *Homo sapiens* counted as a human life, there would be no difficulty in determining whether a fetus inside a human mother was a human life.

The same tendency is found in Judith Jarvis Thomson's article, which opens with the statement: "Most opposition to abortion relies on the premise that the fetus is a human being, a person, from the moment of conception."[7] The same is true of Roger Wertheimer, who explicitly says: "First off I should note that the expressions 'a human life,' 'a human being,' 'a person' are virtually interchangeable in this context."[8]

The tendency to use expressions like "person" and "human being" interchangeably is an unfortunate one. For one thing, it tends to lend covert support to antiabortionist positions. Given such usage, one who holds a liberal view of abortion is put in the position of maintaining that fetuses, at least up to a certain point, are not human beings. Even philosophers are led astray by this usage. Thus Wertheimer says that "except for monstrosities, every member of our species is indubitably a person, a human being, at the very latest at birth."[9] Is it really *indubitable* that newborn babies are persons? Sure this is a wild contention. Wertheimer is falling prey to the confusion naturally engendered by the practice of using "person" and "human being" interchangeably. Another example of this is provided by Thomson: "I am inclined to think also that we shall probably have to agree that the fetus has already become a human person well before birth. Indeed, it comes as a surprise when one first learns how early in its life it begins to acquire human characteristics. By the tenth week, for example, it already has a face, arms, and legs, fingers and toes; it has internal organs, and brain activity is detectable."[10] But what do such physiological characteristics have to do with the question of whether the organism is a person? Thomson, partly, I think, because of the unfortunate use of terminology, does not even raise this question. As a result she virtually takes it for granted that there are some cases in which abortion is "positively indecent."[11]

There is a second reason why using "person" and "human being" interchangeably is unhappy philosophically. If one says that the dispute between pro- and anti-abortionists centers on whether the fetus is a human, it is natural to conclude that it is essentially a disagreement about certain facts, a disagreement about what properties a fetus possess. Thus Wertheimer says that "if one insists on using the raggy fact-value distinction, then one ought to say that the dispute is over a matter of fact in the sense in which it is a fact that the Negro slaves were human beings."[12] I shall argue that the two cases are not parallel, and that in the case of abortion what is primarily at stake is what moral principles one should accept. If one says that the central issue between conservatives and liberals in the abortion question is whether the fetus is a person, it is clear that the dispute may be either about what properties a thing must have in order to be a person, in order to have a right to life—a moral question—or about whether a fetus at a given stage of development as a matter of fact possesses the properties in question. The temptation to suppose that the disagreement must be a factual one is removed.

It should now be clear why the common practice of using expressions such as "person" and "human being" interchangeably in discussions of abortion is unfortunate. It would perhaps be best to avoid the term "human" altogether, employing instead some expression that is more naturally interpreted as referring to a certain type of biological organism characterized in physiological terms, such as "member of the species *Homo sapiens*." My own approach will be to use the term "human" only in contexts where it is not philosophically dangerous.

3. THE BASIC ISSUE: WHEN IS A MEMBER OF THE SPECIES *HOMO SAPIENS* A PERSON?

Settling the issue of the morality of abortion and infanticide will involve answering the following questions: What properties must something have to be a person, i.e., to have a serious right to life? At what point in the development of a member of the species *Homo sapiens* does the organism possess the properties that make it a person? The first question raises a moral issue. To answer it is to decide what basic[13] moral principles involving the ascription of a right to life one ought to accept. The second question raises a purely factual issue, since the properties in question are properties of a purely descriptive sort.

Some writers seem quite pessimistic about the possibility of resolving the question of the morality of abortion. Indeed, some have gone so far as to suggest that the question of whether the fetus is a person is in principle unanswerable: "We seem to be stuck with the indeterminateness of the fetus's humanity."[14] An understanding of some of the sources of this pessimism will, I think, help us to tackle the problem. Let us begin by considering the similarity a number of people have noted between the issue of abortion and the issue of Negro slavery. The question here is why it should be more difficult to decide whether abortion and infanticide are acceptable than it was to decide whether slavery was acceptable. The answer seems to be that in the case of slavery there are moral principles of a quite uncontroversial sort that settle the issue. Thus most people would agree to some such principle as the following: No organism that has experiences, that is capable of thought and of using language, and that has harmed no one, should be made a slave. In the case of abortion, on the other hand, conditions that are generally agreed to be sufficient grounds for ascribing a right to life to something do not suffice to settle the issue. It is easy to specify other, purportedly sufficient conditions that will settle the issue, but no one has been successful in putting forward considerations that will convince others to accept those additional moral principles.

I do not share the general pessimism about the possibility of resolving the issue of abortion and infanticide because I believe it is possible to point to a very plausible moral principle dealing with the question of *necessary* conditions for something's having a right to life, where the conditions in question will provide an answer to the question of the permissibility of abortion and infanticide.

There is a second cause of pessimism that should be noted before proceeding. It is tied up with the fact that the development of an organism is one of gradual and continuous change. Given this continuity, how is one to draw a line at one point and declare it permissible to destroy a member of Homo sapiens up to, but not beyond, that point? Won't there be an arbitrariness about any point that is chosen? I will return to this worry shortly. It does not present a serious difficulty once the basic moral principles relevant to the ascription of a right to life to an individual are established.

Let us turn now to the first and most fundamental question: What properties must something have in order to be a person, i.e., to have a serious right to life? The claim I wish to defend is this: *An organism possesses a serious right to life only if it possesses the concept of a self as a continuing subject of experiences and other mental states, and believes that it is itself such a continuing entity.*

My basic argument in support of this claim, which I will call the self-consciousness requirement, will be clearest, I think, if I first offer a simplified version of the argument, and then consider a modification that seems desirable. The simplified version of my argument is this. To ascribe a right to an individual is to assert something about the prima facie obligations of other individuals to act, or to refrain from acting, in certain ways. However, the obligations in question are conditional ones, being dependent upon the existence of certain desires of the individual to whom the right is ascribed. Thus if an individual asks one to destroy something to which he has a right, one does not violate his right to that thing if one proceeds to destroy it. This suggests the following analysis: "A has a right to X" is roughly synonymous with "If A desires X, then others are under a prima facie obligation to refrain from actions that would deprive him of it."[15]

Although this analysis is initially plausible, there are reasons for thinking it not entirely correct. I will consider these later. Even here, however, some expansion is necessary, since there are features of the concept of a right that are important in the present context, and that ought to be dealt with more explicitly. In particular, it seems to be a conceptual truth that things that lack consciousness, such as ordinary machines, cannot have rights. Does this conceptual truth follow from the above analysis of the concept of a right? The answer depends on how the term "desire" is interpreted. If one adopts a completely behavioristic interpretation of "desire" so that a machine that searches for an electrical outlet in order to get its batteries recharged is described as having a desire to be recharged, then it will not follow from this analysis that objects that lack consciousness cannot have rights. On the other hand, if "desire" is interpreted in such a way that desires are states necessarily standing in some sort of relationship to states of consciousness, it will follow from the analysis that a machine that is not capable of being conscious, and consequently of having desires, cannot have any rights. I think those who defend analyses of the concept of a right along the lines of this one do have in mind an interpretation of the term "desire" that involves reference to something more than behavioral dispositions. However, rather than relying on this, it seems preferable to make such an interpretation explicitly. The following analysis is a natural way of doing that: "A has a right to X" is roughly synonymous with "A is the sort of thing that is a subject of experiences and other mental states, A is capable of desiring X, and if A does desire X, then others are under a prima facie obligation to refrain from actions that would deprive him of it."

The next step in the argument is basically a matter of applying this analysis of the concept of a right to life. Unfortunately the expression "right to life" is not entirely a happy one, since it suggests that the right in question concerns the continued existence of a biological organism. That this is incorrect can be brought out by considering possible ways of violating an individual's right to life. Suppose, for example, that by some technology of the future of the brain of an adult human were to be completely reprogrammed, so that the organism wound up with memories (or rather, apparent memories) beliefs, attitudes, and personality traits completely different from those associated with it before it was subjected to reprogramming. In such a case one would surely say that an individual had been destroyed, that an adult human's right to life had been violated, even though no biological organism had been killed. This example shows that the expression "right to life" is misleading, since what one is really concerned about is not just the continued existence of a biological organism, but the right of a subject of experiences and other mental states to continue to exist.

Given this more precise description of the right with which we are here concerned, we are now in a position to apply the analysis of the concept of a right stated above. When we do so we find that the statement "A has a right to continue to exist as a subject of experiences and other mental states" is roughly synonymous with the statement "A is a subject of experiences and other mental states, A is capable of desiring to continue to exist as a subject of experiences and other mental states, and if A does desire to continue to exist as such an entity, then others are under a prima facie obligation not to prevent him from doing so."

The final stage in the argument is simply a matter of asking what must be the case if something is to be capable of having a desire to continue existing as a subject of experiences and other mental states. The basic point here is that the desires a thing can have are limited by the concepts it possesses. For the fundamental way of describing a given desire is a desire that a certain proposition be true.[16] Then, since one cannot desire that a certain proposition be true unless one understands it, and since one cannot understand it without possessing the concepts involved in it, it follows that the desires one can have are limited by the concepts one possesses. Applying this to the present case results in the conclusion that an entity cannot be the sort of thing that can desire that a subject of experiences and other mental states exist unless it possesses the concept of such a subject. Moreover, an entity cannot desire that it itself *continue* existing as a subject of experiences and other mental states unless it believes that it is now such a subject. This completes the justification of the claim that it is a necessary condition of something's having a serious right to life that it possess the concept of a self as a continuing subject of experiences, and that it believe that it is itself such an entity.

Let us now consider a modification in the above argument that seems desirable. This modification concerns the crucial conceptual claim advanced about the relationship between ascription of rights and ascription of the corresponding desires. Certain situations suggest that there may be exceptions to the claim that if a person doesn't desire something, one cannot violate his right to it. There are three types of situations that call this claim into question: (i) situations in which an individual's desires reflect a state of emotional disturbance; (ii) situations in which a previously conscious individual is temporarily unconscious; (iii) situations in which an individual's desires have been distorted by conditioning or by indoctrination.

As an example of the first, consider a case in which an adult human falls into a state of depression which his psychiatrist recognizes as temporary. While in the state he tells people he wishes he were dead. His psychiatrist, accepting the view that there can be no violation of an individual's right to life unless the individual has a desire to live, decides to let his patient have his way and kills him. Or consider a related case in which one person gives another a drug that produces a state of temporary depression; the recipient expresses a wish that he were dead. The person who administered the drug then kills him. Doesn't one want to say in both these cases that the agent did something seriously wrong in killing the other person? And isn't the reason the action was seriously wrong in each case the fact that it violated the individual's right to life? If so, the right to life cannot be linked with a desire to live in the way claimed above.

The second set of situations are ones in which an individual is unconscious for some reason—that is, he is sleeping, or drugged, or in a temporary coma. Does an individual in such a state have any desires? People do sometimes say that an unconscious individual wants something, but it might be argued that if such talk is not to be simply false it must be interpreted as actually referring to the desires the individual *would* have if he were now conscious. Consequently, if the analysis of the concept of a right proposed above were correct, it would follow that one does not violate an individual's right if one takes his car, or kills him, while he is asleep.

Finally, consider situations in which an individual's desires have been distorted, either by inculcation or irrational beliefs or by direct conditioning. Thus an individual may permit someone to kill him because he has been convinced that if he allows himself to be sacrificed to the gods he will be gloriously rewarded in a life to come. Or an individual may be enslaved after first having been conditioned to desire a life of slavery. Doesn't one want to say that in the former case an individual's right to life has been violated, and in the latter his right to freedom?

Situations such as these strongly suggest that even if an individual doesn't want something, it is still possible to violate his right to it. Some modification of the earlier account of the concept of a right thus seems in order. The analysis given covers, I believe, the paradigmatic cases of violation of an individual's rights, but there are other, secondary cases where one also wants to say that someone's right has been violated which are not included.

Precisely how the revised analysis should formulated is unclear. Here it will be sufficient merely to say that, in view of the above, an individual's right to X can be violated not only when he desires, X, but also when he *would* now desire X were it not for one of the following: (i) he is in an emotional unbalanced state; (ii) he is temporarily unconscious; (iii) he has been conditioned to desire the absence of X.

The critical point now is that, even given this extension of the conditions under which an individual's right to something can be violated, it is still true that one's right to something can be violated only when one has the conceptual capability of desiring the thing in question. For example, an individual who would now desire not to be a slave if he weren't emotionally unbalanced, or if he weren't temporarily unconscious, or if he hadn't previously been conditioned to want to be a slave, must possess the concepts involved in the desire not to be a slave. Since it is really only the conceptual capability presupposed by the desire to continue existing as a subject of experiences and other mental states, and not the desire itself, that enters into the above argument, the modification required in the account of the conditions under which an individual's rights can be violated does not undercut my defense of the self-consciousness requirement.[17]

To sum up, my argument has been that having a right to life presupposes that one is capable of desiring to continue existing as a subject of experiences and other mental states. This in turn presupposes both that one has the concept of such a continuing entity and that one believes that one is oneself such an entity. So an entity that lacks such a consciousness of itself as a continuing subject of mental states does not have a right to life.

It would be natural to ask at this point whether satisfaction of this requirement is not only necessary but also sufficient to ensure that a thing has a right to life. I am inclined to an affirmative answer. However, the issue is not urgent in the present context, since as long as the requirement is in fact a necessary one we have the basis of an adequate defense of abortion and infanticide. If an organism must satisfy some other condition before it has a serious right to life, the result will merely be that the interval during which infanticide is morally permissible may be somewhat longer. Although the point at which an organism first achieves self-consciousness and hence the capacity of desiring to continue existing as a subject of experiences and other mental states may be a theoretically incorrect cutoff point, it is at least a morally safe one: any error it involves is on the side of caution. . . .

4. SUMMARY AND CONCLUSIONS

Let us return now to my basic claim, the self-consciousness requirement: An organism possesses a serious right to life only if it possesses the concept of a self as a continuing subject of experiences and other mental states, and believes that it is itself such a continuing entity. . . . I now want to mention one final reason why my claim should be accepted. Consider the example mentioned in Section 2—that of killing, as opposed to torturing, newborn kittens. I suggested there that while in the case of adult humans most people would consider it worse to kill an individual than to torture him for an hour, we do not usually view the killing of a newborn kitten as morally outrageous, although we would regard someone who tortured a newborn kitten for an hour as heinously evil. I pointed out that a possible conclusion that might be drawn from this is that newborn kittens have a right not to be tortured, but do not have a serious right to life. If this is the correct conclusion, how is one to explain it? One merit of the self-consciousness requirement is that it provides an explanation of this situation. The reason a newborn kitten does not have a right to life is explained by the fact that it does not possess the concept of a self. But how is one to explain the kitten's having a right not to be tortured?

The answer is that a desire not to suffer pain can be ascribed to something without assuming that it has any concept of a continuing self. For while something that lacks the concept of a self cannot desire that a self not suffer, it can desire that a given sensation not exist. The state desired—the absence of a particular sensation, or of sensations of a certain sort—can be described in a purely phenomenalistic language, and hence without the concept of a continuing self. So long as the newborn kitten possesses the relevant phenomenal concepts, it can truly be said to desire that a certain sensation not exist. So we can ascribe to it a right not to be tortured even though, since it lacks the concept of a continuing self, we cannot ascribe to it a right to life.

This completes my discussion of the basic moral principles involved in the issue of abortion and infanticide. But I want to comment upon an important factual question, namely, at what point an organism comes to possess the concept of a self as a continuing subject of experiences and other mental states, together with the belief that it is itself such a continuing entity. This is obviously a matter for detailed psychological investigation, but everyday observation makes it perfectly clear, I believe, that a newborn baby does not possess the concept of a continuing self, any more than a newborn kitten possesses such a concept. If so, infanticide during a time interval shortly after birth must be morally acceptable.

But where is the line to be drawn? What is the cutoff point? If one maintained, as some philosophers have, that an individual possesses concepts only if he can express these concepts in language, it would be a matter of everyday observation whether or not a given organism possessed the concept of a continuing self. Infanticide would then be permissible up to the time an organism learned how to use certain expressions. However, I think the claim that acquisition of concept is dependent on acquisition of language is mistaken. For example, one wants to ascribe mental states of a conceptual sort—such as beliefs and desires—to organisms that are incapable of learning a language. This issue of prelinguistic understanding is clearly outside the scope of this discussion. My point is simply that if an organism can acquire concepts without thereby acquiring a way of expressing those concepts linguistically, the question of whether a given organism possesses the concept of a self as a continuing subject of experiences and other mental states, together with the belief that it is itself such a continuing entity, may be a question that requires fairly subtle experimental techniques to answer.

If this view of the matter is roughly correct, there are two worries one is left with at the level of practical moral decisions, one of which may turn out to be deeply disturbing. The lesser worry is where the line is to be drawn in the case of infanticide. It is not troubling because there is no serious need to know the exact point at which a human infant acquires a right to life. For in the vast majority of cases in which infanticide is desirable, its desirability will be apparent within a short time after birth. Since it is virtually certain that an infant at such a stage of its development does not possess the concept of a continuing self, and thus does not possess a serious right to life, there is excellent reason to believe that infanticide is morally permissible in most cases where it is otherwise desirable. The practical moral problem can thus be satisfactorily handled by choosing some period of time, such as a week after birth, as the interval during which infanticide will be permitted. This interval could then be modified once psychologists have established the point at which a human organism comes to believe that it is a continuing subject of experiences and other mental states.

The troubling worry is whether adult animals belonging to species other than *Homo sapiens* may not also possess a serious right to life. For once one says that an organism can possess the concept of a continuing self, together with the belief that it is itself such an entity, without having any way of expressing that concept and that belief linguistically, one has to face up to the question of whether animals may not possess properties that bestow a serious right to life upon them. The suggestion itself is a familiar one, and one that most of us are accustomed to dismiss very casually. The line of thought advanced here suggests that this attitude may turn out to be tragically mistaken. Once one reflects upon the question of the *basic* moral principles involved in the ascription of a right to life to organisms, one may find himself driven to conclude that our everyday treatment of animals is morally indefensible, and that we are in fact murdering innocent persons.

NOTES

[1] Judith Jarvis Thomson, in her article, "A Defense of Abortion," *Philosophy and Public Affairs* 1, no. 1 (Fall 1971): 47–66, has argued with great force and ingenuity that this conclusion is mistaken. The article appears in the present volume above pp. 331–344.

[2] While this is the position conservatives tend to hold, it is not clear that it is the position they ought to hold. For if the fetus is a person it is far from clear that it is permissible to destroy it to save the mother. Two moral principles lend support to the view that it is the fetus which should live. First, other things being equal, should not one give something to a person who has had less rather than to a person who has had more? The mother has had a chance to live, while the fetus has not. The choice is thus between giving the mother more of an opportunity to live while giving the fetus none at all and giving the fetus an opportunity to enjoy life while not giving the mother a further opportunity to do so. Surely fairness requires the latter. Secondly, since the fetus has a greater life expectancy than the mother, one is in effect distributing more goods by choosing the life of the fetus over the life of the mother.

   The position I am here recommending to the conservative should not be confused with the official Catholic position. The Catholic Church holds that it is seriously wrong to kill a fetus directly even if failure to do so will result in the death of *both* the mother and the fetus. This perverse value judgment is not part of the conservative's position.

[3] Section 230.3 of the American Law Institute's *Model Penal Code* (Philadelphia, 1962). There is some interesting, though at times confused, discussion of the proposed code in *Model Penal Code—Tentative Draft No. 9* (Philadelphia, 1959), pp. 146–62.

[4] A clear example of such an unwillingness to entertain seriously the possibility that moral judgments widely accepted in one's own society may nevertheless be incorrect is provided by Roger Wertheimer's superficial dismissal of infanticide on pages 69–70 of his article "Understanding the Abortion Argument," *Philosophy and Public Affairs*, 1, no. 1 (Fall 1971); 67–95.

5 Compare the discussion of the concept of a right offered by Richard B. Brandt in his *Ethical Theory* (Englewood Cliffs, N.J., 1959), pp. 434–41. As Brandt points out, some philosophers have maintained that only things that can *claim* rights can have rights. I agree with Brandt's view that "inability to claim does not destroy the right" (p. 440).

6 B. A. Brody, "Abortion and the Law," *Journal of Philosophy*, LXVIII, no. 12 (17 June 1971): 357–69. See pp. 357–58.

7 Thomson, "A Defense of Abortion," p. 47.

8 Wertheimer, "Understanding the Abortion Argument," p. 69.

9 *Ibid.*

10 Thomson, "A Defense of Abortion," pp. 47–48.

11 *Ibid.*, p. 65.

12 Wertheimer, "Understanding the Abortion Argument," p. 78.

13 A moral principle accepted by a person is *basic for him* if and only if his acceptance of it is not dependent upon any of his (nonmoral) factual beliefs. That is, no change in his factual beliefs would cause him to abandon the principle in question.

14 Wertheimer, "Understanding the Abortion Argument," p. 88.

15 Again, compare the analysis defended by Brandt in *Ethical Theory*, pp. 434–41.

16 In everyday life one often speaks of desiring things, such as an apple or a newspaper. Such talk is elliptical, the context together with one's ordinary beliefs serving to make it clear that one wants to eat the apple and read the newspaper. To say that what one desires is that a certain proposition be true should not be construed as involving any particular ontological commitment. The point is merely that it is sentences such as "John wants it be the case that he is eating an apple in the next few minutes" that provide a completely explicit description of a person's desires. If one fails to use such sentences one can be badly misled about what concepts are presupposed by a particular desire.

17 There are, however, situations other than those discussed here which might seem to count against the claim that a person cannot have a right unless he is conceptually capable of having the corresponding desire. Can't a young child, for example, have a right to an estate, even though he may not be conceptually capable of wanting the estate? It is clear that such situations have to be carefully considered if one is to arrive at a satisfactory account of the concept of a right. My inclination is to say that the correct description is not that the child now has a right to the estate, but that he will come to have such a right when he is mature, and that in the meantime no one else has a right to the estate. My reason for saying that the child does not now have a right to the estate is that he cannot now do things with the estate, such as selling it or giving it away, that he will be able to do later on.

Active and Passive Euthanasia

James Rachels

The distinction between active and passive euthanasia is thought to be crucial for medical ethics. The idea is that it is permissible, at least in some cases, to withhold treatment and allow a patient to die, but it is never permissible to take any direct action designed to kill the patient. This doctrine seems to be accepted by most doctors, and is endorsed in a statement adopted by the House of Delegates of the American Medical Association on December 4, 1973:

> The intentional termination of the life of one human being by another—mercy killing—is contrary to that for which the medical profession stands and is contrary to the policy of the American Medical Association.

> The cessation of the employment of extraordinary means to prolong the life of the body when there is irrefutable evidence that biological death is imminent is the decision of the patient and or his immediate family. The advice and judgment of the physician should be freely available to the patient and/or his immediate family.

However, a strong case can be made against this doctrine. In what follows I will set out some of the relevant arguments, and urge doctors to reconsider their views on this matter.

To begin with a familiar type of situation, a patient who is dying of incurable cancer of the throat is in terrible pain, which can no longer be satisfactorily alleviated. He is certain to die within a few days, even if present treatment is continued, but he does not want to go on living for those days since the pain is unbearable. So he asks the doctor for an end to it, and his family joins in the request.

Suppose the doctor agrees to withhold treatment, as the conventional doctrine says he may. The justification for his doing so is that the patient is in terrible agony, and since he is going to die anyway, it would be wrong to prolong his suffering needlessly. But now notice this. If one simply withholds treatment, it may take the patient longer to die, and so he may suffer more than he would if more direct action were taken and a lethal injection given. This fact provides strong reason for thinking that, once the initial decision not to prolong his agony has been made, active euthanasia is actually preferable to passive euthanasia, rather than the reverse. To say otherwise is to endorse the option that leads to more suffering rather than less, and is contrary to the humanitarian impulse that prompts the decision not to prolong his life in the first place.

Part of my point is that the process of being "allowed to die" can be relatively slow and painful, whereas being given a lethal injection is relatively quick and painless. Let me give a different sort of example. In the United States about one in 600 babies is born with Down syndrome. Most of these babies are otherwise healthy—that is, with only the usual pediatric care, they will proceed to an otherwise normal infancy. Some, however, are born with congenital defects such as intestinal obstructions that require operations if they are to live. Sometimes, the parents and the doctor will decide not to operate, and let the infant die. Anthony Shaw describes what happens then.

> . . . When surgery is denied [the doctor] must try to keep the infant from suffering while natural forces sap the baby's life away. As a surgeon whose natural inclination is to use the scalpel to fight off death, standing by and watching a salvageable baby die is the most emotionally exhausting experience I know. It is easy at a conference, in a theoretical discussion, to decide that such infants should be allowed to die. It is altogether different to stand by in the nursery and watch a dehydration and infection wither a tiny being over hours and days. This is a terrible ordeal for me and the hospital staff—much more so than for the parents who never set foot in the nursery.[1]

I can understand why some people are opposed to all euthanasia, and insist that such infants must be allowed to live. I think I can also understand why other people favor destroying these babies quickly and painlessly. But why should anyone favor letting "dehydration and infection wither a tiny being over hours and days?" The doctrine that says that a baby may be allowed to dehydrate and wither, but may not be given an injection that would end its life without suffering, seems so patently cruel as to require no further refutation. The strong language is not intended to offend, but only to put the point in the clearest possible way.

My second argument is that the conventional doctrine leads to decisions concerning life and death made on irrelevant ground.

Consider again the case of the infants with Down syndrome who need operations for congenital defects unrelated to the syndrome to live. Sometimes, there is no operation, and the baby dies, but when there is no such defect, the baby lives on. Now, an operation such as that to remove an intestinal obstruction is not prohibitively difficult. The reason why such operations are not performed in these cases is, clearly, that the child has Down syndrome and the parents and doctor judge that because of that fact it is better for the child to die.

But notice that this situation is absurd, no matter what view one takes of lives and potentials of such babies. If the life of such an infant is worth preserving, what does it matter if it needs a simple operation? Or, if one thinks it better that such a baby should not live on, what difference does it make that it happens to have an unobstructed intestinal tract? In either case, the matter of life and death is being decided on irrelevant grounds. It is the Down syndrome, and not the intestines, that is the issue. The matter should be decided, it at all, on the basis, and not be allowed to depend on the essentially irrelevant question of whether the intestinal tract is blocked.

What makes this situation possible, of course, is the idea that when there is an intestinal blockage, one can "let the baby die," but when there is no such defect there is nothing that can be done, for one must not "kill" it. The fact that this idea leads to such results as deciding life or death on irrelevant grounds is another good reason why the doctrine should be rejected.

One reason why so many people think that there is an important moral difference between active and passive euthanasia is that they think killing someone is morally worse than letting someone die. But is it? Is killing, in itself, worse than letting someone die? To investigate this issue, two cases may be considered that are exactly alike except that one involves killing whereas the other involves letting someone die. Then, it can be asked whether this difference makes any difference to the moral assessment. It is important that the cases be exactly alike, except for this one difference, since otherwise one cannot be confident that it is this difference and not some other that accounts for any variation in the assessments of the two cases. So, let us consider this pair of cases:

In the first, Smith stands to gain a large inheritance if anything should happen to his six-year-old cousin. One evening while the child is taking his bath, Smith sneaks into the bathroom and drowns the child, and then arranges things so that it will look like an accident.

In the second, Jones also stands to gain if anything should happen to his six-year-old cousin. Like Smith, Jones sneaks in planning to drown the child in his bath. However, just as he enters the bathroom Jones sees the child slip and hit his head, and fall down in the water. Jones is delighted; he stands by, ready to push the child's head back under if it is necessary, but it is not necessary. With only a little thrashing about, the child drowns all by himself, "accidentally," as Jones watches and does nothing.

Now Smith killed the child, whereas Jones "merely" let the child die. That is the only difference between them. Did either man behave better, from a moral point of view? If the difference between killing and letting die were in itself a morally important matter, one should say that Jones's behavior was less reprehensible than Smith's. But does one really want to say that? I think not. In the first place, both men acted from the same motive, personal gain, and both had exactly the same end in view when they acted. It may be inferred from Smith's conduct that he is a bad man, although that judgment may be withdrawn or modified if certain further facts are learned about him—for example, that he is mentally deranged. But would not the very same thing be inferred about Jones from his conduct? And would not the same further considerations also be relevant to any modification of this judgment? Moreover, suppose Jones pleaded, in his own defense, "After all, I didn't do anything except just stand there and watch the child drown. I didn't kill him; I only let him die." Again, if letting die were in itself less bad than killing, this defense should have at least some weight. But it does not. Such a "defense" can only be regarded as grotesque perversion of moral reasoning. Morally speaking, it is no defense at all.

Now it may be pointed out, quite properly, that the cases of euthanasia with which doctors are concerned are not like this at all. They do not involve personal gain or the destruction of normal healthy children. Doctors are concerned only with cases in which the patient's life is of no further use to him, or in which the patient's life has become or will soon become a terrible burden. However, the point is the same in these cases: the bare difference between killing and letting die does not, in itself, make a moral difference. If a doctor lets a patient die, for humane reasons, he is in the same moral position as if he had given the patient a lethal injection for humane reasons. If his decision was wrong—if, for example, the patient's illness was in fact curable—the decision would be equally regrettable no matter which method was used to carry it out. And if the doctor's decision was the right one, the method used is not in itself important.

The AMA policy statement isolates the crucial issue very well; the crucial issue is "the intentional termination of the life of one human being by another. But after identifying this issue, and forbidding "mercy killing," the statement goes on to deny that the cessation of treatment is the intentional termination of a life. This is where the mistake comes in, for what is the cessation of treatment, in these circumstances, if it is not "the intentional termination of the life of one human being by another?" Of course it is exactly that, and if it were not, there would be no point to it.

Many people will find this judgment hard to accept. One reason, I think, is that it is very easy to conflate the question of whether killing is, in itself, worse than letting die, with the very different question of whether most actual cases of killing are more reprehensible than most actual cases of letting die. Most actual cases of killing are clearly terrible (think, for example, of all the murders reported in the newspapers), and one hears of such cases every day. On the other hand, one hardly ever hears of a case of letting die, except for the actions of doctors who are motivated by humanitarian reasons. So one learns to think of killing in a much worse light than of letting die. But this does not mean that there is something about killing that makes it in itself worse than letting die, for it is not the bare difference between killing and letting die that makes the difference in these cases. Rather, the other factors—the murderer's motive of personal gain, for example, contrasted with the doctor's humanitarian motivation—account for different reactions to the different cases.

I have argued that killing is not in itself any worse than letting die; if my contention is right, it follows that active euthanasia is not any worse than passive euthanasia. What arguments can be given on the other side? The most common, I believe, is the following:

"The important difference between active and passive euthanasia is that, in passive euthanasia, the doctor does not do anything to bring about the patient's death. The doctor does nothing, and the patient dies of whatever ills already afflict him. In active euthanasia, however, the doctor does something to bring about the patient's death; he kills him. The doctor who gives the patient with cancer a lethal injection has himself caused his patient's death; whereas if here merely ceases treatment, the cancer is the cause of the death."

A number of points need to be made here. The first is that it is not exactly correct to say that in passive euthanasia the doctor does nothing, for he does do one thing that is very important: he lets the patient die. "Letting someone die" is certainly different, in some respects, from other types of action—mainly in that it is a kind of action that one may perform by way of not performing certain other actions.

444

For example, one may let a patient die by way of not giving medication, just as one may insult someone by way of not shaking his hand. But for any purpose of moral assessment, it is a type of action nonetheless. The decision to let a patient die is subject to moral appraisal in the same way that a decision to kill him would be subject to moral appraisal: It may be assessed as wise or unwise, compassionate or sadistic, right or wrong. If a doctor deliberately let a patient die who was suffering from a routinely curable illness, the doctor would certainly be to blame for what he had done, just as he would be to blame if he had needlessly killed the patient. Charges against him would then be appropriate. If so, it would be no defense at all for him to insist that he didn't "do anything." He would have done something very serious indeed, for he let his patient die.

Fixing the cause of death may be very important from a legal point of view, for it may determine whether criminal charges are brought against the doctor. But I do not think that this notion can be used to show a moral difference between active and passive euthanasia. The reason why it is considered bad to be the cause of someone's death is that death is regarded as a great evil—and so it is. However, if it has been decided that euthanasia—even passive euthanasia—is desirable in a given case, it has also been decided that in this instance death is no greater an evil than their patient's continued existence. And if this is true, the usual reason for not wanting to be the cause of someone's death simply does not apply.

Finally, doctors may think that all of this is only of academic interest—the sort of thing that philosophers may worry about but that has no practical bearing on their own work. After all, doctors must be concerned about the legal consequences of what they do, and active euthanasia is clearly forbidden by law. But even so, doctors should also be concerned with the fact that the law is forcing upon them a moral doctrine that may well be indefensible, and has a considerable effect on their practices. Of course, most doctors are not now in the position of being coerced in this matter, for they do not regard themselves as merely going along with what the law requires. Rather, in statements such as the AMA policy statement that I have quoted, they are endorsing this doctrine as a central point of medical ethics. In that statement, active euthanasia is condemned not merely as illegal but as "contrary to that for which the medical profession stands," whereas passive euthanasia is approved. However, the preceding considerations suggest that there is really no moral difference between the two, considered in themselves (there may be important moral differences in some cases in their *consequences*, but, as I pointed out, these differences may make active euthanasia, and not passive euthanasia, the morally preferable option). So, whereas doctors may have to discriminate between active and passive euthanasia to satisfy the law, they should not do any more than that. In particular, they should not give the distinction any added authority and weight by writing it into official statements of medical ethics.

NOTE

[1] A. Shaw, "Doctor, Do We Have a Choice?" *The New York Times Magazine*, Jan. 30, 1972, p. 54.

What's Wrong With Rape

Pamela Foa

It is clear that rape is wrong. It is equally clear that the wrongness of rape is not completely explained by its status as a criminal assault. Dispute begins, however, when we attempt to account for the special features of rape, the ways in which its wrongness goes beyond its criminal character. I shall argue against those who maintain that the special wrongness of rape arises from and is completely explained by a societal refusal to recognize women as *people*. I shall offer a different explanation: The special wrongness of rape is due to, and is only an exaggeration of, the wrongness of our sexual interactions in general. Thus, a clear analysis of the special wrongness of rape will help indicate some of the essential features of healthy, non-rapine sexual interactions.

I. THE WRONGNESS OF RAPE GOES BEYOND ITS CRIMINALITY

It is to be expected during this period of resurgent feminism that rape will be seen primarily as a manifestation of how women are mistreated in our society. For example, consider these remarks of Simone de Beauvoir:

> All men are drawn to B[rigitte] B[ardot]'s seductiveness, but that does not mean that they are kindly disposed towards her. . . . They are unwilling to give up their role of lord and master. . . . Freedom and full consciousness remain their [the men's] right and privilege. . . . In the game of love BB is as much a hunter as she is a prey. The male is an object to her, just as she is to him. And that is precisely what wounds the masculine pride. In the Latin countries where men cling to the myth of "the woman as object," BB's naturalness seems to them more perverse than any possible sophistication. It is to assert that one is man's fellow and equal, to recognize that between the woman and him there is a mutual desire and pleasure. . . .

> But the male feels uncomfortable if, instead of a doll of flesh and blood, he holds in his arms a conscious being who is sizing him up. "You realize," an average Frenchman once said to me, "that

447

when a man finds a woman attractive, he wants to be able to pinch her behind." A ribald gesture reduces a woman to a thing that a man can do with as he pleases without worrying about what goes on in her mind and heart and body.[1]

And rape is apparently the quintessential instance of women being viewed as object, of women being treated as entities other than, and morally inferior to, men. It is implicit in the object-view that if men, and therefore society, viewed women as full moral equals, rape would be an assault no different in kind than any other. Thus, it is a consequence of this view that the special wrongness of rape is to be found in the nonsexual aspects of the act.

To this end, Marilyn Frye and Carolyn Shafer suggest in their paper "Rape and Respect" that the wrongness of rape is twofold: first, it is the use of a person without her consent in the performance of an act or event which is against her own best interests; and second, it is a social means of reinforcing the status of women as kinds of entities who lack and ought to lack the full privileges of personhood—importantly, the freedom to move as they will through what is rightfully their domain.[2] What is good about this account is that it provides one way of understanding the sense of essential violation of one's *person* (and not mere sexual abuse), which seems to be the natural concomitant of rape.

This account, further, gives one explanation for the continuous social denial of the common fact of criminal rape. On this view, to recognize rape as a criminal act, one must recognize the domains of women. But if domains are inextricably connected with personhood—if personhood, in fact, is to be analyzed in terms of domains—then it ought to be obvious that where there is no domain there can be no criminal trespass of domain; there can only be misperceptions or misunderstandings. To recognize domains of consent is to recognize the existence of people at their centers. Without such centers, there can be no rape.

Unfortunately, I do not believe that this kind of account can serve as an adequate explanation of what's wrong with rape. I find irrelevant its emphasis on the ontological status of women as persons of the first rank. It is granted that in any act of rape a person is used without proper regard to her personhood, but this is true of every kind of assault. If there is an additional wrongness to rape, it must be that more is wrong than the mere treatment of a person by another person without proper regard for her personhood. Later in this paper, I shall show that there is no need to differentiate ontologically between victim and assailant in order to explain the special wrongness of rape. However, it is important to recognize that rape is profoundly wrong even if it is not an act between ontological equals.

The special wrongness of rape cannot be traced to the fact that in this act men are not recognizing the full array of moral and legal rights and privileges which accrue to someone of equal status. Rape of children is at least as heinous as rape of adults, though few actually believe that children have or ought to have the same large domain of consenting adults (male and female) ought to have. In part, this is what is so disturbing about a recent English decision I shall discuss in a moment: it seems to confuse the ontological and the moral. Men's wishes, intentions, and beliefs are given a different (and more important) weight, just because they are (wrongly in this case, perhaps rightly in the case of children) viewed as different kinds of entities than women.

448

But even if one thinks that women are not people, or that all people (for example, children) do not have the same rights or, prima facie, the same domains of consent, it seems that rape is still especially horrible, awful in a way that other assaults are not. There is, for example, something deeply distressing, though not necessarily criminal, about raping one's pet dog. It is disturbing in ways no ordinary assault, even upon a person, seems to be disturbing. It may here be objected that what accounts for the moral outrage in these two cases is that the first is an instance of pedophilia, and the second of bestiality. That is, the special wrongness of these acts is due to the "unnatural" direction of the sexual impulse, rather than to the abusive circumstances of the fulfillment of a "natural" sexual impulse.

I would argue in response that outrage at "unnatural" acts is misdirected and inappropriate. The notion that acting "against" nature is immoral stems from the false belief that how things are in the majority of cases is, morally speaking, how things always ought to be. Acting unnaturally is not acting immorally unless there is a moral design to the natural order—and there is no such structure to it. This means, then, that if it is reasonable to feel that something very wrong has occurred in the above two cases, then it must be because they are rapes and not because they are "unnatural acts." However, even if this argument is not conclusive, it must be agreed that the random raping of a mentally retarded adult is clearly wrong even though such an individual does not, in our society, have all the legal and moral rights of normal people.[3]

Of course, another very reasonable point to make here may well be that it is not just people who have domains, and that what's wrong with rape is the invasion by one being into another's domain without consent or right. But if something like this is true, then rape would be wrong because it was an "incursion" into a domain. This would make it wrong in the same way that other assaults are wrong. The closer the incursion comes to the center of a person's identity, the worse the act.

The problem here is that such an argument suggests that rape is wrong the same way, and only the same way, that other assaults are wrong. And yet the evidence contradicts this. There is an emotional concomitant to this assault, one that is lacking in nonsexual criminal assaults. What must be realized is that when it comes to sexual matters, people—in full recognition of the equal ontological status of their partners—treat each other abominably. Contrary to the Frye/Shafer theory, I believe that liberated men and women—people who have no doubts about the moral or ontological equality of the sexes—can and do have essentially rape-like sexual lives.

The following case is sufficient to establish that it is not just the assault upon one's person, or the intrusion into one's domain, that makes for the special features of rape. In New York twenty or so years ago, there was a man who went around Manhattan slashing people with a very sharp knife. He did not do this as part of any robbery or other further bodily assault. His end was simply to stab people. Although he was using people against their own best interests, and without their consent—that is, although he is broadly violating domains—to be the victim of the Mad Slasher was not to have been demeaned or dirtied as a person in the way that the victim of rape is demeaned or dirtied. It was not to be wronged or devalued in the same way that to be raped is to be wronged or devalued. No one ever accused any of the victims of provoking, initiating, or enjoying the attack.

Yet the public morality about rape suggests that unless one is somehow mutilated, broken, or killed in addition to being raped, one is suspected of having provoked, initiated, complied in, consented to, or even enjoyed the act. It is this public response, the fear of such a response and the belief (often) in the rationality of such a response (even from those who do unequivocally view you as a person) that seems to make rape especially horrible.

Thus, what is especially bad about rape is a function of its place in our society's sexual views, not in our ontological views. There is, of course, nothing necessary about these views, but until they change, no matter what progress is made in the fight for equality between the sexes, rape will remain an especially awful act.

II. SEX, INTIMACY, AND PLEASURE

Our response to rape beings into focus our inner feelings about the nature, purpose, and morality of all sexual encounters and of ourselves as sexual beings. Two areas which seem immediately problematic are the relation between sex and intimacy and the relation between sex and displeasure.

Our Victorian ancestors believed that sex in the absence of (at least marital) intimacy was morally wrong and that the only women who experienced sexual pleasure were nymphomaniacs.[4] Freud's work was revolutionary in part just because he challenged the view of "good" women and children as asexual creatures.[5] Only with Masters and Johnson's work, however, has there been a full scientific recognition of the capacity of ordinary women for sexual pleasure.[6] But though it is now recognized that sexual pleasure exists for all people at all stages of life and is, in its own right, a morally permissible goal, this contemporary attitude is still dominated by a Victorian atmosphere. It remains the common feeling that it is a kind of pleasure which should be experienced only in private and only between people who are and intend to be otherwise intimate. Genital pleasure is private not only in our description of its physical location, but also in our conception of its occurrence or occasion.

For the rape victim, the special problem created by the discovery of pleasure in sex is that now some people believe that *every* sex act must be pleasurable to some extent, including rape.[7] Thus, it is believed by some that the victim in a rape must at some level be enjoying herself—and that this enjoyment in a non-intimate, non-private environment is shameful. What is especially wrong about rape, therefore, is that it makes evident the essentially sexual nature of women, and this has been viewed, from the time of Eve through the time of Victoria, as cause for their humiliation. Note that on this view the special evil of rape is due to the feminine character and not to that of her attacker.[8]

The additional societal attitude that sex is moral only between intimates creates a further dilemma in assessing the situation of the rape victim. On the one hand, if it is believed that the sex act itself creates an intimate relationship between two people, then, by necessity, the rape victim experiences intimacy with her assailant. This may incline one to deny the fact of the rape by pointing to the fact of the intimacy. If one does not believe that sex itself creates intimacy between the actors, but nonetheless believes that sex is immoral in the absence of intimacy, then the event of sex in the absence of an intimate relationship, even though involuntary, is cause for public scorn and humiliation. For the rape victim, to acknowledge the rape is to acknowledge one's immorality. Either way, the victim has violated the social sexual taboos and she must therefore be ostracized.

What is important is no longer that one is the victim of an assault, but rather that one is the survivor of a social transgression. This is the special burden that the victim carries.

There is support for my view in Gary Wills's review of Tom Wicker's book about the Attica prisoners' revolt.[9] What needs to be explained is the apparently peculiar way in which the safety of the prisoners' hostages was ignored in the preparations for the assault on the prison and in the assault itself. What strikes me as especially important in this event is that those outside the prison walls treated the *guards* exactly like the *prisoners*. The critical similarity is the alleged participation in taboo sexual activity, where such activity is seen as a paradigm of humiliating behavior. In his review Wills says,

> Sexual fantasy played around Attica's walls like invisible lightning. Guards told their families that all the inmates were animals. . . .
>
> When the assault finally came, and officers mowed down the hostages along with the inmates, an almost religious faith kept faked stories alive against all the evidence—that the hostages were found castrated; that those still living had been raped. . . . None of it was true, but guards knew what degradation the prisoners had been submitted to, and the kind of response that might call for. . . .
>
> One has to go very far down into the human psyche to understand what went on in that placid town. . . . The bloodthirsty hate of the local community was so obvious by the time of the assault that even Rockefeller. . . ordered that no correction personnel join the attack. . . . [Nonetheless] eleven men managed to go in. . . . Did they come to save the hostages, showing more care for them than outsiders could? Far from it. They fired as early and indiscriminately as the rest. Why? I am afraid Mr. Wicker is a bit too decent to understand what was happening, though his own cultural background gives us a clue. Whenever a white girl was caught with a black in the old South, myth demanded that a charge of rape be brought and the "boy" be lynched. But a shadowy ostracism was inflicted on the girl. Did she fight back? Might she undermine the myth with a blurted tale or a repeated episode? At any rate, she was tainted. She had, willed she or nilled she, touched the untouchable and acquired her own evil halo of contamination. Taboos take little account of "intention." In the same way, guards caught in that yard were tainted goods. . . . They were an embarrassment. The white girl may sincerely have struggled with her black assailant; but even to imagine that resistance was defiling—and her presence made people imagine it. She was a public pollution—to be purged. Is this [comparison] fanciful? Even Wicker. . . cannot understand the attitude of those in charge who brought no special medical units to Attica before the attack began. . . . The lynch mob may kill the girl in its urgency to get at the boy—and it will regret this less than it admits.[10]

451

Accounts like the one offered by Frye and Shafer might explain why the *prisoners* were treated so callously by the assaulting troops, but they cannot explain the brutal treatment of the hostages. Surely they cannot say that the guards who were hostages were not and had never been viewed as people, as ontological equals, by the general society. And yet there was the same special horror in being a hostage at Attica as there is or a woman who has been raped. In both cases the *victim* has acquired a "halo of contamination" which permanently taints. And this cannot be explained by claiming that in both cases society is denying personhood or domains of consent to the victim.

The victim in sexual assault cases is as much a victim of our confused beliefs about sex as of the assault itself. The tremendous strains we put on such victims are a cruel result of our deep confusion about the place of, and need for, sexual relationships and the role of pleasure and intimacy in those relationships.

In spite of the fact, I believe, that as a society we share the *belief* that sex is only justified in intimate relationships, we act to avoid real intimacy at almost any cost. We seem to be as baffled as our predecessors were about the place of intimacy in our sexual and social lives. And this is, I think, because we are afraid that real intimacy creates or unleashes sexually wanton relationships, licentious lives—and this we view as morally repugnant. At the same time, we believe that sex in the absence of an intimate relationship is whoring and is therefore also morally repugnant. It is this impossible conflict which I think shows us that we will be able to make sense of our response to rape only if we look at rape as the model of all our sexual interactions, not as its antithesis.

III. THE MODEL OF SEX: RAPE

Though we may sometimes speak as though sexual activity is most pleasurable between friends, we do not teach each other to treat our sexual partners as friends. Middle-class children, whom I take to be our cultural models, are instructed from the earliest possible time to ignore their sexual feelings. Long before intercourse can be a central issue, when children are prepubescent, boys are instructed to lunge for a kiss and girls are instructed to permit nothing more than a peck on the cheek. This encouragement of miniature adult sexual behavior is instructive on several levels.

It teaches the child that courting behavior is rarely spontaneous and rarely something which gives pleasure to the people involved—that is, it is not like typical playing with friends. It gives the child a glimpse of how adults do behave, or are expected to behave, and therefore of what is expected in future life and social interactions. Importantly, boys are instructed *not* to be attentive to the claims of girls with respect to their desires and needs. And girls are instructed *not* to consult their feelings as a means of or at least a check on what behavior they should engage in.

Every American girl, be she philosopher-to-be or not, is well acquainted with the slippery-slope argument by the time she is ten. She is told that if she permits herself to become involved in anything more than a peck on the cheek, anything but the most innocent type of sexual behavior, she will inevitably become involved in behavior that will result in intercourse and pregnancy. And such behavior is wrong. That is, she is told that if she acquiesces to any degree to her feelings, then she will be doing something immoral.

Meanwhile, every American boy is instructed, whether explicitly or not, that the girls have been given this argument (as a weapon) and that therefore, since everything that a girl says will be a reflection of this argument (and not of her feelings), they are to ignore everything that she says.

Girls are told never to consult their feelings (they can only induce them to the edge of the slippery slope); they are always to say "no." Boys are told that it is a sign of their growing manhood to be able to get a girl way beyond the edge of the slope, and that it is standard procedure for girls to say "no" independently of their feelings. Thus, reasonably enough, boys act as far as one can tell independently of the explicit information they are currently receiving from the girl.

For women, it is very disconcerting to find that from the age of eight or nine or ten, one's reports of one's feelings are no longer viewed as accurate, truthful, important, or interesting. R. D. Laing, the English psychiatrist and theorist, claims that it is this type of adult behavior which creates the environment in which insanity best finds its roots.[11] It is clear, at least, that such behavior is not a model of rationality or health. In any event, rape is a case where only the pretense of listening has been stripped away. It is the essence of what we have all been trained to expect.

In a sexually healthier society, men and women might be told to engage in that behavior which gives them pleasure as long as that pleasure is not (does not involve actions) against anyone's will (including coerced actions) and does not involve them with responsibilities they cannot or will not meet (emotional, physical, or financial).

But as things are now, boys and girls have no way to tell each other what gives them pleasure and what not, what frightens them and what not; there are only violence, threats of violence, and appeals to informing on one or the other to some dreaded peer or parental group. This is a very high-risk, high-stake game, which women and girls, at least, often feel may easily become rape (even though it is usually played for little more than a quick feel in the back seat of the car or corner of the family sofa). But the ultimate consequences of this type of instruction are not so petty. Consider, for example, the effects of a recent English high-court decision:

> Now, according to the new interpretation, no matter how much a woman screams and fights, the accused rapist can be cleared by claiming he believed the victim consented, even though his belief may be considered unreasonable or irrational.

> On a rainy night seven months ago, a London housewife and mother of three claims she was dragged into this dilapidated shed. Annie Baker says she screamed for help and she fought but she was raped. Mrs. Baker lost her case in court because the man claimed he thought when she said no, she meant yes.

> One member of Parliament [predicts juries will] "now have the rapist saying that the woman asked for what she got and she wanted what they [sic] gave her."

> However, the Head of the British Law Society maintains. "Today juries are prepared to accept that the relationship between the sexes

453

has become much more promiscuous, and they have to look much more carefully to see whether the woman has consented under modern conditions. . . . One mustn't readily assume that a woman did not consent, because all indications are that there is a greater willingness to consent today than there was thirty years ago."[12]

"The question to be answered in this case," said Lord Cross of Chelsea," as I see it, is whether, according to the ordinary use of the English language, a man can be said to have committed rape if he believed that the woman was consenting to the intercourse. I do not think he can."[13]

This is the most macabre extension imaginable of our early instruction. It is one which makes initially implausible and bizarre any suggestion that the recent philosophical analyses of sexuality as the product of a mutual desire for communication—or even for orgasm or sexual satisfaction—bear any but the most tangential relation to reality.[14]

As we are taught, sexual desires are desires women ought not to have and men must have. This is the model which makes necessary an eternal battle of the sexes. It is the model which explains why rape is the prevalent model of sexuality. It has the further virtue of explaining the otherwise puzzling attitude of many that women will cry "rape" falsely at the slightest provocation. It explains, too, why men believe that no woman can be raped. It is as though what was mildly unsatisfactory at first (a girl's saying "no") becomes, over tine, increasingly erotic, until the ultimate turn-on becomes a woman's cry of "rape!"

IV. AN ALTERNATIVE: SEX BETWEEN FRIENDS

Understanding what's wrong with rape is difficult just because it is a member of the most common species of social encounter. To establish how rape is wrong is to establish that we have *all* been stepping to the wrong beat. Rape is only different in degree from the quintessential sexual relationship: marriage.

As Janice Moulton has noted, recent philosophical attention to theories of sexuality seem primarily concerned with sex between strangers.[15] On my view, we can explain this primary interest by noticing that our courting procedures are structured so that the couple must remain essentially estranged from each other. They do not ever talk or listen to each other with the respect and charity of friends. Instead, what is taken as the height of the erotic is sex without intimacy.

As long as we remain uncertain of our legitimacy of sexual pleasure, it will be impossible to give up our rape model of sexuality. For it can only be given up when we are willing to talk openly to each other without shame, embarrassment, or coyness about sex. Because only then will we not be too afraid to listen to each other.

Fortunately, to give this up requires us to make friends of our lovers.[16] Once we understand that intimacy enlarges the field of friendship, we can use some of the essential features of friendship as part of the model for sexual interaction, and we can present the pleasure of friendship as a real alternative to predatory pleasures.

I am not here committing myself to the view that the correct model for lovers is that of friends. Though I believe lovers involved in a healthy relationship have a fairly complex friendship, and though I am at a loss to find any important feature of a relationship between lovers which is not also one between friends, it may well be that the two relationships are merely closely related and not, in the end, explainable with the identical model.

It remains an enormously difficult task to throw over our anachronistic beliefs, and to resolve the conflict we feel about the sexual aspects of ourselves. But once this is done, not only will there be the obvious benefits of being able to exchange ignorance and denial of ourselves and others for knowledge, and fear for friendship, but we will also be able to remove the taboo from sex—even from rape. There will be no revelation, no reminder in the act of rape which we will need so badly to repress or deny that we must transform the victim into a guilt-bearing survivor. An act of rape will no longer remind us of the "true" nature of sex or our sexual desires.

Where there is nothing essentially forbidden about the fact of our sexual desires, the victim of rape will no longer be subject to a taboo or be regarded as dirty and in need of societal estrangement. The victim can then be regarded as having been grievously insulted, without simultaneously and necessarily having been permanently injured.

Further, if the model of sexual encounters is altered, there will no longer be any motivation for blaming the victim of rape. Since sex and rape will no longer be equated, there will be no motive for covering our own guilt or shame about the rapine nature of sex in general by transferring our guilt to the victim and ostracizing her. Rape will become an unfortunate aberration, the act of a criminal individual, rather than a symbol of our systematic ill-treatment and denial of each other.

NOTES

[1] Simone de Beauvoir, *Brigitte Bardot and the Lolita Syndrome* (London: New English Library, 1962), pp. 28, 30, 32.

[2] Frye and Shafer characterize a domain as "where . . . a person. . . lives. . . . Since biological life and health are prerequisites for the pursuit of any other interests and goals, . . . everything necessary for their maintenance and sustenance evidently will fall very close to the center of the domain. Anything which exerts an influence on . . . a person's will or dulls its intelligence or affects its own sense of identity. . . also comes very near the center of the domain. Whatever has a relatively permanent effect on the person, whatever affects its relatively constant surroundings, whatever causes it discomfort or distress—in short, whatever a person has to live with—is likely to fall squarely within its domain" ("Rape and Respect," this volume, p. 337).

[3] This societal attitude, however, that is the mentally retarded are not the equals of normal people is not one with which I associate myself.

[4] Francoise Basch, *Relative Creatures: Victorian Women in Society and the Novel* (New York: Schocken Books, 1974), pp. 8–9, 270–71.

[5] See *The Basic Writings of Sigmund Freud,* ed. A. A. Brill (New York: Random House, 1948), pp. 553–633.

[6] William H. Masters and Virginia E. Johnson, *Human Sexual Response* (Boston: Little, Brown, 1966).

7 It may well be that Freud's theory of human sexuality is mistakenly taken to support this view. See Sigmund Freud, *A General Introduction to Psychoanalysis* (New York: Washington Square Press, 1962), pp. 329–47.

8 What is a complete non sequitur, of course, is that the presence of such pleasure is sufficient to establish that no criminal assault has occurred. The two events are completely independent.

9 Tom Wicker, *A Time to Die* (New York: Quadrangle Books, 1975).

10 Gary Wills, "The Human Sewer." *New York Review of Books*, 3 April 1975, p. 4.

11 See, for example, R. D. Laing and A. Esterson, *Sanity, Madness and the Family* (Baltimore: Penguin, Pelican Books, 1970).

12 CBS Evening News with Walter Cronkite, 22 May 1975.

13 *New American Movement Newspaper*, May 1975, p. 8.

14 See R. C. Solomon, "Sex and Perversion," Tom Nagel, "Sexual Perversion," and Janice Moulton, "Sex and Reference," in *Philosophy and Sex*, ed. Robert Baker and Frederick Elliston (Buffalo, N.Y.: Prometheus Books, 1975).

15 Janice Moulton, "Sex and Sex," unpublished manuscript.

16 See Lyla O'Driscoll, "On the Nature and Value of Marriage." She argues that marriage and the sexual relations it entails should be based on friendship rather than romantic love.

An earlier version of this paper was presented to the Society of Women in Philosophy, Midwestern Division, October 1975, and to the American Philosophical Association, Pacific Division, March 1976. Research for this paper was supported by a generous grant from the University of Pittsburgh. Thanks are due to many colleagues who helped me clarify my views: especially John Cooper, Paul Guyer, Jonathan Himmelhoch, Alexander Nehamas, and, of course, Marilyn Frye and Carolyn Shafer.

Duties Toward the Body in Respect of Sexual Impulse

Immanuel Kant

Amongst our inclinations there is one which is directed towards other human beings. They themselves, and not their work and services, are its Objects of enjoyment. It is true that man has no inclination to enjoy the flesh of another—except, perhaps, in the vengeance of war, and then it is hardly a desire—but none the less there does exist an inclination which we may call an appetite for enjoying another human being. We refer to sexual impulse. Man can, of course, use another human being as an instrument for his service; he can use his hands, his feet, and even all his powers; he can use him for his own purposes with the other's consent. But there is no way in which a human being can be made an Object of indulgence for another except through sexual impulse. This is in the nature of a sense, which we can call the sixth sense; it is an appetite for another human being. We say that a man loves someone when he has an inclination towards another person. If by this love we mean true human love, then it admits of no distinction between types of persons, or between young and old. But a love that springs merely from sexual impulse cannot be love at all, but only appetite. Human love is good-will, affection, promoting the happiness of others and finding joy in their happiness. But it is clear that, when a person loves another purely from sexual desire, none of these factors enter into the love. Far from there being any concern for the happiness of the loved one, the lover, in order to satisfy his desire and still his appetite, may even plunge the loved one into the depths of misery. Sexual love makes of the loved person an Object of appetite; as soon as that appetite has been stilled, the person is cast aside as one casts away a lemon which has been sucked dry. Sexual love can, of course, be combined with human love and so carry with it the characteristics of the latter, but taken by itself and for itself, it is nothing more than appetite. Taken by itself it is a degradation of human nature; for as soon as a person become an Object of appetite for another, all motives of moral relationship cease to function, because as an Object of appetite for another a person becomes a thing and can be treated and used as such by every one. This is the only case in which a human being is designed by nature as the Object of another's enjoyment. Sexual desire is at the root of it; and that is why we are ashamed of it, and why all strict moralists, and those who had pretensions to be regarded as saints, sought to suppress and extirpate it. It is true that without it a man who would be incomplete; he would rightly believe that he lacked the necessary organs, and this would make him imperfect as a human being; none the less men made pretence on this question and sought to suppress these inclinations because they degraded mankind.

Because sexuality is not an inclination which one human being has for another as such, but is an inclination for the sex of another, it is a principle of the degradation of human nature, in that it gives rise to the preference of one sex to the other, and to the dishonouring of that sex through the satisfaction of desire. The desire which a man has for a woman is not directed towards her because she is a human being, but because she is a woman; that she is a human being is of no concern to the man; only her sex is the object of his desires. Human nature is thus subordinated. Hence it comes that all men and women do their best to make not their human nature but their sex more alluring and direct their activities and lusts entirely towards sex. Human nature is thereby sacrificed to sex. If then a man wishes to satisfy his desire, and a woman hers, they stimulate each other's desire; their inclinations meet, but their object is not human nature but sex, and each of them dishonors the human nature of the other. They make of humanity an instrument for their satisfaction of their lusts and inclinations, and dishonour it by placing it on a level with animal nature. Sexuality, therefore, exposes mankind to the danger of equality with the beasts. But as man has this desire from nature, the question arises how far he can properly make use of it without injury to his manhood. How far may persons allow one of the opposite sex to satisfy his or her desire upon them? Can they sell themselves, or let themselves out on hire, or by some other contract allow use to be made of their sexual faculties? Philosophers generally point out the harm done by this inclination and the ruin it brings to the body or to the commonwealth, and they believe that, except for the harm it does, there would be nothing contemptible in such conduct in itself. But if this were so, and if giving vent to this desire was not in itself abominable and did not involve immorality, then any one who could avoid being harmed by them could make whatever use he wanted of his sexual propensities. For the prohibitions of prudence are never unconditional; and the conduct would in itself be unobjectionable, and would only be harmful under certain conditions. But in point of fact, there is in the conduct itself something which is contemptible and contrary to the dictates of morality. It follows, therefore, that there must be certain conditions under which alone the use of the *facultates sexuales* would be in keeping with morality. There must be a basis for restraining our freedom in the use we make of our inclinations so that they conform to the principles of morality. We shall endeavour to discover these conditions and this basis. Men cannot dispose over himself because his is not a thing; he is not his own property; to say that he is would be self-contradictory; but in so far as he is a person he is a Subject in whom the ownership of things can be vested, and if he were his own property, he would be a thing over which he could have ownership. But a person cannot be a property and so cannot be a thing which can be owned, for it is impossible to be a person and a thing, the proprietor and the property.

Accordingly, a man is not at his own disposal. He is not entitled to sell a limb, not even one of his teeth. But to allow one's person for profit to be used by another for the satisfaction of sexual desire, to make of oneself an Object of demand, is to dispose over oneself as over a thing and to make of oneself a thing on which another satisfies his appetite, just as he satisfies his hunger upon a steak. But since the inclination is directed towards one's sex and not towards one's humanity, it is clear that one thus partially sacrifices one's humanity and thereby runs a moral risk. Human beings are, therefore, not entitled to offer themselves, for profit, as things for the use of others in the satisfaction of their sexual propensities. In so doing they would run the risk of having their person used by all and sundry as an instrument for the satisfaction of inclination. This way of satisfying sexuality is *vaga libido*, in which one satisfies the inclinations of others for gain. It is possible for either sex. To let one's person out on hire and to surrender it to another for the satisfaction of his sexual desire in return for money is the depth of infamy. The underlying moral principle is that man is not his own property and cannot do with his body what he will. The body is part of the self; in its togetherness with the self it constitutes the person; a man cannot make of his person a thing, and this is exactly what happens in *vaga libido*. This manner of satisfying sexual desire is, therefore, not permitted by the rules of morality. But what of the second method, namely *concubinatus*? Is this also inadmissible? In this case both persons satisfy their desire mutually and there is no idea of gain, but they serve each other only for the satisfaction of sexuality. There appears to be nothing unsuitable in this arrangement, but there is nevertheless one consideration which rules it out. Concubinage consists in one person surrendering to another only for the satisfaction of their sexual desire whilst retaining freedom and rights in other personal respects affecting welfare and happiness. But the person who so surrenders is used as a thing; the desire is still directed only towards sex and not towards the person as a human being. But it is obvious that to surrender part of oneself is to surrender the whole, because a human being is a unity. It is not possible to have the disposal of a part only of a person without having at the same time a right of disposal over the whole person, for each part of a person is integrally bound up with the whole. But concubinage does not give me a right of disposal over the whole person but only over a part, namely the *organa sexualia*. It presupposes a contract. This contract deals only with the enjoyment of a part of the person and not with the entire circumstances of the person. Concubinage is certainly a contract, but it is one-sided; the rights of the two parties are not equal. But if in concubinage I enjoy a part of a person, I thereby enjoy the whole person; yet by the terms of the arrangement I have not the rights over the whole person, but only over a part; I, therefore, make the person into a thing. For that reason this method of satisfying sexual desire is also not permitted by the rules of morality. The sole condition on which we are free to make use of our sexual desire depends upon the right to dispose over the person as a whole—over the welfare and happiness and generally over all the circumstances of that person. If I have the right over the whole person, I have also the right over the part and so I have the right to use that person's *organa sexualia* for the satisfaction of sexual desire. But how am I to obtain these rights over the whole person? Only by giving that person the same rights over the whole of myself. This happens only in marriage. Matrimony is an agreement between two persons by which they grant each other equal reciprocal rights, each of them undertaking to surrender the whole of their person to the other with a complete right of disposal over it. We can now apprehend by reason how a *commercium sexuale* is possible without degrading humanity and breaking the moral laws. Matrimony is the only condition in which use can be made of one's sexuality. If one devotes one's person to another, one devotes not only sex but the whole person; the two cannot be separated. If, then, one yields one's person, body and soul, for good and ill and in every respect, so that the other has complete rights over it, and if the other does not similarly yield himself in return and does not extend in return the same rights and privileges, the arrangement is one-sided. But if I yield myself completely to another and obtain the person of the other in return, I win myself back; I have given myself up as the property of another, but in turn I take that other as my property, and so win myself back again in winning the person whose property I have become. In this way the two persons become a unity of will. Whatever good or ill, joy or sorrow befall either of them, the other will share in it. Thus sexuality leads to a union of human beings, and in that union alone its exercise is possible. This condition of the use of sexuality, which is only fulfilled in marriage, is a moral condition. But let us pursue this aspect further and examine the case of a man who takes two wives. In such a case each wife would have but half a man, although she would be giving herself wholly and ought in consequence to be entitled to the whole man. To sum up: *vaga libido* is ruled out on moral grounds; the same applies to concubinage; there only remains matrimony, and in matrimony polygamy is ruled out also for moral reasons; we, therefore, reach the conclusion that the only feasible arrangement is that of monogamous marriage. Only under that condition can I indulge my *facultas sexualis*. We cannot here pursue the subject further.

But one other question arises, that of incest. Incest consists in intercourse between the sexes in a form which, by reason of consanguinity, must be ruled out; but are there moral grounds on which incest, in all forms of sexual intercourse, must be ruled out? They are grounds which apply conditionally, except in one case, in which they have absolute validity. The sole case in which the moral grounds against incest apply absolutely is that of intercourse between parents and children. Between parents and children there must be a respect which should continue throughout life, and this rules out of court any question of equality. Moreover, in sexual intercourse each person submits to the other in the highest degree, whereas between parents and children subjection is one-sided; the children must submit to the parents only; there can, therefore, be no equal union. This is the only case in which incest is absolutely forbidden by nature. In other cases incest forbids itself, but is not incest in the order of nature. The state prohibits incest, but at the beginning there must have been intermarriage between brothers and sisters. At the same time nature has implanted in our breasts a natural opposition to incest. She intended us to combine with other races and so to prevent too great a sameness in one society. Too close a connection, too intimate an acquaintance produces sexual indifference and repugnance. But this propensity must be restrained by modesty; otherwise it becomes commonplace, reduces the object of the desire to the commonplace and results in indifference. Sexual desire is very fastidious; nature has given it strength, but must be restrained by modesty. It is on that account that savages, who go about stark-naked, are cold toward each other; for that reason, too, a person whom we have known from youth evokes no desire within us, but a strange person attracts us much more strongly. Thus nature has herself provided restraints upon any desire between brother and sister.

Is Adultery Immoral?

Richard A. Wasserstrom

. . . I propose in this paper to think about the topic of sexual morality, and to do so in the following fashion. I shall consider just one kind of behavior that is often taken to be a case of sexual immorality—adultery. I am interested in pursuing at least two question. First, I want to explore the question of in what respects adulterous behavior falls within the domain of morality at all: For this surely is one of the puzzles one encounters when considering the topic of sexual morality. It is often hard to see on what grounds much of the behavior is deemed to be either moral or immoral, for example, private homosexual behavior between consenting adults. I have purposely selected adultery because it seems a more plausible candidate for moral assessment than many other kinds of sexual behavior.

The second question I want to examine is that of what is to be said about adultery, without being especially concerned to stay within the area of morality. I shall endeavor, in other words, to identify and to assess a number of the major arguments that might be advanced against adultery. I believe that they are the chief arguments that would be given in support of the view that adultery is immoral, but I think they are worth considering even if some of them turn out to be nonmoral arguments and considerations.

A number of the issues involved seem to me to be complicated and difficult. In a number of places I have at best indicated where further philosophical exploration is required without having successfully conducted the exploration myself. The paper may very well be more useful as an illustration of how one might begin to think about the subject of sexual morality than as an elucidation of important truths about the topic.

Before I turn to the arguments themselves there are two preliminary points that require some clarification. Throughout the paper I shall refer to the immorality of such things as breaking a promise, deceiving someone, etc. In a very rough way, I mean by this that there is something morally wrong that is done in doing the action in question. I mean that the action is, in a strong sense of "*prima facie,*" *prima facie* wrong or unjustified. I do not mean that it may never be right or justifiable to do the action; just that the fact that it is an action of this description always does count against the rightness of the action. I leave entirely open the question of what it is that makes actions of this kind immoral in this sense of "immoral."

The second preliminary point concerns what is meant or implied by the concept of adultery. I mean by "adultery" any case of extramarital sex, and I want to explore the arguments for and against extramarital sex, undertaken in a variety of morally relevant situations. Someone might claim that the concept of adultery is conceptually connected with the concept of immorality, and that to characterize behavior as adulterous is already to characterize it as immoral or unjustified in the sense described above. There may be something to this. Hence the importance of making it clear that I want to talk about extramarital sexual relations. If they are always immoral, this is something that must be shown by argument. If the concept of adultery does in some sense entail or imply immorality. I want to ask whether that connection is a rationally based one. If not all cases of extramarital sex are immoral (again, in the sense described above), then the concept of adultery should either be weakened accordingly or restricted to those classes of extramarital sex for which the predication of immorality is warranted.

One argument for the immorality of adultery might go something like this: What makes adultery immoral is that it involves the breaking of a promise, and what makes adultery seriously wrong is that it involves the breaking of an important promise. For, so the argument might continue, one of the things the two parties promise each other when they get married is that they will abstain from sexual relationships with third persons. Because of this promise both spouses quite reasonably entertain the expectation that the other will behave in conformity with it. Hence, when one of the parties has sexual intercourse with a third person he or she breaks that promise about sexual relationships which was made with the marriage was entered into, and defeats the reasonable expectations of exclusivity entertained by the spouse.

In many cases the immorality involved in breaching the promise relating to extramarital sex may be a good deal more serious than that involved in the breach of other promises. This is so because adherence to this promise may be of much greater importance to the parties than is adherence to many of the other promises given or received by them in their lifetime. The breaking of this promise may be much more hurtful and painful than is typically the case.

Why is this so? To begin with, it may have been difficult for the nonadulterous spouse to have kept the promise. Hence that spouse may feel the unfairness of having restrained himself or herself in the absence of reciprocal restraint having been exercised by the adulterous spouse. In addition, the spouse may perceive the breaking of the promise as an indication of a kind of indifference on the part of the adulterous spouse. If you really cared about me and my feelings—the spouse might say, you would not have done this to me. And third, and related to the above, the spouse may see the act of sexual intercourse with another as a sign of affection for the other person and as an additional rejection of the nonadulterous spouse as the one who is loved by the adulterous spouse. It is not just that the adulterous spouse does not take the feelings of the spouse sufficiently into account, the adulterous spouse also indicates through the act of adultery affection for someone other than the spouse. I will return to these points later. For the present, it is sufficient to note that a set of arguments can be developed in support of the proposition that certain kinds of adultery are wrong just because they involve the breach of a serious promise which, among other things, leads to the intentional infliction of substantial pain by one spouse upon the other.

Another argument for the immorality of adultery focuses not on the existence of a promise of sexual exclusivity but on the connection between adultery and deception. According to this argument, adultery involves deception. And because deception is wrong, so is adultery.

Although it is certainly not obviously so, I shall simply assume in this paper that deception is always immoral. Thus the crucial issue for my purposes is the asserted connection between extramarital sex and deception. Is it plausible to maintain, as this argument does, that adultery always does involve deception and is on that basis to be condemned?

The most obvious person on whom deceptions might be practiced is the non-participating spouse; and the most obvious thing about which the nonparticipating spouse can be deceived is the existence of the adulterous act. One clear case of deception is that of lying. Instead of saying that the afternoon was spent in bed with A, the adulterous spouse asserts that it was spent in the library with B, or on the golf course with C.

There can also be deception even when no lies are told. Suppose, for instance, that a person has sexual intercourse with someone other than his or her spouse and just does not tell the spouse about it. Is that deception? It may not be a case of lying if, for example, the spouse is never asked by the other about the situation. Still, we might say, it is surely deceptive because of the promises that were exchanged at marriage. As we saw earlier, these promises provide a foundation for the reasonable belief that neither spouse will engage in sexual relationships with any other persons. Hence the failure to bring the fact of extramarital sex to the attention of the other spouse deceives that spouse about the present state of the marital relationship.

It is possible, though, that a more subtle but pervasive kind of deceptiveness is a feature of adultery. It comes about because of the connection in our culture between sexual intimacy and certain feelings of love and affection. The point can be made indirectly at first by seeing that one way in which we can, in our culture, mark off our close friends from our mere acquaintances is through the kinds of intimacies that we are prepared to share with them. I may, for instance, be willing to reveal my very private thoughts and emotions to my closest friends or to my wife, but to no one else. My sharing of these intimate facts about myself is from one perspective a way of making a gift to those who mean the most to me. Revealing these things and sharing them with those who mean the most to me is one means by which I create, maintain, and confirm those interpersonal relationships that are of most importance to me.

Now in our culture, it might be claimed, sexual intimacy is one of the chief currencies through which gifts of this sort are exchanged. One way to tell someone—particularly someone of the opposite sex—that you have feelings of affection and love for them is by allowing to them or sharing with them sexual behaviors that one doesn't share with the rest of the world. This way of measuring affection was certainly very much a part of the culture in which I matured. It worked something like this. If you were a girl, you showed how much you liked someone by the degree of sexual intimacy you would allow. If you liked a boy only a little, you never did more than kiss—and even the kiss was not very passionate. If you liked the boy a lot and if your feeling was reciprocated, necking, and possibly petting, was permissible. If the attachment was still stronger and you thought it might even become a permanent relationship, the sexual activity was correspondingly more intense and more intimate, although whether the parties (and particularly the girl) accepted fully the prohibition on nonmarital sex. The situation for the boy was related, but not exactly the same. The assumption was that males did not naturally link sex with affection in the way in which females did. However, since women did, males had to take this into account. That is to say, because a woman would permit sexual intimacies only if she had feelings of affection for the male and only if those feelings were reciprocated, the male had to have and express those feelings, too, before sexual intimacies of any sort would occur.

The result was that the importance of a correlation between sexual intimacy and feelings of love and affection was taught by the culture and assimilated by those growing up in the culture. The scale of possible positive feelings toward persons of the opposite sex ran from casual liking at the one end to the love that was deemed essential to and characteristic of marriage at the other. The scale of possible sexual behavior ran from brief, passionless kissing or hand-holding at one end to sexual intercourse at the other. And the correlation between the two scales was quite precise. As a result, any act of sexual intimacy carried substantial meaning with it, and no act of sexual intimacy was simply a pleasurable set of bodily sensations. Many such acts were, of course, more pleasurable to the participants because they were a way of saying what the participants' feelings were. And sometimes they were less pleasurable for the same reason. The point is, however, that in any event sexual activity was much more than mere bodily enjoyment. It was not like eating a good meal, listening to good music, lying in the sun, or getting a pleasant back rub. It was behavior that meant a great deal concerning one's feelings for persons of the opposite sex in whom one was most interested and with whom one was most involved. It was among the most authoritative ways in which one could communicate to another the nature and degree of one's affection.

If this sketch is even roughly right, then several things become somewhat clearer. To begin with, a possible rationale for many of the rules of conventional sexual morality can be developed. If, for example, sexual intercourse is associated with the kind of affection and commitment to another that is regarded as characteristic of the marriage relationship, then it is natural that sexual intercourse should be thought properly to take place between persons who are married to each other. And if it is thought that this kind of affection and commitment is only to be found within the marriage relationship, then it is not surprising that sexual intercourse should only be thought to be proper within marriage.

Related to what has just been said is the idea that sexual intercourse ought to be restricted to those who are married to each other as a means by which to confirm the very special feelings that the spouses have for each other. Because the culture teaches that sexual intercourse means that the strongest of all feelings for each other are shared by the lovers, it is natural that persons who are married to each other should be able to say this to each other in this way. Revealing and confirming verbally that these feelings are present is one thing that helps to sustain the relationship; engaging in sexual intercourse is another.

In addition, this account would help to provide a framework within which to make sense of the notion that some sex is better than other sex. As I indicated earlier, the fact that sexual intimacy can be meaningful in the sense described tends to make it also the case that sexual intercourse can sometimes be more enjoyable than at other times. On this view, sexual intercourse will typically be more enjoyable where the strong feelings of affection are present than it will be where it is merely "mechanical." This is so in part because people enjoy being loved, especially by those whom they love. Just as we like to hear words of affection, so we like to receive affectionate behavior. And the meaning enhances the independently pleasurable behavior.

More to the point, moreover, an additional rationale for the prohibition on extramarital sex can now be developed. For given this way of viewing the sexual world, extramarital sex will almost always involve deception of a deeper sort. If the adulterous spouse does not in fact have the appropriate feelings of affection for the extramarital partner, then the adulterous spouse is deceiving that person about the presence of such feelings. If, on the other hand, the adulterous spouse does have the corresponding feelings for the extramarital partner but not toward the nonparticipating spouse, the adulterous spouse is very probably deceiving the nonparticipating spouse about the presence of such feelings toward that spouse. Indeed, it might be argued, whenever there is no longer love between the two persons who are married to each other, there is deception just because being married implies both to the participants and to the world that such a bond exists. Deception is inevitable, the argument might conclude, because the feelings of affection that ought to accompany any act of sexual intercourse can only be held toward one other person at any given time in one's life. And if this is so, then the adulterous spouse always deceives either the partner in adultery or the nonparticipating spouse about the existence of such feelings. Thus extramarital sex involves deception of this sort and is for this reason immoral even if no deception vis-à-vis the occurrence of the act of adultery takes place.

What might be said in response to the foregoing arguments? The first thing that might be said is that the account of the connection between sexual intimacy and feelings of affection is inaccurate. Not inaccurate in the sense that no one thinks of things that way, but in the sense that there is substantially more divergence of opinion than that account suggests. For example, the view I have delineated may describe reasonably accurately the concepts of the sexual world in which I grew up, but is does not capture the sexual *weltanschauung* of today's youth at all. Thus, whether or not adultery implies deception in respect to feelings depends very much on the persons who are involved and the way they look at the "meaning" of sexual intimacy.

Second, the argument leaves to be answered the question of whether it is desirable for sexual intimacy to carry the sorts of messages described above. For those persons for whom sex does have these implications, there are special feelings and sensibilities that must be taken into account. But it is another question entirely whether any valuable end—moral or otherwise—is served by investing sexual behavior with such significance. That is something that must be shown and not just assumed. It might, for instance, be the case that substantially more good than harm would come from a kind of demystification of sexual behavior: one that would encourage the enjoyment of sex more for its own sake and one that would reject the centrality both of the association of sex with love and of love with only one other person.

I regard these as two of the more difficult, unresolved issues that our culture faces today in respect to thinking sensibly about the attitudes toward sex and love that we should try to develop in ourselves and in our children. Much of the contemporary literature that advocates sexual liberation of one sort or another embraces one or the other of two different views about the relationship between sex and love.

One view holds that sex should be separated from love and affection. To be sure sex is probably better when the partners genuinely like and enjoy each other. But sex is basically an intensive, exciting sensuous activity that can be enjoyed in a variety of suitable settings with a variety of suitable partners. The situation in respect to sexual pleasure is no different from that of the person who knows and appreciates fine food and who can have a very satisfying meal in any number of good restaurants with any number of congenial companions. One question that must be settled here is whether sex can be so demystified; another, more important question is whether it would be desirable to do so. What would we gain and what might we lose if we all lived in a world in which an act of sexual intercourse was no more or less significant or enjoyable than having a delicious meal in a nice setting with a good friend? The answer to this question lies beyond the scope of this paper.

The second view seeks to drive the wedge in a different place. It is not the link between sex and love that needs to be broken; rather, on this view, it is the connection between love and exclusivity that ought to be severed. For a number of the reasons already given, it is desirable, so this argument goes, that sexual intimacy continue to be reserved to and shared with only those for whom one has very great affection. The mistake lies in thinking that any "normal" adult will only have those feelings toward one other adult during his or her lifetime—or even at any time in his or her life. It is the concept of adult love, not ideas about sex, that, on this view, needs demystification. What are thought to be both unrealistic and unfortunate are the notions of exclusivity and possessiveness that attach to the dominant conception of love between adults in our and other cultures. Parents of four, five, six, or even ten children can certainly claim and sometimes claim correctly that they love all of their children, that they love them all equally, and that it is simply untrue to their feelings to insist that all the numbers involved diminish either the quantity or quality of their love. If this is an idea that is readily understandable in the case of parents and children, there is no necessary reason why it is an impossible or undesirable idea in the case of adults. To be sure, there is probably a limit to the number of intimate, "primary" relationships that any person can maintain at any given time without the quality of the relationship being affected. But one adult ought surely to be able to love two, three, or even six other adults at any one time without that love being different in kind or degree from that of the traditional, monogamous, lifetime marriage. And as between the individuals in these relationships, whether within a marriage or without, sexual intimacy is fitting and good.

The issues raised by a position such as this one are also surely worth exploring in detail and with care. Is there something to be called "sexual love" which is different from parental love or the nonsexual love of close friends? Is there something about love in general that links it naturally and appropriately with feelings of exclusivity and possession? Or is there something about sexual love, whatever that may be, that makes these feelings especially fitting here? Once again the issues are conceptual, empirical, and normative all at once: What is love? How could it be different? Would it be a good thing or a bad thing if it were different?

Suppose, though, that having delineated these problems we were now to pass them by. Suppose, moreover, we were to be persuaded of the possibility and the desirability of weakening substantially either the links between sex and love or the links between sexual love and exclusivity. Would it not then be the case that adultery could be free from all of the morally objectionable features described so far? To be more specific, let us imagine that a husband and wife have what is today sometimes characterized as an "open marriage." Suppose that is, that they have agreed in advance that extramarital sex is—under certain circumstances—acceptable behavior for each to engage in. Suppose that as a result there is no impulse to deceive each other about the occurrence or nature of any such relationships, and that no deception in fact occurs. Suppose, too, that there is no deception in respect to the feelings involved between the adulterous spouse and the extramarital partner. And suppose, finally, that one or the other or both of the spouses then has sexual intercourse in circumstances consistent with these understandings. Under this description, so the agreement might conclude, adultery is simply not immoral. At a minimum, adultery cannot very plausibly be condemned either on the ground that it involves deception or on the ground that it requires the breaking of a promise.

At least two responses are worth considering. One calls attention to the connection between marriage and adultery; the other looks to more instrumental arguments for the immorality of adultery. Both issues deserve further exploration.

One way to deal with the case of the "open marriage" is to question whether the two persons involved are still properly to be described as being married to each other. Part of the meaning of what it is for two persons to be married to each other, so this argument would go, is to have committed oneself to have sexual relationships only with one's spouse. Of course, it would be added, we know that the commitment is not always honored. We know that persons who are married to each other often do commit adultery. But there is a difference between being willing to make a commitment to marital fidelity, even though one may fail to honor that commitment, and not making the commitment at all. Whatever the relationship may be between the two individuals in the case described above, the absence of any commitment to sexual exclusivity requires the conclusion that their relationship is not a marital one. For a commitment to sexual exclusivity is a necessary although not a sufficient condition for the existence of a marriage.

Although there may be something to this suggestion, as it is stated it is too strong to be acceptable. To begin with, I think it is very doubtful that there are many, if any, *necessary* conditions for marriage; but even if there are, a commitment to sexual exclusivity is not such a condition.

To see that this is so, consider what might be taken to be some of the essential characteristics of a marriage. We might be tempted to propose that the concept of marriage requires the following: a formal ceremony of some sort in which mutual obligations are undertaken between two persons of the opposite sex; the capacity on the part of the persons involved to have sexual intercourse with each other; the willingness to have sexual intercourse only with each other; and feelings of love and affection between the two persons. The problem is that we can imagine relationships that are clearly marital and yet lack one or more of these features. For example, in our own society, it is possible for two persons to be married without going through a formal ceremony, as in the common-law marriages recognized in some jurisdictions. It is also possible for two persons to get married even though one or both lacks the capacity to engage in sexual intercourse. Thus, two very elderly persons who have neither the desire nor the ability to have intercourse can, nonetheless, get married, as can persons whose sexual organs have been injured so that intercourse is not possible. And we certainly know of marriages in which love was not present at the time of the marriage, as, for instance, in marriages of state and marriages of convenience.

Counter-examples not satisfying the condition relating to the abstention from extramarital sex are even more easily produced. We certainly know of societies and cultures in which polygamy and polyandry are practiced, and we have no difficulty in recognizing these relationships as cases of marriages. It might be objected, though, that these are not counter-examples because they are plural marriages rather than marriages in which sex is permitted with someone other than with one of the persons to whom one is married. But we also know of societies in which it is permissible for married persons to have sexual relationships with persons to whom they were not married, for example, temple prostitutes, concubines, and homosexual lovers. And even if we knew of no such societies, the conceptual claim would still, I submit, not be well taken. For suppose all of the other indicia of marriage were present: suppose the two persons were of the opposite sex. Suppose they had the capacity and desire to have intercourse with each other, suppose they participated in a formal ceremony in which they understood themselves voluntarily to be entering into a relationship with each other in which substantial mutual commitments were assumed. If all these conditions were satisfied, we would not be in any doubt about whether or not the two persons were married even though they had not taken on a commitment of sexual exclusivity and even though they had expressly agreed that extramarital sexual intercourse was a permissible behavior for each to engage in.

A commitment to sexual exclusivity is neither a necessary nor a sufficient condition for the existence of a marriage. It does, nonetheless, have this much to do with the nature of marriage: like the other indicia enumerated above, its presence tends to establish the existence of a marriage. Thus, in the absence of a formal ceremony of any sort, an explicit commitment to sexual exclusivity would count in favor of regarding the two persons as married. The conceptual role of the commitment to sexual exclusivity can, perhaps, be brought out through the following example. Suppose we found a tribe which had a practice in which all the other indicia of marriage were present but in which the two parties were *prohibited* ever from having sexual intercourse with each other. Moreover, suppose that sexual intercourse with others was clearly permitted. In such a case we would, I think, reject the idea that the two were married to each other and we would describe their relationship in other terms, for example, as some kind of formalized, special friendship relation—a kind of heterosexual "blood-brother" bond.

Compare that case with the following. Suppose again that the tribe had a practice in which all of the other indicia of marriage were present, but instead a prohibition on sexual intercourse between the persons in the relationship there was no rule at all. Sexual intercourse was permissible with the person with whom one had this ceremonial relationship, but it was no more or less permissible than with a number of other persons to whom one was not so related (for instance, all consenting adults of the opposite sex). Although we might be in doubt as to whether we ought to describe the persons as married to each other, we would probably conclude that they were married and that they simply were members of a tribe whose views about sex were quite different from our own.

What all of this shows is that a *prohibition* on sexual intercourse between the two persons involved in a relationship is conceptually incompatible with the claim that the two of them are married. The *permissibility* of intramarital sex is a necessary part of the idea of marriage. But no such incompatibility follows simply from the added permissibility of extramarital sex.

These arguments do not, of course, exhaust the arguments for the prohibition on extramarital sexual relations. The remaining argument that I wish to consider—as I indicated earlier—is a more instrumental one. It seeks to justify the prohibition by virtue of the role that it plays in the development and maintenance of nuclear families. The argument, or set of arguments, might, I believe, go something like this.

Consider first a farfetched nonsexual example. Suppose a society were organized so that after some suitable age—say, 18, 19, or 20—persons were forbidden to eat anything but bread and water with anyone but their spouse. Persons might still choose in such a society not to get married. Good food just might not be very important to them because they have undeveloped taste buds. Or good food might be bad for them because there is something wrong with their digestive system. Or good food might be important to them, but they might decide that the enjoyment of good food would get in the way of the attainment of other things that were more important. But most persons would, I think, be led to favor marriage in part because they preferred a richer, more varied, diet to one of bread and water. And they might remain married because the family was the only legitimate setting within which good food was obtainable. If it is impossible to have society organized so that persons will both get married and stay married, such an arrangement would be well suited to the preservation of the family, and the prohibitions relating to food consumption could be understood as fulfilling that function.

It is obvious that one of the more powerful human desires is the desire for sexual gratification. The desire is a natural one, like hunger and thirst, in the sense that it need not be learned in order to be present within us and operative upon us. But there is in addition much that we do learn about what the act of sexual intercourse is like. Once we experience sexual intercourse ourselves—and in particular once we experience orgasm—we discover that it is among the most intensive, short-term pleasures of the body.

Because this is so, it is easy to see how the prohibition upon extramarital sex helps to hold marriage together. At least during that period of life when the enjoyment of sexual intercourse is one of the desirable bodily pleasures, persons will wish to enjoy those pleasures. If one consequence of being married is that one is prohibited from having sexual intercourse with anyone but one's spouse, then the spouses in a marriage are in a position to provide an important source of pleasure for each other that is unavailable to them elsewhere in society.

The point emerges still more clearly if this rule of sexual morality is seen as of a piece with the other rules of sexual morality. When this prohibition is coupled, for example, with the prohibition on nonmarital sexual intercourse, we are presented with the inducement both to get married and to stay married. For if sexual intercourse is only legitimate within marriage, then persons seeking that gratification which is a feature of sexual intercourse are furnished explicit social directions for its attainment: namely marriage.

Nor, to continue the argument, it is necessary to focus exclusively on the bodily enjoyment that is involved. Orgasm may be a significant part of what there is to sexual intercourse, but it is not the whole of it. We need only recall the earlier discussion of the meaning that sexual intimacy has in our own culture to begin to see some of the more intricate ways in which sexual exclusivity may be connected with the establishment and maintenance of marriage as the primary heterosexual, love relationship. Adultery is wrong, in other words, because a prohibition on extramarital sex is a way to help maintain the institutions of marriage and the nuclear family.

Now I am frankly not sure what we are to say about an argument such as this one. What I am convinced of is that, like the arguments discussed earlier, this one also reveals something of the difficulty and complexity of the issues that are involved. So, what I want now to do—in the brief and final portion of this paper—is to try to delineate with reasonable precision what I take several of the fundamental, unresolved issues to be.

The first is whether this last argument is an argument for the *immorality* of extramarital sexual intercourse. What does seem clear is that there are differences between this argument and the ones considered earlier. The earlier arguments condemned adulterous behavior because it was behavior that involved breaking of a promise, taking unfair advantage, or deceiving another. To the degree to which the prohibition on extramarital sex can be supported by arguments which involve considerations such as these, there is little question but that violations of the prohibition are properly regarded as immoral. And such a claim could be defended on one or both of two distinct grounds. The risk is that things like promise-breaking and deception are just wrong. The second is the adultery involving promise-breaking or deception is wrong because it involves the straightforward infliction of harm on another human being—typically the nonadulterous spouse—who has a strong claim not to have that harm so inflicted.

The argument that connects the prohibition on extramarital sex with the maintenance and preservation of the institution of marriage is an argument for the instrumental value of the prohibition. To some degree this counts, I think, against regarding all violations of the prohibition as obvious cases of immorality. This is so partly because hypothetical imperatives are less clearly within the domain of morality than are categorical ones, and even more because instrumental prohibitions are within the domain of morality only if the end they serve or the way they serve it is within the domain of morality.

What this should help us to see, I think, is the fact that the argument that connects the prohibition on adultery with the preservation of marriage is at best seriously incomplete. Before we ought to be convinced by it, we ought to have reasons for believing that marriage is a morally desirable and just social institution. And this is not quite as easy or obvious a task as it may seem to be. For the concept of marriage is, as we have seen, both a loosely structured and a complicated one. There may be all sorts of intimate, interpersonal relationships which will resemble but not be identical with the typical marriage relationship presupposed by the traditional sexual morality. There may be a number of distinguishable sexual and loving arrangements which can all legitimately claim to be called *marriages*. The prohibitions of the traditional sexual morality may be effective ways to maintain some marriages and ineffective ways to promote and preserve others. The prohibitions of the traditional sexual morality may make good psychological sense if certain psychological theories are true, and they may be purveyors of immense psychological mischief if other psychological theories are true. The prohibitions of the traditional sexual morality may seem obviously correct if sexual intimacy carries the meaning that the dominant culture has often ascribed to it, and they may seem equally bizarre when sex is viewed through the perspective of the counterculture. Irrespective of whether instrumental arguments of this sort are properly deemed moral arguments, they ought not to fully convince anyone until questions like these are answered.

Pornography, Sex, and Censorship

Fred Berger

An observer of American attitudes toward pornography faces a bewildering duality: on the one hand, we buy and read and view more of it than just about anyone else, while, on the other, we seek to suppress it as hard as anybody else. I presume that these facts do not merely reflect a judgment of social utilities, namely, that the best balance of goods is achieved by having it available, but under conditions of prohibition![1] I believe, in fact, that this state of things reflects aspects of our attitudes toward sex, and much of the current controversy has tended to obscure this fact, and to ignore important issues concerning sex and freedom to which the pornography issue points.

There is an important reason why the pornography controversy in the American context has tended to be narrowly focused. Our First Amendment prohibits government from abridging freedom of speech and press. Whatever interpretation is to be given that amendment, it is, in fact, stated in absolutist terms, and carries no mention or definition of obscenity or pornography. This difficulty is exacerbated by the fact that in the common-law background of our legal system, there is very little litigation which established clear legal definitions and doctrines. Obscenity convictions in the form we know them seem very much an invention of the 1800s, and the late 1800s at that.[2] Moreover, in our experience with obscenity litigation, we have discovered that an enormous array of serious, even important, literature and art has fallen to the censor's axe. Thus, liberals and conservatives alike have feared that the removal of pornography from the protections of the First Amendment can endanger materials the Constitution surely ought to protect. This has given the constitutional issue great urgency.

The upshot has been that much of the debate has centered on the question of definition, and, moreover, that question has been pursued with legal needs in mind.

In this paper, I want to put aside the First Amendment to ask if there are any justifiable grounds for rejecting the arguments offered for the censorship of pornography independent of First Amendment considerations. Moreover, I shall be concerned with the *censorship* of pornography, not its *regulation*. The regulation of speech often has the same effect as censorship, and that is an important danger; nevertheless, censorship and regulation differ radically in intention, and that is an important difference.[3] I should also indicate that I shall suppose that those who favor censorship (I shall refer to them as "the censors") are not *generally* in favor of censorship, and would not prohibit what they regard as "true" art or literature.

Moreover, to lend further clarity to my discussion I shall propose a definition which is useful for the purposes of this paper, and which picks out most of what is usually regarded as pornographic, and that is all I claim for it. I define pornography as art or literature which explicitly depicts sexual activity or arousal in a manner having little or no artistic or literary value.[4] (I am assuming that scientific and medical texts are a kind of literature, with appropriate criteria of acceptability.)

The definition does, I believe, make pornography a relatively objective classification, insofar as there are clear cases on both sides of the divide, and there are relatively standard literary and artistic criteria by which to judge disputed cases.[5] In this respect, I am somewhat sympathetic to the conservatives who chide those liberals who claim they are not able to recognize standard cases of pornography as such.[6]

1. OBJECTIONS TO PORNOGRAPHY: CONFLICTING VIEWS ON SEX

Generally speaking, there are three forms of argument employed by the conservatives in favor of censorship. First, they simply hold that pornography itself is immoral or evil, irrespective of ill-consequences, which may flow from it.[7] Second, they sometimes assert that, irrespective of its morality, a practice which most people in a community find abhorrent and disgusting may be rightfully suppressed. Finally, they sometimes contend that pornography promotes or leads to certain kinds of socially harmful attitudes and/or behavior.

In this paper, I wish to concentrate on this last form of argument. The proponents of the first kind of claim cannot, for the most part, meet Ronald Dworkin's challenge to specify some recognizable sense of morality according to which their claims are true.[8] Though I am aware of one form of this argument which I think *can* meet that challenge, it is dealt with obliquely in my responses to the other claims. The second form of argument has been widely debated in the literature, and I have little to add to that debate.[9] The arguments do not turn on the nature of pornography as such, and moreover, it is fairly clear that in contemporary America there is not an overwhelming abhorrence of pornography as such.[10] The last form of argument has been given new life, however, by claims based on analyses of pornographic materials as such. These new conservative arguments differ in important ways from the traditional views of the censors, and their arguments have been extremely influential. Each of the articles I shall discuss has been widely referred to; each has been reprinted a number of times, and all but one are cited in support of recent decisions in the courts.[11]

The traditional form of the claim can be labeled the "incitement to rape" theory. It holds that pornography arouses sexual desire, which seeks an outlet, often in antisocial forms such as rape. It is this version of the claim we are most familiar with, and the evidence which is available tends to refute it.[12] I shall have more to say about it later.

The conservative views I want to take up hold that the harms from pornography are somewhat long-range. These commentators maintain that the modes of sex depicted in pornography, and the manner of depiction, will result in altering our basic attitudes toward sex and to one another, so that in the end a climate of anti-social behavior will result. I have isolated four instance of such arguments in the literature of pornography.

The first claim I shall take up is put forth in an essay by George Steiner, entitled "Night Words," which has provoked considerable comment.[13] Though Steiner expressed disapproval of censorship because it is "stupid" and cannot work, his views have been taken as an argument supporting censorship. Steiner holds that pornography constitutes an invasion of privacy:

> Sexual relations are, or should be, one of the citadels of privacy, the night place where we must by allowed to gather the splintered, harried elements of our consciousness to some kind of inviolate order and repose. It is in sexual experience that a human being alone, and two human beings in that attempt at total communication which is also communion, can discover the unique bent of their identity. There we may find ourselves through imperfect striving and repeated failure, the words, the gestures, the mental images which set the blood to racing. In that dark and wonder ever renewed both the fumblings and the light must be our own.
>
> The new pornographers subvert this last, vital privacy; they do our imagining for us. They take away the words that were of the night and shout them over the rooftops, making them hollow. The images of our love-making, the stammerings we resort to in intimacy come prepackaged. . . . Natural selection tells of limbs and functions which atrophy through lack of use; the power to feel, to experience and realize the precarious uniqueness of each other's being, can also wither in a society.[14]

The second claim against pornography is made by Irving Kristol, in an article arguing for censorship. Kristol claims that pornography depersonalizes sex, reducing it to animal activity and thus debases it; that it essentially involves only the readers' or viewers' sexual arousal, and thus promotes an infantile sexuality which is dangerous to society:

> The basic psychological fact about pornography and obscenity is that it appeals to and provokes a kind of sexual regression. The sexual pleasure one gets from pornography and obscenity is autoerotic and infantile; put bluntly, it is a masturbatory exercise of the imagination, when it is not masturbation pure and simple. . . . Infantile sexuality is not only a permanent temptation for the adolescent or even the adult—it can quite easily become a permanent, self-reinforcing neurosis. It is because of an awareness of this possibility of regression toward the infantile condition, a regression which is always open to us, that all the codes of sexual conduct ever devised by the human race take such a dim view of autoerotic activities and try to discourage autoerotic fantasies. Masturbation is indeed a perfectly natural autoerotic activity. . . . And it is precisely because it is so perfectly natural that it can be so dangerous to the mature or maturing person, if it is not controlled or sublimated in some way.[15]

The danger is borne out, he thinks, in *Portnoy's Complaint*. Portnoy's sexuality is fixed in an infantile mode (he is a prolific and inventive masturbator), and he is incapable of an adult sexual relationship with a woman. The final consequences are quite dire, as Kristol concludes: "What is at stake is civilization and humanity, nothing less. The ideal is that 'everything is permitted,' as Nietzsche put it, rests on the premise of nihilism and has nihilistic implications."[16]

Professor Walter Berns, writing in the magazine *The Public Interest*, maintains that pornography breaks down the feelings of shame we associate with sex. This shame, he holds, is not merely a dictate of our society, it is natural in that it protects love, and promotes the self-restraint which is requisite for a democratic polity:

> Whereas sexual attraction brings man and woman together seeking a unity that culminates in the living being they together create, the voyeur maintains a distance; and because he maintains a distance he looks at, he does not communicate; and because he looks at he objectifies, he makes an object of that which it is natural to join; objectifying, he is incapable of uniting and is therefore incapable of love. The need to conceal voyeurism—the concealing shame—is corollary of the protective shame, the shame that impels lovers to search for privacy and for an experience protected from the profane and the eyes of the stranger. . . . Shame, both concealing and protective, protects lovers and therefore love.[17]

The upshot, as we might have suspected, is catastrophic. Under the banner of "the forgotten argument," Berns writes:

> To live together requires rules and a governing of the passions, and those who are without shame will be unruly and unreliable; having lost the ability to restrain themselves by observing the rules they collectively give themselves, they will have to be ruled by others. Tyranny is the natural and inevitable mode of government for the shameless and the self-indulgent who have carried liberty beyond any restraint, natural and conventional.[18]

Finally, Professor Ernest van den Haag, in a series of articles, has argued for censorship on the ground that pornography encourages "the pure libidinal principle," which leads to loss of empathy with others, and encourages violence and antisocial acts:

> By deindividualizing and dehumanizing sexual acts, which thus become impersonal, pornography reduces or removes the empathy and the mutual identification which restrain us from treating each other merely as objects or means. This empathy is an individual barrier to nonconsensual acts, such as rape, torture, and assaultive crimes in general. . . .

> By reducing life to varieties of sex, pornography invites us to regress to a premoral world, to return to, and to spin out, preadolescent fantasies—fantasies which reject reality and the burdens of individuation, of restraint, of tension, of conflict, of regarding others as more than objects of commitment, of thought, of consideration,

and of love. These are the burdens which become heavy and hard to avoid in adolescence. By rejecting them, at least in fantasy, a return to the pure libidinal pleasure principle is achieved. And once launched by pornography, fantasy may regress to ever more infantile fears and wishes: people, altogether dehumanized, may be tortured, mutilated, and literally devoured.[19]

My response to these claims has two parts. First, I shall try to show that they reflect certain attitudes toward sex that are rejected by many, and that pornography will be judged differently by people with different attitudes toward sex. Second, I shall try to show why the gruesome results of these writers foresee as the consequences of the state's failure to suppress dirty books and art are *not* likely consequences. Pornographic materials, *by their nature*, I shall contend, are an unlikely source or means of altering and influencing our basic attitudes toward one another.

Let us begin by noting certain features of pornography on which the conservative claims seem to hinge. First of all, by virtue of its lack of finesse, pornography is stark; it tends to remove those nuances of warmth and feeling which a more delicate approach is more apt to preserve. Second, there is some tendency of much pornography to assault our sensibilities and sense of the private, to estrange us somewhat. This is not difficult to understand, and it is not simply a result of our culture's attitudes toward sex. Sex, quite naturally, is associated with the notion of privacy because in sex we are in a vulnerable state, both emotionally and physically—we are very much in the control of our feelings and sensations, less aware of environmental factors, very much involved in and attending to our state of feeling and present activity.[20] Such vulnerability is the mark of private states—state on which we do not want others to intrude. This is reflected also in our attitudes toward grief and dying. Moreover, because we *want* to be totally taken with the activity itself, we do not usually want others present. So, we can concede that there is some truth to the conservative analyses of the nature of pornography.

These conservative arguments, however, involve and presuppose views on sex that many people reject. I think it is important to make these more explicit. Steiner, as we have seen, regards sex as a source of "inviolate order and repose," in which a sense of our identity is achieved by virtue of the private words, gestures, mental images which are shared with loved ones. (I envisage a hushed atmosphere.) For Van den Haag, sex, or more sex, properly involves the burdens of "conflict, commitment, thought, consideration and love." And Kristol has distinguished mere "animal coupling" from making love, labeling the former "debased." Professor Berns's views about the nature of sex are, perhaps, clarified in a footnote:

> It is easy to prove that shamefulness is not the only principle governing the question of what may properly be presented on the stage; shamefulness would not, for example, govern the case of a scene showing the copulating of a married couple who love each other very much. That is not intrinsically shameful—on the contrary— yet it ought not to be shown. The principle here is, I think, an aesthetic one; such a scene is dramatically weak because the response of the audience would be characterized by prurience and not by a sympathy with what the scene is intended to portray, a beautiful love.[21]

The trouble with these views is that they see sex as normal or proper only within the context of deep commitment, shared responsibility, loving concern, and as involving restraint and repression of pure pleasure. Indeed, Professor Berns's footnote not only carries the suggestion that anything but married love is shameful, but also could be uncharitably interpreted as holding that "a beautiful love" is something which holds between disembodied souls, and in no way involves sexual communion, or the sharing of physical joy and pleasure. It seems to him that if we got some sense of the pleasure the couple take in one another physically, some hint of the physical forms of their communication and sense of mutuality, that this would somehow detract from our sympathy with their "beautiful love."

Now, many in our society reject these analyses of sex, either totally or partially. I want to sketch two possible views so that we might have a sense of the wider context of attitudes within which the pornography problem should be discussed. As many liberals share the conservative attitudes toward sex and many political conservatives do not, I shall label the views I discuss as "radical" and "radical-liberal," with no further political significance to be attached to them.

The radical maintains that the entire facade of sexual attitudes in contemporary society represent sham, hypocrisy, and unnecessary forms of social control. Sexual relations are governed by the nations of duty, shame, guilt. As such, there can be no honest sexuality, since mediating all sexual relations are feelings and associations which have nothing to do with our feelings *for* one another, and, often, little to do really with our sexual natures. The conservative picture of shared communication, in an aura of intimate connection, expressive of tender love, concern, commitment which are involved in mature (preferably married) sex, is an idealized, romanticized, unreal (perhaps even infantile) depiction of what really happens in sex. The fact is that most sex is routinized, dull, unfulfilling, a source of neurosis, precisely because its practice is governed by the restraints the conservatives insist on. Those constraints dictate with *whom* one has sex, *when* one has sex, how *often* one has sex, *where* one has sex, and so on. Moreover, the web of shame and guilt which is spun around sex tends to destroy its enjoyment, and thus to stunt our sexual natures—our capacity for joy and pleasure through sex. The result is a society which is highly neurotic in its attitudes toward and practice of sex—all of which interferes with honest communication and self-realization.

The radical solution to this perceived situation is to treat sex *as* a physical act, unencumbered with romanticized notions of love. Human sex just *is* a form of animal coupling, and to make more of it is to invite dishonesty and neurosis.

It seems to me that it is *this* sort of attitude which the conservative most fears. Though the conservative claims that such an attitude will result in devaluing humans, it is not clear why. He seems to infer that because the radical is willing to treat others as sources of pleasure, without the necessity of emotional commitment, he therefore perceives them as mere *instruments* of pleasure. This, of course, does not follow, either logically or as a matter of probability. Nor have I ever met a conservative who thought that correspondingly, if people are permitted to make profits from others in business dealings, they will come to view them as mere sources of profits. The point is that it is absurd to suppose that one who no longer thinks of *sex* in terms of shame and guilt must lose the sense of shame and guilt at harming others, either through sex, or in other ways.

I do not wish to dwell on the radical position, however, because there is a more widespread view which I have labeled the "radical-liberal" view which I wish to consider. This conception accepts a large part of the radical critique, in particular the notion that guilt and shame, duty and commitment, are not necessary to fully human sex. The radical-liberal agrees that much of our ordinary sexual relations are marred by the inhibitions these impose. He or she need not, however, reject sex as an element in loving relationships, and he or she may well insist that love does engender special commitments and concern with which sex is properly entangled. But, the radical-liberal does not reject physical sex for its own sake as something debased or wicked, or shorn of human qualities. Indeed, he or she may insist that greater concern with the physical aspects of sexuality is needed to break down those emotional connections with sex which stand as barriers to its enjoyment, and as barriers to free open communication with others, and to one's development of a sense of one's own needs, desires, and life-style.

The intensity of such needs on the part of many people is, I believe, well-depicted in Erica Jong's contemporary novel, *Fear of Flying*. In the book, her heroine expresses her reaction to the attitude that a woman's identity is to be found in her relationship with a man. Female solitude is perceived as un-American and selfish. Thus, women live waiting to be half of something else, rather than being simply themselves. These American attitudes are perceived as inhibitions to the woman's self-discovery. The heroine describes her reaction:

> My response to all this was not (not yet) to have an affair and not (not yet) to hit the open road, but to evolve my fantasy of the Zipless Fuck. The zipless fuck was more than a fuck. It was a platonic ideal. Zipless because when you come together zippers fell away like rose petals, underwear blew off in one breath like dandelion fluff. Tongues intertwined and turned liquid. Your whole soul flowed out through your tongue and into the mouth of your lover.
>
> For the true, ultimate zipless A-1 fuck, it was necessary that you never get to know the man very well. I had noticed, for example, how all my infatuations dissolved as soon as I really became friends with a man, because sympathetic to his problems, listened to him *kvetch* about his wife, or ex-wives, his mother, his children. After that I would like him, perhaps even love him—but without passion. And it was passion that I wanted.[22]

She thus concludes that brevity and anonymity are requisite to the perfect zipless fuck. Finally, after describing a sample fantasy, she says:

> The incident has all the swift compression of a dream and is seemingly free of all remorse and guilt; because there is no talk of her late husband or of his fiancée; because there is no rationalizing; because there is no talk at *all*. The zipless fuck is absolutely pure. It is free of ulterior motives. There is no power game. The man is not "taking" and the woman is not "giving." no one is attempting to cuckold a husband or humiliate a wife. No one is trying to

prove anything or get anything out of anyone. The zipless fuck is the purest thing there is. And it is rarer than the unicorn.[23]

Whatever one may interpret as the book's final evaluation of the Zipless Fuck, it is clear that the fantasy is a response to the need for a different attitude toward sex.

The point is that to many people, the conservative's picture of sex, and the sorts of social relations in which he imbeds it, has served to starve them of the unique development of their personalities, or an aspect of it. The antidote they see is a freer, more open attitude toward sex, removed from what they regard as a mystique of duty and guilt and shame.

People with the attitudes of the radical-liberal, or who see themselves as impeded in their full self-realization by the traditional views on sex, may well find pornography something of no consequence, or may even find it beneficial—a means of removing from their own psyches the associations which inhibit their sexual natures. The plain fact is that pornography is used for this effect by various therapists, who have thereby aided people to more fulfilled lives for themselves, and happier, healthier relations with loved ones.[24]

Will such a concern with physical pleasure result in non-attachment, in anti-human feelings, in the loss of loving relationships? It is at least as plausible that just the opposite is the probable result, that by virtue of lessened anxiety and guilt over sex, an important sources of human communion will be enhanced. In a Kinsey-type sex survey sponsored by *Playboy*, there was demonstrated a greatly heightened freedom in sex in America, and a greater emphasis on physical enjoyment, but this has not resulted in a significant lessening of the importance accorded to emotional ties.[25] Greater concern with pleasure has been use to *enhance* those relationships. Thus, it is no accident that among the millions who have lined up to see *Deep Throat, Behind the Green Door*, and *The Devil in Miss Jones*, have been a great many loving, married couples. Indeed, that there has come to be a body of "popular pornography"—porno for the millions—holds out some small hope that our culture will eventually develop a truly erotic artistic tradition, as explicitness becomes more natural, and tastes demand more of the productions.

We have seen that the conservative position presupposes attitudes toward sex which many reject, and that the alternative attitudes are consistent both with the acceptance of pornography and the values of care and concern for others. Let us turn now to the specific points the conservatives make concerning alleged harms.

2. THE RESPONSE TO CONSERVATIVE OBJECTIONS

I want to consider first the argument concerning privacy. It was Steiner's claim that pornography takes the "words . . . of the night," and "by shouting them over the rooftops," robs us of the ability to use them or find them in private—sex becomes a matter in the public domain. Moreover, by dehumanizing the individual, people are treated as in concentration camps. As Steiner expressed it subsequent to the original publication of his essay: "Both pornography and totalitarianism seem to me to set up power relations which must necessarily violate privacy."[26]

If there is any plausibility to the first part of these claims, it must derive entirely from the metaphor of shouting the sacred night words over the rooftops. Were anyone to do such a thing with night words, day words, winter words, and so on, we would have a legitimate gripe concerning our privacy. But in what *way* is the voluntary perusal or viewing of pornography an invasion of privacy? His point *seems* to be that the constant consumption by the public of explicit sexual materials will come to make sex something "prepackaged" for us, so that we will not discover how to do it ourselves, in our own ways. This is extraordinarily implausible, and if it were true, would constitute a reason for banning all literature dealing with human feelings and emotions, and ways of relating to one another. The evidence is that greater sexual explicitness is utilized as a means for people to have greater awareness of their sexuality and its possibilities, and to assimilate the experiences of others into their own lifestyles. The capacity to do this *part* of what is involved in our being the unique individuals we are. At any rate, people who *want* the stimulation of erotic materials, who feel freer in expressing themselves through the influence of sexy art, who do not *want* an environment in which sex cannot be appreciated through explicit literature and art, will hardly be impressed with the manner in which the censor protects *their* privacy.

I want now to turn to Kristol's view that pornography is autoerotic, hence, infantile, and thus promotes a sexual regression which is a danger to civilization itself. The danger which this supposed form of infantilism poses is that it would destroy the capacity for an integral feature of mature relations (and ultimately civilized relations) if "not controlled or sublimated in some way."

Now the ultimate ground for censorship which the argument poses really has only secondary connections with the charges of autoeroticism and infantilism. Lots of things are "self-pleasuring" without being thought infantile or dangerous on that account. Consider the pleasures of the gourmet, or wine aficionado, or devotees of Turkish bath.

Kristol believes that masturbation, and pornography which is its mental form, has an appeal to us as adults, and this is dangerous. Because it *is so* attractive, it is liable to draw us away from real love, and this is why it must be headed off at the pass. The charge of infantilism, then, is only Kristol's way of making us feel bad about masturbating. By virtue of his claiming to know the rationale underlying "all the codes of sexual conduct ever devised by the human race," we are made to feel beyond the pale of civilized adult society. The argument turns, really, on the supposed dangers of an *overly* autoeroticized society, which he thinks the legalization of pornography will help produce.

In criticizing pornography on these grounds, Kristol has surely overshot his mark; for, there is nothing more masturbatory than masturbation itself. If Kristol is right, then his concern with pornography is too tepid a treatment of the danger. What the argument would show is that we must stamp out masturbation itself!

Moreover, Kristol is mistaken if he thinks that censorship of pornography will make one whit of difference to the incidence of masturbation. This is because the masturbatory imagination is perfectly limitless; it does not *need* explicit sexual stimuli. Deprived of that, it can make do with virtually anything—the impassioned kisses of film lovers, a well-filled female's sweater, or male's crotch,[27] even, we are told, a neatly displayed ankle or bare shoulder. The enormity of the problem Kristol faces is shown in the revelation of the *Playboy* survey that: "a large majority of men and women in every age group say that while they masturbate, they fantasize about having intercourse with persons they love."[28] The implications for the censor are staggering!

481

There are two further reasons why reasonable people will not take Kristol's view seriously. First, he underestimates the human capacity to assimilate varieties of sexual experience. People can enjoy pornography and intercourse without giving up one or the other.[29] Second, his entire argument grossly undervalues the appeal and attraction to us of the very thing he wants to preserve—mature sexual love which is fulfilling, rewarding, and integrated into the course of a loving relationship. Pornography may be in some sense autoerotic; it can be pleasant to be sexually stimulated. But it is rarely its own source of ultimate satisfaction; it usually stimulates to acquire further satisfactions. Indeed, this is presupposed by some of the conservative arguments. But there is no reason to assume that such satisfaction will be sought exclusively through masturbation, when a healthy sex relation is available with a loved one. I have *never* heard anyone, male or female, complain that their love life had been ruined by their partner's turn to masturbation as a result of an excess of pornography. On the other hand, I have heard couples rave about sex had after viewing pornographic films.

Still, there does seem to be a lingering problem which the conservatives will regard as not adequately dealt with in anything said thus far. They think that literature and art *can* influence people's attitudes and beliefs, and also their behavior, and they cannot understand why the liberal, who believes this to be true in other cases, is unwilling to admit this with respect to pornography. Now, I believe the liberal *can* admit the possibility of a casual role for pornography with respect to people's attitudes and behavior. Such an admission does not, however, establish a case for censorship.

It would be quite extraordinary if literary and visual materials which are capable of arousing normal men and women did not also have some tendency to arouse people already predisposed to harmful conduct, and especially people with an unstable psychological makeup. It is believable, even apart from any evidence, that such people might act from the fantasies such stimuli generate.

When the conservative is reasonable, however, he recognizes that the stimulation and consequent influence of pornography is a function not merely of the nature of the stimulus, but also of the person's background, upbringing, cultural environment, and his own genetic and personality structure and predispositions.[30] Put *this* way, the conservative has a somewhat plausible claim that pornography can sometimes be implicated as having some causal role in the etiology of social harms.

Put in its most reasonable form, however, the claim makes quite *un*reasonable the censorship of pornography. There are two primary reasons for this: (1) Pornography is not distinguishable from other materials in producing *direct* harms of this kind; it may, in fact, exert a counter-influence to other materials which are more likely to have these effects. (2) The *indirect* harms—those produced through the influence of altered attitudes and beliefs, are highly unlikely, and not of a kind a society which values freedom will allow to become the basis of suppression without strong evidence of probable causal connections. It will seek to counter such remote influences with noncoercive means.

Let us turn to the first point—that other materials which no one would dream of suppressing are as likely to produce harms. Earl Finbar Murphy, writing in the *Wayne Law Review*, has given some graphic illustrations. He begins by pointing out that "everything, every idea, is capable of being obscene if the personality perceiving it so apprehends it." He continues:

It is for this reason that books, pictures, charades, ritual, the spoken word, *can* and *do* lead directly to conduct harmful to the self indulging in it and to others. Heinrich Pommerenke, who was a rapist, abuser, and mass slayer of women in Germany, was prompted to his series of ghastly deeds by Cecil B. DeMille's *The Ten Commandments*. During the scene of the Jewish women dancing about the Golden Calf, all the doubts of his life came clear: women were the source of the world's trouble and it was his mission to both punish them for this and to execute them. Leaving the theater, he slew his first victim in a park nearby. John George Haigh, the British vampire who sucked his victims' blood through soda straws and dissolved their drained bodies in acid baths, first had his murder-inciting dreams and vampire-longings from watching the "voluptuous" procedure of—an Anglican High Church Service!

The prohibition and effective suppression of what the average consensus would regard as pornographic would not have reached these two. Haigh, who drank his own urine as well as others' blood, was educated to regard "all forms of pleasure as sinful, and the reading of newspapers undesirable." Pommerenke found any reference to sex in film, however oblique, made him feel so tense inside that, "I had to do something to a woman." Albert Fish, who has been called the most perverse case known to psychiatry, decided he had a mission to castrate small boys and offer them as human sacrifices to God as a result of reading the Old Testament. Each of these had the common quality of being beyond the reach of the conventionally pornographic. They had altered the range of the erotically stimulating, and each illustrates how impossible it is to predict what will precipitate or form psycho-neurotic conduct. . . . The scope of pornography, so far from being in any way uniform, is as wide as the peculiarities of the human psyche.[31]

These are extreme cases, but they do represent a pattern on the part of people disposed to deviant behavior, as is borne out by studies of the personalities and backgrounds of sex offenders. In their book, *Pornography and Sexual Deviance*, Michael J. Goldstein and Harold S. Kant report:

A problem that arises in studying reactions to pornography among sex offenders is that they appear to generate their own pornography from nonsexual stimuli. . . . The sex offenders deduced a significantly greater number of sexual activities from the drawing (children playing near a tree, figure petting a dog, and three people standing unrelated to each other) than did the nonsex offenders. They also were more prone to incorporate recently viewed sexual pictures into a series of gradually more explicit drawings. These results imply that the sex offender is highly receptive to sexual stimuli, and reads sexual meanings into images that would be devoid of erotic connotations for the normal person. Certainly, this finding was borne out by our study of institutionalized pedophiles (child molesters), who found the familiar suntan lotion ad showing a child, with buttocks exposed to reveal his sunburn as a dog pulls at his bathing suit, to be one of the most erotic stimuli they had encountered.[32]

Indeed, their studies seem to yield the conclusion that pornography itself does not tend to produce antisocial behavior, and that, at least in the case of rapists, other materials are more likely to do so:

> We must consider that sex offenders are highly receptive to suggestions of sexual behavior congruent with their previously formed desires and will interpret the material at hand to fit their needs. It is true, however, that while few, if any, sex offenders suggest that erotica played a role in the commission of sex crimes, stimuli expressing brutality, with or without concomitant sexual behavior, were often mentioned as disturbing, by rapists in particular. This raises the question of whether the stimulus most likely to release antisocial sexual behavior is one representing sexuality, or one representing aggression.[33]

In summarizing the evidence they gathered, and which is supported by other studies, they conclude that pornography does not seem to be a significant factor in the behavior of sex offenders. Moreover, there is some evidence that "for rapists, exposure to erotica portraying 'normal' heterosexual relations can serve to ward off antisocial sexual impulses."[34]

The point is that if we take the conservative's "harm" claim in its most plausible form, we must conclude that while pornography *can* play a causal role of this type, the evidence is that many other ordinary visual and literary depictions are more likely to do so. If we take seriously the claim that having this kind of causal role is sufficient for a case of censorship, then we must do a much greater housecleaning of our media offerings than we had imagined. The problem is that while we know where to begin—with unalloyed portrayals of violence, we can hardly know where to end.

A further serious difficulty of the conservative "harm" argument arises when we ask just what *kinds* of backgrounds and attitudes *do* predispose to the unwanted behavior. The studies of Kant and Goldstein are of help here, especially with respect to rapists:

> The rapists, who found it very difficult to talk about sex, said there was little nudity in their homes while they were growing up and that sex was never discussed. Only 18 percent of the rapists said their parents had caught them with erotic materials; in those instances the parents had become angry and had punished them. (In the control group, 37 percent reported that their parents knew they read erotic materials, but only 7 percent reported being punished. Most said their parents had been indifferent, and some said their parents had explained the materials to them—an occurrence not reported by any other group.)[35]

> For the *rapists*, the data suggest very repressive family backgrounds regarding sexuality.[36]

Moreover: "it appears that all our noncontrol groups, no matter what their ages, education, or occupations, share one common characteristic: they had little exposure to erotica when they were adolescents."[37]

These results at the very least carry the suggestion that the very attitudes toward sex which motivate the censor are part of the background and psychological formation of the personality patterns of sex offenders—backgrounds which include the repression of sexual feelings, repression of exposure to explicit sexual stimuli, an overly developed sense of shame and guilt related to sex. As we have seen, some of the censors advocate *just* this sort of model for all of society, wherein suppression of pornography is just *one* way of safeguarding society. It may well be that they are in the paradoxical position of isolating a possible evil of great extent, and then recommending and fostering a response which will help produce that very evil.[38]

There is, however, a more profound reason why the admission of a possible causal role for pornography in affecting attitudes and behavior need not support the conservative view, and why the traditional liberal may well have been right in not taking pornography seriously.

To begin with, I believe we have granted the conservatives too much in admitting that pornography depersonalizes sex. While there is a measure of truth in this claim, it is not literally true. By concentrating on physical aspects of sex, pornography does, somewhat, abstract from the web of feelings, emotions, and needs which are usually attendant on sexual experience in ordinary life. Nonetheless, people are not depicted as mere machines or animals. Indeed, where there is explicit pornographic purpose—the arousal of the reader or viewer—the end could not be accomplished were it not real fleshy people depicted. In addition, pornography almost always does have *some* human context within which sex takes place—a meeting in a bar, the bridegroom carrying his bride over the threshold, the window washer observing the inhabitant of an apartment. A study of pornography will reveal certain set patterns of such contexts; there is, indeed, a sort of orthodoxy among pornographers. And, there is an obvious reason: pornography springs from and caters to sexual fantasies. This also explains why so little context is needed; the observer quickly identifies with the scene, and is able to elaborate it in his or her own mind to whatever extent he or she wishes or feels the need. That pornography is intimately tied to fantasy—*peopled* fantasy—also accounts for one of its worst features—its tendency to treat women in conventional male chauvinist ways. Pornography, as a matter of sociological fact, has been produced by and for men with such sexual attitudes.

There are further grounds for holding that pornography does not, by its nature, dehumanize sex in the feared ways. It usually depicts people as enjoying physical activity, that is, as mutually experiencing *pleasure*. Typical pornography displays sex as something people take fun in and enjoy. There is usually little doubt the persons involved are *liking* it. All of the censors we have discussed treat *Fanny Hill* as pornographic, but it is obvious to anyone who has read the book that it absolutely resists the claim that the characters are not portrayed as real people with the usual hopes and fears, who desire not to be harmed, and desire a measure of respect as persons. The book concentrates on sex and sexual enjoyment, and *that* is why it is taken as pornographic.[39] Even sadistic pornography, it should be noted, depicts people as having enjoyment; and, it is usually sado-*masochistic* pleasures

485

which are portrayed, with a resultant equalizing of the distribution of pleasure (if not of pain). In this respect, most pornography does not portray humans as *mere* instruments of whatever ends we have. And, in this respect, most pornography does not express or evoke the genuinely immoral attitudes which a great deal of our movies, televisions, and literary materials cater to and reinforce.[40]

Indeed, much of what is found in the media *is* immoral in that it is expressive of, caters to, and fosters attitudes which *are* morally objectionable. People are treated as expendable units by international spies for whom *anything* is permitted in the name of national security; the typical laundry soap commercial treats women as idiotic house slaves; situation comedy typically portrays fathers as moronic bunglers who, nonetheless, rightfully rule their homes as dictators (albeit, benevolent ones); the various detective programs cater to the aggressive, dominating, *macho* image of male sexuality which is endemic within large portions of American society. Pornography cannot get off the hook merely by pointing out that it depicts *people*. On the other hand, most of it does not reflect or cater to attitudes as objectionable as one now finds dominating the output of television alone. And, where it does, it is not a result of the fact it is pornographic, but, rather, that it reflects conventional views widely expressed in other forms.[41]

There remains a final point to be made about the influence of pornography on attitudes. Pornography, when it does attract us, affect us, appeal to us, has a limited, narrowly focused appeal—to our sexual appetite. Such appeal tends toward short-lived enjoyments, rather than any far-reaching effects on the personality.[42] This is why pornography has essentially entertainment and recreational use and attraction; it is taken seriously by almost no one but the censors. It shows us people having sex, and that is it; we must do the rest. Serious literature and art, however, appeal to the whole person—to the entire range of his sensibilities, desires, needs, attitude patterns and beliefs and is thus far more likely to affect our ultimate behavior patterns. Even the limited reaction of sexual arousal is often better achieved through artistic technique. The conservatives deny this, but it is difficult to see on what grounds. Both in the essays of van den Haag and of Walter Berns, there is the claim that aesthetic value would detract from the purely sexual appeal of a work.[43] I can only suppose that they think all people are possessed with, and exercise, the aesthetic sensibilities of literary and art critics, and thus readily separate out and analyze devices of technique in the experiencing of a work. This assuredly is not the case. Moreover, it is hardly plausible that artistic technique should enhance and further every *other* objective of an artist, and *not* be an accessory to the end of evoking sexual arousal. Real artistic value is unobtrusive in this respect.

Of course, television pap may well influence attitudes without having significant artistic value, merely by its sheer preponderance on the airwaves. But it is not *this* sort of role we need envisage for pornography liberated from censorship. Moreover, it is not clear its influence would be worse than that of other materials which now hog the channels.

It seems to me, however, that we have yet to make the most important response to the conservative claims. For, up to now, we have treated the issue as if it were merely a matter of weighing up possible harms from pornography against possible benefits, and the likelihood of the occurrence of the harms. Unfortunately, this is the form the debate usually takes, when it is not strictly concerned with the First Amendment. But, something important is lost if we think the issue resolves into these questions. The more important issue turns on the fact that a great many *like* and *enjoy* pornography, and *want* it as part of their lives, either for its enjoyment, or for more serious psychological purposes. This fact means that censorship is an interference with the freedom and self-determination of a great many people, and it is on this ground that the conservative harm argument must ultimately be rejected. For a society which accepts freedom and self-determination as centrally significant values cannot allow interferences with freedom on such grounds as these.

To give a satisfactory argument for these claims would require another paper. Moreover, I believe (with certain reservations) this has been adequately done in Mill's *On Liberty*. As the conservatives do not regard *that* as enunciating a clear, defensible body of doctrine,[44] I cannot hope to present an entirely convincing argument here. I want at the very least, however, to outline a minimal set of claims which I think bear on the issue, and which can provide ground for further debate.

The idea of a self-determining individual involves a person developing his or her own mode of life according to the person's own needs, desires, personality, and perceptions of reality. This conception has at least three features: (1) the person's desires are (so far are possible) expressions of his or her own nature—not imposed from without; (2) the manner of the development of his or her character and the pattern of the person's life, are, in large measure, a resultant of his or her own judgment, choice, and personal experience; and (3) the person's unique capacities and potentialities have been developed, or at least tried out.[45] Now, *if* one regards this as a valuable manner of living, and freedom as of value, *both* because it is intrinsic to treating others *as* self-determining agents, *and* because it is requisite for the realization of self-determination, then I think one will accept the following propositions concerning freedom:

1. The burden of producing convincing reasons and evidence is always on the person who would interfere with people's freedom and life-styles.

2. The person who would interfere with freedom must show that the activity interfered with is likely to harm others or interfere with their rights as individuals.[46]

3. Those who would deny freedom must show that the harm or interference threatened is one from which others have a superior right to protection.

Though these propositions are subject to considerable interpretation, it seems to me that one who accepts them will, at the least, recognize that the burden of proof is not symmetric either in structure or degree. The person who would deny freedom shoulders the burden, and, moreover, he or she does not succeed merely by showing *some* harms are likely to result. Accepting freedom and self-determination as central values entails accepting some risks, in order to *be* free. We do *not* presuppose that freedom will always produce good. And, insofar as the alleged harms are indirect and remote, we are committed to employing noncoercive means to combat them. Of course, we need not interpret this in a suicidal way—allowing interference only when the harm is inevitably upon us. But, at least, we should require a strong showing of likely harms which are far from remote, and this is a burden which the censors of pornography *cannot* meet. Indeed, on this score, the conservative arguments are *many* times weaker than ones which can be made concerning many other kinds of communications, and such activities as hunting for sport, automobile racing, boxing, and so on.[47] If anyone wants a display of the extent to which our society allows recreation to instigate socially harmful attitudes and feelings, all he or she need do is sit in the stands during a hotly contested high school football or basketball game. And, of course these feelings quite often spill over into antisocial behavior.

Though I have defended pornography from criticisms based on its content or nature, I have certainly not shown that it is always unobjectionable. Insofar as it arises in a social context entirely infested with male sexism, much of it reflects the worst aspects of our society's approved conceptions of sexual relations. Too often, the scenes depicted involve male violence and aggression toward women, male dominance over women, and females as sexual servants. Moreover, there are aspects of the commercial institutions which purvey it in the market which are quite objectionable. My argument has been that this is not necessary to pornography as such; where it is true, this reflects social and sexual attitudes already fostered by other social forces. Moreover, I have maintained that by virtue of a feature which does seem to characterize pornography—its break with certain inhibiting conceptions of sexuality, pornography may well play a role in people determining for themselves the life-style which most suits them. A society which values self-determination will interfere with it only under circumstances which the censors of pornography cannot show to hold.

Of course, I have said almost nothing about the nature of the specific freedoms we incorporate in our notion of freedom of speech. It may well be that that set of rights imposes even stricter obligations on those who would suppress forms of its exercise.

NOTES

A somewhat shorter version of this paper was presented at the meeting of the Society of Philosophy and Public Affairs, held in conjunction with the Pacific Division meetings of the American Philosophical Association, March 28, 1975, in San Diego. Professor Ann Garry delivered a commentary on the paper, for which I am grateful; in several places I utilized points she made. I also wish to thank Susan Denning for her extremely diligent and helpful research assistance.

[1] This proposition is argued for by one advocate of censorship. See Irving Kristol, "Pornography, Obscenity, and the Case for Censorship," *New York Times Magazine* (March 28, 1971): 23.

[2] There are a number of brief summaries available on the development of the common-law approach to obscenity. See *The Report of the Commission on Obscenity and Pornography* (New York: Bantam, 1970), 348–54; Michael J. Goldstein and Harold S. Kant, *Pornography and Sexual Deviance* (Berkeley: University of California Press, 1973), 154–56; and an untitled essay by Charles Rembar in *Censorship: For and Against*, ed. Harold H. Hart (New York: Hart Publishing Co., 1971), 198–227. Apparently, the leading case prior to the 18th century involved Sir Charles Sedley, who, with some friends, had become drunk in a tavern, appeared naked on a balcony overlooking Covent Garden, and shouted profanities at the crowd which gathered below; then he urinated upon, and threw bottles of urine on, the bystanders.

[3] Regulation of speech is one of the most pressing problems for free speech in our contemporary, mass society, in which the control of the media is in relatively few hands, primarily concerned with the use of that media to produce profits. Moreover, the spectre of nonlegal controls, which Mill feared, is very much with us. It is surprising that so little attention has been given to the issue of the principles properly governing regulation. An indication of various forms of control utilized by government for the suppression of pornography is found by studying the development of censorship in the United States. See James C. Paul and Murray L. Schwartz, *Federal Censorship: Obscenity in the Mail* (New York: The Free Press, 1961).

[4] I regard it as a serious drawback of the definition that it rules out by *fiat*, the claim that pornography *can* be, in and of itself, significant literature. This claim is convincingly argued for by Susan Sontag in her essay "The Pornographic Imagination," reprinted in *Perspectives on Pornography*, ed. Douglas A. Hughes (New York: St. Martin's Press, 1970), 131–69; also in her book *Styles of Radical Will* (New York: Farrar, Straus & Giroux, 1966). The argument for a broader, more inclusive definition is made convincingly by Morse Peckham in *Art and Pornography* (New York: Basic Books, 1969), Chapter 1. Anyone with a serious interest in the subject of pornography will find this a most important work.

[5] It is also clear that the definition would be a disaster in the legal context, since there is so great an area of *disagreement*. Moreover, there is a tremendous danger of a secondary form of censorship, in which literary critics come to watch closely how they criticize a work lest the critique be used by the censors. That this in fact has happened is testified in an eye-opening note by the English critic Horace Judson, in *Encounter* 30 (March 1968): 57≠60. To his dismay, a critical review he wrote of Selby's *Last Exit to Brooklyn* was read into the record and used in banning that book in England.

[6] See, for example, Ernest van den Haag, writing in *Censorship: For and Against*, 158. Also, in "Is Pornography a Cause of Crime?" *Encounter* 29 (December 1967): 54.

[7] I believe that the minority report of the Presidential Commission on Obscenity and Pornography reduces to such a view, when it is not concerned specifically with possible harms. See, for example, the rationale given on 498–500 of the report, for their legislative recommendations. Sense can be made of these passages *only* on the assumption the commissioners believe pornography is itself immoral. I might also note that if one looks up "pornography" in the *Readers' Guide*, he is advised "See immoral literature and pictures."

[8] Ronald Dworkin, "Lord Devlin and the Enforcement of Morals," *Yale Law Journal* 75 (1966): 986–1005; reprinted in *Morality and the Law*, ed. Richard Wasserstrom (Belmont, Calif.: Wadsworth, 1971), 55–72.

[9] For starters, one might review the essays in Wasserstrom, *Morality and the Law*.

[10] In surveys done for the Presidential Commission, it was found that a (slim) majority of adults would not object to the availability of pornography if it could be shown it is not harmful. While hardly a declaration of adoration for pornography, this is not a demonstration of utter, overwhelming intolerance for it, either.

[11] See, for example, *Paris Adult Theatre I v. Slaton*, 431 U. S. 49 (1973).

12 Report of the Commission on Obscenity, 26–32, in which the effects are summarized. Also, Goldstein and Kant, *Pornography and Sexual Deviance*, 139–53.

13 George Steiner, "Night Words: High Pornography and Human Privacy," in *Perspectives on Pornography*, 96–108.

14 Ibid., 106–07.

15 Kristol, "Pornography, Obscenity and the Case for Censorship," 113.

16 Ibid.

17 Walter Berns, "Pornography vs. Democracy: The Case for Censorship," *The Public Interest* 22 (Winter 1971): 12.

18 Ibid., 13. Berns cites Washington, Jefferson, and Lincoln as holding that democracy requires citizens of good character and self-restraint, and he seems to think that somehow this is a "forgotten argument" against pornography.

19 Van den Haag, in *Censorship: For and Against*, 146–48.

20 The extent to which feelings of vulnerability can be involved in sex is testified to be the kinds of fears which can inhibit orgasmic response. In her book reporting on techniques she has used with non- or preorgasmic women, Dr. Lonnie Garfield Barbach reports that among the factors which inhibit these women from having orgasms is the fear of appearing ugly, of their partners being repulsed by them, of losing control, fainting, or screaming. See Lonnie Garfield Barbach, *For Yourself: The Fulfillment of Female Sexuality* (Garden City, N. J.: Doubleday, 1975), 11–12.

21 Berns, "Pornography vs. Democracy," 12.

22 Erica Jong, *Fear of Flying* (New York: Signet, 1973), 11.

23 Ibid., 14.

24 In *For Yourself*, Dr. Lonnie Garfield Barbach recommends the use of pornography for preorgasmic women seeking increased sexual responsiveness and fulfillment. See *For Yourself*, 75, 77, 85, 86. Dr. Wardell B. Pomeroy, one of Kinsey's collaborators, wrote *Playboy*, in reaction to a 1973 Supreme Court ruling on pornography:

As a psychotherapist and marriage counselor, I sometimes recommend various erotic films, books and pictures to my patients. Many of them report that erotica helps them to free them of their inhibitions and, thus, helps them function better with their spouses. Now they will have more difficulty in seeing and reading such seriously valuable material, and I am afraid I must enlarge my own library for their perusal. *Playboy* 20 (October 1973): 57.

25 This point is made at length in the report. One example: "Despite the extensive changes that the liberation has made in the feelings that most Americans have about their own bodies, about the legitimacy of maximizing sexual pleasure and about the acceptability and normality of a wide variety of techniques of foreplay and coitus, sexual liberation has not replaced the liberal-romantic concept of sex with the recreational one. The latter attitude toward sex now coexists with the former in our society, and in many a person's feeling, but the former remains the dominant ideal." *Playboy* 20 (October 1973): 204.

26 Steiner, "Night Words," in *Perspectives*, 97.

27 That women look at, and are excited by, the bulges in men's trousers is given ample testimony in Nancy Friday's book on women's sexual fantasies. See *My Secret Garden* (New York: Pocket Book, 1974), the section entitled "Women Do Look," 214–22.

28 *Playboy*, 202.

29 See, for example, *Report of the Commission on Obscenity*, 28–29; also, Goldstein and Kant, *Pornography and Sexual Deviance*, 30.

30 Van den Haag seems to recognize this point. See "Is Pornography a Cause of Crime?" in *Encounter*, 53.

31 Earl Finbar Murphy, "The Value of Pornography," *Wayne Law Review* (1964): 668–69.

32 Goldstein and Kant, *Pornography and Sexual Deviance*, 31.

33 Ibid., 108–09.

34 Ibid., 152.

35 Ibid., 143.

36 Ibid., 145.

37 Ibid., 147.

38 To compound the paradox, if being a remote cause of harms is a prima facie ground for censoring literature, then we have some evidence that the conservative arguments ought to be censored. This is *not* a view I advocate.

39 I do not appeal to its conventional format—girl meets boy, girl loses boy, girl reunites with boy in marriage.

40 Professor van den Haag holds that pornography "nearly always leads to sadistic pornography." It is not clear what this means; moreover, his argument is that this results *because* pornography dehumanizes sex. Since we have grounds for doubting this, we have grounds for doubting the alleged result. Also, since I am denying that pornography significantly dehumanizes sex, I am implicitly rejecting a further conservative argument I have not taken up, namely, that pornography is itself expressive of immoral attitudes irrespective of any further harmful effects. Since some liberals seem to be willing to silence Nazis or racists on such grounds, some conservatives think this argument will appeal to such liberals. I believe that both Kristol and van den Haag maintain this view. See also Richard Kuh, *Foolish Figleaves?* (New York: Macmillan, 1967), 280ff. A position of this sort is maintained by Susan Brownmiller in her book *Against Our Will: Men, Women and Rape* (New York: Simon and Schuster, 1975), 201. Brownmiller regards pornography as an invention designed to humiliate women. I have not responded to her arguments as she gives none. Moreover, she employs a curious "double standard." She gives great weight to law enforcement officials' opinions about pornography, but would hardly be willing to take these same persons' views on rape at face value.

41 In this paragraph I have attempted to bring to bear on the argument some points made by Professor Ann Garry, in her commentary on the paper at the meeting of the Society of Philosophy and Public Affairs in San Diego, March 18, 1975.

42 *Report of the Commission on Obscenity*, 28; and Goldstein and Kant, *Pornography and Sexual Deviance*, 151.

43 Berns, in *The Public Interest*, 12 footnote, and van den Haag, in *Perspectives*, 129.

44 See, for example Gertrude Himmelfarb's recent critical account of Mill, *On Liberty and Liberalism: The Case of John Stuart Mill* (New York: Alfred A. Knopf, 1974). It appears to me that she has not really understood Mill. Ronald Dworkin has picked out some of the most glaring of her errors in his review in *The New York Review of Books* 21 (October 31, 1974): 21.

45 I believe this is Mill's conception. See also Sharon Hill's essay, "Self-Determination and Autonomy," in *Today's Moral Problems*, ed. Richard Wasserstrom (New York: Macmillan, 1975), 171–86.

46 I want to note three points here. First, this view of freedom permits interferences for *moral* reasons; it does *not* insist on the moral neutrality of the law. It does, however, focus on the *kinds* of moral reasons allowed to count as grounds for the denial of freedom. Second, it does not rule out special legal recognition of modes of living which are central to the culture, for example, monogamous marriage. This will have indirect effects on freedom which a liberal theory would have to recognize and deal with, but it need not rule out such recognition out of hand. In addition, the notion of "harm" could be taken to include conduct or practices which are both intrusive on public consciousness, and offensive. This could provide a basis for *regulating* the sale and distribution of pornography, even if *prohibition* is not justified. Important discussion of the principles underlying the treatment of offensiveness in the law is to be found in an article by Joel Feinberg, "Harmless Immoralities and Offensive Nuisances," in *Issues in Law and Morality*, ed. Norman Care and Thomas Trelogan (Cleveland: Case Western Reserve University, 1973). Michael Bayles's commentary on that paper, also found in the same volume, is very useful. Third, valuing self-determination may entail a limited paternalism in circumstances where noninterference cannot possibly further autonomy. That it is at least possible for noninterference to promote self-determination seems to have been conceived by Mill as a presupposition for applications of his principle of liberty. This helps explain some of his "applications" at the end of the essay. Just how to incorporate limited paternalism in a liberal theory is a thorny issue. The pornography issue, however, does not appear to significantly involve that issue. A useful treatment of paternalism is in Gerald Dworkin, "Paternalism," in *Morality and the Law*, 107–26.

47 So far as I can judge, the most telling "evidence" the conservatives have thus far come up with is: (a) *some* reasonable criticism of the studies which have been done, and the interpretations which have been given them; and (b) a few, isolated, contrary studies (which are, coincidentally, open to similar or stronger objections). See especially the criticisms of Victor B. Cline in the minority report of the Presidential Commission on Obscenity and Pornography, 463–89. While I do not think the conservatives need produce ironclad scientific data demonstrating their claims we surely cannot allow the suppression of freedom when the reasons offered are poor, and

the weight of available evidence is heavily *against* those claims. The minority report (it may be Dr. Cline writing in this instance—it is unclear) asserts that the "burden of proof" is on the one who would change current law. This is an indefensible imprimatur of existing law as such; and it is absolutely inconsistent with the recognition of freedom and self-determination as important moral values. The mere *existence* of law cannot be allowed as a ground for its continued existence, if freedom is to have anything but secondary importance.

Supreme Court Decision

Bowers vs. Hardwick

CERTIORARI TO THE UNITED STATES COURT OF APPEALS FOR THE ELEVENTH CIRCUIT

No. 85–140. Argued March 31, 1986—Decided June 30, 1986

After being charged with violating the Georgia statute criminalizing sodomy by committing that act with another adult male in the bedroom of his home, respondent Hardwick (respondent) brought suit in Federal District Court, challenging the constitutionality of the statute insofar as it criminalized consensual sodomy. The court granted the defendants' motion to dismiss for failure to state a claim. The Court of Appeals reversed and remanded, holding that the Georgia statute violated respondent's fundamental rights.

Held: The Georgia statute is constitutional. Pp. 190–196.

(a) The Constitution does not confer a fundamental right upon homosexuals to engage in sodomy. None of the fundamental rights announced in this Court's prior cases involving family relationships, marriage, or procreation bear any resemblance to this right asserted in this case. And any claim that those cases stand for the proposition that any kind of private sexual conduct between consenting adults is constitutionally insulated from state proscription is unsupportable. Pp. 190–191.

(b) Against a background in which many States have criminalized sodomy and still do, to claim that a right to engage in such conduct is "deeply rooted in this Nation's history and tradition" or "implicit in the concept of ordered liberty" is, at best, facetious. Pp. 191–194.

(c) There should be great resistance to expand the reach of the Due Process Clauses to cover new fundamental rights. Otherwise, the Judiciary necessarily would take upon itself further authority to govern the country without constitutional authority. The claimed right in this case falls far short of overcoming this resistance. Pp. 194–195.

(d) The fact that homosexual conduct occurs in the privacy of the home does not affect the result. *Stanley v. Georgia*, 394 U. S. 557, distinguished. Pp. 195–196.

(e) Sodomy laws should not be invalidated on the asserted basis that majority belief that sodomy is immoral is an inadequate rationale to support the laws. P. 196. 760 F. 2d 1202, reversed.

White, J. delivered the opinion of the Court, in which Burger, C. J., and Powell, Rehnquist and O'Connor, JJ., joined. Burger, C. J., *post*, p. 196, and Powell, J., *post*, p. 197, filed concurring opinions. Blackmun, J., filed a dissenting opinion, in which Brennan, Marshall, and Stevens, JJ., joined, *post*, p. 199. Stevens, J., filed a dissenting opinion, in which Brennan and Marshall, JJ., joined, *post*, p. 214.

Michael E. Hobbs, Senior Assistant Attorney General of Georgia, argued the case for petitioner. With him on the briefs were *Michael J. Bowers*, Attorney General, *pro se*, *Marion O. Gordon*, First Assistant Attorney General, and *Daryl A. Robinson*, Senior Assistant Attorney General

Laurence H. Tribe argued the cause for respondent Hardwick. With him on the brief were *Kathleen M. Sullivan* and *Kathleen L. Wilde*.*

Justice White delivered the opinion of the Court.

In August 1982, Respondent Hardwick (hereafter respondent) was charged with violating the Georgia statute criminalizing sodomy[1] committing that act with another adult male in the bedroom of respondent's home. After a preliminary hearing, the District Attorney decided to present the matter to the grand jury unless further evidence developed.

Respondent then brought suit in the Federal District Court, challenging the constitutionality of the statute insofar as it criminalized consensual sodomy.[2] He asserted that he was a practicing homosexual, that the Georgia sodomy statute, as administered by the defendants, placed him in imminent danger of arrest, and that the statute for several reasons violates the Federal Constitution. The District Court granted the defendants' motion to dismiss for failure to state a claim, relying on *Doe* v. *Commonwealth's Attorney for the City of Richmond*, 403 F. Supp. 1199 (ED Va. 1975), which this Court summarily affirmed, 425 U. S. 901 (1976).

A divided panel of the Court of Appeals for the Eleventh Circuit reversed. 760 F. 2d 1202 (1985). The court first held that, because *Doe* was distinguishable and in any event had been undermined by later decisions, our summary affirmance in that case did not require affirmance of the District Court. Relying on our decisions in *Griswold* v. *Connecticut*, 381 U. S. 479 (1965); *Eisenstadt* v. *Baird*, 405 U. S. 438 (1972); *Stanley* v. *Georgia*, 394 U. S. 557 (1969); and *Roe* v. *Wade* 410 U. S. 113 (1973), the court went on to hold that the Georgia statute violated respondent's fundamental rights because his homosexual activity is a private and intimate association that is beyond the reach of state regulation by reason of the Ninth Amendment and the Due Process Clause of the Fourteenth Amendment. The case was remanded for trial, at which, to prevail, the State would have to prove that the statute is supported by a compelling interest and is the most narrowly drawn means of achieving that end.

Because other Courts of Appeals have arrived at judgments contrary to that of the Eleventh Circuit in this case,[3] we granted the Attorney General's petition for certiorari questioning the holding that the sodomy statute violates the fundamental rights of homosexuals. We agree with petitioner that the Court of Appeals erred, and hence reverse its judgment.[4]

This case does not require a judgment on whether laws against sodomy between consenting adults in general, or between homosexuals in particular, are wise or desirable. It raises no question about the right or propriety of state legislative decisions to repeal their laws that criminalize homosexual sodomy, or of state-court decisions invalidating those laws on state constitutional grounds.

The issue presented is whether the Federal Constitution confers a fundamental right upon homosexuals to engage in sodomy and hence invalidates the laws of the many States that still make such conduct illegal and have done so for a very long time. The case also calls for some judgment about the limits of the Court's role in carrying out its constitutional mandate.

We first register our disagreement with the Court of Appeals and with respondent that the Court's prior cases have construed the Constitution to confer a right of privacy that extends to homosexual sodomy and for all intents and purposes have decided this case. The reach of this line of cases was sketched in *Carey v. Population Services International*, 431 U. S. 678, 685 (1977). *Pierce v. Society of Sisters*, 268 U. S. 510 (1925), and *Meyer v. Nebraska*, 262 U. S. 390 (1923), were described as dealing with child rearing and education; *Prince v. Massachusetts*, 321 U. S. 158 (1944), with family relationships; *Skinner v. Oklahoma ex rel. Williamson*, 316 U.S. 535 (1942) with procreation; *Loving v. Virginia*, 388 U. S. 1 (1967), with marriage; *Griswold v. Connecticut, supra*, and *Eisenstadt v. Baird, supra*, with contraception; and *Roe v. Wade*, 410 U. S. 113 (1973), with abortion. The latter three cases were interpreted as construing the Due Process Clause of the Fourteenth Amendment to confer a fundamental individual right to decide whether or not to beget or bear a child. *Carey v. Population Services International, supra*, at 688–689.

Accepting the decisions in these cases and the above description of them, we think it evident that none of the rights announced in those cases bears any resemblance to the claimed constitutional right of homosexuals to engage in acts of sodomy that is asserted in this case. No connection between family, marriage, or procreating on the one hand and homosexual activity on the other has been demonstrated, either by the Court of Appeals or by respondent. Moreover, any claim that these cases nevertheless stand for the proposition that any kind of private sexual conduct between consenting adults is constitutionally insulated from state proscription is unsupportable. Indeed, the Court's opinion in Carey twice asserted that the privacy right, which the *Griswold* line of cases found to be one of the protections provided by the Due Process Clause, did not reach so far. 431 U. S., at 688, n. 5, 694, n. 17.

Precedent aside, however, respondent would have us announce, as the Court of Appeals did, a fundamental right to engage in homosexual sodomy. This we are quite unwilling to do. It is true that despite the language of the Due Process Clauses of the Fifth and Fourteenth Amendments, which appear to focus only on the processes by which life, liberty, or property is taken, the cases are legion in which those Clauses have been interpreted to have substantive content, subsuming rights that to a great extent are immune from federal or state regulation or proscription. Among such cases are those recognizing rights that have little or no textual support in the constitutional language. *Meyer, Prince,* and *Pierce* fall in this category, as do the privacy cases from *Griswold* to *Carey*.

Striving to assure itself and the public that announcing rights not readily identifiable in the Constitution's text involves much more than the imposition of the Justices' own choice of values on the States and the Federal Government, the Court has sought to identify the nature of the rights qualifying for heightened judicial protection. In *Palko v. Connecticut*, 302 U. S. 319, 325. 326 (1937), it was said that this category includes those fundamental liberties that are "implicit in the concept of ordered liberty," such that "neither liberty nor justice would exist if [they] were sacrificed." A different description of fundamental liberties appeared in *Moore v. East Cleveland*, 431 U. S. 494, 503 (1977) (opinion of POWELL, J.), where they are characterized as those liberties that are "deeply rooted in this Nation's history and tradition." *Id.,* at 503 (POWELL, J.). See also *Griswold v. Connecticut*, 381 U. S., at 506.

It is obvious to us that neither of these formulations would extend a fundamental right to homosexuals to engage in acts of consensual sodomy. Proscriptions against that conduct have ancient roots. See generally Survey on the Constitutional Right to Privacy in the Context of Homosexual Activity, 40 U. Miami L. Rev. 521, 525 (1986). Sodomy was a criminal offense at common law and was forbidden by the laws of the original 13 States when they ratified the Bill of Rights.[5] In 1868, when the Fourteenth Amendment was ratified, all but 5 of the 37 States in the Union had criminal sodomy laws.[6] In fact, until 1961,[7] all 50 States outlawed sodomy, and today, 24 States and the District of Columbia continue to provide criminal penalties for sodomy performed in private between consenting adults. See Survey, U. Miami L. Rev., *supra,* at 524, n. 9. Against this background, to claim that a right to engage in such conduct is "deeply rooted in this Nation's history and tradition" or "implicit in the concept of ordered liberty" is, at best, facetious.

Nor are we inclined to take a more expansive view of our authority to discover new fundamental rights imbedded in the Due Process Clause. The Court is most vulnerable and comes nearest to illegitimacy when it deals with judge-made constitutional law having little or no cognizable roots in the language or design of the Constitution. That this is so was painfully demonstrated by the face-off between the Executive and the Court in the 1930s, which resulted in the repudiation of much of the substantive gloss that the Court had placed on the Due Process Clauses of the Fifth and Fourteenth Amendments. There should be, therefore, great resistance to expand the substantive reach of those Clauses, particularly if it requires redefining the category of rights deemed to be fundamental. Otherwise, the Judiciary necessarily takes to itself further authority to govern the country without express constitutional authority. The claimed right pressed on us today falls far short of overcoming this resistance.

Respondent, however, asserts that the result should be different where the homosexual conduct occurs in the privacy of the home. He relies on *Stanley v. Georgia,* 394 U. S. 557 (1969), where the Court held that the First Amendment prevents conviction for possessing and reading obscene material in the privacy of one's home: "If the First Amendment means anything, it means that a State has no business telling a man, sitting alone in his house, what books he may read or what films he may watch." *Id.,* at 565.

Stanley did protect conduct that would not have been protected outside the home, and it partially prevented the enforcement of state obscenity laws; but the decision was firmly grounded in the First Amendment. The right pressed upon us here has no similar support in the text of the Constitution, and it does not qualify for recognition under the prevailing principles for construing the Fourteenth Amendment. Its limits are also difficult to discern. Plainly enough, otherwise illegal conduct is not always immunized whenever it occurs in the home. Victimless crimes, such as the possession and use of illegal drugs, do not escape the law where they are committed at home. *Stanley* itself recognized that its holdings offered no protection for the possession in the home of drugs, firearms, or stolen goods. *Id.*, at 568, n. 11. And if respondent's submission is limited to the voluntary sexual conduct between consenting adults, it would be difficult, except by fiat, to limit the claimed right to homosexual conduct while leaving exposed to prosecution adultery, incest, and other sexual crimes even though they are committed in the home. We are unwilling to start down that road.

Even if the conduct at issue here is not a fundamental right, respondent asserts that there must be a rational basis for the law and that there is none in this case other than the presumed belief of a majority of the electorate in Georgia that homosexual sodomy is immoral and unacceptable. This is said to be an inadequate rationale to support the law. The law, however, is constantly based on notions of morality, and if all laws representing essentially moral choices are to be invalidated under the Due Process Clause, the courts will be very busy indeed. Even respondent makes no such claim, but insists that majority sentiments about the morality of homosexuality should be declared inadequate. We do not agree, and are unpersuaded that the sodomy laws of some 25 States should be invalidated on this basis.[8]

Accordingly, the judgment of the Court of Appeals is

Reversed.

CHIEF JUSTICE BURGER, concurring.

I join the Court's opinion, but I write separately to underscore my view that in constitutional terms there is no such thing as a fundamental right to commit homosexual sodomy.

As the Court notes, *ante*, at 192, the proscriptions against sodomy have very "ancient roots." Decisions of individuals relating to homosexual conduct have been subject to state intervention throughout the history of Western civilization. Condemnation of those practices is firmly rooted in Judeo-Christian moral and ethical standards. Homosexual sodomy was a capital crime under Roman law. See Code Theod. 9.7.6; Code Just. 9.9.31. See also D. Bailey, Homosexuality and the Western Christian Tradition 70–81 (1975). During the English Reformation when powers of the ecclesiastical courts were transferred to the King's Courts, the first English statute criminalizing sodomy was passed. 25 Hen. VIII, ch. 6. Blackstone described "the infamous *crime against nature*" as an offense of "deeper malignity" than rape, a heinous act "the very mention of which is a disgrace to human nature," and "a crime not fit to be named." 4 W. Blackstone, Commentaries *215. The common law of England, including its prohibition of sodomy, became the received law of Georgia and the other Colonies. In 1816 the Georgia Legislature passed the statute at issue here, and that statute has been continuously in force in one form or another since that time. To hold that the act of homosexual sodomy is somehow protected as a fundamental right would be to cast aside millennia of moral teaching.

This is essentially not a question of personal "preferences" but rather of the legislative authority of the State. I find nothing in the Constitution depriving a State of the power to enact the statute challenged here.

JUSTICE POWELL, concurring.

I join the opinion of the Court. I agree with the Court that there is no fundamental right—*i. e.*, no substantive right under the Due Process Clause—such as that claimed by respondent Hardwick, and found to exist by the Court of Appeals. This is not to suggest, however, that respondent may not be protected by the Eighth Amendment of the Constitution. The Georgia statute at issue in this case, Ga. Code Ann. §16–6–2(1984), authorizes a court to imprison a person for up to 20 years for a single private, consensual act of sodomy. In my view, a prison sentence for such conduct—certainly a sentence of long duration—would create a serious Eighth Amendment issue. Under the Georgia statute a single act of sodomy, even in the private setting of a home, is a felony comparable in terms of the possible sentence imposed to serious felonies such as aggravated battery, §16–5–24, first-degree arson, §16–7–60, and robbery, §16–8–40.[1]

In this case, however, respondent has not been tried, much less convicted and sentenced.[2] Moreover, respondent has not raised the Eighth Amendment issue below. For these reasons this constitutional argument is not before us.

JUSTICE BLACKMUN, with whom JUSTICE BRENNAN, and JUSTICE MARSHALL, and JUDGE STEVENS join, dissenting.

This case is no more about "a fundamental right to engage in homosexual sodomy," as the Court purports to declare, *ante*, at 191, than *Stanley* v. *Georgia*, 394 U. S. 557 (1969), was about a fundamental right to watch obscene movies, or *Katz* v. *United States*, 389 U. S. 347 (1967), was about a fundamental right to place interstate bets from a telephone booth. Rather, this case is about "the most comprehensive of rights and the right most valued by civilized men," namely, "the right to be let alone." *Olmstead* v. *United States*, 277 U. S. 438, 478 (1928) (Brandeis, J., dissenting).

The statute at issue, Ga. Code Ann. §16–6–2 (1984), denies individuals the right to decide for themselves whether to engage in particular forms of private, consensual sexual activity. The Court concludes that S16–6–2 is valid essentially because "the laws of . . . many states . . . still make such conduct illegal and have done so for a very long time." *Ante*, at 190. But the fact that the moral judgments expressed by statutes like §16–6–2 may be "'natural and familiar. . . ought not to conclude our judgment upon the question whether statutes embodying them conflict with the Constitution of the United States'" *Roe* v. *Wade*, 410 U. S. 113, 117 (1973), quoting *Lochner* v. *New York*, 198 U. S. 45, 76 (1905) (Holmes, J., Dissenting). Like Justice Holmes, I believe that "[i]t is revolting to have no better reason for a rule of law than that so it was laid down in the time of Henry IV. It is still more revolting if the grounds upon which it was laid down have vanished long since, and the rule simply persists from blind imitation of the past." Holmes, The Path of the Law, 10 Harv. L. Rev. 457, 469 (1897). I believe we must analyze respondent Hardwick's claim in the light of the values that underlie the constitutional right to privacy. If that right means anything, it means that, before Georgia can prosecute its citizens for making choices about the most intimate aspects of their lives, it must do more than assert that the choice they have made is an "abominable crime not fit to be named among Christians.'" *Herring* v. *State*, 119 Ga. 709, 721, 46 S. E. 876, 882 (1904).[9]

I

In its haste to reverse the Court of Appeals and hold that the Constitution does not "confe[r] a fundamental right upon homosexuals to engage in sodomy," *ante*, at 190, the Court relegates the actual statute being challenged to a footnote and ignores the procedural posture of the case before it. A fair reading of the statute and of the complaint clearly reveals that the majority has distorted the question this case presents.

First, the Court's almost obsessive focus on homosexual activity is particularly hard to justify in light of the broad language Georgia has used. Unlike the Court, the Georgia Legislature has not proceeded on the assumption that homosexuals are so different from other citizens that their lives may be controlled in a way that would not be tolerated if it limited the choices of those other citizens. Cf. *ante*, at 188, n. 2. Rather, Georgia has provided that "[a] person commits the offense of sodomy when he performs or submits to any sexual act involving the sex organs of one person and the mouth or anus of another." Ga. Code Ann. §16–6–2(a) (1984). The sex or status of the persons who engage in the act is irrelevant as a matter of state law. In fact, to the extent I can discern a legislative purpose for Georgia's 1968 enactment of §16–6–2, that purpose seems to have been to broaden the coverage of the law to reach heterosexual as well as homosexual activity.[1] I therefore see no basis for the Court's decision to treat this case as an "as applied" challenge to §16–6–2, see *ante*, at 188, n. 2, or for Georgia's attempt, both in its brief and at oral argument, to defend §16–6–2 solely on the grounds that it prohibits homosexual activity. Michael Hardwick's standing may rest in significant part on Georgia's apparent willingness to enforce against homosexuals a law it seems not to have any desire to enforce against heterosexuals. See Tr. of Oral Arg. 4–5; cf. 760 F. 2d 1202, 1205–1206 (CA11 1985). But his claim that §16–6–2 involves an unconstitutional intrusion into his privacy and his right of intimate association does not depend in any way on his sexual orientation.

Second, I disagree with the Court's refusal to consider whether §16–6–2 runs afoul of the Eighth or Ninth Amendments or the Equal Protection Clause of the Fourteenth Amendment. *Ante*, at 196, n. 8. Respondent's complaint expressly invoked the Ninth Amendment, see App. 6, and he relied heavily before this Court on *Griswold v. Connecticut,* 381 U. S. 479, 484 (1965), which identifies that Amendment as one of the specific constitutional provisions giving "life and substance" to our understanding of privacy. See Brief for Respondent Hardwick 10–12; Tr. of Oral Arg. 33. More importantly, the procedural posture of the case requires that we affirm the Court of Appeals' judgment if there is *any* ground on which respondent may be entitled to relief. This case is before us on petitioner's motion to dismiss for failure to state a claim, Fed. Rule Civ. Proc. 12(b)(6). See App. 17. It is a well-settled principle of law that "a complaint should not be dismissed merely because a plaintiff's allegations do not support the particular legal theory he advances, for the court is under a duty to examine the complaint to determine if the allegations provide for relief on any possible theory." *Bramlet v. Wilson,* 495 F. 2d 714, 716 (CA8 1974); See *Parr v. Great Lakes Express Co.,* 484 F. 2d 767, 773 (CA7 1973); *Due v. Tallahassee Theatres, Inc.,* 333 F. 2d 630, 631, (CA5 1964); *United States v. Howell,* 318 F. 2d 162, 166 (CA9 1963); 5 C. Wright & A. Miller, Federal Practice and Procedure §1357, pp. 601–602 (1969); see also *Conley v. Gibson,* 355 U. S. 41, 45–46 (1957). Thus, even if respondent did not advance claims based on the Eighth or Ninth Amendments, or on the Equal Protection Clause, his complaint should not be dismissed if any of those provisions could entitle him to relief. I need not reach either the Eighth Amendment of the Equal

Protection Clause issues because I believe that Hardwick has stated a cognizable claim that §16–6–2 interferes with constitutionally protected interest in privacy and freedom of intimate association. But neither the Eighth Amendment nor the Equal Protection Clause is so clearly irrelevant that a claim resting on either provision should be peremptorily dismissed.[2] The Court's cramped reading of the issue before it makes for a short opinion, but it does little to make for a persuasive one.

II

"Our cases long have recognized that the Constitution embodies a promise that a certain private sphere of individual liberty will be kept largely beyond the reach of government." *Thornburgh v. American College of Obstetricians & Gynecologists*, 476 U. S. 747, 772 (1986). In construing the right to privacy, the Court has proceeded along two somewhat distinct, albeit complementary, lines. First, it has recognized a privacy interest with reference to certain *decisions* that are properly for the individual to make. E. g., *Roe v. Wade*, 410 U. S. 113 (1973); *Pierce v. Society of Sisters*, 268 U. S. 510 (1925). Second, it has recognized a privacy interest with reference to certain *places* without regard for the particular activities in which the individuals who occupy them are engaged. E. g., *United States v. Karo*, 468 U. S. 705 (1984); *Payton v. New York*, 445 U. S. 573 (1980); *Rios v. United States*, 364 U. S. 253 (1960). The case before us implicates both the decisional and the spatial aspects of the right to privacy.

A

The Court concludes today that none of our prior cases dealing with various decisions that individuals are entitled to make free of governmental interference "bears any resemblance to the claimed constitutional right of homosexuals to engage in acts of sodomy that is asserted in this case." *Ante*, at 190–191. While it is true that these cases may be characterized by their connection to protection of the family, see *Roberts v. United States Jaycees*, 468 U. S. 609, 619 (1984), the Court's conclusion that they extend no further than this boundary ignores the warning in *Moore v. East Cleveland*, 431 U. S. 494, 501 (1977) (plurality opinion), against "clos[ing] our eyes to the basic reasons why certain rights associated with the family have been accorded shelter under the Fourteenth Amendment's Due Process Clause." We protect those rights not because they contribute, in some direct and material way, to the general public welfare, but because they form so central a part of any individual's life. "[T]he concept of privacy embodies the 'moral fact that as a person belongs to himself and not others nor to society as a whole.'" *Thornburgh v. American College of Obstetricians & Gynecologists*, 476 U. S., at 777, n. 5 (STEVENS, J., concurring), quoting Fried, Correspondence, 6 Phil. & Pub. Affairs 288–289 (1977). And so we protect the decision whether to marry precisely because marriage "is an association that promotes a way of life, not causes; a harmony in living, not political faiths; a bilateral loyalty, not commercial or social projects." *Griswold v. Connecticut*, 381 U. S., at 486. We protect the decision whether to have a child because parenthood alters so dramatically an individual's self-definition, not because of demographic considerations or the Bible's command to be fruitful and multiply. Cf. *Thornburgh v. American College of Obstetricians & Gynecologists, supra*, at 777, n. 6 (STEVENS, J., concurring). And we protect the family because it contributes so powerfully to the happiness of individuals, not because of a preference for stereotypical households. Cf. *Moore* v. *East Cleveland*, 431 U. S., at 500–506 (plurality opinion). The Court recognized in *Roberts*, 468 U. S., at 619, that the "ability independently to define one's identity that is central to any concept of liberty" cannot truly be exercised in a vacuum; we all depend on the "emotional enrichment from close ties with others." *Ibid.*

Only the most willful blindness could obscure the fact that sexual intimacy is "a sensitive, key relationship of human existence, central to family life, community welfare, and the development of human personality," *Paris Adult Theatre I* v. *Slaton*, 413 U. S. 49, 63 (1973); see also *Carey* v. *Population Services International*, 431 U. S. 678, 685 (1977). The fact that individuals define themselves in a significant way through their intimate sexual relationships with others suggests, in a Nation as diverse as ours, that there may be many "right" ways of conducting those relationships, and that much of the richness of a relationship will come from the freedom an individual has to *choose* the form and nature of these intensely personal bonds. See Karst, The Freedom of Intimate Association, 89 Yale L. J. 624, 637 (1980); cf. *Eisenstadt* v. *Baird*, 405 U. S. 438, 453 (1972); *Roe* v. *Wade*, 410 U. S., at 153.

In a variety of circumstances we have recognized that a necessary corollary of giving individuals freedom to choose how to conduct their lives is acceptance of the fact that different individuals will make different choices. For example, in holding that the clearly important state interest in public education should give way to a completing claim by the Amish to the effect that extended formal schooling threatened their way of life, the Court declared: "There can be no assumption that today's majority is 'right' and the Amish and others like them are 'wrong.' A way of life that is odd or even erratic but interferes with no rights or interests of others is not to be condemned because it is different." *Wisconsin* v. *Yoder*, 406 U. S. 205, 223–224 (1972). The Court claims that its decision today merely refuses to recognize a fundamental right to engage in homosexual sodomy; what the Court really has refused to recognize is the fundamental interest all individuals have in controlling the nature of their intimate associations with others.

B

The behavior for which Hardwick faces prosecution occurred in his own home, a place to which the Fourth Amendment attaches special significance. The Court's treatment of this aspect of the case is symptomatic of its overall refusal to consider the broad principles that have informed our treatment of privacy in specific cases. just as the right to privacy is more than the mere aggregation of a number of entitlements to engage in specific behavior, so too, protecting the physical integrity of the home is more than merely a means of protecting specific activities that often take place there. Even when our understanding of the contours of the right to privacy depends on "reference to a 'place,'" *Katz* v. *United States*, 389 U. S., at 361 (Harlan, J., concurring), "the essence of a Fourth Amendment violation is "not the breaking of [a person's] doors, and the rummaging of his drawers,' but rather is "the invasion of his indefeasible right of personal security, personal liberty and private property.'" *California* v. *Ciraolo*, 476 U. S. 207, 226 (1986) (POWELL, J., dissenting), quoting *Boyd* v. *United States*, 116 U. S. 616, 630 (1886).

The Court's interpretation of the pivotal case of *Stanley v. Georgia*, 394 U. S. 557 (1969), is entirely unconvincing. *Stanley* held that Georgia's undoubted power to punish the public distribution of constitutionally unprotected, obscene material did not permit the State to punish the private possession of such material. According to the majority here, *Stanley* relied entirely on the First Amendment, and thus, it is claimed, sheds no light on cases not involving printed materials. *Ante*, at 195. But that is not what *Stanley* said. Rather, the *Stanley* Court anchored its holding in the Fourth Amendment's special protection for the individual in his home:

> "The makers of our Constitution undertook to secure conditions favorable to the pursuit of happiness. They recognized the significance of man's spiritual nature, of his feelings and of his intellect. They knew that only a part of the pain, pleasure and satisfactions of life are to be found in material things. They sought to protect Americans in their beliefs, their thoughts, their emotions and their sensations."

> These are the rights that appellant is asserting in the case before us. He is asserting the right to read or observe what he pleases—the right to satisfy his intellectual and emotional needs in the privacy of his own home. 394 U. S., at 576–565, quoting *Olmstead* v. *United States*, 227 U. S., at 478 (Brandeis, J., dissenting).

The central place that *Stanley* gives Justice Brandeis' dissent in *Olmstead*, a case raising *no* First Amendment claim, shows that *Stanley* rested as much on the Court's understanding of the Fourth Amendment as it did on the First. Indeed, in *Paris Adult Theatre I* v. *Slaton*, 413 U. S. 49 (1973), the Court suggested that reliance on the Fourth Amendment not only supported the Court's outcome in *Stanley* but actually was *necessary* to it: "If obscene material unprotected by the First Amendment in itself carried with it a 'penumbra' of constitutionally protected privacy, this Court would not have found it necessary to decide *Stanley* on the narrow basis of the 'privacy of the home,' which was hardly more than a reaffirmation that 'a man's home is his castle.'" 413 U. S., at 66. "The right of the people to be secure in their . . . houses," expressly guaranteed by the Fourth Amendment, is perhaps the most "textual" of the various constitutional provisions that inform our understanding of the right to privacy, and thus I cannot agree with the Court's statement that "[t]he right pressed upon us here has no . . . support in the text of the Constitution," *ante*, 195. Indeed, the right of an individual to conduct intimate relationships in the intimacy of his or her own home seems to me to be the heart of the Constitution's protection of privacy.

III

The Court's failure to comprehend the magnitude of the liberty interests at stake in this case leads it to slight the question whether petitioner, on behalf of the State, has justified Georgia's infringement on these interests. I believe that neither of the two general justifications for §16–6–2 that petitioner has advanced warrants dismissing respondent's challenge for failure to state a claim.

First, petitioner asserts that the acts made criminal by the statute may have serious adverse consequences for "the general public health and welfare," such as spreading communicable diseases of fostering other criminal activity. Brief for Petitioner 37. Inasmuch as this case was dismissed by the District Court on the pleadings, it is not surprising that the record before us is barren of any evidence to support petitioner's claim.[3] In light of the state of the record, I see no justification for the Court's attempt to equate the private, consensual sexual activity at issue here with the "possession in the home of drugs, firearms, or stolen goods," *ante*, at U. S., at 568, n. 11. None of the behavior so mentioned in *Stanley* can properly be viewed as "[v]ictimless," *ante*, at 195: drugs and weapons are inherently dangerous, see, *e. g., McLaughlin v. United States*, 476 U. S. 16 (1986), and for property to be "stolen," someone must have been wrongfully deprived of it. Nothing in the record before the Court provides any justification for finding the activity forbidden by §16–6–2 to be physically dangerous, either to the persons engaged in it or to others.[4]

The core of petitioner's defense of §16–6–2, however, is that respondent and others who engage in the conduct prohibited by §16–6–2 interfere with Georgia's exercise of the "'right of the Nation and of the States to maintain a decent society,'" *Paris Adult Theatre I v. Slaton*, 413 U. S., at 59–60, quoting *Jacobellis v. Ohio*, 378 U. S. 184, 199 (1964) (Warren, C. J., dissenting). Essentially, petitioner argues, and the Court agrees, that the fact that the acts described in §16–6–2 "for hundreds of years, if not thousands, have been uniformly condemned as immoral" is a sufficient reason to permit a State to ban them today. Brief for Petitioner 19; see *ante*, at 190, 192–194, 196.

I cannot agree that either the length of time a majority has held its convictions or the passions with which it defends them can withdraw legislation from this Court's scrutiny. See, *e. g., Roe v. Wade*, 410 U. S. 113 (1973); *Loving v. Virginia*, 388 U. S. 1 (1967); *Brown v. Board of Education*, 347 U. S. 483 (1954)[5] As Justice Jackson wrote so eloquently for the Court in West *Virginia Board of Education v. Barnette*, 319 U. S. 624, 641–642 (1943), "we apply the limitations of the Constitution with no fear that freedom to be intellectually and spiritually diverse or even contrary will disintegrate the social organization. . . . [F]reedom to differ is not limited to things that do not matter much. That would be a mere shadow of freedom. The test of its substance is the right to differ as to things that touc' the heart of the existing order." See also Karst, 89 Yale L. J., at 627. It is precis because the issue raised by this case touches the heart of what makes indivi' what they are that we should be especially sensitive to the rights of those choices upset the majority.

The assertion that "traditional Judeo-Christian values proscribe" th' involved, Brief for Petitioner 20, cannot provide an adequate justificat' 6-2. That certain, but by no means all, religious groups condemn th' issue gives the State no license to impose their judgments on the ' The legitimacy of secular legislation depends instead on wheth' advance some justification for its law beyond its conformity to See, *e. g., McGowan v. Maryland*, 366 U. S. 420, 429–453 (196' 449 U. S. 39 (1980). Thus, far from buttressing his case, pet' Leviticus, Romans, St. Thomas Aquinas, and sodomy's her Middle Ages undermines his suggestion that §16-6-2 re' of secular coercive power.[6] A State can no more punish

505

of religious intolerance than it can punish such behavior because of racial animus. "The Constitution cannot control such biases, but neither can it tolerate them. Private biases may be outside the reach of the law, but the law cannot, directly or indirectly, give them effect." *Palmore v. Sidoti*, 446 U. S. 429, 433 (1984). No matter how uncomfortable a certain group may make the majority of this Court, we have held that "[m]ere public intolerance or animosity cannot constitutionally justify the deprivation of a person's physical liberty." *O'Connor v. Donaldson*, 442 U. S. 563, 575 (1975). See also *Cleburne v. Cleburne Living Center, Inc.*, 473 U. S. 432 (1985); *United States Dept. of Agriculture v. Moreno*, 413 U. S. 528 534 (1973).

Nor can§§16–6–2 be justified as a morally neutral" exercise of Georgia's power to "protect the public environment, *Paris Adult Theatre I*, 413 U. S., at 68–69. Certainly, some private behavior can affect the fabric of society as a whole. Reasonable people may differ about whether particular sexual acts are moral or immoral, but "we have ample evidence for believing that people will not abandon morality, will not think any better of murder, cruelty and dishonesty, merely because some private sexual practice which they abominate is not published by the law." H. L. A. Hart, Immorality and Treason, reprinted in The Law as Literature 220, 225 (L. Blom-Cooper ed. 1961). Petitioner and the Court fail to see the difference between laws that protect public sensibilities and those that enforce private morality. Statutes banning public sexual activity are entirely consistent with protecting the individual's liberty interest in decisions concerning sexual relations: the same recognition that those decisions are intensely private which justifies protecting them from governmental interference can justify protecting individuals from unwilling exposure to the sexual activities of others. But the mere fact that intimate behavior may be punished when it takes place in public cannot dictate how States can regulate intimate behavior that occurs in intimate places. See *Paris Adult Theatre I*, 413 U. S., at 66, n. 13 ("marital intercourse on a street corner or a theater stage" can be forbidden despite the constitutional protection identified in *Griswold v. Connecticut*, 381 U. S. 479 (1965)).[7]

This case involves no real interference with the rights of others, for the mere knowledge that other individuals do not adhere to one's value system cannot be a legally cognizable interest, cf. *Diamond v. Charles*, 476 U. S. 54, 65–66 (1986), let alone an interest that can justify invading the houses, hearts, and minds of citizens who choose to live their lives differently.

IV

It took but three years for the Court to see the error in its analysis in *Minersville School District v. Gobitis*, 310 U. S. 586 (1940), and to recognize that the threat to national cohesion posed by a refusal to salute the flag was vastly outweighed by the threat to those same values posed by compelling such a salute. See *West Virginia Board of Education v. Barnette*, 319 U. S. 624 (1943). I can only hope that here, too, the Court soon will reconsider its analysis and conclude that depriving individuals of the right to choose for themselves how to conduct their intimate relationships poses a far greater threat to the values most deeply rooted in our Nation's history than tolerance of nonconformity could ever do. Because I think the Court today betrays those values, I dissent.

JUSTICE STEVENS, with whom JUSTICE BRENNAN and JUSTICE MARSHALL join, dissenting.

Like the statute that is challenged in this case,[1] the rationale of the Court opinion applies equally to the prohibited conduct regardless of whether the parties who engage in it are married or unmarried, or are of the same or different sexes.[2] Sodomy was condemned as an odious and sinful type of behavior during the formative period of the common law.[3] That condemnation was equally damning for heterosexual and homosexual sodomy.[4] Moreover, it provided no special exemption for married couples.[5] The license to cohabit and to produce legitimate offspring simply did not include any permission to engage in sexual conduct that was considered a "crime against nature."

The history of the Georgia statute before us clearly reveals this traditional prohibition of heterosexual, as well as homosexual, sodomy.[6] Indeed, at one point in the 20th century, Georgia's law was construed to permit certain sexual conduct between homosexual women even though such conduct was prohibited between heterosexuals.[7] The history of the statutes cited by the majority as proof for the proposition that sodomy is not constitutionally protected, *ante*, at 192-194, and nn. 5 and 6, similarly reveals a prohibition on heterosexual, as well as homosexual, sodomy.[8]

Because the Georgia statute expresses the traditional view that sodomy is an immoral kind of conduct regardless of the identity of the persons who engage in it, I believe that a proper analysis of its constitutionality requires consideration of two questions: First, may a State totally prohibit the described conduct by means of a neutral law applying without exception to all persons subject to its jurisdiction? If not, may the State save the statute by announcing that it will only enforce the law against homosexuals? The two questions merit separate discussion.

I

Our prior cases make two propositions abundantly clear. First, the fact that the governing majority in a State has traditionally viewed a particular practice as immoral is not a sufficient reason for upholding a law prohibiting the practice; neither history nor tradition could save a law prohibiting miscegenation from constitutional attack.[9] Second, individual decisions by married persons, concerning the intimacie' of their physical relationship, even when not intended to produce offspring, are form of "liberty" protected by the Due Process Clause of the Fourteenth Amendm' *Griswold* v. *Connecticut*, 381 U. S. 479 (1965). Moreover, this protection ey to intimate choices by unmarried as well as married persons. *Carey* v. *Pop' Services International*, 431 U. S. 678 (1977); *Eisenstadt* v. *Baird*, 405 1' (1972).

In consideration of claims of this kind, the Court has emphasized ual interest in privacy, but its decisions have actually been animat' more fundamental concern. As I wrote some years ago:

> These cases do not deal with the individual's interest in '
> from unwarranted public attention, comment, or exploi'
> deal, rather, with the individual's right to make cert'
> important decisions that will affect his own, or his f'
> The Court has referred to such decisions as implic'
> ues," as being "fundamental," and as being dig'

and tradition. The character of the Court's language in these cases brings to mind the origins of the American heritage of freedom—the abiding interest in individual liberty that makes certain state intrusions on the citizen's right to decide how he will live his own life intolerable. Guided by history, our tradition of respect for the dignity of individual choice in matters of conscience and the restrains implicit in the federal system, federal judges have accepted the responsibility for recognition and protection of these rights in appropriate cases. *Fitzgerald v. Porter Memorial Hospital,* 523 F. 2d 716, 719–720 (CA7 1975) (footnotes omitted), cert. denied, 425 U. S. 916 (1976).

Society has every right to encourage its individual members to follow particular traditions in expressing affection of one another in gratifying their personal desires. It, of course, may prohibit an individual from imposing his will on another to satisfy his own selfish interests. It also may prevent an individual from interfering with, or violating, a legally sanctioned and protected relationship, such as marriage. And it may explain the relative advantages and disadvantages of different forms of intimate expression. But when individual married couples are isolated from observation by others, the way in which they voluntarily choose to conduct their intimate relations is a matter for them—not the State—to decide.[10]. The essential "liberty" that animated the development of the law in cases like *Griswold, Eisenstadt,* and *Carey* surely embraces the right to engage in nonreproductive, sexual conduct that others may consider offensive or immoral.

Paradoxical as it may seem, our prior cases thus establish that a State may not prohibit sodomy within "the sacred precincts of marital bedrooms," *Griswold*, 381 U. S., at 485, or, indeed, between unmarried heterosexual adults. *Eisenstadt*, 405 U. S., at 453. In all events, it is perfectly clear that the State of Georgia may not totally prohibit the conduct proscribed by §16–6–2 of the Georgia Criminal Code.

II

If the Georgia statute cannot be enforced as it is written—if the conduct it seeks to prohibit is a protected form of liberty for the vast majority of Georgia's citizens—the State must assume the burden of justifying a selective application of its law. Either the persons to whom Georgia seeks to apply its statute do not have the same interest in "liberty" that others have, or there must be a reason why the State may be permitted to apply a generally applicable law to certain persons that it does not apply to others.

The first possibility is plainly unacceptable. Although the meaning of the principle that "all men are created equal" is not always clear, it surely must mean that every free citizen has the same interest in "liberty" that the members of the majority share. From the standpoint of the individual, the homosexual and the heterosexual have the same interest in deciding how he will live his own life, and, more narrowly, how he will conduct himself in his personal and voluntary associations with his companions. State intrusion into the private conduct of either is equally burdensome.

The second possibility is similarly unacceptable. A policy of selective application must be supported by a neutral and legitimate interest—something more substantial than a habitual dislike for, or ignorance about, the disfavored group. Neither the State nor the Court has identified any such interest in this case. The Court has posited as a justification for the Georgia statute "the presumed belief of a majority of the electorate in Georgia that homosexual sodomy is immoral and unacceptable." *Ante*, at 196. But the Georgia electorate has expressed no such belief—instead, its representatives enacted a law that presumably reflects the belief that *all sodomy* is immoral and unacceptable. Unless the Court is prepared to conclude that such a law is constitutional, it may not rely on the work product of the Georgia Legislature to support its holding. For the Georgia statute does not single out homosexuals as a separate class meriting special disfavored treatment.

Nor, indeed, does the Georgia prosecutor even believe that all homosexuals who violate this statute should be punished. This conclusion is evident from the fact that the respondent in this very case has formally acknowledged in his complaint and in court that he has engaged, and intends to continue to engage, in the prohibited conduct, yet the State has elected not to process criminal charges against him. As JUSTICE POWELL points out, moreover, Georgia's prohibition on private, consensual sodomy has not been enforced for decades.[11] The record of nonenforcement, in this case and in the last several decades, belies the Attorney General's representations about the importance of the State's selective application of its generally applicable law.[12]

Both the Georgia statute and the Georgia prosecutor thus completely fail to provide the Court with any support for the conclusion that homosexual sodomy, *simpliciter*, is considered unacceptable conduct in the State, and that the burden of justifying a selective application of the generally applicable law has been met.

III

The Court orders the dismissal of respondent's complaint even though the State's statute prohibits all sodomy; even though that prohibition is concededly unconstitutional with respect to heterosexuals; and even though the State's *post hoc* explanations for selective application are belied by the State's own actions. At the very least, I think it clear at this early stage of the litigation that respondent has alleged a constitutional claim sufficient to withstand a motion to dismiss.[13]

I respectfully dissent.

NOTES

*Briefs of *amici curiae* urging reversal were filed for the Catholic League for R and Civil Rights by *Steven Frederick McDowell;* for the Rutherford Instit by *W. Charles Bundren, Guy O. Farley, Jr., George M. Weaver, William B Wendell R. Bird, John W. Whitehead, Thomas O. Kotouc, and Alfred* for David Robinson, Jr., pro se.

Briefs of *amici curiae* urging affirmance were filed for the State of by *Robert Abrams,* Attorney General of New York, *Robert H* General, *Lawrence S. Kahn, Howard L. Zwickel, Charles R.* M. *Cohen,* Assistant Attorneys General, and *John Van de Kar* of California; for the American Jewish Congress by *Dani*

Cohen, and *Frederick Mandel*; for the American Psychological Association et al. by *Margaret Farrell Ewing, Donald N. Bersoff, Anne Simon, Nadine Taub* and *Herbert Semmel*; for the Association of the Bar of the City of New York by *Steven A. Rosen*; for the National Organization for Women by *John S. L. Katz*; and for the Presbyterian Church (U. S. A.) et al. by *Jeffrey O. Bramlett*.

Briefs of *amici curiae* were filed for the Lesbian Rights Project et al. by *Mary C. Dunlap*; and for the National Gay Rights Advocates et al. by *Edward P. Errante, Leonard Graff*, and *Jay Kohorn*.

[1] Georgia Code Ann. §16–6–2 (1984) provides, in pertinent part, as follows:

"(a) A person commits the offense of sodomy when he performs or submits to any sexual act involving the sex organs of one person and the mouth or anus of another. . . .

"(b) A person convicted of the offense of sodomy shall be punished by imprisonment for not less than one nor more than 20 years. . . ."

[2] John and Mary Doe were also plaintiffs in the action. They alleged that they wished to engage in sexual activity proscribed by §16–6–2 in the privacy of their home, App. 3, and that they had been "chilled and deterred from engaging in such activity by both the existence of the statute and Hardwick's arrest. *Id.*, at 5. The District Court held, however, that because they had neither sustained, nor were in immediate danger of sustaining, any direct injury from the enforcement of the statute, they did not have proper standing to maintain the action. *Id.*, at 18. The Court of Appeals affirmed the District Court's judgment dismissing the Does' claim for lack of standing, 760 F. 2d 1202, 1206–1207 (CA11 1985), and the Does do not challenge that holding in this Court.

The only claim properly before the Court, therefore, is Hardwick's challenge to the Georgia statute as applied to consensual homosexual sodomy. We express no opinion on the constitutionality of the Georgia statute as applied to other acts of sodomy.

[3] See *Baker v. Wade*, 769 F. 2d 289, rehearing denied, 774 F. 2d 1285 (CA5 1985)(en banc); *Dronenburg v. Zech*, 239 U. S. App. D. C. 229, 741 F. 2d 1388, rehearing denied, 241 U. S. App. D. C. 262, 746 F. 2d 1579 (1984).

[4] Petitioner also submits that the Court of Appeals erred in holding that the District Court was not obligated to follow our summary affirmance in *Doe*. We need not resolve this dispute, for we prefer to give plenary consideration to the merits of this case rather than rely on our earlier action in *Doe*. See *Usery v. Turner Elkhorn Mining Co.*, 428 U. S. 1, 14 (1976); *Massachusetts Board of Retirement v. Murgia*, 427 U. S. 307, 309, n. 1 (1976); *Edelman v. Jordan*, 415 U. S. 651, 671 (1974). Cf. *Hicks v. Miranda*, 422 U. S. 332, 344 (1975).

[5] Criminal sodomy laws in effect in 1791:

Connecticut: 1 Public Statute Laws of the State of Connecticut, 1808, Title LXVI, ch. 1, §2 (rev. 1672).

Delaware: 1 Laws of the State of Delaware, 1797, ch. 22 §5 (passed 1719).

Georgia had no criminal sodomy statute until 1816, but sodomy was a crime at common law, and the General Assembly adopted the common law of England as the law of Georgia in 1784. The First Laws of the State of Georgia, pt. 1, p. 290 (1981).

Maryland had no criminal sodomy statute in 1791. Maryland's Declaration of Rights, passed in 1776, however, stated that "the inhabitants of Maryland are entitled to the common law of England," and sodomy was a crime at common law. 4 W. Swindler, Sources and Documents of United States Constitutions 372 (1975).

Massachusetts: Acts and Laws passed by the General Court of Massachusetts, ch 14, Act of Mar. 3, 1785.

New Hampshire passed its first sodomy statute in 1718. Acts and Laws of New Hampshire 1680–1726, p. 141 (1978).

Sodomy was a crime at common law in New Jersey at the time of the ratification of the Bill of Rights. The State enacted its first criminal sodomy law five years later. Acts of the Twentieth General Assembly, Mar. 18, 1796, ch. DC, §7.

New York: Laws of New York, ch. 21 (passed 1787).

At the time of ratification of the Bill of Rights, North Carolina had adopted the English statute of Henry VIII outlawing sodomy. See Collection of the Statutes of the Parliament of England in Force in the State of North-Carolina, ch. 17, p. 314 (Martin ed. 1792).

Pennsylvania: Laws of the Fourteenth General Assembly of the Commonwealth of Pennsylvania, ch. CLIV, §2 (passed 1790).

Rhode Island passed its first sodomy law in 1662. The Earliest Acts and Laws of the Colony of Rhode Island and Providence Plantations 1647–1719, p. 142 (1977).

Carolina: Public Laws of the State of South Carolina, p. 49 (1790).

At the time of the ratification of the Bills of Rights, Virginia had no specific statute outlawing sodomy, but had adopted the English common law.

[6] Criminal sodomy statutes in effect in 1868:

Alabama: Ala. Rev. Code S3604 (1867).
Arizona (Terr.): howell Code, ch. 10 §48 (1865).
Arkansas: Ark. Stat., ch. 51, Art. IV, §5 (1858).
California: 1 Ca. Gen. Laws, ¶1450, §48 (1865).
Colorado (Terr.): Colo. Rev. Stat., ch. 22 §§45, 46 (1868).
Connecticut: Conn. Gen. Stat., Tit. 122, ch 7, §124 (1866).
Delaware: Del. Rev. Stat., ch. 131, §7 (1893).
Florida: Fla. Rev. Stat., div. 5, §2614 (passed 1868)(1892).
Georgia: Ga. Code SS4286, 4287, 4290 (1867).
Kingdom of Hawaii: Haw. Penal Code, ch. 13, §11 (1869).
Illinois: Ill. Rev. Stat., div. 5, §§49, 50 (1845).
Kansas (Terr.): Kan. Stat., ch. 53, §7 (1855).
Kentucky: 1 Ky. Rev. Stat., ch. 28, Art. IV, §11 (1860).
Louisiana: La. Rev. Stat., Crimes and Offences, §5 (1856).
Maine: Me. Rev. Stat., Tit. XII, ch 160, §4 (1840).
Maryland: 1 Md. Code, Art. 30, §201 (1860).
Massachusetts: Mass. Gen. Stat., ch. 165, §18 (1860).
Michigan: Mich. Rev. Stat., Tit. 30, ch. 158, §16 (1846).
Minnesota: Minn. Stat., ch. 96, §13 (1859).
Mississippi: Miss. Rev. Code, ch. 64, SLII, Art. 238 (18
Missouri: 1 Mo. Rev. Stat., ch. 50, Art. VIII, §7 (185

Montana (Terr.): Mont. Acts, Resolutions, Memorials, Criminal Practice Acts, ch. IV, §44 (1866).

Nebraska (Terr.): Neb. Rev. Stat., Crim. Code, ch. 4 §47 (1866).

Nevada (Terr.): Nev. Comp. Laws, 1861–1900, Crimes and Punishments, §45.

New Hampshire: N. H. Laws, Act. of June 19, 1812, §5 (1815).

New Jersey: N. J. Rev. Stat., Tit. 8, ch. 1, §9 (1847).

New York: 3 N. Y. Rev. Stat., pt. 4, ch. 1, Tit. 5, §20 (5th ed. 1859).

North Carolina: N. C. Rev. Code, ch. 34, §6 (1855).

Oregon: Laws of Ore., Crimes—Against Morality, etc., ch. 7, §655 (1874).

Pennsylvania: Act of Mar. 31, 1860, S32, Pub. L. 392, in 1 Digest of Statute Law of Pa. 1700–1903, p. 1011 (Purdon 1905).

Rhode Island: R. I. Gen. Stat., ch. 232, §12 (1872).

South Carolina: Act of 1712, in 2 Stat. at Large of S. C. 1682–1716, 493 (1837).

Tennessee: Tenn. Code, ch. 8, Art. 1, §4843 (1858).

Texas: Tex. Rev. Stat., Tit. 10, ch. 5, Art. 342 (1887)(passed 1860).

Vermont: Acts and Laws of the State of Vt. (1779).

Virginia: Va. Code, ch. 149, §12 (1868).

West Virginia: W. Va. Code, ch. 149, §12 (1868).

Wisconsin (Terr.): Wis. Stat. §14, p. 367 (1839).

[7] In 1961, Illinois adopted the American Law Institute's Model Penal Code, which decriminalized adult, consensual, private, sexual conduct. Criminal Code of 1961, §§11–2, 11–3, 1961 Ill. Laws, pp. 1985, 2006 (codified as amended at Ill. Rev. Stat., ch. 38 ¶¶11–2, 11–3 (1983) (repealed 1984)). See American Law Institute, Model Penal Code S213.2 (Proposed Official Draft 1962).

[8] Respondent does not defend the judgment below based on the Ninth Amendment, the Equal Protection Clause, or the Eighth Amendment.

[9] Hening's Laws of Virginia, ch. 5, §6, p. 127 (1821) (passed 1776).

[*1] Among those States that continue to make sodomy a crime, Georgia authorizes one of the longest possible sentences. See Ala. Code §13A–6–65(a)(3) (1982) (1-year maximum); Ariz. Rev. Stat. Ann. §§13–1411, 13–1412 (West Supp. 1985) (30 days); Ark. Stat. Ann. §41–1814 (1977) (1-year maximum); D. C. Code §22–2502 (1981) (10-year maximum; Fla. Stat. S800.02 (1985) (60-day maximum); Ga. Code Ann. §16–6–2 (1984) (1 to 2 years); Idaho Code §18–6605 (1979) (5-year minimum); Kan. Stat. Ann §21–3505 (Supp. 1985) (6-month maximum); Ky. Rev. Stat. §51–100 (1985) (90 days to 12 months); La. Rev. Stat. Ann. §14:89 (West 1986) (5–year maximum); Md. Ann. Code, Art. 27, §§553–554 (1982) (10-year maximum); Mich. Comp. Laws §750.158 (1968) (15-year maximum); Minn. Stat. §609.293 (1984) (1-year maximum); Miss. Code Ann. §97–29–59 (1973) (10-year maximum); Mo. Rev. Stat. §566.090 (Supp. 1984) (1-year maximum); Mont. Code Ann. §45–5–505 (1985) (10-year maximum); Nev. Rev. Stat. §201.190 (1985) (6–year maximum); N. C. Gen. Stat. §14–177 (1981) (20-year maximum); Okla. Stat., Tit. 21, §885 (1981) (10-year maximum); R. I. Gen Laws §11–10–1 (1981) (7 to 20 years); S. C. Code §16–15–120 (1985 (5-year maximum); Tenn. Code Ann. §39–2–612 (1982) (5 to 15 years); Tex. Penal Code Ann. §21.06 (1974) ($200 maximum fine); Utah Code Ann. §76–5–403 (1978) (6-month maximum); Va. Code §18.2–361 (1982) (5-year maximum).

[2] It was conceded at argument that, prior to the complaint against respondent Hardwick, there had been no reported decision involving prosecution for private homosexual sodomy under this statute for several decades. See *Thompson* v. *Aldredge*, 187 Ga. 467, 200 S. E. 799 (1930). Moreover, the State has declined to present the criminal charge against Hardwick to a grand jury, and this is a suit for declaratory judgment brought by respondents challenging the validity of the statute. The history of nonenforcement suggests the moribund character today of laws criminalizing this type of private, consensual conduct. Some 26 States have repealed similar statutes. But the constitutional validity of the Georgia statute was put in issue by respondents, and for the reasons stated by the Court, I cannot say that conduct condemned for hundreds of years has now become a fundamental right.

[1] Until 1968, Georgia defined sodomy as "the carnal knowledge and connection against the order of nature, by man with man, or in the same unnatural manner with woman." Ga. Crim. Code §26–5901 (1933). In *Thompson* v. *Aldredge*, 187 Ga. 467, 200 S. E. 799 (1939), the Georgia Supreme Court held that S26-5901 did not prohibit lesbian activity. And in *Riley* v. *Garnett*, 219 Ga. 345, 133 S. E. 2d 367 (1963), the Georgia Supreme Court held that §26–5901 did not prohibit heterosexual cunnilingus. Georgia passed the act-specific statute currently in force "perhaps in response the restrictive court decision such as *Riley*," Note, The Crimes Against Nature, 16 J. Pub. L. 159, 167, n. 47 (1967).

[2] In *Robinson* v. *California*, 370 U. S. 660 (1962), the Court held that the Eighth Amendment barred convicting a defendant due to his "status" as a narcotics addict, since that condition was "apparently an illness which may be contracted innocently or involuntarily." *Id.*, at 667. In *Powell* v. *Texas*, 392 U. S. 514 (1968), where the Court refused to extend *Robinson* to punishment of public drunkenness by a chronic alcoholic, one of the factors relied on by JUSTICE MARSHALL, in writing the plurality opinion, was that Texas had not "attempted to regulate appellant's behavior in the privacy of his own home." *Id.*, at 532. JUSTICE WHITE wrote separately:

"Analysis of this difficult case is not advanced by preoccupation with the label 'condition.' In *Robinson* the Court dealt with 'a statute which makes the "status" of narcotic addiction a criminal offense. . . .' 370 U. S., at 666. By precluding criminal conviction for such a 'status' the Court was dealing with a condition brough? about by acts remote in time from the application of the criminal sanctions c? templated, a condition which was relatively permanent in duration, and a c? tion of great magnitude and significance in terms of human behavior and va? . . If it were necessary to distinguish between 'acts' and 'conditions' for p? of the Eighth Amendment, I would adhere to the concept of 'condition' i? the opinion of *Robinson*. . . . The proper subject of inquiry is whether? acts brought about the 'condition' and whether those acts are sufficient? to the 'condition' for it to be permissible to impose penal sanctions tion.'" *Id.*, at 550–551, n. 2.

Despite historical views of homosexuality, it is no longer v? health professionals as a "disease" or disorder. See Brief for Ame? Association and American Public Health Association as *Ami?* obviously, neither is it simply a matter of deliberate personal?

orientation may well form part of the very fiber of an individual's personality. Consequently, under JUSTICE WHITE's analysis in *Powell*, the Eighth Amendment may pose a constitutional barrier to sending an individual to prison for acting on that attraction regardless of the circumstances. An individual's ability to make constitutionally protected "decisions concerning sexual relations," *Carey* v. *Population Services International*, 431 U. S. 678, 711 (1977) (POWELL, J., concurring in part and concurring in judgment), is rendered empty indeed if he or she is given no real choice but a life without any physical intimacy.

With respect to the Equal Protection Clauses's applicability to §16–6–2, I note that Georgia's exclusive stress before this Court on its interest in prosecuting homosexual activity despite the gender-neutral terms of the statute may raise serious questions of discriminatory enforcement, questions that cannot be disposed of before this Court on a motion to dismiss. See *Yick Wo* v. *Hopkins*, 118 U. S. 356, 373–374 (1886). The legislature having decided that the sex of the participants is irrelevant to the legality of the acts, I do not see why the State can defend §16–6–2 on the ground that individuals singled out for prosecution are of the same sex as their partners. Thus, under the circumstances of this case, a claim under the Equal Protection Clause may well be available without having to reach at the more controversial question whether homosexuals are a suspect class. See, *e. g., Rowland* v. *Mad River Local School District*, 470 U. S. 1009 (1985) (BRENNAN, J., dissenting from denial of certiorari); Note, The Constitutional Status of Sexual Orientation: Homosexuality as a Suspect Classification, 98 Harv. L. Rev. 1285 (1985).

3 Even if a court faced with a challenge to §16–6–2 were to apply simple rational-basis scrutiny to the statute, Georgia would be required to show an actual connection between the forbidden acts and the ill effects it seeks to prevent. The connection between the acts prohibited by §16–6–2 and the harms identified by petitioner in his brief before this Court is a subject of hot dispute, hardly amenable to dismissal under Federal Rule of Civil Procedure 12(b)(6). Compare, *e. g.* Brief for Petitioner 36–37 and Brief for David Robinson, Jr., as *Amicus Curiae* 23–28, on the one hand, with *People* v. *Onofre*, 51 N. Y. 2d 476, 489, 415 N. E. 2d 936, 941 (1980); Brief for the Attorney General of the State of New York, joined by the Attorney General of the State of California, as *Amici Curiae* 11–14; and Brief for the American Psychological Association and American Public Health Association as *Amici Curiae* 19–27, on the other.

4 Although I do not think it necessary to decide today issues that are not even remotely before us, it does seem to me that a court could find simple, analytically sound distinctions between certain private, consensual sexual conduct, on the one hand, and adultery and incest (the only two vaguely specific "sexual crimes" to which the majority points, *ante*, at 196), on the other. For example, marriage, in addition to its spiritual aspects, is a civil contract that entitles the contracting parties to a variety of governmentally provided benefits. A State might define the contractual commitment necessary to become eligible for these benefits to include a commitment of fidelity and then punish individuals for breaching that contract. Moreover, a State might conclude that adultery is likely to injure third persons, in particular, spouses and children of persons who engage in extramarital affairs. With respect to incest, a court might well agree with respondent that the nature of familial relationships renders true consent to incestuous activity sufficiently problematical that

514

a blanket prohibition of such activity is warranted. See Tr. of Oral Arg. 21–22. Notably, the Court makes no effort to explain why it has chosen to group private, consensual homosexual activity with adultery and incest rather than with private, consensual heterosexual activity by unmarried persons or, indeed, with oral or anal sex within marriage.

[5] The parallel between *Loving* and this case is almost uncanny. There, too, the State relied on a religious justification for its law. Compare 388 U. S., at 3 (quoting trial court's statement that "almighty God created the races white, black, yellow, malay and red, and he placed them on separate continents. . . . The fact that he separated the races shows that he did not intend for the races to mix"), with Brief for Petitioner 20–21 (relying on the Old and New Testaments and the writings of St. Thomas Aquinas to show that "traditional Judeo-Christian values proscribe such conduct"). There, too, defenders of the challenged statute relied heavily on the fact that when the Fourteenth Amendment was ratified, most of the States had similar prohibitions. Compare Brief for Appellee in *Loving* v. *Virginia*, O. T. 1966, No. 395, pp. 28–29, with *ante*, at 192–9194, and n. 6. There, too, at the time the case came before the Court, many of the States still had criminal statutes concerning the conduct at issue. Compare 388 U. S., at 6, n. 5 (noting that 16 States still outlawed interracial marriage), with *ante*, at 193–194 (noting that 24 States and the District of Columbia have sodomy statutes). Yet the Court held, not only that the invidious racism of Virginia's law violated the Equal Protection Clause, see 388 U. S., at 7–12, but also that the law deprived the Lovings of due process by denying them the "freedom of choice to marry" that had "long been recognized as one of the vital personal rights essential to the orderly pursuit of happiness by free men." *Id.*, at 12.

[6] The theological nature of the origin of Anglo-American antisodomy statutes is patent. It was not until 1533 that sodomy was made a secular offense in England. 25 Hen. VIII, ch. 6. Until that time, the offense was, in Sir James Stephen's words, "merely ecclesiastical." 2 J. Stephen, A History of the Criminal Law of England 429–430 (1883). Pollock and Maitland similarly observed that "[t]he crime against nature . . . was so closely connected with heresy that the vulgar had but one name for both." 2 F. Pollock & F. Maitland, The History of English Law 554 (1895). The transfer of jurisdiction over prosecutions for sodomy to the secular courts seems primarily due to the alteration of ecclesiastical jurisdiction attendant on England's break with the Roman Catholic Church, rather than to any new understanding the sovereign's interest in preventing or punishing the behavior involved. Cf. Coke, Institutes, ch. 10 (4th ed. 1797).

[7] At oral argument a suggestion appeared that, while the Fourth Amendme' cial protection of the home might prevent the State from enforcing §16-6- individuals who engage in consensual sexual activity there, that protec' not make the statute invalid. See Tr. of Oral Arg. 10-111. The sugg' the point entirely. If the law is not invalid, then the police *can* invad' enforce it, provided, of course, that they obtain a determination of from a neutral magistrate. One of the reasons for the Court's hold' *Connecticut*, 381 U. S. 479 (1965), was precisely the possibilit' of permitting searches to obtain evidence regarding the us' *Id.*, at 485-486. Permitting the kinds of searches that might'

evidence of the sexual activity banned by §16-6-2 seems no less intrusive, or repugnant. Cf. *Winston* v. *Lee*, 470 U. S. 753 (1985); *Mary Beth G.* v. *City of Chicago*, 723 F. 2d 1263, 1274 (CA7 1983).

[1] See Ga. Code Ann. §16–6–2(a)(1984)(A person commits the offense of sodomy when he performs or submits to any sexual act involving the sex organs of one person and the mouth or anus of another").

[2] The Court states that the issue presented is whether the Federal Constitution confers a fundamental right upon homosexuals to engage in sodomy and hence invalidates the laws of the many States that still make such conduct illegal and have done so for a very long time." *Ante*, at 190. In reality, however, it is the indiscriminate prohibition of sodomy, heterosexual as well as homosexual, that has been present "for a very long time." See nn. 3, 4, and 5, *infra*. Moreover, the reasoning the Court employs would provide the same support for the statute as it is written as it does for the statute as it is narrowly construed by the Court.

[3] See, *e. g.*, 1 W. Hawkins, Pleas of the Crown 9 (6th ed. 1787) (All unnatural carnal copulations, whether with man or beast, seem to come under the notion of sodomy, which was felony by the ancient common law, and punished, according to some authors, with burning; according to others, . . . with burying alive"); 4 W. Blackstone, Commentaries *215 (discussing "the infamous *crime against nature*, committed either with man or beast; a crime which ought to be strictly and impartially proved, and then as strictly and impartially punished").

[4] See 1 E. East., Pleas of the Crown 480 (1803) ("This offence, concerning which the least notice is the best, consists in a carnal knowledge committed against the order of nature by man with man, or in the same unnatural manner with woman, or by man or woman in any manner with beast"); J. Hawley & M. McGregor, The Criminal Law 287 (3d ed. 1899) ("Sodomy is the carnal knowledge against the order of nature by two persons with each other, or of a human being with a beast. . . . The offense may be committed between a man and a woman, or between two male persons, or between a man or a woman and a beast.").

[5] See J. May, The Law of Crimes §203 (2d ed. 1893) ("Sodomy, otherwise called buggery, bestiality, and the crime against nature, is the unnatural copulation of two persons with each other, or of a human being with a beast. . . . It may be committed by a man with a man, by a man with a beast, or by a woman with a beast, or by a man with a woman—his wife, in which case, if she consent, she is an accomplice").

[6] The predecessor of the current Georgia statute provided: "Sodomy is the carnal knowledge and connection against the order of nature, by man with man, or in the same unnatural manner with woman." Ga. Code, Tit. 1, Pt. 4, S4251 (1861). This prohibition of heterosexual sodomy was not purely hortatory. See, *e. g., Comer* v. *State*, 21 Ga. App. 306, 94 S. E. 314 (1917) (affirming prosecution for consensual heterosexual sodomy).

See *Thompson* v. *Aldredge*, 187 Ga. 467, 200 W. E. 799 (1939).

⁸ A review of the statutes cited by the majority discloses that, in 1791, in 1868, and today, the vast majority of sodomy statutes do not differentiate between homosexual and heterosexual sodomy.

⁹ See *Loving* v. *Virginia*, 388 U. S. 1 (1967). Interestingly, miscegenation was once treated as a crime similar to sodomy. See Hawley & McGregor, The Criminal Law, at 287 (discussing crime of sodomy); *id.*, at 288 (discussing crime of miscegenation).

¹⁰ Indeed, the Georgia Attorney General concedes that Georgia's statute would be unconstitutional if applied to a married couple. See Tr. of Oral Arg. 8 (stating that application of the statute to a married couple "would be unconstitutional" because of the "right of marital privacy as identified by the Court in Griswold"). Significantly, Georgia passed the current statute three years after the Court's decision in *Griswold*.

¹¹ *Ante*, at 198 n. 2 (POWELL, J., concurring). See also Tr. of Oral Arg. 4–5 (argument of Georgia Attorney General) (noting, in response to question about prosecution "where the activity took place in a private residence," the "last case I can recall was back in the 1930's or 40's").

¹² It is, of course, possible to argue that a statute has a purely symbolic role. Cf. *Carey* v. *Population Services International*, 431 U. S. 678, 715, n. 3 (1977) (STEVENS, J., concurring in part and concurring in judgment) ("The fact that the State admittedly has never brought a prosecution under the statute. . . is consistent with appellant's position that the purpose of the statute is merely symbolic"). Since the Georgia Attorney General does not even defend the statute as written, however, see n. 10, *supra*, the State cannot possibly rest on the notion that the statute may be defended for its symbolic message.

¹³ Indeed, at this stage, it appears that the statute indiscriminately authorizes a policy of selective prosecution that is neither limited to the class of homosexual persons nor embraces all persons in that class, but rather applies to those who may be arbitrarily selected by the prosecutor for reasons that are not revealed either in the record of this case or in the text of the statute. If that is true, although the text of the statute is clear enough, its true meaning may be "so intolerably vague that evenhanded enforcement of the law is a virtual impossibility." *Marks* v. *United States*, 430 U. S. 188, 198 (1977) (STEVENS, J., concurring in part and dissenting in part).

On Racism and Sexism

Richard A. Wasserstrom

INTRODUCTION

Racism and sexism are two central issues that engage the attention of many persons living within the United States today. But while there is relatively little disagreement about their importance as topics, there is substantial, vehement, and apparently intractable disagreement about what individuals, practices, ideas, and institutions are either racist or sexist—and for what reasons. In dispute are a number of related questions concerning how individuals ought to regard and respond to matters relating to race or sex.

There are, I think, a number of important similarities between issues of racism and issues of sexism, but there are also some significant differences. More specifically, while the same general method of analysis can usefully be employed to examine a number of the issues that arise in respect to either, the particular topics of controversy often turn out to be rather different. What I want to do in this essay is first propose a general way of looking at issues of racism and sexism, then look at several of the respects in which racism and sexism are alike and different, and then, finally, examine one somewhat neglected but fundamental issue: namely that of what a genuinely nonracist or nonsexist society might look like.

There are, I think, at least four questions that anyone interested in issues of racism and sexism ought to see as both distinct and worth asking. The first is what I call the question of the social realities. That question is concerned with rendering a correct description of the existing social arrangements, including the existing institutional structures, practices, attitudes and ideology. The second is devoted to the question of explanation. Given a correct understanding of what the existing social reality is, there can be a variety of theories to explain how things got that way and by what mechanisms they tend to be perpetuated. Much of the feminist literature, for example, is concerned with the problem of explanation. Complex and sophisticated accounts have been developed which utilize the theories of Freud, Levi-Strauss, and Marx to explain the oppression of women. Other, equally complex accounts have insisted on the non-reductionist character of the nature and causes of the present sexual arrangements. Although important in their own right, as well as for the solution of other problems, I will have virtually nothing else to say about these explanatory issues in this essay.

The third question, and one that I will concentrate upon, is what I term the question of ideals. I see it as concerned with asking: If we had the good society, if we could change the social reality so that it conformed to some vision of what a nonracist or nonsexist society would be like, what would that society's institutions, practices, and ideology be in respect to matters of racial or sexual differentiation? Here, what I find especially interesting, is the question of whether anything like the ideal that is commonly accepted as a very plausible one for a nonracist society can be as plausibly proposed for a conception of a nonsexist society.

The fourth and final question is that of instrumentalities. Once one has developed the correct account of the social realities, and the most defensible conception of what the good society would look like, and the most comprehensive theory of how the social realities came about and are maintained, then the remaining question is the instrumental one of social change. How, given all of this, does one most effectively and fairly move from the social realities to a closer approximation of the ideal? This, too, is a question with which I will not be concerned in what follows, although it is, for instance, within this context and this perspective that, it seems to me, all of the significant questions concerning the justifiability of programs of preferential treatment arise. That is to say, the way to decide whether such programs are justifiable is to determine whether they are appropriate means by which to bring about a particular, independently justifiable end.

These, then, are four central questions which any inquiry into sexism, racism or any other comparable phenomenon must distinguish and examine. I turn first to an examination of this question of the social realities and then to a consideration of ideals and the nature of a nonracist or a nonsexist society.

1. SOCIAL REALITIES

A. The Position of Blacks and Women

Methodologically, the first thing it is important to note is that to talk about social realities is to talk about a particular social and cultural context. And in our particular social and cultural context race and sex are socially very important categories. They are so in virtue of the fact that we live in a culture which has, throughout its existence, made race and sex extremely important characteristics of and for all the people living in the culture.

It is surely possible to imagine a culture in which race would be an unimportant, insignificant characteristic of individuals. In such a culture race would be largely if not exclusively a matter of superficial physiology; a matter, we might say, simply of the way one looked. And if it were, then any analysis of race and racism would necessarily assume very different dimensions from what they do in our society. In such a culture, the meaning of the term "race" would itself have to change substantially. This can be seen by the fact that in such a culture it would literally make no sense to say of a person that he or she was "passing."[1] This is something that can be said and understood in our own culture and it shows at least that to talk of race is to talk of more than the way one looks.[2]

Sometimes when people talk about what is wrong with affirmative action programs, or programs of preferential hiring, they say that what is wrong with such programs is that they take a thing as superficial as an individual's race and turn it into something important. They say that a person's race doesn't matter; other things do, such as qualifications. Whatever else may be said of statements such as these, as descriptions of the social realities they seem to be simply false. One complex but true empirical fact about our society is that the race of an individual is much more than a fact of superficial physiology. It is, instead, one of the dominant characteristics that affects both the way the individual looks at the world and the way the world looks at the individual. As I have said, that need not be the case. It may in fact be very important that we work toward a society in which that would not be the case, but it is the case now and it must be understood in any adequate and complete discussion of racism. That is why, too, it does not make much sense when people sometimes say, in talking about the fact that they are not racists, that they would not care if an individual were green and came from Mars, they would treat that individual the same way they treat people exactly like themselves. For part of *our* social and cultural history is to treat people of certain races in a certain way, and we do not have a social or cultural history of treating green people from Mars in any particular way. To put it simply, it is to misunderstand the social realities of race and racism to think of them simply as questions of how some people respond to other people whose skins are of different hues, irrespective of the social context.

I can put the point another way: Race does not function in our culture as does eye color. Eye color is an irrelevant category; nobody cares what color people's eyes are; it is not an important cultural fact; nothing turns on what eye color you have. It is important to see that race is not like that at all. And this truth affects what will and will not count as cases of racism. In our culture to be nonwhite—especially to be black[3]—is to be treated and seen to be a member of a group that is different from and inferior to the group of standard, fully developed persons, the adult white males. To be black is to be a member of what was a despised minority and what is still a disliked and oppressed one. That is simply part of the awful truth of our cultural and social history, and a significant feature of the social reality of our culture today.

We can see fairly easily that the two sexual categories, like the racial ones, are themselves in important respects products of the society. Like one's race, one's sex is not merely or even primarily a matter of physiology. To see this we need only realize that we can understand the idea of a transsexual. A transsexual is someone who would describe himself or herself as a person who is essentially a female but through some accident of nature is trapped in a male body, or a person who is essentially a male but through some accident of nature is trapped in the body of a female. His (or her) description is some kind of a shorthand way of saying that he (or she) is more comfortable with the role allocated by the culture to people who are physiologically of the opposite sex. The fact that we regard this assertion of the transsexual as intelligible seems to me to show how deep the notion of sexual identity is in our culture and how little it has to do with physiological differences between males and females. Because people do pass in the context of race and because we can understand what passing means; because people are transsexuals and because we can understand what transsexuality means, we can see that the existing social categories of both race and sex are in this sense creations of the culture.

It is even clearer in the case of sex than in the case of race that one's sexual identity is a centrally important, crucially relevant category within our culture. I think, in fact, that it is more important and more fundamental than one's race. It is evident that there are substantially different role expectations and role assignments to persons in accordance with their sexual physiology, and that the positions of the two sexes in the culture are distinct. We do have a patriarchal society in which it matters enormously whether one is a male or a female.[4] By almost all important measures it is more advantageous to be a male rather than a female.

Women and men are socialized differently. We learn very early and forcefully that we are either males or females and that much turns upon which sex we are. The evidence seems to be overwhelming and well-documented that sex roles play a fundamental role in the way persons think of themselves and the world—to say nothing of the way the world thinks of them. Men and women are taught to see men as independent, capable, and powerful: men and women are taught to see women as dependent, limited in abilities, and passive. A woman's success or failure in life is defined largely in terms of her activities within the family. It is important for her that she marry, and when she does she is expected to take responsibility for the wifely tasks: the housework, the child care, and the general emotional welfare of the husband and children.[5] Her status in society is determined in substantial measure by the vocation and success of her husband.[6] Economically, women are substantially worse off than men. They do not receive any pay for the work that is done in the home. As members of the labor force their wages are significantly lower than those paid to men, even when they are engaged in similar work and have similar educational backgrounds.[7] The higher the prestige or the salary of the job, the less present women are in the labor force. And, of course, women are conspicuously absent from most positions of authority and power in the major economic and political institutions of our society.

As is true for race, it is also a significant social fact that to be a female is to be an entity or creature viewed as different from the standard, fully developed person who is male as well as white. But to be female, as opposed to being black, is not to be conceived of as simply a creature of less worth. That is one important thing that differentiates sexism from racism: The ideology of sex, as opposed to the ideology of race, is a good deal more complex and confusing. Women are both put on a pedestal and deemed not fully developed persons. They are idealized; their approval and admiration is sought; and they are at the same time regarded as less competent than men and less able to live fully developed, fully human lives—for that is what men do.[8] At best, they are viewed and treated as having properties and attributes that are valuable and admirable for humans of this type. For example, they may be viewed as especially empathetic, intuitive, loving, and nurturing. At best, these qualities are viewed as good properties for women to have, and, provided they are properly muted, are sometimes valued within the more well-rounded male. Because the sexual ideology is complex, confusing, and variable, it does not unambiguously proclaim the lesser value attached to being female rather than being male, nor does it unambiguously correspond to the existing social realities. For these, among other reasons, sexism could plausibly be regarded as a deeper phenomenon than racism. It is more deeply embedded in the culture, and thus less visible. Being harder to detect, it is harder to eradicate. Moreover, it is less unequivocally regarded as unjust and unjustifiable. That is to say, there is less agreement within the dominant ideology that sexism even implies an unjustifiable practice or attitude. Hence, many persons announce, without regret or embarrassment, that they are sexists or male chauvinists; very few announce openly that they are racists.[9] For all of these reasons sexism may be a more insidious evil than racism, but there is little merit in trying to decide between two seriously objectionable practices which one is worse.

While I do not think I have made very controversial claims about either our cultural history or our present-day culture, I am aware of the fact that they have been stated very imprecisely and that I have offered little evidence to substantiate them. In a crude way we ought to be able both to understand the claims and to see that they are correct if we reflect seriously and critically upon our own cultural institutions, attitudes, and practices. But in a more refined, theoretical way, I am imagining that a more precise and correct description of the social reality in respect to race and sex would be derivable from a composite, descriptive account of our society which utilized the relevant social sciences to examine such things as the society's institutions, practices, attitudes and ideology[10]—if the social sciences could be value-free and unaffected in outlook or approach by the fact that they, themselves, are largely composed of persons who are white and male.[11]

Viewed from the perspective of social reality it should be clear, too, that racism and sexism should not be thought of as phenomena that consist simply in taking a person's race or sex into account, or even simply in taking a person's race or sex into account in an arbitrary way. Instead, racism and sexism consist in taking race and sex into account in a certain way, in the context of a specific set of institutional arrangements and a specific ideology which together create and maintain a specific *system* of institutions, role assignments, beliefs and attitudes. That system is one, and has been one, in which political, economic, and social power and advantage is concentrated in the hands of those who are white and male.

The evils of such systems are, however, not all of a piece. For instance, sometimes people say that what was wrong with the system of racial discrimination in the South was that it took an irrelevant characteristic, namely race, and used it systematically to allocate social benefits and burdens of various sorts. The defect was the irrelevance of the characteristic used, i.e., race, for that meant that individuals ended up being treated in a manner that was arbitrary and capricious.

I do not think that was the central flaw at all—at least of much of the system. Take, for instance, the most hideous of the practices, human slavery. The primary thing that was wrong with the institution was not that the particular individuals who were assigned the place of slaves were assigned there arbitrarily because the assignment was made in virtue of an irrelevant characteristic, i.e., their race. Rather, it seems to me clear that the primary thing that was and is wrong with slavery is the practice itself—the fact of some individuals being able to own other individuals and all that goes with that practice. It would not matter by what criterion individuals were assigned; human slavery would still be wrong. And the same can be said for many of the other discrete practices and institutions that comprised the system of racial discrimination even after human slavery was abolished. The practices were unjustifiable—they were oppressive—and they would have been so no matter how the assignment of victims had been made. What made it worse, still, was that the institutions and ideology all interlocked to create a system of human oppression whose effects on those living under it were as devastating as they were unjustifiable.

Some features of the system of sexual oppression are like this and others are different. For example, if it is true that women are socialized to play the role of servers of men and if they are in general assigned that position in the society, what is objectionable about that practice is the practice itself. It is not that women are being arbitrarily or capriciously assigned the social role of server, but rather that such a role is at the least *prima facie* unjustifiable as a role in a decent society. As a result, the assignment on any basis of individuals to such a role is objectionable.

The assignment of women to primary responsibility for child rearing and household maintenance may be different: it may be objectionable on grounds of unfairness of another sort. That is to say, if we assume that these are important but undesirable aspects of social existence—if we assume that they are, relatively speaking, unsatisfying and unfulfilling ways to spend one's time, then the objection is that women are unduly and unfairly allocated a disproportionate share of unpleasant, unrewarding work. Here the objection, if it is proper, is to the degree to which the necessary burden is placed to a greater degree than is fair on women, rather than shared equally by persons of both sexes.

Even here, though, it is important to see that the essential feature of both racism and sexism consists in the fact that race or sex is taken into account in the context of a specific set of arrangements and a specific ideology which is systemic and which treats and regards persons who are nonwhite or female in a comprehensive, systemic way. Whether it would be capricious to take either a person's race or a person's sex into account in good society, because race and sex were genuinely irrelevant characteristics, is a question that can only be answered after we have a clearer idea of what the good society would look like in respect either to race or sex.

Another way to bring this out, as well as to show another respect in which racism and sexism are different, concerns segregated bathrooms. We know, for instance, that it is wrong, clearly racist, to have racially segregated bathrooms. There is, however, no common conception that it is wrong, clearly sexist, to have sexually segregated ones. How is this to be accounted for? The answer to the question of why it was and is racist to have racially segregated bathrooms can be discovered through a consideration of the role that this practice played in that system of racial segregation we had in the United States—from, in other words, an examination of the social realities. For racially segregated bathrooms were an important part of that system. And that system had an ideology; it was complex and perhaps not even wholly internally consistent. A significant feature of the ideology was that blacks were not only less than fully developed humans, but that they were also dirty and impure. They were the sorts of creatures who could and would contaminate white persons if they came into certain kinds of contact with them—in the bathroom, at the dinner table, or in bed, although it was appropriate for blacks to prepare and handle food, and even to nurse white infants. This ideology was intimately related to a set of institutional arrangements and power relationships in which whites were politically, economically, and socially dominant. The ideology supported the institutional arrangements, and the institutional arrangements reinforced the ideology. The net effect was that racially segregated bathrooms were both a part of the institutional mechanism of oppression and an instantiation of this ideology of racial taint. The point of maintaining racially segregated bathrooms was not in any simple or direct sense to keep both whites and blacks from using each other's bathrooms; it was to make sure that blacks would not contaminate bathrooms used by whites. The practice also taught both whites and blacks that certain kinds of contacts were forbidden because whites would be degraded by the contact with the blacks.

The failure to understand the character of these institutions of racial oppression is what makes some of the judicial reasoning about racial discrimination against blacks so confusing and unsatisfactory. At times when the courts have tried to explain what is constitutionally wrong with racial segregation, they have said that the problem is that race is an inherently suspect category. What they have meant by this, or have been thought to mean, is that any differentiation among human beings on the basis of racial identity is inherently unjust, because arbitrary, and therefore any particular case of racial differentiation must be shown to be fully rational and justifiable. But the primary evil of the various schemes of racial segregation against blacks that the courts were being called upon to assess was not that such schemes were a capricious and irrational way of allocating public benefits and burdens. That might well be the primary wrong with racial segregation if we lived in a society very different from the one we have. The primary evil of these schemes was instead that they designedly and effectively marked off all black persons as degraded, dirty, less than fully developed persons who were unfit for full membership in the political, social, and moral community.

It is worth observing that the social reality of sexually segregated bathrooms appears to be different. The idea behind such sexual segregation seems to have more to do with the mutual undesirability of the use by both sexes of the same bathroom at the same time. There is no notion of the possibility of contamination; or even directly of inferiority and superiority. What seems to be involved—at least in part— is the importance of inculcating and preserving a sense of secrecy concerning the genitalia of the opposite sex. What seems to be at stake is the maintenance of that same sense of mystery or forbiddenness about the other sex's sexuality which is fostered by the general prohibition upon public nudity and the unashamed viewing of genitalia.

Sexually segregated bathrooms simply play a different role in our culture than did racially segregated ones. But that is not to say that the role they play is either benign or unobjectionable—only that it is different. Sexually segregated bathrooms may well be objectionable, but here too, the objection is not on the ground that they are *prima facie* capricious or arbitrary. Rather, the case against them now would rest on the ground that they are, perhaps, one small part of that scheme of sex-role differentiation which uses the mystery of sexual anatomy, among other things, to maintain the primacy of heterosexual sexual attraction central to that version of the patriarchal system of power relationships we have today.[12] Once again, whether sexually segregated bathrooms would be objectionable, because irrational, in the good society depends once again upon what the good society would look like in respect to sexual differentiation.

B. Types of Racism or Sexism

Another recurring question that can profitably be examined within the perspective of social realities is whether the legal system is racist or sexist. Indeed, it seems to me essential that the social realities of the relationships and ideologies concerning race and sex be kept in mind whenever one is trying to assess claims that are made about the racism or sexism of important institutions such as the legal system. It is also of considerable importance in assessing such claims to understand that even within the perspective of social reality, racism or sexism can manifest itself, or be understood, in different ways. That these are both important points can be seen through a brief examination of the different, distinctive ways in which our own legal system might plausibly be understood to be racist. The mode of analysis I propose serves as well, I believe, for an analogous analysis of the sexism of the legal system, although I do not undertake the latter analysis in this paper.

The first type of racism is the simplest and the least controversial. It is the case of overt racism, in which a law or a legal institution expressly takes into account the race of individuals in order to assign benefits and burdens in such a way as to bestow an unjustified benefit upon a member or members of the racially dominant group or an unjustified burden upon members of the racial groups that are oppressed. We no longer have many, if any, cases of overt racism in our legal system today, although we certainly had a number in the past. Indeed, the historical system of formal, racial segregation was both buttressed by, and constituted of, a number of overtly racist laws and practices. At different times in our history, racism included laws and practices which dealt with such things as the exclusion of non-whites from the franchise, from decent primary and secondary schools and most professional schools, and the prohibition against interracial marriages.

The second type of racism is very similar to overt racism. It is covert, but intentional, racism, in which a law or a legal institution has as its purpose the allocation of benefits and burdens. One particularly good historical example involves the use of grandfather clauses which were inserted in statutes governing voter registration in a number of states after passage of the Fifteenth Amendment.[13]

Covert racism within the law is not entirely a thing of the past. Many instances of de facto school segregation in the North and West are cases of covert racism. At times certain school boards—virtually all of which are overwhelmingly white in composition—quite consciously try to maintain exclusively or predominantly white schools within a school district. The classifications such as school boards use are not ostensibly racial, but are based upon the places of residence of the affected students. These categories provide the opportunity for covert racism in engineering the racial composition of individual schools within the board's jurisdiction.

What has been said so far is surely neither novel nor controversial. What is interesting, however, is that a number of persons appear to believe that as long as the legal system is not overtly or covertly racist, there is nothing to the charge that it is racist. So, for example, Mr. Justice Powell said in a speech a few years ago:

> It is of course true that we have witnessed racial injustice in the past, as has every other country with significant racial diversity. But no one can fairly question the present national commitment to full equality and justice. Racial discrimination, by state action, is now proscribed by laws and court decisions which protect civil liberties more broadly than in any other country. But laws alone are not enough. Racial prejudice in the hearts of men cannot be legislated out of existence; it will pass only in time, and as human beings of all races learn in humility to respect each other—a process not furthered by recrimination or undue self-accusation.[14]

I believe it is a mistake to think about the problem of racism in terms of overt or covert racial discrimination by state action, which is now banished, and racial prejudice, which still lingers, but only in the hearts of persons. For there is another, more subtle kind of racism—unintentional, perhaps, but effective—which is as much a part of the legal system as are overt and covert racist laws and practices. It is what some critics of the legal system probably mean when they talk about the "institutional racism" of the legal system.[15]

There are at least two kinds of institutional racism. The first is the racism of sub-institutions within the legal system such as the jury, or the racism of practices built upon or countenanced by the law. These institutions and practices very often, if not always, reflect in important and serious ways a variety of dominant values in the operation of what is apparently a neutral legal mechanism. The result is the maintenance and reenforcement of a system in which whites dominate over non-whites. One relatively uninteresting (because familiar) example is the case of de facto school segregation. As observed above, some cases of de facto segregation are examples of covert racism. But even in school districts where there is no intention to divide pupils on grounds of race so as to maintain existing power relationships along racial lines, school attendance zones are utilized which are based on the geographical location of the pupil. Because it is a fact in our culture that there is racial discrimination against black people in respect to housing, it is also a fact that any geographical allocation of pupils—unless one pays a lot of attention to housing patterns—will have the effect of continuing to segregate minority pupils very largely on grounds of race. It is perfectly appropriate to regard this effect as a case of racism in public education.

A less familiar, and hence perhaps more instructive, example concerns the question of the importance of having blacks on juries, especially in cases in which blacks are criminal defendants. The orthodox view within the law is that it is unfair to try a black defendant before an all-white jury if blacks were overtly or covertly excluded from the jury rolls used to provide the jury panel, but not otherwise. One reason that is often given is that the systematic exclusion of blacks increases too greatly the chance of racial prejudice operating against the black defendant. The problem with this way of thinking about things is that it does not make much sense. If whites are apt to be prejudiced against blacks, then an all-white jury is just as apt to be prejudiced against a black defendant, irrespective of whether blacks were systematically excluded from the jury rolls. I suspect that the rule has developed in the way it was because the courts think that many, if not most, whites are not prejudiced against blacks, unless, perhaps, they happen to live in an area where there is systematic exclusion of blacks from the jury rolls. Hence prejudice is the chief worry, and a sectional, if not historical, one at that.

White prejudice against blacks is, I think, a problem, and not just a sectional one. However, the existence or nonexistence of prejudice against blacks does not go to the heart of the matter. It is a worry, but it is not the chief worry. A black person may not be able to get a fair trial from an all-white jury even though the jurors are disposed to be fair and impartial, because the whites may unknowingly bring into the jury box a view about a variety of matters which affects in very fundamental respects the way they will look at and assess the facts. Thus, for example, it is not, I suspect, part of the experience of most white persons who serve on juries that police often lie in their dealings with people and the courts. Indeed, it is probably not part of their experience that persons lie about serious matters except on rare occasions. And they themselves tend to take truth telling very seriously. As a result, white persons for whom these facts about police and lying are a part of their social reality will have very great difficulty taking seriously the possibility that the inculpatory testimony of a police witness is a deliberate untruth. However, it may also be a part of the social reality that many black persons, just because they are black, have had encounters with the police in which the police were at best indifferent to whether they, the police, were speaking the truth. And even more black persons may have known a friend or a relative who has had such an experience. As a result, a black juror would be more likely than his or her white counterpart to approach skeptically the testimony of ostensibly neutral, reliable witnesses such as police officers. The point is not that all police officers lie; nor is the point that all whites always believe everything police say, and blacks never do. The point is that because the world we live in is the way it is, it is likely that whites and blacks will on the whole be disposed to view the credibility of police officers very differently. If so, the legal system's election to ignore this reality, and to regard as fair and above reproach the common occurrence of all-white juries (and white judges) passing on the guilt or innocence of black defendants is a decision in fact to permit and to perpetuate a kind of institutional racism within the law.

The second type of institutional racism is that I will call "conceptual" institutional racism. We have a variety of ways of thinking about the legal system, and we have a variety of ways of thinking within the legal system about certain problems. We use concepts. Quite often without realizing it, the concepts used take for granted certain objectionable aspects of racist ideology without our being aware of it. The second *Brown* case *(Brown II)* provides an example.[16] There was a second *Brown* case because, having decided that the existing system of racially segregated public education was unconstitutional *(Brown I)*,[17] the Supreme Court gave legitimacy to a second issue—the nature of the relief to be granted—by treating it as a distinct question to be considered and decided separately. That in itself was striking because in most cases, once the Supreme Court has found unconstitutionality, there has been no problem about relief (apart from questions of retroactivity): The unconstitutional practices and acts are to cease. As is well known, the Court in *Brown II* concluded that the desegregation of public education had to proceed "with all deliberate speed."[18] The Court said that there were "complexities arising from the transition to a system of public education freed from racial discrimination."[19] More specifically, time might be necessary to carry out the ruling because of

> problems related to administration, arising from the physical condition of the school plant, the school transportation system personnel, revision of school districts and attendance areas into compact units to achieve a system of determining admission to the public school on a non-racial basis, and revision of local laws and regulations which may be necessary in solving the foregoing problems.[20]

Now, I do not know whether the Court believed what it is said in this passage, but it is a fantastic bit of nonsense that is, for my purposes, most instructive. Why? Because there was nothing complicated about most of the dual school systems of the Southern states. Many counties, especially the rural ones, had one high school, typically called either "Booker T. Washington High School" or "George Washington Carver High School," where all the black children in the county went; another school, often called "Sidney Lanier High School" or "Robert E. Lee High School," was attended by all the white children in the county. There was nothing difficult about deciding that—as of the day after the decision—half of the children in the country, say all those who lived in the southern part of the county, would go to Robert E. Lee High School, and all those who lived in the northern half would go to Booker T. Washington High School. *Brown I* could have been implemented the day after the Court reached its decision. But it was also true that the black schools throughout the South were utterly wretched when compared to the white schools. There never had been any system of separate but equal education. In almost every measurable respect, the black schools were inferior. One possibility is that, without being explicitly aware of it, the members of the Supreme Court made use of some assumptions that were a significant feature of the dominant racist ideology. If the assumptions had been made explicit, the reasoning would have gone something like this: Those black schools are wretched. We cannot order white children to go to those schools, especially when they have gone to better schools in the past. So while it is unfair to deprive blacks, to make them go to these awful, segregated schools, they will have to wait until the black schools either are eliminated or are sufficiently improved so that there are good schools for everybody to attend.

What seems to me to be most objectionable, and racist, about *Brown II* is the uncritical acceptance of the idea that during this process of change, black school-children would have to suffer by continuing to attend inadequate schools. The Supreme Court's solution assumed that the correct way to deal with this problem was to continue to have the black children go to their schools until the black schools were brought up to par or eliminated. That is a kind of conceptual racism in which the legal system accepts the dominant racist ideology, which holds that the claims of black children are worth less than the claims of white children in those cases in which conflict is inevitable. It seems to me that any minimally fair solution would have required that during the interim process, if anybody had to go to an inadequate school, it would have been the white children, since they were the ones who had previously had the benefit of the good schools. But this is simply not the way racial matters are thought about within the dominant ideology.

A study of *Brown II* is instructive because it is a good illustration of conceptual racism within the legal system. It also reflects another kind of conceptual racism—conceptual racism about the system. *Brown I* and *II* typically are thought of by our culture, and especially by our educational institutions, as representing one of the high points in the legal system's fight against racism. The dominant way of thinking about the desegregation cases is that the legal system was functioning at its very best. Yet, as I have indicated, there are important respects in which the legal system's response to the then existing system of racially segregated education was defective and hence should hardly be taken as a model of the just, institutional way of dealing with this problem of racial oppression. But the fact that we have, as well as inculcate, these attitudes of effusive praise toward *Brown I* and *Brown II* and its progeny reveals a kind of persistent conceptual racism in talk about the character of the legal system, and what constitutes the right way to have dealt with the social reality of American racial oppression of black people.

In theory, the foregoing analytic scheme can be applied as readily to the social realities of sexual oppression as to racism. Given an understanding of the social realities in respect to sex—the ways in which the system of patriarchy inequitably distributes important benefits and burdens for the benefit of males, and the ideology which is a part of that patriarchal system and supportive of it—one can examine the different types of sexism that exist within the legal system. In practice the task is more difficult because we are inclined to take as appropriate even overt instances of sexist laws, *e.g.*, that it is appropriately a part of the definition of rape that a man cannot rape his wife.[21] The task is also more difficult because sexism is, as I have suggested, a "deeper" phenomenon than racism. As a result, there is less awareness of the significance of much of the social reality, e.g., that the language we use to talk about the world and ourselves has embedded within it ideological assumptions and preferences that support the existing patriarchal system. Cases of institutional sexism will therefore be systematically harder to detect. But these difficulties to one side, the mode of analysis seems to me to be in principle equally applicable to sexism, although, as I indicate in the next section on ideals, a complete account of the sexism of the legal system necessarily awaits a determination of what is the correct picture of the good society in respect to sexual differences.

2. IDEALS

The second perspective, described at the outset, which is also important for an understanding and analysis of racism and sexism, is the perspective of the ideal. Just as we can and must ask what is involved today in our culture in being of one race or of one sex rather than the other, and how individuals are in fact viewed and treated, we can also ask different questions: namely, what would the good or just society make of race and sex, and to what degree, if at all, would racial and sexual distinctions ever be taken into account? Indeed, it could plausibly be argued that we could not have an adequate idea of whether a society was racist of sexist unless we had some conception of what a thoroughly nonracist or nonsexist society would look like. This perspective is an extremely instructive as well as an often neglected one. Comparatively little theoretical literature that deals with either racism or sexism has concerned itself in a systematic way with this perspective.

In order to ask more precisely what some of the possible ideals are of desirable racial or sexual differentiation, it is necessary to see that we must ask: "In respect to what?" And one way to do this is to distinguish in a crude way among three levels or areas of social and political arrangements and activities. These correspond very roughly to the matters of status, role, and temperament identified earlier. First, there is the area of basic political rights and obligations, including the rights to vote and to travel, and the obligation to pay income taxes. Second, there is the area of important, nongovernmental institutional benefits and burdens. Examples are access to and employment in the significant economic markets, the opportunity to acquire and enjoy housing in the setting of one's choice, the right of persons who want to marry each other to do so, and the duties (nonlegal as well as legal) that persons acquire in getting married. And third, there is the area of individual, social interaction, including such matters as whom one will have as friends, and what aesthetic preferences one will cultivate and enjoy.

As to each of these three areas we can ask, for example, whether in a non-racist society it would be thought appropriate ever to take the race of the individuals into account. Thus, one picture of a nonracist society is that which is captured by what I call the assimilationist ideal: a nonracist society would be one in which the race of an individual would be the functional equivalent of the eye color of individuals in our society today.[22] In our society no basic political rights and obligations are determined on the basis of eye color. No important institutional benefits and burdens are connected with eye color. Indeed, except for the mildest sort of aesthetic preferences, a person would be thought odd who even made private, social decisions by taking eye color into account. And for reasons that we could fairly readily state we would explain why it would be wrong to permit anything but the mildest, most trivial aesthetic preference to turn on eye color. The reasons would concern the irrelevance of eye color for any political or social institution, practice or arrangement. According to the assimilationist ideal, a nonracist society would be one in which an individual's race was of no more significance in any of these three areas than is eye color today.

The assimilationist ideal in respect to sex does not seem to be as readily plausible and obviously attractive here as it is in the case of race. In fact, many persons invoke the possible realization of the assimilationist ideal as a reason for rejecting the Equal Rights Amendment and indeed the idea of women's liberation itself. My own view is that the assimilationist ideal may be just as good and just as important an ideal in respect to sex as it is in respect to race. But many persons think there are good reasons why an assimilationist society in respect to sex would not be desirable.

To be sure, to make the assimilationist ideal a reality in respect to sex would involve more profound and fundamental revisions of our institutions and our attitudes than would be the case in respect to race. On the institutional level we would have to alter radically our practices concerning the family and marriage. If a nonsexist society is a society in which one's sex is no more significant than eye color in our society today, then the laws that require the persons who are getting married to be of different sexes would clearly be sexist laws.

And on the attitudinal and conceptual level, the assimilationist ideal would require the eradication of all sex-role differentiation. It would never teach about the inevitable or essential attributes of masculinity or femininity; it would never encourage or discourage the ideas of sisterhood or brotherhood; and it would be unintelligible to talk about the virtues as well as disabilities of being a woman or a man. Were sex like eye color, these things would make no sense. Just as the normal, typical adult is virtually oblivious to the eye color of other persons for all major interpersonal relationships, so the normal, typical adult in this kind of nonsexist society would be indifferent to the sexual, physiological differences of other persons for all interpersonal relationships.

To acknowledge that things would be very different is, of course, hardly to concede that they would be undesirable. But still, perhaps the problem is with the assimilationist ideal. And the assimilationist ideal is certainly not the only possible, plausible ideal.

There are, for instance, two others that are closely related, but distinguishable. One I call the ideal of diversity; the other, the ideal of tolerance. Both can be understood by considering how religion, rather than eye color, tends to be thought about in our culture. According to the ideal of diversity, heterodoxy in respect to religious belief and practice is regarded as a positive good. On this view there would be a loss—it would be a worse society—were everyone to be a member of the same religion. According to the other view, the ideal of tolerance, heterodoxy in respect to religious belief and practice would be seen more as a necessary, lesser evil. On this view there is nothing intrinsically better about diversity in respect to religion, but the evils of achieving anything like homogeneity far outweigh the possible benefits.

Now, whatever differences there might be between the ideals of diversity and tolerance, the similarities are more striking. Under neither ideal would it be thought that the allocation of basic political rights and duties should take an individual's religion into account. And we would want equalitarianism even in respect to most important institutional benefits and burdens—for example, access to employment in the desirable vocations. Nonetheless, on both views it would be deemed appropriate to have some institutions (typically those that are connected in an intimate way with these religions) that do in a variety of ways take the religion of members of the society into account. For example, it might be thought permissible and appropriate for members of a religious group to join together in collective associations which have religious, educational and social dimensions. And on the individual, interpersonal level, it might be thought unobjectionable, or on the diversity view, even admirable, were persons to select their associates, friends, and mates on the basis of their religious orientation. So there are two possible and plausible ideals of what the good society would look like in respect to religion in which religious differences would be to some degree maintained because the diversity of religious was seen either as an admirable, valuable feature of the society, or as one to be tolerated. The picture is a more complex, less easily describable one than that of the assimilationist ideal.

It may be that in respect to sex (and conceivably, even in respect to race) something more like either of these ideals in respect to religion is the right one. But one problem then—and it is a very substantial one—is to specify with a good deal of precision and care what the ideal really comes to. Which legal, institutional and personal differentiations are permissible and which are not? Which attitudes and beliefs concerning sexual identification and difference are properly introduced and maintained and which are not? Part, but by no means all, of the attractiveness of the assimilationist ideal is its clarity and simplicity. In the good society of the assimilationist sort we would be able to tell easily and unequivocally whether any law, practice, or attitude was in any respect either racist or sexist. Part, but by no means all, of the unattractiveness of any pluralist ideal is that it makes the question of what is racist or sexist a much more difficult and complicated one to answer. But although simplicity and lack of ambiguity may be virtues, they are not the only virtues to be taken into account in deciding among competing ideals. We quite appropriately take other considerations to be relevant to an assessment of the value and worth of alternative nonracist and nonsexist societies.

Nor do I even mean to suggest that all persons who reject the assimilationist ideal in respect to sex would necessarily embrace either something like the ideal of tolerance or the ideal of diversity. Some persons might think the right ideal was one in which substantially greater sexual differentiation and sex-role identification was retained than would be the case under either of these conceptions. Thus, someone might believe that the good society was, perhaps, essentially like the one they think we now have in respect to sex: equality of political rights, such as the right to vote, but all of the sexual differentiation in both legal and nonlegal institutions that is characteristic of the way in which our society has been and still is ordered. And someone might also believe that the usual ideological justifications for these arrangements are the correct and appropriate ones.

This could, of course, be regarded as a version of the ideal of diversity, with the emphasis upon the extensive character of the institutional and personal difference connected with sexual identity. Whether it is a kind of ideal of diversity or a different ideal altogether turns, I think, upon two things: First, how pervasive the sexual differentiation is, second, whether the ideal contains a conception of the appropriateness of significant institutional and interpersonal inequality, e.g., that the woman's job is in large measure to serve and be dominated by the male. The more this latter feature is present, the clearer the case for regarding this as ideal, distinctively different from any of those described by me so far.

The next question, of course, is that of how a choice is rationally to be made among these different, possible ideals. One place to begin is with the empirical world. For the question of whether something is a plausible and attractive ideal does turn in part on the nature of the empirical world. If it is true, for example, that any particular characteristic, such as sex, is not only a socially significant category in our culture but that it is largely a socially created one as well, then many ostensible objections to the assimilationist ideal appear immediately to disappear.

What I mean is this: It is obvious that we could formulate and use some sort of a crude, incredibly imprecise physiological concept of race. In this sense we could even say that race is a naturally occurring rather than a socially created feature of the world. There are diverse skin colors and related physiological characteristics distributed among human beings. But the fact is that except for skin hue and the related physiological characteristics, race is a socially created category. And skin hue, as I have shown, is neither a necessary nor a sufficient condition for being classified as black in our culture. Race as a naturally occurring characteristic is also a socially irrelevant category. There do not in fact appear to be any characteristics that are part of this natural concept of race and that are in any plausible way even relevant to the appropriate distribution of any political, institutional, or interpersonal concerns in the good society. Because in this sense race is like eye color, there is no plausible case to be made on this ground against the assimilationist ideal.[23]

There is, of course, the social reality of race. In creating and tolerating a society in which race matters, we must recognize that we have created a vastly more complex concept of race which includes what might be called the idea of ethnicity as well—a set of attitudes, traditions, beliefs, etc., which the society has made part of what it means to be of a race. It may be, therefore, that one could argue that a form of the pluralist ideal ought to be preserved in respect to race, in the socially created sense, for reasons similar to those that might be offered in support of the desirability of some version of the pluralist ideal in respect to religion. As I have indicated, I am skeptical, but for the purposes of this essay it can well be left an open question.

Despite appearances, the case of sex is more like that of race than is often thought. What opponents of assimilationism seize upon is that sexual difference appears to be a naturally occurring category of obvious and inevitable social relevance in a way, or to a degree, which race is not. The problems with this way of thinking are twofold. To begin with, an analysis of the social realities reveals that it is the socially created sexual differences which tend in fact to matter the most. It is sex-role differentiation, not gender per se,[24] that makes men and women as different as they are from each other, and it is sex-role differences which are invoked to justify most sexual differentiation at any of the levels of society.[25]

More importantly, even if naturally occurring sexual differences were of such a nature that they were of obvious prima facie social relevance, this would by no means settle the question of whether in the good society sex should or should not be as minimally significant as eye color. Even though there are biological differences between men and women in nature, this fact does not determine the question of what the good society can and should make of these differences. I have difficulty understanding why so many persons seem to think that it does settle the question adversely to anything like the assimilationist ideal. They might think it does settle the question for two different reasons. In the first place, they might think the differences are of such a character that they substantially affect what would be possible within a good society of human persons. Just as the fact that humans are mortal necessarily limits the feature of any possible good society, so, they might argue, the fact that males and females are physiologically different limits the features of any possible good society.

In the second place, they might think the differences are of such a character that they are relevant to the question of what would be desirable in good society. That is to say, they might not think that the differences *determine* to a substantial degree what is possible, but that the differences ought to be taken into account in any rational construction of an ideal social existence.

The second reason seems to me to be a good deal more plausible than the first. For there appear to be very few, if any, respects in which the ineradicable, naturally occurring differences between males and females *must* be taken into account. The industrial revolution has certainly made any of the general differences in strength between the sexes capable of being ignored by the good society in virtually all activities.[26] And it is sex-role acculturation, not biology, that mistakenly leads many persons to the view that women are both naturally and necessarily better suited than men to be assigned the primary responsibilities of child rearing. Indeed, the only fact that seems required to be taken into account is the fact that reproduction of the human species requires that the fetus develop *in utero* for a period of months. Sexual intercourse is not necessary, for artificial insemination is available. Neither marriage nor the family is required for conception or child rearing. Given the present state of medical knowledge and the natural realities of female pregnancy, it is difficult to see why any important institutional or interpersonal arrangements *must* take the existing gender difference of *in utero* pregnancy into account.

But, as I have said, this is still to leave it a wholly open question to what degree the good society *ought* to build upon any ineradicable gender differences to construct institutions which would maintain a substantial degree of sexual differentiation. The arguments are typically far less persuasive for doing so than appears upon the initial statement of this possibility. Someone might argue that the fact of menstruation, for instance, could be used as a premise upon which to predicate different social roles for females than for males. But this could only plausibly be proposed if two things were true: first, that menstruation would be debilitating to women and hence relevant to social role even in a culture which did not teach women to view menstruation as a sign of uncleanliness or as a curse,[27] and second, that the way in which menstruation necessarily affected some or all women was in fact related in an important way to the role in question. But even if both of these were true, it would still be an open question whether any sexual differentiation ought to be built upon these facts. The society could still elect to develop institutions that would nullify the effect of the natural differences. And suppose, for example, what seems implausible—that some or all women will not be able to perform a particular task while menstruating, *e.g.*, guard a border. It would be easy enough, if the society wanted to, to arrange for substitute guards for the women who are incapacitated. We know that persons are not good guards when they are sleepy, and we make arrangements so that persons alternate guard duty to avoid fatigue. The same could be done for menstruating women, even given these implausibly strong assumptions about menstruation. At the risk of belaboring the obvious, what I think it important to see is that the case against the assimilationist ideal—if it is to be a good one—must rest on arguments concerned to show why some other ideal would be preferable; it cannot plausibly rest on the claim that it is either necessary or inevitable.

There is, however, at least one more argument based upon nature, or at least the "natural," that is worth mentioning. Someone might argue that significant sex-role differentiation is natural not in the sense that it is biologically determined but only in the sense that it is a virtually universal phenomenon in human culture. By itself, this claim of virtual universality, even if accurate, does not directly establish anything about the desirability or undesirability of any particular ideal. But it can be made into an argument by the addition of the proposition that where there is a virtually universal social practice, there is probably some good or important purpose served by the practice. Hence, given the fact of sex-role differentiation in all, or almost all, cultures, we have some reason to think that substantial sex-role differentiation serves some important purpose for and in human society.

This is an argument, but I see no reason to be impressed by it. The premise which turns the fact of sex-role differentiation into any kind of a strong reason for sex-role differentiation is the premise of conservatism. And it is no more convincing here than elsewhere. There are any number of practices that are typical and yet upon reflection seem without significant social purpose. Slavery was once such a practice; war perhaps still is.

More to the point, perhaps, the concept of "purpose" is ambiguous. It can mean in a descriptive sense "plays some role" or "is causally relevant." Or it can mean in a prescriptive sense "does something desirable" or "has some useful function." If "purpose" is used descriptively in the conservative premise, then the argument says nothing about the continued desirability of sex-role differentiation or the assimilationist ideal. If "purpose" is used prescriptively in the conservative premise, then there is no reason to think that premise is true.

To put it another way, the question is whether it is desirable to have a society in which sex-role differences are to be retained at all. The straightforward way to think about that question is to ask what would be good and what would be bad about a society in which sex functioned like eye color does in our society. We can imagine what such a society would look like and how it would work. It is hard to see how our thinking is substantially advanced by reference to what has typically or always been the case. If it is true, as I think it is, that the sex-role differentiated societies we have had so far have tended to concentrate power in the hands of males, have developed institutions and ideologies that have perpetuated that concentration and have restricted and prevented women from living the kinds of lives that persons ought to be able to live for themselves, then this says far more about what may be wrong with any nonassimilationist ideal than does the conservative premise say what may be right about any nonassimilationist ideal.

Nor is this all that can be said in favor of the assimilationist ideal. For it seems to me that the strongest affirmative moral argument on its behalf is that it provides for a kind of individual autonomy that a nonassimilationist society cannot attain. Any nonassimilationist society will have sex roles. Any nonassimilationist society will have some institutions that distinguish between individuals by virtue of their gender, and any such society will necessarily teach the desirability of doing so. Any substantially nonassimilationist society will make one's sexual identity an important characteristic, so that there are substantial psychological, role, and status differences between persons who are males and those who are females. Even if these could be attained without systemic dominance of one sex over the other, they would, I think, be objectionable on the ground that they necessarily impaired an individual's ability to develop his or her own characteristics, talents and capacities to the fullest extent to which he or she might desire. Sex roles, and all that accompany them, necessarily impose limits—restrictions on what one can do, be or become. As such, they are, I think at least *prima facie* wrong.

To some degree, all role-differentiated living is restrictive in this sense. Perhaps, therefore, all role-differentiation in society is to some degree troublesome, and perhaps all strongly role-differentiated societies are objectionable. But the case against sexual differentiation need not rest upon this more controversial point. For one thing that distinguishes sex roles from many other roles is that they are wholly involuntarily assumed. One has no choice whatsoever about whether one shall be born a male or female. And if it is a consequence of one's being born a male or female that one's subsequent emotional, intellectual, and material development will be substantially controlled by this fact, then substantial, permanent, and involuntarily assumed restraints have been imposed on the most central factors concerning the way one will shape and live one's life. The point to be emphasized is that this would necessarily be the case, even in the unlikely event that substantial sexual differentiation could be maintained without one sex or the other becoming dominant and developing institutions and an ideology to support that dominance.

I do not believe that all I have said in this section shows in any conclusive fashion the desirability of the assimilationist ideal in respect to sex. I have tried to show why some typical arguments against the assimilationist ideal are not persuasive, and why some of the central ones in support of that ideal are persuasive. But I have not provided a complete account, or a complete analysis. At a minimum, what I have shown is how thinking about this topic ought to proceed, and what kinds of arguments need to be marshalled and considered before a serious and informed discussion of alternative conceptions of a nonsexist society can even take place. Once assembled, these arguments need to be individually and carefully assessed before any final, reflective choice among the competing ideals can be made. There does, however, seem to me to be a strong presumptive case for something very close to, if not identical with, the assimilationist ideal.

NOTES

This is a revised version of Parts I and II of "Racism, Sexism, and Preferential Treatment: An Approach to the Topics," published in *UCLA Law Review Vol 21*, 481–622 (1977), c 1977 by Richard A. Wasserstrom. Some footnotes have been deleted and the remaining ones renumbered. Reprinted by permission of the author.

1 Passing is the phenomenon in which a person who in some sense knows himself or herself to be black "passes" as white because he or she looks white. A version of this is described in Sinclair Lewis's novel *Kingsblood Royal* (1947), where the protagonist discovers when he is an adult that he, his father, and his father's mother are black (or, in the idiom of the late 1940s, Negro) in virtue of the fact that his great grandfather was black. His grandmother knew this and was consciously passing. When he learns about his ancestry, one decision he has to make is whether to continue to pass, or to acknowledge to the world that he is in fact "Negro."

2 That looking black is not in our culture a necessary condition for being black can be seen from the phenomenon of passing. That it is not a sufficient condition can be seen from the book *Black Like Me* (1960), by John Howard Griffin, where "looking black" is easily understood by the reader to be different from being black. I suspect that the concept of being black is, in our culture, one which combines both physiological and ancestral criteria in some moderately complex fashion.

3 There are significant respects in which the important racial distinction is between being white and being nonwhite, and there are other significant respects in which the fact of being black has its own special and importance. My analysis is conducted largely in terms of what is involved in being black. To a considerable extent, however, what I say directly applies to the more inclusive category of being nonwhite. To the extent to which what I say does not apply to the other nonwhite racial distinctions, the analysis of those distinctions should, of course, be undertaken separately.

4 The best general account I have read of the structure of patriarchy and of its major dimensions and attributes is that found in *Sexual Politics* in the chapter. "Theory of Sexual Politics." K. Millett, *Sexual Politics* 23–58 (1970). The essay seems to me to be truly a major contribution to an understanding of the subject. Something of the essence of the thesis is contained in the following:

"[A] disinterested examination of our system of sexual relationship must point out that the situation between the sexes now, and throughout history, is a case of that phenomenon Max Weber defined as *herrschaft*, a relationship of dominance and subordinance. What goes largely unexamined, often even unacknowledged (yet is institutionalized nonetheless) in our social order, is the birthright priority whereby males rule females. Through this system a most ingenious form of 'interior colonization' has been achieved. It is one which tends moreover to be sturdier than any form of segregation and more rigorous than class stratification, more uniform, certainly more enduring. However muted its present appearance may be, sexual dominion obtains nevertheless as perhaps the most pervasive ideology of our culture and provides its most fundamental concept of power.

"This is so because our society, like all other historical civilizations, is a patriarchy. The fact is evident at once if one recalls that the military, industry, technology, universities, science, political office, and finance—in short, every avenue of power within the society, including the coercive force of the police, is entirely in male hands. . . .

"Sexual politics obtains consent through the 'socialization' of both sexes to basic patriarchal politics with regard to temperament, role, and status. As to status, a pervasive assent to the prejudice of male superiority guarantees superior status in the male, inferior in the female. The first item, temperament, involves the formation of human personality along stereotyped lines of sex category ('masculine' and 'feminine'), based on the needs and values of the dominant group and dictated by what its members cherish in themselves and find convenient in subordinates: aggression, intelligence, force and efficacy in the male; passivity, ignorance, docility, 'virtue,' and ineffectuality in the female. This is complemented by a second factor, sex role, which decries a consonant and highly elaborate code of conduct, gesture and attitude for each sex. In terms of activity, sex role assigns domestic service and attendance upon infants to the female, the rest of human achievement, interest and ambition to the male. . . . Were one to analyze the three categories one might designate status as the political component, role as the sociological, and temperament as the psychological—yet their interdependence is unquestionable and they form a chain." *Id.* at 24–26 (footnotes omitted).

[5] "For the married woman, her husband and children must always come first; her own needs and desires, last. When the children reach school age, they no longer require constant attention. The emotional-expressive function assigned to the woman is still required of her. Called the 'stroking function' by sociologist Jessie Bernard, it consists of showing solidarity, raising the status of others, giving help, rewarding, agreeing, concurring, complying, understanding, and passively accepting. The woman is expected to give emotional support and comfort to other family members, to make them feel like good and worthwhile human beings." B. Deckard. *The Women's Movement* 59 (1975), *citing* J. Bernard, *Women and the Public Interest* 88 (1971).

"Patriarchy's chief institution is the family. It is both a mirror of and a connection with the larger society: a patriarchal unit within a patriarchal whole. Mediating between the individual and the social structure, the family effects control and conformity where political and other authorities are insufficient." K. Millett, *supra* note 4, at 33.

[6] "Even if the couple consciously try to attain an egalitarian marriage, so long as the traditional division of labor is maintained, the husband will be 'more equal.' He is the provider not only of money but of status. Especially if he is successful, society values what he does; she is just a housewife. Their friends are likely to be his friends and co-workers; in their company, she is just his wife. Because his provider function is essential for the family's survival, major family decisions are made in terms of how they affect his career. He need not and usually does not act like the authoritarian paterfamilius *[sic]* of the Victorian age. His power and status are derived from his function in the family and are secure so long as the traditional division of labor is maintained."B. Deckard, *supra note 5*, at 62.

[7] In 1970, women workers were, on the average, paid only 59 percent of men's wages. And when wages of persons with similar educational levels are compared, women still were paid over 40 percent less than men. *Id.* at 79–81.

8 "It is generally accepted that Western patriarchy has been much softened by the concepts of courtly and romantic love. While this is certainly true, such influence has also been vastly overestimated. In comparison with the candor of 'machismo' or oriental behavior, one realizes how much of a concession traditional chivalrous behavior represents—a sporting kind of reparation to allow the subordinate female certain means of saving face. While a palliative to the injustice of women's social position, chivalry is also a technique for disguising it. One must acknowledge that the chivalrous stance is a game the master group plays in elevating its subject to pedestal level. Historians of courtly love stress the fact that the raptures of the poets had no effect upon the legal or economic standing of women, and very little upon their social status. As the sociologist Hugo Beigel has observed, both the courtly and the romantic versions of love are 'grants' which the male concedes out of his total powers. Both have the effect of obscuring the patriarchal character of Western culture and in their general tendency to attribute impossible virtues to women, have ended by confining them in a narrow and often remarkably conscribing sphere of behavior. It was a Victorian habit, for example, to insist the female assume the function of serving as the male's conscience and living the life of goodness he found tedious but felt someone ought to do anyway." K. Millett, *supra* note 4, at 36–37.

9 Thus, even after his "joke" about black persons became known to the public, the former Secretary of Agriculture, Earl Butz, took great pains to insist that this in no way showed that he was a racist. This is understandable, given the strongly condemnatory feature of being described as a racist.

Equally illuminating was the behavior of Butz's associates and superiors. Then-President Ford, for example, criticized Butz for the joke, but did not demand Butz's removal until there was a strong public outcry. It was as though Butz's problem was that he had been indiscreet; he had done something rude like belching in public. What Ford, Butz, and others apparently failed to grasp is that it is just as wrong to tell these jokes in private because to tell a joke of this sort is to have a view about what black people are like; that they can appropriately be ridiculed as being creatures who care only about intercourse, shoes, and defecation. What these persons also failed to grasp is how implausible it is to believe that one can hold these views about black people and at the same time deal with them in a nonracist fashion.

10 At a minimum, this account would include: (1) a description of the economic, political, and social positions of blacks and whites, males and females in the culture; (2) a description of the sexual and racial roles, i.e., the rules, conventions and expectations concerning how males and females, blacks and whites, should behave, and the attitudes and responses produced by these roles; and (3) a description of the de facto ideology of racial and sexual differences. This would include popular beliefs about how males and females, blacks and whites, differ, as well as the beliefs as to what accounts for these differences, roles, and economic, political and social realities.

11 The problem of empirical objectivity is compounded by the fact that part of the dominant, white male ideology is that white males are the one group in society whose members are able to be genuinely detached and objective when it comes to things like an understanding of the place of race and sex in the culture. Thus, for example, when a sex-discrimination suit was brought against a law firm and the case was assigned to Judge Constance Motley, the defendant filed a motion that she

539

be disqualified partly because, as a woman judge, she would be biased in favor of the plaintiff. Judge Motley denied the motion. *Blank* v. *Sullivan & Cromwell*, 418 F. Supp. 1 (S.D.N.Y. 1975), *writ of mandamus denied sub nom. Sullivan & Cromwell* v. *Motley*, No. 75–3045 (2d Cir. Aug. 26, 1975). Explaining her decision, Judge Motley stated: "[I]f background or sex or race of each judge were, *by definition*, sufficient rounds for removal, no judge on this court could hear this case, or many others, by virtue of the fact that all of them were attorneys, of a sex, often with distinguished law firm or public service backgrounds." 418 F. Supp. at 4 (emphasis added).

[12] This conjecture about the role or sexually segregated bathrooms may well be inaccurate or incomplete. The sexual segregation of bathrooms may have more to do with privacy than with patriarchy. However, if so, it is at least odd that what the institution makes relevant is sex rather than merely the ability to perform the eliminatory acts in private.

[13] *See, e.g., Guinn* v. *United States*, 238 (U.S. 347 (1915). Such statutes provided that the grandchild of someone who had been registered to vote in the state was permitted to vote in that state; but the grandchild of somebody who had never been registered to vote in the state had to take a special test in order to become qualified to vote. It does not take much knowledge of history to know that in most of the southern states few if any black people had grandparents who before the Civil War were registered to vote. And the persons who enacted these laws knew it too. So even though race was not made a category by the described laws, they effectively divided people on grounds of race into those who were qualified to vote without more, and those who had to submit to substantially more rigorous tests before they could exercise the franchise. All of this was done, as is well known, so as to perpetuate the control of the franchise by whites.

[14] N.Y. *Times*, Aug. 31, 1972, S 1. at 33, col. 3.

[15] All of the laws, institutional arrangements, etc., that I analyze are, I think, cases of racism and not, for example, cases of prejudice. The latter concept I take to refer more specifically to the defective, incomplete or objectionable beliefs and attitudes of individuals. Prejudiced individuals often engage in racists acts, enact racist laws and participate in racist institutions. But they need not. Nor is it true that the only persons connected with racist acts, laws, or institutions need be prejudiced individuals.

A perceptive account of the differences between prejudice and racism, and of the different kinds of racism, including institutional racism of the sorts I discuss below, can be found in M. Jones, *Prejudice and Racism* (1972). *See especially id.* at 60–115 (ch. 4. "Perspectives of Prejudice"); *id.* at 116–67 (ch 5. "realities of Racism"). A somewhat analogous set of distinctions concerning sexism is made in Jaggar, "On Sexual Equality," 85 *Ethics* 275, 276–77 (1974).

[16] *Brown* v. *Board of Educ.*, 349 U.S. 294 (1955).

[17] *Brown* v. *Board of Educ.*, 347 U.S. 483 (1954).

[18] 349 U.S. at 301.

[19] *Id.* at 299.

[20] *Id.* at 300-01.

21 In California, rape is defined as "an act of sexual intercourse, accomplished with a female *not the wife of the perpetrator*, under either of the following circumstances. . . ." Cal. Penal Code § 261 (West Supp. 1976) (emphasis added).

22 There is a danger in calling this ideal the "assmilationist" ideal. That term suggests the idea of incorporating oneself, one's values, and the like into the dominant group and its practices and values. I want to make it clear that no part of that idea is meant to be captured by my use of this term. Mine is a stipulative definition.

23 This is not to deny that certain people believe that race is linked with characteristics that prima facie are relevant. Such beliefs persist. They are, however, justified by the evidence. See. *e.g.*, Block & Dworkin, *IQ, Heritability and Inequality* (pts. 1–2), 3 Phil. & Pub. Aff. 331, 4 *id*.40 (1974). More to the point, even if it were true that such a linkage existed, none of the characteristics suggested would require that political or social institutions, or interpersonal relationships, would have to be structured in a certain way.

24 The term "gender" may be used in a number of different senses. I use it to refer to those anatomical, physiological, and other differences (if any) that are naturally occurring in the sense described above.

25 *See, e.g.*, M. Mead, *Sex and Temperment in Three Primitive Societies* (1935):

> These three situations [the cultures of the Anapesh, the Mundugumor, and the Tchambuli] suggest then, a very definite conclusion. If those temperamental attitudes which we have traditionally regarded as feminine—such as passivity, responsiveness, and a willingness to cherish children—can so easily be set up as the masculine pattern in one tribe, and in another to be outlawed for the majority of women as well as for the majority of men, we no longer have any basis for regarding such aspects of behaviors as sex-linked. . . .
>
> ". . . We are forced to conclude that human nature is almost unbelievably malleable, responding accurately and contrastingly to contrasting cultural conditions. . . . Standardized personality differences between the sexes are of this order, cultural creations to which each generation, male and female is trained to conform." *Id.* at 190–91.
>
> A somewhat different view is expressed in J. Sherman, *On the Psychology of Women* (1971). There, the author suggests that there are "natural" differences of a psychological sort between men and women, the chief ones being aggressiveness and strength of sex drive. *See id.* at 238. However, even if she is correct as to these biologically based differences, this does little to establish what the good society should look like. *See* pp. 611–15 *infra*.
>
> Almost certainly the most complete discussion of this topic is E. Maccoby & C. Jacklin, *The Psychology of Sex Differences* (1974). The authors conclude that the sex differences which are, in their words, "fairly well established," are (1) that girls have greater verbal ability than boys; (2) that boys excel in visual-spacial ability; (3) that boys excel in mathematical ability; and (4) that males are more aggressive. *Id.* at 351–52. They conclude, in respect to the etiology of these psychological sex differences, that there appears to be a biological component to the greater visual-spatial ability of males and to their greater aggressiveness. *Id.* at 360.

[26] As Sherman observes:

"Each sex has its own special physical assets and liabilities. The principal female liability of less muscular strength is not ordinarily a handicap in a civilized, mechanized, society. . . . There is nothing in the biological evidence to prevent women from taking a role of equality in a civilized society." J. Sherman, *supra* note 25, at 11.

[27] *See e.g.*, Paige, "Women Learn to Sing the Menstrual Blues," in *The Female Experience* 17 (C. Tavis ed. 1973).

"I have come to believe that the 'raging hormones' theory of menstrual distress simply isn't adequate. All women have the raging hormones, but not all women have menstrual symptoms, nor do they have the same symptoms for the same reasons. Nor do I agree with the 'raging neurosis' theory, which argues that women who have menstrual symptoms are merely whining neurotics, who need only a kind pat on the head to cure their problems.

"We must instead consider the problem from the perspective of women's subordinate social position, and of the cultural ideology that so narrowly defines the behaviors and emotions that are appropriately 'feminine.' Women have perfectly good reasons to react emotionally to reproductive events. Menstruation, pregnancy and childbirth—so sacred, yet so unclean—are the woman's primary avenues of achievement and self-expression. Her reproductive abilities define her femininity; other routes to success are only second-best in this society. . . .

. . . My current research on a sample of 114 societies around the world indicates that ritual observances and taboos about menstruation are a method of controlling women and their fertility. Men apparently use such rituals, along with those surrounding pregnancy and childbirth, to assert their claims to women and their children.

". . . The hormone theory isn't giving us much mileage, and it's time to turn it in for a better model, one that looks at our beliefs about menstruation and women. It is no mere coincidence that women get the blue meanies along with any event they consider embarrassing, unclean—and a curse." *Id.* at 14.

Robert Hahn is Professor of Philosophy at Southern Illinois University at Carbondale, where he has taught since 1982. He received his Ph.D. degree in Philosophy from Yale University and has previously taught at Yale University, Brandeis University, and Harvard University, among others. He is the author of his new book, *Archaeology and the Origins of Philosophy* (2010), as well as *Anaximander and the Architects*, *Anaximander in Context*, *Kant's Newtonian Revolution in Philosophy*, *Self-Identity and Moral Decisions* and *Formal Deductive Logic: A Logic Workbook*. His journal articles on many topics in the history of philosophy and the history of the philosophy of science have appeared in *Apeiron*, *The Journal of the History of Philosophy*, *The Journal of Chinese Philosophy*, *Phronesis*, *Philosophical Research Archives*, *The Southwest Journal of Philosophy*, *Southwest Philosophical Studies*, and in *New Directions in the Philosophy of Technology*.

Professor Hahn has also won prestigious awards and grants. Besides being elected to *Phi Beta Kappa*, and receiving Yale University's Mady Kady Tew prize in Philosophy and the Jacob Cooper prize in Philosophy and Classics, he also received Southern Illinois University's awards for both The Outstanding Teacher of the College and The Outstanding Educator of the University. Professor Hahn has also won nine research grants from the National Endowment for the Humanities.

ISBN-13: 978-1-269-89261-2
ISBN-10:   1-269-89261-4

90000

9 781269 892612

www.pearsonlearningsolutions.com

PEARSON

ALWAYS LEARNING